SECOND EDITION

PARENTMAKING

A Practical Handbook
for Teaching Parent Classes
About Babies and Toddlers

B. Annye Rothenberg, Ph.D.

Sandra Hitchcock, M.A. ❧ Mary Lou Harrison, M. Ed. ❧ Melinda Graham, M. Ed.

Additional contributions by: Jomary Hilliard, Ph.D. ❧ Karen Friedland-Brown, M.A.,
Rebecca Beacom ❧ Julie Kelsey ❧ Doreen du Celliée, M.S.

Banster Press
Menlo Park, California

Other books by B. Annye Rothenberg, Ph.D.

Parentmaking Educators Training Program: A Comprehensive Skills Development Course to Train Early Childhood Parent Educators (birth to 5) (Menlo Park, CA: Banster Press, 1993).

Understanding and Working with Parents and Children from Rural Mexico. What professionals need to know about child-rearing practices, the school experience, and health care concerns (Menlo Park, CA: CHC Center for Child and Family Development Press, 1995).

Second Edition, 1995
Copyright © 1995, 1983 by Banster Press

10   9   8   7   6   5   4   3   2   1

Library of Congress Cataloging-in-Publication Data

Parentmaking : a practical handbook for teaching parent classes about babies and toddlers /B. Annye Rothenberg . . . [et al.] ; with new revisions by Jomary Hilliard . . . [et al.]. — Rev. ed.
    p.   cm.
    Includes bibliographical references (p.   ) and index.
    ISBN 0-9604620-2-3 (pbk. : alk. paper)
    1. Parenting—Study and teaching—United States. 2. Infants—Care—Study and teaching—United States. 3. Child development—Study and teaching—United States. I. Rothenberg, B. Annye, 1940–
. II. Hilliard, Jomary.
    HQ755.7.P39   1995
    649'.1'07—dc20
                         95-3150
                              CIP

Editor: Carol Whiteley, Los Altos, California
Book Designer: Barbara Ravizza, Portola Valley, California
Cover Designer: Detta Penna, San Carlos, California
Illustrator: Sandra Spiedel, Palo Alto, California
Color Concepts: Carlos Munoz, Hollister, California
Typesetter: WESType Publishing Services, Inc., Boulder, Colorado
Printer: Bookcrafters Inc., Chelsea, Michigan

This work was supported from 1993–1995 by a grant from the Walter and Elise Haas Fund of San Francisco, California.

Revenue from the sale of this handbook and the new **Parentmaking Educators Training Program: A Comprehensive Skills Development Course to Train Early Childhood Parent Educators (birth to 5)** will be used for the continuing support of the Child Rearing Education and Counseling Program at the Children's Health Council in Palo Alto, California.

Banster Press
P.O. Box 7326, Menlo Park, CA 94026
(415) 369-8032

Printed in the United States of America

*To the many parents
who strive to grow
and to their children,
who will surely benefit*

Contents

Preface   xix
Foreword by Alan J. Rosenthal, M.D.   xxiii
Acknowledgments   xxv

PART ONE
DEVELOPING AND LEADING PARENTING CLASSES   1

1. Meeting the Need for Child-Rearing Support and Guidance   3

Support for a Challenging New Role   3
A Comprehensive Child Rearing Education and
   Counseling Program   4
Parent Development as well as Child
   Development   5

2. Deciding on the Structure and Preparing to Lead Groups   7

Determining the Kind of Program to Establish   7
Getting Ready to Lead   8

3. Establishing and Administering the Program   11

Establishing an Affiliation   11
Qualifications and Hiring Criteria for Staff
   Members   11
Publicizing Your Program   13
Handling Inquiries and Registration   14
Expenses and Fees   15

4. The First Class   16

Pre-Class Preparation   16

An Orientation Class Format   17
Post-Class Assessment   18
Formulating a Series Outline   19

5. Ongoing Preparation and Evaluation   21

Class Preparation   21
The Weekly Evaluation   22
Self-Preparation   23

6. Teaching Techniques to Aid in the Development of the Group   25

Establishing Ground Rules   25
Developing Good Discussions   26
Looking at Your Leading Skills   29
Solving Problems Concerning the Group   29

7. Including the Children   31

The Children's Program   31
The Playcarers' (Students') Program   33
Parents' Observation of the Children   34

8. Classes for Fathers 38

Pre-Class Preparation **38**
A Class Format **38**
Developing and Determining the Direction of Future Fathers' Classes **40**

9. Concluding a Series and Providing Further Support 41

Evaluating Reactions to the Series **41**
Continuing Group Support **41**
Continuing Individual Support **42**

10. An Introduction to Parts Two-Six 44

Background/Preparation

Goals to Work Toward in Presenting This Topic **44**
Typical Parental Interests and Concerns About This Topic **45**
Areas of Information You Will Need to Learn About to Teach This Topic **45**
Family Dynamics—What This Topic Means Psychologically to Parent and Child **45**
Sample Concern of Parents **45**
Readings and Other Resources **46**

Teaching/Presentation
Homework **46**
Practical Suggestions or Strategies for Teaching This Topic **46**
Mini-lecture and Lead-off Questions for Discussion **46**
Additional Information for Parents **46**
Handouts **46**

PART TWO
TEACHING ABOUT YOUNG BABIES (1-6 months)[1] 49

1. Crying and Schedules 51
Background/Preparation
Goals to Work Toward in Presenting This Topic **51**
Typical Parental Interests and Concerns About This Topic **51**
Areas of Information You Will Need to Learn About to Teach This Topic **52**
Family Dynamics—What This Topic Means Psychologically to Parent and Child **52**
Sample Concern of Parents **52**
Readings and Other Resources **53**

Teaching/Presentation
Homework: Baby's Current Patterns **54,**
Baby's Crying **55**
Practical Suggestions or Strategies for Teaching This Topic **56**
Mini-lecture and Lead-off Questions for Discussion **56**
Additional Information for Parents **58**
Handout: Average Sleep Patterns in Babies **61**

2. Nutrition 63
Background/Preparation
Goals to Work Toward in Presenting This Topic **63**
Typical Parental Interests and Concerns About This Topic **63**
Areas of Information You Will Need to Learn About to Teach This Topic **64**
Family Dynamics—What This Topic Means Psychologically to Parent and Child **64**
Sample Concern of Parents **64**
Readings and Other Resources **65**

Teaching/Presentation
Homework: Feeding and Nutrition **66**
Practical Suggestions or Strategies for Teaching This Topic **65**
Mini-lecture and Lead-off Questions for Discussion **67**
Additional Information for Parents **70**
Handout: Feeding and Nutrition **71**

1. In addition to the more age-specific topics listed in Parts Two through Five, many other important topics that are of interest to *all* of these age groups can be found in Part Six.

3. Play and Learning 78

Background/Preparation
Goals to Work Toward in Presenting This
   Topic 78
Typical Parental Interests and Concerns About
   This Topic 78
Areas of Information You Will Need to Learn
   About to Teach This Topic 79
Family Dynamics—What This Topic Means Psy-
   chologically to Parent and Child 79
Sample Concern of Parents 79
Readings and Other Resources 80

Teaching/Presentation
Homework: Playing - Learning - Exploring 81
Practical Suggestions or Strategies for Teaching
   This Topic 80
Mini-lecture and Lead-off Questions for
   Discussion 80
Additional Information for Parents 83
Handouts: Cognitive-Motor Development 86,
   Play and Learning 87

4. Adjusting to Parenting 90

Background/Preparation
Goals to Work Toward in Presenting This
   Topic 90
Typical Parental Interests and Concerns About
   This Topic 90
Areas of Information You Will Need to Learn
   About to Teach This Topic 91
Family Dynamics—What This Topic Means Psy-
   chologically to Parent and Child 91
Sample Concern of Parents 91
Readings and Other Resources 92

Teaching/Presentation
Homework: Adjusting to Parenting 93
Practical Suggestions or Strategies for Teaching
   This Topic 92
Mini-lecture and Lead-off Questions for
   Discussion 92
Additional Information for Parents 94
Handouts: A New Mother's Confessions of Am-
   bivalence *by Nancy Kelton* 97, Reflections
   of a Father Who Became a Mother *by Reese
   Sarda* 99

5. Equipment 104

Background/Preparation
Goals to Work Toward in Presenting This
   Topic 104
Typical Parental Interests and Concerns About
   This Topic 104
Areas of Information You Will Need to Learn
   About to Teach This Topic 104
Family Dynamics—What This Topic Means Psy-
   chologically to Parent and Child 105
Sample Concern of Parents 105
Readings and Other Resources 105

Teaching/Presentation
Homework 105
Practical Suggestions or Strategies for Teaching
   This Topic 105
Mini-lecture and Lead-off Questions for
   Discussion 106
Additional Information for Parents 106
Handout: Equipment for Babies 107

6. Speech and Language Development 111

Background/Preparation
Goals to Work Toward in Presenting This
   Topic 111
Typical Parental Interests and Concerns About
   This Topic 111
Areas of Information You Will Need to Learn
   About to Teach This Topic 111
Family Dynamics—What This Topic Means Psy-
   chologically to Parent and Child 112
Sample Concern of Parents 112
Readings and Other Resources 112

Teaching/Presentation
Homework: Speech and Language
   Development 114
Practical Suggestions or Strategies for Teaching
   This Topic 113
Mini-lecture and Lead-off Questions for
   Discussion 113
Additional Information for Parents 116
Handouts: Speech and Language Develop-
   ment 117, Speech and Language
   Skills 118

7. Social-Emotional Development 120

Background/Preparation

Goals to Work Toward in Presenting This Topic 120

Typical Parental Interests and Concerns About This Topic 120

Areas of Information You Will Need to Learn About to Teach This Topic 120

Family Dynamics—What This Topic Means Psychologically to Parent and Child 121

Sample Concern of Parents 121

Readings and Other Resources 121

Teaching/Presentation

Homework: Social-Emotional Development 122

Practical Suggestions or Strategies for Teaching This Topic 123

Mini-lecture and Lead-off Questions for Discussion 123

Additional Information for Parents 126

Handout: Social-Emotional Development 128

PART THREE
TEACHING ABOUT OLDER BABIES (7-14 months) 129

1. Limit Setting 131

Background/Preparation

Goals to Work Toward in Presenting This Topic 131

Typical Parental Interests and Concerns About This Topic 131

Areas of Information You Will Need to Learn About to Teach This Topic 132

Family Dynamics—What This Topic Means Psychologically to Parent and Child 132

Sample Concern of Parents 133

Readings and Other Resources 133

Teaching/Presentation

Homework: Baby's Increasing Mobility 135

Practical Suggestions or Strategies for Teaching This Topic 134

Mini-lecture and Lead-off Questions for Discussion 134

Additional Information for Parents 136

Handout 138

2. Social-Emotional Development 139

Background/Preparation

Goals to Work Toward in Presenting This Topic 139

Typical Parental Interests and Concerns About This Topic 139

Areas of Information You Will Need to Learn About to Teach This Topic 140

Family Dynamics—What This Topic Means Psychologically to Parent and Child 140

Sample Concern of Parents 140

Readings and Other Resources 141

Teaching/Presentation

Homework: Social Development 143

Practical Suggestions or Strategies for Teaching This Topic 142

Mini-lecture and Lead-off Questions for Discussions 142

Additional Information for Parents 145

Handout: Social-Emotional Development 148

3. Patterns and Schedules 149

Background/Preparation

Goals to Work Toward in Presenting This Topic 149

Typical Parental Interests and Concerns About This Topic 149

Areas of Information You Will Need to Learn About to Teach This Topic 150

Family Dynamics—What This Topic Means Psychologically to Parent and Child 150

Sample Concern of Parents 150

Readings and Other Resources 151

Teaching/Presentation

Homework: Baby's Current Patterns 152

Practical Suggestions or Strategies for Teaching This Topic 151

Mini-lecture and Lead-off Questions for Discussion 154

Additional Information for Parents 154

Handout 155

4. Nutrition 156

Background/Preparation

Goals to Work Toward in Presenting This Topic **156**

Typical Parental Interests and Concerns About This Topic **156**

Areas of Information You Will Need to Learn About to Teach This Topic **157**

Family Dynamics—What This Topic Means Psychologically to Parent and Child **157**

Sample Concern of Parents **157**

Readings and Other Resources **158**

Teaching/Presentation

Homework: Feeding and Nutrition **159**

Practical Suggestions or Strategies for Teaching This Topic **161**

Mini-lecture and Lead-off Questions for Discussion **161**

Additional Information for Parents **162**

Handout: Feeding and Nutrition **164**

5. Cognitive-Motor Development 166

Background/Preparation

Goals to Work Toward in Presenting This Topic **166**

Typical Parental Interests and Concerns About This Topic **166**

Areas of Information You Will Need to Learn About to Teach This Topic **167**

Family Dynamics—What This Topic Means Psychologically to Parent and Child **167**

Sample Concern of Parents **167**

Readings and Other Resources **168**

Teaching/Presentation

Homework **168**

Practical Suggestions or Strategies for Teaching This Topic **168**

Mini-lecture and Lead-off Questions for Discussion **168**

Additional Information for Parents **169**

Handout: Cognitive-Motor Development **170**

6. Play and Learning 171

Background/Preparation

Goals to Work Toward in Presenting This Topic **171**

Typical Parental Interests and Concerns About This Topic **171**

Areas of Information You Will Need to Learn About to Teach This Topic **172**

Family Dynamics—What This Topic Means Psychologically to Parent and Child **172**

Sample Concern of Parents **172**

Readings and Other Resources **173**

Teaching/Presentation

Homework: Play and Learning **174**

Practical Suggestions or Strategies for Teaching This Topic **173**

Mini-lecture and Lead-off Questions for Discussion **175**

Additional Information for Parents **176**

Handout: Play and Learning **178**

7. Speech and Language Development 180

Background/Preparation

Goals to Work Toward in Presenting This Topic **180**

Typical Parental Interests and Concerns About This Topic **180**

Areas of Information You Will Need to Learn About to Teach This Topic **180**

Family Dynamics—What This Topic Means Psychologically to Parent and Child **181**

Sample Concern of Parents **181**

Readings and Other Resources **181**

Teaching/Presentation

Homework: Speech and Language Development **183**

Practical Suggestions or Strategies for Teaching This Topic **182**

Mini-lecture and Lead-off Questions for Discussion **182**

Additional Information for Parents **182**

Handout: Speech and Language **186**

PART FOUR
TEACHING ABOUT TODDLERS (15-24 months)   191

1. Emotional Development   193

Background/Preparation

Goals to Work Toward in Presenting This
Topic   193

Typical Parental Interests and Concerns About
This Topic   193

Areas of Information You Will Need to Learn
About to Teach This Topic   194

Family Dynamics—What This Topic Means Psychologically to Parent and Child   194

Sample Concern of Parents   194

Readings and Other Resources   195

Teaching/Presentation

Homework: Emotional Development   196

Practical Suggestions or Strategies for Teaching
This Topic   195

Mini-lecture and Lead-off Questions for
Discussion   198

Additional Information for Parents   199

Handout: Emotional Development   202

2. Limit Setting   203

Background/Preparation

Goals to Work Toward in Presenting This
Topic   203

Typical Parental Interests and Concerns About
This Topic   203

Areas of Information You Will Need to Learn
About to Teach This Topic   204

Family Dynamics—What This Topic Means Psychologically to Parent and Child   204

Sample Concern of Parents   204

Readings and Other Resources   205

Teaching/Presentation

Homework: Discipline—Setting Limits   206

Practical Suggestions or Strategies for Teaching
This Topic   205

Mini-lecture and Lead-off Questions for
Discussion   209

Additional Information for Parents   210

Handout: Setting Limits   213

3. Eating Behavior   214

Background/Preparation

Goals to Work Toward in Presenting This
Topic   214

Typical Parental Interests and Concerns About
This Topic   214

Areas of Information You Will Need to Learn
About to Teach This Topic   214

Family Dynamics—What This Topic Means Psychologically to Parent and Child   214

Sample Concern of Parents   215

Readings and Other Resources   215

Teaching/Presentation

Homework   215

Practical Suggestions or Strategies for Teaching
This Topic   215

Mini-lecture and Lead-off Questions for
Discussion   216

Additional Information for Parents   216

Handout   216

4. Socializing Among Children   217

Background/Preparation

Goals to Work Toward in Presenting This
Topic   217

Typical Parental Interests and Concerns About
This Topic   217

Areas of Information You Will Need to Learn
About to Teach This Topic   218

Family Dynamics—What This Topic Means Psychologically to Parent and Child   218

Sample Concern of Parents   218

Readings and Other Resources   219

Teaching/Presentation

Homework: Socializing Among Toddlers   220

Practical Suggestions or Strategies for Teaching
This Topic   219

Mini-lecture and Lead-off Questions for
Discussion   221

Additional Information for Parents   222

Handout: Socializing Among Children   225

5. Play and Learning 227

Background/Preparation

Goals to Work Toward in Presenting This Topic **227**

Typical Parental Interests and Concerns About This Topic **227**

Areas of Information You Will Need to Learn About to Teach This Topic **228**

Family Dynamics—What This Topic Means Psychologically to Parent and Child **228**

Sample Concern of Parents **228**

Readings and Other Resources **229**

Teaching/Presentation

Homework: Exploring, Playing, and Learning **230**

Practical Suggestions or Strategies for Teaching This Topic **229**

Mini-lecture and Lead-off Questions for Discussion **232**

Additional Information for Parents **232**

Handout: Play and Learning **237**

6. Speech and Language Development 242

Background/Preparation

Goals to Work Toward in Presenting This Topic **242**

Typical Parental Interests and Concerns About This Topic **242**

Areas of Information You Will Need to Learn About to Teach This Topic **243**

Family Dynamics—What This Topic Means Psychologically to Parent and Child **243**

Sample Concern of Parents **243**

Readings and Other Resources **244**

Teaching/Presentation

Homework: Speech and Language **245**

Practical Suggestions or Strategies for Teaching This Topic **244**

Mini-lecture and Lead-off Questions for Discussion **246**

Additional Information for Parents **246**

Handouts: Speech and Language **248**, Speech and Language Concerns **251**, Preschool Speech and Language **253**

TOILET TRAINING (See 2-3 year old section, pp. 317–322.)

PART FIVE
TEACHING ABOUT TWO-YEAR-OLDS (2-3 years) 257

---

1. How Two-Year-Olds Think 259

Background/Preparation

Goals to Work Toward in Presenting This Topic **259**

Typical Parental Interests and Concerns About This Topic **259**

Areas of Information You Will Need to Learn About to Teach This Topic **259**

Family Dynamics—What This Topic Means Psychologically to Parent and Child **260**

Sample Concern of Parents **260**

Readings and Other Resources **260**

Teaching/Presentation

Homework: Children's Thinking **262**

Practical Suggestions or Strategies for Teaching This Topic **261**

Mini-lecture and Lead-off Questions for Discussion **261**

Additional Information for Parents **263**

Handout: How Two-Year-Olds Think—What's Going On Inside? **264**

2. Limit Setting 265

Background/Preparation

Goals to Work Toward in Presenting This Topic **265**

Typical Parental Interests and Concerns About This Topic **265**

Areas of Information You Will Need to Learn About to Teach This Topic **266**

Family Dynamics—What This Topic Means Psychologically to Parent and Child **266**

Sample Concern of Parents **266**
Readings and Other Resources **267**

Teaching/Presentation
Homework: Discipline/Setting Limits **268,**
Conflicts **270**
Practical Suggestions or Strategies for Teaching
This Topic **267**
Mini-lecture and Lead-off Questions for
Discussion **271**
Additional Information for Parents **272**
Handout: Setting Limits **274**

3. Sleep, Fears, and Nightmares **275**

Background/Preparation
Goals to Work Toward in Presenting This
Topic **275**
Typical Parental Interests and Concerns About
This Topic **275**
Areas of Information You Will Need to Learn
About to Teach This Topic **276**
Family Dynamics—What This Topic Means Psy-
chologically to Parent and Child **276**
Sample Concern of Parents **276**
Readings and Other Resources **277**

Teaching/Presentation
Homework **277**
Practical Suggestions or Strategies for Teaching
This Topic **277**
Mini-lecture and Lead-off Questions for
Discussion **277**
Additional Information for Parents **278**
Handout **279**

4. Nutrition **280**

Background/Preparation
Goals to Work Toward in Presenting This
Topic **280**
Typical Parental Interests and Concerns About
This Topic **280**
Areas of Information You Will Need to Learn
About to Teach This Topic **281**
Family Dynamics—What This Topic Means Psy-
chologically to Parent and Child **281**
Sample Concern of Parents **281**
Readings and Other Resources **282**

Teaching/Presentation

Homework **282**
Practical Suggestions or Strategies for Teaching
This Topic **282**
Mini-lecture and Lead-off Questions for
Discussion **283**
Additional Information for Parents **283**
Handout: Eating and Nutrition **285**

5. Play and Learning **292**

Background/Preparation
Goals to Work Toward in Presenting This
Topic **292**
Typical Parental Interests and Concerns About
This Topic **292**
Areas of Information You Will Need to Learn
About to Teach This Topic **292**
Family Dynamics—What This Topic Means Psy-
chologically to Parent and Child **293**
Sample Concern of Parents **293**
Readings and Other Resources **293**

Teaching/Presentation
Homework: Exploring, Playing, and
Learning **295**
Practical Suggestions or Strategies for Teaching
This Topic **294**
Mini-lecture and Lead-off Questions for
Discussion **294**
Additional Information for Parents **294**
Handout: Play and Learning **298**

**SPEECH AND LANGUAGE DEVELOP-
MENT** (See 15-24 month old section, pp.
242–255.)

6. Socializing Among Children **301**

Background/Preparation
Goals to Work Toward in Presenting This
Topic **301**
Typical Parental Interests and Concerns About
This Topic **301**
Areas of Information You Will Need to Learn
About to Teach This Topic **302**
Family Dynamics—What This Topic Means Psy-
chologically to Parent and Child **302**
Sample Concern of Parents **302**
Readings and Other Resources **302**

Teaching/Presentation
Homework: Socializing Among Children **304**

Practical Suggestions or Strategies for Teaching This Topic **303**
Mini-lecture and Lead-off Questions for Discussion **303**
Additional Information for Parents **303**
Handout: Playing with other Children **305**

7. Early Childhood Education Programs (pre-school and childcare) **307**

Background/Preparation
Goals to Work Toward in Presenting This Topic **307**
Typical Parental Interests and Concerns About This Topic **307**
Areas of Information You Will Need to Learn About to Teach This Topic **308**
Family Dynamics—What This Topic Means Psychologically to Parent and Child **308**
Sample Concern of Parents **308**
Readings and Other Resources **309**

Teaching/Presentation
Homework: Early Childhood Education Programs **310**
Practical Suggestions or Strategies for Teaching This Topic **309**
Mini-lecture and Lead-off Questions for

Discussion **309**
Additional Information for Parents **312**
Handouts: Evaluation Checklist for Early Childhood Education Programs **313,** The First Days at School **315**

8. Toilet Training **317**

Background/Preparation
Goals to Work Toward in Presenting This Topic **317**
Typical Parental Interests and Concerns About This Topic **317**
Areas of Information You Will Need to Learn About to Teach This Topic **318**
Family Dynamics—What This Topic Means Psychologically to Parent and Child **318**
Sample Concern of Parents **318**
Readings and Other Resources **319**

Teaching/Presentation
Homework **319**
Practical Suggestions or Strategies for Teaching This Topic **319**
Mini-lecture and Lead-off Questions for Discussion **320**
Additional Information for Parents **320**
Handout **322**

PART SIX
TEACHING ABOUT ONE-MONTH TO THREE-YEAR-OLDS AND THEIR FAMILIES 323
(These topics can be added to class series for any of the ages in Pts. II through V).

1. Sickness and Safety **325**
Background/Preparation
Goals to Work Toward in Presenting This Topic **325**
Typical Parental Interests and Concerns About This Topic **325**
Areas of Information You Will Need to Learn About to Teach This Topic **326**
Family Dynamics—What This Topic Means Psychologically to Parent and Child **326**
Sample Concern of Parents **326**
Readings and Other Resources **327**

Teaching/Presentation

Homework: Sickness and Safety **328**
Practical Suggestions or Strategies for Teaching This Topic **327**
Mini-lecture and Lead-off Questions for Discussion **327**
Additional Information for Parents **331**
Handouts: Handling Sickness **332,** Safeproofing Your Home for Children **334,** Safety Equipment **337**

2. Temperament and Individual Differences **340**

Background/Preparation

Goals to Work Toward in Presenting This
    Topic **340**
Typical Parental Interests and Concerns About
    This Topic **340**
Areas of Information You Will Need to Learn
    About to Teach This Topic **341**
Family Dynamics—What This Topic Means Psy-
    chologically to Parent and Child **341**
Sample Concern of Parents **341**
Readings and Other Resources **342**

Teaching//Presentation

Homework: Observation on Individual
    Differences **343**
Practical Suggestions or Strategies for Teaching
    This Topic **342**
Mini-lecture and Lead-off Questions for
    Discussion **342**
Additional Information for Parents **346**
Handout: Temperament and Individual
    Differences **348**

3. **Family Size 352**

Background/Preparation

Goals to Work Toward in Presenting This
    Topic **352**
Typical Parental Interests and Concerns About
    This Topic **352**
Areas of Information You Will Need to Learn
    About to Teach This Topic **352**
Family Dynamics—What This Topic Means Psy-
    chologically to Parent and Child **353**
Sample Concern of Parents **353**
Readings and Other Resources **354**

Teaching/Presentation

Homework **354**
Practical Suggestions or Strategies for Teaching
    This Topic **354**
Mini-lecture and Lead-off Questions for
    Discussion **355**
Additional Information for Parents **356**
Handouts: Considerations About the Spacing of
    Your Children **357**, Why Have More Than
    One? *by Anne Roiphe* **358**

4. **New Babies and Sibling
    Rivalry 362**

Background/Preparation

Goals to Work Toward in Presenting This
    Topic **362**
Typical Parental Interests and Concerns About
    This Topic **362**
Areas of Information You Will Need to Learn
    About to Teach This Topic **363**
Family Dynamics—What This Topic Means Psy-
    chologically to Parent and Child **363**
Sample Concern of Parents **363**
Readings and Other Resources **364**

Teaching/Presentation

Homework **364**
Practical Suggestions or Strategies for Teaching
    This Topic **364**
Mini-lecture and Lead-off Questions for
    Discussion **365**
Additional Information for Parents **365**
Handout **366**

5. **Baby-Sitters and Returning to
    Work 367**

Background/Preparation

Goals to Work Toward in Presenting This
    Topic **367**
Typical Parental Interests and Concerns About
    This Topic **367**
Areas of Information You Will Need to Learn
    About to Teach This Topic **368**
Family Dynamics—What This Topic Means Psy-
    chologically to Parent and Child **368**
Sample Concern of Parents **369**
Readings and Other Resources **369**

Teaching/Presentation

Homework: Baby-Sitters **370**
Practical Suggestions or Strategies for Teaching
    This Topic **369**
Mini-lecture and Lead-off Questions for
    Discussion **371**
Additional Information for Parents **371**
Handout: Baby-Sitters **376**

6. **Meeting Your Own Needs 379**

Background/Preparation

Goals to Work Toward in Presenting This
    Topic **379**

Typical Parental Interests and Concerns About This Topic **379**
Areas of Information You Will Need to Learn About to Teach This Topic **379**
Family Dynamics—What This Topic Means Psychologically to Parent and Child **380**
Sample Concern of Parents **380**
Readings and Other Resources **380**

Teaching/Presentation
Homework: Feelings and Needs of Parents **382,** Feelings and Needs of Mothers **385**
Practical Suggestions or Strategies for Teaching This Topic **381**
Mini-lecture and Lead-off Questions for Discussion **381**
Additional Information for Parents **381**
Handout: Getting to Know You by Suzanne Massie **389**

7. **Husband-Wife Relationships** **392**
Background/Preparation
Goals to Work Toward in Presenting This Topic **392**
Typical Parental Interests and Concerns About This Topic **392**
Areas of Information You Will Need to Learn

About to Teach This Topic **393**
Family Dynamics—What This Topic Means Psychologically to Parent and Child **393**
Sample Concern of Parents **393**
Readings and Other Resources **394**

Teaching/Presentation
Homework: Parenting and Family Relationships **395,** Feelings and Needs of Parents **382**
Practical Suggestions or Strategies for Teaching This Topic **394**
Mini-lecture and Lead-off Questions for Discussion **396**
Additional Information for Parents **397**
Handouts: Why Fathers Get Jealous by Jean S. Gochros **399,** Men and Women May Speak Different Languages by Constance Rosenblum **402**

8. **Community Resources** **404**

9. **Reading Lists (for parents)** **405**
Handouts: 1-6 months **406,** 7-14 months **409,** 15-24 months **412,** 2-3 years **415**

PART SEVEN
APPENDICES: RESOURCES, INFORMATION, AND FORMS **419**

A. **Readings and Other Information for Instructors** **421**

Books on Group Guidance Techniques **421**
Books on Child and Parent Development and Behavior **421**
Books on Working Parent Families (see Appendix H)
Books on Divorce, Single Parenting, and Stepparenting **422**
Books on Prematurity and Multiple Births **423**
Books on Adoption **423**
Books on Ethnic Minorities **423**
    General Readings **423**

African American Families **423**
Latino Families **423**
Asian Families **424**
Native American Families **424**
Catalogs and Reviews **424**
Organizations Involving Child-Rearing Educators and Education **424**
Journals **424**
Magazines **424**

B. **Sample Publicity and Registration Forms** **425**

Boxed Display Ad to Advertise for Instructors **425**
Newspaper Publicity Article **425**
Informational Flyer for Parents **426**
Initial Information Request Form **427**
Guidelines for Answering Telephone Inquiries **427**
Parenting Program Brochure **428**
Sample Program Philosophy and Purpose **428**
Registration Form **429**
Sample Policy Statement for Program Registration **429**
Confirmation Letter and Attachments: Current Concerns and Parent's Interests Forms (for all age groups) **429–435**
Additional Confirmation Letter Attachments: Separation Experiences (also for working parent classes) **436–438**
Birth or Adoption Experience **439**

C. **Sample Orientation Forms and Series Outlines** **440**

General Information Form **440**
"Welcome to Our Child-Rearing Series" Form **441**
Sample Series Outlines (all age groups) **441**
Sample Working Parents Outline **444**

D. **Sample Class Forms** **445**

Class Session Outline **445**
Homework Assignment **446**

E. **Sample Parent Guide** **447**

Problem-solving Guide **447**

F. **Sample Playcare Forms** **450**

Guidelines for Parents about Playcare **450**
Objectives for Students **451**
Information for Playcarers **451**
Series Curriculum for Playcarers **453**
Possible Observations for Playcarers **453**
Separation Practice Session **454**
Head Teacher/Caregiver **454**
Student Observation Forms **455**
Evaluating Playcarers **460**
Parents' Observations of Playcare **462**

G. **Sample Evaluation Form** **464**
Series Evaluation **464**

H. **Classes for Full-time Working Parents** **466**
Being a Full-time Working Parent **467**
Publicizing These Kinds of Classes **467**
Scheduling Working Parent Series **467**
Registration **468**
Nature of the Working Parent Series **468**
Important Issues to Cover in Teaching a Working Parent Series **469**
Play Care **470**
Observations of the Children **472**
Evaluation of Series **473**
Readings About and for Working Parents **473**

Index 475
About the Authors **481**

Preface

Parenting for each of us has been what it is for most people—a uniquely personal yet universal mixture of experiences and feelings. Being a parent has also been *more* difficult than any of us would have predicted. In those early months and years after our children were born, we each discovered that the kinds of information and support that we needed as new parents were not readily available.

We wondered why it was so difficult to find answers to the questions we had about the many details of child rearing that are the reality of the new parent's life. We waded through the reams of information about the "average" baby, but we could never quite find our own very real children amidst the theories, graphs, and advice. As we looked for support, we realized that our problems and needs were not unique to us as individuals, but were affecting new parents in every part of the country. We wondered why parenting seemed more difficult today than it was for our parents and grandparents.

The answer seems to lie in the sweeping cultural changes (in values, standards, and life styles) that have occurred in our society during the last several decades. Although these changes have promoted individual growth and more freedom of choice for both men and women, they have also resulted in more conflict and uncertainty for parents.

In the past, the extended family provided more of the child-rearing information, philosophy, and support new parents needed. Child-care responsibilities were shared among family members, and parental roles followed traditional lines. There was

greater consistency of thought and a natural assumption of responsibilities.

Society is far different today. Families may be spread out across the country, isolating the new family unit from the support and resources the extended family once provided. Neighbors and friends are often busy with careers and jobs and may live in the same area for only a short time. Though there are an enormous number of books and articles offering child-rearing advice now on the market, their advice often conflicts and their impersonal, general tone cannot hope to speak to the individual values, feelings, and traditions that each new parent brings to his or her child rearing.

Having children, too, is neither the cultural necessity nor the social imperative it once was; it is now a matter of choice for many people. If a couple does decide to have a child, however, parents seem determined to learn the "right way" to have and raise one. In many ways, parents today seem more worried about their parenting than past generations. The difficult feelings they experience when leaving their child with a child care provider, their concerns about how serious a child's problem is, and their inability to comfortably say "no" to their child all seem to be related to a lack of confidence brought on by their being without ties to a family of traditions that work. Many pressures—including financial ones and the faster pace of life—make it seem a formidable task to parent well.

Buffeted by the many choices in their lives, by the variations in philosophies and standards from family to family, and by the loss of "traditional" role models in the extended family, more parents than ever before are asking for better, more consistent, and more realistic child-rearing guidance and information. More organizations and state and federal government are also encouraging parents to participate in parent education. Families and communities today are warned about children growing up feeling alone, feeling like they have no direction or goals, being heavily influenced by peers and turning to drugs, alcohol, and crime. It is these parents' and organizations' underlying belief that early education in parenting/child-rearing skills can have a significant positive effect on both present and future family life and on their child's healthy behavior and emotional development.

In the early 1970s, the Director and Board of the Children's Health Council in Palo Alto, California, provided us an opportunity to develop a program that would address the needs of new parents. Primarily through classes oriented toward information and support, as well as through a telephone "warm-line" service for immediate access to help with parenting concerns and through individual counseling about normal child-rearing problems, this program began by providing education and emotional support for parents of children from one month to preschool age.

The initial focus of the Child Rearing Education and Counseling program and of this book has been the development of a series of classes for parents of young babies, older babies, one-year-olds, and two-year-olds. Each series offers group education and support in the area of child and family development, and integrates both practical and theoretical information, combining traditional instruction with group techniques of problem solving. Thomas, Chess, and Birch's studies on individual differences in temperament, Brazelton's practical, supportive advice to parents, Fraiberg's focus on the child's point of view, and Brigg's theories of self-esteem provide the beginning framework from which the instructors teach, support, and reinforce parenting skills. This eclectic approach ensures our ability to speak to the needs of individual parents and children and provides a forum where parents can share common concerns and experiences. Each series of classes has been taught quarterly since 1973 and has been continually revised through parent evaluations and feedback. Class lecture, homework, and handout material is also updated on an ongoing basis

to include new information relating to child development and family growth.[1] The program has taught more than 7000 families, and achieved a very positive image in the community. A comprehensive three-year longitudinal study reported the program's continued effectiveness for families who participated in the classes in comparison to a group of matched control families who did not.

Since the early 1970s, the national interest in parenting groups and classes has continued to expand dramatically. More communities than ever before now have classes for parents. During the 22 years of our program's work, we have frequently been asked to teach others who would like to teach parents. To broaden our knowledge, we have visited many other parenting classes and learned about still others, and have come to realize that although the goals of most parenting classes are similar to each other, the classes differ greatly in what and how information is taught. The parenting instructors we visited often did not have time to thoroughly investigate all the areas they needed for their teaching; if they did have time, they frequently didn't know where to look. Clearly there was a need for a curriculum or training for parenting class leaders. The problem was to take the developed body of knowledge in child and family development and organize it for teaching.

This handbook has been written to begin to solve that problem and fill that need. It is time to begin to develop a greater consistency among parenting instructors in what and how we teach in our parenting classes. It is also hoped that this greater consistency will encourage a better and more complementary working relationship between parenting educators and pediatricians, much as the relationship between childbirth educators and obstetrician-gynecologists has developed.

Since the beginning, this program has provided services primarily for middle to upper income two-parent families, many of which have part-time and more recently, full-time working mothers. Family structure has and continues to become increas-

---

1. The Child Rearing Program now focuses on parents of children from birth to age 8 years through classes and counseling. The scope of this book is birth through age 2 years.

ingly diverse with many more single-parent families, blended families, and increasing numbers of
working mothers. This greater diversity of family
structure, including inter-racial and same-gender
couples, is found in the parents that currently attend our classes. We have seen that the child-
rearing and parenting information in this handbook is quite relevant and of interest to all of these
parents as well. However, the framework presented in this handbook will need to be modified
for use in parenting programs that are structured
or focused on different parental groups or needs.
(See Appendix H for guidance on teaching full-
time working parent classes).

In addition, parenting programs must also be
tailor-made for ethnic minorities, especially for low
income, low education minorities. Appendix A
provides a resource list to help parent educators
find some of these programs. Resources for single
parents, blended families, multiple birth, and
adoptive families are also in Appendix A.

This handbook is for everyone—both novice
and experienced—who is interested in developing
and teaching parenting/child-rearing classes to
parents of newborns to three-year-olds. (It can
also be of great use to child care center and
nursery school teachers, pediatric, obstetric, and
public health nurses, pediatricians, childbirth
educators, parental stress hotline or talk line
volunteers, mental health staff, cooperative extension specialists, and the many other people who
work with parents who want guidance in raising
their babies and toddlers; it also, of course, can be
of direct value to parents.) It is hoped that the
handbook will provide support and training for
you, and help you more easily and more thoroughly prepare and lead your classes. Beyond
this, the handbook can be a useful source for encouraging better parental guidance.

How to Use This Book

With a book of this length, it can be difficult to
get right to the specific part you're looking for.
The Table of Contents and the Index are quite
detailed and should make this search easier. The
following information can further guide you in an
overall approach to using this handbook.

Part One, Chapters 1 through 9, are the sections you should read **first** for understanding how
to become an organized and effective parenting
group leader. Its related Appendices (A-G) provide sample forms, resources, and further information helpful to the development and leading of
parenting classes.

The last chapter in Part One, 10, provides the
key to the rest of the book. It explains the format
in which the specific child-rearing information for
each topic is presented. All the following chapters
in Parts Two through Five provide the preparation
and presentation material for you to use in
teaching the topics to the four specific age groups.
The chapters in Part Six provide information on
additional topics of interest to *all* of these age
groups. Part Seven, Appendix H provides information on teaching full-time working parent
classes.

B. A. R.
M. S. G.
revised, 1995

Foreword

In the Foreword to the first edition of *Parent-making* in 1982, I wrote the following paragraph from the perspective of a new parent, as well as a clinician at The Children's Health Council. These thoughts remain as true today as they were then:

> Our daughter was born over two years ago, and one of our many decisions during those hectic days was to register for the Child Rearing Education and Counseling Program at The Children's Health Council in Palo Alto. We were educated, concerned parents, but we were *new* parents. We felt alone and uncertain. Our families lived on the East Coast. We had friends, but no one to provide the support, the information, the practical answers from an experienced but broad perspective. And we had many questions—about holding the baby, crying, nutrition, naps, the baby's needs, our own needs. We found we were not alone. Increasing numbers of new parents feel the same confusion, uncertainty and isolation. We met many of these parents at the CHC's Child Rearing Classes. We shared, we supported, we discussed all these issues and more. We were given information, theoretical and practical; our concerns were addressed, as individuals and as a group. This experience made a difference for us and for our daughter. We felt more confident as parents, more confident as a family, and clearer about the directions we wished to pursue. We met other new families, and developed friendships and mutually supportive relationships that we still enjoy.

Since its origin in 1973, the CHC's Child Rearing Program has helped over 7,000 such new families. The program began with a small group of CHC staff members meeting to address a then complicated and controversial question: Could a clinical agency that treated emotionally disturbed children and families develop a program to "prevent" emotional problems? Could we provide meaningful services that would help and support "normal" families in their own development as individuals and as a unit? Not surprisingly, the personal experience each of us had at times of stress in our own lives began to direct our discussion. And it was not long before we could identify the common thread of personal stress that most of us shared: parenthood. The joy that we had with our infants and young children, we recalled, were tempered with feelings of confusion, lack of confidence, inadequate information, isolation, fears of doing or not doing something, and many others. While our clinical experience reminded us that interactions between parents and their infants and young children were of crucial importance in a child's development, it was from our own personal memories and needs as new parents that we envisioned a program that would support others through those first wonderful, frightening, and critical years of parenthood.

Annye Rothenberg quickly emerged as the natural leader of our small group. With a background in developmental and clinical psychology, research experience in child development, and a wife and mother herself, Annye had long been active in parenting concerns, professionally and personally. Her clinical specialty at The Children's Health Council involved work with infants and young children and their parents. She had been instrumental in developing informal parent support groups, children's play groups, and young children's recreational facilities in her community. And it was Annye's devotion, commitment, and perseverance that finally resulted in our "Child Rearing Education and Counseling" program.

Annye recognized that parenting skills were not necessarily innate. She understood that one of the most critical tasks of our social order—child rearing—required learning, practice, and support. She has devoted herself, now for more than twenty years, to developing these services, with the goals of enhancing parent-child interaction, child development, and preventing future emotional and family interactional problems. Her significant efforts resulted in a primary prevention mental health program, noteworthy in the thoroughness of its development; in its acceptance both within a clinical agency and in the greater community; in its stability and support; and in its achievements and success. Its reception by the professional community and by the public has been beyond our expectations. It has contributed to the growing body of literature assessing the values of preventive mental health services with a three year outcome study, using a matched control group, and demonstrating the benefits of these program services.

But developing and implementing our Child Rearing Program was only the "first step". In response to growing requests for instruction in leading new parent groups, and in the absence of any formal or recognized training program for child rearing instructors, the authors produced this Handbook, and along with current staff, a training curriculum and workshop series for leaders of parenting groups. This effort went well beyond a successful parenting program or providing beneficial mental health services. It became an important contribution to the development of a standardized, quality controlled, and eventually regulated course of instruction and training for the rapidly growing field of parent education and counseling.

This preventive program, with its Handbook and training component, has served as a model for the development of similar service and training programs elsewhere. In 1992, the curriculum represented in this Handbook was recognized as the most valuable and recommended curriculum (tied with two others) in parenting education programs in the United States. Further, in response to numerous requests to train others to develop and conduct this model program, our Child Rearing staff produced and published in 1993, the "Parentmaking Educators Training Program". This 410 page text with accompanying instructive videotapes is designed to train and guide the trainers of parent educators in developing and conducting such programs.

While preventive health services have been slow to develop in previous years in this country, the past two decades have seen increasing movement and effort to promote positive health and prevent physical and emotional distress. Certainly increasing economic pressures and the growth of managed health care have contributed to this movement. Child rearing and parenting programs now have joined the growing list of medical, personal, and social programs that includes preparation for childbirth, dietary and physical activity programs, family planning, marital communication workshops, preventive services for populations "at risk", and concerns over food additives, allergies, environmental pollutants, and other practices potentially harmful to our health. These activities emphasize the need for personal effort and commitment to maintain positive health for ourselves and our children. We are optimistic that this movement for the development of medically and socially responsible programs in public health and primary prevention will continue, and that services and training in child rearing education and counseling will be significant among them.

This Handbook has made and will continue to make a critical contribution to this medical and social movement.

ALAN J. ROSENTHAL, M.D.
Medical Director, Children's Health Council

Acknowledgments

So many people have contributed to the development of this book that we would like to say a collective thank you to all the incredibly talented and generous people of the San Francisco mid-Peninsula area who have been involved in this project—especially those who go unmentioned in the following acknowledgments.

We are very grateful to The Children's Health Council, Palo Alto, California—its Board of Directors and its staff—for providing a caring environment in which the Child Rearing Program has been able to grow and flourish. This caring attitude toward children and parents is continually reflected in the work of the agency.

We especially want to thank Dr. Alan J. Rosenthal, child psychiatrist, Medical Director of The Children's Health Council, and Clinical Professor of Psychiatry at Stanford University Medical School. His strong interest and commitment to "primary intervention" in new families has enabled the Child Rearing Program to be developed to its fullest; his encouragement throughout more than 20 years has allowed the program to continue and to expand, and has enabled the idea for this book to become a reality and an important influence in parenting education.

We are also indebted to Dr. Carolyn L. Compton, Learning Disabilities Specialist and Associate Director of The Children's Health Council for all of her helpful support and guidance during the many wonderful years we have worked together.

We are greatly indebted to the Walter and Elise Haas Fund of San Francisco, and particularly Program Officer, Kate H. Godfrey, whose generous support and interest in the Child Rearing Program and this book have been important as well as very much appreciated.

The very talented editor of this book, Carol Whiteley, worked tirelessly and with incredibly good humor—writing and rewriting a very hard-to-work-with manuscript. Its readable style is a tribute to her skill, which we marvel at and are deeply indebted for.

The typing of this manuscript was done in many long, after-hours sessions by two of the most patient, competent, and persevering people we have known—Cheryl Gorewitz and Joan Wolfe. We thank them both for a wonderful job.

The fine design of this book and many related "above and beyond" consultative hours were provided by a very talented and generous person, Barbara Ravizza.

We are grateful for the contributions to the early development of the homework and handout materials made by several of our colleagues at CHC—most especially, Sylvia Woolpert. We are grateful to our current Child Rearing Program colleagues for their excellent revisions to this 1995 edition of *Parentmaking*: Jomary Hilliard, Ph.D., Karen Friedland-Brown, M.A., Rebecca Beacom, Julie Kelsey, and Doreen du Celliée, M.S.

Our knowledgeable and always available colleague in pediatric nutrition at Stanford University Medical Center, JoAnn Hattner, R.D.C.S., M.P.H., has taught us much about nutrition over the years and reviewed and revised the sections in this book that deal with infant nutrition. We thank her for all her help.

We also want to thank Dr. Ann Piestrup, educational psychologist and participating parent in our program, and Dr. Dorothea Ross, psychologist and member of the CHC's professional advisory committee, both of whom—with their wonderfully clear and sharp thinking—helped us whenever we bogged down, from the earliest formulation of the outline for this book through the last detail of publication.

We wish to thank Boyce Nute, member of the Children's Health Council Board and President of Mayfield Publishing Company, who has provided a great deal of valuable advice in many aspects of the production and revision of this book.

Gratitude is also expressed to other of our colleagues—Harry Hartzell, M.D., Edith Studer Rondeau, M.D., Larry Mitchell, and Barry Gevirtz—for their helpful additions and encouraging comments. We also appreciate the support of the California Casualty Group.

Our illustrator, Sandra Spiedel, has made a major contribution in her own skilled way to this book as have the dedicated staff of Bookcrafters, and Ronnie Lynn Moore, Susan Sprouse, Rick Hinrichs, Cindy Marquart, and the late Rolla H. Rieder, Jr. of WESType Publishing Services. Detta Penna has designed a beautiful cover for our second edition and Carlos Munõz has provided the color concepts for the cover art. Thanks also to Detta for redesigning several of the book pages.

The many mothers and fathers who have participated in our parenting classes and whose child rearing and family development we have shared over the years will always be important to us, and it has meant a great deal to each of us to know them.

We also want to express our gratitude to our own parents who have—across the miles— encouraged us as always: (the late) Sam and Fannie Bross, Lloyd and Lorraine Nelson, Bill and Mary Jane Simmermacher, and Robert and Madelyn Strouse.

Lastly, we thank our husbands for so much caring and for not getting *too* upset about our tense and preoccupied days; and our children: Bret Rothenberg, Peter and Nicole Hitchcock, Daryl Harrison, and Erin and Meredith Graham, who were always forgiving and now will be getting their mothers back.

part one

DEVELOPING AND LEADING PARENTING CLASSES

1

MEETING THE NEED FOR CHILD-REARING SUPPORT AND GUIDANCE

Being a parent can be one of the most rewarding experiences of a lifetime. Most parents-to-be look forward with great anticipation to sharing the happy times, the new experiences, the enriched life they believe parenthood will bring. As the birth of their child draws near, they are eager, though somewhat uncertain, about beginning their long-awaited adventure.

With the birth of their baby, many parents—even those who have prepared themselves with relevant courses and information—discover that parenthood is quite different from the experience they expected. Parenting skills, they felt would blossom, need to be learned. Fatigue and pressure to meet their baby's many needs sometimes result in resentment, depression, feelings of incompetence, anger. With no on-the-job training or guidance available for their very challenging new role, parents can find the transition and adjustment to parenting an overwhelming experience.[1] The wide range of choices for today's role as parent can further increase new parents' uncertainty. These

include increased numbers of mothers working outside of the home, older mothers, parenting without a spouse, parenting within a multi-generation family, parenting within a lesbian or gay relationship, and other choices.

Support for a Challenging New Role

As new parents begin to search for help in clarifying and dealing with their roles, feelings, and responsibilities, the pediatrician is often the first person they turn to. Most pediatricians expect to discuss these as well as the many other child rearing and development issues with parents. But a simple discussion may not be adequate, and if the pediatrician has many patients requiring intensive medical care, he or she may not be able to offer the kind of involvement and support some parents want. Even when a pediatrician is able to help, many issues, such as how parents feel when their baby is unhappy or when to begin weaning, cannot always be answered with a statement of fact. Such issues need further thought and perspective, and parents feel the need to gain that perspective by sharing feelings, concerns, and advice with other parents. New parents need to feel that they are not alone, not the only ones who are worried or angry, not the only ones with a child behaving in a way that was

---

1. For a more extensive discussion of the impact of parenthood, see Randy Wolfson and Virginia DeLuca, *Couples with Children* (available only by calling (800) 443-9942); Ellen Galinsky, *The Stages of Parenthood*; T. Berry Brazelton, *On Becoming a Family*; Andrea Boroff Eagan, *The Newborn Mother*; Martin Greenberg, *The Birth of a Father*; Carolyn and Philip Cowan, *When Partners Become Parents*; and Marsha Dorman and Diane Klein, *How to Stay Two When Baby Makes Three* (call (800) 421-0351).

3

not expected. They need the same assurance and emotional support they received when they participated in prepared childbirth classes and other pre-natal activities.

Friends and neighbors who are parents *can* be of assistance by listening, answering questions, and offering support. Similarly, grandparents and other relatives can be good sources of advice and aid, but if they are at a distance geographically or emotionally, they cannot be of much help. Parents turn to child care providers. Most however, are not parents themselves, are not trained in parent guidance, and don't have the time to help. Child-rearing books can also be very helpful—up to a point. Most parents usually feel the need to reach beyond the printed page for personal contact with others going through similar experiences. Such personal contact makes a much more vital and lasting impression than any book.

Out of their need for some form of personal support for their child-rearing concerns, today's more vocal parents—generally those with a positive attitude toward education—are asking for new-parent groups and classes. They want these groups to explore where they and their children stand in relation to other families; they want the classes to help them establish some basic practical approaches they can use in their child rearing; they want to share in these groups their incredibly strong feelings about themselves and their children; they want to find help with specific problems they are currently experiencing; and they want professional feedback about their child's development and their own as parents.

A Comprehensive Child-Rearing Education and Counseling Program

In an attempt to better meet the needs of new parents, the Children's Health Council[2] (CHC) of Palo Alto, California, developed a program of primary prevention, the Child Rearing Education and Counseling Program. Begun in 1973, the pro-

gram focuses most of its resources on helping parents learn about and deal with the first seven years of their child's life—newborn to first grade age—because experience and studies have shown that most parents develop their approach to child rearing and have the greatest influence on their child during these early years. The premise of the program is that a parent's participation in it helps to prevent the development of emotional and, possibly, learning problems in his or her children.[3] As part of this goal of prevention, the program aims to help new parents in a number of ways:

Understand and Develop Their Role. Gain a realistic picture of their parenting role; adjust to being parents; help learn how to best satisfy their child's needs as well as their own.

Obtain Information. Find a source of basic information about their child's current and future development; become aware of established developmental norms with which to evaluate their child's progress.

Understand the Meaning of Their Child's Behavior. Learn to observe and interpret their child's actions; develop the ability to see things from their child's point of view.

Understand Parent-Child Interaction. See more clearly their effect on their child and his or her effect on them; become more relaxed and comfortable with their child.

Share. Discuss questions, concerns, and opinions openly within a group; recognize that each person is important to a group.

Formulate a Comfortable Style. Recognize and change aspects of their child-rearing style that do not satisfy them.

Establish a Philosophy. Develop a realistic, effective child-rearing philosophy; gain skills, confidence, and pride in their parenting role.

The current CHC program consists of child-rearing class series, both comprehensive (10

---

2. The Children's Health Council is a non-profit interdisciplinary center for child and family development that provides clinical services in mental health, special education, and child development, through preventive, diagnostic, treatment, and community outreach programs.

3. An extensive three-year longitudinal study of the program when it focused on newborn to three years compared those parents who took child-rearing classes with parents who did not. Results showed noticeable differences in favor of those who have taken child-rearing classes. We are very grateful to the S. H. Cowell Foundation of San Francisco for their generous support of this evaluation study. (A copy can be obtained by sending $3.50 to CHC-CR, 700 Sand Hill Road, Palo Alto, CA 94304.)

weeks) and brief (3 weeks), and child-rearing counseling/consultation sessions in which families can discuss in detail their specific child-rearing problems and concerns. It is the birth to age three comprehensive child-rearing class series that are the major focus of this book. (The other series and services, however, are discussed in Part I: 9.) The program is staffed by instructors—who are also parents themselves—trained in group leadership techniques and knowledgeable about child rearing and family growth concerns. The methods and philosophy that are the foundations of this program were developed from a wide ranging exploration of many approaches for helping parents. They represent what we have found to work the best.[4] Naturally, changes will continue to evolve in methods over a period of time.

Parent Development as well as Child Development

The philosophy behind the child-rearing program is that the development of the parent as well as the child is important to family contentment and growth and that education can help families in the pursuit of that goal. Experience has shown that there are several major problems confronting parents. First, there is insufficient knowledge of children's development and needs. Not knowing how much you can expect of your child prevents appropriate limit setting by parents. There is also lack of awareness of their own needs and ways to satisfy them which results in difficult feelings for the parents such as anger and guilt. Lastly, there is also more ambiguity about values and beliefs for today's parents.[5] The program strives to help parents in these areas by stressing the following ideas:

Parents need to know what to expect in their child's development, especially what is within the normal range. In addition they should learn that

the growth of such characteristics as sense of humor, curiosity, and how much fun their child is to be with are more important than the age at which he masters many developmental skills. Parents can lose sight of their child's personality development in their anxiety over when their baby can sit up alone, give up his bottle, etc. Societal pressure on parents to accelerate a child's development can be lessened if parents can learn to enjoy each stage for its importance and fun. Parents can deal more reasonably with their child when they understand more about the meaning of his behavior and the importance of each stage he passes through. As parents spend more time at work and less time around other parents and their children, their expectations of their own child tend to be less accurate, sometimes expecting too little but more often expecting too much of their child. As stages and patterns change, the entire family situation needs to be brought up to date to clarify where family members are and to determine their current needs and how the family can best go about meeting them.

Some parents feel they must let their child take the lead on all kinds of issues, many of which the child is often unable to handle. (For example, should a two-year-old be allowed to decide his own bed time?) When a child is given the lead before he's capable of handling it, parents' needs are being disregarded. It is then quite easy for parents to get irritable with their childen and, eventually, with themselves as parents.

Parents need help in analyzing and learning to satisfy their own needs. They could benefit from encouragement to think in terms of what *they* can handle emotionally, as well as what seems best for their child. Parents can use help finding ways to cope with their feelings of GUILT. These feelings can often result from their inability to meet their own—often unrealistic—self-expectations (for example, parents may regret having yelled at their child, having left him with a child care provider too much, having to say "no").

Parents, especially first-time parents, need to better understand the meaning of their child's behavior; in this way they can deal with it more realistically. For example, many new parents often think that a child who constantly gets out of bed at night is insecure and needs more parental contact. This may be true in some situations, but an experienced parent usually discovers that a child who leaves his bed at night is testing the

---

4. Classes that meet on an ongoing basis with a consistent, knowledgeable, and effective group leader dealing with practical concerns and feelings have been the most valuable features for parents.

5. For many families, their energy for and investment in parenting is further limited by lack of time and insufficient income.

ground rules of his environment and is probably signaling for more limit setting and clearer behavior guidelines. Parents need to know that children need parents who have reasons for their behavior and who don't change their reactions every time they're confronted with the same or a slightly varied situation. Children need their parents to be in control, though they, too, have feelings and preferences.

Other parents feel that the child should do what the parent asks without hesitation or question. They have problems seeing the child's perspective or needs. They may be giving the child too little respect.

Parents need help to develop a long-range view of their actions. Such a view can help them become aware of both immediate and future consequences. Parents will be better able to abandon their action-reaction, here-and-now approach to child rearing and focus their sights on the future if their long-term perspective is not lost in the day-to-day issues. They also need to keep working on family values and beliefs and how these are being communicated to their children.

The philosophy of the program reflects some of the more difficult issues in child rearing today and the very real need for support and guidance in this challenging area. The need for well-trained and experienced leaders to help bring support to as wide a range of new parents as possible has become increasingly apparent. Both the Child Rearing program and this book are an attempt to facilitate the development of that support, and the following chapters provide both child-rearing information as well as techniques to use in organizing and leading classes for parents of babies and toddlers.

2

DECIDING ON THE STRUCTURE AND PREPARING TO LEAD GROUPS

Child-rearing classes can provide a great deal for the families involved. They can provide a time to work hard on past, present, and possible future child-rearing concerns. They can also help the parents put real thought and energy into their child rearing, something that is important to do periodically.

Determining the Kind of Program to Establish

The program you develop can provide opportunities for all these things, but since the needs and concerns of parents will be different from those of new parents in other communities and your own interests and experience different from other group leaders, you will need to ask yourself several important questions—about orientation as well as structure—to determine the most effective kind of program to establish and the best match and setting for your skills:

- What kinds of parents would benefit from parenting groups that aren't available or satisfactory in my community now?
- Of these possibilities, what kinds of parents could I work best with? Consider:
  - parents of "normal" children vs. parents of clinically identified children (e.g., high-risk, special needs, etc.)
  - various age groups of parents and children
  - the various income levels

- the various ethnic minorities, including the issue of your bilingualism and biculturalism
- groups that include only mothers, only fathers, or both
- single parents vs. married parents
- full-time working parents vs. those working less than full-time or not at all outside of the home.[1]
- first-time parents vs. second- or third-time
- What organization might be interested in sponsoring a child-rearing class or program? If none is found, can the program be taught privately?
- Where can the groups meet?
- Should the children be included?
- When is the best time to hold group meetings (weekdays, evenings, weekends)?
- What size should the groups be?
- How frequently should the groups meet?
- How long should each session last?
- How long should each series last?

The staff members of the Children's Health Council discussed these questions and from this, as well as their later experience leading groups, the structure for the child-rearing program evolved. It was decided that because of the background, interests, and experience of the instructors, the lack of services available in the community, and a commitment to early interven-

---

1. See Appendix A for readings and resources on single parents, ethnic minorities, etc.

tion, the program would be offered to parents of "well" children up to three years of age.[2]

Staff members initially decided that classes should be held during weekdays so that support could be directed primarily to women engaged in full-time parenting or working not more than part-time outside the home. Having classes during daytime hours have given a boost to these women in what is often a long day with a young child.

Classes meet weekly for two hours over a 10-week period, allowing adequate time for instructors to comfortably and thoroughly cover the topics of concern to the groups. Class size is limited to 12 so that a feeling of closeness could be maintained and each group member have the chance to participate in the discussion. (Experience has shown that eight to twelve members allow for a very participatory group.)

In addition to regular weekly sessions for mothers, it was decided that a weekend class for fathers and children would be offered during each series.[3] The fathers' class was scheduled because instructors felt it important for fathers to see their children interacting with other children and to have a forum to discuss their own parenting concerns and feelings.

The CHC child-rearing program initially offered four class series in the framework just described, each focusing on a particular age range of children: "Learning More About Young Babies" (1-6 months); "Learning More About Older Babies" (7-14 months); "Learning More About Toddlers" (15-24 months); "Learning More About Two-Year-Olds" (2-3 years).[4,5] These divisions attempt to provide a homogeneous background of experiences that are of the most interest and value to the parents, and make the children's time together in group play enjoyable.[6]

Parents are encouraged to bring their children each week. During discussions, a separate play area is provided for all but the young babies, who stay with their parents, and the "playcare" staff plays with and cares for the children. Children are observed by their parents through a one-way window during part of each class and what is learned from and about them is very central to the classes. Meetings are scheduled to avoid typical nap times.

Getting Ready to Lead

The structure of the Child Rearing Education and Counseling Program developed as it did because of the people involved and the needs of the community that was being served. You, of course, will structure your classes based on the way you see things, on your interests, experience, and the available resources in your community. Whatever structure you select and develop, you will need to learn about two important areas before beginning to lead classes: (1) the age group of the children you'll be discussing and (2) group leadership. Preparing yourself thoroughly in these areas will make teaching child-rearing classes very rewarding for both you and the parents. When the series is over, you and your group will know that you have given informed, professional child-rearing and family development assistance to them and their children.

Getting Immersed in the Age Group

As you find out all you can about the age group of the children you'll be teaching about, think about the stage from both the child's and the parent's point of view—the problems, needs, and feelings of both. Doing this will help keep your class from becoming either too child-centered or too adult-centered. Increasing familiarity with the age group and its characteristics

---

2. At present, classes and child rearing counseling/consultations are available for parents of children up to seven years of age.

3. See Part I:8 (p. 38) for details on this topic.

4. During the 1980s, we added Parenting Preschoolers (3 and 4 year olds), Parenting Kindergarteners, and Parenting First Graders. (The elementary school age children do not come to CHC for child care. In addition, we regularly teach evening classes (from 6:00–8:00 p.m.) for working parents of toddlers (15 months to 2½ years) and working parents of preschoolers (2 ½ to 4½ years). Information for teaching parenting classes up through age 5 is included in Rothenberg, B. A. et al., *Parentmaking Educators Training Program* (Menlo Park, CA: Banster Press, 1993).

5. Classes at CHC have been attended almost entirely (90%) by first-time parents. This is probably because first-time parents generally have the most concerns and questions about child rearing. Most of the families have come from middle- to upper-income levels.

6. Provisions for the care of children during group meetings is discussed in Part I:7 (p. 31).

will come after teaching several class series, but some of the following suggestions may help you begin to learn.

• Observe children within the particular age range to see how they act alone, with their parents, and with other children of the same age. What's the general style of the age group? What are the behavior patterns? What do these children need from their parents? What do they play with? How do they handle such activities as sleeping, toileting, and dressing?

• Talk to parents with children in this age range. What do they want to know more about? What areas of development or behavior confuse them? What aspects of their child's needs put stress on them?

• Remember your own feelings when your child was this age. What were your major concerns? What areas of your child's development were particularly confusing or frustrating?[7]

• After you pinpoint major concerns such as limit setting, crying, and stranger anxiety, think about them from the child's point of view. Try to imagine, for example, what strangers mean to a 10-month-old and why they may terrify him. The following books can supplement your observations on the world from a child's point of view:

Brazelton, T. Berry, *Infants and Mothers* (New York: Dell Publishing Co., Inc., 1983).

Faber, Adele and Mazlish, Elaine, *Liberated Parents, Liberated Children* (New York: Avon Books, 1990). 1974).

Fraiberg, Selma, *The Magic Years* (New York: Simon and Schuster, 1976).

Gonzalez-Mena, Janet and Eyer, Dianne, *Infants, Toddlers and Caregivers* (Mountain View: Mayfield Publishing Co., 1989).

Kaplan, Louise, *Oneness and Separateness* (New York, N.Y.: Simon and Schuster, 1980).

• Read books that summarize the age range you intend to discuss as well as those that cover the whole gamut of the pre-school years. This will allow you and your parent groups to have a much broader picture of children's behavior and development. Appendix A provides a basic list of books

that have been found to be helpful. (The work by Rose Bromwich is extremely valuable.)

• For a view of how development proceeds, read the following topics in Parts II-VI of this book (each is covered in several age groups): cognitive-motor development, play and learning (II-3, III-5 and 6, IV-5, V-5), crying and schedules (II-1, III-3), limit setting (III-1, IV-2, V-2), social-emotional development (II-7, III-2, IV-1), language development (II-6, III-7, IV-6), nutrition (II-2, III-4, IV-3, V-4), and adjusting to parenting-meeting your own needs (II-4, VI-6).

Learning About Leading Groups

If you've led groups before, think about your strengths and weaknesses as a leader. What would you like to improve? What feedback did you get from participants in your groups? Pinpointing your weak areas and incorporating class comments can make leading child-rearing series a successful, enjoyable experience.

If you're not an experienced group leader, there are a number of ways you can become comfortable in the role and develop an effective teaching style. Here are a few:

Think about any experiences you've had as a participant in a group:
• What did you like and dislike about the leader's style.
• Did you like his humor or lack of it?
• Did he develop a congenial feeling among group members, and, if he did, how was it done?
• How did the leader focus the discussions and and move them forward?
• Were you given too much information or too little?

Discuss with your friends any small group discussion experiences they've had. Compare their ideas about what makes successful groups and successful group leaders to yours.

Consult an experienced group leader before, during, and at the completion of your series. This person will be your best authority in group leadership and dynamics and can help you solve problems as they occur. Group therapists, rap group leaders, college discussion section leaders, or leaders of groups in which you have participated are good sources.

---

7. Being a parent oneself has been so important in teaching child rearing classes that it is a requirement for all staff in the CHC child-rearing program.

Co-lead the first few series with an experienced group leader. Such a person can give you support and advice while you develop your own teaching style. Even an inexperienced co-leader may be helpful, since each of you can experience the other's style and pinpoint strengths and weaknesses.

Read books that discuss group leadership techniques to obtain an overview of the subject. The following books are recommended for your reading: *Parents Learn Through Discussion* by Aline Auerbach, *Helping Parents in Groups* by Linda Braun, Jennifer Coplan, and Phyllis Sonnenshein, and *Working with Parents* by Dolores Curran. Another source is Part I:6 (p. 25) of this book, which will provide you with information about teaching techniques and group dynamics.

For many parenting educators, however, learning how to lead groups successfully is very complex and therefore very difficult. Parent educators may want to participate in training workshops and other kinds of course work to really develop these skills fully. The Family Resource Coalition in Chicago is an excellent starting point to find out about professional training workshops that are held regionally and nationally. (See Appendix A for their address.)

Another outstanding resource for developing better group leadership skills is the *Parentmaking Educators Training Program: A Comprehensive Skills Development Course to Train Early Childhood Parent Educators* (birth to 5)[8] by B. Annye Rothenberg, Ph.D., et al. This training program was developed by this book's senior author and several colleagues to offer hands-on training to supplement the content of this book. After 10 years of experience of teaching this workshop to parent educators, the entire 36 to 50 hour training program was written up in a 412 page book with 6 hours of accompanying videotapes so that this training can be self-administered at any parenting education site. It teaches all the key components of effective parenting group leadership.

The *Parentmaking Educators Training Program (PETP)* also provides further information on how to learn about an age group, including outlines for a home visit and for interviewing a parent. Lengthy chapters on six content topics are also included: temperament, limit setting, separation, sleep, sibling relations, and husband-wife relationships—all covering birth to age 5 years with additional information for parents, more homework, and handouts.

Many of the resources found in Rothenberg, *PETP* will be referred to in this revised edition of *Parentmaking: A Practical Handbook* as useful for you to know about.

Besides learning about an age group and learning how to lead groups, most parenting group leaders need to know more about couple relationships, divorce, and single parenting, about working parents, and about ethnic minorities. Additional readings on those subjects are listed in Appendix A.

---

8. *Parentmaking Educators Training Program* (book and three videos) can be ordered from Banster Press, P.O. Box 7326, Menlo Park, CA 94026 by sending $155.95 including packing and shipping. (CA residents, add $12.40 sales tax.)

3

ESTABLISHING AND ADMINISTERING THE PROGRAM

If you plan to develop a program that consists of more than just one class based in your home, there are a number of organizational and administrative issues you'll need to deal with.

Establishing an Affiliation

The program described in this book was developed by staff members of a community agency for children; it therefore had access to the agency's resources, facility and reputation. If your program is not an outgrowth of a private or public organization, you will benefit greatly by affiliating yourself with such a group. Social service agencies, hospitals, school districts, daycare centers and nursery schools, churches and synagogues, and community centers are potential sponsoring sources.

The Facility

Wherever you locate your program, you will need a parents' meeting room, an instructors' office or at least a file and supply storage area, and a reception/telephone area. Additional space will be necessary if your series includes a children's program. The organization that sponsors you may be able to provide space for your classes, or at least office space, in its own facility. If it cannot, a community center or church might have acceptable space. A meeting room should be comfortably furnished (more like a living room than a classroom or board room) and be able to accommodate at least 10 to 12 people.

Qualifications and Hiring Criteria for Staff Members

If you plan to offer more than one or two classes, additional leaders/instructors may be needed. If you're not certain of how big your enrollment will be and therefore how many teachers you'll need, you may have to hire instructors on a contingency basis. You will be somewhat aware of community interest, however, if you are in the process of developing classes. Depending on the extent and focus of your program, you may need several other leaders and a program head if *you* do not intend to undertake that responsibility. Though your instructors will be the heart of your staff, a secretary and "playcarers" may prove to be necessary.

Instructors

When you begin to look for additional leaders for your program, look for applicants who—along with other qualifications—are parents. Leaders need experience in what they are teaching, and being a parent provides a necessary part of that experience. (Instructors, however, should not, if possible, have a child who is in the same age group as the one they will be discussing. It's best if the instructor has at least one child older than the age group she is teaching. Instructors need to be able to see an age group in perspective and not feel competitive with the other parents in their class.) Instructors who have similar backgrounds and devote approximately the same time to family commitments (e.g., work outside the home to the same extent) as the prospective group members will be able to relate to them quite well.

In addition to being a parent and someone with interests and a background similar to those of the parents in their classes, it is felt that most successful child-rearing instructors have the following personal qualifications:

- are out-going, warm, and supportive;
- relate easily on a feelings level;
- make people feel good when they're with them;
- are good listeners;
- are good analyzers of other people's problems;
- are able to see things from a child's as well as a parent's point of view;
- enjoy helping other people and sharing their own child-rearing experiences and feelings—the difficult ones even more than the easy ones (people who have experienced a great deal of difficulty while rearing a child and who have had to learn a lot in order to handle these things seem to make the most capable instructors; this is especially true if the very common "forgetting" of these negative experiences hasn't occurred);
- agree with the program's basic philosophy (this helps to keep the program consistent and is especially important for parents who continue to take classes over the years).

It is also felt that effective child-rearing instructors have the following professional qualifications in addition to group leadership skills as mentioned in the previous chapter:

- have education and professional experience in infancy, early childhood, or primary education;

psychology, social work, or counseling; or nursing or childbirth preparation;[1]
- have experience and skills that enable them to be comfortable preparing class content (for example, some people in counseling might not be used to or comfortable researching and organizing lecture material).

To attract potential group leaders, advertising in nursery school association newsletters, childbirth teachers' newsletters, or local newspapers (a box ad is more visible than a general ad in the classified section) should prove helpful (see Appendix B for a sample ad). Also contact friends (professional and personal), parents with similar interests, childbirth preparation teachers, nursery schools, and other parent education programs. The Family Resource Coalition in Chicago has a listing of parenting programs throughout the U.S.

When you begin to interview applicants, screen them on the basis of the criteria that are important to you. Meeting with each person will enable you to determine whether her personal and professional qualifications will match your needs. In addition to other factors, the extent to which you like the applicant and feel she would be able to help parents and work with other staff members will be critical to your evaluation. Observing her teach and interact with parents can be very useful in this interview process.

Most instructors will do more than lead parenting discussions; they may recruit playcare personnel, conduct child-rearing conferences with parents, and handle registration. It is important, therefore, for each applicant to understand the position's responsibilities and time requirements. Experience in the program described here shows that teaching a two hour class and supervising playcare personnel each week involves approximately four hours; preparation for teaching, once the instructor has been trained, usually takes an additional two hours each week;[2] and another one to two hours is devoted to staff meetings. The rest of the responsibilities vary in time requirements each week.

---

1. At this time, formal academic training in child rearing and parent education is not easily available. For those who would like to take some relevant course of study, a degree in any of the above mentioned areas, supplemented by classes in early childhood education, group dynamics, ethnic minorities, couple relationships, child psychology, educational methods, and child and family psychopathology, particularly those including field experience, would be beneficial.

---

2. While in the process of being trained, class preparation alone can easily take five hours each week.

Program Head

If you decide to hire a program head in addition to more instructors, that person will need to have the same skills as the instructors since she will most likely be teaching classes as well as working with the teachers. Staff leadership and training skills will also be necessary, as well as other administrative skills. The program head at CHC handles the following functions, in addition to leading groups:

- trains and consults with instructors, holds weekly staff meetings;
- manages administrative support staff
- is involved in fund raising and budget planning;
- works on public relations and program evaluation;
- plans future program content and direction.

The amount of time required for these various functions is not sharply defined, but usually averages 5 to 10 hours each week.

Secretary

Another essential for your program may be a secretary, or someone to type and copy class material, take messages from interested parents requesting information about the classes,[3] keep program records, arrange for facilities and supplies, and handle registration. Her time commitment will depend on the extent of your program.

Publicizing Your Program

In many communities, parents are requesting child-rearing classes. Publicity needs to be directed toward these parents, but it also needs to reach other parents who are not as aware of the advantages of child-rearing education.

The major problem in attracting sufficient interest and confidence in parenting classes is that parents often do not trust unknown people or programs to help them with their child rearing. Many parents, however, have taken childbirth preparation classes and feel very positively about them, and will generally trust recommendations from their instructors as well as their obstetricians and pediatricians. Informing such professionals in your area and leaving distributable literature with them about the program can be one major source of publicity.

Once your program is functioning, periodic follow-up contacts with obstetricians and pediatricians may be helpful. You can discuss matters that have been of concern to parents in your classes who are also their patients or see if they have any questions regarding the program. There appears to be some potential for "competition" and jealousy between pediatricians and child-rearing instructors, so it may be beneficial for you to get to know and help educate local pediatricians to the idea that your work is actually complementary to theirs, just as the childbirth educator's work complements that of the obstetrician/gynecologist. Pediatricians may be interested to know that parents who have received child-rearing support are likely to call them less often about behavioral questions and show a general decrease in anxiety level.[4]

Hearing about your program through professionals in your area will interest many parents. But they will most likely become more interested if they hear about the program from more than one source. Publicity focused directly at parents can be approached through several means. A month before classes are to start, an announcement of class schedules and content can be submitted to the appropriate local papers (see Appendix B for a sample newspaper article). Press releases distributed to local newspapers can provide a description of the program, discuss its uniqueness, and explain how it meets existing community needs. In turn, the press releases may interest newspaper personnel sufficiently to interview you about your classes.

---

3. At the Children's Health Council in the early years, the secretary took the message and the instructor called the parent back; parents more often followed through on registering for a class if they had spoken directly to the instructor. In more recent years as the program's reputation has become more widely known and as the brochure of classes has become both more descriptive and more widely disseminated, most parents who sign up for classes do not request a call back from the instructor first.

---

4. CHC's parent educator staff now trains community pediatricians and pediatric residents from Stanford University Medical School in parenting guidance and behavioral pediatrics.

A picture of staff members, alone or leading a group, will provide added appeal to the article. Finally, testimonials by parents that tell of the need and/or value of your program usually have a positive impact on readers. It will be necessary to wait until your first class is drawing to a close to get such comments from group members, but publicity for your program will still be valuable at that time. In fact, ongoing publicity is usually important in most communities to help people remember what is available, such as your classes.

In addition to newspaper publicity, parents can be reached directly by hanging posters or by leaving stacks of handouts (see Appendix B for a sample) at libraries, community centers, children's clothes, toy, and book stores, supermarkets, and hospitals. Parents can also be reached by radio. Find out which stations in your area offer free community service announcements and provide them with an appealing statement that fits their time requirements.

A final form of publicity is that which comes from "word-of-mouth" referrals. In the final analysis, this is *the most* effective type of publicity; a parent much prefers to hear about child-rearing classes from other parents who have taken them. If parents who have taken your series are very positive about the experience, hearing about it from

them will help other parents decide to take the classes. The extent to which parents choose to recommend the parenting classes is probably the single best evaluation method. Between 60 and 70% of the parents who have taken classes in the program described here state that they heard about the program "through a friend."

Handling Inquiries and Registration

When your publicity reaches a wide audience and parents begin making inquiries about the classes, several organizational procedures will be necessary. If you or your secretary are not always available, an answering machine, an answering service, or a voice mail system can take each parent's message and ask for the caller's name, telephone number, and child's birth date. When the parent is called back,[5] add her address to your information to complete your file on her. To build

---

5. If your secretary responds to callers' questions in addition to taking initial information, give her a list of commonly asked questions and their answers to keep by the phone. See Appendix B for an example of this type of list.

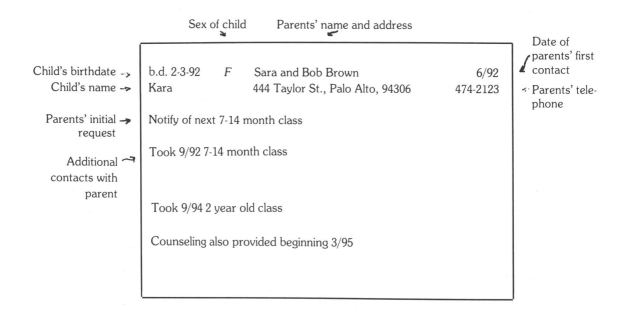

FIGURE 1. Database Information

a mailing list, you may want to enter this information in a computer database (see Figure 1). (You also may wish to keep the form on which the initial information was taken and file it alphabetically or by child's birth date—see Appendix B for a sample form.) Add to the database each time the parent makes a request, is notified of a class, or takes a class. Files can be removed from the database if a caller never takes a class or doesn't telephone a second time within a two-year period.

About two months before each class starts, the instructors of this parenting program decide on the classes to be offered, set up a teaching schedule, write descriptions of each parenting class series, and develop an extensive brochure that will be mailed to all the parents in the computer database. Mailing is done six weeks before the classes begin. Classes are taught in the fall, winter, and spring quarters. (A description of the brochure and registration form is provided in Appendix B.) To register, the parent fills out the registration form and then can call, FAX, mail, or walk in her registration form. An immediate postcard is sent to let the parents know they have a place in the class.

Registration options by phone, FAX, mail, or walk-in were developed to make the process as easy and quick as possible for parents with young children. However, to keep mailing and secretarial costs down, parents could simply send in their checks or credit card information after the announcement of classes appears in the newspaper or elsewhere, saving you time and the expense of mailing a brochure to each interested person. Since any method of registration is likely to arouse some unforeseen issues—as well as some injustices and hurt feelings—a sample statement of a registration policy is shown in Appendix B.

Enrollment is usually on a first-come, first-served basis. If registrations come in after a class has been filled, the secretary sends a letter to those people and attempts to work out a reasonable solution. Solutions can include arranging for the parent to take the series the following quarter,

making an individual appointment with the parent to discuss any of his or her child-rearing concerns, or referring the parent to another child-rearing program.

About a week before the class series begins, a confirmation letter is sent to the parents that includes the information they need to know for the first class. The letter also includes a number of forms that should be filled out and brought to orientation. These include concerns, interests, separation experiences, and birth experiences. (See Appendix B for a sample of each of these forms.)

Expenses and Fees

Another concern you will need to deal with is the expense associated with running your program. Money will need to be provided for instructors' salaries and benefits, facility costs, equipment and supplies, any additional employee salaries you require, publicity, and hiring and training expenses. The initial costs of your program may be paid for by the funding or sponsoring source or instructors may need to volunteer their time at the beginning. Once your program is ongoing, fees can be adjusted to help meet expenses. Since classes can range in cost from free (subsidized by a school district or other sponsoring source) to a minimal cost to those charging a moderate or high fee, it is difficult to discuss what your specific fee might be. Determine local community customs and resources and investigate the fees of other related professions such as private child-birth educators. You can then develop your own fees accordingly.

When you have immersed yourself in the age group you will be teaching about, learned about group management skills, *and* taken care of the administrative details of your program, you are ready to begin thinking about the first class.

4

THE FIRST CLASS

Two important things should happen during the first group meeting: (1) the parents who are participating should get to know each other and (2) the leader of the group should get to know each of the class members, including the parenting issues that are of interest to them.[1] The orientation class is the first step in a gradual building process and it is important to the growth of the group to start it on a positive note. At first, the parents in the class will see each other as strangers, but slowly they will find warmth, openness, and a great deal of valuable help.

Pre-Class Preparation

Once you have received completed registration forms from all group members, you can begin to organize and prepare for the first class.[2] Following are a number of suggestions to help you get ready.

• Since each series will be based on the concerns and interests of its participants, forms will be necessary to determine where these interests lie. (See Appendix B for samples.) You may wish to mail forms to class members prior to the orientation class for completion at home or have the

parents complete them during the first class. Parents' responses will be used as the basis for the major portion of the orientation discussion as well as future discussions.

• If you plan to co-lead the series, discuss with the co-leader which parts of the orientation meeting each of you will undertake.

• Familiarize yourself with the names of the people in your class and with those of their children. You might also note the sex and ages of the children and where the parents live. If you have sent questionnaires about the child's separation experiences or the mother's childbirth experiences (see Appendix B), these will be valuable to read. This information will enable you to feel somewhat knowledgeable about the group before the class begins.

• Determine and prepare any handouts you want to give the group. These could include:
— a class roster or listing to help parents contact one another outside of class and find out who lives in their vicinity;
— a general information sheet (see Appendix C for a sample) that shows the structure of the series and the services that are offered (warmline, counseling, etc.);
— a "welcome" form (see Appendix C for a sample) to help you learn more about each family;
— homework sheets[3] to help the parents focus on the first week's topic.

• Make name tags for the parents and the children

---

1. For more detailed information about the initial expectations of parents when joining groups, see Part II, ch. 17, Group Process in the *Parentmaking Educators Training Program,* Rothenberg et al. (Menlo Park, CA: Banster Press, 1993).

2. Information concerning publicity and registration prior to the first class session is provided in Part I:3 (p. 11).

3. Homework is discussed in Part I:5 (p. 21) and 6 (p. 25).

who will be involved in the program. Write the names in bold letters so they can be read easily from across the room. Include the child's name and age under the parent's.

• Decide if you want to provide food or drink for parents or children and at what time; snacks or juice and coffee can help to keep the atmosphere relaxed. Beverages can be provided by you or by class members on a rotating basis (a variety of caffeinated and decaffeinated coffees and teas along with juice and water could be served).

• Arrange the meeting room in a comfortable, open way, preferably with chairs set in a circle or oval. Be sure group members will be able to see each other easily. Set up a snack table if food or drink is to be provided and a changing table if babies will be in the room.

• Be relaxed. A positive and emotionally at ease instructor can be the keystone for a valuable class session.

An Orientation Class Format

There are a number of ways you can introduce the class content and goals of your series that will interest the participants as well as enable them to feel comfortable in the group setting. Below is one format that has been found to be successful.

1. Greet the parents and children as they enter the room and give each a name tag. Your warmth and interest in each parent and child will make a reassuring first impression.

2. When the group has assembled (most likely they will arrive at different times), introduce yourself and then discuss how the child care, if it is to be away from the room, will operate; before most parents can be comfortable in a group, they must be confident that their children are receiving good care. Some things to discuss are where and how long the children will play, plans for the children's activities, and who will be the caretakers.

3. If the children will be cared for away from the meeting room, let the parents and children become familiar with the play area and playcare staff. After an appropriate time, encourage the parents to part from their children so they can go to their meeting room. Some parents and children will have difficulty separating, but urge parents to

leave their child in a way that tells him all is well.

4. When the parents have settled themselves in the parents' room,[4] ask the group if they have any questions about child-care procedures. Have them consider how they feel about separating from their child and how their child usually separates from them. Let them know that they should not feel guilty if their child has difficulty separating. Encourage them to express their concerns and any negative or positive feelings they may have. This is the best way to establish an honest, open communication system. Let them know that their child will be brought to them if he has trouble being comforted that day.

5. Then tell the group about yourself—your name, child's name and age, what town you live in, and your interests. Ask the group members to do the same. As they introduce themselves, be alert to any direct questions as well as facial expressions that show uneasiness. You may also want to ask them each to tell the group something that is unique about them that will help the members remember them or you can try some other unique way to personalize the introduction.

6. Hand out the class roster and ask the group to check for errors.

7. Give an overview of the parents' children—how many children there are, how many boys and how many girls, their ages.

At this time or possibly after the next item, there should be an opportunity for the parents in the "young baby" class to get to know each other by sharing that very important area of their labor and delivery experience with each other. (New mothers especially have a strong need to do this. Many have had a very different experience than they anticipated and need support and validation from others—especially if the experience was negative and made them feel disappointed in themselves.) The instructor can give a brief introduction about the meaning of the birth experience, share her own, and ask those in the group to share their experiences if they want to. This is also an important way for new parents to get to know each other and begin to feel comfortable together.

---

4. Generally, parents are most comfortable if their children are cared for in a room that is very nearby.

8. Pass out the "welcome" form (if you're using one). This will provide you with more information about the group and may help you work out specific problems with them. (See Appendix C.)

9. Pass out the general information sheet and discuss it. Go over the length of the series, the length of each session, homework, observations of children, the fathers' class,[5] your policy on visitors, and any other services your program offers (counseling services, etc.). When parents are in a new setting and have just left their children, they may be too distracted to remember all the details you give them. The information sheet contains the same information and can be read later. Be sure to ask for questions as you go along.

10. Discuss the goals you have for the class. These could include:
    — to gain confidence as a parent;
    — to understand the particular age range of the children and develop an individual style of parenting within it;
    — to realize that parenting includes problem solving, and to learn which solutions best suit you and your child;
    — to understand that there are no "Super Moms" and "Super Dads," and that every parent has ups and downs;
    — to feel comfortable in a group of parents and be able to offer support to one another;
    — to feel increased satisfaction with your life.

11. Have the group take a short coffee break. This will give them a few minutes to talk among themselves before the major discussion period begins.

12. After the break, explain to the group that the class series will be based on those child rearing topics that are important to them. Have the parents fill out their Current Concerns and Parents' Interests forms if these were not completed at home.

13. Ask each parent in turn to describe her current interests and concerns about her child, herself, and her family. Before the first parent begins, ask the group to listen but try not to give quick solutions to each problem; better help can be given once each topic has been prepared for. Be firm in making sure that each person is allowed to speak

without interruptions and that the discussion does not veer off to a new topic. You can interrupt a remark and guide the conversation back to the original point if necessary. Naturally, no parent should be permitted to be derogatory or condescending to another parent. Remind the group that each family has a unique style and that some concerns of group members will differ and some will be similar.

During this portion of the class, parents find out what is on each other's minds and begin to feel like a group. They also learn that listening to one another and staying with the topic under discussion is beneficial to the group. Encourage this feeling of respect and support. You may want to take notes—in this instance—as parents talk, because frequently, something important will be said that was not written on a form.

14. Summarize the group discussion in a positive way. Let the parents know you have enjoyed their companionship and contributions. Also let them know that they will receive the series outline at the next class.

15. Inform the group of the topic that will be discussed during the next class and pass out the appropriate homework assignment. You can pick the topic prior to the orientation meeting or prepare a variety of homework sheets and then choose one after hearing the group voice its major concerns.

16. Indicate that the class is about to end and it is time to return to the children's play area. Be sure all parents pick up their children at the same time; when one parent is later than the others, her child may become upset.

17. As the group leaves with their children, be available to talk individually with any parent who needs your time.

Post-Class Assessment

After the orientation class has ended, you will need to consider a number of things about it; the group personality, individual group members, and the current concerns and needs of both individuals and the group. This assessment will help you to

---

5. If your classes are directed at women, you may decide to include a weekend meeting for the fathers. Information on fathers' classes is provided in Part I:8.

lead the group well and to develop a course of study that will be meaningful and valuable to its members.

The Group as a Whole

As you think about the group as a whole, ask yourself these questions:

- As the group gathered, was the atmosphere tense or relaxed?
- Did the group respond to the opening comments with warmth or apprehension?
- When did the group relax and seem at ease?
- How many group members knew others in the class prior to the meeting?
- Do the group members have mostly similar or varied backgrounds?
- Did the group ask for very specific information?
- Did the concerns and interests of the group seem mostly similar or varied?
- Were the group members supportive of one another?

The answers to these questions will help you to understand the group and to decide the best way to work with it. For example, if most of the group members are uncomfortable about sharing their feelings, you may have to be *extremely* frank about your own family life to enable them to discuss their own. Or, if several of the parents know each other well and talk constantly, you may have to be firm with them so that other participants are able to speak. Each group you lead will be different from every other and you will probably need to be somewhat different with each. It may take several weeks before you really know what the group is like. (A discussion of group leadership techniques is presented in Part I:6 of this book and in Part II, pp. 51–242 of Rothenberg, *Parentmaking Educators Training Program*.)

Individual Parents

When you have considered the class as a whole, think about each parent in the group, one by one:

- What are her interests and concerns?
- In what areas does she have some intense questions about her child?

- In what areas of child rearing does she seem more relaxed?
- How does she appear to feel about her child in general?
- How does she appear to feel about her parenting?
- How well can she express herself verbally?
- Was she quiet or did she contribute to the discussions?
- Did she speak to you individually before or after the class?
- Did she seem comfortable with the other group members?
- How did she relate to you as the group leader?
- Did she look relaxed or apprehensive?

Asking yourself these questions will enable you to determine how you can best work with each member of the group. You will discover which parent needs to be brought out, the intellectual and emotional level on which each should be responded to, which group members are friends and how they interact, and other important aspects of their personalities and expectations.

Formulating a Series Outline

Now assemble and read the "welcome" forms and the Current Concerns and Parent's Interests forms you received from the group members. These should give you added information about how each individual in the group feels and what each is hoping to gain from the series. You will probably refer to these forms and make additional comments on them as you get to know individuals better.

The next step is to formulate the series outline, basing it on your group's interests and concerns. To pinpoint these areas you will need to group both written and voiced concerns under major topic categories. For example, one parent may say on her Current Concerns sheet, "I do not know how to be consistent. What does consistency mean?" Another may have said during the orientation, "My child wakes up at night. I am tired of getting out of bed." And another may have asked after class, "Should I spank my child?" All of these concerns can be placed under the general topic "Limit Setting." Grouping concerns and interests in this way can help you prepare the information to be presented in specific classes as well as help you to know your group.

Now you can determine which concerns have the highest priorities for your group and should be discussed in the early weeks of the series. First, tally the rank order number given to each item on all the Parent's Interest sheets. Then divide each total by the number of parents in the group to get an average. Arrange the items in order; the most important issues will have the lower scores and the least important issues will have the higher scores. You can also look over the Current Concerns answers to help determine the priorities for the parents.

Once you have determined the priorities of your group, you can assign the topics to particular class sessions. Keep in mind the following considerations as you do this:

• Discuss during the first few classes those topics that are the most pressing to the most parents. However, if a particular topic is too demanding for you to teach early in the series or if you feel that a subject is not urgent though many parents are interested in it, place it later in the outline.

• If certain topics need to be preceded by others for the information to make sense, be sure to do that.

• Include the more emotional topics, such as adjusting to parenting, toward the middle of the series. At that point the group will be sufficiently comfortable with each other to discuss them.

• Include one topic in each session that you enjoy.

• If a class session includes a demanding topic, balance it with a lighter topic.

When you write your outline, personalize it to the group. State the major topic and then follow it with the stated concerns of the group. For example, "Limit Setting: effects of baby's increasing maturity and mobility; coping with baby's negative reactions; consistency." The outline you develop for each group will be different from every other because it will incorporate each group's special needs and concerns. (See Appendix C for examples of series outlines from each class series including two different outlines for one of the series. There is also a sample of a working parents' class outline.) A special chapter devoted to working parent classes begins on p. 466.

In learning some of the many necessary group management skills, you will find Rothenberg, *Parentmaking Educators Training Program* (PETP) to be particularly valuable. Some of the topics it teaches group leaders are how to set basic ground rules for groups, how to help develop the group process over time, and how to balance lecture and discussion including shifting the group when it has become too one-sided.

5

ONGOING PREPARATION AND EVALUATION

Class Preparation

Beginning with the class after the orientation meeting and continuing through the rest of the series, time should be devoted in each session to the following items:

- any points of business (such as when the fathers' class will be);
- concluding the prior week's topic, if necessary, including a verbal summary by you of the written homework on this topic;
- working on the current week's topic(s);
- discussing other topics or problems that are of importance to group members, as time allows;[1]
- observing the children;
- focusing briefly on the major topic(s) of discussion for the following week (distributing homework sheets).

Basing each class on these segments allows you to focus on areas not yet covered, bring up or emphasize issues you feel are important, and

devote time to those questions and concerns that the parents want very much to deal with. Since those questions and concerns will vary from group to group, it is not possible to provide you with an ordered outline of specific areas to be discussed in each class in each series. What is provided, however, is a detailed account of the work that is necessary for developing your weekly class plan.

The Weekly Outline

When you prepare each week's plan, based on the major sections just listed, try to estimate the amount of class time to be spent on each section; this will help you to accomplish what's necessary in a limited time frame. Notes to yourself about specific items, for example, when to distribute a handout or what time the coffee break should be, will be useful. Your outline will only be a guide, however, and is intended to be flexible. (A sample outline for one class session can be seen in Appendix D.) Sections will often take more or less time than anticipated, usually more.

Last Week's Topic. The first item on the outline to consider is the topic that was discussed in the previous week's class. Review the homework turned in by the parents at that time to make sure they understood the essence of the major concerns in that area and to see if any parents need individual help. Decide whether further work needs to be done with the class on that topic, and if it does, allot a small amount of class time to summarize the homework and/or cover individual problems.

---

1. This is especially important in the young baby class where concerns are very pressing and parents' anxiety can be great. In this class, time is alloted *weekly* for "How did the week go?" This is an unstructured time—usually about half an hour—to talk about any problem areas and feelings. In the three older classes, it is useful to have this time at least once every three sessions—although every week is preferable.

Current Week's Topic. Begin to gather information on the topic(s) you have planned for this particular session. Use Parts II-VI of this manual, your own experience, and other suitable resources. The material should be organized into the type of presentation that will be most meaningful to the particular group of parents.[2] The current week's topic usually takes the largest time allotment, so give it ample space.

As you gather information, it will be useful to plan a method of organizing this material. One way to keep track of relevant child-rearing information and be able to consult it easily is to compile file folders for individual topics. Such files can be added to and updated as you research new ideas during class preparation and evaluation. Some or all of the following areas could make up each topic folder:[3]

- notes on areas you wish to cover in class;
- a list of parents' concerns and interests;
- copies of handouts, homework, and other materials to be used in class;
- notes about the kinds of approaches that have succeeded and failed in handling the topic in class (over a period of time, different techniques will be used in presenting a topic, so it's helpful to keep track of what has and hasn't worked; however, an approach that wasn't appropriate for one group may be fine for another);
- notes from other sources—other people, books and so on;
- copies of especially valuable magazine articles;
- a list of sources to reread to refresh your memory about a topic.

Handouts. Review handouts that you have prepared or accumulated pertaining to the particular topic(s) and revise or replace them when necessary. Decide when and how each will be used in conjunction with the presentation of the topic(s). (Handouts are often most useful if they are distributed at the end of a discussion; they aid in summarizing or expanding it. Sometimes, however, you may want parents to read an article before the initial discussion of the topic.)

Observation of Children. If you determine that observing the children will be beneficial to the topic(s), decide: when the observation will take place, if the parents should have a particular focus in mind while they observe, and how the observation will be conducted. A half-hour observation time generally is sufficient.[4]

Next Week's Homework. Plan the homework assignment for the following week and allow a brief time in your outline to introduce its focus. Remember that the point of homework is to allow parents a chance to really learn something about their child and themselves on the topic to be discussed. (See Appendix D for a sample homework assignment. Homework samples can also be found in most chapters in Parts II through VI.)

The Weekly Evaluation

Following each class session, set aside time to review, evaluate, and briefly record what occurred during the meeting. There are two main areas to consider at that time:

Instructional. Focus on how successfully the topics were presented, how the discussion and observation periods went, and what questions or concerns were not answered. Notes on these points will help you to prepare the outline for the next week's class, including what topics you want to cover or specific information you didn't get to and wish to discuss. Recording ideas you may have for updating, revising, or organizing information or the presentation of topics for the next series will also be beneficial.

Emotional/Psychological. This area concerns itself with the dynamics of the class—how the group seemed, how the parents related to each other, and if individuals seemed to need special attention from you as group leader.[5] You may wish to make written notes about the group and its members; however, even if you don't, you will need to give the area thought so that the group can mesh successfully and continue to grow.

---

2. Part I: 6 provides information about the presentation of material to parent classes.

3. Much of the information suggested in the following list can be found in Parts II-VI of this manual.

4. More information on observing the children can be found in I:7, p. 34, and in Appendix F.

5. Details on handling these issues can be found in Part I:6 and in Rothenberg, *PETP*.

Self-Preparation

Leading a parenting group is obviously a large responsibility; during a class session an instructor will be trying to (1) follow the outline for the day; (2) be aware of how the specific topic material is being learned by the parents; (3) watch the flow of the discussion, with particular concentration on the content and feelings of what each person is saying; (4) keep track of how the group is doing as a whole; and (5) notice relevant facts about individuals in the group (for example, a group member may look particularly upset, tired, or confused). Co-teaching one or two series is a very good way for new instructors to slowly take on and feel comfortable with this tremendous amount of work,[6] but whether you will be co-teaching or not, it is very normal to feel tense or anxious before each session begins, especially during the early months of teaching.

Feelings That Can Hinder Effective Teaching

The following section lists feelings that can get in the way of leading—feelings you are likely to encounter during the course of your initial teaching experience. The section also discusses ways to prepare yourself to deal with and understand these feelings, and shows how they can influence your class. Remember, though, that as you gain experience with the very different styles of individuals and classes and gain familiarity with the topics and information, you will most likely find that your tension is easing and that you are growing more skillful and more confident with the style of leadership your work requires.

"I'm incompetent as a parent and can't teach this course." This feeling is especially likely to occur on days when your own child is going

through a hard-to-manage stage or when you are under pressure in your home or personal life. If the feeling occurs, it will be necessary to remind yourself that there are no real experts in child rearing and no real "Super-Parents." Another helpful measure is to share your feelings of incompetence and vulnerability with the group. This will help keep you from imposing unrealistic expectations on yourself, and will also help group members to be more honest and accepting of their own feelings of incompetence.

"I can't teach today, I'm too depressed." During sickness or severe depression, cancelling the class may be the best action to take. However, if you decide to hold a class and later regret it because you feel you didn't handle things well, remember that you still helped and supported the group by simply providing them with an opportunity to talk with each other.

"I don't approve of the way that class member is dealing with her problems." A teacher needs to understand her personal attitudes and biases because her own ideas will influence how she handles people in a group. One teacher realized that she was upset with mothers who were getting up with their toddlers at night as often as the toddlers awakened—often 3 to 4 times a night every night without trying to have the toddlers sleep more of the night. When she later came to terms with her own feelings, she saw that it was not so much what the women were doing about overnight awakenings that she objected to, but how extremely child-centered she felt these women were. She realized that some of the parents were doing what they felt was good parenting even though it placed more demands on them as parents. It is important to try to understand your attitudes and biases but support the right of each parent in your class to find her own style of parenting and her own solution. It is not a teacher's right to dictate solutions to class members. (Working with parents whose philosophy is very different from yours is discussed in Rothenberg, *PETP*, Pt. II, Chapter 9 Advice-Giving.)

"This woman is having problems and really needs my advice. I'd better help her quickly!" The temptation to move quickly to try to solve a parent's problem can be very strong; rescuing, though, doesn't work. Instead, offer support, encouragement and alternatives, and allow each parent to find out she has the strength and courage to determine her own solutions.

---

6. Co-leading after one is experienced, however, has its pros and cons. Continuing to co-lead provides the advantages of dividing some of the work, allowing two complementary styles to best help the group, and having someone to share the experience with. Its disadvantages are that it may be confusing to the parents to relate to more than one instructor, planning and execution take a good amount of collaborative time, it's difficult to be completely in charge, and fees are shared. You'll need to find out if co-leading or teaching alone works best for you.

"I'm spending all my time thinking about and planning for this class." It is *very* easy to do this; it is also emotionally exhausting. Try to compartmentalize the time you spend on teaching—work only during specific times. As you become more experienced and capable in your teaching, it will be easier to separate teaching from other interests.

"I don't like that person." It is impossible to like each person in your class to the same degree, but it is likely you will be able to find at least one trait or quality about *every* parent to like and respect.[7]

Your feelings about yourself and your ability to share these feelings with the group will be valuable tools for you as you teach. In class you will find that examples from your own life, both positive and negative, will be especially meaningful to the other parents. No matter what feelings you are experiencing, your verbal attempts to deal with them and solve problems associated with them will make it possible for each parent in the class to share herself more fully and feel your reassurance, support, and acceptance.

The Importance of Self-Nurturing

In addition to preparing yourself to cope with negative or unexpected personal feelings, you also need to care for your individual needs as you prepare to teach your classes. Self-nurturing is fundamental to the philosophy of the child-rearing program; it's much easier to be a successful leader when you learn to care for yourself. To avoid neglecting yourself as you become involved in caring for others, periodically ask yourself the following questions:

- How do I feel? How am I?
- What is troubling me or making me feel good?
- How is my balance in a typical week in terms of time alone, romantic time, social time, fun time, physical exercise time, intellectually stimulating time—in other words how well am I taking care of myself?
- How is my family?
- What steps can I take to become more satisfied with myself and my family?

A good way to care for your needs is to become affiliated with a source of support. One source could be found in weekly meetings with other parenting instructors. The major purposes of the meetings could be two-fold: (1) to share how the groups are going and get peer consultation as needed, and (2) to share yourselves and your families and get help from each other on your own child-rearing, individual, or family concerns. Time to talk with other instructors allows you to share on an open, deep, and trusting basis and to receive help in areas of your personal life that are concerning you. Close friends and family members, growth groups and other classes can also provide personal support.

In addition to preparing yourself to work with a group, you will also be finding ways for the group to work with itself. Appropriate teaching techniques, problem solving techniques, and operational guidelines are discussed in the following chapter.

---

7. Discussions concerning difficult feelings we have toward group members and vice-versa are discussed in Rothenberg, *PETP,* Pt. II, Chapter 17 Group Process.

6

TEACHING TECHNIQUES TO AID IN THE DEVELOPMENT OF THE GROUP

Learning to lead successful, comprehensive child-rearing groups requires time and the development of good teaching techniques. The instructor's role can best be seen as that of a guide, a person who has had more experience in most child-rearing areas than the parents in her classes but who is still willing to help parents find answers she can't give them. In her classes, she teaches parents to use a basic problem-solving approach that is applicable to many aspects of child rearing. By the end of a series, she usually finds that she does not need to participate as actively as she did at the beginning, because the group has learned how to have comprehensive, in-depth discussions and problem solve almost on their own.

Below you will find ground rules with which to guide your groups and teaching techniques that will enable you to lead quality discussions. Further in the chapter you will find information that deals with helping parents problem solve—work on their interests and concerns—and a discussion of problems you may encounter while leading a group.

Establishing Ground Rules

To keep your groups functioning smoothly and effectively, and to help parents develop a trusting atmosphere within a group, basic ground rules will be necessary. These guidelines should be rein-

forced by you either directly or indirectly and as often as necessary.

Respect Other Class Members. Through your own attitude and behavior, you can convey respect for every parent in the group and emphasize each person's individuality and strengths. Since there may be differences in life style, values, mannerisms, and so on among the parents in your classes, teaching and modeling respect for each of them is essential to the value of the class. Discourage group members from judging and evaluating each other. For example, if one parent in the group acts quite differently or puts forth a different set of values than the rest of the class, the other parents may tend to disregard what she says. Instead of allowing them to judge her as someone not to be taken seriously, you can help her to become more a part of the group; point out her contributions to the class. Try to engage that parent in a full discussion during class to help emphasize any similarities she has with the rest of the group. Quote her, if possible, at other times during other discussions. By working in this way, the rest of the class may change its attitude toward her and begin to hear what she has to say. Your role is to try and help parents care for each other; you can do this by showing how you care for all of them. Discourage competition and the image of a "Super-Mom" or a "Super-Dad" raising a "perfect" child.

Keep to a Topic. Many parents have a tendency to bring in extraneous issues during a discussion. Be alert to this; if you feel the focus or topic is starting to shift, bring the parent who is changing the subject back to the main focus being discussed by the group. Class members will appreciate this, and it will prevent the discussion from becoming rambling and unproductive. Comments such as "Let's focus on Sandy's concern first" or "That sounds important—let's talk about it a little later" are tactful yet effective ways to keep the topic under control. Occasionally a digression from a topic can prove beneficial, but it is best to set an early goal of one topic at a time.

Listen to One Another. Parents are often so eager to speak that they don't pay attention to what others are saying. A parent may interrupt and take over a discussion, or she may engage the person next to her in a separate conversation. As leader you need to be firm in these situations and allow the person who was speaking first to continue. It may be necessary to say to someone who interrupts a speaker, "Let's let Gail complete what she was saying" or "Let's continue what we were working on." If two or three people carry on a side conversation while someone else is speaking to the group, you might say, "I'm sorry, but it's hard to hear what Gail is saying"; this will remind the group that they need to respect each other's contributions. If you are consistent in listening to speakers and avoid interrupting them yourself, you will set a helpful example and will need to remind the group less often to listen to others.[1]

Developing Good Discussions

In order for group members to be open and relaxed with each other—something necessary for a valuable discussion—they need to know each other. At the orientation class, they learn each other's names, share concerns, and see each other's children. This is a positive beginning. In the next few sessions that follow the orientation, continuing to provide name tags and using the parents' names as much as possible will encourage the group to get better acquainted.

Homework assignments consisting of several questions for the parents to consider and answer will also add to the value of the discussion. Such assignments enable parents to assess their concerns and questions in relation to the next week's topic, help them gain more understanding about the subject, and focus their thoughts deeply enough on the topic so that they are ready for the next group discussion.

Starting Discussions

Good lead-offs are essential for quality discussions—they are your way to ensure that a valuable discussion will follow an informative lecture.[2] Specific lead-off suggestions for each topic in Parts II through VI of this handbook will be included in that topic, but to understand the reasons for those specific suggestions, it is important to know that there are several basic approaches that tend to enhance discussions.

For "feelings"-oriented topics (adjusting to parenting, husband-wife relationships, needs as a parent and as an individual): If you begin a discussion with *typical patterns* that occur in many families, such as "Many families have experienced . . . . since becoming parents" and follow this up with some honest vignettes about your own difficult experiences in this area, you will allow parents to feel more comfortable when you ask, "Have any of you experienced similar feelings?" or "I can tell from your laughter that all of you have had some of these feelings (experiences) too."

For major topics with clearly defined concerns (toilet learning, nursing, nutrition, socializing among children, limit setting, etc.): Begin by asking the group what they would like to cover within this subject; this allows you to focus on particular needs. Take a few notes and decide how much emphasis to give each. You can do this by looking over the points the parents indicated interest in and group the subtopics by

---

1. Teaching a group the basic ground rules is covered in detail in Rothenberg, *Parentmaking Educators Training Program (PETP),* Pt. II, Chapter 3.

---

2. Brief (5-minute) mini-lectures should be prepared in advance to formally explain certain kinds of important topic information to the group; long lectures are not recommended because they inhibit discussion. Mini-lectures that may be used as guidelines are provided in Parts II-VI of this book. Thorough practice on giving mini-lectures, developing lead-off questions, and guiding the flow of the discussion can be found in Rothenberg, *PETP,* Pt. II, Chapter 4.

category. Deal first with those areas that you feel need immediate attention because of the logic of the topic and their importance to the greatest number of parents. If the topic is one where you need to know how far people have gotten before you begin to find out their concerns, ask them first, for example, "Let's take a moment to find out at what point all of you are in the process of toilet training." (*Note:* Although you learned the group's current concerns at the beginning of the series, it is important to check with the parents again on the day you are discussing the particular topic. Concerns can often change during a period of a few weeks—especially with babies.)

For topics that parents have difficulty knowing what to ask about (play and learning, handling sickness in children, emotional development, having more than one child, etc.): Some groups formulate questions on a topic more easily than others, but occasionally parents will be completely unable to express or focus on concerns in an area. Begin, in this event, by suggesting many subtopics that have been of interest to parents in previous classes (see Parts II-VI of this handbook) and ask for other areas that may interest them on this subject. List them on a board or paper. Then find out which of all the subtopics the group would like to focus on, and begin there.

For topics that require background information or that are more theoretical ("What is a child's thinking like?"): Begin with some introductory background information and then a well-phrased question, such as "Let's try to draw a verbal picture of what is going on inside a two-year-old's head—how does he see things? Doing this will help us to better understand his behavior." Be prepared to give an example to get this kind of discussion started.

In addition to using examples and background information to start a discussion, you can also utilize material from the previous week's homework assignment. If you read and summarize the work during the week, you can use it to continue or reopen a topic. You might say, for example, "As I looked at your last week's homework, I noticed that several of you are interested in _____ . If one of you who has that interest will ask your question to the group, we'll go from there." Using examples from parents' homework makes them feel cared about and personally heard.

Keeping Discussions Flowing

Group discussions should follow from the concerns and questions the parents have; after you lead off a discussion, parents usually bring up areas of interest (for example, how and when to wean a baby) and concerns (for example, "I am trying to wean my baby—I've tried and nothing works."). At times, however, you will need to help a parent rephrase a question or see a concern in broader terms so that it will be informative to the group as well as help the particular parent understand her concern and find ways to resolve it.

When an interest (an area a parent wants to learn more about to avoid later problems) or a concern (an area where the parent is already experiencing problems) is expressed, reflect on the important issues that all the parents need to learn about:

Interests. Here you must first determine what the parents in the group have accomplished or decided about in this area, for example, how many have not started to wean and how many are in the process. Then you help them learn more by using:

- brief lecture notes that you have prepared on this topic but not used in your mini-lecture may be of help here in dealing with the parents' interests. (If you have no information on this interest, you can tell the parent that you will see what you can find out for her that week or suggest a source she can check herself).
- information from other parents about their experiences;
- vignettes from your own experience (personal examples that seem very relevant);
- handouts that you have prepared or obtained;
- articles that parents have brought into class.

When you discuss an interest, use your sources of information and support in an informal and spontaneous way; be aware of the nature of the discussion and how much additional help is needed. Be sure that group members have the opportunity to be helpful instead of assuming that everything of value must come from you. You can provide such opportunities by asking the group, "Have any of you been in a similar situation (or had a similar experience)?" Parents usually like to learn from peers as well as from the group leader in parenting classes.

Concerns. When a concern is voiced, usually after basic lecture material has been presented, the discussion should revolve around the parent finding out for herself how the problem developed and what is causing it to continue. By teaching parents to ask themselves questions and employ problem-solving techniques, you can help many parents learn how to analyze and resolve their own concerns. As the series proceeds, parents tend to help one another by asking some of the probing questions that are needed to clarify a situation. A great deal of class time is often spent helping an individual learn how to analyze a problem in detail. After a problem or concern has been analyzed, various suggestions can be made by the group and by you to help resolve the problem. When dealing with concerns, sharing real-life experience seems to be more useful than lecture notes or handouts.

Helping Parents to Problem Solve

A major goal of the program here is to help new parent groups learn more about problem solving; this will enable them to cope more successfully with the child rearing problems they will encounter in the future. It will also allow parents to go beyond a superficial solution, to learn how to look beneath a child's behavior to understand its meaning and come up with useful resolving techniques. Asking the group to explore their own experiences with expressed concerns can add to parents' understanding of problem solving.[3]

When a parent voices a problem or a question, it is easy for other group members to offer quick solutions at the symptom level. Questions from you that examine the whole concern on a deeper level, however, will enable all participants to get a fuller picture of the problem. The following kinds of questions promote discussion that result in increased understanding of a problem.

What? What is the expressed problem? What are the details of the specific incident?

How long? How long has this problem existed? How has it been handled up until the present?

Where? Where does the problem occur? (Only at home? Other places? Certain rooms?)

When? Does the problem occur at a certain time of day? Is there a time pattern to the problem or the child's behavior? To your feelings? Does the problem surface when you or your spouse is busy? When the activity level of the family is high? Or when the family is tired?

Who? Who is around when the problem occurs? Only one parent? Both parents? Are your child's friends involved? Other adults?

Why? What is the child's state of mind? How do you think he's feeling? What is the child trying to communicate? How are you, your spouse, or others responding? What are your (their) feelings? What circumstances lead up to the incident? Is there a pattern? What is expected from the child? Is this expectation realistic for his developmental stage? Have your expectations been made clear to the child? What are you and your spouse expecting from yourselves? Are there circumstances in your or your spouse's life that could be influencing this problem? Do you or your spouse have important needs of your own that aren't being met? (Appendix E is a guide for parents to use in their problem solving.)

Summarizing the major points of a discussion can be a useful follow-up for increasing the understanding of a problem. At this point you can ask the parent who voiced the concern if she feels it was addressed sufficiently. If it was not, or if the concern is particularly detailed or problematic, you may wish to arrange a separate meeting or telephone conversation to successfully analyze and help resolve it.[4] Talking with parents individually during coffee breaks also allows you an opportunity to discuss in detail those issues that are immediately important to them.

Note: Occasionally a parent will offer ideas or

---

3. In Parts II-VI, typical concerns have been analyzed in terms of underlying issues as well as the key questions to ask the particular parent and the group. In addition, Rothenberg, *PETP* book and videotapes has a detailed chapter on using this problem-solving technique. (See Pt. II, Chapter 1 in *PETP*. Also, see Bromwich (App. A) as an excellent content and process resource.)

---

4. For parents taking our 10 week, comprehensive, age-divided parenting classes, there is a *free* warm-line call available so that the instructor can complete something that wasn't finished with a parent or individualize the help. These are half-hour telephone calls by appointment. (Telephone counseling is described on p. 43.)

opinions to the group that you realize are incorrect or inappropriate. Correcting the misinformation is, of course, necessary, and it can be tactfully done by saying something like, "Although this certainly has been so for some people, I think we will generally find that . . . ."

Looking at Your Leading Skills

As you progress in your teaching, you may discover that some areas of your presentation or style need further work or refinement. Periodically asking yourself the following questions can help you to solve leadership difficulties you may encounter:

• Am I usually quiet or talkative during group meetings? Do I need to assert myself more than is natural to help the group keep its focus? Or do I need to be quieter and remember that I am a group leader, not a group member?

• How well am I listening to the parents and comprehending what they are actually saying? Do I tend to give quick solutions to problems? Do I tend to be analytical?

• Do I know how to ask meaningful questions to enable parents to find solutions to their concerns?

• How opinionated am I? Do my opinions come through easily in my communication with other people? Can I be open to other people's ideas without accepting them as my own?

• Do I offer a lot of information during a class or is it easier for me to flow with the way the group is moving, commenting in appropriate places?

• How is the balance of time for information versus feelings? Am I allowing both to happen?

Your own judgment on these questions, as well as feedback from parents at the end of a series and comments from co-leaders or other observers, should help you to focus on areas of group leadership you need to improve. (See Part I: 9 for further information on using group feedback to improve your classes and see *PETP* for more training.)

Solving Problems Concerning the Group

Even after discovering a group's characteristics and how to lead it, you should expect that some meetings will not go as well as others. There are many variables that may change and affect the group from week to week, including:

• how you feel;
• how the group feels;
• how the children are adjusting to playcare;
• what the discussion topic is.

Holidays, even extremes in weather, can have an impact on the way you and the group function.

Despite the many variables, you can use your experience and a variety of teaching techniques to provide most parents and most groups with satisfying class experiences. However, an occasional hard-to-manage situation may also arise, and it will be necessary to do something specific to prevent yourself from beginning to dislike a group member or even the group as a whole. Problems can result from disturbing individual styles or group styles.

Individual Styles

Individual styles can present a problem for the group or for the parent herself. Problems for the group include:

• the over-talkative person who monopolizes the discussion—this person needs firm limits imposed on her so she can learn from and learn to respect others;

• the person who interrupts—this person needs firm limits too;

• the person whose comments never refer to the topic at hand—this person needs to learn to think about what she says before she says it;

• the negative person who criticizes others—this person often has a poor self-image and needs to feel liked by the instructor;

• the "perfect" parent who, of course, has the "perfect" child—this person has usually not been able to face the discrepancy between expectations and reality and needs some gentle introduction to reality;

• the person who tries to assume your role—this person likes to be the expert, and needs to learn how to become a class member so she can benefit from ideas being given in the class.[5]

When parents with these characteristics unsettle a class, reminders of the "ground rules" may be helpful. Talking to these parents individually, perhaps during a coffee break, and telling them tactfully but directly about the problem is usually a successful approach.

Individual style problems can also affect the parent herself. Problems are likely to occur for:

• the parent who is "different," that is, looks, dresses, speaks, or acts differently from the other group members, is less educated, comes from a distinctly different area, or the like—this person needs to become more comfortable and involved in the group and the other parents need to be made aware of her value to the group;

• the parent who is very quiet and rarely participates—she, too, needs to be made more comfortable in the group;

• the parent who thinks in very narrow, specific, or concrete terms—this person needs help in thinking in broader terms, but her viewpoint may be basic to her personality or cognitive style, and if so, it may be impossible to change;

• the person you take a dislike to emotionally—*you* need to determine the causes for your dislike and think of the person's strengths.

Group Styles

Some types of groups can be difficult as a whole; several of them are listed below, along with techniques to help you enable the group to grow and learn.[6]

Group Style	Technique for Instructor
Very talkative but congenial.	Firm leadership is necessary in this case to allow everyone's participation.
Very talkative but critical of each other.	Try to prevent criticism, increase respect, and talk individually to members about their behavior and how it affects others.
Unusually interested in either emotional, philosophical, or concretely informational areas.	Since the group has expressed its major concerns, try to cover the preferred focus first and then strive to balance this during the series.
So diverse that group members have trouble talking about child rearing.	Emphasize the value of differences in the group and the similarities of feelings among group members.
Tense, tight; unwilling to share.	Since the members of this type of group tend to talk a lot but only at a superficial level, provide the parents with a great deal of individual support; you can encourage more sharing by using examples from your own personal experience.
Quiet.	Work with parents individually to bolster their confidence in the group; prepare to be more active and "information-oriented" than usual.

5. See Rothenberg, *PETP,* Pt. II, Ch. 12 on Managing Difficult Group Member Problems for details and practice on handling these and many other group member styles.

6. See Rothenberg, *PETP,* Pt. II., Chapter 12 and Chapter 17; also Chapters 5, 6, and 8 to develop your skills in these areas more fully.

7

INCLUDING THE CHILDREN

Providing a program in which the children of the parents in your groups participate during class times can be a particularly worthwhile component of your child-rearing program. Including the children enables their parents to observe and learn from them, and it gives you and the other parents an opportunity to get to know the children first-hand. It also gives the parents some relief from child-care responsibilities during the day; makes it easier for the parents to attend class (no need to find and pay a baby-sitter); and allows the children time to be with each other. (See Appendix H for information about children in working parent classes.)

The Children's Program

In the program described here, the playcare staff for the children is made up of experienced teachers and college student volunteers. A nominal fee is charged each family to cover the costs of the teachers and of the playcare staff's supervision by the parenting instructors. The program is divided into two parts: the Young Babies' Program *and* the Older Babies', Toddlers', and Two-Year-Olds' Playcare Program.

The Young Babies' Program

All young babies remain in the meeting room with their parents during class, unless a parent wishes a student to take her child—usually when the child is extremely fussy. During class, the babies often sleep in infant seats brought from home, but when the babies are awake they lie or play on a rug in the center of the parents' group. Many toys are available for the babies to play with, as well as a changing table with necessary supplies and a portacrib. A second room, next to the parent room, contains another changing table and more portacribs that the sitters put into use whenever a parent wishes them to. The room is near enough to the parents' room so that parents can feel comfortable about being near their babies. This baby-sitting arrangement not only allows class sessions to continue with minimal interruptions but also provides an opportunity for the parents to begin a gradual process of separation from their infants in a positive way and at a level they can tolerate. (Usually one experienced teacher/caregiver and three students are necessary for a a class of twelve babies.)

"Playcare" for Older Babies, Toddlers, and Two Year Olds

For the children of parents in the 7- to 14-months, 15- to 24-months, and 2- to 3-year-old classes, a separate play room with an adjoining playground is provided. The children in these age groups do not stay with the parents during the class. The indoor room is equipped with a large variety of toys and play equipment, a table and small chairs to use for snack (or crafts) time, a changing table with the necessary supplies, and a potty chair. A ramp leads from the play room to the playground, which is a grassy area containing a sandbox and toys, some crawl-through tunnels, and some bigger outdoor toys.

It is important that any playcare area provide both indoor and outdoor play space and that the toys and equipment suit the ages of the children who will be using them.[1] Though all your supplies for every age group may be on hand, it is most beneficial to offer only those toys and equipment the particular age group is interested in and can manipulate, and to rearrange the room so that the needs and activities of each particular group can be handled. Music boxes, toys that make a response when touched, soft toys, records, nesting toys, and stackers are probably best suited to 7- to 14-month olds; push toys, dolls, books, simple puzzles, surprise toys, records, balls, and a small slide for 15- to 24-month olds; and records, puzzles, dolls, trucks, material for imitative play (for example, hats and brooms), construction toys (for example, Lego sets), blocks, balls, a slide, and books for 2- to 3-year-olds.

Another important feature is an observation window into the play room. Watching their children when they are not with them can add a valuable dimension to your program by providing a unique learning experience for the parents. To accomplish this, a "one way" window and viewing room with a sound system would be useful. Observation in this manner enables parents to see their children from a very different—usually a less emotionally involved and more realistic—perspective. (See the section "Parents' Observation of the Children" on p. 34 for more on this area.)

Upon their arrival in the play area, children are greeted by the head teacher and the student who has been assigned to them,[2] and are helped to get involved in playing by the teacher, the student and/or the parent (parents may wish to come a few minutes early to help settle their child). At the appropriate time, parents leave for the meeting room, assisted in separating from their child by the teacher, if necessary. (See Appendix F for parents' guidelines for playcare. Also see Rothenberg, *PETP* chapter on separation, pp. 291–318.) The different age groups then follow their own particular routines.

Older Babies (7-14 months). Since the babies in this age group spend much of their time sitting or crawling, toys are set up on the floor (which is covered with a rug). Snack time occurs midway through the period and also takes place on the rug. The babies enjoy finger foods and juice or a bottle from home. Play time continues throughout the time the older babies are in the play areas. Each playcare student is responsible for caring for one or two babies, offering them specific toys, giving comfort, playing with them, changing their diapers, and seeing to their other needs.

Toddlers (15-24 months). The children in this group are comfortable using all the play equipment in both the inside and outside areas, and do so throughout the play time. In addition, the playcare staff lead games such as "Ring Around the Rosie," read stories to the children, take small groups of toddlers on walks, play records and encourage music-related activities. Each student usually feels comfortable caring for two children in this age group.

Snack time for these children is at a table, inside or outdoors. Juice, milk, and finger foods are provided and parents often bring bottles or cups with lids for their toddlers' familiarity and comfort. Children are encouraged to stay at the table while eating to prevent spills or stickiness in other parts of the room.

Two-Year-Olds (2-3 years). Like the toddlers, children in this age group can use all the available play equipment and enjoy a snack at an indoor or outdoor table. They enjoy stories and music. They also become involved in many kinds of crafts activities, such as drawing with felt-tip pens, using playdough, blowing in water with straws, tearing paper and pasting, and painting. They are able to do more climbing than the younger children and also enjoy walks. Each student is usually assigned to two or three two-year-olds.

---

1. For more detailed information on the organization of and provisions for play areas, see *Developmentally Appropriate Practice in Early Childhood Programs,* Sue Bredekemp, ed., and *Setting Up for Infant Care,* Annabelle Godwin and Lorraine Schrag—both titles available by calling (800) 424-2460—and *Toddler Day Care,* Robin Leavitt and Brenda Eheart (800) 423-8309.

2. Students are assigned to specific children for the length of the series. See the next section for details concerning the student program.

The Playcarers' (Students') Program

The desire to include children in the parenting program described here provided the impetus to find an ongoing source of people who would enjoy being with young children, take good care of them, and receive personal or academic benefits as the children received good care. Over a period of time, the most mutually beneficial relationship developed between this program and several local colleges. It is of course possible, however, to employ suitable community volunteers or members of service organizations, professional baby-sitters, retired people, or pregnant women interested in gaining experience with babies and young children if student volunteers are not available.

Finding a Playcare Staff

The plan for student involvement in this child-rearing program was developed through meetings with instructors in psychology and related courses at local colleges and universities. It was determined that course credit would be available for the students involved, to encourage their commitment to the program and to guarantee high-quality care for each child. Students work with the children depending on their class schedules; you will need to schedule parent classes in relationship to this factor if you wish to have a student staff (for example, the young baby and older baby classes in the CHC program are scheduled in the afternoon; the toddler and two-year-old classes are scheduled on the one morning each week that local college students are least likely to have classes.)

Students learn about these "field experiences" through presentations at their classes and through handouts.

When you interview students or other potential care providers for your program, you will need to explain the objectives (see Appendix F for the details) of the students' experience. Since you will be looking for loving yet responsible people to care for the children—people who will enable the parents to feel comfortable and confident that their children are being well taken care of—you will be looking for students who are capable of being:

- reliable in their attendance;
- responsible in their child care functions (including being able to take and follow instructions from you and the parents);
- alert to the safety and well-being of all the children for whom care is being provided;
- flexible in their approach to children;
- a member of a team.

You should assume that students know little about caring for infants and young children and let them know that they will have training before the first class and throughout the series. After an initial interview with each student, those who will be participating in the series are asked to meet with the two teacher/caregivers and the parenting instructor one hour before the parents' orientation session to begin training.

Training the Playcare Staff

Training is provided primarily by the two teacher/caregivers. Written handouts (see Appendix F), modeling and coaching, and verbal information are offered. Training is enriched by questions students ask. A variety of topics is generally covered, including:

- the need to treat children in a calm, gentle, supportive, and careful fashion;
- the basics of child care, such as diapering and feeding;
- how to play with children;
- how to handle conflicts;
- limit setting (no sand throwing and the like);
- ways to help parents and children separate;
- the need to be objective, rather than subjective, when talking to parents and to defer the more difficult feedback to the teacher/caregiver or parenting instructor;
- the schedule for the day, including when an observation will take place and when to provide food for the children;
- the assignment of specific children to students.

During training, it is important for the teacher/caregivers and the parenting instructor to relate your program's philosophy to the students so that they may function smoothly within it. It is also important to present information to students in a manner that will encourage their commitment to the program and make them feel they are part of a professional team providing an important service.

Providing a Playcarers' Curriculum

In this child-rearing program, students are encouraged to sharpen their observation skills by watching and reporting on the children they are caring for, and are introduced to the problem-solving techniques that the parents are learning. Instruction is given before, during, and after every class during a series. The teacher/caregivers and the parenting instructor are responsible for teaching the students about the general normal development of children in that specific age range. The individual development of the children and parents in the class—stressing each person's uniqueness—is also discussed. Through coaching, discussion, questions, shared observations, and readings, the students gain a broader grasp of child and family development (a suggested curriculum is shown in Appendix F). Below are a number of ways to increase students' awareness, have informative discussions, and meet the curriculum objectives.

• Have each student keep an ongoing diary or journal about one or two of the children in the class. Ask the students to describe them and their activities from week to week and distinguish between the two children. This activity can help students sharpen their observation skills and can give you valuable information about each child in the group.

• Have one student at a time rotate out of the play area to observe the entire group for a short period. This assignment will again aid observation skills and offer students an overview of the group, as well as enable them to watch children other than those each is caring for. With unpressured time to observe, students will be able to focus on individual differences among children.

• Give the students a topic, question, or area of development to focus on during the time they care for the children. They can rotate out of the group to observe the children and answer the relevant questions, or write up answers and/or observations just after the children leave. The topics and questions can be the basis for post-class discussion. (See Appendix F for a list of possible observations and several sample student curriculum observation forms.)

As the series progresses, students generally develop warm relationships with the children and their parents, enabling the post-class discussion to become broader and deeper in scope. As students become more aware of parent-child interactions, discussion can extend into such areas as family dynamics and philosophies and theories of parenting. It is useful to connect their course learning to that in the field experience. Students become invested in the families they work with and are pleased as the family members show growth.

Evaluating Playcarers' Skills

At the end of each series or period of time a college student has been volunteering, the teacher/caregiver and the parenting instructor who have worked with him or her evaluates the student's performance in the program. This usually entails a short written report that is sent to the student's college instructor. The report may include comments on the student's reliability, willingness, and competency, as well as other points important to the college. A more detailed method of evaluating the student's attainment of the curriculum objectives can be found in Appendix F.

Parents' Observation of the Children

Observing the children each week gives most parents in child-rearing classes a great deal of pleasure and knowledge. Watching their children function in a group setting allows parents to discuss the children's actions, acquire observational skills, gain more knowledge about the development of the age group of the children, discover differences and similarities in children and parents, and have a better understanding of their own child. Observation of both young babies and older children can be a unique part of your program.

Observation of Young Babies (one to six months)

Since little babies will most likely remain with their parents during class time in any parenting program, observation of their activities will be ongoing. If the class structure is flexible, it will be possible to interrupt a discussion or any part of the class time to watch what the babies are doing. You can try to focus observations on activities that relate to the topic under discussion, but the babies' actions may not always fit your plans; for example, the babies could be sleeping when you are discussing language development and you want to listen to them. You may decide instead to stop a class and observe the babies at any time you feel they are doing something that is appropriate to any of the topics that will be covered in the class, for example, stop to listen when a baby begins to make babbling sounds (language development) even though you're discussing nutrition. The most important part of observing, however, can be simply taking time to appreciate and enjoy the babies, pointing out a light moment or an interesting action.

During periods of observation, you can help the parents in your class to appreciate the uniqueness and individuality of each baby by avoiding any comparisons or statements that would make one parent feel her baby was "behind" the development of another baby of the same age. All babies grow at their own rate and babies often concentrate on only a few skills at any one time in their development. Parents will often note that their child is doing something he or she was unable to do at the last class, and this kind of self-comparison can be informative.

Observation of Older Babies, Toddlers, and Two- to Three-Year-Olds

The ideal way to observe children who are cared for in their own playroom is to watch them from an adjacent room that has a large one-way window and a sound system. In such a room, parents are free to observe the children and to talk, without the children or the caregivers being aware of their presence. If this kind of observation is not possible, there are several alternative ways to consider:

- Arrange playthings in the center of the parents' room and let a few of the children at a time play there for short periods of time each week and be observed;
- Have several parents observe in the children's play area each week;

- Have several parents care for the children each week and observe them during that time;
- Take the children to an outdoor setting and have all the parents observe the children at play.

No matter where the observation takes place, be sure that all the parents involved can see all the children and hear one another's comments.

If the class is to observe the children through a one-way window, you will need to decide at what point in the class this will be done. In general, when an observation of the children is made *at the beginning of a session,* parents see how their children are adjusting to the playcare situation and are usually calmed by what they see; they relax and are more likely to participate comfortably in the discussions that follow. Immediate observation, however, does not work well with a group of children who find it hard to adjust to the new routine or separate from their parents.

Observing the children *in the middle of a session* can be interesting and valuable because the children are usually quite involved with activities at this point. However, you will most likely be discussing the week's topic at that time, and the observation will disrupt the discussion. If the discussion is riveting, the group will not be ready to stop. But, if two topics are being presented during that session, observing between them can be a valuable break. (If children are observed in the parents' room, the middle of a session is the least valuable time to schedule it, since this would involve a second separation time during the class.)

When the topic has been lengthy and the observation is intended to be short, the *end of the session* is the most valuable time to observe the children. However, by the end of the class, both the children and the playcare staff are frequently tired. Although all of the observation times have certain drawbacks, the parents enjoy and value this experience at any time it occurs.

Topics for Discussion

When the parents observe their children, you may wish to tie the observation to a specific topic. The topic can be one under discussion in the class that day or relate to a wide variety of concerns, skills, and feelings. Below are a number of topics that observations could center around.

- How children separate from their parents and how their parents feel when separating from their children.
- Parents' feelings about observing and discussing their children.
- The individual style of each child in the group.
- Communication by children of their needs to caregivers.
- Learning to watch other children beside your own.
- Emotional occurrences and how they are handled by the children.
- Play interests and activity level.
- Curiosity.
- Sex differences.
- Motor development.
- Social skills.
- Language.
- Current questions of parents in the group.
- Changes of the children over the duration of the series.

During the first few classes in a series, parents may be so fascinated and intent on watching their children that it may be too difficult for them to concentrate on a single question or topic. In this case, simply let the parents observe and ask you or each other any questions that come to mind. When appropriate, you may wish to structure the observation somewhat, using one of the following techniques. It is wise to vary the structure throughout the series, since this helps to hold the parents' interest and helps them discover different ways to observe their children.

- Mention a number of things that could be observed such as activity level and play interests, and make some observations about each child. This shows parents how to observe the children and how to discuss what they are viewing.
- Pair the parents and let them talk to one another, in free discussion or in discussion guided by specific questions. Have them observe their own child and their partner's. This technique allows parents some time to get to know one another better, and it is often easier for parents to talk about their child with one person than an entire group.
- Ask a question and have each parent respond to it verbally. For example, "How does your individual style compare with that of your child?"

"What did your child do when he separated from you today? How is he now?"

Appendix F shows the details of how to conduct playcare observations with parents using various techniques and several observation topics.

Flexibility and Unpredictability in Observing Children

Most parents enjoy observing the children because they can talk and be open with each other—they can share positive and negative feelings about their child and parenting in general. On occasion, however, parents can become anxious or defensive about their child's behavior during the observation, and the observation time then will not be as enjoyable. Parents may find the child care inadequate or not to their liking, or say that their child is tired and normally does not act this way. Parents, too, can become so engrossed in watching their own child that they do not hear what the other group members are saying. When parents become angry, defensive, or withdrawn, it is often helpful to ask them what they would like to see done at that point. Depending on how they react, you would then decide to help them with their feelings about the handling of their child, help bring their child out of playcare if he or she seemed very upset or very tired, or whatever seems appropriate.[3]

Individual children, too, will have both pleasurable and difficult times during observation periods. A child feeling sad at separation may be bursting with joy three minutes later when his parent is watching through the observation window, or a happy child may being crying after a toy is pulled from his hands. Remember that children will have ups and downs and that all

---

3. For ease of communication, a phone is set up for the parenting instructor to use during observations to call the teacher/caregivers and vice-versa.

observations will not go according to plan.[4] If you are focusing on a particular topic and the child does something special, such as walking for the first time, you will obviously want to observe this instead of the planned observation.

Since the observation time can vary greatly, you need to be prepared for a variety of occurrences as well as be flexible in your approach. Observations will not always tie in with the class discussion, and the feelings of the group or behavior of the children can sometimes change your plans. If the tone or direction of the observation changes in a meaningful way, allow your plans to flow with it; if the discussion moves in a negative or valueless way, bring it back to the central topic. Demonstrating and verbalizing good observation skills will help parents to develop them as well.

4. More information on observing children can be obtained from *Observing and Recording the Behavior of Young Children* by Dorothy H. Cohen and Virginia Stern (New York: Teacher's College Press, Columbia University, 1983), *A Guide to Observing and Recording Behavior* by Warren Bentzen (Albany, N.Y.: Delmar Publishers, 1993), and *Infants, Toddlers, and Caregivers* by Janet Gonzalez-Mena and Dianne Eyer (Mountain View, CA: Mayfield Publishing Co., 1989).

8

CLASSES FOR FATHERS

If the child-rearing classes you decide on are focused primarily on mothers, you may wish to include a meeting for fathers sometime[1] during each series. Fathers need a chance to discuss their child-rearing concerns just as mothers do. Holding a class for them will give them an opportunity to share their fathering experiences with others in their same situation and to explore the question of "how to be a good father."

Pre-Class Preparation

You will most likely need to do a number of things before holding the fathers' class: do some refresher reading on "being a father,"[2] think through an outline of areas to cover, and perhaps send a letter home to the fathers a week or so in advance to determine the areas they would like to discuss. (You may want to suggest some topics.)

The most convenient time to hold a fathers' class is usually on a weekend morning. Expect this class to last the same length of time as your usual classes. The meeting room and playcare facilities should remain as they are organized for the mothers' classes. Relevant books and copies of handouts from the series can be displayed for the men to look at.

_____
1. It is helpful to know the mothers and children before holding the fathers' class. This often takes three or four weeks; the fathers' class could be held anytime from that point on.

2. See p. 40 for some suggested readings.

A Class Format

The most beneficial format for a fathers' class is likely to be a general, flexible one that allows you to structure the time but deal with the fathers' interests and concerns as they arise. After you greet and give name tags to each participant and after the children are settled in the playcare room (the young babies stay with the fathers), the following items might be included in your agenda:

1. _An explanation of the parenting program—why it was started and how it's organized._ This introduction enables fathers to understand that the program represents an attempt to put together information about children that is often haphazardly obtained by new parents. It also tells them that the class series provides a support group where new parents can share ideas and talk with each other about problems, solutions, and feelings.

2. _An explanation of how the topics were chosen for the mothers' class, i.e., how the series outline was formed._ The fathers will learn that each class series is organized around topics of interest to the mothers in that group. They may be interested to know which topics their wives have chosen to discuss.

3. _Introductions._ You can introduce yourself in a little more detail at this time; tell about your background and the ages of your children, etc. Have the fathers introduce themselves by telling

their names and their children's names and ages. It is also useful at this time to let the fathers know some of your expectations. For example, "We hope you will try to share your experiences as openly as possible. We know that all of us have more we can learn as parents and that there are no Super-Dads or Super-Moms. We are going to try to learn from each other today rather than impress each other with how 'great' we and our children are." (Since it seems to be harder for men to share openly at first than it is for women, you may have to find a method to use to remind the fathers of your expectations as the class proceeds.) You could also enable the fathers to have their opportunity to 'boast' during the introductions by also asking them to tell about something that really pleases them about themselves and/or their children.

4. *A discussion of the fathers' concerns.*[3] To begin a discussion, you might start with "Since the purpose of this session is to help you with some of the child-rearing issues you're confronting, I'd like to ask each of you to think for a minute about what you'd like to learn more about and discuss with the other fathers. Then let's go around our group and find out what's on your mind." At the appropriate time, ask one of the fathers to start, and then continue around the group until each man's interests have been discussed with the group. Keep the discussion on one topic and be sure one father is finished before going on to the next. Some of the questions fathers often ask are:

- What do other men do when they're with their children? What does a good father do?
- What changes have occurred in other couples' social lives now that they're parents?
- What changes are occurring in other couples' marriages because of their new roles?
- How do different families share child care and household chores?
- How do other men feel about being fathers?
- When and how do other fathers discipline and set limits for their children?

- When fathers work long hours, how can they spend quality time with their children and also have time for themselves?
- What do other fathers expect from their child? Are their expectations in line with the behavior appropriate to the child's age?
- What kinds of differences are occurring between husbands and wives in their approaches to child rearing?
- What changes in the family can be expected as a couple has more children?
- Why do children behave the way they do?
- How do things look from a child's point of view?

Letting the fathers decide the areas to be discussed seems to help them talk about what is really on their minds. Although the men generally do want to hear what you know about children's behavior and development and parent-child relationships, avoid being the only one to offer information. *Encourage the fathers to respond to and ask questions of each other.* If fathers ask you specific questions, you may feel it is more appropriate to turn them back to the group at least some of the time, asking, "How do the rest of you feel about this issue?" This approach encourages the fathers to learn from each other, something especially important here, and to work out their own individual approaches to parenting. In addition, a female instructor's approaches to problems under discussion may not be appropriate or plausible for the men.

5. *A coffee break.* If the discussion begins to move in a non-productive or confusing direction, a coffee break can be helpful before bringing the conversation back to a useful focus. Breaks provide fathers with further opportunity to relax and get to know each other.

6. *Observation of the children.* If the class is for fathers of young babies, the children will be in the room and the observations can be ongoing and flexible. (See Part I: 7 for information on observing young babies in mothers' classes.) For the other classes, a specific time should be planned for the fathers to observe the children, using the same facilities as those used for the mothers' classes. Observing at the beginning of the class gives fathers who are uncomfortable about leaving their child with the sitters time to watch the children adjust to separation. It also gives them a chance to discuss with each other how it feels to separate. This early observation can be very effec-

---

3. The men often feel more comfortable during the discussion when there is a printed outline and other material to refer to; you can use some of the handouts that have been prepared for the mothers' classes, especially those on children's development and play.

tive for "breaking the ice" by allowing each father to introduce and describe his child. Observing at the end of the class gives the fathers a chance to first complete their discussion and then end the class by watching the children, who have adjusted by then to the setting.

During the observation, ask each father to point out his child and comment on what he observes. The resulting discussion during the observation time and later can then be based on questions and comments the father have about the children. Encourage the fathers to comment and question freely. If they don't have many questions, you can direct some of the following to the group:

- What signs of comfort or discomfort do you see in the children?
- How occupied or unoccupied are the children?
- What interests do they show in their play?
- To what extent are the children involved with each other and with adults?

In addition to the questions you or the fathers address to the group, you can also provide a brief description of norms in several areas, such as language, social, and motor development. This kind of information enables the fathers to see how the children are similar and individually different.[4] It also gives them a broader perspective on behavior and a better understanding of how children progress through the various stages of development.

7. *A summarization of the major topics discussed.* Conclude the session by commenting on why the areas that were discussed are valuable to think about as the men work to define their own styles of parenting. This can help to put the discussion into perspective. You may wish to distribute pertinent handouts or refer the fathers to appropriate sections of child-rearing books.[5] It is also possible that the fathers would like to meet again as a group.

---

4. Fathers may be bothered if their child behaves differently than the other children (e.g., cries more, doesn't eat his snack, etc.). You should be alert to this so you can help the father with something troubling him.

5. Suggested books for fathers to read are: *On Becoming a Family* by T. Berry Brazelton; *Birth of a Father* by Martin Greenberg; *Fathers and Babies,* also *Fathers and Toddlers* by Jean Marzollo; *The Gift of Fatherhood* by Aaron Hass; and *Finding Time for Fathering* by Mitch and Susan Golant. Additional references can be found in Part II:4 (p. 90). Part VI:6 (p. 379) and 7 (p. 392) and Appendix H.

Developing and Determining the Direction of Future Fathers' Classes

Separate classes for fathers were started in the program described here after groups were initially offered to mothers and fathers together. The couples' groups were discontinued because they did not adequately support or meet the needs of both parents. During the classes, the mothers did not develop relationships with each other since each husband and wife tended to relate primarily to each other and usually one of them spoke for both to the group. The women also avoided delving into their practical, everyday concerns about child rearing because they felt such concerns would not be of interest to their husbands. The men tended to talk about theoretical and future-oriented kinds of child-rearing concerns and these were concerns that were not of immediate interest to the women. When it was seen that the couples' program was not workable, classes directed toward women were established and a one-time or, if requested, two-time class for fathers was incorporated into each series.

If fathers in your area seem interested in fathers' series, it is possible to develop other kinds of child-rearing classes to involve them in. An ongoing fathers' series in which they could discuss their concerns, perhaps meeting twice a month or as frequently as desired could be developed. The group could be led by a female or a male parenting instructor.

At this time, we find that there is still value for mothers and fathers to take parenting classes separately sometimes and at other times together. Brief topic-focused series tend to work well for couples to learn together; also, when couples share child rearing responsibilities more evenly, taking any-length series together tends to be very successful for the parents. Moms and dads frequently take our full-time working parent series together.

Brief series could focus on limit-setting, raising difficult children, sibling relationships, changes in marriages with children.[6]

---

6. See "Husband-Wife Relationships," Part VI:7 of this manual for details on devoting a class to this topic.

9

CONCLUDING A SERIES AND PROVIDING FURTHER SUPPORT

When a series draws to an end, parents may have a great deal on their minds. You will need to evaluate their reactions to the series as well as discuss their feelings and suggest ways for them to receive continued support.

Evaluating Reactions to the Series

It is helpful to determine how well you worked with a particular group and what the positive and negative areas were for each parent. This information can be obtained by using evaluation forms. Parents' responses can then be used as a guide to develop future series. For example, you can discover if there is a particular area of your teaching style that needs work (this will be evident if you receive many comments suggesting that the instructor talked too much and didn't allow enough time for group discussion *or* allowed a few parents to monopolize the discussion) or if you need to learn the content of some areas better (this will be indicated by comments that imply specific questions were not answered adequately or not covered). You will also hear if parents were not pleased with the time the classes were held (nap schedules were interrupted), if husbands should have been more involved, and other individual remarks. Be aware that evaluations can be excellent reasons for making changes in your classes, but before you make any changes, be sure that many parents

would benefit from them. (If no negative consensus occurs in your evaluation, there probably was no major flaw in the presentation of the series and you are to be congratulated. It usually takes some time and experience, however, before this happens.)

Evaluation forms can be completed by the parents at home *before* the last class or at some point during the last class session. If you ask the group members to complete the forms during class time, do not engage them in a discussion of how the series went *before* they fill out the forms; avoiding previous discussion will encourage honest and uninfluenced replies. It is generally not useful to have parents take the forms home after the last session and plan to mail them back; few are actually returned that way.

There are a number of evaluation forms that can suit your purposes, and naturally you should develop or select the one you feel will be most useful. Appendix G shows a suggested form that measures overall satisfaction with the course and also asks participants specific questions about how the series went for them.

Continuing Group Support

Discussing Further Classes

At the end of a series, parents are often interested in learning about child-rearing classes that will be offered in the future, how to enroll in them, and when they will be offered. It is very important to listen to their questions and have specific answers when possible. Usually parents find child-rearing classes helpful, and once they have attended some, they realize that the classes meet an important need. If you will be unable to provide later classes within your program, it will be important to determine where such classes will be offered or find people who are interested in developing them.

Reunions

You can help a group plan a reunion by suggesting a number of formats for it: an informal get-together, a question and answer period, or a time to discuss a topic that was not covered in class. Reunions are generally held at a group member's home, with or without the instructor present, and occur a few weeks or up to a month after the series ends. Whether or not the class decides on a simple gathering or a discussion period, homework assignments that were turned in during the series can be returned to the parents during the reunion. Most parents enjoy keeping their work and think of it as something like a diary.

Encouraging Continuation Groups

It is hard for many parents to separate from a "caring" group. You will need to talk with the group about their feelings and help them determine if they would like to keep meeting after the series ends. You can make suggestions, such as who should lead the group (members probably should rotate), what the focus for discussion could be (help them to think of a few), where to meet (probably in homes on a rotating basis), and what time of day to gather (perhaps evenings without children or the same time the classes have been meeting). This process can help continued meetings become a reality and lessen the group's feelings of abandonment. Groups that worked well with each other and with the parenting instructor are offered the opportunity to continue with the instructor, usually on a once-a-month basis. The topic is planned ahead but the structure is more informal; a fee is charged.

Continuing Individual Support

Parents will benefit greatly from the information and support your program provides, but after a series ends they may still need occasional advice or assistance. In the program described here, this support has been made available in two ways: continuation groups as already mentioned and child-rearing counseling—usually in-person.

In-person Child-Rearing Counseling

Individualized help is provided in child-rearing counseling for parents who are finding themselves concerned about aspects of their child's behavior, their relationship with their child, or relationships within the family unit. These conferences deal with concerns that are considered to be normal or typical child-rearing problems. Specific concerns can include parents being upset and guilty over their inability to feel as happy as they expected to in their new role; not really knowing what to do with a new baby beyond basic physical care; not knowing how to play with a child or what a baby or young child should be learning; problems in setting limits; understanding and handling a child who "whines"; being bothered by a child's way of playing with others; wondering if a child is too passive or too aggressive, and what to do about it; deciding if a child is ready for preschool; problems in changing expectations or understanding of a child as he grows older; and differences in child-rearing approach between husbands and wives. Each session is tailored to the style of the family involved, and is an ideal step between a psychoeducational group and psychotherapy. A fee is charged for these sessions.

Parents who come to counseling are seen by a member of the child-rearing staff. During a conference, the staff member helps the parents to identify the problems and begin to look at some of the reasons behind their concerns. They also try to help parents understand what their child's behavior means and develop some changes and solutions for their concerns. Parents are seen for one or several sessions, and, if it would be useful, a staff member makes a home or school visit where direct observation of difficulties is possible and realistic solutions for the particular family or teacher can be devised.

If the parenting educator/counselor feels a particular parent needs more assistance than she can give, she recommends a number of other sources the parent can call (for example, pediatricians for medical problems, psychologists or psychiatrists for emotional problems, speech and language therapists for speech problems, marriage counselors for marriage problems).

Some of the ways that a good list of local referral sources can be developed are:

1. Networking with other parent educators and early childhood educators to learn which specialists they use and why they use them, and to share our own sources and impressions.
2. Talking to the clinical directors of private or public mental health agencies.
3. Talking with pediatricians.
4. Going to community talks given by professionals in the area.
5. Using our own experiences as parents as well as those of our friends.

Parenting educators need to know *when* to refer a family for additional help, *how* to refer them, and *who* to refer them to. In Rothenberg, *PETP,* pp. 231–242 cover these questions in the chapter on Making Referrals.

Telephone Warm-line/Counseling Service

The warm-line or telephone counseling service offered by this parenting program provides advice for child-rearing problems that a family with young children often experiences. The service is provided at no cost only for parents currently taking a comprehensive parenting class series. For all other parents, there is a fee for the telephone counseling just as for the in-person counseling.[1]

Parents of newborn to first-grade-age children are also the focus of this service. When a parent needs more limited help with a problem (e.g., a baby's or young child's poor sleeping habits, limit-setting problems, handling the adjustment to a new baby, or just a general need for support), she calls the office coordinator and asks for a counselor. Counselors are assigned on the basis of whether they know the family, the age group they specialize in, and the nature of the problem. This is true for the in-person counseling as well. The assigned instructor returns the call to make an appointment. Phone counseling appointments are usually in the evening when the children are most likely asleep and the parents can concentrate better. Calls typically take about half an hour.

Staff members use information given in Parts II-VI of this manual and their general knowledge and experience to help parents with their concerns. They question the parents (appropriate questions can also be found in Parts II-VI) to pinpoint their concerns. Information on children from birth to age 5 years can be found in *PETP,* Pt. III. Instructors may also suggest that a parent meet with her for an in-person child-rearing conference.

---

1. Unless a family is known to the parent educator/counselor, parents are encouraged to come in-person to the counseling session.

10

AN INTRODUCTION TO PARTS TWO THROUGH SIX:

THE FORMAT FOR PREPARING AND PRESENTING CLASS TOPICS

In the following pages, information is presented that will enable you to provide your parenting groups with an in-depth understanding of child rearing. The pages are divided into five parts: Part II, the major topics that are of importance to parents (especially first-time parents) of one- to six-month-olds; Part III, the topics for parents of 7- to 14-month-olds; Part IV, the topics for parents of 15- to 24-month-olds; Part V, the topics for parents of 2- to 3-year-olds; and Part VI, those more general topics that are of interest to parents of children anywhere between one month and three years. Each topic in each age range provides important background information on the subject as well as the materials and strategies to use while teaching about the topic. The topics in Parts II through V appear in the order in which they are generally covered in Children's Health Council classes. In addition, many of the topics in Part VI are always included in each of the four age classes.[1] Below you will find the format in which the information about each topic is presented and an explanation of each area's importance.

background/preparation

Goals to Work Toward in Presenting This Topic

This section offers an explanation of the importance of the subject. It describes the goals to be accomplished during the coverage of the topic, enabling you to focus your thoughts on specific points as you study and prepare to lead the discussion.

---

1. Much additional content information on the topics of temperament, separation, limit-setting, sleep, sibling relations, and husband-wife relationships focusing on birth to five years of age can be found in Rothenberg, *Parentmaking Educators Training Program* (PETP) book and videotapes. These include additional homework, handouts, and lectures.

Typical Parental Interests and Concerns About This Topic

Here are listed, in parents' own words, the main issues that most parents have questions about.[2] Knowing these major concerns will help to guide you toward the areas you will need to learn about.

Areas of Information You Will Need to Learn About to Teach This Topic

This section outlines the information you need to know to lead a valuable discussion. For example, before leading a discussion on nutrition, you will need to learn the following basic information: foods that make up a balanced diet, normal patterns of weight gain in children, ways to introduce new foods, and so on. You will need to be completely familiar with the subheadings in this section because the parents in your groups will expect you to have both perspective and knowledge about the topic.

Family Dynamics—What This Topic Means Psychologically to Parent and Child

There is constant interplay among family members; a child's behavior affects his parents just as the parent's behavior influences the child. Looking at the topic from both the child's and the parent's point of view will take the discussion to a new level and encourage greater understanding of parent-child interactions.

Sample Concern of Parents

In this section, a very common concern that many parents have is described. The format, ex-

plained in detail below, is designed to help you guide group members through a discussion of the concern in a way that will help them learn to problem solve on their own.

Concern

The *Concern* stated is a composite of the most typical concerns many parents have on this subject and is written in the way parents usually phrase their questions about it.

Critical Issues

Critical Issues highlights the points that are involved in the statement of the concern, showing that questions and concerns often have several parts. Breaking down the concern to its elements enables you to know which areas you must deal with to help the parent resolve the problem. (In an actual group situation you should identify the issues not only from the concern as stated, but also from any background information you know about the parent stating the concern.)

Key Questions

Key Questions contains suggestions for the kinds of questions you can use to elicit more detailed information from the parent. This information is necessary to enable parents to get a more complete understanding of the problem at hand. (Some questions are designed to involve the whole group so that discussion and in-depth thinking are encouraged.) It is important to choose appropriate questions and to phrase them so that they give understanding and support to the parent.

---

2. The issues presented throughout Parts II-VI have been distilled from concerns mothers have voiced during the last ten years of classes at the Children's Health Council; many of the concerns, however, are those of fathers as well.

Readings and Other Resources

Included in this section are a number of books, articles, and videotapes that can provide you with additional background information for the development and greater understanding of the topic. Asterisks indicate those resources that are highly recommended. Page numbers for books are inclusive; only the beginning page of a magazine article is indicated.

teaching/presentation

Homework

The focus of the homework for the particular topic, to be given out the week before the topic will be discussed, is described in this section. Working on the material will help parents prepare their thoughts for a more productive discussion the following week. It is helpful for both parents to do the homework. The homework assignment typically used by the instructors in this program is found in this section. (Others can be found in Rothenberg, *PETP*.)

Practical Suggestions or Strategies for Teaching This Topic

Presented in this section are practical ideas for preparing to teach the topic. The unusual or special aspects of the particular topic are focused on since your awareness of them can contribute to the success of the discussion.

Mini-lecture and Lead-off Questions for Discussion

This section contains a sample lecture and presentation of the topic, and mentions some of the attitudes and information about the topic that are helpful for parents to gain. Each mini-lecture will need to be adapted to your own style and wording, however, since you will probably not be comfortable using another person's words. Specific ways to begin a discussion on the topic and particular ideas on how to keep a discussion going are also included. (Mini-lectures are printed in boldface.)

Additional Information for Parents

Some of the information and attitudes you'd like parents to grasp will be presented in your lecture. Much of the information you'd like them to know, however, will come from you and the group members during the discussion. This section offers you more of the information parents should be learning.

Handouts

Printed handouts are a way to extend or summarize information presented in a mini-lecture and discussion. The specific purpose of the handouts that accompany topics is explained in this section. The handouts are reprinted at the conclusion of each topic section, and are generally empirical and practical rather than theoretical. (Additional handouts can be found in *PETP*.)

After you read about and study each topic for your particular age group, also read about the topic in the preceding age range. This will give you a good picture of the focus and development of the subject as it relates to younger children, and can help you determine how to tie in the topic to where the children currently are. Depending on the stage the children are in and on the information (or concerns) the parents have, particular handouts from the younger age may be appropriate.

As part of a primary interest in the prevention of later problems, some of the handouts used in these classes provide screening devices and charts or information concerning norms, particularly in developmental areas. These handouts are included to make parents aware of expectations in particular areas and to enable them to be alert for signs of irregular growth or behavior.

Note: You will find it important to read some of the resources mentioned in each topic and to continue your own child and family observations. Without doing some of your own "spade" work, you will not have the depth of understanding to really be that "knowledgeable" person the parents need.

part two

TEACHING ABOUT YOUNG BABIES

(1–6 months)

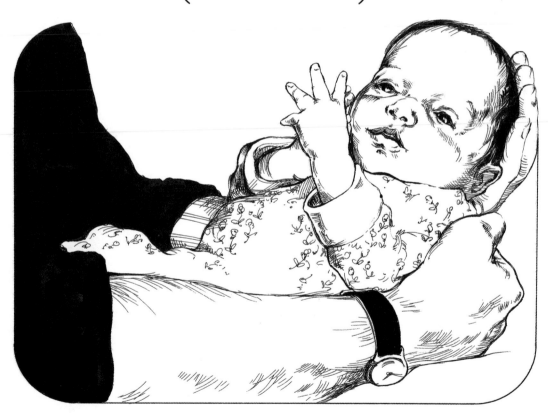

1

CRYING AND SCHEDULES

background/preparation

Goals to Work Toward in Presenting This Topic

Many parents say crying and schedules are two of their biggest concerns. Listening to a baby cry can be incredibly painful, and getting used to the complete unpredictability of life with a new baby can be difficult as well.

The goals to work toward on this topic are: (1) to help parents understand and gain perspective on the fact that all babies fuss and cry and on why they cry; (2) to help parents become aware that many babies are unpredictable, some more, some less; (3) to help parents cope with the difficulties of listening to their baby cry; (4) to inform parents of the broad range of normal sleeping and eating patterns in babies and gain some ideas about ways to handle crying and fussing, structure sleeping and eating patterns, and balance a whole day.

Typical Parental Interests and Concerns About This Topic

Crying

1. Jenny cries a lot—several hours every evening.
We can't find anything to help her stop and it's awful to listen to her. Is something wrong?
2. Since David is sleeping on his back, he startles and then wakes up and cries. I know it's best to have him on his back for now, but I worry that this is causing a sleep problem.
3. Our five-month-old is becoming fussier and often seems either frustrated or bored. Just a few weeks ago our days were relatively peaceful. What happened?
4. One minute Katie is happy and the next she's screaming. Why does she change moods so quickly?
5. No matter what time we have dinner, James fusses so we can never eat in peace.
6. I've heard that I should be able to distinguish cries and tell which ones mean hunger, fatigue, and so on. They all sound the same to me.
7. Is it possible to overfeed my baby if I nurse her every time she cries?
8. How long should I let Joshua cry before he goes to sleep?

Schedules

1. How much should I allow Daniel's schedule to decide what I do during the day? Is it necessary to always be consistent?
2. How long should we let the baby sleep in our bedroom?
3. My baby sleeps too much (or too little).

4. Our baby doesn't fall asleep easily, so we rock him. Then he wakes up when we put him down. I'm getting tired of all this holding and rocking.

5. Should I wake Brooke to feed her?

6. Erin wakes up at 5:00 a.m. and won't go back to sleep. Help!

7. Our baby was sleeping through the night for several weeks. Then this week he's started waking up wanting to be fed.

8. I worry that I'm not concerned enough about our schedule. I just stay flexible, but there must be something wrong since I feel tongue-tied when someone asks about our schedule.

9. I'll return to work when Matthew is 3 months old. Is there any way I can make sure he sleeps through the night by that time?

10. I can't figure out when my baby should eat or take naps.

Areas of Information You Will Need to Learn About to Teach This Topic[1]

- Reasons why babies cry and how the reasons change as babies grow.
- Routines for comforting babies and coping with periods of crying.
- Common patterns of sleeping, eating, and crying and ways these "schedules" change as babies grow.
- Ways to establish routines and structure for a day with an infant.

Family Dynamics—What This Topic Means Psychologically to Parent and Child

---

Parents are often very confused about crying and schedules because their baby's crying is so painful to hear and because their daily schedules are often so unpredictable. Crying seems to demand a response but responding to constant needs can be terribly tiring. Demands and con-

fused days can make the early months with a child very trying.

New parents also receive (often unsolicited) daily advice from others about crying and schedules. The ideas are often conflicting: 'Don't pick the baby up every time she cries or you'll spoil her"; "Be sure to pick the baby up when she cries so she feels secure and loved"; "Let the baby tell you when she's tired or hungry since she can set her own schedule"; "Be sure to establish a consistent schedule and don't feed her more than every 3 to 4 hours." The advice can be confusing or unsettling. In the face of people who are sure they are communicating the right thing to do, a new parent can feel inadequate and incompetent about her own ideas regarding crying and schedules.

Often parents look to the baby to decide what he wants or needs but this often doesn't work since the baby doesn't know himself. Babies at this age need guidance to learn the patterns, the language, the customs of their world. Without this guidance the baby can become demanding and come to expect constant parental time and attention. Babies can learn either to mostly amuse themselves or to mostly be entertained; that they can get attention at any hour of the night or that parents are regularly available only during the day; that they need to find ways to comfort themselves or that their parents will provide comfort at their slightest whimper. Babies need a great deal of warmth, comfort, love, and attention in the early months, but they also need the guidance of a flexible routine.

Sample Concern of Parents

Crying Concern	*Critical Issues*
Our six-week-old baby cries for several hours every evening. Nothing seems to stop her. We can't stand to hear her cry and we worry that something is wrong, especially since the crying seems to be lasting longer and longer.	—Crying more frequent than parents anticipated. —Parents are unable to calm baby. —Crying upsets and worries them. —Crying is getting worse.

---

1. Much of this information, for this topic and all others in this part, can be found in the "Additional Information for Parents" sections of the topics.

Key Questions

1. At what time do the crying spells start?
2. How long do they last?
3. Are there other fussy times during the day? How do you deal with these?
4. What is the baby eating, how often does she eat, and how much does she weigh?
5. What patterns have you noticed in the crying? Have these changed in the last few weeks?
6. What do you do about crying? What do you feel about what you've tried?

For the group

7. How have you handled periods of crying?
8. What's going on inside of you that concerns you about giving too much or too little to your child?

Schedules Concern	*Critical Issues*
When I went to visit a friend yesterday, the baby fell asleep in the car. So, instead of having his usual two-hour nap, he only slept 10 minutes. As a result he was really cranky and fussy last night. I feel I should be consistent and let him sleep in his own bed during regular naps, but then I'm cooped up in the house all day.	—Parent's concern about meshing baby's schedule with activities she wants to do. —Parent's attempt to find a workable schedule. —Parent's confusion over planning a day with her baby.

Key Questions

1. What's bothering you about your day?
2. What kinds of days have been most satisfactory for you in terms of patterns and schedules? Do you know why?
3. How many times a day do you go out with your baby?

4. What kind of daily structure feels right to you?
5. Think of the balance of a whole day. Does your baby have time by himself as well as with you? Does he have time outside the house as well as inside? Do you have some kind of time to yourself, to be with friends and with your spouse? What areas do you feel need more planning?

Readings and Other Resources[2]

*Brazelton, T. Berry, *Infants and Mothers* (New York: Dell Publishing Co., 1983).

Cuthbertson, Joanne, and Schevill, Susan, *Helping Your Child Sleep Through the Night* (New York: Doubleday, 1985).

*Kitzinger, Sheila, *The Crying Baby*, New York: Viking Penguin, 1990).

*Leach, Penelope, *Your Baby and Child* (Westminster, Md.: Alfred A. Knopf, 1989).

*Kitzinger, Sheila, *The Crying Baby*, New York: Viking Penguin, 1990).

Sears, William and Sears, Martha, *The Baby Book* (Boston, Mass.: Little, Brown & Co., 1993)—(*Dr. Sears' guidance on crying and schedules reflects a more child-centered approach than most other resources. Offers support to parents who are committed to this philosophy*).

American Academy of Pediatrics, "Positioning and SIDS" (policy statement on sleep position for infants). To order, send a self-addressed stamped envelope with a request for publication RE9254 to: American Academy of Pediatrics, 141 Northwest Point Blvd., P.O. Box 927, Elk Grove, Ill. 60009-0927 or call (708) 228-5005.

2. Readings marked with an * are the most highly recommended. The work of Rose Bromwich is highly recommended for information on the topics in this part and is cited in Appendix A. Articles from *Working Mother, Parents, Parenting*, and *American Baby* are often good sources of current information on the topics in this part.

teaching/presentation

Homework

The homework assignment "Baby's Current Patterns" helps parents become more aware of their baby's daily patterns. Keeping a simple journal like this can help parents see patterns that might otherwise not be obvious. "Baby's Crying" helps parents think more broadly about the reasons for crying and ways they can cope with it

BABY'S CURRENT PATTERNS

(1–6 months)

An important method for you to learn to use to help you understand more about your baby's patterns and behavior is making notes about his or her day.

1. Use this paper to record the times your baby ate and slept during a three-day period. You can also record awake times, outings, or anything else you would like to keep track of. For example:

7:10	wakes up
7:20 - 7:45	nursed
7:45 - 9:20	awake (had bath, played, had fussy time, etc.)
9:20 - 10:15	nap

Parent's name _____ Date _____ Child's age _____

BABY'S CRYING

(1–6 months)

1. There are any number of reasons for babies to cry. What seem to be some of the reasons for your baby's fussing?

2. A situation: It is 3:30 p.m. Your baby has been crying for the last 20 minutes. The crying is getting louder. You have tried everything you could think of. How do you feel?

   What could you do?

3. What specific concerns do you have about your own baby's periods of crying or fussing?

Parent's name _____ Date _____ Child's age _____

Practical Suggestions or Strategies for Teaching This Topic

• The topics of crying and schedules work well together since in young babies crying is frequently related to patterns of sleeping and eating. The two topics generally can be included in one class session with time enough to deal with each separately and to discuss their overlapping points.

• Since parents' concerns about crying and schedules generally occur most frequently between their child's birth and four months of age, the discussion works well as the first in the class series. The discussion is often long, and questions about the topic may arise in other classes during the series.

Mini-lecture and Lead-off Questions for Discussion

Sample Mini-lecture on Crying

If parents had a guaranteed solution to the problems of crying and schedules, we'd all be a good deal more relaxed and confident. Though there are no prescribed answers for the concerns related to these two areas, there is a lot of information available to help us understand them. Let's talk first about crying and then go on to schedules and patterns.

Several current authors have written some strict commandments about crying: "Never ignore a baby's crying" and "Never let him cry it out." As parents, we know we need to try to respond to a baby's crying so he doesn't feel panicked and isolated. We also know that if our baby's needs are met at the right times, babies begin to find their world predictable and caring, both of which are important. Premature efforts to develop a baby's powers of self-reliance can result in a baby's demandingness or apathy.

All babies in their first 3 to 4 months of life fuss or cry even without apparent physical cause. The amount of crying varies from baby to baby but the reported average is be-

tween 1 and 3 hours a day. As babies become more "settled" —around the 3rd or 4th month of life, the amount of time spent crying decreases.

The intensity of babies' crying also varies among individual babies and may provide some insight into a given baby's style of expressing himself. Some babies are more sensitive than others and less tolerant of stimuli. A warm, loving environment that responds to a baby's needs and sensitivities can help minimize baby's crying but some crying is inevitable regardless of how a parent responds. Most experienced parents and professionals feel there are no serious ill effects if a baby is not picked up each time he cries. It is the loving and overall, responsiveness of the environment that they feel is more important.

At this point you can ask the group what they've found to be some of the reasons their babies cry. Discuss their answers, and then talk about any of the following reasons that haven't been mentioned.

Hunger. Many parents automatically assume that every time their baby cries he's hungry; it's often hard to tell a hunger cry from other cries. Parents need to know that it usually takes at least two or three hours for a baby's stomach to empty, and if a baby cries before this time it can be for other reasons. Parents need not offer food automatically each time their child cries.

Fatigue. Fatigue is a very common cause of crying during the early months. An overtired baby, for whatever reason, becomes cranky and irritable. Sometimes nothing works to stop the crying—not feeding, rocking, a diaper change, or holding. Dr. T. Berry Brazelton in his book *Infants and Mothers* feels an infant's tendency to cry for certain periods (often at certain times of the day or night) is strong evidence that the baby is expressing some inner need to cry or let off tension. Also, the tension of a tired family can contribute to the crying of a tired infant at the end of a day. A fussy period may be what enables a baby to sleep for a long period afterward. Parents can try calming methods first—feeding, changing, cuddling, rocking, a pacifier—but if the attempts seem only to lengthen the crying, it's time to let the baby alone. Brazelton's solution is to have the parents let their baby cry for 20 minutes, then pick him up, love him, burp him, and put him back down to cry again.

A change from wakefulness to sleep or vice versa. Picking up a child has an alerting effect on her so it's really hard for a sleepy, crying child to sleep after being picked up. As painful as it is for parents, letting their baby cry for a few minutes before sleep can be crucial.

Loneliness. Babies can cry because they're lonely and want physical closeness. They may miss the warmth, closeness, and rhythm of the womb.

Too cold or too warm. Too much cold or warmth can result in crying. A baby's back should feel comfortably warm, not cold or sweaty.

Pain or discomfort. Causes of discomfort can be gas, air bubbles, irritated skin, or wet diapers. (Most babies don't care about this last possibility unless they have a diaper rash that's irritated by a wet diaper or when a wet diaper makes them feel cold.)

No cause. Parents can look for a cause for crying, but shouldn't feel badly if they can't pin it down or soothe their baby as quickly or as easily as they expected. Letting a baby cry when a reason for it can't be found is fine, as long as the baby has something to look at, to listen to, or touch; it gives the baby a chance to figure out how to get comfortable and depend on himself a little. Nothing may be wrong; perhaps just an off day such as adults have. Psychologists also tell us that a "bad" day of crying and fussing may indicate tension before a thrust into a new developmental stage. The quiet, peaceful days are usually those when a baby is operating on a consistent level and not responding to any kind of change.

Lead-offs for Crying

• Crying was one of the hardest things for me to cope with. The crying felt like someone was stabbing me and often my husband came home to find me crying along with the baby. What are some of the feelings you've experienced when you've had to listen to crying?
• How to handle fussiness in a baby greatly depends on what the baby's typical behavior is like (even though most books usually cite one kind of behavior and fail to mention the wide variety of babies). What have some of you done

about crying? How do you feel about what you've tried?
• What causes you to pick up a crying baby?
• Do you have any theories about crying that influence your handling of it?
• What patterns have you noticed in your baby's crying? Have these changed in the last few weeks?

Sample Mini-lecture on Schedules

In thinking about schedules, your first reaction probably is "What schedule?" Mention an example from your own experience such as the one that follows. **One of the hardest things for me to get used to when I first became a parent was the complete unpredictability of my life with a new baby. It would have been a luxury to know when I'd have time to take a shower and brush my teeth. During our first months with the baby, it never failed but that her schedule would change as soon as I thought I could predict it.**

I have some information to share with you about general sleeping and eating patterns of young babies. But I want you to remember that whenever I talk about the age at which things tend to occur, I'm only talking about averages and showing you the direction in which your babies are heading. If I say that something is listed as occurring at six months, it may occur earlier or not until much later for your particular baby. And even with some guidelines for patterns of eating and sleeping, no baby is truly on a consistent schedule until around six months, and then usually only if he's been guided into one.

Now is a good time to distribute the handout "Average Sleep Patterns in Babies" and ask the parents to follow along as you expand on its information.

Babies usually sleep from five to six hours at a stretch at two months of age and ten or more hours some time between four and six months. As the length of each sleeping period increases, babies begin to take fewer naps; at two months they may sleep five hours spread out over three naps while at four to six months they may sleep two to four hours spread out over two naps. While

the newborn may have a total of six to eight sleep periods a day, by six months these have decreased to about three or four. With each increasing month, you will need to think more about his awake time rather than just the sleeping and feeding of a newborn.

Young babies' feeding patterns are similar to their sleep patterns in that newborns have many more feedings a day than do six-month-olds. During the first month, babies tend to eat about six to ten times a day with two of those feedings generally occurring during the night. By the second month, babies begin to need closer to six feedings a day. In the third month they eat five times a day and can generally wait a little longer for each feeding. By four months they are down to about four feedings a day, including perhaps some solids one or two times a day. At six months they usually eat three or four times a day, beginning to aim toward a three-meals-a-day schedule.

As far as differences between nursing and bottle feeding go, babies who are bottle fed tend to sleep longer than nursing babies; breast milk is more easily digested than formulas and the stomach therefore empties faster. However, some nursing babies sleep through earlier than others if their mothers are nursing fewer times (in other words, about the same number of times a day as bottle-fed babies) and the babies are getting larger amounts at each feeding, enabling them to go longer between nursings.

Most parents start out with a complete "demand" pattern in which they meet their baby's need at the time he expresses it. Later, some babies pattern themselves so that their schedule fits fairly well with the rest of their family's, but if this does not happen, parents may have to try to adjust their baby's schedule so their own needs can also be met. This isn't a negative manipulation of a baby but is a way to balance each day so that everyone's needs are taken care of. Even if a baby is placed on a very rigid schedule with precise times for feeding, sleeping, bathing, playing, and so on—something that isn't very common these days—he will do very well as long as he is in a warm, loving environment.

Some parents, particularly mothers, spend so much time with their baby during his first six months that he begins to demand a continuance of the same amount of attention, even at just a few months of age. It is very helpful if you can establish a comfortable pattern—for you and your baby—before this happens, somewhere between two and five months, that will be comfortable throughout your child's young years. Remember, though, as you establish a schedule, that it should be a very flexible one in the beginning, one that can be interrupted by teething, illness, house guests, and many other things.

Lead-offs for Schedules

• Discussing schedules is important because it has something to do with the whole of your relationship with your baby as well as with the atmosphere in your home. Since there is such a wide range of patterns among babies, let's find out how things proceed in each of your homes. Then, let's take as much time as we need to help each other with any sleeping, eating, and awake-time patterning problems.

Additional Information for Parents

Crying

• A certain amount of crying is inevitable for all babies between three and 12 weeks of age. The peak period for length of crying per day is around six weeks.
• There's no easy solution to crying, but it helps to know that during the first three months it's a channel for releasing tension and getting exercise. The end of the crying periods tends to come when the baby can do other things, such as coo, babble, and smile.
• Some parents have found modern devices such as "white noise" machines, crib attachments that vibrate or rock the crib, infant seats that also allow for bouncing or rocking, mechanical baby swings, etc. to be helpful in soothing their young baby. Soothing music (lullaby tapes, etc.) and holding and rocking a baby eases tension for parent *and* child.
• Parents can make their children have certain needs. For example, if they feed their baby every

time she cries, she'll want to be fed whenever she cries.

• Parents often do more for a child (especially a first child) than the child needs, and then the child isn't as able to cope herself. Some child-centered theories imply that if children are given all they want, they'll become less demanding. This doesn't seem to work in practice. Instead, babies become usually more demanding and parents become very resentful.

• The age and development of a child has a great deal to do with how a parent should respond to crying.

Schedules

• The concern for their child's present and future welfare often means that parents must make demands and impose restrictions on him when he is able to handle them, even though these demands may not coincide with what he wants. Parents need to balance their baby's needs with those of other family members.

• The whole day doesn't have to revolve around a baby. Parents may bear the brunt of fussiness if regular naps are interrupted, but that may be far better than feeling resentful or frustrated about being cooped up.

• Parents often don't impose any structure or schedule on their child, thinking the baby knows what he wants. He doesn't, and may be guided into conforming with a reasonable schedule after the first few months.

• It's easy for new parents to be sufficiently overwhelmed by their new roles and responsibilities that they aren't aware of their baby's sleeping schedule unless they write it down for at least a 24-hour period. This may help them get oriented.

• If parents keep their house very quiet for their newborn, she may later be disturbed by any noise at all. Babies are usually quite adaptive, and if they are exposed to noise in the beginning, they will learn to sleep through it. The exposure can move them early on toward the pattern the parents want.

• Sleeping through the night is one of the most common problems parents face in the second half of their child's first year. Sleeping through may never have been established or the child may have gotten sick, had discomfort from teething,

traveled, or in some way had his nighttime pattern disrupted. Babies will not go back to their former pattern or begin to sleep through the night unless their wakefulness is not reinforced, and the longer one waits to do this, the worse the problem gets. Thus, it is helpful for parents to encourage their baby during his first half year to sleep through the night. Even when a baby is a few months old, parents usually find that if they put their baby to bed at a reasonable hour, follow a soothing bedtime routine, and put their baby down drowsy yet still awake, he'll soon learn to sleep through the night. For additional information on sleep schedules and guidance, see Rothenberg, *PETP,* pp. 384–410).

• More pediatricians are recommending a side-lying or on-their-back (supine) sleep position for most newborns as recent research reveals a reduction in overall SIDS rates when babies are put down to sleep in this way. A very young baby may startle and awaken more in the supine position than if it were placed on its stomach, but this tendency decreases rapidly and rarely causes a lasting problem.

• Putting a baby down for sleep while he's drowsy may be followed by a period of fussing or crying. It's hard for parents to ignore this fussiness and a baby's learning to fall asleep on its own may be prevented if the parent intervenes. Encouraging a parent to "give it a few minutes" before going in may be just enough time for baby to do what she needs in order to fall asleep.

• Babies being guided to "sleep through" will often cry angrily in response to this new way of doing things. How quickly they learn involves many factors—age (6 mos and up), adaptability, consistency of parents, etc., but most babies learn to sleep through by the third or fourth night of guidance.

• If a baby is 6 mos. or older and is still waking at night for comfort or feeding, it can bring parents to "their limit." At this point parents may seek help to guide them and their baby toward wakeless nights (i.e., read books on sleep, seek a parent educator or doctor's advice) or they may decide that bringing baby to their own bed is the best decision for their family. Regardless of what course parents may take, success and overall satisfaction relies on both parents agreeing on and supporting each other through their chosen course of action.

Handouts

The handout for this topic, "Average Sleep Patterns in Babies," shows the direction of sleep changes as babies grow during the first year. In addition, there are several useful handouts from Rothenberg, *PETP:* "Average Sleep Needs/Typical Sleep Requirements in Childhood," page 395; "Guiding Sleep Patterns of 4-14 Month-Olds," page 397; "Helping Your Child Learn to Fall Asleep" R. Ferber M.D., pg. 399; and "Mom's Exhausted, Baby Won't Sleep," T. B. Brazelton, M.D., pgs. 406–408. Useful articles on the topic of crying, and sleep and schedules appear frequently in issues of Parents' Magazine, Working Mother, Parenting Magazine, etc.

AVERAGE SLEEP PATTERNS IN BABIES

(1–6 months)

Newborn

—The baby sleeps an average of 15 hours per day with a range of 9-18 hours.

—He may have 6-8 sleep periods during 24 hours.

—He usually sleeps the longest stretch during the day at first, waking often at night.

—The books say babies "sleep from feeding to feeding" (about every 2-4 hours) but this discounts all the crying, burping, changing, bathing, etc., that goes on in the meantime.

—Babies get the amount of sleep they need (wide variation).

Sometime within the next one to two months

—The baby sleeps for longer stretches and less frequently. He's awake more during the day. This trend continues until about 6 months.

—He can sleep as long as 5 or 6 hours at a stretch (at night, hopefully).

—He may sleep 5 hours in 3 naps during the day.

Sometime within the next two to three months

—The baby begins to sleep about 10 hours at night.

—Sleep patterns become much more predictable, and the baby can go to sleep on his own without being rocked, walked, etc.

Sometime within the next one to four months

—Around this time the baby's sleep decreases to 2 naps per day (usually one of the naps is 1 hour long and the other 2 hours).

—He begins to sleep 11-12 hours per night (uninterrupted).

About one year

—The baby typically sleeps about 13½ hours per day (range is from 9-18 hours), most of that uninterrupted sleep at night. He's beginning to move from 2 naps per day to one.

—When the baby's nap time is changing, or when the baby is teething or sick, his nap schedule or his whole sleeping schedule may be very erratic.

2

NUTRITION

background/preparation

Goals to Work Toward in Presenting This Topic

The feeding relationship that is established in a child's first year is important because the psychological patterns that result will influence a child's lifetime eating habits. A baby's nutrition also affects his mental and physical growth. Discussion of the whole range of nutritional issues with particular emphasis on what typically happens during the first year can help parents feel more confident with the way they are managing the feeding of their baby.

The goals for this topic are: (1) to help parents gain up-to-date information on nutrition for babies; (2) to help parents become more aware of the direction their feeding patterns are taking and of any feeding problems during the first year; (3) to give parents the opportunity to think about their own attitudes toward food; and (4) to give parents support and encouragement in their efforts in food-related areas.

Typical Parental Interests and Concerns About This Topic

1. How often should I feed my four-month-old baby?

2. Even after I've just fed Sarah, she tries to get her fingers in her mouth and seems hungry again. How can I know if she's hungry? Why else would she be frantically trying to suck her fingers?

3. My baby seems to be a little underweight. Should I be concerned?

4. My baby seems chubby to me. I'm concerned about what I've heard about fat cells. Should I do something about his weight?

5. When should I give Amanda milk when she's eating solids too—before or after or in between solids?

6. Is it OK to use commercial baby foods or should I make all my baby's food at home?

7. Is there any point in avoiding additives such as sugar and salt during the first year since my baby will be eating what adults eat after that?

8. When can I start using cow's milk instead of formula?

9. Do I need to sterilize bottles?

10. My baby refuses to take a bottle. Since I'm nursing, I can't get away. Help! What do I do?

11. I have a problem with nursing (cracked nipples, low milk supply, weaning, etc.).

12. How do foods that I eat affect my breast milk?

13. How often should I give a bottle if I'm nursing so I'm sure my baby will continue to accept one? Should I use breast milk or formula?

14. How do I freeze breast milk?

15. If I'm breast-feeding, how long should I wait before starting solids?

16. What does an allergic reaction to food look like?
17. Should I give my baby vitamins and/or fluoride?
18. Should I use iron-fortified formula or give my baby iron drops?
19. How should I handle teething discomfort?
20. Should I worry if my baby sucks her thumb?

Areas of Information You Will Need to Learn About to Teach This Topic[1]

Breast-feeding.
— How to handle common problems.
— Use of supplemental bottles.
— Community resources to aid nursing mothers.
Formula feeding.
— Kinds of formula that are good to use.
— When to switch to regular milk.
Introducing solids.
— Age to start.
— How to start introducing the cup and spoon.
— Kinds and amounts of foods to use first.
Menu planning.
— Schedules for feeding and ways these change as the baby grows.
— How to work toward offering a balanced diet.
— Patterns of weight gain during the first three years of life and how these influence the baby's appetite.
— Use of growth charts.
Sucking needs of babies.
— Pacifier.
— Thumb sucking.
Teething.
— How to handle a baby's reaction to new teeth.
— Care of teeth.
Allergies.

---

1. Much of the information in this chapter has been provided by JoAnn Hattner, R.D.C.S., M.P.H., Nutritionist, Pediatrics, Stanford University Medical Center, Stanford, California.

Family Dynamics—What This Topic Means Psychologically to Parent and Child

For most parents, the way their baby eats is closely tied to their feelings about how well they are raising their baby. Food becomes even more important to them when so much emphasis is placed on getting feeding established and on having their child achieve a certain weight gain. Parents receive a great deal of advice about feeding from friends and their pediatrician, so much so that they can have difficulty deciding what's best for their baby and themselves.

For babies, learning to eat (liquids, then solids) is sometimes difficult, but in general eating itself is pleasurable and comforting, providing a variety of new experiences. The exception is when feeding time becomes a battleground—when parents assume or expect certain behavior (for example, the baby will keep sucking until he's full) and the baby acts in a different way (keeps falling asleep or turning away during feeding, even though he had seemed to be very hungry).

Sample Concern of Parents

Concern	Critical Issues
I don't know how often I should feed my four-month-old baby. It seems like she wants to eat all the time— often every two hours—but I feel like her feedings should be more scheduled and less frequent.	—Parent's need for information on how feeding schedules change as a child grows. —Need to listen to inner feelings and attitudes. —Parent needs to think about long-term feeding pattern.

Key Questions

1. How often does your baby eat in a typical day? Is she waking at night for feedings?
2. What is your baby eating and how much is she eating? (Nursing mothers, of course, can't tell

how much milk their child is getting.) Has she started solids?

3. When your baby cries, what kinds of things do you do to try to comfort her?

4. What does your pediatrician say about your baby's pattern of weight gain?

5. What are your feelings about your baby's eating patterns now?

Readings and Other Resources

Eisenberg, Arlene, and Murckoff, H. E., and Hathaway, S. E., *What to Expect the First Year,* (New York: Workman Publishing, 1991).

Huggins, Kathleen, *The Nursing Mother's Companion* (Boston: Harvard Common Press, 1991).

*Kitzinger, Sheila, *Breastfeeding Your Baby* (Westminster, Md.: Alfred S. Knopf, 1989).

*Leach, Penelope, *Your Baby and Child* (Westminster, Md.: Alfred A. Knopf, 1989), pp. 117–137.

Renfrew, Mary, Fischer, Chloe, and Arms, Suzanne, *Bestfeeding: Getting Breastfeeding Right* (Berkeley, Cal.: Ten Speed Press/Celestial Arts, 1989).

*Satter, Ellyn, *Child of Mine: Feeding With Love and Good Sense,* (Menlo Park, Cal.: Bull Publishing, 1991).

Satter, Ellyn, *Feeding With Love and Good Sense* (videotape—a useful tool for classes; dramatic examples of the "feeding relationship," supplements information from Satter's book, *Child of Mine*), (Menlo Park, Cal.: Bull Publishing, 1989).

Further information on nutrition can be obtained by:

- Contacting a pediatric nutritionist at a local medical center for relevant information.
- Obtaining "Healthy Start" brochure by sending a self-addressed stamped envelope to:
  American Academy of Pediatrics
  Dept. C, ("Healthy Start" brochure)
  P.O. Box 927, Elk Grove, Ill. 60009-0927
- Contacting your local dairy council for a catalog of nutrition-education material or phone (800) 426-8271 (the National Dairy Council).

---

teaching/presentation

Homework

The homework for this topic helps parents to evaluate their present feeding situation and think about questions they want to raise in the group.

Practical Suggestions or Strategies for Teaching This Topic

• Parents have many specific questions about feeding and nutrition. They will be better able to have those questions answered if you present a brief overview of the topic first, letting them know which areas of nutrition will be discussed. Then ask the group to bring up their concerns during the appropriate discussion.

• Concerns about nutrition-related subjects, particularly breast- or bottle-feeding and the introduction of solids, will come up again and again throughout the series, often when you ask parents how the past week has gone for them. Let parents know that this is fine and that they should not worry if they don't think of all their nutrition questions during the scheduled meeting or if they find they have questions when their child progresses to a new phase.

• Try to be sensitive and supportive to both breast- and bottle-feeding parents, pointing out the positive points of both types of feedings.

• The week before the class on nutrition, you may wish to ask parents to bring in for that class any food implements they are using, such as a spoon, grinder, cup, or food warmer. These can be discussed and shared.

• Try to prepare yourself well on the topic of breast-feeding, and have on hand the phone numbers of local breast-feeding support groups.

FEEDING AND NUTRITION

(1–6 months)

Recalling the last few times you fed your baby, please answer the following questions:

1. How do the feedings seem to be going for you? For your baby?

2. What does your baby do to let you know he/she is hungry?

3. In thinking about such things as techniques of breast- or bottle-feeding, use of pacifiers, and introducing solid foods, what sorts of questions come to mind on these or related issues?

Parent's name _____ Date _____ Child's age _____

Mini-lecture and Lead-off Questions for Discussion

In our discussion of nutrition today, I'll be covering the following topics: milk, weight gain, solids, allergies, using a spoon and cup, thumb sucking and pacifiers, and other topics you'd like to discuss. I have information on each of the subjects so please ask related questions while we're on the particular topic. (Before you begin talking, you may wish to pass out the handout "Feeding and Nutrition" (p. 68) so the parents can refer to it during the presentation.

Milk[2]

Milk is the primary food of the young baby during his first year. If he is not yet on solids, he'll drink about 1½ to 2½ ounces of milk per pound of body weight. Breast- or formula-feeding as opposed to using cow's milk is recommended through the whole first year because cow's milk is allergenic for many babies. Although formulas have a cow's milk base, they are heat treated and less allergenic for babies. Your pediatrician may suggest a soy-based formula for your baby if there's a history of cow's milk protein allergy in your family.

There are several kinds of milk available. If you'll look on p. 3 of your handout, we can discuss each kind. Continue on after you have compared the various milks. You may be wondering what to expect in terms of your baby's growth. Of course, every baby will develop in her own way, but on the average many babies will grow half again their length at birth by the end of the first year. They will also double their birth weight around four-five months and triple it by the time they're a year old. They gain the most during the first half of the first year—about two pounds a month during the first three months, and one pound a month during the next three months.

For the next six months, a gain of three-quarters to one pound a month is typical. Around a year a baby's appetite decreases. On the average she'll gain only about five or six pounds during the entire second year and grow less than five inches.

How much your baby grows in weight, height, and head circumference will be charted by your pediatrician on "normal growth" charts as part of regular medical check-ups. You can ask to see these charts and have your pediatrician explain how this visual summary of height and weight relates to your own baby's growth.

Your own attitude, plus your baby's appetite, should be taken into account when you make the decision about when to start feeding solids. We're talking about introducing solids now not to urge you to start but simply to give you information for when you need it. Here are a few guidelines that can help you decide:

• If your baby is drinking about 35 to 40 ounces of formula a day and is still hungry, it's a good time to start solids.
• The weight of your baby and his calorie needs ought to be evaluated in the decision to introduce solids. Solids can add a variety of nutrient sources to your baby's diet. Begin solids when your baby has developed head control, can sit up, lean forward in anticipation, and pull back when satisfied.
• Several growth spurts occur during the period of time a baby nurses. You can increase your milk supply and probably meet the greater demand by nursing your baby more frequently for a day or two. But, if your child seems hungry in spite of more frequent nursings (after he's about four months), you may wish to introduce solids.
• By the fifth or sixth month, a baby's store of iron begins to be depleted. Iron can be found in meats and iron-fortified baby cereals.
• From a nutritional standpoint, there's no urgency to introduce solids during the first few months of life. Depending upon the baby's growth, you may want to begin solids around four to six months for bottle-fed babies, while breast-fed babies may wait until five to six months. Adding solids to a bottle-fed baby's diet, however, is important because formula

2. When milk is mentioned in reference to a baby's first year, it is meant to stand for either breast milk or formula.

may not contain all the trace elements that breast milk contains.

How to introduce solids is another consideration. One method is described on p. 4 of your handout, but you can check with your pediatrician and find a pattern that's good for you and your baby. Here are a few points on introducing solids and meal planning and preparation:

• At first, solids are just experiences and tastes, and most parents have little interest in how much their baby eats. Sometime between six and ten months, however, you may find yourself working toward a three-meals-a-day schedule in which your child is beginning to have less milk, and solids are being substituted for some of the milk.
• The purpose of introducing solids is to help a child get used to different tastes, to the spoon, to begin to add a variety of nutrients to his meals, and eventually to be able to eat balanced meals of baby food and then balanced meals of regular food. Parents usually introduce cereals, fruits, vegetables, meats, cottage cheese, eggs, juices, and so on so their child will be able to eat many kinds of food.
• As your child moves toward three meals a day, he may still want small snacks, which should be given about 1½ to 2 hours before a meal. Page 5 of your handout gives the breakfast, lunch, and dinner servings that make up a balanced diet. Since each baby uses food differently, it's impossible to give exact amounts. The figures given are only guidelines. The emphasis should be on balanced variety, not on amount, except if your baby doesn't give clear signals about when he's had enough.
• Page 4 of your handout discusses the pros and cons of commercial versus home-prepared foods. Fresh foods have the highest nutritive value but most commercially prepared baby foods are now made without excessive salt, sugar, or additives.
• Gradually introduce lumpier foods to your baby's diet. If babies get too used to strained baby foods (even "junior" foods are fairly smooth), they'll refuse more textured foods. Babies don't need teeth to chew, so they can

eat tiny pieces of cut-up "adult" foods by eight months. You can offer pieces of such finger foods as teething biscuits, graham crackers, toast, bananas, and cheese.

Allergies

Each time you introduce a new food, it's a good idea to wait about three days before adding another new food. This allows you time to tell if your child is reacting to the food and makes it easier to pinpoint the cause of any reaction. If there's a history of allergies in your family, you'll probably want to watch closely for signs of allergy in your child. If you suspect an allergy, take your child to your pediatrician for diagnosis. If an allergy exists, you'll be able to work out a plan with the doctor to handle it. Here are a few symptoms that *may* indicate an allergy:

• Colic or gas pain, loud constant crying and pulling legs up.
• Rash or hives. This may be an allergic reaction to a specific food that can be eliminated for a month or so. A light dusting with cornstarch will relieve any itching. Often a baby of one or two months develops a pimply rash that looks like acne. This isn't a food allergy but is caused by clogged pores from changes in the baby's oil glands.
• Diarrhea, or loose, watery bowel movements (not the normal breast-fed baby's stools, which are usually loose), can be a sign of teething, an oncoming illness, or a reaction to a specific food. Frothy, foul-smelling bowel movements containing undigested food may also be a reaction to a specific food.
• Constipation may be caused when certain solid foods are introduced; however, babies often strain and fuss with bowel movements and adults sometimes interpet this straining as constipation when it's a normal method of evacuation as muscles develop. If constipation persists, it could be a sign of allergy.
• Vomiting, or forceful throwing up of a large amount of food, may be caused by illness, may be a reaction to a certain food, or a sign that a baby is eating too much.

If you're concerned about allergies, delay introducing foods such as egg whites, wheat, beef, citrus fruits, and, of course, cow's milk until your baby's first birthday. Good foods to start with are yellow vegetables, potatoes, pears, bananas, lamb, rice cereal, and oat cereal.

Using a Spoon

Because of the tongue thrust needed to swallow liquids, babies under 4 months don't take solids well from a spoon. When you begin to use a spoon, you may have to put it on the side or on the back of your child's tongue. You may find that your baby sucks food off the spoon at first or sucks your knuckle in between bites until she learns to swallow.

Babies may reach out to grab the spoon as they learn to connect it with feeding. A good solution is to feed with two spoons so your baby has one to hold as well. You may find yourself playing the "Spoon Trade" game since your baby will probably want the one you're using. Steps in the process of learning to use a spoon begin early, but your child will probably be about a year and a half before she can dip the spoon, take it to her mouth, and get most of the food into her mouth.

Using a Cup

A child is usually about 15 months old before she is able to lift a cup and drink from it; it doesn't seem to matter if she starts using a cup at four months or eight months. If your breast-fed baby refuses to take a bottle, however, you may want to start having her use a cup early on so she can have some milk during a meal while you're away.

When she starts, a baby can only take sips from a cup while someone else holds it. But as she learns to hold it, you'll need to expect lots of spills. A good place for your child to practice drinking is in the bathtub.

Miscellaneous Ideas

These are a number of miscellaneous points that may help you with your feeding:

• Feed your baby at his own rate and look for cues that show he's had enough (some babies don't give such cues with solids but some close their mouth, turn their head away, spit food, or play with it). Feed him in a comfortable place, such as in an infant seat or your lap. When your baby is seven to eight months (or whenever he can sit up well), you can start feeding him in a highchair. Non-skid strips on the seat prevent sliding and a strap or a bar between the baby's legs can keep him from falling out.

• Serve foods separately so each flavor can be enjoyed. Try to keep yourself from thinking that your baby needs to eat a certain amount; focus instead on balance and variety of foods.

• You may want to feed your baby on a modified demand feeding schedule. This entails keeping track of the intervals at which your baby seems to be hungry and planning to feed him around those times. As your baby gets older, you can gradually lengthen the intervals. Your baby will get used to the regularity and you will be able to plan your day more easily.

• By about a year, eating is not so central to children and can be put in perspective as it is for adults. Babies can wait longer for their meals and sleeping patterns no longer depend on how much babies eat.

• Babies can learn to use food as a tension reducer if parents feed them each time they fuss. Parents may then have a difficult time later helping children find ways to comfort themselves.

• Look at how you feed. Are you sitting down and relaxed or are you up and hopping around?

• Most sucking occurs during the first three months of life. The need to suck gradually decreases and is often nearly over by 15 to 18 months. Some oral babies, however, still suck their thumb, fingers, or knuckles at that age and older, but suck less as the need diminishes. At two years, about 40% to 50% of all children suck their thumbs, but usually only during times of fatigue or frustration.[3]

---

3. You may wish to refer to pp. 64–67 in *Touchpoints* by T. Berry Brazelton or pp. 204–206 in *What to Expect the First Year* or pp. 114–115 in *What to Expect the Toddler Years* both by Eisenberg et al. for more information on thumb sucking.

Additional Information for Parents

• The time between feedings increases as babies get older, but this doesn't always happen automatically. If babies continue to be fed every two hours, they get used to eating frequent, small meals; however, if the time between feedings is gradually increased to every four hours, babies learn to eat enough to last until the next meal.

• Parents often get so caught up in the urgency of a newborn's need to eat that they don't notice when the baby is able to wait longer and eat less frequently.

• Parents should check to be sure they're not using food to comfort their baby or to stop his crying. Putting together a list of other things to try before offering food would be helpful.

• A parent's feelings influence the feeding pattern she establishes for her baby. She should be sure her schedule is comfortable and as structured or as flexible as she needs.

• Parents of a baby who is being nursed should be encouraged to acquaint the baby with a supplementary bottle between 4 and 6 weeks of age. The regular use of two or three bottles a week helps the baby stay familiar with the bottle. Sometimes parents find that when they decide to use a bottle, their baby refuses it. Some ideas to try are:

— Have the father give the bottle; the baby may not accept another kind of feeding style from her mother.

— Enlist the help of someone who has recent experience with bottle feeding to feed the baby away from his parents a few times. Nursing mothers and their husbands usually feel so positive about breast-feeding that they may have negative feelings about the bottle despite their desire for occasional freedom from nursing. Babies pick up these ambivalent feelings and may react by refusing the bottle.

— Mothers can try different nipples and different milks (breast milk or formula).

— Some babies completely refuse to take a bottle. Parents can try a cup instead or give cereal and applesauce for one feeding to enable the mother to miss an occasional nursing.

Some of the above choices may have negative connotations that have to be weighed against the parents' desire for some time away from their child.

Handouts

One lengthy handout, "Feeding and Nutrition," has been developed for this topic. The information covers feeding patterns, introduction and preparation of solid foods, menu planning, feeding abilities, and weaning. You may also wish to hand out pp. 64–67 in *Touchpoints* by T. Berry Brazelton or pp. 204–206 in *What to Expect the First Year* or pp. 114–115 in *What to Expect the Toddler Years* both by Eisenberg et al. for more information on thumb sucking.

FEEDING AND NUTRITION*

(1–6 months)

CHANGES IN FEEDING PATTERNS

Newborns	—Most newborns need about 8-10 feedings a day including 2 feedings during during the night. Especially with breast-fed babies, time lapses between feedings during a baby's wakeful time may sometimes be quite short (1 to 2 hours from the beginning of one feeding to the beginning of the next) but longer (4 to 6 hours) during restful times.
Within another month or two	—Most bottle-fed babies are on a 3 to 4-hour schedule with about 5 feedings in 24 hours. A breast-fed baby may not be comfortable with a 4-hour feeding pattern until his second or third month. The interval between feedings gradually lengthens as babies grow bigger and older, but individual babies differ widely in how soon they can comfortably settle in to a regular pattern.
Within another month or two	—By this time, many babies have given up the 2 a.m. feeding. There is wide variation, however, in the age at which babies begin sleeping through the night—anywhere from 6 weeks to 6 months, depending upon the baby's individual temperament and on the parents' feelings about either providing the night feedings or encouraging the baby to sleep through. Babies can wait longer for a feeding since they have learned to expect it and to trust it will be provided.
Within another month or two	—Most babies move to about 4 feedings in 24 hours (5-hour intervals). They may give up the 10 p.m. feeding. They are more distractable at feedings.
Somewhere between 6 and 10 months	—Most babies move toward a three-meal-per-day pattern.

From 8 to 10 months on, your baby's daily menu could include the following servings (an average serving for an eight-month-old is 2-3 tablespoons):

2 protein foods (including 3 egg yolks/week)
2-3 cereal, grain
3-4 fruit/vegetable (including 1 juice, 1 dark green or yellow vegetable)
5-6 milk (approximately 28-32 oz. of breast milk or formula)

*This handout has been reprinted with permission of and/or consultation from JoAnn Hattner, R.D.C.S., M.P.H., Nutritionist, Pediatrics, Stanford University Medical Center, Stanford, California.

Your baby could have a mid-morning and mid-afternoon snack of juice, milk, crackers, or the like. The choice of snack depends on what he is able to eat safely.

During this first year, your baby will progress from milk to pureed foods, chopped foods, and, by a year, table foods. He will be able to sit in his highchair at about seven months of age. Until then, try feeding your baby in an infant seat or on your lap.

DEVELOPMENTAL FEEDING ABILITIES**

Birth to 1 month
Rooting reflex
Sucking reflex
Swallowing reflex
Tearless hunger cry

1-2 months
Looks at mother's face

3-4 months
Sucking—swallowing in sequence
Head erect
Mouth poises for nipple
Some ability to wait for food

4-5 months
Tongue projects after spoon, nipple
    removed
Good head control

5-6 months
Brings hand to mouth
Ejects food with tongue
Strong hand-to-mouth response as spoon
    or nipple removed
Pats bottle or breast
Closes in on bottle with hands

6-6½ months
Grasps and draws bottle to mouth (re-
    leases when nipple in mouth)
Grasps spoon, cup rim
Smacking noises with lips
Sucks liquid from cup

6½-7½ months
Sits leaning forward
Pulls food off spoon with lips
Keeps lips closed while chewing
Lingers over food for companionship
Vocalizes eagerness during feeding
    preparations
Brings toys to mouth, bites and explores

7-9 months
Feeds self cracker
Bites, chews toy
Reaches toward dish
Holds feeding bottle
Acquiring sitting balance

** Adapted from B. Umbarger, The Children's Hospital Research Foundation.

FEEDING AND NUTRITION (continued)

COMPARISON OF MILKS

Food	Cal./Oz.	% of Calories			Supplementation and Additional Information
		Protein	Carbo-hydrate	Fat	
Breast	22	6	38	56	Varies. May give Vitamin D, fluoride.
Evaporated & Sugar	20	14	49	37	Usually contains Vitamin D, may give Vitamin C, fluoride. Not used unless child is on solids and preferably not in first six months.
Formula (Cow's milk base)	20	10-12	42	46	Fluoride. Formulas are closest to breast milk in percentages of proteins, fats, and carbohydrates, and therefore are recommended if breast milk isn't used.
Cow—whole	20	21	29	50	Fortified milks contain Vitamin D, may give Vitamin C, fluoride. Cow's milk may cause allergy and isn't recommended for use during the baby's first year. Only whole milk is recommended until age 2.
—low-fat	16	26	38	36	
—extra light	15	36	50	15	
—skim (non-fat)	11	40	57	3	
Goat	23	20	27	60	Vitamins D and C, fluoride, and folic acid.
Soy	20	16	40	44	Fluoride. For use with vegetarian diets.

RECOMMENDED DAILY DIETARY ALLOWANCES*

	Calories	Protein	Vitamin D	Vitamin C	Iron
0-6 months	108/kg. 50/lb.	2.1/kg.	400 IU	30 mg.	6 mg.
6 months - l year	98/kg. 43/lb.	1.5/kg.	400 IU	35 mg.	10 mg

*Food and Nutrition Board, National Academy of Sciences, 1989.

WEIGHT GAIN GUIDE

Birth-3 mo.—Approximately 2 lbs./mo, 1 oz./day
4-6 mo.—Approximately 1 lb./mo, ½ oz./day
Double birth weight 4-5 mo.
Triple by 1 year.

Solids

1. It is not necessary to introduce solids to a nursing baby until he is around 5-6 months; this is when his own iron supply begins to be depleted.
2. Questions are often raised about the pros and cons of commercially prepared and home-prepared baby foods. Here is some information about this subject.

- Food prepared from fresh ingredients has the highest nutritive value but is often higher in calories than frozen or canned foods because of its density; it may need to be diluted.
- Many commercially prepared baby foods are now made without excessive sugars or salts.

(Sugars and salt occur naturally in fruits, vegetables, and other basic foods and do not need to be added.) Some contain modified starches to preserve consistency but these aren't needed for a baby's nutrition. Since different brands and kinds of food vary in the number of additives, read the labels to pick the foods with fewest unnecessary additions. The plainer the commercial food, the higher its nutritive value, for example, plain meat and plain vegetables are more nutritious than the "combination" jars. Combination dinners and desserts are not especially recommended for babies because of their high starch and sugar content.

- Using commercially prepared adult food (such as canned peas) and mashing or blending it for a baby may be less expensive than prepared baby foods, but the food value is usually the same. Again, check the labels.

3. The following chart is *one* means of introducing solids to your baby. Bear in mind that foods should be introduced one at a time and in small amounts every few days so that an allergic reaction can easily be attributed to a single food.

RECOMMENDED PATTERN OF INTRODUCTION OF SOLID FOOD

Age	Food	Instructions
4-6 months (or by 6 months)	Iron-fortified baby cereal	Start with 1-2 t. *rice* cereal mixed with water or formula. Increase amount gradually. Other baby cereals may be added later.
6-8 months	Strained or pureed vegetables and fruits	Start with 1-2 t. and increase gradually. Introduce *one* new fruit *or* vegetable every 2-4 days (watch for allergic reaction). Avoid orange juice because of high allergic incidence. First foods should be cooked since raw foods are more difficult to digest and are allergenic.

FEEDING AND NUTRITION (continued)

RECOMMENDED PATTERN OF INTRODUCTION OF SOLID FOOD (continued)

Age	Food	Instructions
8-10 months	Strained or pureed meats, beans, or egg yolks	Start with 2-3 t. and increase gradually. Avoid vegetable-meat combination dinners because of small protein content. Avoid egg white as it may cause allergic reaction.
8 months	Mashed potatoes, soups, zwieback,	Start with 1-2 t.
12 months	Orange juice,	1-2 t. diluted with water. Increase gradually.
	whole eggs, cottage cheese, small curd.	Start with ¼ cooked egg and increase gradually.

MENU PLANNING GUIDE

Age	Breakfast	(Snack)	Lunch	Snack	Dinner
5-6 months	Cereal Milk (formula or breast milk)		Milk		Cereal Milk
6-8 months	Cereal Fruit Milk		Fruit Milk (Vegetable)		Cereal or Protein Fruit Milk
8-10 months	Cereal (or breakfast finger foods) Fruit Egg yolk (not daily) Milk		Fruit Vegetable cut up, chopped table foods Protein Milk		Protein Starch Fruit or Vegetable Milk

PARENTMAKING: A Practical Handbook for Teaching Parent Classes About Babies and Toddlers by B. Annye Rothenberg, Ph.D., et al.
© 1995 Banster Press, P.O. Box 7326, Menlo Park, CA 94026. Can copy for parent classes if this notice is included in full.

MENU PLANNING GUIDE (continued)

Age	Breakfast	(Snack)	Lunch	Snack	Dinner
10-12 months (begin using cut-up, chopped table foods)	Cereal (or breakfast finger foods) Fruit Egg yolk (not daily) Milk		Protein Starch Fruit Vegetable Milk		Protein Starch: mashed potato, pasta Fruit, Vegetable Milk

Directions for Preparing Infant Foods

1. Scrub all equipment with hot water and soap and rinse well.
2. Prepare food for cooking, remove skin, pits, and seeds. Bring to full boil and cook until tender, or steam in vegetable steamer until tender.
3. If using blender, add one cupful of food at a time with ¼-cup liquid (cooking liquid). With meats, more liquid may be needed to allow blades to operate.
4. You may use a food grinder, food mill, or a regular strainer; the most important thing is that the particle size of the food is initially very small. You can ensure this by putting a small amount of the food in the palm of your hand. Rub it with your finger; if any large particles can be felt, process or strain food again.
5. If you prepare more than one day's feedings at a time, you may freeze food by putting small amounts in small plastic bags in the freezer. You can also freeze in an ice cube tray, each cube being about one serving.
6. To reheat: Place food in a glass custard cup or jar and heat until very hot in a covered pan of boiling water. Cool before feeding.

RECIPES

Meats

½ cup cubed, cooked meat
2 tablespoons liquid

Place ingredients in blender and mix at high speed until smooth. *Note:* For liquid, use cooking liquid, water, or formula.

Vegetables

½ cup freshly cooked vegetables

Remove any remaining skin, pits, or seeds. Add liquid as necessary and blend or mash through strainer or food mill.

Fruits

Fresh banana: ¼ very ripe (brown-flecked) banana. Mash until smooth.

¾ cup cooked or canned fruits (peaches, pears, apricots).

Remove any remaining skin, seeds, or pits. Mix with liquid as necessary and strain or blend.

Weaning

1. The age of your baby influences whether you wean her (1) to formula or milk, and (2) to a cup or a bottle. Around a year your baby may switch to cow's milk. Before that, you'll need to use formula or heat-treated milk (e.g., evaporated milk). Check with your pediatrician. By 9-10 months a baby can meet her daily milk needs with about 6 oz. of milk at each meal. Before this age, it may be difficult for her to drink this amount using only a cup.

2. Wean your baby gradually, introducing a bottle or cup of milk as a substitute for one nursing (probably the mid-day feeding). After a few days, repeat this procedure with another nursing. (For detailed information on weaning, see the books in Readings and Other Resources, p. 65.)

3

PLAY AND LEARNING

background/preparation

Goals to Work Toward
in Presenting This Topic

Parents are often concerned about how to play with and how much time to spend playing with their child. They wonder if their interactions with their baby and the time they spend with him are giving him the kind of play that he needs.

The goals to work toward on this topic are: (1) to help parents better understand the stages of motor development; (2) to help parents identify their own attitudes about their baby's play and how they view their role in it; (3) to inform parents about activities and toys their babies will enjoy; (4) to offer parents techniques to use in organizing a day with a baby.

Typical Parental Interests
and Concerns About This Topic

1. What should I be doing when I play with my baby?
2. What kinds of toys do babies enjoy?
3. How can I make some of my own toys?

4. What kinds of research have been done on play and learning? Aren't there facts, not just theories, about how parents can help a child learn?
5. Now that Aaron is awake more hours of the day, how can I keep him occupied when his attention span is so short?
6. How do I know when I should introduce new toys?
7. Erica wants to be held all the time. How can I encourage her to play by herself?
8. How can I avoid pushing my child while still enabling him to grow to his full potential?
9. What can I expect as far as the stages of motor development? In what sequence will they occur?
10. Our baby was premature. Will his development be behind that of full-term infants?
11. What should a parent do if her baby isn't doing something that other babies her age are doing?
12. Claire is large for her age. Will this affect her development?
13. What is my role as a parent in terms of encouraging my baby's development?
14. I want to help my baby learn as much as I can but I'm not sure how or what to do. Can you help or stimulate a child too much? How much encouragement is right?

Areas of Information You Will Need to Learn About to Teach This Topic

- Stages of motor and intellectual development in young babies.
- Toys and activities babies tend to enjoy at each stage and why these things are interesting to them.
- How to make toys for babies.
- Activities and games that are fun for parents and babies.
- How to set up a play environment, or several places inside and outside for a baby to play in.
- Attitudes toward play and learning—philosophies about the meaning and use of play and interaction for parents and children.
- Ways to provide balance in a baby's daily activities—time for parents or caregivers to play with the baby, time for the baby to be alone; time to rest, time for activity; time inside, time outside.

Family Dynamics—What This Topic Means Psychologically to Parent and Child

Many parents are burdened by the feeling that the way they play with their baby and the toys they provide for him determine their child's intelligence. A great amount of guilt goes along with this feeling. Parents often think they're the architect of their child's world, but they're not very sure of what the child needs within it. They're confused about the kinds of toys to provide at certain ages and about what their own role is in relation to their child's play.

Play is vital to the child's total growth; it is how he practices his skills and develops his theories about the world. Play helps a young baby develop basic skills such as focusing his eyes, coordinating his eyes and hands, shaking and banging things, and rolling over. Through play he becomes aware of how he can use his skills to explore the world around him. And as he explores, he learns that learning is fun. He gets satisfaction not only from the activity itself, but from the result of it—his increased ability to handle the world.

Parents will learn a great deal about their baby by watching him play and being aware of what he's trying to do. By understanding the signals, parents can figure out what their child is ready for next. But in addition to watching, parents need to play with their child. This interaction is as important, if not more so, than the specific game or toy the child uses. It's not just what the parents have bought or made for their child that affects his learning, but how the child feels, the messages the parents send when their child plays, and how the parents feel when they play with and care for him. In play with his parents, a baby's self-confidence in what he can do is enhanced by his trust in the people around him. Love, learning, and play are all intertwined.

Sample Concern of Parents

Concern	Critical Issues
I've read several books that indicate that the amount of stimulation we give our baby determines his I.Q. I want to help him achieve his maximum potential (as the books phrase it) but I don't know what to do. How much stimulation is too much? Not enough? How can parents know what's right?	—Parent's concern about her role in her infant's development and about how to play with her baby.

Key Questions

1. What are you doing now to stimulate your baby? How do you feel about this?
2. What kinds of activities or play would you like to be doing with your child?

For the group

3. What do some of you do when you play with your babies?
4. How do you define your own role in relation to your baby's play?

Readings and Other Resources

Allison, Christine, *I'll Tell You a Story, I'll Sing You a Song* (New York: Dell/Bantam Doubleday Dell, 1987).

*Berends, Polly, *Whole Child, Whole Parent* (New York: Harper Collins, 1987), pp. 99–147.

Caplan, Theresa, and Caplan, Frank, *The First Twelve Months of Life* (New York: Perigree/Berkley, 1993).

Consumer Guide, *The Complete Pregnancy and Baby Book* (New York: NAL/Dutton, 1991).

Early, George H. et al., *Growing Child* (Lafayette, Ind.: Dunn & Hargitt, updated annually).

Oppenheim, Joanne and Stephanie, *The Best Toys,* *Books and Videos for Kids* (New York: Harper Perennial/Harper Collins, 1994), pp. 3–23.

*Segal, Marilyn, *Your Child at Play: Birth to One* (New York: Newmarket Press, 1985).

Pamphlets:
- "Toys: Tools For Learning" (excellent pamphlet on developmentally appropriate toys and activities from birth to age 8).
- "Toys and Play," (another valuable pamphlet focussing on birth to age 12).

(See p. 85 for ordering information for both of these pamphlets.)

teaching/presentation

Homework

The homework assignment helps parents to focus on those kinds of play that interest their child and on the different ways different people play with babies.

Practical Suggestions or Strategies for Teaching This Topic

- A good approach for organizing this topic is to first give a brief overview of the motor and intellectual development that takes place during the first seven or eight months of life and then open the discussion to questions. This gives parents an overall view of play abilities which they can then apply to their concerns and questions.
- One way to focus the discussion is to ask group members for broader kinds of questions first—those dealing with theories about play and learning, goals of play, and the parent's role in play—and then ask them for their more practical ques-

tions, such as those about the kinds of toys babies like, when to introduce new toys, ways parents can connect their daily routine with a baby to the larger goals of play. You may also wish to go into specifics of where to buy certain toys and similar focuses but be sure to keep the discussion from settling too heavily into this area. Questions can be categorized for discussion.

Mini-lecture and Lead-off Questions for Discussion

Sample Mini-lecture

During the first month or so, most of a baby's actions are related to reflexes. For instance, if you stroke a baby's cheek or mouth, her head turns toward the stroking and she tries to suck. If an object is placed over her nose or mouth, she tries to remove it by working her mouth, twisting her head, and flinging her arms across her face. There are many other reflex movements besides these.

PLAYING · LEARNING · EXPLORING

(1–6 months)

1. What are the things your baby enjoys playing with? (Include things like mobiles that he/she may not be able to reach but likes to look at.)

2. Describe how he/she plays. (Watch your baby for a while at home.)

3. What are some of the kinds of things you think your child is getting from this play?

4. In what ways do you and your spouse differ in how you play with your baby?

What are some of the styles of play you see in yourself?

Your spouse?

Baby's grandparents?

Baby's other caregivers?

Parent's name _____ Date _____ Child's age _____

During the first month and up until four or five months of age, a baby's activity is centered on her own body as the relationship between visual and grasping skills begins to grow. During the first months she becomes aware of movement and begins to follow objects and watch her hands. Reflex movements gradually disappear, and she slowly gains some control over kicking and arm waving. A baby during this time is developing patterns of movement on which she'll build the later skills of crawling, reaching, and other motor actions. She is beginning to locate where sounds come from and also finds pleasure in sucking her hand or an object in her hand, although she doesn't yet know that the object is separate from her. She's learning that she feels something when she squeezes her own hand—a circular response that doesn't happen when she holds an object.

When an infant is between four and eight months, her interest shifts away from the body and toward toys and objects. She begins to connect her movements, such as batting her hand, with making things happen. She learns that if she does something to a toy, she may see movement or hear a noise. (Action-reaction toys offer opportunities for powerful learning.) She also learns about the permanence of objects and begins to realize that an object doesn't cease to exist just because she doesn't see it. She watches to see where a rattle goes when she drops it or shakes it to hear the noise. She inspects objects carefully. As she reaches out to people and things, she finds interaction pleasurable. She's building confidence to reach out toward more complex tasks. During this entire period, babies are also developing social skills through their play. Play with vocalizing and interaction with family and friends teaches babies how to relate to other people.

During the period of eight to twelve months, babies begin to explore more and relate means to ends, for example, moving one toy or object to get to another. Later, somewhere between 12 and 18 months, babies will start to use old toys in new ways. Grasping and looking are no longer ends in themselves but are skills for reaching other goals. For instance, grasping may now be used for the purpose of learning to put things in and take things out of a container. By 18–24 months, children can visualize solutions to problems and can use their minds, not only their bodies, to problem solve.

I'm now going to distribute a chart that shows some examples of cognitive-motor development during the first six months. Let's take a few minutes to look at it and discuss any questions you have about cognitive-motor development. Then let's make a list of the areas you'd like to cover when we talk about play and learning so we're sure to get to all your questions.

Lead-offs

• Now that we have a list of the kinds of areas you'd like to talk about in our discussion of play, let's talk first about your own feelings about your baby's play.
• How comfortable are you with the time you spend with your baby in play and the time your baby plays by himself?
• Do you have any feelings about play that bother you? Some that please you? Where do you think these feelings come from? What do they tell you about yourself?
• How do you see your own role as a parent in terms of play?

_____

Additional Information for Parents

_____

• Some child rearing-related books raise the issue that parents can "maximize their child's potential" by following certain well-defined patterns of play and parenting. Parents often get the feeling that there's a right way to play with their child and then feel confused if they don't know what that is. They can also feel guilty if they don't follow recommendations from an "expert" or from a highly promoted book.

Parents need to know that no person or study has proven that any particular stimulation is more valuable than any other. Although parents would like you to quote research to know if they're giving their child enough stimulation, they should understand that theories are not facts, and that

1–6 months

they need to suit their approach to their baby's play and learning to what fits their particular family.

• Most parents want to know how much time they should spend playing with their baby. Again, there is no one answer—there is no set time because all parents are different. Some like to play on the floor for an hour with their child while others don't enjoy more than two minutes at a time. Also, parents enjoy different stages of development more than others; play may be more fun for them when their child is two or three. Parents should know that short interactions can be as meaningful as long ones. Play should be as long as both parent and child feel good about and enjoy it.

• Parents should remember to look at the messages they're sending their child during play. Often it's, "Don't bug me, try this toy instead."

• When offering new toys, parents can look at their baby's cues to see what principles he's intrigued with at that time. Maybe it's batting at objects, arm waving, or learning to control movement. Maybe it's kicking, or mouthing objects. Parents can connect what their child likes to do with objects that help him learn more about that activity. Parents can provide the tools and the love babies need to discover and learn about their world.

• When exposed to excessive or inappropriate stimulation, babies may withdraw and build up a strategy for dealing with the person providing the stimulation. When parents play with their baby, they should watch his reactions—is he responding or is he withdrawing? Parents need to watch their own reactions as well—they can become discouraged by failure to reach their baby and withdraw themselves. If certain play is not fun for both parent and child, something else should be tried or play should be postponed until a better time.

• Shaping an environment with "correct" learning materials at the "correct" time seems not to be as important as providing conditions that are most likely to encourage a baby to discover for herself the physical properties of objects and the logical relationships among them. A child's construction of theories about the world takes time, practice, and opportunities for spontaneous exploration and discovery.

• An unencumbered, friendly, warm relationship between parent and baby may be an essential background for the baby's intellectual development; it can provide a secure base from which she can risk abandoning old solutions for newly discovered ones.

• Babies pick up parents' feelings about how they are doing, including how they stand in terms of norms of development. Since every baby is different, it's probably best to just enjoy them where they are, and watch them develop naturally at their own pace.

• Parents sometimes worry that their child may be delayed if they notice he hasn't acquired a specific skill when other babies his age have or when someone implies the baby should have that skill by now. Pediatricians watch for signs of slow development, and during baby check-ups will usually ask a range of questions about skill acquisition. Since some of the skills are well beyond a baby's age, all parents will have to say "no" to some of the skills asked about. If a parent is bothered by thoughts of retardation, she should certainly talk with her pediatrician about them. Six months of age is the earliest that retardation can usually be diagnosed. At that point a baby would have to be two or more months behind in *everything*. At one year he would have to be three to four months behind in *everything*.

During the first three months, babies are pretty even in terms of skills. Starting at three months, patterns of skills diverge and get wider and wider.

• Parents should know that babies don't need to have every toy or piece of equipment on the market. One mobile can offer plenty of opportunity for visual practice; it's not necessary to have three mobiles, ten posters, and six bright, patterned scarves.

Handouts

There are two handouts included here for this topic:

"Cognitive-Motor Development." This handout has a chart that shows month by month the ways that visual, hand, and mouth skills develop and interrelate. The information can help parents gain perspective on the ways infant play is related to development. It can also reassure parents that their baby is really giving cues about the things he's interested in learning about.

The Play and Learning handout has three parts:

"Toys for the Young Baby." In this section of the Play and Learning handout, parents can tell the kinds of play their baby will enjoy. By watching his interests, parents will be able to give their child the toys and objects that will help him practice and learn about those interests.

"Sensory Stimulation." This section of the handout lists the five developing senses in the young baby and the kinds of toys that can stimulate their growth. Parents can work toward a balance in what they provide so all senses are stimulated sometime during each day.

"Guidelines for Parents When Playing with Their Baby." The information in this section can lead parents into a discussion of their own theories of play and of places to buy toys that have the best selection and lowest prices.

You may also wish to recommend or order and distribute:

—"Toys: tools for learning". This valuable pamphlet provides a thorough discussion on the importance of play, types and use of toys and play materials. A chart matches a child's developing skills with appropriate toys and activities from birth to age 8. Available from the National Association for the Education of Young Children, 1509 9th St. N.W., Washington, D.C. 20036-1426 or call (800) 424-2460; 100 copies for $10.

or

—"Toys and Play". Another valuable pamphlet focussing on birth to age 12. Available from Toy Manufacturers of America by writing to: Toy Booklet, P.O. Box 866, Madison Square Station, New York, N.Y. 10159 or call (800) 851-9955; free to parents and qualified organizations.

1–6 months

COGNITIVE-MOTOR DEVELOPMENT

(1–6 months)

	VISUAL	HANDS	MOUTH
Newborn	Sees best close up. Tonic-neck reflex (fencing position).	Fists closed. Hands and arms move in a jerky way.	Sucks.
•	Stares at things but doesn't reach for them.	Body is still in tonic-neck reflex (fencing position). Hands still tightly closed.	Sucks.
•	Primarily exploring through eyes. Can follow things briefly with eyes. Begins to recognize mother.	Random movements. Holds objects briefly. Very little hand control.	Thumb sucking. Some finger sucking.
3 months	Follows objects from side to side. Aware of strange situations. Interest in hand watching. Doesn't visually follow object that goes out of sight. Very excited by visual stimulation.	Reaches out to bat at objects. Fists open more. Starting to use hands to play.	Can look and suck at the same time but stops to listen.
•	Turns head at sound of voice. Vision begins to be similar to adults.	Hands grab each other. Active reaching. Beginning to wave things around and to recover toys.	Beginning teething and chewing—in some babies. Mouthing of things. Sucking need *begins* to diminish.
•	Begins to look carefully, inspecting things in his hand. Begins to discriminate strangers. Looks around in new situations. Alternately glances between hand and object.	One-handed reaching for toys still not totally accurate. Persistence in reaching. Grasps objects as though he had on a mitten.	Mouths and sucks on toys, clothes, toes. Drooling.
6 months	Tends to keep looking for an object that goes out of sight (peek-a-boo). Enjoys mirror image. Eyes can still be used better than hands.	Purposeful and coordinated reaching for toys. Manipulation and exploration of objects. Transfers from hand to hand. Free rotation of wrist. Enjoys banging toys.	Mouth is now extremely important for learning more about objects. Baby sees object, reaches for it, mouths it, looks at it, etc.

PLAY AND LEARNING*

(1–6 months)

Toys for the Young Baby

Age	Babies like to:	Give your baby:	Age	Babies like to:	Give your baby:
1 and 2 months	Suck. Listen to sounds.	Wind chimes, music, ticking clock, your talking and singing. In later months he'll enjoy toys that make noise.	5 and 6 months	Be sociable and laugh.	Games he plays with you (rattles, mirrors, peek-a-boo), funny sounds.
	Look at patterns, movement, and light.	Change of positions around the house and outside, bright posters, colored fabric, mobiles, your face near his.		Kick.	Toys near his feet, bag filled with paper, jumper.
	Be touched and rocked.	Body rub with different textures of materials, lots of cuddling and holding.		Touch, grasp, let go.	All kinds of objects he can safely handle, squeak toys, toys with noisy moving parts, toys that can be grasped easily and put into mouth, sponge, wooden spoon, fabric.
3 and 4 months	Smile.	Your smile.	7–9 months	Sit and roll over.	
	Touch different textures.	Material to hold, nylon netting, soft toys.		Begin crawling.	Toys on the floor he can reach for.
	Reach and bat at nearby objects.	Cradle gyms, hanging objects, weighted toys, toys he can activate, rattles placed in his hand.		Shake, feel, bang, gum, and drop things.	More objects to handle, spools on a string, nesting cups, water play with sponges, cups, and washcloth.

*Use caution when selecting toys and suitable play materials for babies and young children. Check toys for sharp, small and/or loose parts (i.e. buttons, eyes, strings on stuffed animals) that might present a choking or injury hazard.

Sensory Stimulation

Tactile

- Balls made of different material
- Patchwork quilt with different textures and buttons, bells, etc., around edges
- Small, light-weight toy he can pick up
- Board or cardboard with fabrics, etc., glued on (sandpaper, foam rubber, foil, etc.)—to use with parents or other caregivers during play time
- Toys or objects hanging from frame or bars for baby to "bat" and reach.
- Unused powder puff, etc., rub his body with contrasting textures

Kinesthetic

- Toys he can wave around
- Toys out of reach for baby to reach for
- Drum or paper at baby's feet
- Manipulate baby's body; dance with baby

Visual

- Mobiles—any type of hanging object (bright, intense colors, light-reflecting and lightweight). Use elastic and/or string, tin foil, balloons, ribbons, bright paper, rattles, two small mirrors glued back to back with string between
- Unbreakable mirror attached to outside of crib
- Bright pictures by the crib and changing table
- Fish bowl or aquarium
- Infant seat near "busy" window or in kitchen
- Red mitten on hand
- Peek-a-boo
- Crystal "sun-catcher" in window to make rainbows; spin!

Oral

- Different textures, lightweight, small enough to hold and put in mouth (use with safety guidelines)
- For teething and oral exploration: leather, ivory, rattles, gold and silver bracelets, tongue depressors, plastic can lids, spoon (with adults)
- Thick, soft cord with knots
- Rings, etc., snapped to bib with ribbon

Auditory

- Music—not all the time, however; wind-up toys
- Toys that demonstrate cause and effect (e.g., baby hits bell, cradle gyms)
- Elastic across playpen with bracelets, bells, plastic containers with lids, spoons, etc., on them (must be removed at 5 months)
- String that baby pulls to make noise, with clothes pin or the like tied at the end to make it easier to grab (with adult supervision)

Guidelines for Parents When Playing with Their Baby

1. The parent's role is that of a facilitator who sets up the opportunity to play; she helps with the play if necessary.
2. Try to tune in to your child and allow him to play with toys or objects in his own way rather than the way you think he should. Avoid playing for him.
3. Allow your child to solve his own problems as much as possible (rather than always retrieving toys for him, for example). Realize you're giving your child an important opportunity to learn.
4. Your baby's attention span may be longer than yours. Let him play with a toy as long as he's interested in it.
5. Rotate the toys you have so there's a "controlled variety" rather than a confusing bombardment of stimuli. This method extends the length of time the toys will be interesting.

Considerations When Purchasing Toys

1. Safety.
2. Durability.
3. Interesting color.

PLAY AND LEARNING (continued)

4. Multi-purpose (many senses are stimulated or different skills are involved when using toy).
5. Multi-age (child's current skills and interests are tapped now, but toy will be fun for other reasons later).
6. Child does something with the toy rather than wind it up and have it work independently.
7. Toys for young babies should be easy to manage with one hand and easy to grab from any angle. There should be no detachable parts.
8. Many wonderful toys are in your home now (measuring cups, spools, bright paper, bells, pots and pans, etc.). Don't feel you must find toys only at the store. (Always keep safety and supervision in mind when selecting materials).

4

ADJUSTING TO PARENTING[1]

background/preparation

Goals to Work Toward in Presenting This Topic

Every parent has ambivalent feelings about her child and about herself. While it's easy to find opportunities to share the joy, beauty, and excitement of life with a new baby, it may be difficult to find an opportunity to share the negative feelings that are a normal part of parenting. Unless these feelings are faced and discussed, however, it will be difficult for parents to work toward new ideas and solutions that will make child rearing rewarding.[2]

The goals to work toward on this topic are: (1) to help parents feel more capable of understanding themselves and life with a baby; (2) to let parents know that other parents share the same feelings, doubts, and frustrations that they feel; (3) to help parents gain some insight into why the marriage relationship often changes with the arrival of a baby; (4) to help parents feel that they are doing a good job of parenting.

Typical Parental Interests and Concerns About This Topic

1. I have no time to myself.
2. I feel isolated from my friends. It seems impossible to get out of the house.
3. My husband and I have lost our spontaneity. We can no longer go out on the spur of the moment.
4. My husband has suddenly started to work longer hours. We have no time to talk. It almost seems like he doesn't like to be home any more.
5. How can I get my husband to help with the baby?
6. I feel guilty when I want to do something besides hold the baby. Should he have my complete attention all day?
7. I don't understand what's happening to me. I just don't feel like myself.
8. Even though we're both back at work now, I still feel like I have all the responsibility for the baby and the house. I'm not happy.
9. Our home life has become a wreck. Sometimes I wish we had never had a baby.

---

1. The presentation of this topic in the young baby class has been to groups of women only, but the information can be adapted to meet the needs of fathers' or couples' groups.

2. As their children pass through and beyond the young baby stage, you will find further information on this topic in Part VI:6 (p. 379) and 7 (p. 392).

Areas of Information You Will Need to Learn About to Teach This Topic

- The common emotional stages parents go through as they adjust to a new child.
  - The kinds of feelings that are typical when men and women become parents.
  - Ways parents' feelings change as their child gets older.
  - Typical feelings parents have toward their baby and their spouse.
- Ways couples can maintain a close relationship during their baby's first year.
- Ways a woman can help her husband develop his relationship with his baby.
- Ideas about ways to make adjustment to parenting easier.
- Variety of feelings expressed by mothers who are returning to work.
- Ways couples can make a smooth transition when a mother returns to work.

Family Dynamics—What This Topic Means Psychologically to Parent and Child

Becoming a parent and adjusting to that new role can be two of the most difficult endeavors in a person's life. New parents typically have feelings of fatigue, confusion, inadequacy, and anger, along with—and sometimes at the same time as—feelings of elation, love, wonder, and joy. The combination of feelings and the extremes of highs and lows can add tension and frustration to an already hectic time. Parents can be so overwhelmed by the adjustments they must make and the learning they must absorb that they feel unhappy with their life and in need of some "mothering" themselves.

While parents are experiencing great emotional turmoil, babies have no comprehension of their parents' difficulties. They are only aware of their own needs and wants, though they are aware on some level of their parents' feelings toward them. Babies are not as affected by their parents' adjustment to their new roles as they are by their parents' long-term relationship with them.

Sample Concern of Parents

Concern	Critical Issues
My husband and I waited a long time for our baby, but in spite of our happiness, things seem to be falling apart at home. We bicker frequently, nothing gets done around the house, I'm tired all the time, and I hate myself for sometimes wishing we had never had a baby.	—Surprise at strength and ambivalence of feelings. —Husband-wife relationship is strained. —Feelings of inadequacy. —Parent feels guilty over resentment of baby. —Parent finds it difficult to cope with constant fatigue. —Parent feels lack of accomplishment since her life isn't as organized as it was.

Key Questions

1. What are you expecting of yourself? Are you setting yourself up for disappointment by expecting the impossible?
2. What are you expecting of your husband? How do things look from his point of view?
3. What are you doing to make yourself feel good? Are you meeting some of your own needs? Can you do anything else for yourself?

For the group

4. Have others of you experienced similar feelings? How have you dealt with them?

Readings and Other Resources

Belsky, Jay, *Transition to Parenthood* (New York: Delacorte, 1994).

*Boroff-Eagan, Andrea, *The Newborn Mother: Stages of Her Growth* (New York: Henry Holt, 1985).

Brazelton, T. Berry, *Infants and Mothers* (New York: Dell Publishing Co., Inc., 1983).

Brazelton, T. Berry, *On Becoming a Family* (New York: Delacorte, 1992).

Brazelton, T. Berry, "Working Parents," *Newsweek* (Feb. 13, 1989), p. 66.

*Cowan, Carolyn P. and Cowan, Philip A. *When Partners Become Parents* (New York: Basic, 1993).

Dorman, Marsha, and Klein, Diane, *How To Stay Two When Baby Makes Three* (Buffalo, New York: Prometheus Books, 1984).

Galinsky, Ellen, *The Six Stages of Parenthood* (New York: Addison-Wesley, 1987).

Golant, Mitch and Susan, *Finding Time for Fathering* (New York: Fawcett, 1993).

Greenberg, Martin, *Birth of a Father* (New York: Avon, 1986).

Hochschild, Arlie, *The Second Shift* (New York: Avon, 1990).

Marzollo, Jean, "After the Baby: Easing Your Return to Work," *Parents* (October, 1989), p. 106.

Marzollo, Jean, *Fathers and Babies* (New York: Harper Collins, 1993).

Massie, Suzanne, "Getting to Know You," *Family Circle* (this article is reprinted in its entirety in "Meeting Your Own Needs," pp. 389–391.

Rothenberg, B. Annye, et al., *Parentmaking Educators Training Program* (Menlo Park, Cal.: Banster Press, 1993), pp. 245–269.

Sarda Reese, "Reflections of a Father Who Became a Mother," *Redbook* (this article is reprinted in its entirety in the "Handouts" section of this topic.)

Tannen, Deborah, *You Just Don't Understand: Women and Men in Conversation* (New York: Morrow, William & Co., 1990).

===

teaching/presentation

Homework

The homework observation for this topic was developed to encourage parents to think about and try to accept the kinds of adjustments they are experiencing.

Practical Suggestions or Strategies for Teaching This Topic

• It is generally better to schedule this topic later in the series. By then, group members will know each other fairly well and feel more comfortable discussing personal issues.

• A warm, supportive, free-flowing discussion is more important to this topic than a long and specific agenda of issues.

• It is important to cover as many feelings new parents experience as possible. If certain feelings aren't brought up, you can summarize those that have and then ask about other feelings that the group has found hard to cope with. Offering

examples from your own experience can be very helpful.

• Parents of young babies often have difficulty verbalizing their feelings. The whole experience is so new that they may feel upset, tired, or confused and not really know why. Gentle encouragement and appreciation are important responses for you to make to any ideas group members feel able to share.

• Since parents continually gain insight about parenting as they gain more experience, new parents will not have the depth of understanding you have. However, your ideas and information will help them gain perspective on what's happening, on what's coming later, and on the continuing nature of the process of learning about parenting.

Mini-lecture and Lead-off Questions for Discussion

Sample mini-lecture

Becoming a parent entails learning a new role. It also entails undergoing changes, accepting new responsibilities, and feeling

ADJUSTING TO PARENTING

(1–6 months)

Please spend some time thinking about these homework questions and then discussing them with your spouse. They will be a guide for our class next week when we talk about what the first months of parenting have been like for you and your spouse or partner.

1. Please read the following paragraph and describe some of your reactions to what this author says.

"No matter how much you have read about babies or how many Red Cross courses you have taken to try to get ready for the experience of caring for your new baby, it is still a totally new experience. The reality of it all doesn't hit you until you come home from the hospital and are actually face to face with this brand new, living, breathing thing: your new baby. There it is, twenty-four hours a day, and it won't go away!" (Dodson, *How to Parent*).

2. The arrival of a new baby is the beginning of real changes in your life. What are these changes like for you *and* your spouse (or partner), as individuals and as a couple?

Parent's name _____ Date _____ Child's age _____

new and often unsettling emotions. We can feel elated with our new son or daughter, but we can feel unhappy, too, with the way our lives have changed. Negative feelings are perfectly normal for new parents, but they need to be accepted and discussed to keep them from taking too great a hold on us. Let's talk today just about us and about our adjustment to becoming parents.

You can begin the discussion if no one volunteers a statement or question with a lead-off such as the one that follows and use any of the rest of the lead-offs to continue the discussion..

Lead-offs

• Adjusting to parenting is difficult. Some days you may find yourself saying, "Now what were all those reasons that we decided to have a child?" From your own personal experience, what feelings about being a parent have been difficult for you to deal with?

• We've been talking about some of the feelings associated with becoming a parent. In our adjustment, a lot of us get mixed up about our role because we can't separate what we know about ourselves from the myths of what we think a good parent should be. What are some of the myths about parenthood? How do these differ from its reality?

• How do things look from your spouse's point of view? What are some needs he is finding hard to meet now that he's a father?

• What are some of the things you and your spouse are finding hard to continue or maintain in your relationship? What concerns do you have about the way your time is spent together?

• How do you feel about your spouse's (or partner's) relationship with your baby and about his participation in baby care?

• What are some of the ways you have found to deal with the adjustment to becoming a parent? What are some of the ways you're finding to meet some of your own needs? When confidence and self-esteem are low, what do you do?

Additional Information for Parents

• Things do get better. The first months of parenting really are the hardest.

• There are many myths about parenting that have nothing to do with its reality. Parents are not naturally patient, loving, always giving, and totally responsible for *every* aspect of their child's development.

• New parents often shut off their own needs. Several times a year parents ought to reevaluate their own needs to see how much of themselves they really "turn their backs on" and if there are more needs that can be met. Sometimes parents' needs for nurturing can be met by simply setting aside five minutes to do something special for themselves.

• Parents will always have some negative feelings to cope with, but they may become more accepting of them if they can learn to appreciate their diagnostic value. A period of depression, for example, may indicate that a personal need is asking to be recognized.

• Some parents may not be able to implement proposed solutions to parenting adjustment problems for some time. Knowing about the possibilities, however, will give them options to choose from at the appropriate time.

• Most new parents feel some difficult emotions. The most common are:

Guilt, Resentment, and Anger.

• Parents may feel at times that they don't love their baby, especially until they feel that they are meeting their baby's needs. Since babies can't send clear signals and often don't know what they want, it's hard to figure out what they need. Parents can feel guilty over what they think is their failure, and anger at the child who is causing these emotions. Parents need to remember that it often takes a while to love a child and much longer to get used to being a parent.

Lack of Confidence

• Parents start on their new career with little or no training. They feel there are answers to their questions somewhere but they don't know where to go to find them. It seems like they're experimenting with their baby, not knowing what to do. A great deal of anxiety can result from this confusion.

• Parents may feel inept when attempts to soothe don't work; they may blame themselves when their baby is fussy. It helps parents to know that all babies fuss, no matter what kind of parenting they experience.

Burden of Responsibility

- Many parents feel a great, almost overwhelming responsibility to help develop *every* aspect of their child's behavior. This feeling of responsibility usually comes from cultural or societal pressure to be all things to one's child. The sensation of having one's existence be the source of nourishment for another is a good feeling, but sometimes it can be frightening and the expectations that accompany it unreasonable. It helps for parents to remember that although they do structure a great deal of the environment for their child, the child develops at his own rate according to his own interests and temperament. Development is his responsibility, guidance the parents'.

Lack of Organization and Sense of Accomplishment

- With a young baby's constant needs, it's hard for a parent to feel in control and confident. Even simple things like making phone calls, writing notes, paying bills, and shopping can seem like huge tasks. It's hard for parents of a young baby to plan because they never know if or when there will be time to do anything. If time is available, parents often feel absent-minded or unable to get going. This is a time when all those routine chores *are* huge tasks. No one breezes through this period without some help and support from family, friends, cleaning services, and so on. Though parents are used to thinking, "How can I help?" they now need to think, "How can I accept offers and services from others to make this time easier?"
- It's hard for parents to give so much to their baby and get so little back. It's also hard to put their own needs last. Most parents of infants wonder if their lives will ever have a comfortable, rewarding routine again.

Feeling Isolated

- Many new mothers often feel neglected. Shortly after their baby is born, there are no more childbirth classes to attend and no visits to their doctor. The baby receives a great deal of attention and the mother may feel like she's no longer important. Parks, YMCA's, churches, parenting classes, and other community resources offer ways for new parents to meet each other. It's well worth the effort to find another parent of a young baby to talk with.
- There's no praise for a job well done or for the incredible effort that goes into parenting. In addition, mobility may be limited, especially for mothers, and there can be little stimulation from or interaction with other adults.

Fatigue

- After weeks or months of getting up during the night, fatigue can make parents feel like zombies. They can literally fear going off the deep end, really falling apart and not being able to cope. Parents need to figure out how to get more rest and temporarily relax some housework-related standards.
- Most parents don't realize that emotional exhaustion is worse than physical exhaustion. They may not even recognize or understand it when they're experiencing it, but the emotional adjustment to the new situation can be extremely difficult and continue for at least six months. Women aren't used to giving serious thought to pampering themselves, but this is the time to figure out how to get more rest. The house doesn't have to be clean; standards can be temporarily relaxed.

Change in Friends

- Often, good friends of new parents may not understand the new situation. It can be hard for them to fully know the changes or problems when they haven't experienced them. Parents need to seek out parents with young babies who understand the experiences. Again, it's crucial to find other parents of young babies who *do* understand.

No Time Alone

- With their new responsibilities, parents can suddenly find that they have no time to themselves. As soon as feasible, they should try to set up an arrangement that enables them to have time alone. A mother can arrange for a weekly sitter, exchange sitting with a friend, or get help from her husband. Finding time to meet personal needs can make parents feel a great deal better.

Ambivalence

- Having a child seems to broaden the range and intensity of one's emotions. Parents may feel incredible love and happiness one minute and extreme anger and resentment the next.

Loss of Warmth and Closeness with Spouse

- Some couples have been together a long time before their baby is born, and are used to having lots of time with each other. During pregnancy, they may even increase their shared time and communication by going to classes together and working on the joint goal of delivery. They feel close, optimistic, and excited. When their baby is born, many fathers may stay home to help the first few days but soon, in most households, it's back to work for the husband and the start of total child care and home management for the wife. Even if a mother plans to return to work, "traditional roles" have a way of "happening" during maternity leave. If these roles are set, parents begin to operate in different worlds and have different types of work schedules. The husband may not understand what is happening to the wife and the wife may lose touch with what the work world is like for her husband. Even when both parents are participating in child care, communication between them can be subject to all kinds of restraints and limitations. Parents need to try to arrange some time each week to spend alone together. This can give them time to concentrate on each other, talk about each other's needs, and have fun together.
- Couples need all the support they can get to remember who they are as people. All too often, however, they are helped to become the kind of parents others feel they should be, not helped to keep a sense of personal adventure in their lives. Couples need to be overly assertive in their goals and expectations because it is likely they will encounter opposition from other people.

And About Working Parents

- Dual career families and single working parents need to be even more careful of their family time and individual needs.
- New parents who are also working outside the home often feel guilty or conflicted about the amount of time they spend away from their baby. Simplifying their lives and schedules at home and at work will allow for more quantity *and* quality time as a family.
- When both parents work, their baby's caregivers can be a valuable source of insight and perspective about their baby. Sharing the events and activities that shapes the baby's day, caregivers can help fill an otherwise uncomfortable "gap" for parents.

Handouts

Two magazine articles, "A New Mother's Confessions of Ambivalence" by Nancy Kelton and "Reflections of a Father Who Became a Mother" by Reese Sarda, are the handouts for this topic.

For more content and additional handouts and exercises, see Rothenberg, *PETP,* "Husband-Wife Relationship" topic, pp. 245-269 particularly the newborn mother: stages of her growth, pp. 256-258, and "Diary of a Very New Father," pp. 261-264. Also see the beginning on p. 466 in this book for additional content on Working Parents issues.

A New Mother's Confessions of Ambivalence

by Nancy Kelton

Sometimes when I walk down the street with my child in her carriage and my husband beside me, I feel so detached from them that I want to turn around and face off in the opposite direction to be alone with my thoughts. At other times, in the same situation, I feel we are so close to one another that I want nothing more than to continue walking along in silence, sharing what is ours alone.

Shortly before I decided I wanted to get pregnant, I had a dream that I was called to do substitute work at a public school. The job was to take the place not of a teacher but of an absent third-grade student, and I found myself sitting at a small desk in a classroom with 20 eight-year-olds.

In the next part of the dream, it was the following day and I was substituting for the teacher of the same third-grade class. When I stood in front of the room to begin the day's lessons, the children did not know how to respond. They could not figure out whether I was a teacher or a student.

At the same time, I was not sure whether I was an adult wanting nurturing. Now I am still not sure, although I often find myself struggling to be both.

When my daughter, Emily, and I are together in the house for an entire day, somewhere between five and six o'clock, when she is tired and hungry and cranky, and I am tired and hungry and cranky, I want to run away from home. I am resentful that my husband gets such a thrill when he comes in and sees her little face light up.

When Emily and I are apart during the day, somewhere between five and six o'clock I want to get home. When I come in, I can understand precisely how my husband feels, and I am no longer resentful. It is an incredible thrill to see my daughter's little face light up.

One day when I took Emily shopping, a woman stopped beside the carriage to admire her. "Enjoy her now," the woman advised me. "Before you know it, she'll be all grown up and leave you." I didn't say anything, but I was secretly wishing that Emily would grow up and leave me already. It isn't easy to enjoy someone who cries when she should be napping and who spits out her cereal when she should be swallowing it.

Later, when I was changing Emily's clothes, I started to put her in a T-shirt, and I noticed it was too tight across the chest. I got up on the stepladder to put it away, feeling a slight pang of sadness. My little girl had already outgrown something.

During my pregnancy, I dreamed that I took off my old, faded jeans and gave them to an older woman friend who handed me a pair of well-tailored, stylish slacks to wear. I did not put the new pants on. I remained in my underwear, staring at both pairs, trying to decide which were right for me.

At the time I was frightened that I would soon have to replace the parts of myself with which I felt most comfortable with what others expected of me. I have discovered that, as a mother, I did not have to give away my favorite jeans. It is just a little more difficult to wear them all the time these days. They always seem to need washing.

Recently when my parents came up to visit us from Florida, they kissed me rather quickly when they arrived and then lavished their attention on Emily. After a few moments, my mother apologized for neglecting me. I told her I didn't mind. Everyone doted on Emily. It was only natural. She then looked at me and said, "I guess now it's your turn to live vicariously."

Her remark went through me like a knife, and although I remained silent, I felt enormous waves of anger and fear rising inside of me. Anger that my own role model, who spent what could have been her most creative years, in frustration, living vicariously through her daughters, had no qualms

Nancy Kelton is an author of children's books. Reprinted from the *New York Times*.

about passing on this legacy to me. And fear that I might find myself accepting it.

Sometimes when Emily is getting up from a nap, I stand over her crib, watching her and smiling. She looks up at me and smiles back. Then I tickle her or talk to her or kiss her and she smiles even more or else she starts to giggle. Sometimes her giggling makes me laugh out loud. These moments when we are sharing and connecting are the ones that make me say "yes" when someone asks me if I am glad I decided to become a mother.

One Friday afternoon, not too long ago, after Emily had spent a good portion of the week teething and crying and refusing to eat, nap, be quiet, or give me one minute to myself, I sat down on the floor beside her intending to play, when I felt big tears streaming down my cheeks. I began to sob. And I could not stop.

To gain my composure, I walked over to the window and looked out, pretending for a few seconds that I was alone. It didn't work. I was still crying. When I turned around Emily was staring at me. And smiling. Her smiling made me sob even louder. Her eyes were fixed on me and she started laughing and waving her arms about, responding to my outburst of frustration as if it were a game or song.

Suddenly my sobbing turned to laughter. I picked up my little daughter and held her very tightly, realizing that there will be many more times in our lives when we will unwittingly inflict pain on each other, and many more times when we think we understand each other but don't. And it won't always be easy. But nothing worthwhile ever is.

REFLECTIONS OF A FATHER WHO BECAME A MOTHER

by Reese Sarda

Our first child, Sigrid, was born in the spring, and for some months afterward our family appeared cast from the standard American mold. My wife Lynn did all those things a young housewife and mother is supposed to do. She cooked the meals, did the housework and cared for the baby. I went off to work each day, doing either carpentry or house painting.

There were only two slight drawbacks to our otherwise-pleasant situation. Lynn didn't feel she was cut out to be a housewife; she was a teacher and wanted to teach. Although I was successful at it, I didn't feel I was meant to be a builder or a house painter; I wanted to write and would gladly have kept house and cared for the baby in exchange for that privilege.

Our decision to reverse roles took place in June, when Lynn was offered a teaching position at a school for retarded children. We did no debating or soul-searching; within three days our minds were made up.

"You'll have to start weaning Sigrid," I said.

"I'll talk to Dr. Zipser," Lynn replied. "We should probably start now with a bottle for one feeding." And: "You can always call Mrs. Campbell or Mrs. Peterson if you run into trouble."

Unnecessary advice! I thought. I felt perfectly competent to take care of the house and the baby.

By September, Sigrid, now five months old, had become a bottle baby, Lynn began going out to work and I became the "houseperson," doing my writing at night when Lynn and the child were asleep.

Eleven months later our second daughter, Inga, was born, and after seven weeks at home Lynn went out to work again. Sigrid was now a mischievous, active 18-month-old.

Now I had two children to care for, and I found it to be extremely hard work. And after over a year of being a houseperson I began to wonder: Am I suited to this job? Is parenting strictly a woman's occupation after all? Do women have some natural bent for the work that I, a man, lack? Is my maleness what is making the work more difficult than it logically should be?

I thought those questions over and concluded that to accept the premise they implied would be a paltry rationalization. Talking to some housebound mothers and reading a few magazine articles thoroughly dispelled any remaining doubts I might have had. We, the housebound parents, all were in the same situation. To some extent we all exhibited the same symptoms. It had to do with the job, not the gender.

That fact was further established by observing Lynn. She would come home tired after a day of teaching, but her tiredness was entirely different from the dragged-out feeling she'd experienced when she held the houseperson job. Now it was a very direct tiredness, easy to pinpoint and easy to cope with. She would come home and say: "We did numbers all morning. I don't want to see another number today." Easy enough. Shut down the math segment of the brain. Let it rest. By the time she went to bed, the exhaustion would be gone. It had been the same for me when I was out working.

But parenting was different; it was an over-all wearing down. One never quite caught up with the attrition of continuous wear and tear.

At first I thought the two hours I spent writing every night might be taking away needed sleep. But I knew I had never required, until about two years ago, more than five hours of sleep. As for the writing itself, I realized it had a reverse influence: It wasn't wearing me out; it was giving me energy. It was something all my own. It was an activity that relaxed me and bore fruit, and I looked forward to doing it.

Without seeming to be "work," parenting was actually a physically demanding and mentally consuming job. The physical aspects were easiest to understand. I didn't have that nice aching-muscle tiredness that comes from expending large amounts of energy in a relatively short time. When I painted a house, I worked fast and intensely. I carried ladders and climbed up and down, using my legs as well as my arms. At the end of the day I was worn out, but I knew when and where I had earned my tiredness and I could feel my body being replenished as I ate a good meal and relaxed in a soft chair.

When and where does a homebound parent get tired? How, by the end of the day, had I earned the dull stiffness in my legs, the kink in my back? Was it the result of my 14th trip upstairs? Perhaps it was the 23rd trip that did it. Maybe it was from having my leg tugged at by Sigrid while I was trying to do the dishes. And how about the heaviness in my arms? Did that come from tying Sigrid's shoes, or from spooning out petite servings of pablum to Inga?

So much for the physical side of parenting. There is the mental side too.

The mental effort needed for parenting is also different from that needed for other jobs. Most work demands a type of concentration that focuses on just one area or on a few specifics at any given time. A plumber running copper tubing through a house concentrates on the soldering of one joint before moving on to the next. Should he run into an unusual problem, he can take a short break.

A computer programmer concentrates on a specific problem too. If he has solved it or not, when his mind tires he can walk down the hall and find an idle co-worker with whom to discuss the upcoming title fight or the grim realities of rising mortgage rates.

In most jobs ample opportunities exist to switch off concentration and then switch it back on—periods of action and rest, wear and refreshment. But the concentration required for good parenting, especially when handling more than one young child, is different. The parent is *always* on the job.

Even when the parent is asleep a state of being "on call" exists. The sound of coughing, steps in the hall, doors closing—any and every sound must be heard and evaluated before it can be dismissed. The mind is prevented from getting so involved in some one thing that it shuts out the surroundings.

The proverbial housewife, who has so much to do all day that she wishes she had a third hand, would do better to wish for a second head instead. That way, when one brain got overworked she could switch it off for a while and switch on the other.

In my case there have been moments—many of them—when I could have used a third hand and a third head! A not-so-hypothetical 15-minute segment of a typical day shows how that could help:

It is afternoon. There is bread baking in the oven. It will be done in five minutes. Suddenly Inga wakes up and begins crying. She's a half hour early. Sigrid is sitting peacefully by the toy box, puttering with something. Should I take out the bread early and hope it won't be soggy inside? Or should I leave it in the oven and go up and change Inga and bring her down and hope the bread won't dry out? Or should I get her bottle ready and let her wait the five minutes that it takes? The last is the most practical. As long as she's crying, "Hey, I'm hungry!" I know she is safe and sound. A parent quickly learns to distinguish the meanings in a baby's different cries.

The baby is crying lightly, the bread is baking and the bottle of formula is being heated. I open the oven, take out one loaf, turn it out of the pan and thump it. A nice, resonant sound—the bread is finished. I've just reached in for the second loaf when out of the corner of my eye I see Sigrid dashing across the room, shoelaces flapping dangerously. That's why she's been so quiet! She's been fastidiously working on the bows I'd tied 30 minutes before.

Sigrid is going too fast for comfort. I put the second loaf of bread, still in the pan, on the counter and rush into the living room and grab Sigrid before she trips. While I'm tying her left shoe in a more challenging combination of bows, the water in which the formula is heating suddenly boils over the saucepan.

At that instant the baby stops crying, arousing my suspicions—and the telephone rings, arousing exasperation. I finish with Sigrid's left shoelace and rush to get the stove before the boiling water puts out the gas flame. Then I pick up the phone.

Sigrid glares at me. She is furious. First I've undone the beautiful job she'd done of untying her left shoe and now I am completely ignoring her untied right shoe, thus saddling her with a terrible case of lopsidedness. She starts sobbing as if the world's greatest tragedy had just occurred.

"Hold on a minute," I say into the telephone—it's my favorite telephone phrase—and I dash upstairs to see why Inga has stopped crying. She's asleep. By the time I get back, Sigrid has forgotten about her shoe and is using the phone receiver and cord as a yo-yo, whacking the receiver on the floor. I get the phone back, which means more tears from Sigrid.

Lynn, who is usually very thoughtful about not disturbing me at my work (unlike the majority of providing mates), is on the phone. She has called for no other reason than to be friendly.

"What's going on there?" she asks.

I sense an accusatory tone and snap, "Everything's fine."

At that moment Sigrid notices the bread pan and tries to reach it. I call, "No, no! It's hot!" She pauses in her efforts. A teasing grin crosses her face. I can hear the wheels turning as she wonders: Does Daddy mean it?

There are some lessons you let your child learn through experience after she's failed to heed a warning, but burning her hand isn't one of them. "Hold on a minute," I tell Lynn, and then carry Sigrid out of the kitchen. She's crying again. I return to the kitchen, push the bread well out of reach and win the race with Sigrid back to the yo-yo. She storms off. Everything she wants to do today I mess up.

Before I get the phone to my ear Inga begins crying again. An alarm goes off inside me. This time it's not because she's hungry or wet. It is something else—something that can't be put off. "I'll call you later," I tell Lynn, and race upstairs. One of Inga's legs is caught between the crib bars. I free her and pick her up, comfort her, and change her diaper. All the while I listen carefully to Sigrid's progress on the stairs. As long as she's going up, she's fine. She reaches the top just as we are ready to go down. With Inga over my shoulder and Sigrid under my arm, we head for the living room. A moment later I'm sitting down, holding the baby's bottle in one hand and struggling to untie a knot in Sigrid's right shoelace with the other.

The scene took about 15 minutes. It could hardly be called a crisis—it was just one series of nonscheduled involvements that fill the parenting schedule daily. I was mentally alert every minute; yet what was I thinking about? I don't know what I was thinking about.

Life went on that way. There were hardships. There were moments of joy. The baby was crawling; then she was walking. Sigrid had become a chatterbox. The demands on me didn't diminish. But my writing sustained me.

When Inga was two and Sigrid about three and a half, I went through a crisis. The years had passed, and somewhere along the way I had started to feel that I was being consumed by those around me. It wasn't a particularly dramatic feeling, but I felt it just the same. Somehow I didn't have enough energy to combat the sensation that I was starting to shrink, to disappear.

There seemed to be tangible reasons connected with my mood, but they were of the which-came-first-the-chicken-or-the-egg? variety. One of these reasons was the first serious cold I'd had since I was a child. It took hold of me in autumn and held on until spring. Another was that I'd been unable to get started on a second book—the first, at long last, was finished. The mounting pile of rejection slips wasn't nearly as distressing as my not being able to write. I needed the escape and the sense of accomplishment that writing afforded me. Writing was my private tranquilizer.

I knew that somehow I had to muster the energy to get rid of my cold and begin writing again, but there didn't seem to be enough energy for everything and everyone. Lynn, Sigrid, and Inga had first claim on me. I didn't want to skimp on whatever portion of me each of them needed to keep fit and happy. The bigger they all grew—

101

both inside and out—the more of me and my energy each seemed to require. It had reached a point where there was hardly any of me left for me. I was becoming, I feared, a faded nonperson.

I had had advance warning that the homeperson's identity gets a little fuzzy during those intense years of dealing with small children. All my life I had seen, read, and heard about women in various degrees of fuzziness, but it had never occurred to me that such a problem wasn't just one of those "female weaknesses" we men tend to dismiss without a second thought.

Up to now Lynn and I had faced some problems that came about simply because I was a male in the home or because Lynn was a female out of the home. It was *because* I was a male, for example, that I sometimes had a self-conscious time dealing with infants when my men friends were around. It was *because* Lynn was a female that her parents refused to accept her position as provider in our family. But my fuzziness problem was completely different. This problem came about not because I was male, but *in spite of the fact* that I wasn't female.

I was going through a traditionally female identity crisis—the one in which the very existence of a clearly defined self is threatened because of a woman's constant service to her provider and her children. Whoever heard of such a thing happening to a man? It meant just one thing: The emotional condition of the housebound mate has nothing to do with the sex of that person.

Now, I certainly don't want to deny males their hallowed right to such a crisis: the male's seeking his own identity is an intricate part of growing up and away from parents and past. But while the traditional female crisis is one of losing an identity, the traditional male crisis is one of searching for something as yet unfound. Men are always roaming around looking for their identities; women are always clinging to their identities so that they don't lose them.

Until that winter I had been able to dismiss moments of discomfort by saying, "That's the way men are" or "That's the way women are." I realized now that the psychic state of the dependent adult—the housebound mate charged with parenting—transcended sex and simply slammed the door on a lot of easy answers. I could no longer think in conventional male-female terms.

Why do women so often feel consumed?

Traditionally a woman is the sustenance of her family. She's the one who gives of herself for the growth of a family and its individual members. It's a completely supportive role. Whatever success comes, comes in the shape of laurels won by those she's nourished. The sensation of having one's existence be the source of nourishment for other people is a good feeling, but sometimes it can be frightening.

A case in point was what was happening to me. (I was not a woman, but a mother all the same.) I was fighting a cold on the physical front. On the mental side I had made several false starts on a new book. After two and a half years of 24 hours a day of parenting, my sense of myself and my defenses were low. Something had got past my guard, sneaked into my spirit, and pulled the drain plug. It was a slow drain, but constant. I was being quietly consumed, and the rest of the family was so busy growing that they didn't even notice.

Not that I wanted them to notice. Surely if I became openly moody and loaded down my wife and children with my private frustrations, it would be counterproductive for us all. Lynn would feel lousy about going out to work; the girls would feel lousy about growing up; and I'd get even more frustrated because not only was I being consumed but also I wasn't doing my job properly. How could I be doing a good job if everyone felt lousy?

Why doesn't a man feel consumed in the same way his wife does? I think it's because he tends to get so caught up in the material commitment to his wife and children that he loses sight of his potential for deep emotional commitment and involvement. We males have unwittingly grown so complacent about our positions and the material comforts we provide that many of us are no longer capable of giving a pure and spiritual part of ourselves to those we love. We have somehow permitted ourselves to become emotional stiffs.

A man works hard. He contributes a lot of energy and devotion to earning a living for his family. He gives his family tangible support by the truckload and intangible support by the thimbleful. He allows his family to nourish off him—but only in nibbles, seldom in feasts, unlike the woman at home who gives herself without stint.

In thinking about the roles of men and women I realized that unconsciously I had always judged men and women in pat terms. Men gave and women took on the material and physical level, but on the spiritual and emotional plane men were the takers and women the givers. Fair exchange: Men gave prosperity and women gave comfort. What could be more natural? It was hardly worth a thought. The species thrived.

Now I was forced to give it some conscious thought. I no longer took comfort; I gave it. That changed matters.

The situation Lynn and I were in made the standard provider-parent area of our relationship less rigid than in a lot of other families. It didn't matter that in the past we'd been fed substantial doses of social indoctrination regarding male-female roles. Both of us were able to give and take support; we each had worn the other's shoes.

I knew how Lynn felt in most instances. On the other side, Lynn knew what I meant when I said, "Inga's getting another tooth" or, "Sigrid followed me everywhere today."

Just knowing that Lynn was able to understand allowed me to feel not quite so helpless and without identity or control of my destiny as many women must feel along about midway through the third winter, housebound with two small children. Thanks to Lynn with her understanding and her emotional generosity, I began to feel less helpless.

One night in early March I awakened with a throat that was sorer than it had been for the last four months (probably from talking too much; I had doubled the amount of my talk, almost as if doing that would prevent me from disappearing). The left side of my face was stiff, as if Muhammad Ali had given me his best left jab to the cheek. I felt awful. Still half asleep, I couldn't keep the thought from my mind that if I didn't get better soon, I was going to die. I was going to die before my children could grow up. It made me so sad that I almost cried.

I think the fact that I—a man—had almost cried scared the cold right out of me. It left a few days later. In its place came a small bolt of inspiration. Nothing big—just enough to get my fingers moving on the typewriter keys again. Now, again, I had a place other than my own mind and body in which to deposit my daily frustrations. It had been a long stagnation, but I emerged a little wiser.

When Sigrid was four and a half and Inga was three, they stepped out into the world; they entered nursery school. For me it was like the end of an era that had lasted a hundred years and was over in a minute. Those are the years, so all the baby- and child-care books proclaim, that shape the child. Those years also shape the parent. They are difficult years, but the sensation of accomplishment is just overwhelming. Like the work itself, the parent can't put a finger on any one thing and say, "Look what I've done! Look what I've accomplished!" There just isn't any tangible reward involved—and that's the beauty of parenting. You reach a point where you no longer need tangible rewards to feel rewarded.

5

EQUIPMENT

background/preparation

Goals to Work Toward in Presenting This Topic

Many parents are interested in the various pieces of baby equipment that are available in today's market. With the wide number of choices, parents can be uncertain as to which are beneficial, which are unnecessary, or simply what is obtainable.

The goals to work toward on this topic are: (1) to review for the parents the different kinds of baby equipment that are available, including those pieces that are essential and what to look for when buying; (2) to provide information about safe and appropriate uses of baby equipment; (3) to provide parents with information about places where they can buy, borrow, or trade equipment.

Typical Parental Interests and Concerns About This Topic

1. When can I start having Meredith use a highchair, a jumper, a backpack, and the other standard pieces of baby equipment?
2. Will I hinder my baby's development if I let her use a walker? What *are* the safety concerns about walkers?

3. How do I keep John from slipping out of his highchair?
4. Is a wooden playpen better than a mesh playpen?
5. Am I restricting Bret's freedom too much if I put him in a playpen?
6. Where can I find used baby equipment?
7. Is it possible to rent baby equipment to try before buying?

Areas of Information You Will Need to Learn About to Teach This Topic

The kinds of equipment available for babies.
— How to tell which brands are the safest and most durable.
— Local stores that carry baby equipment, especially those with the best selection and the lowest prices.
— Appropriate ages for babies to be when using different kinds of equipment.
— How to use the different pieces of equipment.
— The kinds of equipment that are most necessary.
The ways certain pieces of equipment influence development.
— The effects of the use of walkers and automatic swings.
— Different ways to use a playpen.

Family Dynamics—What This Topic Means Psychologically to Parent and Child

The subject of baby equipment can be yet another area in which parents can feel uncertain. With so many kinds and models of equipment available, parents may not know what is beneficial[1] or suitable for their child, when the appropriate time is to provide it, or how to use it. Many parents want to be sure that their child has appropriate experiences and is properly stimulated, but most don't feel they know what their baby needs. When they provide equipment, however, they find it enjoyable to see their baby use it and to see him have new experiences.

Being in different types of equipment can provide babies with pleasure and new learning. It can expand their world and sometimes decrease their fussiness. In some situations, however, babies can be frightened by certain equipment or need time to adjust to it.

---

1. At the time of this printing (1995), the American Academy of Pediatrics had called for a ban on the manufacture and sale of "infant walkers" due to their high incidence of injury and lack of apparent benefit to the child. See readings for ordering information on the official policy statement.

Sample Concern of Parents

In-depth analysis of a particular concern is not necessary for a discussion of equipment.

Readings and Other Resources

American Academy of Pediatrics, For the policy statement on infant walkers, and/or "Parent Fact Sheet on Infant Walkers" write: American Academy of Pediatrics, 141 Northwest Point Blvd., P.O. Box 927, Elk Grove, Ill. 60009-0927 or call (708) 228-5005.

Burck, Frances Wells, *Babysense* (New York: St. Martin's Press, 1991).

Consumer Guide, *The Complete Pregnancy and Baby Book* (New York: NAL/Dutton, 1991).

*Consumer Product Safety Commission, "The Safe Nursery" (a comprehensive guide to safety information in regard to infant equipment). To order, send a postcard to: CPSC Publication List, "The Safe Nursery", Washington, D.C., 20207 or call 800-638-CPSC.

*Jones, Sandy, *Guide to Baby Products* (Yonkers, N.Y.: Consumer Reports books, 1991).

teaching/presentation

Homework

There is no written homework for this topic, but you may wish to ask parents a week before the discussion which pieces of equipment they are interested in learning more about. Then the group can pool its resources and bring to class equipment they already own that others wish to see and familiarize themselves with.

Practical Suggestions or Strategies for Teaching This Topic

• The discussion of this topic can be very informal, especially if equipment is brought in for demonstration. Parents can share ideas about which kinds of equipment they feel are most helpful, where to buy them, and how to use them.

• You may wish to collect catalogs from places

that sell, rent, or exchange equipment and make them available during the break.

• You may find that many parents already have a good deal of equipment, either received as gifts or purchased. Be careful not to let parents become overly concerned that their equipment is not the "best," for example, if their car seat is not the highest rated.

• Be ready with ideas on equipment exchanges or ways to sell equipment.

Mini-lecture and Lead-off Questions for Discussion

Before you begin your talk, you may wish to distribute the handout "Equipment for Babies" (see the "Handouts" section of this topic) so that the group can refer to it as you speak.

With so many pieces of baby equipment available, most of us would like to know just what is necessary and what we can do without. I would say that a crib, a car seat, a highchair, and a stroller are the most important pieces to consider. The rest of the pieces listed on the handout can be helpful or practical, depending on your needs and your life style. Let's go over the list one by one and talk about what's important to look for when purchasing or renting each.

As you discuss equipment, ask the parents if they have any questions or pointers to share. Be sure to include safety information about each item. Then ask if they'd like to talk about any items that haven't been mentioned.

Now that we've talked about the various pieces, let's discuss where to obtain them. Remember as we mention places, that finding the store that offers the lowest prices may not be the answer for all of you. It may be easier to obtain something at a nearby store for a higher price or borrow a used item than
to drive a long distance in order to find a better price. Practicality should always balance cost.

You can mention a number of stores in your area that sell or rent new and used equipment. Ask the parents about stores they've frequented or other ways they've obtained what they needed.

Parents may want to talk about the various catalog services that they could order equipment from. Encourage parents to bring in catalogs that they have purchased from so they can tell the group about their experiences with mail ordering baby equipment.

A final step in the discussion can be the demonstration of pieces of equipment parents have brought in to show each other.

Additional Information for Parents

• The *Guide to Baby Products* (Consumer Reports, 1991) is a good resource for determining which brands of equipment are recommended and what to watch for when purchasing equipment.
• There seem to be about the same number of pros and cons for wooden playpens and mesh playpens. Wooden playpens allow a baby to pull himself up to a standing position more easily, but he can hit his head on the bars and toys can fall out. A mesh playpen doesn't allow a baby to pull himself up, but his toys will stay inside it and he can't hit his head.

Handouts

The handout for this topic, "Equipment for Babies," lists the kinds of equipment available, appropriate ages for their use, and things to watch for when buying equipment.

EQUIPMENT FOR BABIES*

Equipment	Age	Use	Buying Tips
Cribs	Infancy on.	For baby to sleep in.	1. Be sure the crib meets all current federal safety standards. 2. Buy a hardwood crib rather than pressed wood. 3. The crib should offer adjustable mattress height so that as your child grows, you can lower the mattress to prevent falling or climbing out. 4. Crib prices vary according to type of wood and style. 5. Standard crib size is 27¼" by 52⅝". 6. Put bumpers around side of crib for softness and keeping out drafts. 7. Crib slats should be spaced no more than 2⅜ inches apart. 8. Corner posts should be no higher than 1/16" to prevent entanglement. (1995 CPSC recommendations) 9. There should be no cutouts in the head and/or footboard.
Crib mattress	Infancy on.	For baby to sleep on.	1. Make sure the mattress is firm; either foam or innerspring. 2. The mattress should have a triple laminated waterproof cover. 3. The mattress should fit snugly into the crib. (There should be no more than two fingers space between the mattress and crib frame.)
Portacrib	Newborn to 1½ years old.	Sleeping and as small play-pen.	1. Get one with casters so it can be easily moved through house. 2. Be sure it folds up for travelling.

* Prepared with consultation from Lullaby Lane Children's Store, San Bruno, California 94066.

Equipment	Age	Use	Buying Tips
			3. Adjustable height allows ease in picking baby up and putting him down and allows crib to double as changing table. 4. Portacribs come in mesh and wood—get bumpers for wooden ones. 5. Watch that mesh is continuous around bottom of portacrib so arm or leg can't slip through.
Infant seats	Infancy to approximately 4-5 months.	A place for baby to be to watch what's happening; can be used for feeding, as a carrier, and for visiting.	1. Cheaper ones have weaker construction. 2. Infant seats can topple easily, especially when baby pushes against a surface with his legs. 3. Many infant car seats are designed to serve this function also.
Playpen ("Play-yard")	Early—approximately 3 months and up. The earlier the better so child becomes accustomed to it. The more mobile the baby, the less use you'll get.	Safe place for baby to play. Room to stretch, exercise, crawl, practice standing. Can use outdoors also. Don't use as a "prison." Baby also needs larger crawling space.	1. Wooden ones have advantage of sturdy rings for baby to pull up against, but are harder if baby bumps himself. (Slats should be less than 2⅜″ apart.) 2. Make sure mesh ones have a pad of good quality that ties down to its base. (Mesh ones should have a small weave with less than ¼″ openings.) 3. Both kinds are equally convenient as wooden ones roll on wheels and mesh ones lift easily.
Swings	From 6 weeks until baby wants to move around and exercise more.	Baby sits passively; motor (or parent) pushes; many infants fall asleep in one.	Built with seat or cradle and seat, simple or elaborate styles.
Jumper, Baby Bouncer	Beginning at 5 months when baby has	Pre-walking exercise—baby learns that his own actions (pushing feet against floor)	1. Be sure springs are covered so fingers cannot be caught. 2. Bouncers are like a chair.

EQUIPMENT FOR BABIES (continued)

Equipment	Age	Use	Buying Tips
	strong back and can sit up for a few minutes.	make something happen. Exercises feet and legs.	3. Jumpers suspend from a door jamb.
Walkers*	Parents are strongly cautioned against the use of walkers. The American Academy of Pediatrics has called for the ban of manufacturing and sales of walkers due to their high rate of injury and lack of any apparent benefit.		
Highchair	From 6-8 months— whenever baby's back is strong enough to sit for length of feeding time.	Place to feed baby; play place—tie toys to aid in retrieval problems.	1. Wood and metal chairs are equally safe. Chair can't tip unless baby stands up and pulls at something outside chair. 2. Check on ease and safety of getting baby in and tray off and on. 3. Could baby flip tray? 4. To make seat less slippery, paste bathtub non-skid strips on it. 5. Footrest is not essential and parents often remove it to cut down on kicking noises.
Front and back packs	Infancy on, depending on style and size of baby in relation to strength of parent's back.	To carry baby around and still have two arms free. Great for hiking, shopping, etc.	1. Two types: Infant to 4 months and aluminum frame type for older baby. 2. Consider length of useable time vs. price. 3. Try on pack with your baby in it. 4. Decide whether you want style that lets baby face front or back. 5. Some infant styles require parent to use one arm to support baby. 6. Be sure there's no strap to push baby's head or face.

*The American Academy of Pediatrics will be issuing a policy statement in 1995 calling for a ban on the manufacture and use of infant walkers. High injury rates among infants and lack of any developmental benefits have prompted their position.

Equipment	Age	Use	Buying Tips
			7. Be sure infant style has head support for baby. 8. Both types should be adjustable.
Car seats	Three types: • Infant (birth–20 lbs.) • Infant/toddler (birth–40 lbs./4 yrs.) • Booster seat (30–65 lbs.)	Taking baby or toddler with you in car.	1. Required by law until child is 4 years old and 40 lbs. 2. Label should give size, height, and weight of child seat can carry. 3. Get one that's easy to install if you will need to switch it from car to car. 4. Make sure the car seat fits well in your car before it is purchased.
Stroller	From newborn on, if stroller reclines into bed or if infant seat fits in securely, until child resists the ride, usually around 2 to 3 years old.	Transporting baby.	1. Consider how easily it collapses for getting in and out of car; umbrollers are great on this. 2. Be sure it has a seat belt. 3. Compartments or baskets are handy for packages. Can buy or make big bag for umbroller that attaches over handles. 4. Some people like "flexible" wheels in front for guiding stroller. Umbrollers don't have this but are lightweight enough to guide easily. 5. Many strollers come with awnings to shade baby. Can get them with wind and rain protection too.
Tubs	First 3-6 months.	Bathing or rinsing baby.	1. This is used only briefly, so it's best to spend as little as possible. 2. Some have canvas, foam, or sponge pad to support baby.

6

SPEECH AND LANGUAGE DEVELOPMENT[1]

background/preparation

Goals to Work Toward in Presenting This Topic

Most parents realize the importance of speech and communication and are interested in knowing how they can help their baby learn to talk.

The goals to work toward on this topic are: (1) to help parents learn to recognize the main stages of language development in infants; (2) to help parents gain perspective on their role in encouraging language development; and (3) to encourage parents to relax about language and remind them that different babies focus on different developmental skills at different times.

Typical Parental Interests and Concerns About This Topic

1. Julia used to "talk" a lot but all of a sudden she's not doing it any more. Is something wrong?
2. I love to talk "baby talk" and gurgle and coo with Ryan but feel very foolish if someone overhears us playing. Will I hinder his language development if I don't always speak in complete sentences?

3. What can my spouse and I do to further Katie's language development?
4. How can I tell if my baby's hearing is normal?
5. I don't feel like I talk to my baby enough.
6. I try to give Tamara my full attention all the time so she knows how important communication is, but often that's not possible. Will there be problems if I can't be totally with her all the time?
7. Allison is at daycare until 2 p.m. every day. I know they don't talk to her as much as we do at home. I worry that being at daycare will delay her language development.

Areas of Information You Will Need to Learn About to Teach This Topic

- The main stages of speech and language development.

---

1. Speech *and* language are not the same as each other. Speech refers to the mechanics (in the throat and mouth), i.e., the movement of the vocal musculature to form sounds and eventually words. Language refers to the thought processes (in the brain) and encompasses the meaning of words (semantics), memory, and word order and grammar (syntax). In our Speech and Language chapters, we generally use "Language" when we are referring to both at once.

— Ways babies differ in language development.
— How to recognize the sounds that differentiate the stages.
— The role of nonverbal communication between parents and baby.
- How to recognize and handle delays in speech and language development.
- Ways parents can stimulate their child's speech and language development.
— Games and activities.
— Attitudes toward language and communication.

Family Dynamics—What This Topic Means Psychologically to Parent and Child

It is important to most parents that they feel they are doing everything they should to help their baby's language develop normally and fully. While they're encouraging their child's speech, however, they can feel foolish talking to him, using complete sentences to respond to coos and gurgles or imitating the baby and responding with like sounds. Parents sense the importance of their own speech in encouraging language development, but they may feel confusion about the proper way to go about it.

Although the first sounds babies make are involuntary and in response to bodily conditions, babies slowly gain control over their sounds and come to realize that they are making the sounds they hear. This is an exciting discovery, and sounds and later speech come to be an enjoyable way to communicate with parents. Language becomes a fun way for babies to play.

Sample Concern of Parents

Concern	Critical Issues
My six-month-old seems to have lost his interest in cooing and babbling. He used to vocalize for long periods at a time but lately seems uninterested in speech play.	—Baby has lost interest in language expression.

Key Questions

1. What does your baby seem interested in doing now? Did he do this when he was vocalizing a lot?
2. What kinds of communication patterns are happening now between you and your baby?
3. Does your baby vocalize around other people? How does he react to new faces?
4. What are your feelings when your baby does other things besides "talk"?

Readings and Other Resources

*Allison, Christine, *I'll Tell You a Story, I'll Sing You a Song* (New York: Dell/Bantam Dell Doubleday, 1987).

*Baron, Naomi, *Growing Up With Language* (New York: Addison-Wesley, 1992).

Caplan, Theresa, & Caplan, Frank, *The First Twelve Months of Life* (New York: Perigree Books/Berkley Publishing, 1993).

Helleberg, Marilyn Morgan, "Check Your Baby's Hearing," *Parents Magazine* (this page is reprinted in the "Handouts" section of this topic).

Leach, Penelope, *Your Baby and Child* (Westminster, Md.: Alfred A. Knopf, 1989).

Maurer, Daphne, *The World of the Newborn* (New York: Basic Books, Inc., 1988), Chapter 7.

Shelov, Steven P., *Caring For Your Baby and Young Child* (New York: Bantam Books, 1991) p. 529 (excellent section on hearing loss).

For information and pamphlets on speech and language development issues, contact American Speech-Language-Hearing Association (ASHA), 10801 Rockville Pike, Rockville, Maryland 20852 or call (800) 638-8255 or (301) 897-8682.

teaching/presentation

Homework

The homework developed for this topic helps parents observe their baby's present language pattern and think about related questions they have for the class discussion.

Practical Suggestions or Strategies for Teaching This Topic

• Since young babies vocalize frequently during class but never seem to when you'd like to illustrate a certain language stage, it's helpful to have a tape recording of examples of the different stages of language development babies go through in the first year and a half. You can make the recording yourself with a cassette recorder and visits to babies of different ages. A cassette of representative sounds and words can help parents have a better idea of what each stage sounds like.

• Some groups may want detailed information about language development while other groups may be more interested in sharing their own feelings and ideas on the topic. Knowledge of the group helps you decide how to focus the presentation.

• Some parents may feel foolish discussing how they communicate with their child (talking about the words or sounds they use). Sharing a funny story with them that tells about how you "spoke" with your baby may help them to relax and share their own stories.

• Some parents do not know very many word games or songs/rhymes to share with their baby. Having parents demonstrate their songs is fun for the group and increases everyone's repertoire.

Mini-lecture and Lead-off Questions for Discussion

Sample Mini-lecture

Today we are going to talk about the main stages of language development, and I'll play a tape to illustrate each one. As we go over the stage, feel free to add comments or examples of your own. My comments will follow the handout I'm passing around now— "Speech and Language Development" (from the "Handouts" section of this topic) **so you can follow it too as I talk. Remember that the ages on the chart are approximate, and the exact month when each stage is reached isn't as important as knowing the direction in which your baby is heading. Also, some babies simply are more interested in language than others. When we've talked about the various stages, we'll discuss any questions you have.**

When a child is born, crying is his first means of communication. Other noises that accompany the crying—grunts, belches, squeals, and the like—are spasmodic and uncontrolled. They're bodily expressions of hunger, cold, dampness, and discomfort.

Most babies are born hearing, and respond to sounds with blinks, jerks, and drawing in of their breath. Some fussy babies can be calmed by human voices, music, or the hum of motors. They also may startle or shudder at a loud noise, then shut it out when it happens again. Studies indicate that even newborns tune in to language-related sounds (vs. nonsense syllables), suggesting that there is an inherent capacity to discriminate language sounds from other sounds.

By the time a child is one month old, small throaty sounds are made in addition to crying. These first sounds are accidental and usually made as the baby breathes out, the result of unintentional muscle changes. Soon

SPEECH AND LANGUAGE DEVELOPMENT

(1–6 months)

1. What sorts of sounds is your baby playing with? What's he/she trying to do with the sounds?

2. What do you find yourself doing in regard to your baby's speech and/or language?

3. In thinking about your baby's speech and language development, what questions come to mind?

Parent's name _____ Date _____ Child's age _____

the child begins to make more of these sounds since he finds them pleasurable.

Somewhere between six weeks and three months, babbling starts—cooing and gooing sounds and vowel vocalizations that gradually lead to large numbers of indescribable sounds and sound combinations. Babies at this age experiment and play with sounds for pleasure and to master a new skill. And during the first year, every sound in every language is produced by a baby. The ones pertinent to the child's particular culture are reinforced and therefore repeated more often.

At two months, it's important for a baby to direct his smiling and vocalizing to a responsive face. Speech becomes associated with comfort and communication. Also, the reinforcement of sounds by parents provides feedback to the baby that is important in early speech learning. Parents babble to imitate the baby's sounds and play word games, and in this play teach their child to produce a response to the expression of others. Through sound and word play, parents also show their baby that his own verbal behavior produces pleasant consequences. This early imitation of a baby's speech encourages his later imitation of adult sounds.

Around three months, babies begin to laugh and chortle. They also whimper, gurgle, squeal, chuckle, and cry less. They listen to voices and are more and more pleased when spoken to and imitated. They watch faces and mouths when people are talking, and seem to study the whole process.

Somewhere around four months, cooing includes more pitch changes and sounds more musical. Babies "talk" for longer periods of time, some 15 to 30 minutes of syllable-like vocalizing. There's usually a real belly laugh by the end of the fourth month.

Between four and six months, a higher level of babbling occurs when a baby begins to imitate the babbling he hears—his own and his parents'. Before this time he seemed to vocalize because it felt good to him in his throat and mouth, but now he is aware that the sounds he makes and the sounds he hears are related. Imitation of his own sounds is the beginning of the memory neces-

sary to learn words, matching what the sound feels like and what it sounds like when it's made. Babies enjoy this early form of "chatting," of responding to babbling, even though their imitation may be inaccurate because the necessary skills aren't developed yet. There are many sounds during this experimental period—clicks, smacks, yells, screeches, and all sorts of faces (tongue stuck out, a "fish" look). Every type of emotion has been expressed by six months.

Babies begin to use sounds at this age to initiate social interaction. Sounds and events also become associated, for instance, the sound of footsteps becomes associated with being picked up. Babies are now more aware of intonations and inflections in voices and are increasingly interested in human sounds. They begin to turn to look for sounds.

By about seven months, babies have special, well-defined syllables, usually four or more, that they practice over and over again. These could be ma-ma, da-da, ga-ga. Babies try to imitate sounds or sound sequences and babble several sounds in one breath.

Around eight months they babble with a variety of sounds and inflections, spontaneously, for fun, or alone. This babbling is still primarily for themselves, but they begin to impose adult intonations on it. When they hear a familiar sound nearby, such as their name, the phone, or the vacuum cleaner, they turn their head toward it. They can listen selectively to familiar words and begin to recognize some.

Somewhere around nine months, a baby may say a syllable or a longer sequence repeatedly, and his intonation patterns become distinct. He may use "mama" or "dada" as specific names.

By ten months he has picked up the lilt and intonation of adult speech, and the sounds of real speech replace the earlier flat monotones. Jargon occurs when the baby makes real speech sounds and sounds like someone talking in a foreign language.

To sum up, I'll give you some information that's not on the chart. It will give you an idea of how fast speech develops once a baby begins to use actual words (those that the child's parents understand, even if a stranger doesn't). If the first word occurs at

around 12 months, by 18 months the baby
has a 5- to 20-word vocabulary. At 24 months
he may have a 200- to 300-word vocabulary.

You may now wish to play a tape of the various
sounds made at each stage, and then ask the
group to bring up any questions they'd like to ask
about language.

Lead-offs

* What are some of the sounds your babies are
  making now? What are your babies doing with
  the sounds? Are the sounds involuntary or are
  the babies showing more voluntary control?
* What kinds of communication are your babies
  perfecting?
* What sounds are your children playing with?
* When do your babies talk the most? When do
  they do their practicing?
* What have you done to encourage your babies'
  talking?

Additional Information for Parents

Encouraging Speech and Language Development

* Parents often create a rich verbal environment
  for their child without even realizing it. Simply
  exposing a child to everyday sounds and words—
  clocks ticking, wind chimes ringing, voices speaking—is helping him become acquainted with his
  world.
* Parents and baby's other caregivers need to talk
  to their baby. Even before babies understand,
  they respond to tone of voice, facial expressions,
  and gestures. Later, actual words become important as the child begins to develop a memory for
  sounds.
* Parents and caregivers should be encouraged to
  ask their baby questions and converse with him as
  though they expect him to reply. Any response

can be treated as a real one and conversation can
continue. Researchers suggest that how well a
baby imitates or responds to speech will depend
to a large extent upon the response his speech get
from his listeners.
* Sounds and words can be used as a form of
play, hamming it up and enjoying the nursery
rhymes and word games.
* By imitating the adults that care for them, babies get the idea that their own verbal behavior
produces pleasant consequences. Early imitation
of a baby's speech encourages his later imitation
of adult sounds.
* Parents can stimulate their child's environment
by providing mobiles, bright shapes, and other
interesting and attractive objects. Studies show
that the more appealing the environment, the
more the baby learns and the more he wants to
learn. (This doesn't mean overdo it—see the
topic "Play and Learning" (pp. 78–89) for more
information).

Handouts

There are two handouts for this topic. The
handout, "Speech and Language Development,"
shows the main stages of receptive and expressive
language development during the first year of life.
The section in "Speech and Language Skills" of
"Suggested Activities" offers ideas for activities
that further language growth. The section on
"Simple Tests to Check Your Baby's Hearing" offers some suggestions for parents who would like
to be sure their baby can hear. You may also wish
to refer to "Finger Plays" which gives the words
to simple songs and word games as well as nota-
tions about the hand or finger motions that go
with them (see pp. 163–181 in *I'll Tell You a Story,
I'll Sing You a Song* by Christine Allison (New
York: Dell/Bantam Doubleday Dell Publishing
Group, 1987).

Speech and Language Development

(newborn–1 year)

	RECEPTIVE	EXPRESSIVE
(Newborn)	Responds to voice by quieting.	Cries.
•		
•	Listens to voices. Smiles when talked to.	Laughs. Produces vowel sounds (e.g., ahhh, eee).
(3 mo.)		Experiments with inflection, rhythm, pitch, and sounds. Babbles, coos, gurgles.
•		
•	Reacts to different intonations and inflections. Listens to own vocalizations.	
(6 mo.)		Imitates sounds. Uses vocalizations to express feelings more and more.
(7 mo.)		Babbles several sounds in one breath.
•	Responds to own name. Recognizes some simple words.	
(9 mo.)		Imitates simple sounds. Speaks with intonations, rhythm, and emphasis.
•		
•	Understands some words.	
(12 mo.)	Recognizes words as symbols. Follows some simple directions.	Uses single words meaningfully. 1 to 2 word vocabulary. Jabbers in jargon. Imitates extensively.

SPEECH AND LANGUAGE SKILLS

(1–6 months)

Suggested Language Activities*

Emotional Development. The way you talk to your baby, the way you treat him, and the way he gets along with other people in the family are very important in his learning to talk. The things you say to your baby will influence how he thinks about himself. He will learn to like himself better if you talk to him with a soothing voice that lets him know that he is part of a secure and loving home. Hold him close and show that you enjoy being with him. Teach him that you and the rest of the family are fun to be with. Help him learn to like other people.

"A baby's great need early in life is for love, affection, and good physical care. Being loved and cuddled helps a baby learn to live in the world." (From the John Tracy Clinic's Language Program, "Getting Your Baby Ready to Talk.")

Before your baby will want to talk he must first be convinced that talking is something that he wants to do. Do things that will convince him that it is worth the effort he has to make. Hold your baby and let him hear friendly and affectionate talk. This will help him associate speech and language with something pleasant and enjoyable.

Imitation. Teach your baby to imitate. The first step is to copy the things *he* does. *Don't* expect him to imitate you, at least not yet. Imitate his smiles and other movements and the kinds of sounds he makes. If he says "mmmmbah," then you say "mmmmmbah." This will help him develop an interest in imitation and will encourage him to imitate your sounds later on. This is not *baby talk.* When your child is at this age, you should

repeat these sounds and help him to develop imitation skills. When he begins to use *meaningful* words, don't repeat his incorrect attempts. Instead use the word correctly in your own speech.

Basic Talking Times. "Talk" to or imitate your baby when you dress, feed, bathe, or change him, or when the two of you just decide to sit down and chat. Be sure he is able to watch you talk and can hear you during these times. Remember to keep your gestures and the tone of your voice consistent. These times provide opportunities for you and your baby to associate pleasure with talking.

Learning How to Listen. Let your baby hear as many different sounds as possible to help him develop his listening skills. When you leave your baby alone in his crib, he will be soothed by such things as the tinkling of wind chimes, a clock that ticks quietly near his bed, or soft music from a radio or music box.

Pictures and Crib Mobiles. Because your baby spends a lot of time in his crib, you should give him interesting things to look at. Hang brightly colored pictures on nearby walls. They don't have to be expensive; an older child's art work or pictures cut from magazines are fine.

Simple Tests to Check Your Baby's Hearing*

These are some simple, effective tests that can be used at home:

Birth to Two Months. Choose a quiet time when your baby is sleeping. Gently touch one eyelid—if it quivers even slightly or his body moves, you know he is in that light stage of sleep

---

*Reprinted with permission from *Teach Your Child to Talk,* by David Pushaw (Fairfield, N.J.: CEBCO/Standard Publishing Co., out-of-print).

*Taken from "Check Your Baby's Hearing at Home" by Marilyn Morgen Helleberg, *Parents Magazine.*

most favorable for testing hearing responses. Next, take a sheet of onionskin paper, crush it near one of the baby's ears, and watch for a strong, immediate eye-blink followed by a stirring movement of the body and the opening of both eyes.

Once your baby is quiet again, repeat the test near the other ear. On another occasion, using a high-pitched bell, rattle, or loud voice, follow the same procedure. This will help determine whether or not your child hears the full range of sound frequencies. Some children hear low- but not high-pitched sounds; for others the reverse is true. You should discount reaction to door slamming, foot stamping, and other noises that create vibrations which can be discerned through the sense of touch.

Two to Four Months. When your baby cries or frets, stand where he can't see you and make a loud noise. If he suddenly stops what he's doing or changes his behavior, you'll know that he has responded to the sound. Then, distracting him with a stuffed animal or doll, hold him on your lap facing you. Have another person stand behind him and ring a bell, or shake a rattle. If the baby's hearing is normal he should respond with a head-wobble in the direction of the sound, or open his eyes wider.

Five to Eight Months. Repeat the sequences of testing for a four-month-old child. Now the baby should turn his head towards the source of the sound. Listen to him babble—does he make more than one or two sounds? A hard-of-hearing baby may babble as much as one who hears normally during the first few months, but at six to eight months, he should use at least four distinctly recognizable sounds.

Eight to Thirteen Months. Stand where your baby cannot see you; call his name or say "shhh." He should turn toward you immediately. Listen closely to his babbling during these months. Does he use different pitches? Is he sounding consonants? Even profoundly deaf babies appear to be saying "mama" at one year and mothers often interpret this as an indication that their children hear normally. But all babies make these sounds; they seem to be a basic utterance, not dependent on hearing. So reevaluate your testing to make sure he really hears you.

Thirteen Months to Two Years. By this time, you can give your child a verbal command such as "Bring me the ball" but do not help him by pointing toward the object or looking in its direction. If he hears, he should be able to follow simple directions or understand simple questions like "Where's your shoe?"

7

SOCIAL-EMOTIONAL DEVELOPMENT

background/preparation

Goals to Work Toward in Presenting This Topic

By looking at the broad issues of a child's social and emotional development, parents can begin to formulate their own philosophy of child rearing. What are their expectations for their child? Do these fit with what they know about their child? Are the expectations realistic both for their baby and themselves?

The goals to work toward on this topic are: (1) to help parents begin to think about long-term social and emotional influences on their child; (2) to help parents gain perspective on the kinds of social and emotional changes that are occurring within their baby; (3) to help parents understand that the philosophical framework of their parenting changes and will be revised as they continue to grow as parents and as individuals; (4) to help parents become aware of which characteristics are a part of various temperaments and how much babies differ from each other.

Typical Parental Interests and Concerns About This Topic

1. How can I nurture my child's spirit?
2. How can I avoid passing on my own bad character traits to my child?
3. Will Ryan suffer emotional damage if I don't pick him up each time he cries?
4. My friend's baby sleeps and eats on a regular basis. Why is it so difficult for me to tell when my baby is tired or hungry?
5. With me working so much I worry that Emma may care more for her nanny than for me. What can I do?

Areas of Information You Will Need to Learn About to Teach This Topic

- Stages of social and emotional development in infants.
- Practical techniques for parents to use as they deal with these different stages.
- How babies differ in temperament.

- How the temperament of the child and that of of the parent influence their relationship and interaction.
- Ways parents can be beneficial influences on their child's emotional development.

Family Dynamics—What This Topic Means Psychologically to Parent and Child

Parents often feel that they must be all things to their child—such a beneficial influence that the child will grow up free of any emotional traumas or difficulties. In the early months, parents may think that they'll be able to raise a "perfect" child if they provide the "right" parenting. It seems to them that each of their actions will have a long-term effect on their baby's emotional development. This makes it difficult for parents to relax with their learning of parenting skills.

The child's social and emotional development—how she feels about herself—is greatly influenced by how she is treated and cared for by others. However, her inborn temperament also accounts for much of why she becomes the person she does.

Sample Concern of Parents

Concern	Critical Issues
I've always been a worrier. I worry about everything. I don't like this part of myself and wonder if I'm passing the trait on to Melissa.	—Parent's concern about negative influence on child. —Parent's definition of her concern. —Parent's need to be a "good" parent.

Key Questions

1. What steps can you take to help yourself grow as a person?
2. Think about your strengths. In what ways will your child benefit from these?

For the group

3. Do you have any suggestions for ways to handle personal weaknesses so that they have little influence on your child?
4. How much can parents realistically expect of themselves?

Readings and Other Resources

*Brazelton, T. Berry, *Infants and Mothers* (New York: Dell Publishing, 1983).

Brazelton, T. Berry, *On Becoming a Family* (New York: Delacorte Press, 1992).

Brazelton, T. Berry, *The Earliest Relationship* (New York: Delacorte, 1990).

Brazelton, T. Berry, *Working and Caring* (New York: Addison-Wesley, 1992).

*Briggs, Dorothy, *Your Child's Self-Esteem* (Garden City, N.Y.: Doubleday and Co., Inc., 1975).

Chess, S. and Thomas, A., *Know Your Child* (New York: Harper Collins, 1989).

Greenspan, Stanley, *First Feelings* (New York: Viking Penguin, 1989).

*Greenspan, Stanley, *The Essential Partnership* (New York: Viking Penguin, 1990).

*Kaplan, Louise, *Oneness and Separateness* (New York: Simon & Schuster, 1980).

La Farge, Phyllis, "Team Up With Your Caregiver," *Parents*, February, 1993, p. 87.

teaching/presentation

Homework

The homework assignment for this topic helps parents begin to look at their child as an individual and at how they can positively influence and support his development. It also asks parents to examine their pre-natal expectations of what heir baby would be like and to compare that to the actual baby they now have. This helps parents see their child more clearly as a unique individual.

SOCIAL-EMOTIONAL DEVELOPMENT

(1–6 months)

1. When your baby was first born, what were some of the expectations you had for him/her in terms of what you thought he/she would be like as a person? Think mostly in terms of behavior and personality and secondly, about developmental expectations if any of these occur to you.

2. Have your initial expectations changed now that you've gotten to know your baby? If so, in what ways?

3. What do you feel are some important ways that you and your husband can be a beneficial influence on your baby's personality development? Also, what about your baby's other caregivers?

Parent's name _____ Date _____ Child's age _____

PARENTMAKING: A Practical Handbook for Teaching Parent Classes About Babies and Toddlers by B. Annye Rothenberg, Ph.D., et al. © 1995 Banster Press, P.O. Box 7326, Menlo Park, CA 94026. Can copy for parent classes if this notice is included in full.

Practical Suggestions or Strategies for Teaching This Topic

• Parents of a young baby are caught up in the immediacy of a newborn's demands and often can think only as far ahead as the next feeding or the next crying episode. Their baby is such an unknown in the first weeks that it's impossible for them to plan ahead or visualize long-term influences. Consequently, discussing emotional influences and child-rearing philosophies is most beneficial if it is undertaken at the end of the series. Most parents will then be starting to have some knowledge of themselves, their new role, and their interaction with their baby.

• While aspects of individual temperaments may be discussed, it's best to avoid labeling specific babies. The parent of a child who cries often may fear that the child will grow up to be a negative person, especially if someone labels the baby as fussy; she may find as time goes on that the crying is due to colic rather than to temperament. Parents can watch for general ways babies differ but should also be aware that regular patterns of characteristics may not be determined until later.

• Since parents at this stage are still getting to know their baby and since personality patterns aren't established yet, the discussion of social and emotional development may be fairly brief. However short, the discussion can help parents to realize that as their child's temperament becomes more apparent and familiar (somewhere between 12 and 20 months), knowledge of it will help to guide them in their goals for parenting.

• Parents may need a gentle reminder that every baby is an individual with his or her own unique personality. Sometimes new parents become so involved in the day-to-day concerns of child care that they need help taking time to learn the distinctive and special qualities of their child.

Mini-lecture and Lead-off Questions for Discussion

The presentation of information related to social-emotional development can be divided into three parts: (1) a summary of development; (2) a description of individual differences, and (3) a discussion of child-rearing philosophies. The summary of development expands on material listed in the handout for this topic ("Social-Emotional Development") so it will be valuable if this handout is distributed prior to the discussion.

Summary of Development

Social-emotional development is crucial to the well-being of any infant and is very much involved in a parent's interpersonal relationship with the child. In the early months, the parent-child relationship is quite intense. The baby quickly learns the sounds, smells, touch, footsteps, face, and other signals that mean pleasure, food, protection, and satisfaction. This early form of learning—associating the parent (generally the mother) with nurturing—results in a sense of trust. Even before a child can identify her parent's face, certain cues lead her to a feeling of security. The initial bond between parent and child is a prerequisite for all future close ties. It's no wonder that a baby's early smiles are a product of the association of satisfaction and a special face. When both mother and father work outside the home, a baby's relationship with his or her caregiver also influences this developing sense of trust. A consistent and responsive caregiver during this first year of life provides baby with both separation experience and an emerging sense of security with caregivers other than its parents.

Since there are so many changes that occur in the first few months of life, I'd like to break them down into stages. You can follow along on the handouts you've just received.

During the *newborn* stage:

Emotions are not directed toward any person. This is because babies can't distinguish themselves from the environment and aren't aware of people as objects to whom to express emotion or need. New parents usually find this fact contrary to their beliefs. They think that when their baby screams, he's screaming at them. Actually, he's simply reacting to his own needs.

Babies usually quiet when they are comforted.

They adjust their posture to the body of the person holding them. They also watch a person's face, rather than any other part of the body, from their first moments.

A baby functions on an instinctive level. A newborn's whole world revolves around reflexes and needs that must be satisfied. The book *The First Twelve Months of Life* (by Theresa and Frank Caplan) has a chart of these reflexes.

Around *six weeks:*

Babies begin to smile socially. This action results in a good deal of positive reinforcement which, in turn, causes a baby to associate smiling with pleasant occurrences.

Babies become visually interested in people and more interested in people than toys. Although at this stage of development the most significant forms of stimulation are tactile (being rocked, held, touched, and so on) and oral (sucking), the baby's awareness of and interest in people is steadily increasing. The six-week-old baby cries to express a growing number of emotions and also smiles and coos.

During the *three- to four-month* stage:

Babies recognize their parents, and begin developing an awareness of themselves as separate beings. A baby at this age begins to discover himself (hands, feet, body, sounds he can make, familiar people) and has more mastery over his body (reaching, batting, cooing) than he has had before. He also begins to notice textures and his own body vs. other objects. This discrimination is part of the "scientist" aspect of an infant—he processes and organizes all sensory data, laying the foundation for an awareness of self and a development of ego.

Babies express emotions with their entire body. In the first three months, a baby changes from a bundle of reflexes and instincts whose emotions are basically contentment or distress to a very sociable, interacting individual who displays a multitude of feelings.

Infants become more and more interested in others. The sequence of development from three months on is fairly predictable, yet within that sequence individual variations make each child unique.

Babies are able to entertain themselves for longer periods.

Around *five months:*

Babies are able to anticipate. They know which actions follow other actions and can demand more.

They begin to protest, wailing if play is disrupted and more overtly showing likes and dislikes. At four months a baby may indicate enjoyment, indecision, protestation, and excitement while at five months he may add fear, disgust, and anger to his repertoire. The feelings of a six-month-old are often very easy to read.

Babies this age want to be part of social activities. By four months they have differentiated family members and can sense appropriate behavior for each. This is more clearly seen if siblings are around. They are friendly toward everyone, although special smiles and shows of excitement are saved for parents. Around five months of age, they begin to form attachments to people and things, but by six months the differentiation of self and others is so distinct that the baby is often disturbed by strangers. This stranger anxiety can increase during the first year until the child cries if approached too rapidly or held too soon by someone he isn't familiar with.

Babies around this age begin to show they understand "cause and effect." This becomes apparent by their behavior, i.e. if a parent walks past the baby's door, the baby may make happy, encouraging sounds. If the parent doesn't go in to the child, he may scream, then calm down if the parent returns and goes in to him.

Around *six months:*

Babies want to interact with other children; they like to watch and be around them.

They are interested in playing with toys for longer periods of time.

They may reach to be picked up. Love for their parents has changed from mostly gratification (material love) to satisfaction from simply being in their presence. In the next half year, a baby's tie to her parents grows. They are her link between her new-found "self" and the world. When a parent is not around, a baby can feel somewhat confused and disoriented.

Around *seven months:*[1]

Babies are clearly aware of themselves versus the world. As their motor skills improve and they have the option of physically moving away from their parents, their dependence increases. It's as though the prospect of being on their own is scary, and they know there's a compelling force within them that will make them move out on their own. The seven-month-old clearly prefers people and enjoys cooperative games like "peek-a-boo" and "come and get me."

Around *seven to eight months:*

Babies begin to show signs of independence. They want to feed themselves and resist being pressured into doing something they don't want to do (for example, having their diapers changed). Humor is appearing to a greater extent and babies this age like to tease and be teased.

Around *nine months:*[2]

Babies clearly dislike being separated from their mother. Separation is easier for both parent and baby if familiar sitters are used and if the parent is leaving the baby often enough for him to get to know the sitters. The nine-month-old is usually a busy explorer who rejects confinement, has a mind of his own, and is highly social and charming. His imitative behavior is budding, keeping all around him entertained and happy.

Individual Differences[3]

Babies are known to be very different from each other at birth, and even more different a day or two later. Your parenting goals can become more specific as your child's temperament emerges further and as you learn more about that temperament's unique characteristics.

The first 3 to 4 months of any baby's life are busy spent getting organized and adjusted to life outside the womb. But people who have worked with lots of babies have been able to distinguish several kinds of temperament differences that pertain mostly to babies *over* four months of age. Among them are:

People who have worked with lots of babies have been able to distinguish several kinds of temperament differences that pertain mostly to babies over four months of age. Among them are:

Regularity.—the rhythm of biological functioning. Some babies have very predictable rhythms while others seem to be hungry and sleepy in very irregular patterns.

Accepting of changes—how adaptable the baby is in reacting to new experiences (new food, new people, and so on). Some babies have a terrible time when parents attempt to shape their behavior to conform to schedules that are more convenient for the family.

Persistence—the ability of babies to concentrate. Some are easily diverted while others can continue an activity in the face of difficulties or resume an activity after interruption.

Mood—happy, neutral, or fussy and crying.

Activity level—the amount of energy expressed in the baby's behavior, his intensity of response.[4]

We feel parents need different kinds of guidance based on the nature of their baby and on their own individuality as well. Different parent tempos interact in different ways with tempos of the baby. For instance, a

---

1. Though the information regarding 7-, 8-, and 9-month-olds *exceeds* the age range for this topic, it is meant to give parents a brief look ahead.

2. For a thorough discussion and treatment of "Separation" including useful handouts and exercises as well as content materials, refer to *PETP,* pp. 291–318.

3. For a more complete discussion of individual differences, see pp. 340–351. Rothenberg, *PETP* also discusses the area of temperament in great detail (pp. 272–284) and includes handouts for parents.

4. From *Know Your Child* by Stella Chess and Alexander Thomas, chapter 2, pp. 28–31.

slow-moving, relaxed parent may feel over-whelmed by an extremely active child. Sug-gestions can be useful to help this parent develop a positive relationship with the child by meshing the two diverse temperaments.

Lead-offs

• Are there certain personality characteristics that seem to be unique to your baby and that could influence the kind of person he could become?

• What expectations did you have for your baby before he was born? Have these changed now that you know him?

• What have you learned about your own temperament? How might your own traits influence your parenting?

Child-rearing Philosophy

Sometimes we need to raise our sights beyond the immediate routine of each day and look at the values and ideas that are important to us in our long-term relationship with our child. As we appraise our relationship, we need to remember that the philosophy or framework within which we operate is a changing thing. We'll probably change our outlook many times because we're growing as our child grows.

No matter what our philosophy, we will all have times that seem like huge failures. It will be helpful if we accept the fact that we will have successes and failures. Most of us may want to be "perfect" parents and have a "perfect" child, but we need to make our expectations for ourselves and our child realistic as well as appropriate.

Lead-offs

• What kinds of guidelines for emotional development do you feel are important to apply to your parenting on a day-to-day basis?

• How do you feel you can be a beneficial influence on your child?

• How child centered is your home? How adult centered? Are you meeting your own needs as well as your child's?

• What might be the long-term consequences of today's patterns of parenting? (It's hard to back-track once we've gotten into habits.)

Additional Information for Parents

Awareness

• Parents are only human. They have problems, strengths, and weaknesses and, no matter how hard they try to do things "just right," their children will have similar successes and failures. Instead of expecting perfection from themselves, parents would do better to set an example for their children of facing problems and attempting to work through them toward a solution.

• Parents should try to handle their baby calmly and with respect, and minimize his exposure to very angry or depressed feelings expressed by adults.

• Parents should try to accept and enjoy their baby for her uniqueness, not try to mold her into someone else.

• Knowledge of developmental stages can expand acceptance and awareness of "stages" and personality. It can also give parents an opportunity to reexperience growing up by seeing things through their baby's eyes.

• Parents can provide stimulation by giving their baby frequent opportunities to see other people and places.

• Working parents may be away from their baby for a good deal of the baby's awake hours. Care-givers can be a valuable source of insight and perspective in regard to the baby.

The Young Baby as an Individual[5]

• Parents should treat their child with respect and as a person.

• Quality time, not quantity time, is what is important for parents to spend with their baby.

• Babies need time to be alone so that they can experience themselves and the world on their own terms.

• Parents should allow their child the opportunity to struggle and fail, and struggle and succeed. Effort, not achievement, should be rewarded.

• Parents need to provide time (once their child is

---

5. A good resource for this area is the *Neonatal Behavioral Assessment Scale* developed by Dr. T. Berry Brazelton.

around 5 to 6 months) when they are available to play with their baby but are not initiating play. Babies need the opportunity to set the pace and tone of play and have the freedom to explore.
• Parents need to keep in mind their baby's basic needs and meet them soon enough to reduce crying and discord during the day.

Parents as Individuals

• Parenting can be exhausting. Parents need to remember to nurture themselves and have respect for themselves as they meet their child's needs. Proper self-care can enable parents to continue giving while remaining satisfied with their lives.
• Everyone makes mistakes. Children are highly resilient, durable, and adaptable.
• In order to enjoy their baby fully, parents need to have:
— sufficient rest;
— enough time to be with each other;
— the chance to pursue outside interests and have other adult contacts;
— the flexibility to pick up their baby's cues about changing stages;
— sources to contact to learn about child rearing;
— the ability to look at their own habits and behavior and realize that they can't expect their child to behave any better than they do (parent's behavior and expectations are

models for their children's behavior—especially beginning around age one);
— a good sense of humor.

Planning for the Whole Family

• Parents can help their baby experience order in his world by having a fairly predictable routine and a familiar place for him to sleep.
• When parents work outside the home, or spend time away from their baby, it's best for baby's (and parents') sense of security to have one, or only a few, consistent care providers. This predictability helps baby learn and trust adults other than its parents. (See Appendix H beginning on p. 466 for the chapter concerning Working Parent classes.)
• Limits and plans that meet *all* family members' needs should be arranged.
• Parents would do well to plan ahead and give themselves lots of time to reach a goal—preparing a dinner or going to a friend's—so that they and their baby can feel relaxed during the day.

Handouts

The handout developed for this topic is entitled "Social-Emotional Development." It highlights growth from the newborn to the six-month stage.

SOCIAL-EMOTIONAL DEVELOPMENT

(1–6 months)

(Newborn) Emotions are not directed toward someone.
Cries; quiets when comforted.
Usually placid, vague expression.
Adjusts posture to body of person holding him.
Functions on instinctive basis.

• Smiles socially.
Visually interested in people.
• More interested in people than in toys.

• Recognizes mother and father. (May show preference if one
parent has a greater share of caregiving); begins devel-
oping awareness of self as separate being.
Begins to recognize siblings and consistent caregivers.
Expresses emotions with entire body.
Social stimulation becoming important.
Smiles back when smiled at.
Able to entertain self for longer periods.

(4 months)

• Anticipates.
Protests.
Wants to be a part of social activities.
Begins to understand cause and effect so behavior that
seems manipulative becomes apparent.

(6 months) Wants to interact with children.
Plays with toys for longer periods of time.
May reach out to be picked up.

part three

TEACHING ABOUT OLDER BABIES

(7–14 months)

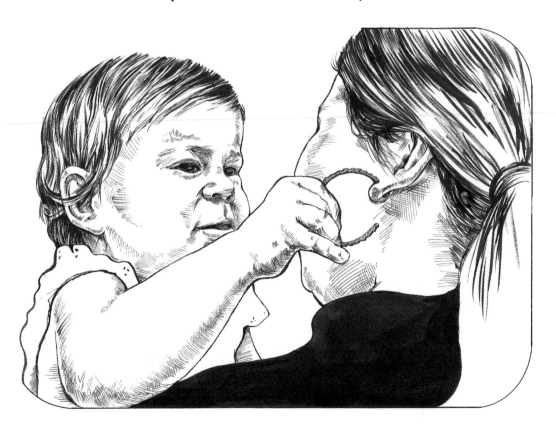

1

LIMIT SETTING

background/preparation

Goals to Work Toward in Presenting This Topic

It is during the 7- to 14-month stage that many infants begin to move about independently—crawl, stand, possibly walk—and to explore their surroundings. Quite suddenly (or so it seems), parents find they must constantly "supervise," or at least be alert to what their child is doing. It is at this point that most parents find it necessary to begin to set limits, to discipline. Because this is new and often difficult for both parent and child, it is a major topic for the older baby group.

The goals to work toward on this topic are: (1) to introduce parents to the concepts of discipline and limit setting—what they mean to parent and child, and the necessity for them; (2) to have parents become aware of and learn to implement a variety of limit-setting techniques; (3) to alert parents to the need for child-proofing and safety precautions, and to inform them of ways to child-proof their environment; (4) to help parents understand what their child is feeling and how to cope with his reactions to limit setting; (5) to help parents understand and cope with their own feelings and beliefs about limit setting and discipline; (6) to help each family begin to develop a "philosophy" of discipline.

Typical Parental Interests and Concerns About This Topic

1. Now that my baby can walk and really get around the house, he is literally into everything. How can I avoid saying "no" to him all day long?
2. When I say "no" to my daughter, she often stops and grins at me. Other times she cries. I don't know what to expect when I say "no." Is this normal?
3. Why can't Alex remember that he can't touch the stereo, even after I've told him a hundred times? Is he ever going to learn?
4. Saying "no" and trying to distract my baby with a toy don't seem to work any more. What do I do now?
5. It is really hard for me to be consistent about the limits I set, especially if I'm tired. What can I do to be more consistent?
6. Tyler keeps trying to crawl into the fireplace over and over. It's dirty and it's dangerous, but obviously we can't move it. How do I handle this?
7. Is it all right to slap my baby's hands if she touches something dangerous or valuable? What about spanking a child?

131

8. When I take something away from Kate that she's not allowed to have, she screams so hard I'm afraid she'll make herself sick. How do I cope with her reactions?

9. Our sitter is middle-aged and very "old-school." While she is never harsh, she has a lot more limits than we do. Will this confuse our child?

10. My husband and I have very different ideas about how to discipline our son. How do we decide which way is better?

11. What do I do to keep my very active and mobile child safe, short of putting him in a "padded room"?

12. My little girl just started to walk and she's so unsteady on her feet that I find myself hovering over her every time she stands to walk. How can I avoid being so overprotective?

13. The daycare center is completely child-proofed; there is almost nothing that's off-limits. Do we need to make our house like that too or is it okay to have some "adult-only" areas?

14. After I've disciplined my baby, she dissolves into tears and wants to be held. Is it okay to comfort her?

Areas of Information You Will Need to Learn About to Teach This Topic[1]

Setting limits for older babies.
— Why it's necessary (baby's mobility and curiosity—the problems they cause).
— What to limit.
— Limit-setting techniques.
— Consistency in limit setting.
— Coping with babies' reactions.
Child-proofing and safety precautions.
— Indoors—kitchens, bathrooms, plants, fireplaces and heating units, etc.
— Outdoors—plants, stairs, pets, stones, etc.
Parents' feelings about setting limits.
Discipline (definition of the concept).
— Different styles of discipline.
— Conflicts between parents over beliefs and styles (how to compromise).

---

1. Much of this information, for this topic and all others in this part, can be found in the "Additional Information for Parents" sections of the topics.

Family Dynamics—What This Topic Means Psychologically to Parent and Child

Parents often appear to be taken by surprise at the need to set limits during their baby's first year. The whole area of discipline may not have been considered or discussed until the need for it had already arisen. Then many parents find they are uncertain within themselves and sometimes in disagreement with their spouse about how to set limits and enforce them. (Everyone retains memories and feelings from childhood about how they were disciplined. These memories tend to color beliefs about the "right" way to train a child.) One of the major tasks confronting parents in this area is that of working together to create a philosophy and style of discipline that will work for their new family unit.

Parents usually do not find the area of discipline a very satisfying one. Mothers, in particular, are often uncomfortable in the role of "disciplinarian." Much has been made of "meeting your child's needs" during the first year of life. But when the baby's needs turn to demands and begin to interfere with the daily functions of the family, parents are understandably confused about setting limits. Many times, parents feel as though they are in a maze of conflicting ideas, advice, and feelings.

The baby is no less confused by the introduction of limits into his world. He does not understand the meaning of "no" and is much too young to comprehend danger to himself. So, he gives inconsistent responses to his parents' limit setting. And, if he senses uncertainty or inconsistency in his parents' behavior, he will repeatedly test the same limits in order to learn exactly what is expected of him. An older baby can comprehend that "no" means "not at this moment" but he cannot grasp that "no" means "never. Thus, his limit-testing behavior is not usually meant to tease or annoy, but is simply his way of getting information about the "house rules."

Sample Concern of Parents

Concern	*Critical Issues*

I'm at my wit's end with Greg (9 months) and his fascination with electrical cords. There is one in the family room that can't be hidden behind anything and he goes straight for it *every* time we're in there. We tried putting pillows over it and that worked for a while, but he's discovered how to get under them now. I say "no" and move him and try to distract him with a toy, but that doesn't work either. He just crawls right back. When I say "no," he usually stops and looks at me—sometimes he even grins, which really gets me—then he goes right ahead. My husband says a good swat on the bottom would settle the whole issue, but I have really mixed feelings about doing that. I am terrified he will pull the whole lamp over on himself or bite through the cord and get shocked.

—Baby's curiosity.

—Attempt to child-proof.

—Parent's need for other limit-setting techniques.

—Baby's limit testing.
—Baby's inconsistent response and parent's feelings about it.

—Parents' different styles of limit setting.

—Parent's uncertainty about physical punishment.

Key Questions

1. Why do you think Greg is so fascinated with cords? What is he trying to accomplish?
2. Have you tried any others ways of letting Greg know that he *cannot* do this? What happened?
3. Since Greg doesn't seem to have gotten your message, can you think of ways to make it clearer that playing with cords is unacceptable?

4. It can be upsetting and irritating when your child responds this way. How do *you* feel when he grins at you? Why do you suppose he does it? How are you coping with your feelings?
5. Have you and your husband talked about your different approaches to limit setting? What kinds of conclusions did you reach?

For the group

6. Can you think of other ways to child-proof in this situation?
7. What techniques have you used to let your child know he cannot do certain things?
8. Let's discuss physical punishment and your feelings about it.

Readings and Other Resources[2]

*Brazelton, T. Berry, *Infants and Mothers* (New York: Dell Publishing Co., Inc., 1983).

Brazelton, T. Berry, *Touchpoints* (Reading, Mass.: Merloyd Lawrence/Addison-Wesley, 1992), pp. 121–123.

Burck, Frances Wells, *Babysense* (New York: St. Martin's Press, 1991). Chapter 19.

Dodson, Fitzhugh, *How to Parent* (New York: The New American Library, Inc./Dutton, 1971) Chapter 9.

Eisenberg, Arlene, Murkoff, H. E., Hathaway, S. A., "Babies Need Discipline Too", *Working Mother Magazine*, February 1989, p. 57.

*Green, Martin, I., *A Sigh of Relief* (New York: Bantam Books, 1994), part 1.

Leach, Penelope, *Children First* (New York: Random House, 1994), Chapter 6.

Miller, Jeanne, *The Perfectly Safe Home* (New York: Simon & Schuster, 1991).

Sunset Books, *Making Your Home Child-Safe* (Menlo Park: Lane Publishing Co., 1988; out of print, available in libraries.)

---

2. Readings marked with an * are the most highly recommended. The work of Rose Bromwich is highly recommended for information on the topics in this part and is cited in Appendix A. Articles from *Working Mother, Parents, Parenting,* and *American Baby* are often good sources of current information on the topics in this part.

teaching/presentation

Homework

The homework for this topic is intended to help parents focus on how their baby's mobility has created the need to set some limits for him. It also encourages parents to look at what their child is trying to accomplish from his point of view. (See ch. 4 on Limit Setting in Rothenberg, *PETP,* Pt. III for additional homework.)

Practical Suggestions and Strategies for Teaching About This Topic

• Since the topic of discipline and limit setting is of great interest and concern to parents, it should be scheduled early in the series. (It will probably take two sessions to cover.) If it is not discussed then, it will most likely be brought up again and again during the discussion of other topics.

• Discussion that occurs around this topic is usually complex. As a parent describes what her child is doing, she will also be giving you information about how she feels about it. You will need to be aware of both levels of communication in order to help the parent understand what is happening and why.

• The topic of discipline is an excellent one for demonstrating the problem-solving techniques you want parents to learn. Try leading one or two of the group members through detailed accounts of their specific limit-setting concerns as you problem solve with them using the techniques discussed in Part I: 6. As other parents outline their problems, encourage the group to assume your role, questioning, leading, and supporting one another. (This is a very satisfying experience for parents to have early in the series since it gives them confidence in themselves and each other.) Also read *PETP,* Part II, chapter 10.

• Because so many parents feel confused and uncertain about how to handle limit setting, be sure to monitor the group's discussion closely,

preventing comments that are judgmental or derogatory. Watch especially for signs that a parent is becoming very uncomfortable or defensive.

• It may be helpful to handle the mechanics of child-proofing and safety in a short discussion following the more general one on discipline and limit setting. This structure keeps the group from getting bogged down in details about installing plug covers and drawer latches.

Mini-lecture and Lead-off Questions for Discussion

Since setting limits is usually a relatively new experience for most of the parents, it helps to introduce them to the whole topic by first defining the concepts of discipline and limit setting and giving them an overview of what these mean for parent and child. With such an introduction, the group has the opportunity to see the topic as a whole, rather than viewing it as a stream of isolated incidents (which is how many parents think of their concerns at this stage). See *PETP,* Pt. III, ch. 4 on limit-setting. Defining the concepts also sets a non-judgmental tone for the discussion.

If we were to look up the word "discipline" in a dictionary, we would find that it means to lead, to train, to guide, to teach. Using this definition, we could say that discipline is the overall guidance that you give your child as she matures, the goal being the child's eventual ability to impose limits on herself. Effective discipline helps produce desired change or growth in a child, maintains the child's self-esteem, and keeps a close relationship between parent and child. Discipline is one of the foundations of the parent-child relationship, and continues to be one as the child moves toward adulthood and independence. Limit setting is just one part of the teaching process that is discipline.

It is impossible *not* to have some limits for your child. Limits help your child understand the world around her and how it operates.

BABY'S INCREASING MOBILITY

(7–14 months)

1. Describe your baby's ability to get around (for example, rolls over, is beginning to crawl).

2. What is your baby trying to accomplish with his/her increasing ability to move around? (Watch your baby and list some of the things.)

3. What problems are you experiencing as your baby becomes increasingly mobile? Give examples of them.

4. What problems are you encountering in "child-proofing" your home (that is, in making your home safe for your child)?

Parent's name _____ Date _____ Child's age _____

They also help insure that your child's behavior will be "acceptable" to others and that she can be an integral part of society. You will not foster happiness if you give your child license to do whatever she wants.

Unfortunately for us as parents, there is no "magic formula" for setting limits. There are no universal rules that can be applied to every child. So, even though each of us will be setting limits for our child, the limits imposed will be different within each family unit.

Most babies' curiosity and their urge and new-found ability to explore become evident in the second half of their first year, bringing parents face to face with concerns and conflicts about limit setting. What do these new developments mean to your baby and to you?

From your baby's point of view, there is obvious joy in his ability to move about independently—you can see it on his face. For the first time, he is able to influence the world around him. As he crawls and explores, he achieves his first real taste of "mastery" over himself and his environment. This is very exciting, and sometimes frustrating. He is now aware that he influences *your* behavior, too. He sees it in your reactions to what he does and this is fascinating for him. All of his curiosity, urge to explore, and need to practice his new skills are drives toward maturity (which he can't stop, though you may sometimes wish he would).

It is important to realize and remember that "no" is just a sound to your baby during this stage. He does not know what the word means until he learns from you. (He also has no sense of danger or caution at this point.) As he begins to understand "no," an older baby can grasp that you mean "No, not right now," but he cannot comprehend that you mean 'never."

From your point of view, there is joy in each new skill your child acquires—one of the real thrills of parenthood is watching your child achieve developmental milestones. But contrary to what you may have expected, once a child is mobile he needs a great deal more supervision than he used to. He can't just be put on the floor or another "safe" place while you go about your activities.

When he is able to move about, you will find you have real concerns about his safety—and your sanity! (How can one child get into so much?) You will probably want to help him satisfy his glorious curiosity, but not at the expense of his (or your) well-being. So, you may be searching for a middle ground where you both can be satisfied. This means that you will need to use your special knowledge of your special baby to find a creative approach to limit setting that is right and comfortable for your family.

Before you ask the parents to discuss their concerns, you may wish to review the problem-solving techniques found in Part I: 6. This can help the group to better understand and deal with the problems that will arise. (Also *PETP*, Pt. I, ch. 10).

Now you can start the discussion by saying, **Let's begin the discussion here with any questions or concerns you have about limit setting in your house.** If the parents seem reluctant to volunteer a concern, you might begin by relating to them an experience of your own in which you found yourself confused or upset about setting limits for your child. Doing this usually breaks the ice by reassuring the group that you really understand their concerns and will not judge them. Another option is to refer to a concern that you know one of the parents has, asking her if she will share it in more detail with the group. (Many other ideas can be found in *PETP*, Pt. III, ch. 4).

Try to allow every group member a chance to voice her most pressing concerns and then try to satisfy all questions as completely as possible. You may wish to summarize possibilities for each parent who has voiced a detailed concern and ask her to share the outcome of her problem solving during the next class session.

Additional Information for Parents

Limit-setting Techniques

• It is impossible to work from a distance with an older baby. Parents should remove their child from an unacceptable area or put the forbidden object away.

• When parents say "no," they should say it

firmly. Sometimes parents say "no" so gently that the child cannot distinguish it from ordinary conversation. A simple reason for the "no" should be given—"That's hot," or "That's sharp."

• Parents should try to redirect their baby's attention when they want her to stop doing something. Showing her something fun to do in another part of the room or the house often helps.

• If a baby is so fascinated that he seems compelled to return over and over to a forbidden object, parents should try to figure out what is so appealing about it. If possible, the baby should be offered a safe alternative or substitute. (For example, if he crawls into the fireplace, he could be given a big box to crawl into. If he pulls hair or pokes at eyes, a doll that has hair or eyes that open and close could be offered, and the child could be told, "You can't pull Mommy's hair but you can pull dolly's." This allows a child the opportunity to satisfy the urge to explore in a way that is acceptable for both of you.)

• Isolation can be used. Before a parent becomes truly angry with her child, she should try putting him in the crib or playpen for a few minutes, telling him that this behavior is *not* to continue. This is a very clear message to the child that what he did is not acceptable. It also provides a "cooling-off" period for parent and child.

• Using physical punishment (slapping hands, spanking, and so on) is a very individual decision. It is usually used by parents who were spanked as children. Overall, physical punishment is rarely a good approach and often tells you that parents are frustrated and need to learn other good approaches.

• Sometimes a change in environment or schedule decreases the need for limit setting.

Consistency in Setting Limits

• Being consistent in imposing limits will help a child because it diminishes the need for her to check and recheck them quite so often.

• It is hard to be consistent. Initially, parents should try saying "no" to only those few things that are so important to them that they will follow through on them, no matter what kind of day they've had.

• It helps to keep valuable and breakable objects out of the child's reach, or perhaps put away for a time. This makes everyone more relaxed, and lessens the chance of someone's being upset if a treasured item is broken or damaged.

• If possible, furniture that can cause problems, such as chairs that tip easily or sharp-cornered tables, should be removed. Babies will pull themselves up to stand using anything they can reach.

• It helps if parents (and also caregivers) can decide between them what limits they should set. This allows no room for indecision and the baby will benefit from observing a "united front."

• Even though parents and also caregivers may have agreed on what limits to set, they may find differences in the way they communicate these limits to the child. But having different styles is not being inconsistent. A child needs to learn that people are different. For example, mother may be more patient and father quicker to react, or vice-versa. If the child is in day care, the care provider's style must also be carefully considered. While learning about adults' different styles can enhance the baby's development, being exposed to conflict between them will not; thus the shared goal of the various caregivers need not be consistency, but should be harmony, excellent communication, and mutual support.

Baby's Inconsistent Reactions and Limit-testing Behavior

• Parents can expect a variety of reactions from their baby when they tell her "no"—she may scream with anger and frustration, sob as though she is broken-hearted, smile, or even laugh aloud. A child is starting out with no information about why her parent is acting the way she is. A "no" may startle her because it seems "out of character" for the parent. Whether she laughs or cries depends a lot on her individual temperament.

• When a baby tests limits, she is trying to find out what the rules are. Usually, she does not do it to tease or annoy in the beginning. If, however, she seems to be making a game out of the situation, she may be using her limit testing as an attention-getting device. This is more often true of toddlers than babies under a year old.

• Babies are often bewildered by the introduction of limits into their worlds. Each situation seems different to them and they test over and over again to try to sort out what is expected of them. Repetition is the best way to communicate expectations—and patience is a necessity.

• For the time being, parents are setting limits on activities and objects, not on behavior. A baby cannot control his feelings or his drives toward development but parents can control his environment and what he has access to.

• The *Parentmaking Educators Training Program* by B. A. Rothenberg (Menlo Park, CA: Banster Press, 1993) has an extensive chapter on Limit Setting (pp. 319–349). Refer to this chapter for information on basic principles of limit setting, helping parents learn why setting limits can be so hard, and strengthening a parent's ability to set limits. The *PETP* chapter also covers prevention and discipline techniques and helps teach about husband-wife differences in limit setting.

Child-proofing and Safety

• Everything interests older babies, and parents and also caregivers need to be continually alert to the child's safety. Many babies of this age use their mouth as the primary tool of exploration.

• Babies in the second half of the first year have no sense of danger or caution. The handouts on pp. 334–339 can help parents make their homes as safe as possible.

• Parents should try to anticipate their child's development and keep one step ahead of him in child-proofing.

• Parents need to be particularly aware of how quickly their child can endanger herself. Babies should not be left unattended, especially in the kitchen or the bathroom.

Handouts

The handouts for this topic—"Safeproofing Your Home for Children" and "Safety Equipment," both concern childproofing and safety precautions. They can help parents become more aware of areas of potential concern or danger. The handouts themselves and information on how to send for other useful safety handouts can be found in the topic, 'Sickness and Safety" (p. 331).

Handouts on limit-setting that help parents identify their style of discipline, understand basic principles of limit setting, look at themselves as limit setters, and learn useful limit setting techniques can be found in *PETP,* Pt. III, chapter 4.

2

SOCIAL-EMOTIONAL DEVELOPMENT

background/preparation

Goals to Work Toward in Presenting This Topic

Sometime during the second half of their first year, children begin to discover that they are separate beings, distinct from their mother and father and from the world around them. Every child makes this discovery in his own unique way, and the knowledge he gains manifests itself in a variety of behaviors that influence both parent and child. Because of the unique nature of the process of social and emotional growth and because of the long-term implications of each child's development, the topic of social and emotional development is of great concern to most parents.

The goals to work toward on this topic include: (1) to provide parents with information about social-emotional development and its meaning for parent and child; (2) to help parents recognize and understand the kinds of behavior that indicate social-emotional growth in the older baby; (3) to help parents become aware of the unique and individual way each child may express the changes and growth occurring within him; (4) to help parents learn to cope comfortably with the changes in their child and with their feelings

about these changes; (5) to give parents the opportunity to share ideas about fostering self-esteem in their child.

Typical Parental Interests and Concerns About This Topic

1. Every time I leave my little boy with anyone except my husband, he cries and screams the whole time I'm gone. What did I do to make him feel so insecure?
2. Roni has always been such a friendly baby. She enjoyed being held and would go to anyone. Now she cries when anybody (but us) even *looks* at her or smiles. Why does she act this way?
3. When I drop Erin off at the daycare home she's fine, and the sitter says she has a good day there, but when I come back she screams and falls apart. Does she hate me?
4. Whenever my husband and I try to carry on a conversation in the evening, our daughter begins to fuss and whine and tries to climb in my lap. It's very annoying! How do we handle this?
5. Is it possible to "spoil" a baby this age?
6. Alex seems to need so much *more* of my time and attention than he did before. I know it's

important to meet your child's needs so that he'll feel secure, but where do you draw the line?

7. I'd like to go back to work. I tried Ben at a sitter's for a few days, but he cried a lot. Should I give up for now?

8. Diapering my son—and dressing him, too—is like working with a tornado! He is furious, yelling and kicking—and frankly, so am I! What can I do?

9. How do my moods affect my baby? Should I try to hide my own negative feelings?

Areas of Information You Will Need to Learn About to Teach This Topic

---

Social-emotional development in older babies.
— Behaviors that indicate social-emotional growth in older babies.
— The meaning (or explanation) of these behaviors from a child's point of view.
— Differences in children's ways of expressing social-emotional growth.
  Parents' attitudes and feelings.
— How to cope with a baby's behavior.
— How to cope with feelings, especially negative ones, about a child's behavior.
Self-esteem.
— How to encourage positive influences.
— How to identify undermining influences.

Family Dynamics—What This Topic Means Psychologically to Parent and Child

---

The social and emotional growth that occurs in a child during the older baby stage is not visible to parents in the same way that other development, such as learning to walk, is. Because this is so, parents usually report what they feel are sudden and surprising changes in their baby's personality or behavior. Unfortunately, some of these changes manifest themselves in negative ways, such as stranger anxiety and separation anxiety. Many parents do not recognize the changes in their child as indications of growth but see them rather as signs that they have somehow failed in their attempt to meet their child's needs

or to make him feel secure. When parents, most of whom have eagerly awaited this age as a time of increased independence in their child, find their child clinging, refusing to separate, or making *increased* demands upon their time and energy, they may be confused, resentful, and/or angry.

All of this is distressing and of real concern to parents. At the same time that they are struggling to find ways to cope with their baby's new behavior and his emerging personality, they must also deal with their own feelings about these changes.

Because she cannot yet express herself well, the older baby must use her behavior to communicate her new feelings and awareness to her parents. She may appear to be "stranded" between dependence and independence and can be inconsistent both in her demands and responses. The intensity of this dilemma and her expression of it are unique to each child, given her individual temperament. Her behavior mirrors her struggle to cope with the changes. In most babies, some degree of stress is evident. If her reactions and behavior change considerably, she may find that her parents do not readily understand and can no longer anticipate her needs as well as they used to. This adds to the intensity of the child's feeling of separateness.

The period of social and emotional growth in the 7- to 14-month-old is a period of upheaval and change in the relationship between parent and child. Although social and emotional development are obviously desirable, the time during which it occurs can be difficult to live through on a day-to-day basis. As the older baby works to consolidate the gains she has made in discovering herself and the world around her, her parents begin the process of learning to know and accept the "person" inside their child.

Sample Concern of Parents

Concern	Critical Issues
It seems like Sarah (12½ months) has been a different baby since her first birthday. She used to play quite happily while I worked around the house, but now she cries whenever I leave	—Separation anxiety.

Concern	*Critical Issues*
the room. She seems to need me to play with her *all* the time and I feel like I can't get anything done. The worst time of all is when I'm trying to cook dinner! She crawls after me and actually hangs on my leg and whines and fusses to be picked up. That really drives me up a wall! At first I thought she was sick because she was acting so strangely. But the doctor says she's fine and this is just a stage. Even so, what really concerns me is that she seems so insecure, needing all this time and attention. I really thought I had done such a good job of meeting her needs, and now this!	—Baby's dependence and use of attention-getting devices. —Parent's feelings about child's behavior. —Parent's inability to recognize signs of social-emotional growth. —Parent's interpretation of child's behavior. —Parent's sense of inadequacy.

Key Questions

1. When do you play with Sarah and how do you feel about these times?
2. Why do you think Sarah cries when you leave the room? What do you do to reassure her?
3. Late afternoon is the low point of the day for a lot of us, and it can be really aggravating when your baby acts this way. What is she trying to tell you when she does this? How do you handle it? How are you handling *your* feelings?
4. Now that you know Sarah isn't sick, how do you account for the changes in her behavior?
5. You seem to feel that you are responsible for the way Sarah is acting right now. Given what you have learned today about social-emotional growth, can you see other reasons for her behavior? How does that make you feel?

For the group

6. What are realistic limits that a parent can set during the day that would be good for her and also help her child feel she's liked?
7. How have you coped when your child cries as you leave the room?
8. What do you do to avoid your child's fussing and clinging in the late afternoon pre-dinner time?
9. Can you think of ways to describe Sarah's behavior other than "insecure"?

Readings and Other Resources

Ames, Louise Bates, Ilg. Frances I., & Haber, Carol Chase, *Your One-Year-Old* (New York: Dell Publishing Co., Inc., 1982).

*Brazelton, T. Berry, *Infants and Mothers* (New York: Dell Publishing Co., Inc., 1983).

Briggs, Dorothy, *Your Child's Self Esteem* (Garden City, N.Y.: Doubleday & Co., 1975), Parts I and II.

Chess, Stella and Thomas, Alexander, *Know Your Child* (New York: Harper Collins, 1989).

*Fraiberg, Selma, *The Magic Years* (New York: Charles Scribner's Sons, 1959), Part II.

Greenspan, Stanley and Greenspan, Nancy Thorndike, *First Feelings: Milestones in the Emotional Development of Your Baby and Child* (New York: Viking Penguin Books, 1989.)

Greenspan, Stanley, *The Essential Partnerhip* (New York: Viking Penguin, 1989).

*Kaplan, Louise, *Oneness and Separateness* (New York: Simon & Schuster, 1980).

Rothenberg, B. Annye et al., *Parentmaking Educators Training Program* (Menlo Park: Banster Press, 1993), Pt. III—"Separation", pp. 291–318.

Stern, Daniel, *Diary of a Baby* (New York: Harper Collins/Basic Books, 1990), pp. 81–108.

teaching/presentation

Homework

The homework for this topic is to be used *after* the discussion so that parents can watch for specific areas of social-emotional development and focus on their reactions to these changes.

Practical Suggestions and Strategies for Teaching This Topic

• There is not a great deal of "factual" information for you to work from in this topic area. Instead you will need to rely on parents' descriptions of their child's behavior and on your own experiences with children. It may be difficult to lead the discussion on this topic at first, but as you continue to lead classes your experiences with a wide variety of children will increase your proficiency and skill.

• Since the concepts of social-emotional development may be unfamiliar or new to your group, it will be important for you to give group members an in-depth understanding of the changes occurring in their children. If you can help each parent explore her concern fully, she will be better able to recognize and pull together the various aspects of it. As you work with each parent, you will be illustrating to the group how feelings and behavior (in both parent and child) interact and influence each other.

• Since each baby's growth in this area can be very different from any other child's, it is important to give each parent an opportunity to describe and discuss her experiences and concerns. Hearing a variety of concerns will emphasize to the group how unique the social-emotional development of each child is. It will also help to reassure parents who may feel they have somehow caused negative behavior in their child.

• The discussion of this topic is often complex, with parents communicating information on one

level and feelings on another. Your awareness of the various levels of comment can help group members learn more about themselves, and therefore contribute to their ability to handle their babies more effectively.

• Reassurance and support are major instructor responsibilities during this discussion. Parents often view indicators of social-emotional growth, such as separation anxiety, as signs that they have not met their child's needs effectively though they have worked hard to do so. It will be reassuring if you interpret each child's behavior in terms of social-emotional development, and explain what is happening from the child's point of view. Parents need to know that growth is desirable, even though it may be difficult to cope with at the present. Letting parents know that separation anxiety and other "negative" behaviors are normal can help to stave off unnecessary feelings of failure. (See *PETP*, Pt. III, ch. 5 on Separation.)

• The behavior changes springing from social-emotional growth in a baby will affect the everyday patterns of his and his parents' lives. The group's recognition and understanding of social-emotional growth will most likely enhance a discussion of patterns and schedules, especially in the parents' ability to use problem-solving techniques on day-to-day problems. "Patterns and Schedules" should therefore follow this topic in the series' schedule. In-depth knowledge of each child's behavior will help you to lead the latter discussion.

Mini-lecture and Lead-off Questions for Discussion

Parents may be unaware that many of the changes in behavior they see in their older babies are due to social-emotional growth. An effective way, therefore, to introduce the topic would be to give the parents a handout highlighting the most common indicators of social-emotional development in the older baby (see p. 148 for a copy of this handout). You can then describe each area

SOCIAL DEVELOPMENT

(7–14 months)

Before beginning this homework observation, read through the first part of the handout "Social-Emotional Development" to note the changes that generally occur in babies this age. Then describe the changes that you have noticed in your own baby and your reactions to them.

1. What are some of the social-emotional changes you've seen in your baby?

   a.

   b.

   c.

2. What was your first reaction to these changes?

   a.

   b.

   c.

3. Have you and your baby now come to accept and live with these new stages? How have you done this?

   a.

   b.

   c.

Parent's name _____ Date _____ Child's age _____

in greater detail. This method helps the parents to fix in their minds the various behaviors they may encounter and to keep track of those about which they have concerns.

During your child's first months, other people are his primary source of information and satisfaction. Somewhere in the middle of his first year, however, your baby begins to differentiate himself from the outside world. This is a crucial step in his social-emotional development. He discovers his separateness, his "self." He begins to discover and experience himself and the world around him. This new phase of self-discovery is a gradual process that will continue to take place over the next few years. (Distribute the handout.)

Here are some of the highlights of social and emotional development in the older baby. We'll discuss them all and you may wish to take notes about those areas that are of particular interest to you in the spaces available on the handout. Remember, each baby will experience developmental stages at different times and with varying degrees of intensity.

• Separation anxiety is very common at this age. With mobility comes the realization that a baby can go away from other people. You may find that your baby needs to "check in" with you frequently if you're in the next room or even just across the room. You may also find that your baby still does not have much capacity to realize that people and objects exist when she cannot see them. Out of her sight, they cease to exist for her. So, when you leave her, she fears that you are gone forever. During this period, a baby learns that you *will* come back because it happens over and over again. This is an important lesson! (It also accounts for some babies bursting into tears at their parents' return. The return reminds them that the parent was gone and that the child was upset.) One of the reasons that playing "peek-a-boo" is so popular with the older baby is that it allows a child to try out a short separation from her parent under her own control. It's a good way to help a child deal with her anxiety on a small scale.

• Your baby may react negatively to people and places that are strange to him. He is less "portable" than in earlier months in the sense

that he will probably need time to adjust to new surroundings. He may have trouble sleeping in a strange place. He also may refuse to "perform" or "show off" any of the new skills he has acquired. He responds favorably to regular scheduling, a daily routine he can count on. Most babies of this age are definitely more at home with familiar people in familiar surroundings.

• Most older babies become increasingly assertive, something that may show itself in negativism. They will begin to demonstrate definite likes and dislikes, and resist pressure to do anything they do not want to do, such as nap, eat new foods, or have their diaper changed. (They may use "persuasion" or loud protest to try to get you to change your mind.) Older babies dislike being hurried or rushed. In addition, they may complain about confinement, like the playpen or a gate across a door. Anger begins to be apparent and may even flare into what might be called a tantrum.

• The older baby's curiosity and urge to explore are insatiable. His increasing mobility and upright posture give him a three-dimensional view of his world for the first time, and everything looks new and different from this perspective. He has to see and touch and begin to sort it out.

• The older baby can recognize herself and her parents in a mirror. She responds to her own name. She becomes interested in exploring her body when she is undressed. She may also be fascinated by other people's faces, poking her fingers into eyes, noses, and mouths or pulling hair. This is all part of her growing awareness that she is a separate person.

• Imitation of parents and other family members—an activity that is developed to a "high art" during the second year—can be seen in older babies' actions and heard in their vocalizing during play. Around their first birthday, most babies enjoy following simple directions and being enthusiastically congratulated when they carry them out. Babies begin to "perform" for family members when they laugh at their actions; their capacity for repetition is truly awesome.

• A budding sense of humor becomes more apparent at this time. Babies enjoy being chased and caught, and may laugh aloud at anything unusual or mildly surprising that you do (like wearing a shower cap, sneezing, or tripping). Babies also enjoy making funny faces and strange sounds, such as coughing.

• The older baby is becoming more interested in observing other children. He learns by watching them but still does not play *with* them. He is sensitive to their moods and may be upset if he hears or sees another child crying. He may react negatively to your holding or playing with another baby.

• The older baby is beginning to evaluate and sort out the moods of other family members by watching their facial expressions and listening to their various tones of voice. By the end of her first year, she is able to show moods on her own face. She also shows affection for people and favorite toys by hugging, patting, stroking, and kissing.

All of these changes in older babies are signs of growth, not signs that parents have failed.

Following your opening remarks, group members might wish to have a few moments in which to finish their notes and look over the handout. When they're ready, ask who would like to discuss any of the behaviors just mentioned in more detail or as it pertains to their child. This is usually sufficient to get the discussion started.

You will most likely find that you will need to participate more in this discussion (in the sense of explaining, interpreting, and supporting) than in most other topic discussions. Most parents have not had enough experience to enable them to recognize social-emotional growth in their babies for what it is.

As the discussion moves on, questions about the effects of a child's new behavior on daily routines (such as bathing, diapering, and dressing) will probably be raised. These questions can be handled here or in the discussion of patterns and schedules.

After the discussion of the group's concerns, you can move on to a related area: **We've talked about the older baby's growth, socially and emotionally. A long-term influence on this growth is the parents' attitude toward their child's development, since it will affect the child's self-concept and self-esteem. How can we encourage healthy emotional growth and self-esteem in our day-to-day parenting? What gets in the way of this encouragement?**

The length of the discussion of social and emotional growth varies widely from group to group. It will be helpful if you are prepared to move on to "Patterns and Schedules" should the developmental discussion be short. Sometimes a group may seem unable to work with the rather subjective aspects of social-emotional development. If this is so, move immediately to "Patterns and Schedules" and try to weave the information on social-emotional development into that discussion. This technique works particularly well with a group that is very information- or detail-oriented.

Additional Information for Parents

Since every baby will express his or her social-emotional growth differently in terms of intensity, age, and behavior, the general information that follows will need to be tailored to fit individual situations within each group you lead.

Social-Emotional Development

• Separation anxiety and stranger anxiety usually peak in intensity in a majority of babies at 12 to 13 months. Whenever a baby experiences these fears, it is *not* a signal to stop leaving him with other people. He needs support and encouragement, but he also needs the repeated experience of his parent's going away and *coming back* to learn that he *can* cope. If a child is having a very difficult time, a parent can try leaving him for short periods (1 to 2 hours) more frequently, as opposed to leaving him less often but for a long period of time. Parents should try to be cheerful and confident when they leave their child even if they don't really feel that way. Their trust will communicate itself to their baby. Parents should try not to linger because this only prolongs the leave-taking that is painful for their child. Parents may wish to use only sitters or friends whom they trust to give the child calm and confident care during his anxious period. (see *PETP*, Pt. III, ch. 5.)

• It is probably best for parents to take only short (weekend) vacations and not to return to full-time work during a period in which it is very difficult for their baby to separate from them.

• If a baby has developed a fear (of men, uniforms, mustaches, beards, glasses, or whatever), parents need to be patient and reassuring. Fears do not usually arise from a frightening or negative experience, but are usually attributable to the child's heightened awareness and recognition of differences. Parents should not prevent their child from having contact with the object of his fear, but they should not push their baby to accept it either. Fears will generally subside naturally if they are not overemphasized. (See p. 147 for a discussion of temperament.)

Coping with Baby's Behavior

• The 7-month-old to 14-month-old stage of development may be a difficult one for parents to live through on a daily basis. They will need to be open to signs of social-emotional growth in their child and aware of the inner turmoil the changes can cause. Parents should try to experiment with different approaches and responses to their child's behavior until they find those that are both comfortable and effective. Parents will also need to keep their sense of humor intact.

• A review of limit-setting techniques may help parents to cope with specific behaviors—pulling hair, biting, poking eyes, whining, and so on—that they are now encountering in their child.

Parents' Attitudes and Feelings

• The intensity with which children express their social-emotional growth (especially separation anxiety and stranger anxiety) is a function of their individual temperament, not a sign that parenting has somehow been inferior (or superior).

• It is helpful to know that anxiety (fussiness, irritability) sometimes precedes a major developmental step such as walking. Once the task has been mastered, the anxiety usually recedes.

• Dealing with a baby's swings between dependence and independence can be frustrating. The older baby tends to be inconsistent in his needs and in his responses to his parents' help until he learns to cope with his new feelings. In the meantime, he probably will need more reassurance, support, and time with his parents than most parents thought would be necessary at this age. This does not mean that parents should return to a "newborn" pattern of being available to every demand 24 hours a day. Parents need to work *with* their child to encourage his independence and his confidence in his ability to cope with the

world around him. At the same time, they need to let their child know that they are there for him when he is overwhelmed by the confusion around and within him.

• It is possible for parents to allow their child little by little to "take over" much of their day and to find themselves unable to accomplish much of anything other than meeting the child's needs. How can a parent tell if her child's needs have become demands? The parent's own feelings are probably the best indicators. If parents often find themselves feeling resentful, angry, or manipulated, it's time for them to reevaluate the situation.

• Sometimes it is necessary for a parent to restructure *her* day so that she makes time for her tasks and for herself, as well as for her child. (It helps parents to know that they are *not* fostering independence in their child by being at his beck and call every minute.) Accomplishing tasks that she has planned on doing helps a parent to alleviate tension and negative feelings and creates a more realistic balance in her relationship with her child. Restructuring or establishing a more equitable schedule takes time, just as it took time to create the situation that presently exists. A child may not be pleased with his parent's move to take care of her needs as well as his, but both parent and child will benefit in the long run.

• A child's personality begins to emerge during the older baby stage, and parents may want to examine the way they relate to their child as a person. It is important for parents to understand and consider their child's feelings, and realize he now needs to be included in conversation and activity. Parents need to spend more time getting to know the "person" in their baby—they will likely find that it is time well-spent in terms of personal enjoyment and rapport within the family.

Baby's Self-Esteem

• A child's feeling good about himself is influenced by whether his parent feels good about herself and by how the parent acts toward him, letting the child know that she really likes him.

• Parents need controls and limits for their child so the baby doesn't continually do things that make the parents angry.

• A child's demands increase at this age so he naturally seems more like a tyrant. Parents need to learn to say "no" to their child, not just to dangers but to their baby's demands for excessive attention as well.

• A parent's concern should not be just with what kind of child her baby will become. She also needs to remember that she is building a lifetime relationship with her child and in her relationship establishment she is setting the groundwork for other relationships her child will have. If a parent likes her child, it is probable that other people will, too. Parents can help their child develop into a likeable person.

Temperament[1]

• Every baby is a unique little person from the very beginning. Research on temperament reveals that children differ from one another in terms of their activity level, their sensitivity to stimuli and to changes in their environment and/or routine, their attention span, persistence and distractibility, and their intensity in expressing positive and negative reactions. Children do best when their parents are aware of their unique style of temperament and respond to it with appropriate support and guidance. Some parents have a great deal of difficulty with the emotional development of the older baby who is very active, sensitive, intense and persistent; these children can be seen as extremely demanding and will quickly exhaust the parent who cannot distinguish demands from needs and set some limits. Parents also should be informed about the special needs of the very quiet child; parents and caregivers may fail to give this child adequate stimulation and responsiveness to his needs unless they learn to read his low-level signals and guide him toward expressiveness and involvement. The child who is "slow to warm up" to new foods, people, places, etc. also will need patient and persistent guidance in order to learn to accept and enjoy a rich variety of experiences.

Separation[2]

A baby learns that mommy and daddy always come back, not by having them never leave but by experiencing one short separation and reunion after another. She learns that other adults are O.K., not by being protected from them but by being gently introduced to them over and over again. Thus, while their baby is in her early months, the task for parents is to master parent-child attachment; soon, however, their task becomes one of *balancing* attachment with gradual, gentle *detachments,* in order to meet their child's complex needs and to help her develop on many levels. Gradually increasing both the amount of time (up to several hours) with other caregivers and the repertoire of caregivers results in greater confidence for both children and parents. This sort of gentle guidance toward growth in a difficult area is an essential building block of a child's self-esteem. (From *PETP,* Rothenberg et al., 1993, p. 297.)

Handouts

The section on "Typical Changes in Babies" is the basis for part of the mini-lecture on p. 142 and lists the highlights of older babies' development. "Developing a Positive Relationship" may be used as an effective summary of the discussion. It may also be given out during the last class in the series to summarize attitudes and feelings you hope have been imparted throughout the series.

Rothenberg, *PETP* includes an entire chapter (pp. 291–318) on separation issues and helping parents with difficult problems in this area. The handouts focus on the differing questions of parents who stay home, parents working full-time, and parents working part-time; and on ways to help children and parents with separation.

---

1. For additional information on temperament, see pg. 340–351 and in Rothenberg, *PETP,* see Pt. III, chapter 2.

2. For a full discussion of separation issues, see *PETP,* Pt. III, chapter 5.

SOCIAL-EMOTIONAL DEVELOPMENT

(7–14 months)

Typical Changes in Babies

The following are some of the social-emotional changes that often occur in babies between 7 and 14 months. Remember that these stages of development will be experienced by different babies at different times and with varying degrees of intensity.

1. Separation anxiety

2. Negative reaction to unfamiliar people and places

3. Increasing assertiveness and independence

4. Insatiable curiosity and urge to explore

5. Recognition of and interest in himself as a separate person

6. Imitation of parents and other family members

7. Budding sense of humor

8. Increasing interest in observing other children

9. Recognition and evaluation of moods of family members and self.

Developing a Positive Relationship

Communication. Be aware of what you are communicating to your child with your words and your actions. Encourage him to express himself; handle him calmly; tell him what you're going to do. Minimize his exposure to *very* angry or depressed feelings in adults.

Acceptance. Show respect for his feelings and yours. Recognize that he has his own unique style and try to enjoy his specialness.

Flexibility. Remind yourself to stay flexible enough to pick up your child's cues about the changing stages he's going through.

Expectations. Try to keep your expectations in line with your child's age and his developmental stage.

Accessibility. When you're with your child, be with him totally. Give him some undivided attention and try to let him set the pace and tone of your play together.

Privacy. Both parents and children need time by themselves. Your child needs opportunities to experience himself and his world on his own terms; you need these times to take care of *your* own needs, to be with your spouse and other adults, and to pursue other interests.

Anticipation. Try to plan ahead and allow lots of time for activities; this can help produce a relaxed atmosphere in your home.

Learning. Allow your child the opportunity to struggle and fail, struggle and then succeed. Reward his effort, not his achievement. Try to give yourself the same opportunity in your role as a parent and don't be too hard on yourself.

Reality. It helps to realize that children can't be expected to behave any better than their parents. Remember that you're a role model for your child—and try to maintain your sense of humor!

3

PATTERNS AND SCHEDULES

background/preparation

Goals to Work Toward in Presenting This Topic

The older baby's continuing growth and development often necessitate changes in the patterns and schedules her family has been accustomed to. Babies are developing needs in many new areas, including emotional, social, cognitive, and motor development. These newer, more exciting needs can often overwhelm the baby and distract him from his more straightforward physical needs such as eating and sleeping. It becomes the parents' job, then, to structure and balance the day. Many parents need to gain comfort with "taking charge" in these areas before they can begin to master more complex limit-setting skills.

Goals to work toward on this topic are: (1) to help parents consider and evaluate the patterns and schedules of their child's day and night in the light of her present stage of development; (2) to provide parents with a forum for sharing a variety of ideas, alternatives, and information about handling the daily activities and patterns of older babies; (3) to encourage parents to work toward finding and establishing a daily pattern (life style) that is as balanced and comfortable for all members of the family as possible.

Typical Parental Interests and Concerns About This Topic

1. My baby doesn't seem to be able to sleep through the night anymore. I've been nursing her back to sleep, but now she's waking three or four times a night. I feel like a zombie at work! What can I do to get her to sleep through again?
2. We've always put Robert to bed in the evening when he seemed sleepy, usually about 7:30 p.m. But lately he's been staying up later and later. We don't really enjoy having him with us *all* evening, but he doesn't act tired or fussy. How should we determine a bedtime for him?
3. I've always nursed my little girl to sleep before putting her into bed. Now that I've weaned her, she cries and carries on until I come in and rock her to sleep. She won't even let my husband do it! How can we teach her to go to sleep on her own?
4. Whenever my little boy wakes in the night, he pulls himself up to stand at the side of his crib and stands there screaming because he doesn't know how to get down again. I can't stand to let him cry like that, but if I go in and put him down, he just stands right up again. Help!
5. Jennifer's nap times are different every day. I think she's trying to move toward one long nap in

the afternoon. How can I help her make the changeover?

6. David keeps standing up in the highchair (bathtub, car seat) and it really scares me. How can I stop him from doing this?

7. Our baby is waking up every morning at 5 and she refuses to go back to sleep. She may be ready to get up then, but we sure aren't! What can we do about it?

8. I really need some information about schedules. What's rigid? What's flexible? How do I know what's right for Tami?

9. We have to wake our baby each morning to take her to day care and she's grumpy while we feed and dress her. Is there a better way?

Areas of Information You Will Need to Learn About to Teach This Topic

---

Typical daily patterns of older babies:
— Daily sleep needs, sleep/wake cycles, and typical nap times and night sleep times.
— Play and activity patterns.
Impact of baby's development on daily patterns:
— Social-emotional development.
— Motor development.
— Individual Temperament differences.
Balancing of needs within the family:
— Evaluating needs and demands of family members.
— Structuring new patterns and ways of meeting the family's—parents' and child's—needs.
— Helpful approaches to solving sleep problems.

Family Dynamics—What This Topic Means Psychologically to Parent and Child

---

When their child reaches the older baby stage, parents often find that the practice of structuring her days and nights by following her cues becomes increasingly difficult. They find that their baby's internal controls are not the totally reliable indicators of fatigue, hunger, and other bodily conditions that they were in the newborn months, yet many continue to rely solely on their baby's cues in setting daily patterns. When their baby's

"needs"—or what they still feel to be her needs—expand to cover much of the day and night, parents feel manipulated and not in control. If parents feel forced to ignore their own feelings in favor of what they perceive to be their child's best interests, they experience real frustration.

By the time a baby has reached the second half of the first year, her growth and development have given her some mastery over her internal controls. She is no longer at the mercy of biological needs to sleep and eat but is now driven by more complex needs to explore, to satisfy curiosity about the world, and to develop in every area. If she is excited, engrossed in play, or enjoying the company of her parents, she does not want to eat or go to sleep. She is not, however, capable of limiting her drives or activities in the sense of knowing when or how to stop. If, for example, it is left to her to indicate when she is ready for bed, she may be unwilling and/or unable to do so. Instead, she may continue her activity until she can sustain it no longer and then fall apart with exhaustion. With no effective internal or external boundaries to help her, the older baby finds herself in an uncomfortable situation.

Sample Concern of Parents

Concern	Critical Issues
We are having a real problem at night. Paul (11½ months) still goes to bed at 7 p.m., just as he's always done. But three weeks ago he began waking every night about 1 a.m. At first I assumed he was hungry, since he's grown a lot recently, so I would just nurse him back to sleep. But now he's started to get up again about 4 a.m. He can't possibly be that hungry, can he? It's almost like when he was a new baby. Last night we decided not to go in	—Change in baby's sleep pattern. —Parent's initial response to pattern change. —Baby's response to parent's "rewarding" action.

| *Concern* | *Critical Issues* | *For the group* |

to him and to let him cry it out. After he'd screamed for 30 minutes I just couldn't take it, so I went in and nursed him. It seemed so cruel to stay away deliberately when he needed me. On the other hand, I can't keep this up indefinitely. I'm tired and my husband is disgusted and we're both upset. I don't know what to do now.

—Parent's attempt to change baby's pattern.

—Parent's interpretation of baby's needs and of her own role.

—Parent's need for re-evaluation and alternative responses.

For the group

7. Why do we have so much difficulty imposing our own requirements on our baby's schedule? Where does this difficulty and conflict come from?
8. How do some of you feel about being alone? Do you really believe that a baby should be alone all night?

Readings and Other Resources

Arsons, Sarah, "Changing Times: Making Diapering a Special Moment", *Working Mother,* August 1986, p. 97.

Brazelton, T. Berry, *Infants and Mothers* (New York: Dell Publishing Co., Inc., 1983).

*Cuthbertson, Joanne & Schevill, Susan, *Helping Your Child Sleep Through the Night* (New York: Doubleday, 1985), Introduction pp. 1–26, Chapters 2 & 3, pp. 53–134.

Ferber, Richard, *Solve Your Child's Sleep Problems* (New York: Avon, 1985).

*Health Education Associates, Inc., "Helping Your Baby Sleep through the Night" pamphlet, 1988. To order write: Health Education Associates, Inc., 8 Jan Sebastian Way, Sandwich, Mass. 02563.

Leach, Penelope, *Your Baby and Child* (Westminster, Md.: Alfred A. Knopf, 1989), pp. 207–217.

Rothenberg, B. Annye et al., *Parentmaking Educators Training Program* (Menlo Park, Cal.: Banster Press, 1993), Part III, Chapter 6, "Sleep Topic", pp. 383–410.

Key Questions

1. What is Paul's sleep schedule during the day? How many naps does he take? How long does each nap last?
2. Can you describe Paul's eating pattern during the day? How much does he eat at each meal?
3. Can Paul fall asleep on his own during the day?
4. Have you noticed any ways Paul has of comforting himself?
5. Where does Paul sleep? (What are the sleeping conditions?)
6. What do you feel are your options for dealing with Paul's nighttime waking?

teaching/presentation

Homework

The homework assignment helps parents to discover and focus on the current patterns of their baby's daily life. Question 3 is included to make parents aware of how their baby's patterns and their own needs can be at odds and cause frustration.

Practical Suggestions and Strategies for Teaching This Topic

• It will be valuable to the parents if you encourage them to consider the emotional climate or atmosphere surrounding the daily activities in their homes. Parents need to be aware of the fact that babies are sensitive to the feelings and attitudes of their parents whether or not these emotions have been expressed verbally to them.

BABY'S CURRENT PATTERNS

(7–14 months)

Try to keep some sort of record of your baby's activities and behavior for a few days to see if you notice any kinds of patterns in his/her days and nights. Then answer the following questions.

1. During the last several days, what have you noticed about your baby's patterns of fussiness and contentment during the day?

What relationship do you see between your activities and your baby's behavior?

When he is fussy, what have you found that calms him?

BABY'S CURRENT PATTERNS (continued)

2. What are your baby's current sleeping patterns (nap time and night)?

3. Given your baby's patterns and your needs, what do you find most difficult or frustrating about organizing the day?

What is most difficult about organizing the night?

Parent's name _____ Date _____ Child's age _____

• Encourage the group members to show respect and tolerance for other families' life styles. It is fine for the group to discuss options and suggest alternative actions but it is not appropriate to criticize or judge another's decisions about how her family will live.

• You may wish to reintroduce limit-setting techniques when discussing such "activities" as standing in the highchair.

Mini-lecture and Lead-off Questions for Discussion

Because family life styles can differ so widely, there is not a great deal of general information that can be presented about this topic. Instead of offering many facts, the mini-lecture should simply get the group ready to begin the discussion.

Some of you have no doubt discovered that you can no longer rely on your baby's internal controls to effectively regulate her daily activities. Perhaps her naps are erratic or she's staying up later and later or waking at the crack of dawn. Even though scheduling may be a negative term for you, you may be wondering about how to set up some routines, some boundaries for the day and night that both you and your baby can rely on.

That's exactly what we're going to discuss today—the questions and concerns you have about daily patterns of sleeping, eating, and playing and how to integrate those patterns and your baby's needs with those of the rest of the family. In addition, let's include any questions you have about everyday activities you're involved in while caring for your child—bathing, diapering, dressing, riding in the car, and so on. (See *PETP*, Pt. III, ch. 6 on Sleep.)

With the introductory remarks spoken, you can then ask who would like to open the discussion. If no one volunteers, provide an example of a scheduling problem from your own experience or direct a specific question to a parent whom you know has a concern in this area. If many questions are not voiced, don't be overly concerned. Many of the concerns that revolve around this topic (particularly those about sleep patterns) are nearly universal for this age group

and the information and ideas exchanged can be used by the parents to fit their own situations.

It will be helpful to the parents if you briefly summarize at the end of this discussion the main points that were raised. The group may have jumped back and forth from one area of daily life to another, and summarizing will clarify the entire topic area.

Additional Information for Parents

Patterns and Schedules

• There are many reasons why babies wake more frequently and have changing sleep patterns during the second half of the first year. Some of these are teething, excitement over developmental changes (crawling, standing, etc.), awareness of separateness, increasing assertiveness, and sickness.

• A schedule is nothing more than a routine for the day, an outline or pattern that underlies daily activities. (Most people operate on one whether they realize it or not.) If parents are finding that every day and night with their baby is different and that they're never sure what will happen when, it may be helpful for them to create a daily pattern that they and their baby can count on. This does not mean that activities should be scheduled into 15-minute blocks and checked off as they're covered; the goal is a general outline only, or steps toward one. Every family's pattern will be different.

• Some babies are, by nature, more adaptable than others, and fit themselves easily into their family's routine. A baby's temperament will play a big part in this.

• This is a stage of development in which parents also establish patterns of relating to their child around the "business activities" of each day. Many parents find it helpful now to begin teaching their baby to play alone for a bit each day and to accustom the baby to becoming a partner in such routines as washing up, diapering, toy pick-up, etc.

• Some children just are not getting enough sleep. (Refer to charts in *PETP*, Pt. III, ch. 6.) In some cases, these same parents describe their children as fussy, clingy, demanding, needing constant attention, and not having a schedule. These may very well be children who are not getting enough sleep. Such children may not have routines and habits conducive to sleep and, paradoxically, their overtiredness may inhibit sleep. Overtired children often have trouble falling asleep, having unbroken sleep during the night, sleeping long enough in the morning, and catching up on lost sleep. While some parents say that their children who get up a lot at night or have other sleep problems seem fine during the day, when the sleep problems are worked out almost all children sleep more, are less easily upset, and are more content throughout the day—often to the amazement of their parents.

• When parents are working to change a pattern or establish a new one (especially at night), they should give it time to take hold. They should not try one "solution" one day and another one the next. For instance, if their baby is waking at night, they should not go to him one night and not the next. This would be very confusing for the child. When parents make a decision, they need to stick to it. In that way, their baby will know what is to be expected. (See *PETP*, Pt. III, chapter 6 for a full discussion of sleep. This chapter includes specific guidance for parents on sleep covering the newborn to five year old age range in age-divided detail. It covers parents' feelings and attitudes as well as baby's and children's needs.)

• Parents should aim toward balance in their baby's days—time alone and time with parents, time outside and time inside, new activities and familiar ones, and so on.

• Working parents should work closely with their child's other caregivers to make sure that the schedule including feeding and sleeping times fits for the child's whole day and evening.

• Over the last decade, a great deal of research has been conducted regarding young children's sleep patterns. This research has led to the development of several systems (e.g. Ferber, Cuthbertson & Schevill, and others) that provide helpful advice for parents who wish to guide their children in establishing healthy sleep patterns. Some parents are able simply to use one of these systems as a "cookbook" for solving sleep problems. Many others have strongly felt conflicts about what their child really needs and require a high level of support from the group and/or the leader in order to be able to commit themselves to a plan and follow through with it.

Evaluating Family Needs

• Flexibility is important. As a child grows, parents need to periodically evaluate and update patterns.
• A baby is a social being and it is necessary and desirable for him to learn about the give-and-take of family life. Parents, therefore, should not ignore their own needs and feelings when they evaluate daily patterns. (For further information on this point see "Social-Emotional Development," p. 139.)

Handouts

Several useful handouts on the topic of sleep can be found in Rothenberg *PETP,* Pt. III, pp. 383–410. These are typical sleep requirements charts and several articles on approaches to guiding sleep patterns in older babies.

4

NUTRITION

background/preparation

Goals to Work Toward in Presenting This Topic

A number of nutrition-related changes for both parent and child generally occur when a baby reaches the second half of his first year. This is the time when babies begin the transition to table foods and parents often feel uncertain about how to handle it and how to help their baby through it. Information on nutrition and the changing physical needs of children is sought as babies' appetites and attitudes toward food change and as they begin to be weaned from the breast or bottle. There is more to mealtime now than nursing or bottle feeding, and it is important to discuss all the changes—nutritional as well as emotional—that are involved.

The goals to work toward on this topic are: (1) to provide parents with information concerning nutrition and food-related changes in the older baby; (2) to help parents learn techniques to cope with their child's new eating habits and patterns; (3) to help parents understand and feel good about their child's growing independence.

Typical Parental Interests and Concerns About This Topic

1. My baby refuses all food but breast milk. How can I encourage him to try solids without turning meals into a battleground?
2. My baby won't let me feed him at all with a spoon. He wants to do it himself. Can he really get enough to eat that way?
3. What's a "balanced diet" for a baby this age?
4. My baby refuses all vegetables (meats, cereals, fruit). What can I do?
5. Anna has always been a good eater, but now she doesn't even seem interested in food. What's the matter?
6. Do I have to feed my baby fruits and vegetables every day?
7. What can my son eat, since he has only a few teeth?
8. How will I know when Elizabeth is ready for finger foods?
9. Kirsten would rather play with her food than eat it. The mess really bothers me. What do I do?
10. When should I wean my baby from the breast (or bottle)?
11. How do I teach my baby to drink from a cup? When I offer it, he acts like it's poison!

156

12. When James gets fussy, I often give him a cracker if I'm busy. I know he's learning a bad habit but what can I do to avoid this?

Areas of Information You Will Need to Learn About to Teach This Topic

Nutrition for older babies.
— Daily requirements for a balanced diet.
— Food sources for major vitamins and minerals.
— General information on allergies, food sensitivities, and hyperactivity in children.
How to handle the transition to solids and table foods.
— Increasing the array of solids and lumpier foods.
— Finger foods—suitable foods, how to prepare them, how to offer them.
— Beginning to use the cup and spoon.
— Food safety—how to handle choking, what foods are unsafe.
Typical changes in appetite and eating habits.
— Normal growth patterns and weight gain in older babies.
— Varieties of learning experiences that accompany meals.
— Parents' feelings about eating changes—coping with messiness, etc.
— How to develop good eating habits and patterns in children with small appetites.
Issues concerning independence.
— Child's need to learn to feed himself.
— Weaning from breast or bottle.
— Parents' feelings about baby's independence in feeding.
Typical feeding problems.
— Overweight children.
— Use of food, breast, or bottle as a "pacifier."
— "Picky" eaters.

Family Dynamics—What This Topic Means Psychologically to Parent and Child

Feeding is so closely tied to parenting in the early months of a child's life (especially for mothers) that it is often difficult for parents to gradually relinquish control of it as their child grows older. Parents worry that their child cannot get enough to eat without their help, which is often refused from the older baby period on. Feeding is no longer smooth and easy—the child's appetite may decrease, he plays with food, drops or throws it, will eat only certain foods. All these new and confusing behaviors can combine to make mealtimes tense or uneasy for both parent and child, especially if the parent resorts to interfering, coaxing, or force-feeding.

For the older baby, mealtimes now offer much more in the way of experience than just the satisfaction of hunger. Many kinds of learning and development, such as eye-hand coordination, occur during experimentation with food and utensils. Along with learning come new demands for more independence in feeding himself, including control over the amount of food he eats. This independence is supremely messy. It is also necessary and valuable to his development; a child can become angry and frustrated if he is not allowed to experiment. No healthy child will choose to starve himself. Even though it may not seem so to parents, children can and do get enough to eat—provided their parents do not turn mealtimes into a "battleground."

The older baby stage is a time of transition. For everyone's well-being, families must work out a balance in which the parents are still responsible for the nutrition of their child—the kinds of food that are offered and when—and the child is increasingly in charge of feeding himself.

Sample Concern of Parents

Concern	Critical Issues
I don't know what to do about feeding Hannah (9 months) any more. She's always been a good eater and really looked forward to meals, but suddenly she won't let me feed her at all with a spoon. She just clamps her mouth shut and turns away. I've been giving	—Baby's independence.

Concern	*Critical Issues*	*For the group*
her a few finger foods like Cheerios, bananas, and cooked carrots, but that's not much of a diet and half of it gets mashed in her hair or dropped on the floor anyway. She only has four teeth and I don't know what kinds of foods she can handle. Now I find myself giving her little snacks, like a piece of graham cracker, all day long because I'm worried that she's not eating enough to keep a bird alive!	—Parent's concern about good nutrition.

—Baby's play with food and her messiness.

—Parent's need for suitable finger food ideas.

—Parent's concern about baby's appetite decrease. | 7. Let's have some suggestions from the group of healthy finger foods that babies enjoy.
8. What kinds of foods would *not* be suitable or safe for a baby with just a few (or no) teeth?
9. How do you cope with the mess your baby makes at meals?
10. What do some of you do when your child won't let you feed her? |

Key Questions

1. Why does Hannah seem to be refusing help with a spoon?
2. Does her refusal occur at *every* meal, even when your spouse feeds her?
3. What do you do when Hannah refuses to let you feed her?
4. What do you think Hannah is really doing when she plays with her food? How are you feeling about all the messiness that goes with her learning to feed herself?
5. What happens with the snacking? Does it change Hannah's meal behavior?
6. How do you feel about giving Hannah "snacks"? What other ways of dealing with her smaller appetite can you think of?

Readings and Other Resources

Burck, Frances Wells, *Babysense* (New York: St. Martin's Press, 1991), Chapters 3, 4, and 5.

Green, Martin, *A Sigh of Relief* (New York: Bantam Books, 1994).

*Leach, Penelope, *Your Baby and Child* (Westminster, Md.: Alfred A. Knopf, 1989), pp. 194–206.

*Satter, Ellyn, *Child of Mine: Feeding With Love and Good Sense* (Menlo Park, Cal.: Bull Publishing, 1991).

*Satter, Ellyn, *"Feeding With Love and Good Sense"*— Video (Menlo Park: Bull Publishing, 1989).

*Sears, William, and Sears, Martha, *The Baby Book* (Boston, Mass.: Little, Brown & Co., 1993), Chapter 12 (general nutrition) and pp. 250–256 (allergies).

Further information can be obtained by:
1. Contacting a pediatric nutritionist at a local medical center.
2. Contacting a local children's dentist.

teaching/presentation

Homework

The homework encourages parents to go beyond their feelings about how their baby is eating to examine specifics of amounts of food eaten, the eating atmosphere, and independence.

Focusing on their baby's mealtime activities can also demonstrate graphically the wide variety of learning experiences that food provides for their child.

FEEDING AND NUTRITION

(7–14 months)

1. What changes have you noticed in your baby's interest in food and in his/her eating patterns over the last month or so?

2. How does your baby seem to feel about food? About eating? (Think about the atmosphere that surrounds him/her while eating.)

3. How much is your baby presently doing on his/her own in the way of eating and drinking?

4. In what ways do you need to help your baby with feeding?

5. Note any concerns you're having about the foods your child eats or his/her eating patterns.

Parent's name _____ Date _____ Child's age _____

Practical Suggestions or Strategies for Teaching This Topic

• This topic is almost always one that parents discuss readily, so keeping the discussion moving should not be a problem. It is helpful, however, to pass out the nutrition handouts immediately following the mini-lecture so that you can refer to them throughout the discussion without interrupting its flow.

• Try to deal with specific concerns about weaning from the breast or bottle with a separate discussion following the general one on nutrition. This helps parents focus on each area more completely

Mini-lecture and Lead-off Questions for Discussion[1]

Since parents are most often responsible for the meal planning and preparation of foods during their child's early years, there are some overall nutritional guidelines and facts for developing adequate eating patterns that you should know about.

One fact is that Americans eat too much refined sugar—over 100 pounds per year—and too much salt. There is strong evidence that the overconsumption of these two foods can lead to many serious health problems such as obesity and hypertension. It's important, then, to know what we're eating, what's in the food products we buy. If you become a label reader, you'll find that some foods contain not only extra sugar and salt but a number of chemical additives that are controversial; you'll also find that many products are made without extra sugar, salt, or additives. If you're an aware, informed consumer, you can make intelligent decisions about what you do and do not want your family to eat. Your best bet is to use fresh, unprocessed, unrefined foods.

Though you may plan your meals to provide a healthy, balanced, and tasty diet, you will find that your baby's appetite fluctuates from day to day and from meal to meal. Try to trust his judgment about how hungry he is and how much he wants to feed himself. He'll be wanting to do more and more on his own, and eating is part of this. Remember that you're not equally hungry for every meal you sit down to.

As your child becomes more aware of different foods, watch for signs of boredom with the "same old thing," like cereal for breakfast. (Remember he's probably had it every morning for months now.) Try new choices. I'll be handing out a list of appropriate finger foods to try. Experiment a little. Don't be deterred by thinking certain foods are only for certain meals.

You may notice a decrease in your child's appetite—this is normal for children this age. Babies eat the most in the first half of their first year. They gain about two pounds a month during the first three months, and about one pound a month for the second three months. They gain three-quarters to one pound a month from 6 to 12 months. By a year, most babies have tripled their birth weight and are half again their length at birth.[2]

Your baby's rate of growth slows considerably in his second year when he gains on the average about five to six pounds and grows less than five inches. A decrease in appetite seems contradictory because a child's activity level and mobility increase so much during the second year, but it does occur.

Mealtime is often the place where the older baby makes his first "declaration of independence" by refusing food he's always liked or by refusing to be spoon-fed by you any longer. Since this can be unsettling and because this transition time can last a while, let's talk about what you can do to make it easier for both of you. What techniques have you found to cope with your baby's changing patterns and behaviors?

---

1. Much of the information in this topic has been provided by JoAnn Hattner, R.D.C.S., M.P.H., Nutritionist, Pediatrics, Stanford University Medical Center, Stanford, California. (Also see pp. 63–77 for additional information and handouts dealing with older baby nutrition).

---

2. Parents should be referred to their pediatricians for any concerns about their child's weight and length.

Additional Information for Parents

• When a baby won't eat, parents shouldn't panic. Hunger will turn the tide eventually. Children of this age normally show a decrease in appetite; teething can cause a lack of interest in eating as well. Forcing, coaxing, or making an issue of eating usually makes matters worse. If a child becomes aware of parental tension, he may turn meals into "power plays." This can cause real feeding problems for the child.

• Parents should experiment with different attitudes about feeding, as well as different amounts and textures of foods. (See pp. 63–77 for more details on what and when to feed older babies.)

Attitudes

— If mealtime is a battleground, the baby will sense it. Parents need to relax and to be aware of the messages they're sending: "Mealtime is pleasant," or "Be quiet and entertain yourself with food."

— Parents should try to be companionable. They should sit down with their child while he eats, not move around the kitchen, eager to have him finish so they can clean up.

— If a child is so interested in the social interaction between himself and his parent that he can't be bothered to eat, the parent should try a *little* inattention. Being busy in the vicinity can let a baby know that it's time to eat, not time to play.

— Often a child will allow a parent to help feed him if he's *really* hungry. Parents may be able to figure out when that is. One "good" meal out of *every* five or six is not an unusual pattern for children this age.

Amounts

— Balanced meals are important. Parents should offer similar amounts of food, for example, one tablespoon, from the different food groups at each meal.

— Sometimes more than a few pieces of food at a time are overwhelming to a child. He may react by sweeping everything off onto the floor or by stuffing every piece into his mouth and choking. Parents can try two or three pieces

of food at a time, then add two or three more. Patience is the key.

— If several kinds of food are too much, parents can try one kind of food at a time—a few pieces of fruit, then bread, then cheese, and so on.

— It may be possible to spoon-feed while a baby is manipulating finger food.

Textures

— It is important to introduce lumpy foods to a baby. Toddler foods in jars or finger foods can provide a variety of textures. If a child has no experience with food textures as a baby he may reject all attempts later, which will severely limit his diet.

— Babies with no teeth or just a few can still eat grated foods—raw apples, pears, zucchini, cheeses. Grated pieces are easily handled even before a baby can bite or chew larger pieces of the same foods.

• If a baby is offered food all day long, even tiny amounts, he will never have a chance to get really hungry or become interested in meals. Parents should try to feed their child primarily at mealtimes with a small snack at mid-morning and mid-afternoon. This pattern may produce a better appetite for meals and will help to keep a child from learning poor eating habits.

• If a child's appetite is very small, he should be offered only the highest quality foods. In that way whatever he eats will be sure to be good for him. His liquid intake should also be watched—if he's drinking too much milk or juice, he'll have no room left for food. (At this age, milk—breast or bottle—no longer provides enough nutrition to be the majority of a diet.) At a year a child should be drinking only 16 ounces of milk a day. Generally, no low- or non-fat milk until age 2.

• It is going to be messy while a baby learns to feed himself, so parents need to resign themselves to the fact. A large vinyl tablecloth, plastic runner, or beach towel can be placed under and around a child's highchair for easier clean-up and a big bib with pockets can be used.

• During meals, a baby experiences many different types of learning—fine finger dexterity, eye-hand coordination, comparisons of textures, colors, sizes, and shapes of pieces of food—as well as the considerable joys of dropping, throwing, and feeding the dog! Handling food is just as fascinating to a baby as tasting it.

• There are several foods that are *not* suitable for babies this age. These are nuts, seeds, popcorn, large chunks of raw or firm fruits or vegetables, and anything else that could lodge easily in the throat or be inhaled.

• Parents should be familiar with the Heimlich maneuver for dislodging food caught in the throat. The technique is described in Martin Green's *A Sigh of Relief.*

• If a parent cannot dislodge food from her child's throat, she should call the local fire department or emergency number. People trained for this type of emergency will respond quickly.

• When weaning from the breast, parents should consider the following:

— If weaning occurs long before the first birthday, it is advisable to wean to both bottle and cup. One note of caution: Parents should not get into the habit of leaving a bottle in bed with their child unless it contains only water. Milk or juice that remains in the mouth is extremely damaging to teeth. Also, a child may come to expect a bottle at bedtime and rely on it as a part of going to sleep.

— Parents should watch for cues in themselves and in their baby that indicate that one or the other is ready for weaning. Prolonging the nursing relationship when mother or child is ready to give it up will only sour what has probably been a lovely experience. This applies particularly to the mother who feels somehow guilty that she wants to stop nursing before her baby seems ready. A parent has just as much right to make the decision to end nursing as the child does. It is important, though, that no tension develops between mother and child because of the decision.

— When weaning is to occur, it should be done gradually. Mothers can begin by eliminating one feeding, then waiting several days and dropping another feeding. It helps to begin by eliminating the feeding that seems to mean the *least* to the child, usually the mid-day feeding. By gradually reducing the number of feedings, mothers will lessen the physical discomfort they can feel.

— When a mother is down to nursing only once or twice a day, her baby is no longer dependent on her for adequate nutrition. At that point, nursing becomes more of a social and emotional bond between parent and child than a nutritional need.

• When weaning from the bottle, parents can consider the following:

— Weaning from the bottle is often thought of as a "socially derived" developmental step— one that is used to denote "maturity." There is no "best" time to wean as far as a child's development is concerned. Each parent must decide the best time for herself and her child.

— Parents should watch for cues that their child is ready to give up the bottle. They should also watch for signs of their own negativity toward their child's use of a bottle.

— A young child may refuse to use a cup if it contains milk. Often children act as though a cup is a ludicrous place to find milk (and for them maybe it is) and reject it. If this happens, parents can further their child's use of the cup by offering him fruit juice, or water, or something other than milk. A child can also be given a cup in the bathtub to experiment with.

Handouts

The first section of the handout developed for this topic, "Feeding and Nutrition," suggests a daily meal plan for older babies. The second section lists a number of suitable finger foods for breakfast, lunch, dinner, and snacks. There are also a number of nutrition-related handouts that you may wish to refer to in the other nutrition sections of this book: "Suggested Daily Food Plan for Children 13 Months to Three Years" (p. 286), "Major Nutrients: Their Roles and Sources" (p. 290), and the handouts beginning on p. 71 that also refer to older babies. Selected pages from Satters or Sear's books (see p. 158) can also be useful handouts.

FEEDING AND NUTRITION

(7–14 months)

Suggested Daily Meal Plan for Children 7 Months and Older*

Breakfast   serving size: 2 to 3 tablespoons

Yogurt or cottage cheese and fruit, pancakes,
    eggs, cereal, French toast, etc.
Formula or breast milk (8 oz.)

Mid-morning

Fruit juice
Whole grain crackers

Noon Meal

Meat, fish, cheese, peanut butter, etc.
Starch
Vegetable
Fruit
Formula or breast milk (8 oz.)

Mid-afternoon

Milk or juice and/or finger food (e.g. crackers,
    cheese, fruit, or vegetable)

Evening Meal

Meat, fish, cheese, etc.
Starch
Fruit
Vegetable
Formula or breast milk (8 oz.)

---

*Reprinted with permission of JoAnn Hattner, R.D.C.S.,
M.P.H., Nutritionist, Pediatrics, Stanford University Medical
Center, Stanford, California.

Finger Foods

Breakfast

Cereal—dry, unsweetened, o-shaped such as Cheerios

Eggs—soft-boiled or poached, tossed with cubes of buttered toast
  —scrambled semi-firm (with milk to make fluffy)
  —hard-boiled and diced
  (all eggs should be yolk only)

Bread with yogurt, cottage cheese, peanut butter, etc.

Pancakes, French toast, or waffles—cut into strips (no syrup)

Fruit breads (heavy, not crumbly) cut into sticks (oatmeal, banana, etc.)

Fruit—melon or orange, sliced or cut into eighths, strawberries (after 9 months), peach, plum, canned fruit (drained and dried to remove syrup and to make less slippery)

Lunch & Dinner

Protein

Chicken or turkey—slivered or diced

Roast beef, etc.—diced

Fish—cooked and flaked
  —canned tuna or salmon (drained)

Hamburger—cut into small pieces (ground veal, ground beef, etc.)

Pureed meats—spread on bread to make small sandwiches

Cottage cheese—large curd

Cheese—grated or sliced or sticks
  —casseroles such as macaroni and cheese
  —melted on bread under broiler, cut into quarters

Peanut butter—spread on toast, bread, or crackers (can be thinned with milk)

Tofu—cut into pieces

Vegetables

Carrots, peas, green beans, beets, asparagus tips, celery, broccoli, zucchini, cucumber—steamed until tender, not mushy

Potatoes, sweet potatoes, yams—baked or boiled and diced

Cherry tomatoes—cut in half (after 9 months)

Pickles—sweet or dill

Fruits

Apples, pears—grated or very thinly sliced

Avocado—diced

Peaches, pears (very ripe), nectarines, plums, bananas, apricots—fresh or canned, peeled and diced.

Starches

Rice (brown or converted)—can be cooked in chicken or beef broth instead of water

Macaroni—different shapes and sizes add interest

Noodles—(whole wheat and vegetable as well as egg)

Ravioli, tortellini

Beans—baked, lima, kidney, or garbanzo

Potatoes—small pieces, well-cooked

Bread—bread sticks, crackers, zwieback, bagels, teething biscuits, etc.

Rice cakes

5

COGNITIVE-MOTOR DEVELOPMENT

background/preparation

Goals to Work Toward in Presenting This Topic

The developmental milestones that the older baby achieves in the cognitive and motor areas are fundamental to her exploration of the world around her; they also provide the foundation for later learning. Because of this, these areas of development are of interest to parents. Even though parents recognize developmental milestones (such as walking) as they appear, they may not be familiar with the overall patterns of cognitive and motor growth.

Goals to work toward on this topic are: (1) to provide parents with information concerning cognitive and motor development in the older baby and to make them aware of the importance of the changes; (2) to help parents become aware of the individual differences in growth patterns among older babies.

Typical Parental Interests and Concerns About This Topic

1. My baby only crawled for two weeks before he began to walk. Is there any reason to be concerned that he did not crawl long enough?
2. Our daughter has been side-stepping along the furniture for six weeks now, but she will not walk by herself yet. Is something the matter?
3. Jason puts absolutely everything he finds or or touches into his mouth! Why does he still do this? How can I get him to stop?
4. My baby loves to climb up on things. But getting down is something else again, even when she can easily reach the floor. I'm curious about why there seems to be such a difference to her.
5. What should parents do to help a child learn to walk?
6. Alexa isn't crawling yet and she's 10 months old. Is something wrong?
7. Nicole isn't following the development charts exactly. Why?

Areas of Information You Will Need to Learn About to Teach This Topic

- Motor development in the older baby.
- Cognitive development in the older baby.
- Individual differences in developmental growth patterns.

Family Dynamics—What This Topic Means Psychologically to Parent and Child

Parents often do not realize how small a role they play in their baby's cognitive and motor development. They can interact with their child and provide the environment and experience that will stimulate him, but they cannot override the individual pattern of growth that dictates when his body and mind will be ready to achieve each milestone. This inability to change or hurry developmental stages sometimes leads to impatience, worry, or frustration in those parents who seem to feel that their baby should have achieved a certain stage of growth.

Regardless of his parents' feelings, every baby follows his own particular growth pattern at his own particular pace. (He must follow the pattern because physiologically and neurologically he is unable to do otherwise. If he is not "ready" to walk, for example, he simply cannot do it.) Achieving *every* developmental milestone is exciting for the older baby since he invests a great deal of time and energy into the mastery of each. He is pleased with this increased control of himself and his environment and is hungry for new experiences and accomplishments.

The second half of the first year is a period of intense work and accomplishment for children and should be one of pride and excitement for their parents. As parents watch their child's body and mind develop, they can support and encourage him, but the real work is up to the baby.

Sample Concern of Parents

Concern	*Critical Issues*
Brooke (13 months) seems slow in learning to walk and I'm a little worried. She has always been a quiet, happy baby. She will sit with her toys for what seems like hours, mouthing and fingering and studying each one intently. But she doesn't like to crawl much and has just now begun to pull herself up to stand. I guess I really want to know if I should be concerned.	—Parent's concern about motor development. —Baby's development of small-motor area and attention span. —Beginning of large-motor achievement. —Parent's need for information.

Key Questions

1. How do you feel about Brooke's ability to play quietly? Does she seem to enjoy herself?
2. What do you think Brooke wants to learn about as she plays with her toys?
3. How much time does she spend on the floor?
4. What kinds of play areas are available for Brooke in your home? Would she have any reason to want to crawl from one area to another?
5. How do *you* play with her?
6. What are you doing to encourage Brooke to move about more?
7. Have you talked to your pediatrician about your concern? Are there other areas of development that Brooke has been concentrating on recently?

For the group

8. As you look at what your baby is doing now, how many areas is she working on at once? (Attempt to get the group to see that babies don't develop equally in all areas at the same time.)

Readings and Other Resources

Ames, Louise Bates, and Ilg, Frances, I., *Your One-Year-Old* (New York: Dell Publishing Co., Inc., 1982).

Brazelton, T. Berry, *Infants and Mothers* (New York: Dell Publishing Co., Inc., 1983).

Eisenberg, Arlene, Murkoff, Heidi E., & Hathaway, Sandee E., *What To Expect the First Year* (New York: Workman Publishing, 1989).

Caplan, Theresa, and Caplan, Frank, *The First Twelve Months of Life* (New York: Perigree/Berkley Publishing, 1993).

Hickey, Mary C., "Little Explorers", *Working Mother*, May, 1993, p. 50.

*Jessell, Camilla, *From Birth To Three* (New York: Delta/Bantam Doubleday Dell, 1990.)

*Leach, Penelope, *Your Baby and Child* (Westminster, Md.: Alfred A. Knopf, 1989), pp. 230–251.

Segal, Marilyn, *Your Baby at Play: Birth to One* (New York: Newmarket Press, 1985).

---

teaching/presentation

Homework

No homework has been developed for this topic.

Practical Suggestions and Strategies for Teaching This Topic

• A discussion of cognitive and motor development is an excellent introduction to the topic "Play and Learning," since it lays the groundwork for understanding the meaning of play for the older baby. The former is generally a short discussion and can lead right into the "play" topic.

• The discussion of this topic is usually straightforward and fact-oriented. As such, it is not an extremely complex topic to teach.

Mini-lecture[1] and Lead-Off Questions for Discussion

Through your lecture, it is hoped that the parents will better understand the overall patterns of cognitive and motor development and recognize where their individual children are within these

---

1. More detailed information can be obtained by reading the resources mentioned in the "Readings and Other Resources" section of this topic.

patterns. It will be helpful if the handout "Cognitive-Motor Development" is distributed as you begin.

Your child's mental and motor development are laying the groundwork for the learning that will characterize his childhood. They are the foundation for and the prelude to the play and learning experiences that will teach him about himself and the world around him. Seen in this light, it is apparent why cognitive and motor achievements are extremely exciting and stimulating for your child and why he invests so much time and energy in them. He uses his cognitive and motor abilities even during the night—he may be driven to waking from sleep to continue practicing his crawling, standing, or walking.

During the first year of life, your child is engrossed in discovering the physical properties of the world around him. He asks, in essence, of each object he encounters, "What is it made of?". He then attempts to answer this question by using the cognitive-motor skills he is currently practicing. In the beginning, many children make their evaluations by using their mouths—everything goes in to be tasted, to be mouthed for texture, shape, and so on. But as they become more mobile and more skilled, children begin to use their eyes and hands for more detailed discovery making. During the second year of life, they're familiar with the textures and properties of objects and they begin to think about what to do with the objects they've discovered.

A child's cognitive, or mental, development during the first year seems to fall into three major areas:

Reasoning ability. Your child is beginning to be aware of basic cause-and-effect relationships. (If he squeezes a certain toy, there is a noise. If he cries, someone will come to him.) He is also beginning to realize that he does not cause everything that happens in his world; that some things and people operate independently of him and his actions.

Space orientation. Your baby is developing an awareness of the space around him and how to work with and within it. His eye-hand coordination is rapidly developing. (A number of examples of this are listed under "Small-Motor Achievements" in your handout.) He is aware of heights and may develop fears in this area. (His awareness may make him cautious of climbing up or down on furniture or the like.) He is beginning to experiment with concepts such as near and far, in and out. He is becoming aware of differences in size and shape. Things look different from various angles and he turns each object so that he can observe it fully. If you hand him his bottle upside down, he will turn it right-side up. He *knows* that is how it is supposed to be.

Memory. As memory begins to develop, your child is able to recall events and information that allow him to build on his previous experiences. He is now able to recognize objects that are familiar to him, and that is often why a new toy or plaything is more interesting than an old one. He is also realizing that objects have permanence, that they exist from day to day and don't change even though he comes and goes. His attention span is lengthening little by little. He will become more and more persistent about reaching a goal, and less easily distracted from it.

Cognitive and motor development are somewhat difficult to isolate from the entirety of your baby's development because they are a fundamental part of its every facet. You can observe how developmental achievements influence your child's play, his language, his social interaction—the whole of his personality as it develops. That's what makes every

achievement so exciting for you and your child.

Now that we've had a general overview of the subject, let's discuss the specific questions you have about your baby's development.

During the discussion, it is often helpful to use anecdotes from your own experience to illustrate and clarify points for the group. Sharing examples also serves to emphasize the wide range of individual differences in growth and temperament among normal babies.

Additional Information for Parents

• Parents should not judge their baby's rate of development solely on her large-motor achievements. Small-motor development, attention span, and cognitive development may not seem as dramatic, but are just as important for the child.
• Parents need to keep their baby's temperament in mind. Some babies learn more through observation than they do by trial and error.
• If parents are concerned about their child's cognitive or motor development, they should try to keep some records of what their baby is doing from week to week. Encourage them to look back over these records and to observe their child's progress in all areas. The time to be concerned is when a baby seems to have made *no* gains in any area (motor, language, and so on) over a period of a month or two. Then the baby's doctor should be consulted.

Handouts

The handout, "Cognitive-Motor Development," is best used with the mini-lecture as an overview of the two areas.

COGNITIVE-MOTOR DEVELOPMENT

(7–14 months)

Small-Motor Achievements

1. Uses thumb and finger like pincers to pick things up.

2. Holds an object in each hand—may bang them together—and may transfer objects from hand to hand.

3. Still uses mouth for exploration, also to hold a third object when both hands are full.

4. Begins to use index finger to point, poke, hook, and pull.

5. Begins to use hands in sequence, one following the other; turns pages of a book (several at a time).

Large-Motor Achievements

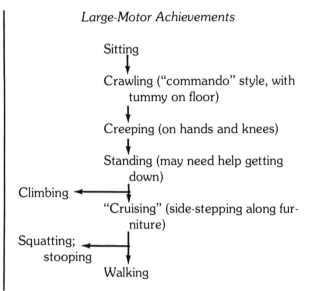

Sitting

↓

Crawling ("commando" style, with tummy on floor)

↓

Creeping (on hands and knees)

↓

Standing (may need help getting down)

Climbing ← ┐

"Cruising" (side-stepping along furniture)

Squatting; stooping ← ┐

Walking

6

PLAY AND LEARNING

background/preparation

Goals to Work Toward in Presenting This Topic

Play and learning are interwoven in the life of the older baby because play *is* learning for her. Her waking hours are filled with exploration and discovery of herself and the world around her. Most parents recognize the importance of their children's play and want to encourage and stimulate this activity. Because they are eager for information on how to accomplish this, play and learning are included for discussion.

The goals to work toward on this topic are: (1) to help parents become aware of the meaning of play for the older baby; (2) to outline for parents the goals and developmental steps that older babies strive for in their play; (3) to provide a forum for parents to exchange ideas and information about all aspects of their children's play; (4) to help parents explore their roles in their child's play and learning.

Typical Parental Interests and Concerns About This Topic

1. Lauren seems content to play by herself most of the time and I worry that I'm not playing with her enough. How much time should a parent spend playing with her child?
2. My son refuses to play by himself. It almost seems like he expects me to entertain him! How can I get him to spend more time playing independently?
3. What kinds of toys are appropriate for babies this age?
4. Jessica acts bored with all her toys right now. We can't afford to keep buying new ones all the time. What can we do?
5. I'd like Gregory to play with things that are interesting, stimulating, and safe for him to have. Can you give me some guidelines to go by?
6. What sort of play environment should I look for in a day-care setting for my child?
7. What about playing outdoors? What can a baby this age do outside?
8. We have two incomes but too little time with our child? What's wrong with buying him whatever he wants?
9. What toys can I make?

Areas of Information You Will Need to Learn About to Teach This Topic

- Significance of play for the older baby.
- Types of play and playthings appropriate for older babies.
- The parent's roles in child's play and learning.

Family Dynamics—What This Topic Means Psychologically to Parent and Child

Parents often think of play in an entirely different way than their child does—they don't see the purpose of what their child is doing in his play, don't feel he plays enough by himself, and don't feel he uses his toys in the way they were intended (by the manufacturer). This can lead them to put pressure on their child to modify what he plays with and the ways in which he plays.

Parents often feel, too, that their child should be "learning" while he plays, but they sometimes only think of learning in the adult sense of the word. They don't understand that the explorations babies make during their play are teaching them many things and will help them to "learn" later on.

From the baby's point of view, play is his doorway to the world. He uses every experience to add to his growing store of information about himself and his environment. He experiments with pushing and poking things, squashes and throws his food, watches his parents and begins to imitate their actions. The older baby's focus is on the physical properties of his world, discovering what objects are made of. His marvelous curiosity and his obvious joy in each new discovery seem to make every day a new opportunity for him.

Babies encounter play-related problems primarily in the nature of their play environment and in their parents' attitudes and expectations for their play. If the play environment is not relatively free of hazards, a baby will receive such frequent discipline that he'll learn that it's not a good idea to explore. He can also receive negative messages if he is not playing as long as his parents feel he

should or he does not play in the ways they expect him to.

Where play and learning are concerned, parents do well to follow their child's lead and allow themselves to be caught up in his exploration of the world. Looking at the world through a child's eyes can bring parents a heightened awareness and rekindle a sense of wonder that is all the more satisfying because it is shared.

Sample Concern of Parents

Concern	Critical Issues
Chris (10 months) doesn't seem very interested in playing with his own toys, even the really good educational ones. But he will sit for almost an hour on the kitchen floor with pots and pans all around him. When we're in the car, he insists loudly on having *my* car keys, even though he has a set of brightly colored ones of his own. I really don't mind his playing with things from around the house (except for my keys) but I wonder why he isn't more interested in the toys specifically made for children his age.	—Baby's preference for "real" playthings. —Beginning of imitative behavior and, again, preference for the real. —Parent's need for information.

Key Questions

1. Why do you suppose *your* keys are so much more fascinating to Chris than his own?
2. What is your definition of play? How do you think this differs from the way Chris looks at it?

For the group

3. Why do you think Chris enjoys the pots and pans so much?
4. What can we learn about play from Chris as far as what's important to a child this age?

Readings and Other Resources

*Allison, Christine, *I'll Tell You a Story, I'll Sing You a Song* (New York: Dell, 1991).

Berends, Polly, *Whole Child, Whole Parent* (New York: Harper Collins, 1987), Chapter 3, pp. 99–147.

Burck, Frances Wells, *Babysense* (New York: St. Martin's Press, 1991), Chapter 22.

Growing Child newsletter (Lafayette, Ind.: Dunn & Hargitt, updated annually).

Leach, Penelope, *Your Baby and Child* (Westminster, Md.: Alfred A. Knopf, 1989), pp. 259–267.

*Marzollo, Jean, *Fathers and Babies* (New York: Harper Collins, 1993).

*Segal, Marilyn, *Your Baby at Play: Birth To One Year* (New York: Newmarket Press, 1985).

Pamphlets: "Toys: Tools for Learning" (National Association for the Education of Young Children) "Toys & Play" (Toy Manufacturers of America) (See p. 177 for ordering information for both of these pamphlets.)

teaching/presentation

Homework

The homework for this topic helps parents gain insight into their babies' play and learn more about its meaning for them. Questions 2 and 3 focus on differences in the ways parents play with children.

Practical Suggestions and Strategies for Teaching This Topic

• You will need to be prepared to handle the discussion of this topic in a number of ways, since groups differ widely in their approach to it. Some group approaches to play and learning are:

Learning-oriented. Parents with this orientation want to know how children learn and want to find out what they can do to provide stimulation and learning experiences for their babies. There will be questions about educational toys, books, and activities. Parents will need help to broaden their definition of play and learning, and will need to become aware of other parental roles in play besides "teacher." Learning-oriented parents should be shown how *all* play is really learning for their child.

Toy- and environment-oriented. This group of parents likes to focus on the details of play—what their babies play with and where they play. Here again, you will need to help them broaden their definition to include the deeper significance of play for children. You should also try to show them that they can provide a variety of experiences as well as toys and playthings for their babies.

Role-oriented. Parents with this approach to the topic are concerned with *how* to play with their children. Their questions generally center around how much time should be spent playing with their babies and what their roles should be ("teacher," "entertainer," "playmate," and so on). This group is usually receptive to a combination of information described in the two preceding approaches.

• It will be helpful if you develop a list of toy alternatives to suggest (for example, metal keys from the hardware store, small pots and pans, and so on). All playthings should of course be safe and preferably inexpensive.

PLAY AND LEARNING

(7–14 months)

1. What seem to be your baby's favorite playthings right now?

   Why do you think he/she enjoys them so much?

2. How does your spouse's way of playing with your baby differ from yours?

   How does your baby handle these differences?

3. What aspects of your child's play or your play with him/her are not going as smoothly as you had hoped?

Parent's name _____ Date _____ Child's age _____

• Many groups seem to enjoy sharing with each other their baby's favorite toys and activities. You might consider asking them to bring things from home to show to the group; this could provide a wealth of new ideas for you and the other parents.
• It is helpful to list parents' questions on the board and group them by category. They can then be discussed as broad, theory-based questions (parent orientation) or as practical questions (actual toys and activities).

Mini-lecture and Lead-off Questions for Discussion

It is usually most productive (in terms of the discussion) to first talk with the group about the significance of play for the older baby. This helps the parents recognize that it is the child who is the central focus of the topic.

Play is vital to a child's total growth. In play he practices his skills and develops his theories about the world; he investigates and experiments; he gains control and, eventually, mastery of himself and parts of his world; he learns about success and failure; about what he is good at and what he is interested in; he imitates behavior, preparing himself to be a part of our society; he begins to be creative and develops his own unique and individual style.

As a child grows, his intellectual and motor development occur together. There's a direct relationship between what a baby knows and what he can do. As he learns to sit and crawl, he becomes aware of how to use his new skill to explore the world around him. The learning process is fun, and enjoyment comes not only from the activity itself but from its results—his increased ability to handle the world.

There are three kinds of skills that are very much related to play and are necessary for successful learning, independent behavior, and effective communication with people. These are:

Cognitive Skills

• attention skills such as persistence, curiosity, and exploration;
• perceptual skills, including the ability to notice discrepancies and to learn from observation;
• **conceptual skills such as anticipating consequences, taking the perspective of another person, planning and carrying out activities, developing strategies for problem solving, and acquiring basic knowledge.**

Behavioral Skills

• **motor skills such as manipulation of objects and control of body position.**
• **control skills, including the ability to carry out instructions and to inhibit impulsive behavior;**
• **self-care skills such as toileting and eating in a regular manner.**

Social Skills

• **being able to understand and use language;**
• **being able to use adults as resources by getting their attention and asking for their help when necessary;**
• **developing personal skills such as feelings of self-worth and independence, the ability to express feelings, being able to feel and express warmth, be flexible, and to cooperate with others.**

This summary of the specific abilities babies are working on in their play is actually the summary of the same abilities we all work on during our entire lives. Babies don't complete this learning through their play but rather begin their life-long path of learning.

You may be wondering how you can connect your daily routine, your enjoyment of your baby, and his toys to this large goal of continuous learning. You may be wondering, as I did, how to know just what a child needs. Here are a few suggestions:

• **Be aware of the stages of development to know the direction in which your baby is heading; knowing the general pattern is more important than expecting the baby to achieve certain skills by a certain age. If you know where your baby is heading, you can provide opportunities for her to discover for herself the physical properties of objects and the logical relationships among them.**
• **Watch your baby's signals about what he's trying to do. By reading the signals, you can figure out what the child is ready for next.**

The cues are fascinating and become easier to read as the child gets older.

• **Watch the balance of your child's day to see that she has time with you and other people, time alone, time inside and time outside, time for resting and time for quiet and active play.**

• **Remember that love, learning, and play are all related, and that interaction between parent and child is more important than a specific toy or skill. When a parent shows her enjoyment of an activity her child is involved in, her message encourages her baby's confidence and self-esteem. In turn, self-esteem positively influences a child's skill development.**

Can any of you tell us about techniques you use to connect your developmental goals for your child to his daily activities? Do you have any theories about play and learning that influence your day-to-day parenting?

As the discussion moves on, try to keep it focused on the child and the parents, rather than on the details of play, such as specific toys. (If you have asked parents to bring things to share, ask them to talk about them after the general discussion of the topic.) Listing and grouping parents' questions before the discussion (see Practical Suggestions and Strategies for Teaching This Topic) can prevent the discussion from becoming bogged down in minor details. As various aspects of play and learning are brought up, you can distribute the handout for this topic.

Additional Information for Parents

Types of Play and Playthings

• Some parents may have already noticed that their babies often prefer "real" objects to toys. This is the beginning of imitative behavior—children want to use what parents use. There are a lot of creative alternatives to store-bought toys that are available in the home as well as in the houseware and hardware sections of stores; these are usually less expensive than commercial toys. Parents can fill a cupboard or drawer with *safe* kitchen utensils and let their child know that they are his.

• Encourage parents to keep their child's play

area relatively uncluttered. A jumble of toys is confusing to a baby and hazardous to him and to others. Encourage parents to think of toys as children's "tools" and to organize them in ways that make sense and enable the baby and his caregivers to find what they need to engage in meaningful play. It is helpful to the baby's developing sense of order as well as his cognitive development to play "cleaning up" games like "Toss it in!" or "Does the puppet go with the balls? No-o-o, (silly laughter); the puppet goes with the puppets!"

• Parents should try to offer a wide variety of experiences to their baby. Children are extremely curious at this age and a good range of activities—water play, enclosed spaces or boxes to crawl into, opportunities to climb—can be fun for parent and child.

• Many parents tend to have a rather restricted definition of play. This is often because they have forgotten or misplaced their child-like sense of wonder at the world and all its marvels, and tend to concern themselves in the extreme with the more obvious trappings of play. By concentrating on toys and play environment, parents can overlook the wealth of experiences and playthings their home and daily life have to offer. Toy merchandisers, too, discourage this rich view in favor of focusing attention on specific functions of purchased objects. Parents can be encouraged to expand their ideas about play and learning by thinking of playthings as things to USE, in many different and creative ways, rather than as things to OWN. As one parent educator put it, "the ideal plaything is 90% child and 10% toy."

Parents' Roles in Play

• Parents should take their cues from their child and his interests. A child should set the tone and the pace of play and the parent should then play *with* him.

• Older babies don't usually respond well to directive "teaching" from their parents. They seem to sense that parental involvement is very intense and they refuse to "perform"; for example, they won't wave "bye-bye" on command until the other person is out of sight. If parents find themselves tense and insistent that their baby "learn" something, it's time for them to back off and examine why they feel that way. Parents need to remember that they "teach" their child all the time in the sense that they are models for him.

• If a baby insists that her parents entertain her constantly, she needs encouragement (and a little less involvement) from them to play more independently. Parents may have to be "very busy" in the vicinity, and tell their child that they'll play with her in a little while. It is useful to determine the time of day when such an attempt would be most successful. Often babies are more rested in the morning and a small amount of independent play can be fostered then. Babies may object at first, but if parents stick with it, the children will get the idea.

Handouts

The four sections of this handout, Developmental Goals in Play, Considerations When Selecting Toys, Types of Play, and Play Guide-lines, cover various aspects of play and learning. You may also wish to recommend or order and distribute:

— "Toys: tools for learning." This valuable pamphlet provides a thorough discussion on the importance of play, types and use of toys and play materials. A chart matches a child's developing skills with appropriate toys and activities from birth to age 8. Available from the National Association for the Education of Young Children, 1509 9th St. N.W., Washington, D.C. 20036-1426 or call (800) 424-2460; 100 copies for $10.

or

— "Toys and Play." Another valuable pamphlet focussing on birth to age 12. Available from Toy Manufacturers of America by writing to: Toy Booklet, P.O. Box 866, Madison Square Station, New York, N.Y. 10159 or call (800) 851-9955; free to parents and qualified organizations.

7–14 months

PLAY AND LEARNING

(7–14 months)

Developmental Goals in Play

1. banging
2. poking
3. twisting things (knobs, dials)
4. pushing and pulling things
5. crawling under things
6. getting into things
7. opening and shutting doors
8. pulling drawers in and out
9. getting in and out of things
10. climbing
11. squeezing things (water out of sponges)
12. dropping objects from heights

*From Sutton-Smith, Brian and Sutton-Smith, Shirley, *How to Play With Your Children* (New York: Hawthorn Books, Inc., out of print).

Considerations When Selecting Toys

SAFETY—Read the label and instructions. Pay particular attention to parts or pieces that could be inhaled or swallowed. Also remove plastic wrappings, staples, pins, etc., before allowing your child to play with the toy.

DURABILITY—Can the toy stand up to banging, dropping, poking, pulling, etc.? Can it be washed or easily cleaned in some way.?

SENSORY APPEAL—Consider how the toy will stimulate your child. (Is it colorful? Does it move? Does it make noise? Can it be "mouthed"? Does it offer a variety of textures for touching?)

AGE RANGE—Will the toy "grow" with your child? Does it appeal only to his current interests and skills or does it also stimulate and encourage him to try new combinations of skills? (The midpoint of an age range listed on a toy box is often the most appropriate age for that toy.) Will the toy be fun for other reasons as your child grows older?

INDEPENDENT PLAY—Consider whether your child can *use* the toy by himself. Toys that your child can work and play with independently are more satisfactory for him (and for you) in the long run than toys that require your intervention and assistance.

VARIETY—Try to provide different kinds of toys that will give your child a wide range of experience. Consider also your child's temperament and whether he will respond to the experiences the toy will offer.

"REAL" TOYS—Many of the best playthings can be found in the kitchen or other rooms in the home. The housewares and hardware departments of discount and hardware stores are excellent places to find a wide variety of relatively inexpensive "real" toys. These are very appealing to children and help to encourage the development of imitative play.

Types of Play

Large motor (moving around)

rolling around
crawling
standing up and walking around furniture

7–14 months

pushing things—furniture, toddler ride-on toys, push-pull toys

climbing

walking on own

pulling things—pull toys

rocking—rocking horse

running

Fine motor

mouthing, chewing, teething

banging, waving things around—metal cup, pie tins, wooden spoons, Band-aid box, keys

squeezing, poking, feeling, manipulating

dumping things out of containers—boxes inside boxes

turning pages of books, etc., tearing things

nesting—cans, pots, margarine tubs

throwing—balls (different sizes, textures, colors)

opening and shutting doors, drawers

dropping things

stacking

push toys—cars, little trucks

Interactional games

peek-a-boo; hide 'n seek

chasing

reading—books

talking

singing/nursery rhymes

Messy play

sand

water: bath toys, sponge, washcloth, floating toys, ball, cups, plastic bottles

dirt

Surprise toys

Imitation—social play

large cardboard boxes

Dance/music

Play Guidelines

Exploring. Young children need a chance to do a lot of exploring. They learn the basic properties of many objects during their first year of exploration and they want to know how to use all these things during their toddler year.

Toys. Too many toys to choose from and a big jumble of toys can be very confusing for a child and decrease his attention span; too many things that are difficult to play with can be frustrating; "non-toys" are often more appealing than toys; toys should be rotated (some put away for a while) and moved to different play areas from time to time to keep things interesting. (You can borrow toys from friends and loan them some of yours.)

Learning. Help a child develop his attention span by letting him play as long as he's interested in something. Expect and encourage him to solve as many problems as he can for himself. (Some frustration is necessary for learning, so when you help, try to help only part-way sometimes and do your part slowly so the child can learn from what you're doing.) When you use his toys, don't always do everything fast and "right." Children enjoy seeing grown-ups make mistakes once in a while. Show your child some ways to use materials but, of course, he'll use materials in his own way much of the time. Use your sense of humor to help develop his.

Balance. Remember to think about your whole day—have you both had enough change of scenery for that day? Have you and your child had some balance in your day's activities—has he had time to be indoors and outdoors, time for energetic play and relaxing play (like baths), time to play by himself, with you, and near other children? (See Rothenberg, *PETP,* p. 310 for ways to provide balance in the day for the child who has been home much of the time and for the child who has been away in child care much of the day.)

7

SPEECH AND LANGUAGE DEVELOPMENT[1]

background/preparation

Goals to Work Toward in Presenting This Topic

The emergence of expressive language is a major, exciting milestone that is reached around the end of a baby's first year. Once language occurs, its development moves predictably from one step to the next in normal babies; the timing of these steps, however, is highly variable since every child moves through the developmental pattern at his own pace. Most parents generally have great interest in the topic of language development.

Goals to work toward on this topic are: (1) to provide parents with detailed information on language development in older babies; (2) to help parents become aware of the influence they have on their baby's developing speech; (3) to give parents a variety of techniques they may use to encourage and stimulate language development.

Typical Parental Interests and Concerns About This Topic

1. When should a baby say her first word?
2. How can I help Molly learn good speech habits?
3. How do I stimulate Daniel's language development?
4. How can I judge whether my baby's language development is normal?
5. Is there anything wrong with "baby talk" or nicknames?
6. This may sound funny, but what's the best way to talk to Sam to help him learn what words mean?
7. I'm a fairly quiet person. Will my baby learn language more slowly than the baby of a mother who talks more? Should I try to talk more?
8. Our full-time nanny speaks only Spanish. How will this affect my child's language development?

Areas of Information You Will Need to Learn About to Teach This Topic

Language development in older babies.
— Stages of development.
— Individual differences in development.
Parents' roles in language development.
— "Modeling."
— Stimulation.
— Interpretation and encouragement.

---

1. Speech *and* language are not the same as each other. Speech refers to the mechanics (in the throat and mouth), i.e., the movement of the vocal musculature to form sounds and eventually words. Language refers to the thought processes and encompasses the meaning of words (semantics), memory, and word order and grammar (syntax). In our Speech and Language chapters, we generally use "Language" when we are referring to both at once.

Family Dynamics—What This Topic Means Psychologically to Parent and Child

It is a great thrill for parents when their baby begins to use language. (Along with the ability to walk, the ability to speak signifies for many parents the transition of their child from baby to toddler.) But along with the excitement, many parents may experience frustration because the child's speech is not clear and they have difficulty interpreting it. These problems disappear, however, as the baby's language ability and vocabulary increase.

The baby, too, may experience some frustration as he tries to make himself understood. But with the reinforcement of his parents' attention and the models of their everyday speech in the home, these frustrations are transitory. Babies can become quite pleased with their new words (and their parents' pleasure in them) and with the reactions they bring about.

For both parent and child, language development usually produces feelings of pride and excitement as it adds a new dimension to the family's relationships. The emergence and progression of speech usually provide much satisfaction and parents' concerns are generally few.

Sample Concern of Parents

Concern	Critical Issues
When should a baby say his first word? I'm a little concerned that Chip (12 months) isn't talking yet. He makes a lot of noises and babbles to himself, but there aren't any "real" words. When he wants something, he says, "Uh, uh, uh" and looks in the general direction of whatever it is. It's like a guessing game, but when I can't figure out what he wants, he cries. It is really frustrating because we're both trying so hard. What can I do to help him hurry up and talk?	—Parent's need for information about normal language development. —Baby's attempt to "talk." —Baby's frustration. —Parent's frustration. —Parent's need for ways to encourage and stimulate speech.

Key Questions

1. What kinds of noises is Chip practicing?
2. When does he vocalize most during the day?
3. What kinds of vocal interactions with Chip are satisfying to you? Does he also seem to enjoy these times?
4. How do you deal with your own frustrations about language?
5. Is Chip in day care? What are his opportunities for language stimulation?

For the group

6. How do you respond to your children when they are trying to tell you what they want?

Readings and Other Resources

Arnberg, Lenore, *Raising Children Bilingually* (Philadelphia: Multilingual Matters, 1987).

*Baron, Naomi, *Growing Up With Language* (New York: Addison-Wesley, 1992).

Brazelton, T. Berry, *Infants and Mothers* (New York: Dell Publishing Co., 1983).

Caplan, Theresa, and Caplan, Frank, *The First Twelve Months of Life* (New York: Perigree Books/Berkley, 1993).

Growing Child newsletter (Lafayette, Ind.: Dunn & Hargitt, updated annually) 7 to 14-month issues.

*Jessell, Camilla, *From Birth To Three* (New York: Delta/Bantam Doubleday Dell, 1990), pp. 76–87.

*Leach, Penelope, *Your Baby and Child* (Westminster, Md.: Alfred A. Knopf, 1989), pp. 260–266.

For further information and pamphlets on speech and language development issues, contact American Speech-Language-Hearing Association (ASHA) 10801 Rockville Pike, Rockville, Maryland, 20852 or call (800) 638-8255 or (301) 897-8682.

A local speech and language specialist can also be a resource for further information.

teaching/presentation

Homework

The homework assignment for this topic helps parents focus not only on specific sounds their child makes, but also on the ways they already stimulate language and on what the baby already understands even though he can't yet verbalize.

Practical Suggestions and Strategies for Teaching This Topic

• Since language development is a complex physiological and neurological process, there may be questions from group members that you are not able to answer. A local speech therapist or other language-related professional can probably provide explanations and answers for you to take to the group.

• The discussion of language development generally does not require a full class period and does not involve complex emotional concerns. Because of this, you will probably encounter more questions and fewer issues to problem solve. However, you should be prepared with an outline of issues you want to raise in case the group does not bring them up.

Mini-lecture and Lead-off Questions for Discussion

It will help the parents to follow the typical pattern of language development if you distribute the handout "Normal Speech and Language Development" at the beginning of the discussion.

The emergence of language in your child is tremendously exciting. It is the first verbal indication of the interests your child has, and it gives you a view of what's going on inside him. It is also a producer of change in your
relationship with your child. No longer will you be just speaking *to* him—now you will be speaking *with* him. The first time your child actually answers a question you ask him can be truly startling, and may suddenly make you feel that your son or daughter is no longer a baby, but is a child.

You may find, however, that language may cause frustration. Your child may find it hard to express himself. You may not be able to understand him. When this happens, perhaps the most important thing you can do is to talk to your baby. Label everything around him. And let him know that you're trying to understand him. Encourage and praise his efforts. When you cannot understand, help him to show you physically what he wants. Have him point to the object. Tell him, "Show me." This kind of positive reinforcement will give him the drive to keep on trying to communicate verbally and will show him how much you value him as a person.

The handout I've distributed to you describes the various developmental stages of speech. As you raise the questions you have about your child's language and your communication with him, let's refer to the handout.

As the discussion moves on, show the parents the sections of the handout that are most helpful. They will then be able to review the material later.

Additional Information for Parents[1]

• Parents should be encouraged to label things for their baby and to talk about what she's doing. They should also tell her what they're doing and how they're feeling. When they're upset because they cannot understand their child, they should

---

1. This section notes the major points that are covered in the handout "Normal Speech and Language Development." You will most likely wish to expand on them.

SPEECH AND LANGUAGE DEVELOPMENT

(7–14 months)

Try to notice different patterns of sound that your baby makes during the day. Then answer these questions.

1. What sounds does your child have that you don't have in your language?

2. What does it seem like your child is doing when he/she is making sounds?

3. Do you involve yourself with your child when he/she is practicing sounds? How?

4. Do you give your child any clues besides your words that help him/her understand what you're saying? What are these clues?

5. How do you know when your child understands what you say?

Parent's name _____ Date _____ Child's age _____

tell her. This will help the child begin to comprehend intangibles as well as physically concrete objects.

• Most children's first meaningful words come between 9 and 18 months, and by 15 months most children have a vocabulary of several words. As a group, girls usually talk one or two months before boys. Current research also shows that girls have a larger vocabulary than boys until the middle school years. If a child has no words by the age of two, parents should be concerned and seek professional help.

• Anticipating a child's needs too quickly and too often can actually retard her speech development. If needs are immediately met, the child will have no reason to speak. It's important to try to strike a balance between responding too quickly and not quickly enough.

• A child's speech patterns will be like his parents' because that is what he hears. He will also copy his parents' intonations and gestures, accompanying a "no" with finger-shaking or saying "OK" for "yes."

• A baby may use "mmm" sounds or say "mama" to register complaints or needs and "d" sounds or "dada" for playtime. The associations may reflect parental roles.

• It is natural and very helpful for adults to speak to babies differently than they speak to other adults. Babies give increased attention and responsiveness to high-pitched tones, utterances with a musical or sing-song quality with lots of repetition of key words or phrases (e.g. "Where's your NOSE? THERE it is! THERE'S your NOSE?") and an added emphasis of word sounds by the addition of an "ee" ending, as in "DOGgie," "HORsey," etc. Conversely, parents and caregivers should avoid either directly correcting or directly reinforcing the child's imperfect utterances. Thus when the child points and says "baba", the adult should avoid responding with a correction, such as, "No, not 'baba,' say 'BOTTLE!' or with a mirroring of the child's sounds as in "Here's your baba." The adult can best encourage and foster language growth by saying something like "Yes! That's your BOTTLE! You want your BOTTLE? Here's your bottle!"

• Studies show no correlation between a child's early speech (how early or late his first word emerges or how rich his vocabulary) and later intelligence.

• The babbling and sounds a baby makes are practice for expressive speech. Babies should be provided with some quiet time for experimenting with language.

• It is important to encourage a baby's attempts to use words to communicate. When a child is unable to express a word, parents can pick him up and help him point to the object he wants, saying, "Is it the *cup*? Is it the *ball*? Is it the *cookie*?

• Current research shows that children's language development may be hampered by too little time in active verbal interaction with an adult. This is an important consideration for parents whose children are in group day care or have several small siblings. While important for social development, interaction with other children by itself will not enhance language development. Neither will passive exposure to spoken language as in being addressed in a group or listening to television. Thus parents should make sure that their children, wherever they are cared for, have frequent opportunities for active engagement in verbal exchanges with an adult who uses language in an appropriate and developmentally facilitative manner.

Handouts

There is one handout developed for this topic. The first section on "Normal Speech and Language Development" is an overview of language development in the older baby, and should be used during the discussion. The second section on "Suggested Activities for Language Growth" provides parents with excellent ideas for stimulating and encouraging language growth and development. You may also wish to refer to the section on finger plays in *I'll Tell You a Story, I'll Sing You a Song* by Christine Allison (New York: Dell/Bantam Doubleday Dell Publishing Group, 1987, pp. 163–181). There, both words and hand motions for singing games and rhymes are provided.

7–14 months

SPEECH AND LANGUAGE*

(7–14 months)

Normal Speech and Language Development

There are two important principles to keep in mind as your baby's speech begins to develop:

1. Speech development is an orderly process with milestones following each other in a logical and predictable sequence.
2. The timing of each of the steps in the sequence will vary from child to child.

6-12 months

As your baby approaches six months of age, you will hear him repeating syllables. He will say a consonant-vowel sound and then repeat it—"ba, ba, ba, ba, ba" or "me, me, me, me, me." This is called babbling. Through these "pre-words" your baby explores the world of sound and increases the efficiency of his tongue, lips, and throat muscles. Babbling is enjoyable for babies and is practiced primarily for their own satisfaction; it occurs only when they are happy and contented. It's important to give your baby a chance to practice his sound play. If you hear him babbling away in his crib after a nap or while he's playing alone, let him continue until he tires of it. He needs time to practice sound making alone as well as time to imitate and interact verbally with others.

Babies seem to enjoy both feeling and listening to what happens when they make repeated sounds. This is good. They need to associate a sound they make with the feeling for it if they are going to remember how to make it again.

As they vocalize, babies gradually become aware that they have the power to attract attention to themselves with their sounds. They already know that crying will bring someone to care for them. And now they discover that babbling often brings a delighted response from those around them. This is a strong incentive to babble more and more.

Babbling changes when a baby reaches approximately eight months of age. You will notice at that time an increase in the variety of syllables your child says as well as a broadening of the inflections he uses. He will sound as if he's making a statement, giving a command, or asking a question. Shouting, coughing, hissing, and tongue clicking may appear about this time, too. He is also likely to try to imitate your gestures and facial expressions as well as the sounds you make. He will begin to respond to familiar sounds such as his name or the ring of the telephone by turning toward them.

The change in babbling is important because it means that your baby is close to saying his first meaningful word. Not only is he saying more, but he is understanding more. An eight-month-old baby will understand what you say by how you say it. He will react by being interested, afraid, or happy. He is in the process of learning what words mean by identifying them within the context of a whole situation, that is, by your tone of voice, inflection, gestures, your "body English."

Don't be puzzled if your baby temporarily loses interest in babbling or imitation at some point. He is probably getting ready to learn something else, perhaps to crawl, stand, or walk. Since he can concentrate on only one thing at a time, the babbling takes a "back seat." When your baby is ready, you will find he'll return to babbling again.

When your baby babbles something to you, "babble" the same thing back to him. If you say something like "Ma-ma" and he repeats it, then you can consider this as another sign that he is getting close to saying his first meaningful word.

Your baby understands words and phrases before he can say them with any meaning. He will respond to some words with gestures to show his

---

*Adapted from *Teach Your Child to Talk* by David Pushaw (Fairfield, N.J.: CEBCO/Standard Publishing, out of print).

understanding. For example, he may clap his hands when he hears you say, "Pat-a-cake."

Around his first birthday, your child should be able to follow one simple direction at a time. This direction might be, "Come here," "Get down," or "Open your mouth." He may also understand "No," "Bye-bye," "That's mine," "Where's your coat?" He will best understand the words you use most. He should now be more aware that sounds make up words. He will gradually associate the words you say with the correct object, feeling, or activity they represent.

Children normally say their first meaningful word somewhere between nine months and a year and a half. It's quite difficult to pinpoint exactly when it happens. The timing is probably more important to you, as a parent, than to your child because of your delight and pride and the reinforcement you give your baby. Reward your baby's efforts to use a word meaningfully. Be sure to show your enthusiasm. He should be made to feel extremely proud of his first words. Give him a smile or a hug to show him how happy you are. If his attempts to talk are not appreciated, he will not try very hard to learn new words. Baby's first words usually are those that are easy to hear and make, for example, caca, ball, wawa, etc. ("er" is not in the vocabulary of a young child—thus *wawa*, not *water*). When a baby first begins to use "Mama" and "Dada," it is interesting to note that "Dada" usually refers to the adult present (whether it's mother or father) but "Mama" is used to register a complaint or a request.

The time when your baby begins to use meaningful words is the time for you to stop imitating exactly what he says (if it's not a real word) and begin to supply him with the correct word. For example, if he says, "Aw gaw," you should not repeat what he says. Say instead, "All gone."

When your baby says one of his first words, remember he is trying to tell you a complete thought. If he says "Go," for example, he may mean, "Where did Daddy go?" or "I want to ride in the car" or any number of other things.

Help your child to combine gestures with his single words if you don't understand him. His first words will normally be one-word puzzles to be figured out, but lack of precision in speech is not something to be concerned about at this stage. This is because speech is learned, not automatic. It takes a lot of practice before all the tiny muscles in a child's mouth, lips, and tongue work together perfectly. Most errors will correct themselves as the child grows older.

12-18 months

Your child will explore his world more and more as he learns to climb and walk. When he begins to stand up and move around, he will see things he has never seen before. He will be eager to investigate and learn the names for everything. Although a child of this age probably says some meaningful words, he needs his parents' help to learn more.

Give him a new word (or short phrase, if it applies) every time he experiences a new feeling (for example, the first time he gets the hiccups); discovers a new object (such as the toilet bowl); or when he is puzzled about something (such as how a toy works). Saying simple words or phrases at the time your child needs them will make the learning experience a stronger one for him.

Your child may need to hear things again and again before he tries to imitate them. This is normal and should be expected. You will probably grow tired of repeating words to him long before he gets tired of listening, but he needs to keep hearing them. Then, suddenly, he may begin to repeat many of the things you say. This is not a sign that he no longer needs you to help him learn to talk. Interest in imitation is only a normal stage of speech and language development and gives a child practice in making speech sounds. Imitating, however, teaches very little or nothing about what words mean or how to use them.

As your child approaches 18 months, he should be able to say the names of several common objects. His pronunciation won't be perfect, but it will be close. He might say *baw* for *ball*, *poon* for *spoon*, *tup* for *cup*. Speech errors are normal.

Your year-old child will scream, shake his crib, or do anything else he can to get your attention.

He is not trying to be naughty during this stage, but his limitations in expressing himself often create much frustration. Fortunately this problem improves at around 18 months when he has a larger vocabulary to express himself.

Suggested Activities for Language Growth

7-12 months

Your Talking. Try to use short words and phrases when you talk to a baby this age. Use gestures along with words to help him better understand what the words mean. For example, say, "Bye-bye" and wave your hand; say, "Come" and hold out your hands to him as you pick him up; or say, "No, no" and shake your finger.

Your six- to twelve-month-old baby is not able to repeat every sound you make. After all, he's just getting started. Give him time to respond, but don't pressure him to do so. Wait several seconds for him to "talk." It sometimes takes a baby this age quite a while to get things going.

Listening. Help your baby learn to listen. Playing music for him is one way to begin.

Imitation Games. You will notice that at this age your baby is becoming interested in imitating you. For example, he may enjoy imitating your tongue movements, rolling a ball back and forth, clapping hands, or playing "Peek-a-boo." Try the following rhymes and gestures and see if he shows interest in imitating you.

This little pig went to market, This little pig stayed home, This little pig had roast beef, This little pig had none, This little pig cried, "Wee, wee, Wee, wee!" all the way home.	Have your baby point to his toes as you point to them, one by one.
Pat-a-cake, pat-a-cake, baker's man, Bake me a cake as fast as you can.	Encourage him to imitate the hand clapping and pat-a-caking.

Pat it and prick it and mark it with "B"
And put it in the oven for baby and me.

"How big are you?" "So-o-o big!"	Say, "How big are you?" and then help your child answer by saying, "So-o-o big!" as you raise his hands above his head. He should learn that when you say, "How big are you?" he's to raise his hands above his head.

A baby this age will use repeated syllables and a variety of voice gestures. Before he's using meaningful words, be sure to copy what he says just as he says it. After he begins to use meaningful words, provide him with the correct model. Don't forget to imitate the tone and mood of his talking, too.

Reading. Show books and magazines to your baby. Let her have a cardboard book of her own. Colorful pictures and a few words from you will interest her for short periods of time, though perhaps not longer than two minutes. That's fine; two minutes of looking and listening in happy interaction with the adult are worth more than 20 minutes of squirming. On the other hand, literary (written) language is richer in structure and vocabulary than ordinary spoken language, and babies need exposure to both. Some older babies will enjoy sitting in a parent or caregiver's lap and listening to simple stories, looking at and pointing to the pictures. Parents of babies who are too active to enjoy books for long may still want to expose them to written language by reading simple, rhythmic stories or poems (Goodnight, Moon is a fine example) while they play, or using lots of nursery songs and rhymes in interactive play.

Your Baby's Name. Teach your baby his name by saying it often for him. Use the name you want him to be called when he grows up. Don't call him "Junior" unless you want him to be "Junior" when he's 39. It is often difficult to drop nicknames.

A Baby's First Words. Your baby will probably say his first meaningful words somewhere between 9 and 18 months. They may be *bye-bye*, baw (ball), *no, mama, hi, mine,* or *go.* Use the words when you talk to your baby and repeat them slowly over and over. Give him time to answer you. Remember to add a gesture whenever possible. Even though we recommend that you use gestures when talking to your baby, be careful not to respond to his gestures too quickly. Try to convince him that talking is a better way to communicate.

If he doesn't say a word right, don't correct or criticize his speech. Simply use the word again, pronouncing it correctly as a model for him to copy. Eventually he will use words correctly if you show him each time what you expect him to say.

12-18 months

Good Teacher. You are the model for your child's speech. Therefore, it is important that you speak very clearly, slowly, and simply. If you want to understand a little better what it's like to learn to speak, imagine yourself listening to a foreign language. At first, you would try to understand the meaning in all those strange sounds. The foreigner to whom you're listening would do well to use as few words as possible and be sure to add plenty of gestures. Also, if his words were pronounced slowly and clearly, you would have an easier time learning to repeat them yourself. You would need to hear the words many times before you would feel comfortable about trying to say them.

In talking with your child when he's this age, some important rules should be kept in mind:

- Use simple, clear, slow speech when talking to him.
- Prepare him for events by talking about what you're going to do before you do it, while you're doing it, and after it's all over.
- Make him feel that he is part of what is going on and not just an observer.
- Talk with him and give him a chance to add his vocalizations, even if you can't understand him. Listen to what he says and make him feel that what he says is definitely important.
- Do not expect or demand perfection.

Self-Talk. Talk out loud about what you are hearing, seeing, doing, or feeling when your child is nearby. Let him know there are words to describe all sorts of activities and feelings. The things adults take for granted are new adventures for young children. For example, as you are hanging up clothes, dusting the furniture, repairing a faucet, or washing the car, talk about the things you are doing. Be sure to use slow, clear, simple words and short phrases. The "Mr. Roger's Neighborhood" TV program uses this technique of self-talk. Watch it to see how it is done.

Parallel Talk. Parallel talk differs from self-talk because you talk about what is happening to your child, not what is happening to you. Use words that describe what she is doing, seeing, hearing, or feeling. This gives her words to think with. She will use them later when she wants to talk about similar things.

Listening. Listening is a skill that you can continue to help your child develop. He needs to understand what he hears. Call his attention to sounds, then show or explain to him what made them. Good examples of outdoor sounds that can be called to his attention are noises of engines running, trucks braking, dogs barking, leaves rustling, birds singing, and the wind blowing. Inside the house, you and he will hear doors closing, water running, someone walking upstairs, the microwave running, the furnace starting, the clock ticking, the vacuum cleaner running, or the teakettle whistling. Make listening to these sounds a game: "Can you hear that noise? What is it?" Then help him answer the question by showing him what it was.

Many other activities can help build listening skills. Here are a few:

- Your child should be eager to show that he understands you. Give him directions such as, "Bring me the paper." Each time, make it a different object, something that is familiar to him. Praise his accomplishments and be sure to use parallel talk.
- Use the tune "Here We Go 'Round the Mulberry Bush" and add your own lines such as: "This is the way we wash our hands, wash our hands, wash our hands. This is the way we wash

our hands so early in the morning." Other short phrases such as "eat our soup," "comb our hair," or "brush our teeth" can also be used. Teach your child a gesture to go with each phrase.

- Let him listen to people on the telephone. Let him say a few words back. Children this age are curious about voices on the telephone but say very little themselves until they become more familiar with it.
- Play "Follow the Leader." Several children can line up and the leader can give directions like, "Pat your head," "Clap your hands," or "Go behind the chair." Even a one-year-old child can play this.

- Encourage your child to play "Ring Around the Rosey." This is a good listening game. If there are older children, they can help teach the younger ones.
- "Hide and Seek" is a game that little children usually enjoy. Call to your child from your hiding place if she takes too long to find you. This is another good time to use parallel talk as she tries to find the people who are hiding.
- Language development activities can be very enjoyable for children and their parents as it encourages a great deal of interpersonal interaction and reaction.

part four

TEACHING ABOUT TODDLERS

(15–24 months)

1

EMOTIONAL DEVELOPMENT

background/preparation

Goals to Work Toward in Presenting This Topic

Parents of toddlers are frequently uncomfortable about their child's emotional development. They are not sure if their child's emotional responses are "normal" and to be expected, and wonder how to respond to their toddler when he or she is frustrated, sad, withdrawn, or in any but a "happy" state. Many parents want their child to be happy all the time and tend to forget that everyone needs to experience a variety of feelings.

To enable parents to feel comfortable with and understand their child's emotional development, the discussion on this topic should help them to: (1) be aware of the normal range of emotional development in 15- to 24-month-olds; (2) develop a comfortable way to separate from their child; (3) learn how to sometimes be apart from their child at home; (4) understand the reasons behind toddler emotional and physical outbursts and look at them from the child's point of view; (5) find ways to acknowledge and handle their own uncomfortable emotions; (6) develop their child's self-esteem.

Typical Parental Interests and Concerns About This Topic

1. I have difficulty leaving my daughter without feeling guilty. She cries and screams if I leave her with a baby-sitter. Sometimes she even does this when I leave her with her father.
2. I find that my daughter clings to me when I'm in the kitchen. I try to ignore her or have someone else come and distract her if other people are around. I find that I am busy in the house and being with her constantly drives me up a wall and makes me feel impatient.
3. When my son bangs his head against the floor, I don't know what I should do. Sometimes I pick him up. Other times I try to put a pillow under his head. I am afraid he will permanently injure himself.
4. What is the effect of our emotions and personalities on our son? Are we passing on our hangups to him already? How much is his behavior and temperament a reflection of our personalities? Is he intense because we are?
5. How can I help my child have a good self-concept?
6. How can I get time for myself? I always feel like someone is hanging on me or pulling at me.
7. My toddler is afraid of adults he doesn't know.

Areas of Information You Will Need to Learn About to Teach This Topic[1]

- Characteristics of normal emotional development in toddlers.
  - Separation anxiety.
  - Independence and dependence of toddlers.
  - Emotional responses (for example, kicking feet on floor and screaming, sucking thumb with sad eyes).
- How individual styles of children and their parents affect their emotional behavior.
- Ways parents and toddlers can separate from one another for short and long periods.
- Techniques parents can use to get time away from their toddlers at home.
- Anger outbursts.
  - Why they occur.
  - What they are like from a child's point of view.
  - Ways parents can handle them.
- The reasons for toddlers' biting, hitting, and scratching adults, and how adults can redirect this behavior.
- Ways for parents to acknowledge and handle their own uncomfortable emotions.
- How to help toddlers develop self-esteem.

Family Dynamics—What This Topic Means Psychologically to Parent and Child

The toddler is at a stage when he is undergoing rapid physical, mental, social, and emotional changes. He is aware of the changes but often cannot cope with them in a rational fashion. One moment he may demand to do things for himself and in a second may desperately need the help of an adult. When he loses emotional control, he often tries to regain it with physical responses or screaming and yelling. When he gets frustrated or angry, he may need help to come back to a rational state.

----

1. Much of this information, for this topic and all others in this part, can be found in the "Additional Information for Parents" sections of the topics.

A toddler's irrational outbursts and responses can be frightening to the child's parents and they are often anxious to confirm that such behavior is normal. They are also concerned to know if their own emotional responses are appropriate. When parents of toddlers experience uncomfortable emotions, many feel that they are doing an inadequate job of parenting. They also sometimes feel that if they were doing something different, all of the uncomfortable feelings would disappear. Most parents dislike stress for themselves or their child, but often they forget to consider their child's and their own temperament and how the two affect each other.

Sample Concern of Parents

Concern	Critical Issues
My toddler wants to be with me all the time. She tugs on my pants, puts pots and pans in my path, and cries to be picked up. When I don't pick her up or give her what she wants, she lies down on the floor and screams. I can't play with her all day, but I feel guilty when I let her cry. When she does play by herself, she usually gets mad at her toy and bangs it on the floor with great fury.	—Toddler wants to be with parent. —Anger outbursts occur when she does not get her way. —How much time does a parent need to spend with her toddler? —Parent's feelings of guilt. —Toddler's inability to play for a long time without frustration.

Key Questions

1. What would you like your toddler to be doing?
2. What do you expect?
3. How do you get your work done when your daughter is awake?
4. How much time do you feel a toddler should spend alone?
5. How much time do you feel you should devote to your toddler?
6. Is this picture realistic?

7. Have you been able to break the cycle of whining and crying and frustration on previous occasions? How have you done this?
8. Does your spouse handle similar situations differently?
9. Are there patterns to what happens before, during, and after an emotional outburst?
10. Does your daughter have toys that are appropriate for her developmental level?
11. Have you noticed a difference in your toddler's behavior on weekday nights vs. weekends when things are less rushed?
12. On a work day, how have you been able to fit in some relaxed time with your toddler?

For the group

13. What have others of you done in situations like this?
14. How does a toddler feel when she wants to be picked up all the time?
15. How does the parent feel?
16. After a day at work, what have you found that helps to ease the transition to being together again?

Readings and Other Resources[2]

Ames, Louise, et al., *Your One-Year-Old* (New York: Dell, 1993).

*Briggs, Dorothy, *Your Child's Self Esteem* (Garden City, N.Y.: Doubleday and Co., Inc., 1975).

Caplan, Frank and Caplan, Theresa, *The Second Twelve Months of Life* (New York: Bantam, 1982).

*Fraiberg, Selma, *The Magic Years* (New York: Macmillan, 1966).

Greenspan, Stanley and Greenspan, Nancy. *First Feelings* (New York: Viking Penguin, 1989).

*Greenspan, Stanley and Greenspan, Nancy, *The Essential Partnership* (New York: Viking Penguin, 1990).

Growing Child (Lafayette, Ind.: Dunn & Hargitt, 1995 [updated annually]). To order call (800) 927-7289.

*Kaplan, Louise, *Oneness and Separateness* (New York: Simon & Schuster, 1980).

Leach, Penelope, *Your Baby and Child, Rev. Ed.* (New York: Knopf, 1989), pp. 328–337.

Lieberman, Alicia, *The Emotional Life of the Toddler* (New York: Simon & Schuster, 1993).

Rothenberg, B. Annye, et al., *Parentmaking Educators Training Program* (Menlo Park, Cal.: Banster Press, 1993), Pt. III, Chapter 3 on Separation.

2. Readings marked with an * are the most highly recommended. The work of Rose Bromwich is highly recommended for information on the topics in this part and is cited in Appendix A. Articles from *Working Mother, Parents' Magazine, Parenting,* and *Child* are often good sources of current information on the topics in this part.

teaching/presentation

Homework

"Emotional Development" helps parents to focus on the emotional outbursts that toddlers are having that make them uncomfortable. It can help parents to problem solve the cause of outbursts and what to do about them. It can also help parents to see if they are intensifying the outburst or helping their child with the uncomfortable response.

Practical Suggestions or Strategies for Teaching This Topic

Parents need to discuss their own and their toddler's emotional development early in the series. Such a discussion brings a feeling of openness to the group and allows you and the group members to have a better understanding of one another; it also frees the group to have better discussions in other areas. Emotional development

EMOTIONAL DEVELOPMENT

(15–24 months)

1. What are some of your toddler's emotional reactions that are hard for you (for example, anger, frustration, tendency to give up, withdrawal)?

2. What types of circumstances seem to provoke these emotional reactions?

3. What kinds of responses do you have to these emotions in your child?

4. How do you *feel* about how you respond?

5. Have you noticed any kind of change in your child's emotional reactions over the last few months? If yes, why do you think this change has occurred?

6. What questions do you have about emotional development in toddlers?

Parent's name _____ Date _____ Child's age _____

is a particularly exciting and rewarding topic for parents of this age group.

Some parents are very comfortable discussing this topic and others do not want anyone to know that stress exists in their family. You will need to help the latter group feel that your class is a safe place to discuss emotions, and this can be done in a number of ways.

• Provide the group with information about the normal emotional development of toddlers. For some families, knowing that their experience is within the usual boundaries enables them to relax.
• Share your own experiences with the group. This will tell them that you are real and not a perfect parent, and will encourage others to talk about their own experiences.
• Be supportive. If the group is going well, questions you ask will lead right into a discussion of the emotional responses the parents are presently experiencing. You will need to help them cope with their feelings and help them to learn how to channel them in a positive direction.

Mini-lecture and Lead-off Questions for Discussion[3]

Sample mini-lecture

Before we discuss the emotional development of your toddlers and answer your questions, I would like to talk a bit about what to expect from your toddlers emotionally. Feel free to comment as I go along.

Toddlers like to be with their parents! How many of you already know that? All of you most likely—and you wonder if you will ever get your own space back again.

But as much as your toddler likes to be with you, he is also practicing his separateness. He is often eager to make choices and exercise his independence, but he certainly does not have the skills necessary for many of his actions. Giving a toddler too many choices can make him frustrated.

---

3. Further information for conducting the discussion can be found in "Additional Information for Parents" (p. 199).

You may be hearing the word "No" a lot from your toddler. He says "no" because he hears it, because he's becoming more independent and wants his own way, and because "no" is a word usually learned before "yes."

Your toddler might be having more anger outbursts than he did in his first year. He may cry, yell, bang his head on the floor, stamp his feet and turn blue or any number of strong reactions in response to frustration. His frustration may come from his inability to get what he wants, his inability to make something operate the way he wants it to, or simply from fatigue or hunger.

Toddlers can be demanding. They want things right now! Your toddler has no concept of the term *later*. He also is most concerned with himself. Who could be more important?!

Because toddlers are changing and growing so rapidly in all ways, they enjoy rituals. The ritual of baths, eating, naps, and bedtime all contribute to helping them cope better with daily life, something which is at present very busy. Toddlers need to feel that there are stable, predictable parts in their world to explore and learn about.

What are some other emotional actions and responses that your toddlers are experiencing that I haven't mentioned?

Lead-offs

For Emotional Responses and Actions to Expect from Toddlers.

• Use mini-lecture.
• Summarize the parents' homework on toddlers' emotional development that they completed the previous week.
• Ask group members to contribute one fact that they feel is important about toddler's emotional development. Encourage parents to use examples.

For Separation.

• Ask several parents, "How do you feel when you separate from your toddler?" "How does your toddler seem to feel?"
• Ask, "What are the advantages of leaving your toddler?" "What are the disadvantages?"

For Clinging Toddlers.

- Use a personal example, such as, "I remember when my son was a toddler. I felt like I would have handprints around my knee forever. Sometimes I would shake my body just to free myself from his clutch. What I really needed to do sometimes was to free my worrying mind from his presence. He always wanted me, but I didn't want him around me all the time, and I felt guilty. How many of you have toddlers that want to be with you all the time?"
- Ask the group how they get time away from their toddler when they're at home.

For Toddler Frustrations.

- Use a personal example, such as, "When my son was a toddler he used to bang his head on the floor. I was sure he was ready to see a psychiatrist, but I never knew which one to call." How do your toddlers show their frustrations?
- Ask the group what questions they have about toddler frustration. Then categorize the questions and order them according to interest level. Help them see the child's perspective.

For Difficult Days at Home.

- Use humor. Ask, "Do you ever have difficult days at home?" Then offer a personal example or let an anxious group member expound on her bad day last week. Keep the discussion light; humor can often bring out the deepest of feelings in a comfortable fashion.

For Handling Parents' Emotions.

- Ask the group to describe the emotions they are experiencing as parents. These may be positive as well as uncomfortable.
- Discuss some of your own feelings as a parent and ask the group if they have ever experienced similar feelings.
- Lead the group into a discussion of ways to handle uncomfortable negative feelings by asking them how they presently do this.

For Developing Self-Esteem.

- Note how much interest the group has shown in this topic and ask them what questions they have.
- Be prepared with specific information for this subtopic. Parents generally like facts and resources to turn to when discussing the area of self-esteem.

Additional Information for Parents

The Need to Be With Parents. Toddlers like to be with their parents, and they need some direct play time with them. However, at other times they can simply play alone in the same room. For example, when a parent is busy making dinner, the toddler can work beside or near her, perhaps taking kitchen utensils in and out of a large pan or playing in water. He might sit on the floor and take things out of a "special" cupboard or drawer.

Separation. Toddlers handle their growing awareness of their own separateness in different ways. Some withdraw and observe, others go forward and play, some cling, and some cry heartily when left. All of these responses are within the normal range of emotional development.

Parents, too, handle separation in various ways, and they need to find a way that enables them to feel comfortable when leaving their child. If parents are hesitant or uncomfortable about parting, their toddler becomes very uncertain, too. Parents need to realize that body messages count as much as words. You can discuss some of the points involved in bringing about a comfortable separation:

- Begin by leaving the toddler for several times for short periods rather than for a larger period once a week.
- Let parents know that children can manage some discomfort.
- Ask mothers how they feel when they return to their children and how the children respond.
- Reinforce the point that employing a familiar care-giver or providing a consistent nurturing situation will encourage confidence in the separation. (See *PETP*, Pt. III, ch. 3 on separation.)

Here are other points about separation that parents should be aware of:

Why leave a toddler?
- To enable the child to learn to trust other adults.

- To help the toddler begin to establish a bond with other people.
- To enable the toddler to experience a new environment and learning situation.
- To allow the parent time to renew her own spirit and/or pursue her career goals.
- Because no one can be on call every minute of the day and do a quality job; everyone can become frustrated and fatigued.

What makes it difficult to leave a toddler?
- The child's care-giver may not adequately meet his needs.
- The child may be left with an inappropriate peer group.
- If left too long or when sick, the toddler may become upset.
- Parents may feel guilty.
- If a toddler is fatigued or upset by the separation, he will be difficult to manage when he and his parents are reunited.

Developing Independence in the Toddler. The toddler learns to be independent and self-sufficient over a period of time. He needs his parents' help to learn how to do things for himself, but he needs to be allowed to work at his own pace. Toddlers can learn by doing one part of a task, such as taking off a sock while being undressed or mashing a potato while the rest of the dinner is being prepared. Toddlers can help the family as they learn, and love to be involved beside you in a meaningful task.

Obtaining Time to be Alone.[4] Before a parent can be successful in obtaining time for herself or in returning to work she needs to ask herself certain questions:

- What kind of time do I need?
- What am I trying to do at home or in the workplace?
- What does my toddler do when I try to spend time alone?
- How much time am I away from my child because of work or other activities?
- How do I handle this?

While trying to find time for themselves, parents of toddlers should also try to do the following:

---

4. For a fuller discussion of this topic, see p. 211 of the topic "Limit Setting."

- Pinpoint their attitude. Do they really believe they need and deserve time away from their child?
- Balance taking time for themselves and/or working with spending time with their child.
- Structuring and scheduling the day helps parents feel they are meeting their child's needs as well as their own.
- Praise their toddler when he gives them time alone.
- Teach their child to play alone. At the best time of day, encourage him to play outside alone, or get him started with a great activity such as water play or dumping and filling and quietly walk away.

Toddler's Outbursts. This subject needs to be studied from the child's point of view. When toddlers lose total control, they need adult help to come back together.

What can an adult do during an outburst?
- Stand and wait.
- Take the child to his room.
- Decide when the toddler needs you to come to him and give comfort.
- Be calm and consistent.
- Try to see if there is a pattern. What triggers the outburst? What does the child do? What does the parent do?

Before such outbursts occur, parents can try to encourage some physical outlets for frustration such as water play, jumping, hammering, running, or pounding a pillow.

Biting. To help parents learn more about this situation, you can ask them the following questions:

- When does biting usually occur—when your child is tired? At a certain time?
- Who is present during the occurrence—does it happen more when you are alone with your child or when you and your spouse are together?
- When large groups are present? When he is with older children?
- What precipitates the bite?
- What reaction does the bite get from you or your spouse?

How can you help your child to release frustration in another way? Some suggestions you can

2

LIMIT SETTING

background/preparation

Goals to Work Toward in Presenting This Topic

How well parents define and put into practice the limits they wish their child to be guided by affects their total relationship with their child. If parents establish positive limit-setting patterns early in their child's development, the child will be able to grow at a more relaxed and successful pace and the parents will most likely feel more comfortable and assured in their role. Limit setting is an important topic for parents of toddlers and will involve them and their child over a long period of time.

As you lead the discussion concerning limit setting, direct it toward achieving the following goals: (1) to help parents understand what they can expect from toddlers when setting limits; (2) to help parents develop an awareness of how their toddler feels about limits; (3) to help each family develop a general philosophy for setting limits; (4) to help parents find positive limit-setting techniques; (5) to work with each family on its specific limit-setting problems.

Typical Parental Interests and Concerns About This Topic

1. How much discipline should I use?
2. Where do I draw the line? I don't want to stifle my child's creativity or make her feel negative about herself.
3. How flexible should I be?
4. I worry because my daughter minds her father well but at times is hostile and defiant toward me. It's as if she does not need my approval.
5. I'm not sure how to follow through when I say "no" and Sarah ignores me.
6. Frequently Ben will stop what he's doing when I say "no" while at other times he'll laugh, keep doing it, and make my discipline into a game.
7. My overriding concern is consistency. I find it very difficult to say "no" to Mark when he wants something to eat or drink. I feel extremely frustrated and unsuccessful in disciplining him because he is so adorable. I am truly enjoying his antics right now and don't know if I should be restricting him more.
8. What about setting limits in public? Everybody stares at you when your child has a tantrum.
9. How can my husband and I agree on discipline rules and a consistent manner of reinforcement?
10. Is spanking bad?

11. After working all day, I'm often too tired to discipline. I also feel guilty saying "no."
12. My child gets very frustrated when not allowed to do certain things. She'll do anything to get her way, like pretend to forget and play with you and the minute you get distracted go back to the original object.

Areas of Information You Will Need to Learn About to Teach This Topic

---

- What can be expected from toddlers when setting limits.
  — How much he can understand.
  — How much the parents should control the environment.
- How toddlers feel about having limits.
- How to help parents work on their differences of opinion in setting limits.
  — What rules to establish.
  — How to teach a toddler to follow the limits.
- Limit-setting techniques that work with toddlers.
- Knowledge of types of specific problems parents have when setting limits with toddlers (for example, dropping food on floor, not going to bed, repeatedly returning to an electrical outlet.)
- Ways to help parents work with their specific problems, including the unique issues of working parents.

Family Dynamics—What This Topic Means Psychologically to Parent and Child

---

When babies become of toddler age, they begin a process of separating from their parents and finding out their own identity. They test things over and over again, to see how they work, how they are made, and how they affect them. Toddlers want to see how their parents will respond to them in a variety of situations. If the response is different each time the same action takes place, toddlers can become very confused and tense.

During this period of their life, toddlers are eager to explore and control. They want what they want and they want it immediately. When children at this stage are denied their wishes, they often show anger, frustration, or sadness, and it is difficult for them to go on to something else without help from an adult.

Some parents feel very comfortable about setting limits for their child. Others find limit setting difficult because they do not know what limits to set, how to set them, or what to do when their toddler becomes frustrated with or does not want to abide by them. Parents may sometimes feel that if they impose too many limits on their toddler, he will lose his creativity as well as his desire to explore.

In some families, toddlers follow limits very easily. This may be because of the child's own accepting style or the way her parents established the limits or both. In other families, limit setting can be more difficult, as when gentle parents must set guidelines for a persistent toddler with a high energy level. How parents and toddlers respond to setting limits depends upon the personalities, emotional make-up, and temperament of each family member.

Sample Concern of Parents

Concern	Critical Issues
I want to get myself into a more positive, creative routine of dealing with my son's tremendous increase in energy and physical ability. There are times when he seems interested in checking out every one of his limits. I end up feeling like all I say is "no." I want to balance his needs and my needs when we're both at home. I worry because he does mind his father better than me.	—Parent needs knowledge of limit-setting techniques to use with a busy toddler. —Parent needs to be aware of normal activity level of toddlers. —Parent's disappointment in how she deals with her toddler. —Parent needs knowledge of the point that toddlers often favor one parent.

Key Questions

1. What does your son do when he checks out all his limits? What do you do? How does your child respond to what you do? What does your husband do? How does your son respond to that? What are you doing that works well? What techniques never work?

2. What would you like your son to be doing during the day whether he is with you or in another caregiving situation?

3. How much time are you getting for yourself, at home and away from home? How do you find time for yourself at home?

4. Do you and your husband agree on what limits to set for your child? Do you agree on how to enforce the limits?

5. How do you handle transitions from being away from your child to being with him at home?

For the group

6. What do your toddlers do during the day?

7. What do you offer your toddlers, indoors and out, that helps them with their drive for action?

8. How can you work with your schedule to provide time for your child's need for active play?

Readings and Other Resources

---

*Cherry, Clare, *Parents, Please Don't Sit On Your Kids* (Carthage, Ill.: Fearon Teacher Aids, 1985).

*Crary, Elizabeth, *Without Spanking or Spoiling, 2nd Ed.* (Seattle, Wash.: Parenting Press, 1993).

Dodson, Fitzhugh, *How to Parent* (New York: Dutton, 1971).

Eisenberg, Arlene, Murkoff, Heidi and Hathaway, Sandee, *What To Expect the Toddler Years* (New York: Workman Publishing, 1994) pp. 119–132.

Galinsky, Ellen and David, Judy, *The Preschool Years* (New York: Random House, 1988) Chapter 1.

*Leach, Penelope, *Children First* (New York: Knopf, 1994) Chapter 6.

*Rothenberg, B. Annye, et al., *Parentmaking Educators Training Program* (Menlo Park, Cal.: Banster Press, 1993), Pt. III, Chapter 4 on Limit Setting.

===

teaching/presentation

Homework

The homework for this topic asks parents to focus on how and why they disciplined their child. Going through this process helps parents become more aware of the sequence of events, the learning, and the feelings that took place. Additional limit-setting homework can be found in *PETP*, pp. 337–341.

Practical Suggestions or Strategies for Teaching This Topic

Parents of toddlers are generally very eager to discuss the subject of limit setting and often come to the meeting on this topic hoping to have their current problems solved. Some members of your group will want to talk about their immediate problems as soon as possible, so it will be helpful to outline for the group how you plan to run the discussion and when individuals may bring up their concerns. Even group members who find it very difficult to wait for their concern to be discussed usually find they have more perspective on the problem after hearing the presentation.

Before you can hold an effective discussion on limit setting, you need to be familiar with the parents in the group, how they feel about parenting, how they feel about their child, what the different families are like, which group members can help one another, and which group members sometimes stop others from bringing up their problems. This means that at least one or two class sessions should be held before scheduling the limit setting topic.

Discipline—Setting Limits

(15–24 months)

this week's observation, we'd like you to focus on two situations where you had to discipline your
d: one situation in which you were pleased about the outcome and the other in which you weren't
ased.
What was your child doing that caused you to discipline him/her?

a.   b.

2. Why was your child behaving that way?

a.   b.

3. What did you do to discipline him/her?

a.   b.

PARENTMAKING: A Practical Handbook for Teaching Parent Classes About Babies and Toddlers by B. Annye Rothenberg, Ph.D., et al.
© 1995 Banster Press, P.O. Box 7326, Menlo Park, CA 94026. Can copy for parent classes if this notice is included in full.

4. What were your child's reactions?

   a.   b.

5. Why do you think your child reacted in the way he/she did?

   a.   b.

6. What do you think your child learned from this experience?

   a.   b.

7. How do you feel about the whole thing?

   a.   b.

8. What do you think you learned about handling your child?

   a.   b.

Parent's name _____ Date _____ Child's age _____

Group members usually like this discussion to run from the specific to the general, but you will have a more effective discussion if you direct it from the general to the specific. When you start with general information, parents first learn how toddlers think, what to expect from them, and some good limit-setting techniques, and are then better equipped to study the responses of all family members and deal with specific problems on a more educated level. Specific limit-setting issues may continue to be brought up throughout the series. (See *PETP*, Pt. II, ch. 4, pp. 319–349.)

Mini-lecture and Lead-off Questions for Discussion[1]

Sample mini-lecture

Setting limits is a difficult job for parents because we must constantly redefine our limits as our child grows. Things that toddlers are not permitted to do today may be acceptable for them tomorrow. Throughout all this change, however, the books all say that we need to be consistent to be good parents, and this sometimes seems impossible, since every day with a toddler is unpredictable.

As toddlers grow, they gain new competence. We applaud when they learn to turn a light on and off and then two days later wonder when they will quit this new trick. It is hard for us to know where each new discovery will lead, but when we do not feel good about a developing pattern we need to change it in a kind and constructive way, letting our children know what they can do.

While our toddlers are exploring and changing, many of us find ourselves going through discipline cycles with them. When they are meeting our expectations and we are in a good mood, we allow them more freedom; when they displease us, we often tend to be harsher. Sometimes we make more demands on our children, and some-

times less. These cycles and fluctuations can make us feel uncomfortable.

Despite the ups and downs, one thing in setting limits is certain. It is a full-time job that goes on as long as we are raising our children.

Let's begin our discussion on limit setting in a general fashion, talking about what can be expected from a toddler when setting limits, what limits are like from the toddler's point of view, how to establish limits, and which techniques to use when establishing limits. Then we can go on to discuss each of your specific limit-setting concerns, such as what to do when your toddler throws his food on the floor. (Detailed sections on each of these subtopics can be found in *PETP*, pp. 319–349.)

Lead-offs

For What to Expect from a Toddler When Setting Limits.

- Ask the group what they expect from their toddlers. What rules must their toddlers follow?
- Distribute the handout (see p. 213) as you tell the parents what they can expect from their toddlers when limits are set for them.
- Ask the parents which areas of limit setting make them uncomfortable because they do not know appropriate limits to set.
- Give a personal example of an instance in which you were unsure about what you could expect from your child, such as, "I picked up my child every time he fussed because I did not know that fussiness and whining were normal responses from a toddler, and that it was all right for them to express their feelings that way." Ask group members if something similar has happened to them.

For Limit Setting from the Toddler's Point of View.

- Ask the parents how their children are responding to the limits established for them.
- Pretend you are a toddler repeatedly returning to an electrical outlet or purposely spilling a cup of milk and try to let the parents see what you might be thinking and why.

---

1. Further information for conducting the discussion can be found in "Additional Information for Parents" (p. 210) and in *PETP*, Pt. III, chapter 4, Limit-Setting.

For How to Establish Limits.
- Offer the information contained on p. 210 under "Establishing a Philosophy on Limit Setting."
- Ask the group how they developed their present rules for limit setting.

For Techniques for Setting Limits.
- Discuss the handout section on techniques on p. 213.
- Ask the parents to refer to their homework on the topic and discuss a technique they used that worked.
- Ask the group to discuss techniques they have tried that do not work.

For Individual Concerns.
- Have the parents bring up their specific questions about limit setting.
- Assure them that everyone has concerns about setting limits—which limits to set, how to set them—and that parents often dislike something their child does but cannot always find a good way to stop the behavior.

Additional Information for Parents

How Toddlers Feel About Limits

When toddlers say "no" to the limits set for them, their response and defiance may indicate their growing awareness of their separateness. They may also be in a period when their immediate response to most things is "no."

Toddlers don't like too many no's, hurry ups, or come ons. Toddlers become frustrated when they are asked to wait. It is very frustrating for them at this age not to be able to do what they want immediately.

What Can Be Expected from Toddlers When Limits Are Set for Them

Additional information on this topic is contained in the handout on p. 213.

How to Establish a Philosophy for Limit Setting

Parents and caregivers need to learn that it is often easier to establish general limits first, then work on more specific problems. Some general limits might be:
- Rules that must always be followed. For example, Don't go in the street.
- You may not harm yourself or others to meet your own needs.
- Be considerate of others' property.

Some guidelines for establishing more specific limits might be:
- Limits should not be thought of as restraints, but as a channeling of children's energy from areas of restriction to areas of freedom.
- A reasonable number of reasonable limits are good for children. They let children know where they stand, and show them that parents are people who can be understood and relied on.
- Limits should not be subtle or inconsistent. If something is not allowed, it should be plainly stated and not be allowed at all times. Children need definite rules and definite responses.
- Limits should be as few in number as possible. Constant no's and don'ts are frustrating to both parents and children, and expectations and environment should be questioned if no's are in abundance.
- Toddlers need to do things that they like.

Questions husbands and wives should ask themselves when determining their philosophy on general and specific limits:
- What can each of you cope with? What bothers you?
- Can you usually retain your sense of humor or do you get upset easily?
- Are you generally firm or lax about rules?
- Are you rigid or flexible once you have set a limit?
- Do you often feel that you are in a contest with your child to see who is in charge?

Considerations that husbands and wives need to discuss to determine their differences about limit setting:
- Discuss the things you disagree about. Can you discover the reasons behind the differences— upbringing, personal experience?
- Take the time to clarify your limits. It may be possible for each of you to have your toddler obey limits in different fashions, but be sure the limits are the same. Remember that patterns are different, and spouses are different.

- Husbands and wives need respect for one another. Think about the things you like that your spouse does as part of his or her limit setting.
- If you differ with how your spouse or caregiver is setting a limit, speak about your feelings after the action has taken place. If one person sets a limit for the child, the limit should be enforced at that time.

Consider your child's style when determining your philosophy on limit setting. Refer to the section on "Individual Differences" on p. 340 and the *PETP* chapter on Temperament (pp. 271–289).

Good Limit-setting Techniques

Refer to the information on the handout on p. 213.

No matter what technique you use, keep these three points in mind: (a) have a calm, firm attitude, and believe in yourself; (b) always teach your children what they **can** do; (c) be specific and immediate.

If the best techniques fail to elicit the proper response, parents become very frustrated so you may want to discuss less acceptable forms of discipline, such as:

- Social Isolation. Putting a child in his room or crib by himself for a short period of time. Ask the group how they feel about this technique.
- Spanking. Discuss with the group, using these questions, how they feel about spanking:
    How comfortable are you with spanking?
    How do you feel after you have spanked your child?
    How frequently do you spank your child?
    How were you raised?

Spanking. Spanking is not a recommended technique; it can make children angry, can teach them to hit, can cause humiliation if used frequently, can make parents feel angry and guilty, and leaves nothing left to try if it fails to bring about the desired action. (See *PETP*, pp. 320–330 for information to teach about *prevention* versus *punishment* and pp. 344–347 for *prevention* handouts for parents.)

Unsuccessful Limit-setting Techniques

These are:
Belittling or name calling;
Threats;
Bribes;
Overprotective supervision;
Excessive talking;
Parental loss of all control, including spanking;
Using rules inappropriate for a toddler's age;
Giving a command you will not enforce.

Why Children Resist Cooperating With Parents More Than Other People

Our parental emotional involvement gets in the way. We are more emotional and can get out of control when actually calm firmness works the best.

How to Discipline Children Without Stifling Their Creativity

Examine the limit-setting techniques being used. Do you have creative techniques? Do you teach your child?

Remember that wild children will not be accepted by society. You may accept them, but no one else will.

Teach your child what she can do and can't do; for example, she may climb on the stepping stool but may not climb on the couch.

Having confidence in your child and an awareness of her special qualities will allow her to be creative or free; for example, if you know your child is very active, you will need to take her to the park and allow her to run, and if your child is quiet, you will need to allow her time to sit and observe.

Determining What Toddlers May Be in Charge Of

Each family needs to determine what the toddler should be in charge of and what the parents should be in charge of. Often control is passed back and forth, and families find themselves in a game of tug of war. Toddlers enjoy this game as much or more than its outcome, and parents need to question whether or not they are turning negative behavior into fun for the child.

Often parents let their child go too far to avoid an uncomfortable confrontation and then blow up when their child's behavior becomes too much to handle. Angry outbursts can be avoided if you think of yourself as a teacher and guide your toddler through difficult situations.

*Keeping the Environment from Controlling
Your Standards*

Sometimes parents look to see which actions
are acceptable or what a situation will allow. For
instance, when a family is at a restaurant, parents
often wait for others to let them know if it is
acceptable for their child to wander about.
Instead of waiting for outside opinions, it is
generally best to decide how you feel about an
issue and then let your child know.

*How to Get Time for Yourself When Your
Toddler Is Awake*

To help parents determine their needs, ask
them these questions:
• What kind of time do you need? Do you really
  feel that you deserve this time? Do you feel
  guilty for wanting the time?
• What are you trying to accomplish during time
  alone? How much time do you feel you should
  have for this task? Can you realistically expect a
  toddler to be without you for this length of time?
• What are you doing to keep your toddler occupied during your alone time?

Suggestions for obtaining time alone:
• Start by taking short periods of time for yourself, then build up and take the time on a regular
  basis. When you set up a pattern for your time
  alone, it will eventually become a habit for your
  child.
• Let your child be with you but give him something to do. If you want to read, let him read
  beside you. If you want to rest, let him lie down
  with you.
• Spend some quality time with your toddler prior
  to the time you take for yourself. Doing this
  will help to ease any feelings of guilt.
• Praise your child for giving you time alone.
• Consider putting your toddler in his room or in
  an outdoor area for a scheduled period each
  day and using this time for alone time for yourself. You can start with a short time span and
  gradually build up. Choose a time of day when
  your child is rested, well fed, and usually content. Think of this time as a chance to teach

(See Appendix H, p. 466 for a chapter on Working
Parent classes.)

your toddler to rely on himself to find pleasurable tasks, as well as time for you. Be sure that
the area in which you ask your child to play is
safe and well-supplied with playthings.

Making Use of Preventive Strategies

• Preventive strategies are an important aspect of
  discipline. Be sure your child has some undivided attention from the parent and/or caregivers daily; inside and outside time; and quiet and
  active time each day. Children will feel more
  cooperative when adults have balanced their
  day.

*How to Set Limits When Your Child
Won't Pay Attention to Them*

 Ask the parents these questions:
• Are you yelling or are you calm when establishing limits? Do you overreact to certain behavior, making it a pleasure for your child to
  disobey?
• Do you get down to your child's level, look in his
  eyes and speak with a calm assured voice, or do
  you talk across the room at him?
• Do you help your child find a meaningful substitute activity for an unacceptable one?
• Do you guide your child physically if this is
  necessary?

Handouts

There are two parts to the handout for the topic
of limit setting. The first, "What to Expect,"
deals with what can be expected of toddlers when
limits are set for them. The second, "Techniques,"
offers techniques to use to help toddlers and parents feel comfortable with limits.

Refer to Rothenberg, *PETP* chapter on Limit
Setting (pp. 319–349) for many additional hand-
outs, "Basic Principles of Limit Setting," "Under-
standing the Need for Setting Limits," "Identify
Your Style of Discipline," "Why It's So Hard for
Parents to Set Limits," "Stubbornness, Arguing,
and Not Listening in Preschoolers," "Techniques
for Beginning Limit Setting with Older Babies,"
"Limit-setting Techniques for Toddlers/Preschool
Children," and "Limit Setting: Possible Discipline
Techniques to Use With Young Children."

SETTING LIMITS

(15–24 months)

What to Expect

What can be expected from the 15-month- to two-year-old when you are setting limits?

1. Many toddlers will continually test the limits to be sure they do not change.
2. A toddler cannot be expected to visibly like limits, but he can be expected to obey the most important ones.
3. He can understand the feelings you are radiating. Your face and body probably tell him more than your words.
4. By one-and-a-half, the toddler can understand you when you use plain and straightforward language, especially if the words are associated with an object.
5. The toddler does not respond well to lengthy verbal dissertations on why he cannot do something. Long, involved, explanations are very confusing for him.
6. Your toddler may have difficulty making choices. He can become frustrated if you frequently ask him to choose. He can also become difficult when given a choice if it is not really a choice, for example, "Do you want lunch now?" "Do you want to come now?" He can, however, make a specific choice, for example, "Do you want a pear or an apple?".
7. Usually toddlers are easy to distract. They are distracted by themselves and by others.

Techniques

1. Use substitutions and distractions in an immediate way. Tell your toddler what he *can* do, not what he can't. For example, "You can climb on your slide," not "You can't climb on that table."
2. Give advance notice; talk to your child as you are about to change what he is doing. For example, "Good-bye park . . . *see you later!*"
3. Motivate your toddler toward the next activity; don't take "no" too seriously if it's the automatic kind. Think of something appealing about what's ahead—"Let's go get your bear in the car" rather than "It is time to go home."
4. Talk in simple language, using *few* words. Be specific, be immediate, and give clear and consistent directions. It is fine to sympathize with your child's feelings, but do not be afraid to physically move your child.
5. Give your toddler dramatic praise when he is following the limits you have established. Be specific.
6. Toddlers like to do things for themselves, such as getting in the car seat or pushing open a door; follow their lead and let them lead when they are ready.
7. Children learn a little at a time. The toddler forgets easily—much repetition is needed. Encourage and reward his progress.
8. Toddlers must have things to do, places to go, and times and places in which to make a racket. It is important to go at their pace sometimes.
9. Be aware of your own feelings; often inner tenseness gets in the way of discipline. Be friendly, not angry, in your firmness. (Keep your feelings under control—you'll have a child who is more under control.)

3

EATING BEHAVIOR

background/preparation

Goals to Work Toward in Presenting This Topic

Parents of toddlers, just like parents of older babies and two-year-olds, are concerned about their children's eating patterns as well as their eating behavior. This section will cover only information dealing with toddlers' eating behavior, but if information about nutrition or eating patterns is needed you may refer to pp. 156–165 in the older baby topic section and pp. 280–291 in the two- to three-year-old topic section.

The goals for this presentation are: (1) to help parents learn more about the eating behavior of toddlers; (2) to help parents understand the dynamics of eating together.

Typical Parental Interests and Concerns About This Topic

1. Allison does not want to eat in her highchair. She has a renewed interest in playing with her food and throwing it on the floor. I am not sure how firm I should be with her.
2. I feel that Laurel should eat with us at the table, but my husband feels that this is too exhausting an experience after a day at work.

Areas of Information You Will Need to Learn About to Teach This Topic

- The range of physical development in toddlers, including their drive to dump and fill and their love of water and sensual experiences. How long can they sit still?
- The kind of manners that can be expected from toddlers when eating alone and when eating with the family.

Family Dynamics—What This Topic Means Psychologically to Parent and Child

The eating behavior of toddlers can become a battleground for both parents and child. Toddlers are at a developmental level where dumping liquid from a cup or dropping food to the floor is a pleasure, even a right. It is difficult for them to sit still for very long periods of time, and they enjoy playing with their food as they sit. Parents become very frustrated at having to constantly clean up spilled milk or sticky oatmeal, but they also feel very guilty if they take away their child's food when they feel he might still be hungry.

When the family eats together, the toddler can become very stimulated. He soon finds that certain actions bring immediate attention from one or both parents. He finds that certain behavior can result in his not being "left out" of the conversation. He would prefer to eat food from his parents' plates or to be held by one of his parents while he eats. Sitting with the food that's on his own plate quickly becomes boring. He likes to be in control.

If a family eats every dinner together, it can be particularly difficult for both parents. Parents can be torn between pleasing their child and their spouse; each wants the toddler to eat appropriate foods and learn good manners, but also wants to share conversation with his/her spouse. Most parents want a quiet and relaxed meal time with good conversation. They find it very stressful to watch or take part in helping their toddler eat with the family.

Sample Concern of Parents

Concern	Critical Issues
I need help in disciplining Sam not to throw his cup, spoon, or bowl off the tray when he is through eating (or when he really doesn't	—Developmental level of toddler —Techniques to help the toddler have better eating habits.

like the food). I get upset, yell at him that it was very wrong and that I am angry. I am at a loss for new ideas.

Key Questions

1. What is your toddler doing before he throws his bowl on the floor?
2. What are you doing during this time?
3. Then what occurs?
4. What do you wish your toddler would do instead of throwing utensils?

For the group

5. What are you doing to help your children with their drives to dump, throw, and spill?

Readings and Other Resources

*Brazelton, T. Berry, *Toddlers and Parents, Rev. Ed.* (New York: Dell, 1989).
Caplan, Frank and Caplan, Theresa, *The Second 12 Months of Life* (New York: Bantam, 1982).
Eisenberg, Arlene, Murkoff, Heidi and Hathaway, Sandee, *What To Expect the Toddler Years* (New York: Workman Publishing 1994) Chapter 18.
Leach, Penelope, *Your Baby and Child, Rev. Ed.* (New York: Knopf, 1989) pp. 291–304 and 389–394.
*Satter, Ellyn, *How to Get Your Kid to Eat . . . but not too much* (Menlo Park, Cal.: Bull Publishing, 1987).

teaching/presentation

Homework

This particular topic does not have a homework assignment.

Practical Suggestions or Strategies for Teaching This Topic

• A discussion of toddler eating behavior can successfully conclude a discussion on limit setting since parents will be talking about problems they are having with their toddlers.

• Parents need to realize that they may be expecting their toddlers to eat the way much older children do.

• Once a parent brings up her toddler's eating style, the entire group will most likely bring up all of the eating problems and situations they have encountered with their children. This kind of discussion can be humorous, meaningful, and filled with good examples of problem solving.

Mini-lecture and Lead-off Questions for Discussion

There is no mini-lecture for this particular topic. The best lead-off is to simply ask the group members about their toddlers' eating behavior or begin with a humorous example and demonstration of how a toddler eats. This will encourage parents to talk about their concerns.

Additional Information for Parents

How to Handle Toddlers Playing With Food. Parents need to determine the point in the meal when their toddler begins to play with or spill his food. Is it at the beginning or the end of the meal?

Ask the parents: What do you do when your toddler spills his food? Do you give him more because he has not eaten or do you remove him from the table? Are you annoyed or are you entering into a game with your child? When do you feed your toddler again?

If parents don't like it when their children play with their food, they may consider providing only small portions and small amounts of liquid to drink at a time. The children can always be given more later. Parents might also consider removing all food from their toddler's reach as soon as he begins to play in it, and going on to another activity.

Sometimes children play with their food when they are left to eat alone or have little supervision from an adult. Playing with their food helps them to get attention.

Eating Dinner As a Family. Toddlers like to be with their family, but many are not capable of waiting for the rest of their family to sit down to the evening meal. Toddlers may be ready to eat at five o'clock but their parents may not wish to eat until seven. Such problems with timing can produce uncomfortable feelings. Parents may believe that dinner time should be a family time, and that excluding the toddler from the meal is a sign of poor parenting. To help with this problem, ask parents to:

• Find out how other families handle the dinner hour. It is usually different from their own way—perhaps the time itself is different—and it helps parents to see that most families have difficulties at this time and that there is more than one way to handle it.

• Acknowledge that it is important for families to eat together, but it is much easier to do when children are more mature. Families do not need to eat together every night.

• Note their child's style. Some children need to eat earlier than others and if they are not provided for, become very fussy.

• Realize that some parents, including those with two working parents, enjoy eating as a family group and some don't. If dinner cannot be enjoyed as a group, other times can be considered family time, such as a game or story time or a family outing.

• Work to find ways to manage their toddler if he eats early but is not in bed when they eat. Some techniques are giving the child a special book or puzzle by the table and giving him a dessert or favorite food. Remind parents of the importance of talking to and acknowledging their toddler while they eat.

• Consider eating breakfast together.

Handouts

For handouts about toddler nutrition, see pp. 285–291 of the two- to three-year-old nutrition topic.

4

SOCIALIZING AMONG CHILDREN

background/preparation

Goals to Work Toward in Presenting This Topic

Toddlers are at a stage where they are just beginning to have an interest in other children, and it is important for parents to understand that children do not instinctively know how to socialize with other children. Toddlers may want to interact with other children, but parents must teach and work with them to make this happen. Parents are also interested at this time in socializing with other families who have toddlers, but they are often not sure how to handle groups of young children.

The goals for this discussion are: (1) to help parents learn about the social skills of toddlers; (2) to help parents share what they find uncomfortable about their toddler's social style (for example, hitting, possessiveness) and help them find constructive ways to encourage their child to develop; (3) to give parents an opportunity to talk about specific kinds of conflicts the toddlers have gotten into and to provide them with a variety of ways these conflicts can be handled and how the parents can work on these issues with the child's other caregivers; and (4) to help parents develop play groups for their toddlers as appropriate.

Typical Parental Interests and Concerns About This Topic

1. My son always has to have things his own way when he plays with other children. The day care center staff find this to be a problem also.
2. Since we know few people in this area and there are no children in our neighborhood, I worry about Sara's ability to learn to get along with other children.
3. We have a friend with a very physically aggressive child. He bites and pinches. Katie is not at all this way. She does not retaliate and instead cries.
4. What should I do when my child is fighting with another toddler over a toy?
5. We are starting a play group and I could use some helpful hints.
6. Joshua is very possessive when other children come over. He wants whatever toys his friends are playing with, so I've started letting them work it out themselves. Is that a good approach or is there something I should be doing?
7. How do you set limits for other children when they're at your house?
8. It's hard enough to set limits for other children playing at our house but when their parents are there too, I'm at a complete loss about who's in charge and what to do.

Areas of Information You Will Need to Learn About to Teach This Topic

- Expectations for toddlers regarding their social development—how they play with others, how much time they should spend with other children, what to expect in their future development.
- Social styles of children—the aggressive child and how to deal with him, and the passive child and how to deal with him.
- Ways to handle toddler conflicts.
  — How to know to whom to give a toy.
  — How to make both children feel better.
  — How to handle a hitter or biter.
- The effect of parents' presence on other parents when children are together.

Family Dynamics—What This Topic Means Psychologically to Parent and Child

Parents today are very anxious for their child to have appropriate social behavior. Often, their expectations are too high. Parents have their memories of how they played as four- and five-year-olds, but sometimes they have forgotten the steps that come before this degree of sophistication. They forget that what they consider to be normal social behavior takes a long time to develop.

Many parents are dissatisfied with their child's social style—he is too passive or too aggressive. Most parents are not aware of the sequence of social development or of the need to instruct children about appropriate social behavior.

Most parents of toddlers feel it is very important for their child to play with other children. Yet, because of their limited experience with groups of young children, parents are often surprised by what occurs. They can feel uncomfortable with the behavior of the children but indecisive about whether to intervene or let the children work it out. They find it tiring to teach young children to interact, yet feel it is important. At times, they may wonder if their child is developing in a normal manner. Parents of children in

childcare also get feedback about their child's social skills. If the child is doing well and/or if the caregiver is skilled, the feedback can be helpful. Sometimes, however it is just disturbing for parents.

The toddler doesn't know how to socialize. At times all he can think about is himself—what he is playing with, where he is moving, or how he feels. It is very frustrating for him to deal with others. He is usually more comfortable with adults because he knows what to expect—other children are very unpredictable. When a toddler does something to another child (gives him a toy, hits, smiles), he is trying to find out what response will occur. In many instances the toddler finds out about others by watching. Then, when he feels ready, he joins in.

Sample Concern of Parents

Concern	*Critical Issues*
Emily is always taking a toy from another child. I tell her not to do this, but she still pushes and pulls to get what she wants. I am in a play group with other mothers and I am very embarrassed when she does this and I don't know what else to do besides tell her no.	—Toddler wants other child's toys. —Toddler pushes and pulls to get what she wants. —Parent feels uncomfortable with toddler's behavior. —Parent does not know how to handle this behavior.

Key Questions

1. How does your toddler behave in the play group setting and what does she do? Give me a detailed description.
2. What do the other parents in this setting do?
3. Does the pushing and pulling occur only at play group or also when other children are in your home?
4. When the behavior occurs, are you involved in adult conversation? In the same room?
5. How do you feel about the way you handle your daughter when she is "pushy"?

6. How many other members of the play group have toddlers who take toys from others? How do they handle this?
7. Is the play group set up so that the parents can talk with one another about play group problems and ways to handle them?

For the group

8. Ask group members if they feel that because a child is "pushy" and possessive at this age that it will go on forever.

Readings and Other Resources

Domash, Leanne, *Wanna Be My Friend?* (New York: Hearst, 1994).

Eisenberg, Arlene, Murkoff, Heidi and Hathaway, Sandee, *What To Expect the Toddler Years* (New York: Workman Publishing, 1994) pp. 107–110 and 183–197.

*Gonzalez-Mena, Janet and Eyer, Diane, *Infants, Toddlers and Caregivers* (Mountain View, Cal.: Mayfield Publishing, 1989) Chapters 10 and 11.

*Lieberman, Alicia, *The Emotional Life of the Toddler* (New York: Macmillan, 1993) Chapter 10.

*Van der Zande, Irene, *1, 2, 3, . . . The Toddler Years* (Santa Cruz, Cal.: Toddler Center Press, 1986).

teaching/presentation

Homework

The homework for this topic helps parents to focus on their toddler's interaction with other children.

Practical Suggestions or Strategies for Teaching This Topic

Before you begin your lecture, you will first need to determine how interested your group is in this topic. Some parents are very anxious to hear about social development because they participate frequently in social experiences. Other parents have had little experience with other families and groups and will not know what to ask about the social development of toddlers. If many of the members of your group have older toddlers—children 19 to 22 months of age—their interest level should be higher. If interest is low, the topic can be placed later in the series when group members and children have had more time to interact.

It is usually helpful to begin the discussion with a mini-lecture or a series of suggestions concerning the kind of social behavior to expect from toddlers. Parents need to know if their child is operating within the appropriate boundaries before they will feel comfortable with the discussion.

Some groups will need a lot of in-depth information from you, while others will be much more interested in how the group members are handling their toddler-related social situations. You will need to listen carefully to what parents are saying to lead the discussion in the right direction.

Parents who use child care centers will have additional impressions of toddler's social development in general and of their child's, specifically. Child care providers often teach parents about this important area. If the information does not seem developmentally accurate, you will need to address this with the parent. On the other hand, the parent may have a lot of helpful information to share with the group.

Discussing the social development of toddlers is not the only important area to cover. Talking about how parents respond and react to different children's social styles is also critical. The parent of an aggressive child needs to hear how the parent of a more passive child feels when her child is hit. The parent of a passive child needs to hear

SOCIALIZING AMONG TODDLERS

(15–24 months)

In this week's observation, we'd like you to focus on your toddler's interactions with other children.

1. How often is your toddler with other children? (Please mention whether he/she gets together regularly with any other children and how old they are.)

2. What is your toddler like with other children? How does he/she behave?

3. Give an example of a conflict situation involving your toddler and another child and also describe what *you* or the caregiver did. (Are there other things that are commonly done when your child is in conflict with another child?)

4. What kinds of questions do you or your spouse have about your child's relationships with other children?

Parent's name _____ Date _____ Child's age _____

how the parent of an aggressive child feels when her child hits or bites someone. Hearing other parents' perspectives can enable group members to help one another and one another's children.

As the discussion draws to a close, summarize what the group has talked about and add any information you feel is pertinent to this particular group of toddlers and parents.

Mini-lecture and Lead-off Questions for Discussion[1]

Sample mini-lecture

It is difficult for toddlers to socialize with their peers; other children are much less predictable than toys, adults, and the rest of the world. Other children, however, are intriguing to toddlers and they may spend a lot of time observing them. They sense a special kinship with other children but they need to learn how to make friends. Toddlers do not know how to make ordinary attempts at being friendly. They may use pushing or touching as a way of making contact.

Often, toddlers are intensely involved in their own play and with themselves. They do not seem particularly aware of other children, but enjoy finding out how their own bodies feel and move as well as about the world around them. Watch toddlers move down a street, stopping to investigate a leaf or look between their knees or whatever. They enjoy themselves immensely.

Toys usually have more importance for a toddler than the child next to her. As toddlers approach two, however, they see other children more as people and less as objects and may begin to copy them. Toddlers can learn how to walk and turn on the TV by watching other children. Children may be seen as easier role models than adults.

Toddlers do not understand the concept of sharing. When you tell them to share their toys, you are expecting too much of them. The concept of sharing does not usually

begin to form until two-and-a-half to three years of age, and even then and for some years to come it is difficult for children, as well as for some adults. (Children in group child care often show an earlier awareness of the relationship between an object and the person using it.) Toddlers can understand who had a toy first and can begin working on trading toys or finding something for a friend, but the idea of sharing is typically too incomprehensible to them. Therefore, offering opportunities to be with other children affords them a chance to experience simple sharing of toys.

Many toddlers will try to grab a toy from another child, especially when the child is playing with one of their toys. Often they don't want to play with the particular toy until they see it in the other child's possession. Arguments over toys can look very intense, but after they are over the children can forget them immediately. However, during arguments, biting, hitting, or banging over the head can and does occur. But you should not assume that certain children are really very angry or mean because of the intensity of what they do to each other during this and following stages. Children can usually shrug off more than adults would, but they must be told loud and clear when they are exhibiting unacceptable behavior. They should also be told what kind of behavior is acceptable.

Toddlers need time with other children, preferably at least two times a week and not always in a play group. They do need some group experience, but time spent with one other child is very beneficial. It is good for toddlers to have relationships with older children, younger children, and children of the same age, and strong and valuable relationships can develop if toddlers see the same children on a regular basis. It may take toddlers a while to warm up in new situations, so if your child doesn't jump right in, give him time to feel comfortable before demanding too much of him. Remember, too, that your toddler may show jealousy toward other children when you are caring for them.

I've just given you a great deal of information to digest. What kinds of questions do you have about points I've brought up?

---

1. Further information for conducting the discussion can be found in "Additional Information for Parents" (p. 222).

Lead-offs

For What to Expect from a Toddler on a Social
Level.
- Use a mini-lecture and then ask the parents if
  they have any questions about what you have
  said.
- Ask the group what their children are like when
  they are playing with other children. (See Question 2 of the homework on p. 220.)

For The Social Styles of Toddlers.
- Give a brief and objective overview of the social
  style of toddlers. Then ask the parents to relate
  the social style of their child and how they feel
  about this style.
- Lead the group into discussion on this topic
  after a group member asks about her child's
  aggressive or passive style and how she should
  handle it.

For Toddler Conflicts.
- Ask the group to give some examples of toddler conflicts they encountered during the past
  week and how they handled them.

For How Frequently Toddlers Should Play and in
What Settings.
- Ask the parents the types of social settings their
  children are part of on a regular basis. Ask them
  to talk about both the group situations and
  those in which only one other child is present.
- Ask parents whose children are in group child
  care to also talk about their experiences and
  feelings.
- Ask the parents how frequently they feel their
  toddlers should be in contact with other
  children.

For Play Groups.
- Ask the group if they have any questions about
  play groups.
- Ask the parents if any of their children are in
  play groups. If they are, ask how the groups
  were established and what problems were
  encountered.

Additional Information for Parents

---

*What to Expect from Toddlers on a Social
Level.*   It will be a long time until toddlers are

able to share easily. But for a child to begin to
share he needs an awareness of which things are
his and a secure feeling about those things. He
also needs to gain pleasure from his first play
experiences with other children.

Parents need to remember that sharing needs
to take place voluntarily. It cannot be forced by
practical necessity or by parents bent on instruction. Sharing is not coercion. It is give and take.

Children's Social Styles. In our society, parents tend to want their children to be out-going,
talkative, and self-assured in social situations.
They tend to forget that quiet or shy children can
have very rewarding relationships too, especially
if they are understood and appreciated.

Social problems can occur when parents
expect more than what is reasonable for their
child's age and personality, for example, if parents take a very quiet child daily to a variety of
large-group settings and expect him to participate
upon arrival, or if parents or caregivers expect an
active toddler to sit quietly in a circle with other
toddlers who are listening to a story.

Parents need not worry about a toddler's
aggressive behavior becoming permanent. They
do need to keep toddlers from being hit or bitten
and from hurting other children. Parents and caregivers need to understand that hitting and biting
at this age are not always aggressive acts, but can
be experimental and that some aggressiveness is
normal and necessary for all people. Learning to
stand up for one's own rights in a socially acceptable manner can take time.

Parents should ask themselves some questions
to further understand aggressive behavior in
toddlers:
- What is happening to my toddler right before he
  grabs, hits, pushes, or bites?
- Is he usually with one child or in a group? (Some
  children begin to feel uncomfortable when too
  many children are close to them.)
- At what times does the aggressive behavior occur? Does it coincide with nap or mealtimes?
- Is the play supervised?
- How do I respond to this behavior in my child?
  Am I calm and helpful or do I find myself losing
  control when her behavior is unacceptable?
  Does my response to my toddler have meaning
  for her? Do I tell her what acceptable behavior
  for the situation is?

- Is there any time this behavior does not occur?
- Do I talk to my child about his behavior at times when the behavior is not in evidence? (Telling your child and modeling for him what he can do when somebody angers him is an effective technique. It does however need to be repeated as it takes time to be successful.)
- Who does my toddler play with? Does he always play with children who let him bite, hit, or grab? (If so, you might consider older playmates so that your child is not always in the position of being a bully.)

Parents should ask themselves some questions to further understand passive behavior in toddlers:

- In what setting is my child more aggressive? Why? More passive? Why?
- What do I like about my child's style? What do I dislike?
- Who does my child play with? Is he always with older or larger children?
- What do I do when someone grabs a toy from my child? (Do you always help him? You might want to model for your toddler at home what he can do when someone tries to take his toy.)

How to Handle Toddler Conflicts. Discuss with the group the information contained in the section of the handout on toddler conflicts (see p. 225). If conflicts between toddlers seem to occur primarily with a caregiver, a discussion of family rules and expectations would be helpful.

When toddlers are in a continuous conflict and you cannot see a pattern or a reason for it, try diversion or a change of pace. Take the children to neutral territory, perhaps a park, or take them for a walk, initiate water play, provide a snack, or engage them in a music activity. Drastically changing the setting can help the toddlers go on to something more constructive.

When a toddler is possessive about his toys:

- Give each child a short turn with the toy—30 seconds to 1 minute. Let the child holding the toy play with it first, then tell him it is the other toddler's turn. If the exchange goes on for a long time, change the pace.
- Ask your child, "If you want the ball, what can Sam have?" Often, when a child is not in his own home, he will be happy to play with any-

thing. You could also say, "If you want to play with the train that Sam's holding, get the car and trade him for it. Here, let's get the car for Sam." Model for your toddler with words and actions.

- Teach your toddler to share when no other toddlers are around. Show him how to wait by getting yourself a drink before you get one for him. Explain to him the difference between now and later in a situation that is not emotionally laden.
- Do not always allow your child to have his own way when he is in an adult-child play relationship. If adults always give way to him, he will assume that all children will do the same.
- Look for a pattern in your child's possessiveness.
- Prepare for another child's visit by:
  — Having the guest bring a bag of special toys.
  — Not planning to make your child share everything. With your toddler's assistance, put his most special toys away.
  — Having materials that can be divided between the children.
  — Planning to move to neutral territory when play is to begin.

How Frequently Toddlers Should Play and in What Settings. Toddlers need to be with other children and other families, but they need to be in their own home with their own family even more.

When toddlers begin to establish one-to-one relationships, taking turns, sharing, and caring for other children become a natural way of life.

If you enjoy being a part of a play group, it is likely your toddler will, too. But if a group does not work for you or your toddler, do not feel obligated to stay. Other forms of group play, such as visiting one other parent and one other child, playing in a park, or baby-sitting for other children, can be substituted.

Play Groups. A play group is a small group of children who meet regularly at each other's homes to play, with the parents or caregivers supervising or taking turns at supervising. The advantages of play groups are:

- Children are able to see each other on a regular basis.
- Children get to know other adults well.

15–24 months

- Participation in play groups is a good way to begin the process of gaining independence.
- Toddlers can have a variety of experiences and a good time.
- If parents take turns supervising, play groups can offer parents some free time with the knowledge that their child is in a stimulating and safe environment.

Parents may benefit from asking themselves these questions before joining a play group:

- What are my goals for and philosophies about the group? Is my philosophy compatible with those of the other members?
- Do I enjoy having groups of children in my home?
- Do I want a group in which all the parents stay each time or do I want one in which the parent/supervisor rotates?
- Is my child ready for play in a group setting?
- What are the other children like? Are their styles compatible with my child's style?

Parents may wish to ask themselves these questions when organizing a play group:

- How many children should participate?
- What ages should they be?
- Should there be an equal number of boys and girls?
- Should all the parents participate each time or should only one or two be present?
- How often should the group meet? (Once a week is usual for toddlers.)
- During what time of day should the group play and for how long? (Toddlers often meet for one and a half hours in the morning.)
- When should parents meet without the children present to discuss how the play group is going?
- What kind of structure should there be? (A typical daily plan is:

     9:30 - 10:30—Free time
     10:30 - 10:45—Snack
     10:45 - 11:30—Outside play, circle game, stories, music)
- What activities should be offered? (Typical activities are sand and water play, chalk and play-dough play, listening to and using rhythm instruments, listening to and singing along with records, singing games, and story reading.)

Talking to young children is very important. While participating in a play group, talk to them about what you are doing and what they are doing. Speak with a warm, soft, calm, and assured voice. Positive words and eye contact will get their attention.

Don't expect startling social development in your child from participation in a play group. Cooperative play is rare before four years old unless children see each other several times a week on a continuous basis.

You may need to comfort or reassure your child during group play at your home. If necessary, let him have a security object, and hold or touch him when possible. Put away toys that could frustrate him if other children handled them. Comfort and be with him after the rest of the group has gone.

Early Childhood Education Programs. Some children attend programs outside of the home to allow parents time to pursue other activities and/or career interests on a regular basis. These settings provide most of the advantages of play groups in meeting children's social development needs. It is important for parents of children in these settings to work closely with the care providers to stay aware of how their child's social interactions are going.

At-Home Child Care. When the child is cared for at home, ongoing discussions between caregivers and parents about what to expect and how to resolve toddler conflicts are also necesssary and can be helpful in providing more continuity of approach between parents and caregivers.

Handouts

The first part of the handout "Socializing Among Children" helps parents understand the kind of social behavior they can expect from their toddler. The second part describes ways to deal with conflict.

Socializing Among Children

(15–24 months)

Development

Following are some of the highlights in the social development of the toddler:

One to two years

1. Often is involved in his own play and with himself, and does not seem to be particularly aware of other children.
2. Toys usually have much more importance to him than the child nearby.
3. Learns about children and adults from observation.
4. Pushing, poking, and touching are ways of making contact. The toddler does not know how to make friends. Parents need to help toddlers get along.
5. Some toddlers will grab a toy away from another toddler if the child allows him to do this.
6. The terms "mine" and "no" will be heard in a group of toddlers at play.
7. May need warm-up time in unfamiliar situation.
8. Likes to show and offer adults his toys. This is one of his ways to make friends.
9. Enjoys the company of his parents.
10. Likes to be chased and caught by adults.
11. Enjoys playing "Pat-a-Cake" and "Ring Around the Rosy" with his parents.
12. As he approaches two, may favor one parent over the other.
13. Begins to enjoy daily rituals such as bath time.
14. Imitates the world of adults by sweeping, cooking, reading, and doing other adult activities.
15. Enjoys himself as he walks, stooping to pick up sticks, bending over to look between his legs.

16. Talks more to himself than to others, and more to adults than to other children.

Two to 2½ years

Many characteristics just listed carry over into this period. Other characteristics of the two-year-old are listed below.

1. Has a definite sense of himself and what he wants.
2. Can be very attached to his possessions. It is difficult to *share* toys.
3. Likes to play side by side (parallel play) but not often *with* another child.
4. Begins to develop interest in his special friends.
5. Considers most men and women to be mommies and daddies.
6. Can be shy with strangers, particularly adults.
7. Begins to identify himself by his first name.
8. Continues to need supervision while at play.
9. Needs to begin to establish meaningful relationships with other children and other adults outside of the immediate family.

Techniques for Handling Conflicts

---

1. When one child takes something from another child *and* the second child is not bothered, try not to intervene.
2. If the toddler is upset by something being taken away from her, let her try to solve the situation in her own way. If she cannot solve the conflict, you can step in. The limit usually set is that the toddler who had the toy first may play with it. The toddler who wants the toy may play with it next. Try to help the child who grabbed the toy to get interested in something else, but be sure he soon receives his turn with the toy he tried to take. You might say, "Ashley had the toy, John.

You may play with it when she is finished. You may play with the stuffed dog now. Look, he can bark. I will be sure you get your turn to play with the truck." (Or something shorter!)

3. If the same toddler tries to take the same toy again, explain things to him again.

4. If the toddler tries to take the toy *again,* it is best to take him from the room and try to get him interested in something else. Bring him back to the play area when he is ready. It helps not to get angry. Try to be calm, but firm and assured.

5. Many toddlers do tend to be physical in the way they interact with others. Try not to condone toddlers physically harming each other. You could say, for example, "No, I can't let you bite. Biting hurts." Then with words and actions, comfort both children.

PARENTMAKING: A Practical Handbook for Teaching Parent Classes About Babies and Toddlers by B. Annye Rothenberg, Ph.D., et al. © 1995 Banster Press, P.O. Box 7326, Menlo Park, CA 94026. Can copy for parent classes if this notice is included in full.

5

PLAY AND LEARNING

background/preparation

Goals to Work Toward in Presenting This Topic

Play is very important to toddlers—it is really their way of life. And because play is involved in so much of what these children do, it is also a very important subject for their parents. Parents' concerns about play, however, often differ. Some parents need to know more about appropriate play areas and toys; others are concerned about how much to play with their toddler; still others are concerned about playing too much with their toddler and learning how to teach him to play alone.

There are numerous goals for the play and learning section, but you will need to select those that are appropriate to the interest and concerns of your particular group of parents. The goals are: (1) teaching parents about cognitive and motor development of toddlers; (2) helping them to understand toddlers' play styles; (3) helping them to determine appropriate play environments; (4) helping them to determine appropriate toys for toddlers; (5) helping them to determine how much to play with their toddler; (6) showing parents how to teach their toddler to play alone; (7) teaching parents how to plan a day with a toddler; (8) helping parents understand the different play styles parents use; (9) informing parents about what toddlers learn from their play; (10) showing parents how to stimulate a toddler; (11) helping parents understand the importance of reading to toddlers.

Typical Parental Interests and Concerns About This Topic

1. What are some good ideas for play activities?
2. What are the best educational toys?
3. How can I get Max to play by himself so I can get something done?
4. How often should I play with my child?
5. My husband plays so roughly with our son he cannot go to sleep at night.
6. My toddler will not sit still when I try to read to her.
7. I don't like to stay home with my toddler. If we go places, she is fine, but at home she always wants my attention and cannot entertain herself.
8. How far should I go trying to stimulate my child?
9. I'm often so tired after working all day; I wonder what can my child and I do together that we can both enjoy?
10. What can I do with my child on a rainy day?
11. What is a good play environment for my toddler?.
12. How can I tell what toys to buy for my child?

Areas of Information You Will Need to Learn About to Teach This Topic

- Toddlers' large- and small-motor development. (Look for realistic and specific examples in books and observe toddlers at play.)
- Cognitive development of toddlers. (You will need information that is meaningful to parents, not to research psychologists.)
- The variety of toddler play styles. (Observe children at play and watch how their styles affect what they pursue.)
- How adults play with children—its importance and the various play styles adults use.
- How toddlers and parents spend their days together; how toddlers and working parents spend their evenings and weekends together.
- What toddlers learn from their play.
- The kinds of toys toddlers play with.
- Appropriate books for toddlers and the importance of reading to young children.
- Ideas to pursue if toddlers are not interested in being read to.

Family Dynamics—What This Topic Means Psychologically to Parent and Child

Parents of toddlers want to feel that their child's play is constructive. They can be bothered by his wandering, observing, and clinging, and seem to be much more satisfied if their toddler is doing a puzzle or digging in the sand. Parents feel they are doing a good job when they play with their toddler, but often feel frustrated or impatient when play goes on too long. Some read about how important the first three years of a child's life are and feel pressured to provide superior play experiences now so their toddler will function at a high intellectual level in later years. Parents do not seem to be very relaxed about their children's play. Working parents often feel even less confident about what experiences they need to provide for their children. Further, they can be unclear on what is reasonable to expect.

Toddlers, however, do not differentiate between constructive and "nonconstructive" play.

They want to explore, touch, interact, observe, and simply "be," as well as play at meaningful games. Toddlers like to go at their own pace while learning about the world, and become very frustrated when required to do tasks above their developmental level. They will let a parent know when they are ready to move on by their actions and responses to new activities and situations.

Sample Concern of Parents

Concern	*Critical Issues*
Sarah seems to need constant stimulation, and particularly likes to read, read, read. I worry that I am not giving her enough, but at the same time she is demanding too much of my life and the more I give the more she wants. She enjoys playing with her father in a more physical way, but still wants me if anything goes wrong.	—Toddler likes parent to keep her occupied.

—Parent does not know how much stimulation she should provide.
—Parent wants time for herself.

—Toddler has a different play style with her father. |

Key Questions

1. How much time are you spending with your toddler?
2. What do you do with her?
3. What does she do when you do not want to play with her?
4. What is your child's play environment like? What playthings are available for your toddler to use?
5. How does your husband play with your daughter? What does your daughter do when he does not have time to play with her?
6. How do you plan your day with your toddler if you're at home together?
7. If you are away from your toddler during the day, how do you structure your evening and weekend time?
8. What kinds of play experiences do you provide for your toddler?

9. How much time do you need for yourself? What do you do during this time?

10. How do you manage your toddler when you are attending to household tasks?

Readings and Other Resources

Allison, Christine, *I'll Tell You a Story, I'll Sing You a Song* (New York: Bantam Doubleday Dell, 1987).

*Bredekamp, Sue, Ed. *Developmentally Appropriate Practice in Early Childhood Programs Serving Children from Birth to Age Eight, Expanded Ed.* (Washington, D.C.: NAEYC, 1989).

Caplan, Frank and Caplan, Theresa, *The Second Twelve Months of Life* (New York: Bantam Doubleday Dell, 1982).

*Gonzales-Mena, Janet and Eyer, Diane, *Infants, Toddlers and Caregivers* (Mountain View, Cal.: Mayfield Publishing, 1989) Chapter 4.

Growing Child (Lafayette, Ind.: Dunn & Hargitt, 1995 [updated annually]) To order, call (800) 927-7289.

Miller, Karen, *Things to Do With Toddlers and Twos* (Marshfield, Mass.: Telshare Publishing Co., 1984).

NAEYC, *Toys: Tools for Learning* [Pamphlet][1] (Washington, D.C.: NAEYC, 1985).

Oppenheim, Joanne and Oppenheim, Stephanie, *The Best Toys Books and Videos for Kids* (New York: HarperCollins, 1995).

*Segal, Marilyn and Adcock, Don, *Your Child at Play: One to Two Years* (Newmarket Press, 1985).

Toys and Play [pamphlet][1] (New York: Toy Manufacturers of America, 1993).

---

1. Please see page 236 for ordering information.

teaching/presentation

Homework

The homework for this topic helps each parent focus on her child's play style, her own play style and her spouse's, and any questions she may have concerning the area of play.

Practical Suggestions or Strategies for Teaching This Topic

Parents do not always know what they want to learn about the subject of play. To them, *play* is often synonomous with the word *toys*, and the discussion of play can quickly deteriorate into talking about what specific toys are good for toddlers. This is not the most useful way to use class time since toddlers will soon be two-year-olds and their need for certain toys will change. Parents will need more general guidelines when they discuss toys, learning experiences, and play environments.

When you begin the discussion, offer a broad picture of play to the group and then work into specifics. If parents learn about the cognitive and motor development of toddlers and the children's different play styles, they will be better equipped to work with the group's particular concerns. If parents' interests are limited, suggest some topics to discuss.

You will need to inform and reassure the parent of an active child with a short attention span. Parents often think that children who are quiet and able to sit still at their play for a long period of time are very bright. Parents of more active children who cannot concentrate can be fearful that these children are slow learners or hyperactive. (Highlighting children's temperament is helpful.)

Concrete examples and sharing of experiences help the play discussion become even more effective. If you are able to relate a real example of how a toddler with a certain play style has developed now that he's of school age, this can help the parents see where their children are heading. It is important for parents to get a more relaxed and realistic picture of play with their toddler and how it influences later development.

EXPLORING, PLAYING, AND LEARNING

(15–24 months)

1. What are the activities your child enjoys at home as well as away from home (e.g. at childcare). Include places, people, toys, and so on.

2. How have the skills that your child has developed recently influenced his/her play?

3. Are there any special interests or skills that your child tends to focus on more than other children the same age do?

4. Think about what your child did during the last few hours he/she was awake and describe the learning that you think has been going on through that play.

5. What aspects of your child's play or your play with him/her are you finding troublesome (i.e., are not going as smoothly as you had hoped)?

6. How does your spouse's (as well as other adults') way of playing with your child differ from yours?

How does your child handle these differences?

Parent's name _____ Date _____ Child's age _____

Mini-Lecture and Lead-off Questions for Discussion[1]

Sample mini-lecture

Play is our children's life. It teaches them what the world is—how high is up, what is meant by down, what is soft and what is hard, what is solid and what is hollow, the meaning of the inside and the outside, of wet and dry and shape and form. Play also teaches children about themselves. They learn what they can do and what is harder and easier for them.

While toddlers play, they strengthen their muscles, improve their perceptions, learn new skills, let off excess energy, try out different solutions to problems, practice the tasks of life, learn how to deal with other people, and come to know the values and symbols of the world. All of this can be done in a variety of styles, and it is a mistake to assume that there is one good way to play and that all others are abnormal. Child's play, like adult's work, expresses what the person is, what he likes, and what is on his mind.

To begin our discussion, let's first review toddlers' cognitive and motor development and their various styles of play, and then go on to the specific questions you may have about play.

Lead-offs

For Toddlers' Motor Development and Cognitive Development. Use the information provided in the sections of the handout "Some Developmental Motor Skills" and "Developmental Goals for Toddlers" (see pp. 237 and 239) and offer a simple description of pertinent facts. Then ask the parents to ask any questions they may have about their child's development, or to add any information about development they feel is typical for the age group.

For Toddlers' Play Styles. Discuss the information on p. 233 with the group, and use any personal examples you may have.

For Concerns and Interests of the Group. Ask the group to bring up the areas of concern they have, and make an informal outline to structure the discussion.

For Appropriate Toys. Ask the group to discuss toys in a general way and do not allow the conversation to turn to the pros and cons of specific toys. Use the information from the section of the handout "Buying Toys."

For How to Help Toddlers Learn to Play Alone. Ask the parents how much their toddlers play alone and how much they play with their toddlers. Ask them if they feel they have a good balance or if they would like to change the way things are going.

For Differing Play Styles of Parents and Caregivers. Use the homework responses or examples of how spouses and other adults play with their child to get this discussion going. Let the parents talk among themselves to see how other families play with their children.

For What Toddlers Learn from their Play. Tell, instead of ask, parents what toddlers can learn from their play. Most parents will not be informed on the subject since they have not parented very long.

For Reading to a Toddler. Begin the discussion by asking what types of books toddlers enjoy; how long their toddlers will sit while being read to; or when do parents read to their toddlers. Do not stress the importance of reading to a child until the end of the discussion, or a parent who reads little or not at all to her child may not contribute to the conversation.

Additional Information for Parents[2]

Motor Development of Toddlers

Children develop at different rates. The information in the handout on p. 237 is to be used only as a guide.

When toddlers learn a new motor skill, they often want to practice it over and over.

---

1. Further information for conducting the discussion can be found in "Additional Information for Parents."

2. A summary of some of the following information is contained in the handout for this topic.

Cognitive Development of Toddlers

12- to 15-month-olds

- Begin imitation of what others—especially parents—are doing.
- Spend time jabbering, experimenting with conversational inflection.
- Occasionally imitate sounds they know well. Are able to place circle in form board.
- Able to do some building, perhaps stacking 2 blocks; much more able to knock things down.
- Use gestures to make wants known (language is limited, and children get frustrated because people don't understand them).
- Look at books, turn pages, point to individual pictures, want to know pictures' names.

15- to 18-month-olds

- Show or point to specific object when asked where it is.
- Follow simple directions, such as, "Where is your bottle?" and "Get the ball."
- By 18 months, say "no" even if they mean "yes."
- Imitate, model.
- May know words for some things, but may not know what the words mean.
- Repeat words or actions.
- Can learn and then forget.
- Desire to dump things out.

18- to 21-month-olds

- Begin to use a few words to make wants known.
- Able to point to parts of a doll when asked where they are.
- Able to find things hidden under cups.
- Begin to use two-word sentences.
- May begin to use "mine."
- Use one word to indicate everything in a category.
- Can be told what is happening next.
- Know where things are and where they left them.
- Want to know how to use things.

21- to 24-month-olds

- Able to stack several blocks.
- Begin to group things by size, color, or form.

Play Styles of Toddlers

Toddlers have very different ways of playing. Some are more energetic than others, some con-

centrate longer than others, some play longer by themselves, some have very specific interests. Often parents find that their child's way of playing is very different from what they expected.

Every child progresses through stages of play and learning at her own pace. Parents need to help their toddler along by building on their child's play strengths and working with her in areas where she is not as interested or as strong.

Parents can gain insight by asking themselves, "What are some things I do with my toddler to help him use a lot of energy? To concentrate? To develop fine-motor skills?"

Appropriate Play Environments

A specific section of the handout is provided for this topic on p. 237. Parents need to become aware of the information it contains.

Types of Play

There are several types of play a toddler should encounter during the course of a day or a several day period:

Playing alone. This type of play can last from 5 to 30 minutes but could be more or less, and should not be interrupted by an adult.

Playing beside an adult. Toddlers learn from watching adults.

Playing beside other children. Toddlers enjoy observing and imitating them.

Playing in an organized way, such as working with playdough or a special puzzle, listening to a record, or taking a walk in the yard.

Playing away from home. This might be walking about the block or going to the park or grocery store.

Playing actively. This is time to run, jump, pound, and enjoy large-motor activities.

Playing quietly. This is time to dream, imagine, and think, and often occurs before or after a nap.

Playing with a parent. This is when the parent concentrates on the child and not on other activities, and plays with the child in a relaxed manner.

How Much Time Should Be Spent Playing with a Toddler

There is no definite information on exactly how much time a parent should spend playing with a toddler. It is important for parents to know, however, that they need to play with, read to, and be responsive to the needs of their child every day.

Parents can gain insight into their own play styles and philosophies about playing by asking themselves these questions:
- How long can I play with my toddler and remain interested?
- How important do I feel play is for my child?
- How comfortable am I playing with my child?
- What do I like to play with my toddler?
- Am I using my leisure time to show my child how to relax or am I always busy?
- Do I play with my child at a specific time each day?

How to Teach a Toddler to Play Alone

Parents can gain insight into how to enable their toddler to learn to play alone by asking themselves these questions:
- How long does my toddler play alone?
- When does he play alone?
- How long would I like him to play alone?
- Given the rest of his day, is it realistic for him to play alone?
- Where do I want him to play alone? In a separate room? Outside?
- What do I do when my toddler is playing alone? Do I worry about him? Do I check him constantly? Do I go to him immediately when he fusses or do I wait and listen?

Toddlers can spend a short time away from their parents in a separate room, but do not like to spend long periods of time in this way. No matter how long toddlers spend playing away from parents, it must be certain that:
- The environment is a safe one.
- There are toys available that they can handle and enjoy.
- They are asked to play alone at a time of day when they are at their best (the dinner hour is not a time toddlers want to be separated from their family).
- Before they are asked to play alone, parents have first given them some quality time during which they have had undivided attention. (This may be especially true for children who have been away from their parents for several hours or the whole day.)

Children can be trained to play alone. Parents can train them by not going in and getting their child immediately after a nap, finding a set time each day for their child to play alone, and setting up a play situation near each other but where the parent remains unavailable for play—and building on the amount of time they expect their toddler to play alone (they can begin with 5 minutes and work up to 30 minutes or so). It is easier for the toddler to accept the parents "unavailability" if the parent is physically active versus, e.g., reading the newspaper. Parents need to remember to praise their toddler when he has played awhile by himself.

Guides for Planning a Day with a Toddler

Parents need to know their child's schedule to successfully plan a day—when the child eats, sleeps, is fussy, is in a good frame of mind.

Days should be allowed to flow naturally, but they also need some guidelines to work well. Times should be scheduled for a child to play alone, play with a parent, have a special activity, and take a walk.

Parents should be encouraged to get more of their own tasks accomplished early in the day when their toddler is fresh and more able to be on his own. Establishing a routine for the morning, perhaps having the child listen to a record or do puzzles beside a parent while she is working, should help the time go more smoothly.

Naps and bedtime should be at a set time.

Children dislike hurry. Parents should check their words and body movements for signs of unnecessary rushing, which can make a toddler unsettled or frustrated.

If parents are playing with their child, callers could be told their call will be returned later in the day. If a child's time with his parents is respected, it is more likely the child will respect the parent's time alone.

Including the different types of play described on p. 238 will make a day more interesting as well as successful.

How Spouses Play with Their Toddler

Parents need to think about how they play with their toddler and how their spouse plays with the toddler. They should note what they both enjoy doing with their toddler and what types of play work well.

Children do not seem to be bothered by different parental play styles; they come to accept the differences and enjoy them. Parents who play in very different ways are still providing for their child's development.

Some children cannot tolerate a high level of stimulating play for too long a period of time. Parents need to be aware of the point at which play becomes too stimulating, and stop.

It is beneficial if both parents participate in active and quiet play with their child, even though they may prefer one of the types of play.

What Children Learn and Obtain from Play

Refer to the section of the handout on p. 240, "Learning Through Toddler's Play."

In active play, children develop their physical selves. They learn bodily control, running, pushing, pulling, and throwing. They also develop hand-eye coordination, the concept of left and right, bodily feel, and an awareness of spatial relationships.

Play helps toddlers begin to fit themselves into the social world. People who are important to toddlers will begin to figure in their play.

Play helps toddlers begin to develop their powers of concentration. They have a natural urge to explore and discover and learn about the material world—sand, water, soft, hard, rough, liquid, solid, and so on—as they are able to study objects for longer and longer periods of time.

Toddlers learn about adult roles through imitative play. They talk and practice their language as they play.

Play affords toddlers an opportunity to use their judgment.

Play leads toddlers into later work with academics.

Play provides toddlers with opportunities to develop their creativity.

Play puts toddlers in a position of power—they are in charge of what they do while they play.

How to Stimulate a Toddler

Parents should let their toddlers lead them at times. Children will show parents what they are capable of handling, and it may not be what parents expect.

Children need to be talked to. Parents should label, repeat, talk about what they are doing.

Children should be allowed to do things for themselves when they are ready.

Toys should be appropriate for a child's style and developmental level. Children should not be required to play with toys that are too frustrating for them to handle, even though parents feel such toys will raise the child's intellectual level.

Toys that are too sophisticated can make a toddler feel inadequate.

Experience with large-motor activities can help toddlers to gain confidence in their bodies. Play environments should be big enough to move around in.

Children need to be taught so they can learn how to explore their environment on their own. Parents should expect and encourage toddlers to solve as many problems by themselves as they can.

Parents should provide their children with sensory experiences—touching, smelling, feeling, talking about sizes, shapes, and colors.

Reading to a Toddler

Parents should read to their child as soon as they can hold him in their lap.

When parents read to toddlers they should keep the following considerations in mind:

- Don't demand that your toddler sit and listen. Allow him to point and verbalize.
- When your child does not want to sit still any longer, stop reading to him and let him get down.
- Hold your child on your lap or next to you when you read to him. Make reading time cozy, warm, and calm, and instill it with love and a sense of caring.
- Read yourself. Your child will model you.

Handouts

The lengthy handout included in this section focuses on helping parents formulate a philosophy of play, obtain a working knowledge of the skills and learning play provides, and understand the necessities for a healthy play environment. The titles of the sections are "Some Developmental Motor Skills," "Play Environment," "Types of Play," "Developmental Goals for Toddlers," "Buying Toys," "Play Guidelines," and "Learning Through Toddler's Play."

You may also wish to recommend or order and distribute:

— "Toys: tools for learning." This pamphlet focuses on birth to age 8. Available from the National Association for the Education of Young Children, 1509 9th St. N.W., Washington, D.C. 20036-1426 or call (800) 424-2460; 100 copies for $10.

or

— "Toys and Play." Another valuable pamphlet focussing on birth to age 12. Available from Toy Manufacturers of America by writing to: Toy Booklet, P.O. Box 866, Madison Square Station, New York, N.Y. 10159 or call (800) 851-9955; free to parents and qualified organizations.

8. Wants to see what things fit inside of others ~~~~ 10. E~~~~ ~king at books, turning the pages
He is beginning to ~~~~ ne), and pointing out objects in the
locks, simple puzz~~~~ the beginning of representational

9. Likes things ~~~~
This helps him to ~~~~ in imitative play (enjoys keys,
him. ~~~~ s, etc.). He is learning adult roles.

6

SPEECH AND LANGUAGE DEVELOPMENT[1,2]

background/preparation

| **Goals to Work Toward in Presenting This Topic** | **Typical Parental Interests and Concerns About This Topic** |

Parents are eager to learn about the language development that takes place during the toddler stage and how they can help to stimulate it in their own child. Though the majority of parents seem to accept the way and pace in which their child is gaining language, a few are anxious. Parents can become more relaxed about language development when they realize the wide range of what is considered normal and when they hear how other parents of toddlers are coping with their inability to always understand their child.

The goals for this discussion are: (1) to inform group members about what can be expected from toddlers in the area of language development; (2) to help parents learn ways to stimulate their child's language development; (3) to help parents determine what to do when they feel their child's language is not developing at the proper rate; (4) to help parents learn how to respond to misarticulated words and/or stuttering.

1. I do not have any concerns about my child's language development but I would like to know how toddler language develops.
2. What should I do when my toddler mispronounces a word?
3. What are some ways I can encourage Matthew to talk instead of pointing or using his own words?
4. My friend's 19-month-old daughter uses many words and *my* child isn't speaking yet.
5. When my toddler wants something, I usually cannot understand him, and he and I get very frustrated.
6. My two-year-old has started to stutter in the last few weeks. What could this be due to? Do you think he'll just grow out of it?

---

2. Speech *and* language are not the same as each other. Speech refers to the mechanics (in the throat and mouth), i.e., the movement of the vocal musculature to form sounds and then words. Language refers to the thought processes and encompasses the meaning of words (semantics), memory, and word order and grammar (syntax). In our speech and language chapters, we generally use "language" when we are referring to both at once.

---

1. This material is meant to be used in both the toddler (15-24 months) and two-year-old (two- to three-year-old) classes.

7. My child used to say many more words but we haven't heard him use them for some time now. Is that normal?
8. My 2-year-old is with a bilingual caregiver all day. Should she be introduced to a second language at this young age?
9. I can understand my 2½-year-old but other people can't.
10. My child imitates words of others but doesn't seem to use words spontaneously.

Areas of Information You Will Need to Learn About to Teach This Topic

---

- How speech and language develops from infancy through the pre-school years.
- The norms for and range of speech and language development.
- Various ways parents can work with their children to help them develop both speech and language.
- What to do when children mispronounce words.
- How to help the toddler who points but cannot use words to tell what he wants.
- How to teach children new words.
- What to do if a child begins to stutter.
- What a family can do when their toddler is not talking at all.

Family Dynamics—What This Topic Means Psychologically to Parent and Child

---

When parents have a toddler whose language is well developed, they feel very proud and think that perhaps their child is very bright. When parents have a toddler who has little language, they wonder how bright the child is, and often feel guilty that they have not helped him enough. Each time the latter parents encounter a toddler who is more verbal than their own, they feel uncomfortable. Parents often cannot understand what their toddler is saying and feel frustrated and guilty that they do not know what he means. Some parents get very tense and try too hard to correct their child's speech instead of continuing to provide good speech models.

It is easier for the toddler who has more language to deal with his world because he can make his wants and desires known. The toddler with a limited vocabulary, however, can become frustrated because it is more difficult for the people around him to understand his thought processes. That toddler knows what he is trying to express and often gets very upset when people don't respond to him.

Sample Concern of Parents

Concern	*Critical Issues*
Daniel seems to be able to understand a great deal and has since he was much younger. But he has shown little interest in spontaneously using words. I have not really been concerned about it nor have I made any special effort to "teach" him. I may be inhibiting him by anticipating his needs and understanding his gestures.	—Parent comfortable with child's receptive language. —What should be expected from a toddler this age? —What verbal vocabulary does the toddler have? —Is there a need to stimulate a toddler's language development? —Parent's guilt over possible role in child's lack of language development.

Key Questions

1. What, in detail, is your child's expressive language like?
2. What kind of vocabulary do you feel your child should have?
3. How do you work with your toddler's language development at home?
4. What do you feel you have done well with in the area of language development and what mistakes do you think you have made?
5. When do you feel you should try to figure out your toddler's needs and when should you let him try to tell you what he needs?
6. How does he tell you what he wants?
7. Does he play with language in his crib?
8. Does he interact with people, verbally or otherwise?

15–24 months

9. Is your TV or stereo always on? (A lot of background noise makes it hard for a toddler to distinguish sounds.)

10. How much do you talk with your child?

Readings and Other Resources

Ames, Louise B. et al., *Your One-Year-Old* (New York: Dell, 1983).

Ames, Louise B. and Ilg, Frances, *Your Two-Year-Old* (New York: Dell, 1983).

*Baron, Naomi, *Growing Up With Language* (New York: Addison-Wesley, 1993).

*Caplan, Frank and Caplan, Theresa, *The Second Twelve Months of Life* (New York: Bantam, 1982).

*Caplan, Frank and Caplan, Theresa, *The Early Childhood Years* (New York: Bantam, 1984).

Growing Child (Lafayette, Ind.: Dunn & Hargitt, 1995 [updated annually]). To order, call (800) 927-7289.

Harding, Edith and Riley, Philip, *The Bilingual Family: A Handbook for Parents* (New York: Cambridge University Press, 1986).

Leach, Penelope, *Your Baby and Child, Rev. Ed.* (New York: Knopf, 1989).

For help in locating a qualified audiologist or speech-language pathologist in your area, write the American Speech-Language-Hearing Association, 10801 Rockville Pike, Rockville, Maryland, 20852 or call (800) 638-8255 or (301) 897-8682.

teaching/presentation

Homework

The homework for language development asks parents to spend time thinking about how they encourage their toddler's language development so they can later share their methods with the group; some parents are using techniques to develop language that other parents have never considered, but might enjoy learning about. The homework assignment also helps parents to focus on their concerns and the usual sequence of events in speech and language development.

Practical Suggestions or Strategies for Teaching This Topic

The language development discussion goes best if you structure it around the questions group members have. Some groups may have few questions, however, and only want to hear about the norms of development and how other families are encouraging language skills. Keep in mind that parents with language concerns want to know if their child's language is progressing at a normal rate.

Depending on the questions group members have, you may want to first discuss the normal sequence of steps and the norms for speech and language development, stressing that a child's future academic success is not indicated by the rate at which he develops effective language skills. Be sure to stress that parents are important in the language socialization process. Then it will help to give examples, if you can, of children you know who developed language early and some who developed language later and describe how they are doing as pre-school or elementary school children. This can calm parents' fears as they learn about variation in normal language development.

Be sure that the language discussion is non-competitive. If a parent is worried about her toddler's language and the other group members have made it sound as if they have children with superior language skills, the parent will remain quiet. If you think a parent is worried about a language-related area and she does not speak up in the group, talk with her after class or arrange a time to call her. A parent may wonder what it means for the future if her child is linguistically precocious. Again, personal sharing of your own children or children you know will help to reassure them.

Handouts (see p. 248) can be used in a variety

SPEECH AND LANGUAGE

(15–24 months)

1. How do you and your husband help your toddler with speech and/or language development?

2. What do you find frustrating in your toddler's speech and/or language development? How do you handle this?

3. List any concerns you have about your child's speech and/or language skills.

Parent's name _____ Date _____ Child's age _____

of ways: as a lead-off for discussion, as a summary, or as additional information.

Mini-lecture and Lead-off Questions for Discussion[3]

Sample mini-lecture

You can use the section of the handout entitled "Speech and Language" (see p. 248) as a guide and tell parents the kinds of toddler language development that can be expected.

Lead-offs

For How to Encourage Toddler Language Development. Ask the parents to discuss how they stimulate their toddler's language development at home. This is a particularly effective technique if the group members get along well and are not competitive.

For Parental Interests and Concerns. Ask the group how many of them have toddlers who point to what they want and become frustrated when their meaning is not understood. Then ask the parents to describe what occurs. This query generally results in humorous anecdotes and gets the parents started with their own questions and concerns.

When you feel you have answered and worked on all of the group's questions, review your notes for points that have been left out and ask the parents if any of these areas interest them. Sometimes group members have questions in the back of their minds that need to be brought to the surface.

Additional Information for Parents

What Can Be Expected in Toddler Language Development

• Refer to the information in the handouts on p. 248 and p. 250.

---

3. Further information for conducting the discussion can be found in "Additional Information for Parents."

• The norms for expressive vocabulary size are:
1 year — 1 to 2 words
1½ years — 5 to 10 words
2 years — 25 to 100 words or more (two word combinations occur during this stage).
2½ years — 200 to 400 words or more
By 3 — 500 words or more
• If a child is not talking at all by his second birthday, most authorities advise consulting a specialist.

Stimulating a Child's Language Development
• Refer to the information in the handout on p. 248.
• Parents can stimulate development by responding in any of these ways when their child talks to them:
— Smiling.
— Repeating what is said and expanding on it.
— Answering the question.
— Repeating the word and giving the child what was asked for.
— Not talking baby talk.
— Making good eye contact, bending down or sitting down while speaking.
— Not interrupting.
— Having fun with language—humor is a great stimulator.

When a toddler points to instead of says what he wants, parents should:

Not anticipate his needs. Instead they should hold back and give him a chance to gesture, point, and talk. Then they should ask, "Do you mean milk? Juice? Water? Parents should touch each object as they say its name and speak slowly and clearly.

Use the "show me" method. Parents should let the child lead them to whatever he is talking about. Once they see what he means, they need to talk about it with him. This kind of action stimulates language development in a secure and warm environment.

After a toddler tries to ask for and find something, parents should help him find it. They should repeat the name of the thing being sought, perhaps *water*, in a sentence as they begin to look: "Oh, you would like some water." Then they should talk about water during the course of the day, let the child drink some, and talk about it again when it's in use, perhaps during the child's bath.

Stimulating a Child's Speech Development

When a child does not say a word correctly[4], parents should repeat very casually and in the correct form what was said. Doing this enables the child to hear the correct pronunciation and lets you and the child know if you are understanding what he has said.

Teaching New Words

When teaching new words, parents need to know that they should:
— Talk about people, objects and events that are a part of their lives.
— Engage a child in conversation.
— Teach words in context. Adjectives help children to know what words mean.
— Say words slowly and clearly and establish eye contact when they speak.
— Encourage a child to express herself. The parent then remembers to listen.

Children want to learn words that are important to them. Toddlers will want to learn words for body parts, food, eating utensils, clothing, favorite toys, and people. Most of children's early words are names for things.

When a Child Does Not Talk

• Be sure the child has and continues to be developing increased receptive language. Is he able to follow simple directions, for example "Go and get your shoes."
• Talk to the child with simple words in a friendly manner.
• Give the child opportunities to be around other children.
• Encourage him to ask for things by name; do not anticipate all his needs.
• Parents with speech and/or language concerns should consult with a speech-language pathologist.

---

4. Faulty articulation is the rule rather than the exception for toddlers—they can't always get the right sound in the right place. Sounds in the middle and at the ends of words are missed more frequently than those at the beginning. The section of the handout on p. 250 lists the sequential development of sounds and when they are normally mastered.

Bilingualism

Many working parents have secured a caregiver who speaks a different first language. This can be an advantage if the child will have continuing contact with someone who speaks that language as it offers the opportunity for a child to become bilingual. Bilingual aptitude offers the child social and conversational advantages. It is helpful if each person uses only one language with the child, or if the second language is used only at home. These teaching methods are thought to reduce any confusion in language learning. The best way for a young child to learn another language is through exposure: casual conversation in everyday activities. In a bilingual situation, parents should be aware that the child will be juggling two vocabularies and will therefore learn fewer words in the early stages of exposure. However, it is felt that a child who was exposed to two languages early in life on a consistent and continuing basis does not have a deficit in vocabularies in either language after 3 years of age.

Handouts

The three handouts deal with different aspects of language development and provide a summary of and an addition to the detailed information presented in class. The first handout is "Speech and Language," which includes sections on Toddler Development (15 to 24 months), Helping the Toddler with Speech and Language Development, Two-year-old Development (Two to three years), and the Sequential Development of Sounds. The second handout is "Speech and Language Concerns" and includes sections on Possible Speech and Language Problems, and Normal Non-Fluency. This handout is useful in classes dealing with children from about 15 months of age through the pre-school years. The last handout is "Preschool Speech and Language" and includes sections on Language Help at Home and A Guide for Parents. This is useful in classes dealing with children from two years of age through the pre-school years.

SPEECH AND LANGUAGE

(15–36 months)

Toddler Development

Speech and language development differs with each child. The *rate* at which a child acquires new skills and the way he *learns* about language will be unique to him. Some of the steps in speech and language development that a child uses between the ages of one and two-and-a-half are listed below, roughly in chronological order.

From *one to two years* the child:
- Knows much more about the world than he has words to express this knowledge.
- Can obey simple commands such as "Come," "Go," "Open your mouth."
- Will give you something upon request, such as a toy, ball, or food.
- Uses single words meaningfully. When the toddler says the word *ball*, he might mean, "Where is the ball?", "I see a ball," or "Give me the ball."
- Has a vocabulary associated with his experiences, things, and people important to him.
- Will mix real words with many words that have no real meaning.
- Talks to himself as much as to others.
- Can indicate his wants with a word or gestures and a vocalization.
- Can point to objects when their name is stated.
- Points to his *eyes, mouth, nose,* and *feet* when named by someone else.
- Talks about what he can see and what he is doing, but does not talk about the past or future.
- Will acquire verbs and adjectives after knowledge of some nouns. May say, "All gone," "More," and "Hot."
- Enjoys imitating the sounds of cars, animals, and horns.

- May refer to himself by name rather than by a pronoun—"Aaron do it."
- Begins to use pronouns in the order of me, you, and I.
- Will ask you to name objects.
- Starts to make two-word sentences.
- Will practice his language while alone (in crib).
- Imitates your language.
- Talks much less in a group setting.
- Has several speech articulation errors.

From *two to two-and-a-half years* the child:
- Usually has rapid speech acquisition if this did not happen between 18 months and two years.
- Says the same thing over and over.
- Talks more when playing by himself.
- Enjoys saying parts of songs and rhymes.
- Has speech that shows interest in himself: "Give me a cracker," "Me do it."
- Does NOT have fluent articulation; sounds at the middle and ends of words are missed most frequently.
- Acquires verbs that match his actions: "Climb up," "Slide down."
- Begins to use time-related words: day, night, now, first.
- Uses longer sentences with nouns, verbs, and adjectives.
- Is "word hungry!"
- Asks many, many questions.

Helping the Toddler with Speech and Language Development*

1. As you talk with your child when she's this age, keep these ideas in mind:

---

*Adapted from *Teach Your Child to Talk,* by David Pushaw (Fairfield, N.J.: CEBCO/Standard Publishing, out of print).

- Use simple, clear, slow speech.
- Prepare her for the future by talking about what you're going to do before you do it, while you're doing it, and after it's all over.
- Start with words that are useful—foods, body parts, clothing, toys, family names.
- Make her feel that she is part of what is going on and not just an observer.
- Talk with her and give her a chance to add her words and expressions, even if you can't understand them. Listen to what she says and make her feel that what she says is definitely important.
- When using new words, make sure she can see the way you're saying them as well as be able to hear them.
- Do not expect or demand perfection.
- Make your child feel as if she is being understood. Avoid using "what?" over and over.

2. There are two ways to talk with your toddler—self-talk and parallel talk.

- Self-Talk. Talk out loud about what you are hearing, seeing, doing, or feeling when your child is nearby. Let her know there are words to describe all sorts of activities and feelings. The things adults take for granted are new adventures to young children. For example, as you are preparing dinner, folding clothes, or grocery shopping, talk about the things you are doing. Be sure to talk slowly and clearly and use simple words and short phrases.
- Parallel Talk. Parallel talk involves talking about what is happening to your child. Use words that describe what she is doing, seeing, hearing, or feeling. This gives her words to think with. She will use them later when she wants to talk about similar things.

3. Listening is a skill that you can continue to help your child develop. She needs to understand what she hears. Call her attention to sounds, then show or explain to her what made them. Good examples of sounds that can be called to her attention are noises of engines running, trucks braking, dogs barking, or birds singing. Make it a game: "Can you hear that noise? What

is it?" Then help her answer the question by showing her what it was and talking about it. Many activities can help build listening skills. Here are a few:

- Give your child directions, such as "Bring me the ball." Each time, make it a different object, something that is familiar to her. Praise her accomplishments and be sure to use parallel talk.
- Try the tune "Here We Go 'Round the Mulberry Bush" and add your own lines, such as, "This is the way we wash our hands, wash our hands, wash our hands. This is the way we wash our hands so early in the morning." Other short phrases, like "eat our soup," "comb our hair," or "brush our teeth" can also be used. Show your child how to act out each new line.
- Let her listen to people on the telephone. Let her say a few words back. Children this age are curious about voices on the telephone but say very little themselves until they become more familiar with the phone.
- Play "Follow the Leader." Children in the family or your child and her friends can line up and the leader can give directions, such as, "Pat your head," "Clap your hands," or "Go behind the chair."
- Encourage her to play "Ring Around the Rosy." This is a good listening game. If there are older children, they can help teach the younger ones.
- "Hide and Seek" is a game that little children usually enjoy. Call to your child from your hiding place if she takes too long to find you. This is another good time to use parallel talk as she tries to find the people who are hiding.

4. Read to your child. Sometimes the toddler likes you to read by simply stating the name of an object seen on the page. Often she will try to repeat what you say and point to the picture herself. She may enjoy having the same story read over and over. Rhymes and poetry also contribute to language development; finger plays are enjoyed by the toddler and older children.

5. Give your toddler practice in following directions. Have her point out her own body parts as you say, "Where are your eyes?" "Where is your

nose . . . mouth . . . hair (and the other parts)?" Be sure not to demand the answer. If she does not know the answer, show her.

Be aware of the fact that all children of this age mispronounce words and articulate some words in different ways. This is because their verbal abilities are not fully developed; most errors will correct themselves as the child grows older. Not until three years of age can you expect most children to be able to correctly pronounce words that contain the following sounds: m, n, ng, p, f, h, and w. (It can be useful to repeat what you thought you heard your child say just to check that out with her—and then you can pronounce her word correctly; don't talk baby talk.)

6. Add to your child's vocabulary when she is ready; when she wants and needs a word, tell it to her. When your child is not interested in learning new words, stop for a while. Encourage your child to make words or sounds for what she wants rather than just allowing her to point.

7. If your child is not talking, some useful approaches might be to: talk with her using simple words and a friendly manner; give her chances to be around other children and to hear and to participate in their interaction; and encourage her to ask for things by name.

8. *Relax* and enjoy talking with your child and be interested in what she's saying.

Two-year-old Development

Speech and language development differs with each child. The rate at which a child acquires a new skill and the way he learns about language will be unique to him. Some of the steps in speech and language development are listed below, roughly in chronological order.

From *two to three years* the child:
- Usually has rapid speech acquisition if this did not happen between 18 months and two years.

- Says the same thing over and over.
- Talks more when playing by himself; talks much less in a group setting.
- Enjoys saying parts of songs and rhymes.
- Has speech that shows interest in himself: "Give me a cracker," "Me do it."
- Does NOT have fluent articulation; sounds at the middle and ends of words are missed most frequently. Pronunciation problems are common.
- Acquires verbs that match his actions: "Climb up," "Slide down."
- Begins to use time-related words: day, night, now, first.
- Uses longer sentences with nouns, verbs, and adjectives.
- Is "word hungry"!
- Asks many, many questions—why, how, how come, etc.
- Understands longer sentences and some simple stories in books.
- Often asks a question because he wants it asked of him.
- Uses plurals.
- Use of his long-term memory becomes more apparent in his speech.
- Uses sentences with two parts, suggesting the relationship he sees between two events.
- Wants to know more about colors and numbers.
- Learning word opposites, but mixes them up.

Sequential Development of Sounds

Age*	Sounds
3	mmm, nnn, ng, f, p, h, w
4	y, k, b, d, g
4½	sss, sh, ch, r
6	t, v, l, th
7	zzz, zh, j
8	wh

*The following ages are those by which most children have mastered the sound in question. In addition to these sounds, most vowels are expected to be mastered by three years of age. The information presented here is from the *Reference Manual for Communicative Sciences and Disorders* by Raymond D. Kent (Austin, TX: Pro-Ed, 1994).

SPEECH AND LANGUAGE CONCERNS*

(15 months–5 years)

Delayed Speech and Language

When Is Speech and Language Delayed?

We know that all children do not talk at the same age, but most children begin to use simple words when they are about 15 months old. Usually by the age of three, a child has a word for almost everything and strings words along in 2-3 word (or longer) "sentences." If speech has not developed satisfactorily by this time, parents should consult a speech pathologist to see what is causing the delay.

This late development in talking is known as delayed speech and language. It can be caused by many factors, including hearing loss, slow development (retardation), emotional problems, poor environment, lack of stimulation, frequent or prolonged illness, etc. Most of the time the child is normal in all areas except for speech and language development.

What Is Delayed Speech and Language?

Delayed speech and language is often no speech at all; grunts and gestures may be used as a method of communicating after age 2½. The child may still be using only single words. Sentences, when present, are often incomplete or of poor quality. The child may have difficulty understanding and/or following directions.

If the child has speech it is usually very difficult to understand. In addition to the fairly common habit of substituting one sound for another (wake/lake), the child often omits a number of sounds (up tai/upstairs). Often, too, the words are so distorted that one must guess at their meaning. In this type of speech, the child may

lack coordination of the lips, tongue, jaws, and/or soft palate.

The speech pathologist evaluates the child's speech, language, and hearing, attempts to find and remove, whenever possible, the cause of the difficulty, and institutes a program of speech and language training when indicated.

Helping the Child with Delayed Speech and Language

The speech pathologist will make suggestions to the parents for improving speech and language development at home. For the child three years and older, preschool placement may be recommended along with, or in place of, speech therapy.

There is much the family can do to help speech and language development, even when the child is receiving speech and language therapy.

Possible Speech and Language Problems

Referral for a speech and language evaluation should be made if difficulty in any of the following areas is noted:

1. The child is not talking *at all* by the age of two, i.e., doesn't say "ma-ma" or "no," etc.
2. He is still not using two- to three-word sentences by the age of three.
3. His speech is largely unintelligible after the age of three.
4. The child is leaving off many beginning consonants after the age of three.
5. Sounds are more than a year late in appearing in the child's speech according to their developmental sequences.
6. The child uses mostly vowel sounds in his speech after the age of two and one-half years.
7. His word endings are consistently missing after the age of five.

---

*Reprinted with the permission of the Speech Pathology and Audiology Department, Fairmont Hospital, San Leandro, California.

8. Sentence structure is noticeably faulty at the age of five.
9. He is making speech errors after the age of seven.
10. The child is noticeably non-fluent.
11. Voice is a monotone, too loud or too soft, or of a poor quality that may indicate a hearing loss.
12. Voice is too high or too low for his age or sex.
13. The child sounds as if he were talking through his nose, or as if he had a cold all the time.
14. His speech has abnormal rhythm, rate, and inflection after the age of five.
15. The child is having learning problems in school, especially with reading and writing.
16. He is embarrassed and disturbed by his speech at any age.

Normal Non-fluency

This section discusses one of the phases of normal speech development—"normal non-fluencies"—and offers suggestions for helping the child during this period.

During the early years of language development, there are times when a small child finds it difficult to talk. He often repeats sounds, words, or phrases and sometimes has difficulty in getting words out at all. This usually occurs during periods of stress, excitement, illness, or rapid language development. Since this is a normal part of growing up, and the child is getting the feeling of speech, his attention should not be directed to his manner of speaking. Those in his environment should not become too concerned and try to correct him with such remarks as "Say that over again," "Say that without stuttering," "Take a deep breath," "Slow down," or similar well meant, but frequently harmful advice. If his attention is called to his way of speaking, he is likely to feel that his speech is different from that of others. He might begin to react in ways that may cause serious trouble in speaking. He may hear himself labeled a "stutterer" and begin to think that his way of talking is very wrong and unacceptable.

Recommendations

To aid those in the child's environment in handling the child during speech development, we recommend the following:

1. Keep the child in as good physical condition as possible.
2. See that he gets plenty of rest.
3. See that his meals are regular and well balanced.
4. Let him choose which hand he wishes to use.
5. Make the home situation as pleasant as possible by avoiding friction and conflict in his presence.
6. Avoid comparisons between him and other children.
7. Make certain you are not expecting too much or setting too high standards for a child of his age and ability.
8. Eliminate emotional strain and undue excitement as much as possible.
9. Accept his way of talking without showing disapproval, fear, embarrassment, irritation, or surprise. Advise all relatives, friends, and acquaintances to do likewise.
10. Let him talk without interrupting him and without making suggestions as to how he should speak.
11. Give him time to express himself without supplying words.
12. Encourage him to take part in all school and family activities without forcing him to speak or "show off."
13. Find ways to make talking a pleasant experience for him. Games, rhymes, and stories may be used to encourage speaking.
14. Remember that easy repetitions and prolongations are normal in the speech of young children and should not be called "stuttering."

PRESCHOOL SPEECH AND LANGUAGE*

(2–5 years)

Language Help at Home

1. Build your child's self-confidence by praising him for his successes, no matter how minor. Don't compare him to other members of the family or friends.
2. Talk to him about his ideas, opinions, and experiences. Let him know that you consider his thoughts and experiences important.
3. Read stories to your child and ask him questions as you read. For example, "What do you think will happen next?" "Why did the children go into the house?"
4. Take your child on planned trips. Point out road signs, places, and things of interest. Encourage him to talk about what he sees.
5. Build on what your child already knows. Make references to objects or experiences that he is familiar with. Tell him stories based on his experiences.
6. Develop your child's vocabulary during family activities. For example, when in a department store, point out the elevator, sales person, money.
7. Demonstrate the meaning of words. Hop while saying "hop"; hold a book while saying "book."
8. Discuss colors, shapes, and sizes. Ask your child to point out similarities and differences. "What color is this apple?" "Which pencil is longer?" "Who is taller, Mommy or Daddy?"
9. Work on rhyming words. Have your child select one word from a series that does not rhyme. "Hay, play, top, say. Which word is different from the others?"
10. Work with words that start with the same sound. Have your child choose the word that does not start with the same sound. "Man, mother, house, mouse. Which word starts with a different sound?"
11. Encourage your child to discriminate between pictures, "Which picture has more people?" Show him pictures of varying numbers of animals and talk to him about what he sees. Ask him simple questions, such as, "This paper has a picture of one dog, doesn't it? How many dogs are there on this paper? Are there more dogs here or there?"
12. Play simple games to help your child develop memory. Show him three objects, have him turn away, remove one, and then ask him which one is missing.
13. Talk with your child about the position of one object in relationship to other objects. The food is *in* the refrigerator. The pencil is *on* the table. The ball is *under* the chair. Play games where your child is asked to put the block in the box, under the table, behind the chair, etc.
14. Let your child practice coordination between eyes and hands through tracing, coloring, cutting, pasting, and working with playdough. Have him feel, hold, and trace familiar shapes, including squares, triangles, rectangles, circles, and ovals. Ask your child to draw pictures and cut them out. Have him assemble puzzles. Draw an incomplete picture and ask your child to fill in the missing part.
15. Encourage your child to speak in complete sentences.
16. If your child watches television, try to view as a family and discuss what you see.
17. Check your child's physical condition periodically. Pay particular attention to hearing and sight ability.
18. Maintain a relaxed and calm atmosphere in the home. Your child should not be pressured to learn rapidly.

*Reprinted with permission of the Speech Pathology and Audiology Department, Fairmont Hospital, San Leandro, California.

A Guide for Parents

The speech of young children is frequently not understandable. Many children do not have perfect speech for some time after entering kindergarten. During the pre-school years it is more important for your child to have a happy personality and be able to express his ideas than to say words correctly. However, there is a great deal you can do to help him improve his speech. The following suggestions are given to aid you in helping your child to develop good speech.

Good Health Promotes Good Speech Development. Your Child Will Develop Better Speech If He Has:

1. A well-balanced diet.
2. A reasonably regular mealtime routine.
3. A happy mealtime atmosphere without stress and strain.
4. A regular bedtime routine (children of this age should sleep approximately 10-12 hours).
5. Quiet times or a regular nap routine.
6. Opportunity for active play and companionship with children.
7. A variety of healthful outdoor play activities.
8. Independence from the family commensurate with age.

You Can Expect Your Pre-school Child To:

1. Be interested in any activity for only a short time.
2. Be energetic and restless.
3. Have negative behavior.
4. Be more difficult to handle when he is tired, hungry, or ill.
5. Display his temper when he is unable to make you understand his speech.
6. Be unaware of his speech difficulty.
7. Cry, be unhappy, refuse to talk, walk away, or be generally negative if you try to correct his speech errors.
8. Say new words better than words he learned at an earlier age.

9. Use isolated words better than continuous speech.
10. Change his speech only gradually.

You Can Help Your Child Improve His Speech If You Will Avoid:

1. Correcting errors in his speech.
2. Making him aware of his speech problem.
3. Discussing his speech problem in his presence.
4. Trying to force your child to talk.
5. Using penalties or threats to make him talk.
6. Asking unnecessary questions to make him use speech.
7. Showing signs of being disturbed or embarrassed when others comment on his speech.
8. Making your child say words over to say them better.
9. Comparing his speech with that of other children.
10. Holding your child to adult standards of behavior, such as table manners or sitting still.
11. Holding your child to adult speech standards. At this age, ability to express ideas is more important than correct pronunciation, grammar, or adult vocabulary.

It Will Hasten Your Child's Speech Improvement If You:

1. Listen for the thought he is trying to express rather than for the speech errors.
2. Take the time to listen to his conversation.
3. Try to recognize as much of your child's speech as possible. Listen for vowels and parts of words. Ask him to show you what he wants if you don't understand him upon repetition.
4. Make all speech enjoyable—correction of speech responses at this age may delay the speech development.
5. Are satisfied with the speech your child uses; being corrected is not fun.
6. Occasionally help your child by casually talking for him if he cannot make himself understood.
7. Allow all talking to be voluntary, but encourage conversation.
8. Provide opportunities for your child to help you and help himself. This may take more of the adult's time but provides a good learning situation.

9. Substitute picture books and recommended games for roughhousing or wrestling, especially at bedtime.

10. Give your child the feeling that you accept him as he is—including his speech—and that you are entirely satisfied with him.

11. Give your child love and affection freely and build a home situation in which your child feels secure.

12. Gain the understanding and cooperation of family, relatives, friends, and child care providers, in carrying out suggestions to improve your child's speech.

13. Give your child an equal opportunity to express his thoughts without interruption at family gatherings such as dinner time.

part five

TEACHING ABOUT TWO-YEAR-OLDS

(2–3 years)

1

HOW TWO-YEAR-OLDS THINK

background/preparation

Goals to Work Toward in Presenting This Topic

Many parents are eager to learn what is going on inside their child's mind—how he or she thinks. Knowing this, they feel, can help to explain some of the major changes they see in their two-year-old's behavior and make it easier for them to set limits in a flexible and patient manner.

The general goals to work toward in this topic are: (1) to help parents learn how the world looks from a child's point of view; (2) to help parents understand why a child does what he does. The specific goals are: (1) to help parents discuss what their child is asking about or showing interest in, that is, what is on their child's mind; (2) to have parents share with each other some of the common misunderstandings between parent and child; (3) to have parents begin to understand why child-parent differences can contribute to many kinds of difficult behaviors and conflicts.

Typical Parental Interests and Concerns About This Topic

1. Overnight, my child changed personality; she used to be very agreeable and now we have a clash of wills constantly. Is she going to grow out of this?

2. We have been clashing a lot over who is going to have their way. What is going on inside my child's head?

3. How do you handle all those questions that they ask over and over again?

4. We try to give Mara choices whenever possible so she doesn't feel we're always telling her what to do; sometimes this works fine and other times she gets very upset.

5. David gets upset when he sees something very different or broken like when a manikin's arm was off in the department store. Actually, he likes things to always be the same. He really seemed frightened one day when he saw me with sunglasses and a big floppy hat.

Areas of Information You Will Need to Learn About to Teach This Topic[1]

- The meaning and purpose of the two-year-old's struggle for autonomy and why there is a change in the personality of many two-year-olds.
- The sequence of events in this struggle and how long it lasts.

1. Much of this information, for this topic and all others in this part, can be found in the "Additional Information for Parents" sections of the topics.

- What two-year-olds are trying to learn about, for example, why things happen and what makes things work.
- The nature of a two-year-old's language development and the limitations of this "concrete" phase.
- The specific difficulties parents of two- to three-year-olds must deal with in their children, for example, frustration, the tendency to demand, the struggle for independence, rigidity.

Family Dynamics—What This Topic Means Psychologically to Parent and Child

During the two- to three-year-old stage, parents must deal with the problems their child comes up against as she tries to understand all about her world. Many parents find this a difficult task and feel impatient or unable to understand what their child is trying to learn. Parents often find their answers aren't satisfying to their child, and feel frustration and anger with their child's narrow meanings of words.

A two- to three-year-old child has a tremendously limited cognitive understanding of the world and only a rudimentary control of her emotions. She wants to know things now; has a great deal of trouble waiting for things; misunderstands a great deal; and has *many* inaccurate assumptions about things (for example, Mommy and Daddy know everything, like the name and destination of *everyone* walking down the street).

Sample Concern of Parents[2]

Concern	Critical Issues
My child asks questions over and over. First, I try to repeat my answers. Then I say it in other words. Sometimes I get sarcastic,	—Child repeats questions. —Parent tries to answer him, and works at it.

and eventually, I just get angry. Why can't he understand me the first time? Is he just doing it for attention?

—Parent gets frustrated and angry.
—Parent wonders why child can't comprehend the answer. Is that the child's way of getting parents to focus on him?

Key Questions

1. What are some of the possible reasons children ask questions?
2. What are the possible reasons they keep repeating their questions?
3. Why do you think you're getting frustrated?
4. What is the balance of your child's day like, especially in terms of time with you? Does he have other ways of being with you besides asking you questions over and over?

For the group

5. What are some of the reasons children ask questions over and over?
6. What are your feelings when you can't seem to find a way to satisfy your child's questions?
7. What have you found to be helpful to your child and yourself when he repeats questions?

Readings and Other Resources[3]

Ames, Louise and Ilg, Frances, *Your Two-Year-Old* (New York: Dell, 1983), Chapter 1, 2, 4 and 5.
Dodson, Fitzhugh, How to Parent (New York: Dutton 1971), pp. 98–106.
*Fraiberg, Selma, *The Magic Years* (New York: MacMillan, 1966).
Growing Child (Lafayette, Ind.: Dunn & Hargitt, 1995 [updated annually]). To order, call (800) 927-7289.
*Hussey-Gardner, Brenda, *Parenting to Make a Difference* (Palo Alto, Cal.: VORT, 1992), Chapter 1.
Leach, Penelope, *Your Baby and Child, Rev. Ed.* (New York: Knopf, 1989), pp. 334–355 and 422–434.

2. Usually there are *few* concerns about this topic. Parents have interest in the subject but not many real concerns.

3. Readings marked with an * are the most highly recommended. The work of Rose Bromwich is highly recommended for information on the topics in this part and is cited in Appendix A. Articles from *Working Mother, Parents' Magazine, Parenting,* and *Child* are often good sources of current information on the topics in this part.

teaching/presentation

Homework

The homework assignment "Children's Thinking" aims at encouraging parents to pay close attention to what their child is saying. This can help them to begin to understand what their child is trying to learn about and what occupies his thoughts and catches his attention.

Practical Suggestions or Strategies for Teaching This Topic

• This topic is one of the very few that has been made part of the series because *the instructor* feels it provides an important foundation for work with all later topics. For this reason and because of the nature of the topic itself, it can be difficult for parents to really get into this discussion. Examples from you are particularly important to its success.

• There is a tendency for this topic to veer off into a problem-solving session on limit-setting issues. Prevent this by telling the parents, before you begin, when specific limit-setting issues will be dealt with and why it's important to understand children's thinking and behavior first. If a parent brings up a discipline problem anyway, lead her back to the topic under discussion by saying, "What does that tell us about what's going on inside your child's mind?"

Mini-lecture and Lead-off Questions for Discussion

A good way to lead into the discussion of this topic is to start with a mini-lecture and then ask questions that encourage parents to report aspects of their homework observation. By the end of the session, you can help them summarize some of the major issues that explain how two-year-olds think; hopefully the discussion will shed some light on why some difficult parent-child conflicts exist.

Two-year-olds are often difficult to understand, both in their language and their behavior. Some don't have much language and those that do often make many associations but may not truly understand meanings, for example, they've just learned how to use a phrase or expression at the right moment but don't understand what it says. From the words they use, it seems they should understand the things we're saying, but often they don't. Moreover, two-year-olds often get confused about causality, and when things happen coincidentally, children of this age may believe they caused it. Their understanding of what is possible in the physical world is quite tenuous, as those of you who have tried to explain to your child why you can't get him the moon will recognize. It's very interesting, in fact, to watch two-year-olds at a magic show. From their point of view, nothing surprising is happening. Not for several years after this age will a child really find a magic show to be "magic."

Let's begin our work by trying to get inside the mind of a two-year-old and seeing how things look from his point of view. Using your homework, what have you found that interests your child? What did he or she comment on or ask about during the past week?

As parents begin to volunteer observations about their child, such as, She always wants to know where Daddy is (Grandma, her friend) or She tells what she is doing as she is doing it or He wants to know what each sound he hears is and what's making it—comment on each and try to put the statement into perspective. (After the group gets the idea, you can let other parents make those comments if you think it would be helpful.) Your comments on the above examples could be as simple as, **She's trying to check out what these important**

CHILDREN'S THINKING

(2–3 years)

In order to help us all understand the way two-year-olds think, take some time during a period of several days and write down some of your child's comments, observations, and questions. If your child does not have many words yet, just note down some of the things that seem to be on his/her mind.

1. What kinds of questions is your child asking?

2. What comments or observations has your child made which demonstrates his concrete thinking?

3. What are some misunderstandings you have experienced with your child because of your different points of view?

Parent's name _____ Date _____ Child's age _____

people's worlds are like when she can't see them, putting them somewhere so they don't just disappear; **She is building a concept of who she is through what she does, and is practicing her rapidly expanding vocabulary; He wants to do a thorough and immediate investigation of unknowns so he can really find out what is in this world and what everything does.** This type of simple but clear comment can be very helpful toward decreasing parents' confusion. After you have summarized both the areas the children in your group are showing interest in, such as parts of the body and important people in their lives, and the meaning of some of these interests, go on to the next part of the discussion as follows.

Now try to think of any times you may remember when your child understood something in a completely different way than you meant. (Give examples to help the parents understand what you mean, for example, **Did you drop your fork on purpose? —No I dropped it on the floor; "I have a frog in my throat" —"Is it going to jump out on me?"**

After the parents have shared some of the misunderstandings they've experienced, begin to summarize, asking the parents to contribute ideas on what's going on inside a child's mind and how hard he is working to try to understand the people and the world around him. As you talk, distribute the handout "How Two-Year-Olds Think" but mention only those points on it that haven't already been summarized.

If you think the group is really benefiting from the discussion, you may wish to work toward the goal of having the parents relate the way two-year-olds think and behave to some of the major behavior difficulties parents of two-year-olds must cope with. Say something like: **What kinds of behavior in your children have you found to be particularly difficult to deal with?** After parents have contributed some examples of this type of behavior (repetitious questions, tantrums, and so on), ask them, **What light can we shed on why children behave in each of those ways now that we understand more of what's going on inside them?** Help the parents brainstorm each problem behavior, guiding them to further insight into the problem.

Now you can deal with any of the group's concerns that have not been spoken to (see the "Typical Parental Interests and Concerns" section

[p. 259] for examples). Concerns that are related to limit-setting issues are best saved for that topic's discussion.

Additional Information for Parents

• Children are exploring all kinds of areas in their expanding world. Some of their main interests are:
— People—where they are; who they are; where they are going; when they are coming back; how they feel;
— Themselves—what they can do; how they affect people; how they can get others to do what they want;
— Predictability—if they can count on things looking and staying the same;
— The physical world—what makes things work; why things do what they do; what things *they* can make work;
— Control—finding out if their parents control everything; what they themselves control;
— Labeling—giving names, colors, etc., to things; practicing new words and phrases.
• Children learn a great deal from people's responses to their behavior and from answers to their questions. They will repeat questions for many reasons but one of the least appreciated by parents is that a child's question doesn't always mean what an adult asking the same question would mean. Parents may need to try to figure out what was meant, and the child may keep repeating his question because it wasn't answered. This can be frustrating for parent and child, but it's good for a child to feel that his parents are trying to help him figure out some answers.
• Difficult behavior is not necessarily a permanent characteristic of a child. It is more likely related to the two-year-old's tendency to function in the present and his inability to wait for things.

Handouts

The handout for this topic, "How Two-Year-Olds Think—What's Going on Inside?" summarizes some of the major aspects of two-year-olds' emotional and cognitive functioning, helping to make them more understandable.

HOW TWO-YEAR-OLDS THINK—WHAT'S GOING ON INSIDE?

(2–3 years)

1. Two-year-olds tend to function in the *present*; they want things now and there often isn't much value to telling them what will be happening much later or on another day. It is, however, helpful to begin to talk in sequences: e.g. "After we go to the library, we'll have lunch and then go to grandma's." This gives them experience with time-oriented vocabulary, and helps support their need for predictability.

2. The "two's" tend to think *concretely,* for example, when you say you're "all tied up" or "I'm going to eat you all up" they may take you literally. At two, parents and caregivers need to increase their awareness of what and how they are speaking when their child can overhear them.

3. Halfway between the age of two and three is known to be the most contrary age. Children have times of being very assertive, domineering, and "dictatorial."

4. Two-year-olds can see two alternatives, but they can't inhibit themselves to try only one, that is, they can't think of one to the exclusion of the other. As a result, some can have great difficulty making a choice between two things you offer.

5. Two-year-olds can't handle lengthy verbal "dissertations" explaining things. Most children of any age have little tolerance for wordy explanations, especially in a discipline situation. Limit yourself to a few words.

6. "Two's" have a strong drive for independence but often can't manage the things they want to do. It is helpful to balance their day so there are opportunities for taking the time to let a child try to do things for herself.

7. "Two's" often like things to be done in the same way each time and have problems making transitions from one activity to another. It's hard for them to go from something familiar to something different. They often want things "just so" and seem to function "as a conservative who combats innovations."

8. When a two-year-old wants something and can't have it, he often gets frustrated and blocked. Sometimes he can't think of anything else unless you help him.

9. By the age of three, negativism has generally decreased quite a bit and most children are more eager to please again.

2

LIMIT SETTING

background/preparation

Goals to Work Toward in Presenting This Topic

Limit setting is a major topic to be covered in a two-year-old series because so many children of this age are engaged in a strong battle of wills with their parents, struggling over control. Parents can become quite disturbed by this parent-child entanglement.

The specific goals to work toward on this topic are (1) to teach parents general guidelines about limit setting, including its purpose and the importance of consistency; (2) to have parents share how it feels to set limits and what gets in the way of being consistent; (3) to have parents be able to integrate what they have learned about the way children think with their own limit-setting attitudes and techniques; (4) to have parents learn how much they can expect of two-year-olds and how a variety of two-year-olds behave; (5) to help parents develop strategies for identifying and solving recurring and future discipline problems; (6) to help parents learn a number of useful limit-setting techniques.

Typical Parental Interests and Concerns About This Topic

1. My child used to be easygoing; overnight he's turned into a tyrant. I don't know how to deal with him.
2. Jason and I are often involved in power struggles. He's determined to have his way and I'm determined he won't. At times he even hits us.
3. Some days quickly degenerate into one battle after another. How can I turn the situation around when I'm so angry?
4. Caitlin is very opinionated about her clothes and if I want her to wear a particular outfit she doesn't like, it's fireworks. If she's wearing something she likes, she won't take it off without a fight either.
5. Scott often wants to do everything "all by myself." But so often he can't and that makes him very frustrated.
6. After a long day at work, I often find I'm too exhausted to discipline or I just want to please Jesse. Being away all day makes it hard to be consistent.
7. Jenna contradicts everything we say, even when we're answering her questions. She is much more cooperative with her sitter.

Areas of Information You Will Need to Learn About to Teach This Topic

- General principles of limit setting.
- What can be expected of two-year-olds in terms of their ability to control their behavior and their developmental skills.
- How to analyze problems that parents have (see the "Sample Concern" section on this page.)[1]
- The most useful limit-setting techniques for dealing with children of this age.

Family Dynamics—What This Topic Means Psychologically to Parent and Child

At the time a child approaches the age of two, society warns parents that the "Terrible Two's" are about to begin. Although the anticipation of this stage can be frightening, most parents usually find out that their anxiety is quickly replaced by confusion about what their child's behavior means. Parents often worry about the extent of their child's negativism and often feel they have created some sort of tyrant. They are then faced with the moment-to-moment question of how to work with their child—how much to bend and when to stay firm. Parents frequently feel frustration and anger in confrontations with their child, and are not pleased with their own behavior.

While parents feel frustration, confusion, and anger, two-year-olds feel the need to have more control over what happens to them. Things have been done *to* them for two years, and now they want to change that pattern. During this year, language develops into a powerful tool, and two-year-olds enjoy determining just how much of an impact it can have on the people around them (for example, seeing what happens when they say "no" or "Mommy, *sit down*"). Children of this age see the world quite differently than adults, as far

as what catches and absorbs their attention; often they have a different sense of time as well. Since two-year-olds have trouble being denied what they want, have trouble making transitions, and don't have the skill to be as independent or as capable as they want to be, all kinds of parent-child conflicts are likely.

Sample Concern of Parents

Concern	Critical Issues
Sara is terribly bossy. I find myself listening to her and then starting to let her do things she shouldn't. When I refuse her, she reacts with anything from grumpiness to a tantrum. When I try to get her to do something, she says "no," even when I think she'd want to cooperate because it's something she likes. I find myself more angry than I've ever been in my life.	—Child demands control. —Parent initially responds to commands with compliance. —Refusal by parent brings on child's negative behavior. —Child tends to say "no" to many of parent's initial requests. —Parent is disturbed by the amount of anger she is experiencing.

Key Questions

1. What is Sara's temperament like compared to yours? Let's explore this while trying to remember why two-year-olds are bossy, and see if you can figure out a new way to respond to Sara when she gives you a command.
2. When you refuse to go along with Sara's commands, what do you say or do? Can you think of a particular example?

For the group

3. How can we get our children to cooperate when we ask them to do something? What do we know about why they tend to refuse?
4. Have any of you experienced an extreme amount of anger? What do you think it came from? Why was it so strong? (Help parents get at the feelings of incompetence that arise

---

1. The problem-solving suggestions in Part I:6 (p. 28) and the guide in Appendix E should also be useful for parents who are trying to understand how to analyze and deal with limit-setting issues.

when even a two-year-old won't listen to them. See if they can work through this feeling so the struggle is taken less personally.)

Readings and Other Resources

Ames, Louise Bates and Ilg, Frances, *Your Two-Year-Old* (New York: Dell, 1983), Chapters 2, 4, 6 and 8.

*Cherry, Clare, *Parents, Please Don't Sit On Your Kids* (Carthage, Ill.: Fearon Teacher Aids, 1985).

*Crary, Elizabeth, *Without Spanking or Spoiling, 2nd Ed.* (Seattle, Wash.: Parenting Press, 1993).

*Faber, Adele and Mazlish, Elaine, *How to Talk So Kids Will Listen and Listen So Kids Will Talk* (New York: Avon, 1982).

Galinsky, Ellen and David, Judy, *The Preschool Years* (New York: Ballantine, 1991), Chapter 1.

*Kurcinka, Mary, *Raising Your Spirited Child* (New York: Harper Collins, 1992).

Leach, Penelope, *Children First* (New York: Knopf, 1994), Chapter 6.

Nelsen, Jane, *Positive Discipline* (New York: Ballantine, 1987).

*Rothenberg, B. Annye, et al., *Parentmaking Educators Training Program* (Menlo Park, Cal.: Banster Press, 1993) Part III, Chapter 4 on Limit Setting.

teaching/presentation

Homework

There are two homework assignments for this topic. The first, "Discipline/Setting Limits," is used to help parents analyze in detail exactly what happens when they discipline their child. This kind of analysis usually makes parents much more aware of the sequence of events, the learning, and the feelings involved.

The second homework topic, "Conflicts," has two purposes: (1) to help parents obtain an overall picture of the major areas of conflicts they are experiencing; (2) to think about some new ways to deal with conflict situations. The second objective may make the discussion of limit-setting techniques more interesting to parents since they will be working on and improving problem areas, not waiting for their child to "grow out of them." (Also, see *PETP,* pp. 337–341 for additional homework sheets.)

Practical Suggestions or Strategies for Teaching This Topic

• The same sorts of suggestions made in the Toddler section on limit setting (see p. 205) would apply here as well. This topic should be placed in the series as soon as possible after "How a Two-Year-Old Thinks."

• The discussion should allow group members to learn how other parents deal with limit setting and how those parents feel about it.

• Limit setting actually involves so many parental interests and concerns that the topic can encompass nearly everything in the series. Use group member's home work to help them focus on *recurring conflicts* between parent and child. It can be helpful to look at problem solving from a preventitive standpoint, and then discuss intervention strategies.

• Find out, then group the kinds of problems the parents want to discuss. Then choose a few concerns and do some detailed problem solving with them. (This will keep the discussion from seeming like 10 private back-to-back counseling sessions.) Help the parents to see how each problem relates to their families as well, and strategies that can be applied in different situations.

DISCIPLINE/SETTING LIMITS

(2–3 years)

In this week's observation, we'd like you to focus on two situations where you had to discipline your child: one situation in which you were pleased about the outcome and one in which you weren't.

1. What was your child doing that caused you to discipline him/her?

   a.   b.

2. Why was your child behaving that way?

   a.   b.

3. What did you do to discipline him/her?

   a.   b.

4. What was your child's reaction?

   a.   b.

5. Why do you think he/she reacted that way?

   a.   b.

6. What do you think your child learned from this experience?

   a.   b.

7. How did you feel about the whole thing?

   a.   b.

8. What do you think you learned about handling your child?

   a.   b.

Parent's name _____ Date _____ Child's age _____

CONFLICTS

(2–3 years)

1. What are some of the main types of conflict that you find yourself involved in regularly with your two-year-old?

   a.   d.

   b.   e.

   c.   f.

2. What are some of your usual methods of handling these conflicts?

Parent's name _____ Date _____ Child's age _____

Mini-lecture and Lead-off Questions for Discussion[2]

When working with this topic, it is helpful to first relate "How Two-Year-Olds Think" to limit setting, and then go on to general limit-setting guidelines. This can avoid problems when parents begin to apply the guidelines at home and find they do not always work (because of the nature of two-year-olds, and because of the particular home situation). Specific problems can then be worked on, followed by a summary of realistic and useful techniques for setting limits with two-year-olds.

Sample mini-lecture

Last week we talked about how two-year-olds think and the common parent-child misunderstandings that can often lead to frustration, anger, tantrums, and guilt. This week we're going to focus on limit setting. First I'd like to talk about some major principles that are involved, such as firmness, consistency, and realistic expectations. The focus will be on parent-child conflicts—we'll save child-child conflicts for the session on relationships (or socializing) among children. After discussing the principles, I'd like to talk with you about specific issues you're currently facing with your children, and useful techniques you can use in your limit setting.

Discipline is a teaching process in which we instruct, train, and educate our children toward self-regulation. We must teach our children the rules of social behavior since it is these rules, regulations, and expectations that will regulate our children's conduct. When we set limits we are:

---

2. See the "Mini-lecture and Lead-offs" (p. 209) and "Additional Information (p. 210) in the 15 to 24 months section on limit setting for more information. Also, see Rothenberg, *PETP* for a chapter on Limit-setting (pp. 319–349). Beginning on p. 320, the presentation covers basic principles of limit-setting, what gets in the way of being consistent, and helping parents strengthen their limit-setting skills. Also included are prevention/intervention techniques, how to teach about husband-wife differences in limit-setting and problem-solving techniques.

- **Teaching children to avoid danger;**
- **Helping children to attain socially acceptable behavior (to have regard for others as well as for themselves);**
- **Showing our children that we care for them—children feel more secure with limits to follow (for example, keeping a child safe and within the range of socially acceptable behavior by not letting him climb on the dining room table);**
- **Helping children to control themselves;**
- **Putting a sense of organization and predictability into children's worlds;**
- **Helping ourselves and our children know what to expect of each other.**

Having a good parent-child relationship is the best basis for effective discipline. When a child knows you care he will most likely want to please you. Your child needs your focussed attention on a regular basis.

It is important to remember that the general rules and expectations you begin to establish now may remain in effect for many years, although the specific limits will change as your child acquires more skills and can control himself better. You might like to offer an example here, then go on: **Limit setting can be predominant in your relationship with your child at certain times, and it is sometimes hard to determine what the limits should be. It seems best to establish broad limits and then work on specific rules as the need for them arises. Each of your families will need to establish its own stance on limit setting.**

When you impose limits, try not to allow yourself to become trapped in a battle of wills. You may win the battle at the expense of your child's curiosity, enthusiasm, and self-esteem, or you may lose to a determined child's tantrums and negativism.

Guilt can do much to make limit setting ineffective. It can make us have poor expectations of our child and make us expect too much from ourselves. It can urge us to be unrealistically patient and cause us to vacillate when we need to be firm. We need to realize that it isn't always wrong to say 'no' and to remember to take time for ourselves— setting and enforcing limits is hard work and guilt should not be allowed to force parents into a tension-filled situation. Children need

well-defined and consistent limits. They forget easily and therefore need many repetitions or answers from their parents. When rules are being established, the child's developmental level and his style need to be considered; the rules should be reasonable, protective, and enforceable. Children will keep checking your limits until they're sure you really mean to keep them. It's harder on you when you break your own rules than if you don't. Also, it takes time for discipline strategies to work.

If you choose to, you can have parents get involved in your presentation by adding ideas on general limit setting guidelines. This helps avoid being lectured to.

After talking about ideal guidelines, talking about reality is very important to parents' feelings about themselves:

At our home, things can be very different on different days. Sometimes our children are in great shape, sometimes in terrible shape. The same is true for my husband and myself—some days are just terrible. Would someone be willing to describe a particularly bad day they've had? (Have one or more parents describe a bad day, including how they felt. Then have someone describe a good day, and go on to a discussion of how parents feel during and at the end of both of those kinds of days. Talk with parents about ways they deal with expectations and guilt.) When the group seems ready to go on, continue with the next section.

Now, let's find out from each other some of the major conflicts between our children and ourselves that are going on in our homes, and let's try to work on them, using the information and guidelines we've talked about so far. (You can provide some examples from the homework observations to give the group some concrete ideas of what you're talking about.) Take notes as the parents talk, and let the group know what you're doing. Explain that the class will spend several sessions working on the conflicts that have been described. Try to group the concerns and plan to devote the most time to those of more general interest. Very unique or difficult concerns may need to be handled in a phone consultation. (Ideas for dealing with a concern in detail can be found in the "Sample Concern" section, p. 266.)

When you have finished discussing the subject of limit setting (this may take several weeks), ask the group to help you summarize the techniques that have been talked about. Pass out the handout "Setting Limits" (see p. 274) and have the group bring up other ideas they've learned about. Tell them that as the series continues, there will be many opportunities to talk about setting limits in other areas.

Additional Information for Parents

• Parents and caregivers need to learn that there is a reason why many two-year-old children behave in an oppositional way, and that if they take a less personally involved attitude when such behavior occurs they will be able to feel less intense and upset with their children.

• A useful way to help parents with limit setting is to look first at preventitive strategies. For example, encourage parents to balance their child's day, making room for active and quiet times, social and alone times, structured and unstructured times, play and family business. Emphasize the importance of giving their child some uninterrupted attention each day, where no demands are being made on the child by the parent.

• Parents and caregivers need to develop motivational techniques they can use to make it easier for their child to cooperate. For example, instead of saying, "We *have* to go now" they could say, "Let's say good-bye to the flowers . . . bye-bye, see you another time; now let's say good-bye to the slide . . ." and so on. Such techniques are especially necessary for the primary caretaker. Help parents identify what motivates young children, e.g. play, independence, being with people, etc.

• Both parents and children have feelings and rights, but parents and caregivers need to remember that *they* are in charge even if their children have louder and more commanding voices. When parents start to feel "pushed," *that* moment is an appropriate time for a limit to be placed. All parents and caregivers have to decide for themselves, based on their own gut reactions, how much they can bend. They must also remember that their personal feelings are legitimate guides for limit setting.

3

SLEEP, FEARS, AND NIGHTMARES

background/preparation

Goals to Work Toward in Presenting This Topic

Most parents have some problems with or concerns about their child's sleep, both nap and nighttime. They are also concerned about the impact frightening experiences can have on their child. Sleep and fears are dealt with together in this section because fears can have significant effects on children's sleeping patterns in the form of nightmares and other manifestations.

The goals to work toward on these topics are: (1) to help parents learn more about the range of sleeping patterns in children and what is realistic to expect of their child; (2) to teach parents techniques with which to guide their child's sleep so that it will be more acceptable to the whole family; (3) to help parents learn about common fears in children and their causes; (4) to help parents learn how to diminish the impact on their child of the child's fears and nightmares.

Typical Parental Interests and Concerns About This Topic

1. My child is having trouble falling asleep at nap time. She finally falls asleep so late in the after-

noon and sleeps so long that she is up all evening.
2. My child is having a problem falling asleep at bedtime. The bedtime rituals are getting longer and longer and I'm just exhausted. Then she comes out again after we've finally said goodnight.
3. By the time my husband and I get home from work, make dinner, and give Krista some attention, it is ten o'clock. I worry she's not getting enough sleep but if we put her to sleep earlier, when will we ever see her?
4. Sam is waking up several times during the night. I don't think he's hungry or thirsty, but just seems to want company. After we've comforted him, he goes back to sleep but I don't like getting up all night.
5. My child has started to be afraid of the dark, dogs and other animals, and even some people. I'm not sure what to do about it.
6. Ariel wakes up about once a month at night screaming. She's really frightened. I console her but she can't tell me what made her scream. Is this normal? What could be frightening her?
7. My child has started to talk about monsters a lot. I wonder what this means. She seems preoccupied but not really frightened.
8. My child was badly frightened on Halloween two weeks ago by all the children coming to the door in costume. Since then he

screams every time the doorbell rings. What should I do?

9. Evan will go to bed at naptime or bedtime easily when he's with his sitter but is very resistant with me. What can I do?

Areas of Information You Will Need to Learn About to Teach This Topic

- Typical sleep problems of two-year-olds.
- How individual styles influence sleep needs.
- Useful techniques for improving children's sleep patterns.
- The development of fears in pre-school children.
- Common childhood fears.
- Techniques for helping children master their fears and nightmares.

Family Dynamics—What This Topic Means Psychologically to Parent and Child

Sleep

Sleep problems are extremely common in young children. They are related to both the child's temperament—his activity and energy levels—and the parents' ability to set sleep-related limits. Parents are sometimes unwilling to set firm limits in this area because they feel their child wouldn't wake up or stay up unless he really needed to, and he must therefore need to see them during the night.

Children have little control over their sleeping and waking up, but they may see sleep as a separation from their parents and develop negative feelings about it. If their pattern of sleep becomes less regular, as it very easily can, they may feel some negativism from their parents about it and a demand by them for a return to former patterns. This may intensify the problem, which is difficult for children to do anything about.

Fears

When a child experiences fears, parents may sometimes feel that they are raising an overanxious son or daughter, and this is worrisome. Even when parents have a less guilty perspective on their child's fears, they still feel the need to help overcome the fear so they and their child will not have to live in a very restricted world—one that avoids the sound of vacuum cleaners or fire engines or the sight of dogs, or whatever.

From the child's point of view, certain things frighten him. He doesn't really know why, but he does want to avoid these things and have his parents protect him from them. He strives for control of his fears—sometimes acting them out in his play—and derives comfort from those who have mastered them and can lend him some of their strength and acceptance of the situation.

Sample Concern of Parents

Concern	Critical Issues
My child just suddenly seemed to start to be afraid of things. She's afraid of the dark and of unexpected noises. She says there are monsters in her room. We try to explain to her and show her that there aren't really any and there's nothing to be afraid of. She continues to be fearful and these fears certainly aren't going away. Do you think this is just a stage? Is there something I can do that will be more helpful to her?	—Sudden onset of fears. —Specific fears. —Parent's attempt to talk child out of fears. —Fears not decreasing. —Is child normal? Will fears pass? —Parent's desire to help child; frustration.

Key Questions

For this type of concern, parents need additional information more than questions. (See the "Additional Information" section, p. 278.)

Readings and Other Resources

Ames, Louise B. and Ilg, Frances, *Your Two-Year-Old* (New York: Dell, 1983), pp. 79–82 and 109.

*Cuthbertson, Joanne and Schevill, Susie, *Helping Your Child Sleep Through the Night* (Garden City, N.Y.: Doubleday and Co., 1985).

Ferber, Richard, *Solve Your Child's Sleep Problems* (New York: Simon and Schuster, 1985).

Galinsky, Ellen and David, Judy, *The Preschool Years* (New York: Ballantine, 1991), pp. 107–112 and 216–223.

Growing Child (Lafayette, Ind.: Dunn & Hargitt, 1995 [updated annually]), issues 2 years 4 months and 2 years 8 months. To order, call (800) 927-7289.

Hyson, Marion, "Lobster on the Sidewalk," *Young Children* (Vol. 35, July 1979) pp. 54–60. (To order, call NAEYC: (800)-424-2460).

*Leach, Penelope, *Your Baby and Child, Rev. Ed.* (New York: Knopf, 1989) pp. 305–314, 328–332, 395–400 and 415–417.

Rothenberg, B. Annye, et al., *Parentmaking Educators Training Program* (Menlo Park, Cal.: Banster Press, 1993), Part III, Chapter 6 on Sleep.

What's A Parent to Do? A one hour video from the television show "20/20" (order by calling (800) 222-7500; cost, $19.98 plus $3.95 shipping and handling.) The 20-minute segment on sleep is the second of three segments in this video.

teaching/presentation

Homework

No homework observations have been developed for this topic since parents are generally very aware of any sleeping problems their children have. Describing details surrounding fears is usually somewhat harder for them to do, however, and you may wish to develop a homework assignment that asks parents to think about one or two fear situations their children have experienced and then describe them along with what provoked them. Parents could note what they feel might be useful approaches for helping the child with his fear, and why.

Practical Suggestions or Strategies for Teaching This Topic

Since interrupted sleep can cause a great deal of stress to family members, it is recommended that this group of topics be discussed during the first few weeks of the series.

Mini-lecture and Lead-off Questions for Discussion[1]

Discussion of the topic of sleep can be easily begun by summarizing some of the various concerns about sleep that parents have expressed during orientation, on their limit setting homeworks, or elsewhere, and mentioning that you'd like to begin work on any of the group's individual concerns. If no one brings up a concern, call on one of the parents whom you know had a sleep concern and see if she'd like to describe it to the group. Then you can deal with specific sleep concerns as they come up.

At some point during the discussion of sleep, nightmares and fears are usually brought up. When this happens, or when you feel ready to turn to this topic, begin with a talk that includes the normalcy of fears, common fears in young children, and why fears develop (see the readings section above for information on these areas). Then find out the kinds of questions the parents want to work on, organize them, and begin working through them.

---

1. Rothenberg, *PETP* includes a chapter on sleep (pp. 383–410). Refer to suggested presentation (pp. 384–393) for important information on guiding parents in common sleep problems and changing sleep patterns for toddlers and pre-schoolers.

Additional Information for Parents

Fears

Sometimes a potential fear can be made less intense by the parents before it becomes a reality. For example, when a train the child is riding in suddenly goes through a dark tunnel and is likely to frighten him, a parent can hold the child and try to speak in ways that will decrease the scariness of the situation: "It's getting dark, dark, dark. Soon it will be light, light, light." Often the child will join in the assuring words and actions instead of being paralyzed with fear. In that way he can do or say something that decreases the depth of his fear.

When a child is already fearful, perhaps of gorillas in his bedroom, a logical investigation to prove there are no gorillas in the room does little good. What the child needs instead is some way to gain control over his fears. One way could be by the parent teaching the child that he can make the gorilla stay away and showing him how to do it: "Let's tell the gorilla that he has to stay outside because Mommy and Daddy don't allow gorillas inside; I'll walk him outside now and lock the door. Do you want to come with me?" Whatever way is used, the parent needs to show the child that she accepts the fear—is not afraid of the gorilla but accepts the child's fear of it—and wishes to help the child achieve some mastery or control over it.[2] Suggest approaches the child can use on his own.

When a child's fears are extreme—perhaps she screams every time the doorbell rings because of a frightening experience when the doorbell rang on Halloween—it is helpful to try to gently desensitize the child to such an experience. This can be done by taking the source of the fear—someone coming to the door and ringing the doorbell—breaking it down into small steps, and introducing them again one at a time in a non-threatening way. For example, parents could make a playhouse with a door but not call it a door and play games with the house with their child; use a small

bicycle bell and let the child practice making it ring; play games with an interior door in the house when the child knows it's Mommy or Daddy on the other side, and so on.

Sleep

Since the major concern of most parents in this area is that their child is not sleeping as well as expected, it is helpful for you to know what normal sleep patterns are as well as the history of individual children's sleeping. You will also need to know the parents' limits and previous methods of handling sleep problems.

As children reach the age of two, they can often stay up longer in the afternoon before falling asleep for a nap. Parents or caregivers *may* need to start a nap earlier and wake a child up from it so his bedtime doesn't become too late. Many children are very grouchy at the end of a long afternoon nap and an appealing snack or project can help both the child and the parent or caregiver at this time.

As a child gets closer to the age of three, he may not be ready for his nap until *very* late in the afternoon. This is a very difficult transition period—from taking a nap to not taking one—for everyone concerned, because if a child starts his nap at 4:30 or 5:00 p.m. he may sleep until between 6:30 and 8:00 p.m. and not be ready for sleep again until the end of the evening. A good strategy is to enforce "rest time" for up to an hour, when the child is expected to stay in his room, but does not necessarily fall asleep. Families also sometimes solve this problem by letting their child doze off for a few minutes during the late afternoon and then waking him for supper.

The length of bedtime rituals need to be controlled by parents. Children do want their parents to stay with them as long as possible or come back in with a drink for them, so parents need to be kind but firm when bedtime comes. This can be hard because parents are often tired themselves and hate to end the day thinking of their child being unhappy. Encourage parents to have a very defined routine which can include bath, story, backrub, etc.

It seems that a child's "biological clock" can easily be "set" to waken him at regular times during the night. These awakenings can begin because of colds, teething, hot nights, bad

---

2. A similar principle applies to nightmares but it usually takes several years for a child to feel any kind of mastery or control over them.

weather outside, or a number of other reasons, and they are very resistant to stopping. Parents usually first try to wait out the awakenings, hoping the child will soon start sleeping through the night again. Many parents have very ambivalent feelings about setting limits around sleep. It is important for parents to understand that children sometimes cry and call for their parents in the night because they don't know *how* to put themselves back to sleep, not because they are emotionally insecure, or they want to play. Parents can become motivated to work on sleep issues when they become aware of how their own fatigue takes away from the quality of family life, and when they realize that sleeping independently is a *skill* that can actually be taught to the child.

In a parenting group, frequently there are one or more parents who have successfully overcome a sleep issue like getting out of bed at bedtime or middle-of-the-night waking. It is helpful to have parents share their stories, emphasizing key ingredients such as:

1. an attachment to a lovey (e.g. blanket or stuffed animal). Parents can encourage this by giving the child a lovey during the day for comfort.
2. a bedtime routine which is nurturing and not rushed

3. a regular bed time so child becomes accustomed to falling asleep at that hour, and does not become overtired.

When a child seeks attention after bedtime, parents should check in with the child without being reinforcing. Having a phrase like "It's nighttime, we are all sleeping now. I'll see you when it's light out" is helpful, as well as keeping a monotonous, "robot-like" tone and demeanor. (See Rothenberg, *PETP* chapter on sleep for more detailed sleep guidance, pp. 383–410).

Handouts

The *Parentmaking Educators Training Program* (Menlo Park, Cal.: Banster Press, 1993) has a chapter on sleep (pp. 383–410) that includes handouts to identify children's sleep requirements at different ages, factors which influence a child's sleep, and strategies for implementing a sleep plan. Parents also can be referred to sections of Molly Mason Jones' book *Guiding Your Child from Two to Five* (pp. 228–241 for material about sleep, pp. 274–296 for information about fears).

4

NUTRITION [1]

background/preparation

Goals to Work Toward in Presenting This Topic

Most parents of two-year-olds have long-standing concerns about their child's eating patterns and attitudes and find many of these problems hard to change by themselves.

The goals to work toward on this topic are: (1) to help parents learn the real norms, not just what books call norms, of what and how much children eat; (2) to help parents get support and ideas for working on their "real" problems; (3) to help parents identify their own attitudes toward food and their child's need for and feelings toward food; (4) to help parents learn more about good nutrition and other related areas (for example, how to improve food appeal and taste for their child).

Typical Parental Interests and Concerns About This Topic [2]

1. My child eats only a few kinds of food. I'm afraid he isn't getting a very balanced diet. Should I give him some vitamins? When can we expect him to try new foods like he used to?
2. Shira says she's hungry (or thirsty) all day long. How is it possible that she needs so many snacks? She's started to climb into the kitchen cupboards and help herself to all kinds of things.
3. My daughter loves to eat—at meals and any time. She just keeps eating and can't seem to stop herself.
4. Michael is still taking a bottle when he goes to sleep at nap time and nighttime. I'm thinking I'd like to wean him but I don't know the best way or even if this is the right time.
5. Jordan eats well at his daycare I'm told, but at home he will barely touch his dinner, and begins to act out at the table. How can we have a meal together at the end of a long day for all of us?

---

1. Eating behavior is not included here as part of the broad topic of nutrition but is discussed within the 15- to 24-month section on nutrition (p. 214). Most of the information and handouts in this topic are for parents of 15- to 24-month-olds as well as two- to three-year-olds.

---

2. At the two- to three-year-old level, parents' concerns about nutrition usually are related to a particular problem they are having with their child's eating, rather than to an interest in general development norms.

6. When can we expect our daughter to eat what we serve so I don't have to cook separately for her?
7. My husband wants to know whether we can expect Alex to sit with us through a whole meal. What can we expect in the way of manners from him?

Areas of Information You Will Need to Learn About to Teach This Topic

- The typical amount of growth—height and weight—in a child this age, and how a two-year-old's appetite is different from that of a younger and an older child.
- The amount and kinds of food two-year-olds typically eat, and how they like their food prepared and served (for example, small portions, moist meat, and so on).
- What makes for a balanced diet, a safe diet, and an appealing diet.
- The highly allergenic foods and the very healthy foods.
- Realistic expectations for a two-year-old's table manners and for his behavior as it relates to nutritition (for example, brushing teeth).
- How the home environment, including the parent's own attitude toward eating, influences two-year-olds.
- Things that can be done to change unsatisfactory eating habits.
- Ways to include in a parent's expectation the individuality of her child.

Family Dynamics—What This Topic Means Psychologically to Parent and Child

Parents feel that proper nutrition is critical to the life and well-being of their child. More and more, current books on nutrition are supporting this feeling, sometimes making food even more of an emotional issue. Often a parent feels that how well her child is fed is a real indication of how good a parent she is. Therefore, when a child does not eat something a parent has prepared for her, the parent can become very upset.

On the other hand, children sometimes feel that they are being asked to perform at meal

times, to meet their parent's needs rather than their own. Depending on how food and meal times are handled in their homes, meals can be a source of tension two-year-olds want to get away from as soon as possible; a source of relaxation and closeness that they want to prolong; or a battleground that is exhilarating but exhausting.

Sample Concern of Parents

Concern	Critical Issues
My child isn't interested in eating at all. Occasionally she'll eat an enormous amount and then won't eat at all for several days. Since I never know when she's going to be hungry, I try hard to prepare an attractive, well-balanced meal. Most of the time I end up angry and frustrated because she doesn't eat what I about her health and wonder if she should be getting some extra vitamins.	—Child's lack of appetite. —Unpredictable interest in food. —Parent tries to give child nutritious diet. —Parent's anger and frustration. —Child's health; parent worried. —Need for dietary supplements.

Key Questions

1. What does your child actually eat and drink during the course of a day? How balanced is it?
2. How long has your child's lack of interest in food been evident?
3. What does food mean to your child? To you and your spouse?
4. What is your child's body type or size? What is her activity level?
5. How do you feel when your child isn't eating? How do you decide when and what she eats? How is food served? Who eats with your child?
6. Does your child eat differently with different people at home? In different places?
7. What does your child's pediatrician say about your child's health and her need for vitamins? (Note: Medically related questions are always

referred to a pediatrician because instructors are not medically trained.)

For the group

8. Have any of you felt that your child was eating much too little? How did you handle that?
9. How do you feel when your child doesn't eat what you've prepared for her?

Readings and Other Resources

Healthy Start [pamphlet] (To order, send a self-addressed stamped envelope to: American Academy of Pediatrics, Dept. C, (Healthy Start Brochure), P.O. Box 927, Elk Grove Village, Ill., 60009-0927).

Leach, Penelope, *Your Baby and Child, Rev. Ed.* (New York: Knopf, 1989), pp. 291–304.

*Satter, Ellyn, *Child of Mine* (Menlo Park, Cal.: Bull Publishing, 1991).

*Satter, Ellyn, *Feeding With Love and Good Sense* [video] (Menlo Park, Cal.: Bull Publishing, 1989).

*Satter, Ellyn, *How to Get Your Kid to Eat . . . But Not Too Much* (Menlo Park, Cal.: Bull Publishing, 1987).

*Sears, William and Sears, Martha, *The Baby Book* (Boston, Mass.: Little, Brown and Company, 1993), Chapter 12 on nutrition and pp. 250–256 on allergies.

Further information on nutrition can be obtained by:
• Contacting a local pediatric nutritionist
• Contacting your local dairy council for a catalog of nutrition education material or phone (800) 426-8271 (the National Dairy Council).

---

teaching/presentation

Homework

The topic of nutrition usually is discussed during the limit setting class meeting, since it pertains to this area. Therefore, parents who have major concerns around nutrition usually have dealt with them in one of the limit setting homework assignments, and no separate homework on nutrition is provided.

Practical Suggestions or Strategies for Teaching This Topic

• Parents sometimes forget they have concerns about nutrition unless someone in the group mentions a similar one or makes a statement that brings the concern to mind. This is most likely because parents have often lived with this slowly evolving problem since their child was a baby and a problem that has existed two or three years is hardly extraordinary any more.

• Discussions of nutrition tend to become very specific, but will be more valuable if they have a broader focus. If too much detail is provided on exactly what other children eat or how to make food more attractive, for example, the discussion can bog down or some of the broader issues, such as family dynamics and individual differences, may be neglected. Parents seem to get more from a discussion of nutrition if the focus has been on the family dynamics and individual differences involved in it. Helping parents look at how nutrition and mealtime were handled when they were children can add to their understanding of their feelings about this issue.

Mini-lecture and Lead-off Questions for Discussion[3]

Since everyone in the group will most likely have a great deal of firsthand experience with and longstanding attitudes toward nutrition, your job for this topic will entail getting the discussion started and keeping it directed toward the goals, rather than doing a great deal of lecturing. A good way to get the discussion going is to review ahead of time all the nutrition concerns parents have previously noted and select those you feel have the broadest interest to the group. (You may wish to include some of those noted in the "Typical Parental Interests and Concerns" section on p. 280.) Then you can begin as follows:

During the first two years of their lives, children go through many stages in their eating behavior, and parents go through some stages too. At first, parents need to help their babies get their initial liquid feeding established; then they begin introducing their children to all kinds of solids and watch closely for allergies; then the children want to feed themselves; and then, for many children, appetites start to slow down. When children reach the age of two or three, parents often want their children to eat with them and eat the kinds of food adults eat, although that may not be what the children want. For most parents of two-year-olds, then, there are still many unsettled and unsettling issues that relate to eating, for their children and thus for themselves. Let's begin our discussion by hearing about your major interests in nutrition.

If the group is a quiet one and no one volunteers an interest, think back to the parents' concerns on eating and nutrition and say, for example, **Several parents in our group feel their children are very picky eaters. Could one of you who feels that way tell the group about it in more detail?** You could also: (1) let the parents know that nutrition and eating behavior can be dis-

cussed under limit setting and use a parent's concern to get the discussion going at that time, or (2) develop a homework assignment on nutrition to hand out the week before the topic will be discussed, which will help the parents be more prepared for the discussion.

After the discussion gets started, keep your goals for the topic in mind. It is important for the parents to talk to each other in detail about many of the concerns they have; it's also important for you to guide the discussion so that all group members learn about the normal range of the amounts and kinds of food two-year-olds eat, as well as what to expect in eating behavior. Parents can help each other by sharing techniques they use to handle some of the problems of limited diet, bottles, and so on.

Once the discussion is under way, try to summarize information about norms and ideas that have been discussed to help with specific problems. Gently correct views you think are not helpful and supplement them with other suggestions as needed. You can also help one or two parents problem solve their concerns in detail (see the "Sample Concern" section on p. 281 for an example of this). During this problem-solving time, these parents are asked questions—by you and some of the other parents—that help alert *all* group members to think about their own attitudes toward food. Encouraging parents to think about their attitudes and appreciate what their child's behavior suggests about *his* attitude can be the major contributions of the discussion. (Many parents will go home and figure out their attitudes and expectations after hearing the issue raised in regard to another parent in the class.)

Additional Information for Parents

There is much information to be learned from the handout included for this topic (see p. 281): the norms of feeding skills; balanced meals and how much to expect a child to eat; helpful hints about the four major food groupings and about how to make food less of a major problem area for two-year-olds; information on milk products and other protein foods to help in making substitutes in a child's diet; nutritious and appealing snack foods; and a list of the major nutrients— why they're needed and what foods contain them.

---

3. Much of the information for this topic has been provided by JoAnn Hattner, R.D.C.S., M.P.H., Nutritionist, Pediatrics, Stanford University Medical Center, Stanford, California.

Other important information for parents to learn on this topic is as follows.

• Parents need to be in charge of what foods are in the house and what's available for a child to eat.
• Parents can also set rules on the frequency of snacks; if too many are eaten, meal time appetites can be ruined. Children often say they are hungry or thirsty when they really mean that they are at loose ends. (By the way, the snacks that are served can be "healthy" foods, including, for example, the vegetables you were going to serve an hour later at dinner.)
• When a parent is concerned about how balanced her child's diet is, she can keep track of what her child eats and see if her child is getting an adequate nutritional balance. She can also learn what foods make good nutritional substitutes for those her child doesn't like.
• Some foods do ruin appetites and prevent the possibility of balanced diets. For example, two-year-olds may fill up on two or three 8-ounce bottles of milk a day and have little appetite left for other food.
• Parents should really learn what their own attitude about food is since their feelings about food and eating are conveyed to their child. Children can easily learn the extremes—disliking to eat and eating too much—and can be helped toward a more reasonable attitude if their parents answer some food-related questions, such as those in the "Sample Concern" section (see p. 281) for themselves.
• Lots of children are not as interested in eating as their parents had expected. Many parents expect their child to eat more than he wants, and this attitude can make a child even less interested in eating. In a power struggle over how much a child will eat, the child always wins.
• Most parents too, are frustrated with how little

of the food they prepare is really eaten by their child. Children's appetites vary from day to day, and it often helps to prepare small amounts of food so both children and parents can feel more successful. Food can be frozen in very small containers.
• Parents, particularly those who are working full-time, often need guidance in establishing family mealtimes, and having reasonable expectations for their two-year-olds. Suggestions such as having the sitter feed the child earlier, having family breakfasts occasionally instead of dinner together, and planning earlier meals on week-ends, can help parents broaden their options. Also, parents can be encouraged to allow their children to leave the table (or high chair) when they start to be disruptive or are clearly done eating, to avoid conflict at meal-time.
• Nutritionists usually recommend vitamins at this age, because of the extreme fluctuations with food amounts and variety. Supplements offer consistency of vitamin intake, but don't take the important place of food in the diet.

Handouts

The handout for this topic "Eating and Nutrition" for one- to three-year-olds, includes "Child's Feeding Abilities," "What Does a Day's Diet Look Like," "Suggested Daily Food Plan for Children 13 Months to Three Years," "Additional Information About the Major Food Groups," "Information on Milk Products and Other Protein Foods as Guides for Making Substitutes in a Child's Diet" (see Table 1), "Feeding Guidelines," "Suggestions for Children's Snacks," and "Major Nutrients: Their Roles and Sources" (see Table 2).

EATING AND NUTRITION*

(15–36 months)

The following is some general information to keep in mind when planning meals for your child. Your child may well differ from the developmental norms described below since there are wide ranges in individual development, but the sequence of developing skills is generally correct and may give you some ideas on what to expect from your child.

Child's Feeding Abilities**

Between 12 and 14 months, a child usually:
— can hold a cup with both hands; may need help in drinking.
— uses spoon poorly; finds it hard to fill, spills, turns it in mouth.
— dumps cup and food; throws utensils.
— demands to feed himself.
— handles finger foods well.

Between 15 and 18 months, a child usually:
— can hold a cup or glass well with both hands.
— can fill a spoon, still turns it in mouth, and usually returns to finger feeding before meal is finished.
— can drink and lower cup without spilling.

Between 18 and 24 months, a child usually:
— can fill a spoon, eat without turning it over.
— has increased ability to feed himself, with some spilling.
— handles a cup well.
— can discriminate between foods.
— asks for food, refuses food, says "all done," "more," and the like.
— can drink with a straw.

By three years, a child usually:
— spills little.
— pours well from a pitcher.
— feeds himself well using utensils.
— easily combines eating and talking.
— can obtain drink of water from faucet.

Balanced Meals

Foods from the following four groups are necessary to ensure the essentials for health and growth.

1. Dairy foods—milk and milk products.
2. Protein foods—meat, fish, poultry, and eggs.
3. Vegetables and fruits.
4. Breads and cereals.

What Does a Day's Diet Look Like?

The basic food pattern for the day includes
4-5 servings*** of breads and starches
2-3 servings of protein or protein equivalents (i.e. vegetable protein)
2 small servings of vegetable
3 small servings of fruit
3-4 servings of milk and dairy foods

Sample Menu

Breakfast: 1/2 cup whole grain, iron enriched cereal (e.g. raisin bran)
4 oz. milk
1/2 small banana
Snack: One tablespoon peanut butter with two whole grain crackers
1/2 cup citrus juice

---

*This entire handout has been printed with permission of and/or consultation with JoAnn Hattner, R.D.C.S., M.P.H., Nutritionist, Pediatrics, Stanford University Medical Center, Stanford, California.

**Adapted from B. Umbarger, The Children's Hospital Research Foundation.

***See next page for serving size.

PARENTMAKING: A Practical Handbook for Teaching Parent Classes About Babies and Toddlers by B. Annye Rothenberg, Ph.D., et al.
© 1995 Banster Press, P.O. Box 7326, Menlo Park, CA 94026. Can copy for parent classes if this notice is included in full.

Lunch: 2/3 cup noodle, chicken, pea soup
     1/2 slice oatmeal bread
     4 oz. milk
     1/2 ripe, soft pear in chunks with strawberries
Snack: 1 oz. string cheese
     1/2 apple sliced

Dinner: 1 oz. meatloaf
     1/3 cup mashed potato with butter or soft margarine
     1/4 cup raw carrot-pineapple salad
     4 oz. milk
Snack: 1/2 cup fruited yogurt
     graham cracker

SUGGESTED DAILY FOOD PLAN FOR CHILDREN 13 MONTHS TO 3 YEARS****

Foods	Amount Each Day	Average Serving Size	Foods	Amount Each Day	Average Serving Size
Milk and dairy foods Milk fortified with Vitamin D, regular, low-fat, evaporated. Cheeses or yogurt may be used in place of milk. Soy milk and tofu are substitutes if milk is not tolerated.	3-4 servings	1/4-1/2 cup (2-4 oz.)	**Vegetables and fruits** Raw or cooked, use dark green or deep yellow for Vitamin A.	5 or more servings/day 1 serving at least every other day	2-4 tablespoons
			Fruit or vegetable high in Vitamin C (citrus).	1 per day	1/4-1/2 cup
			Other fruits and vegetables, including potato.	2 servings	2-4 tablespoons
Protein foods Meat, poultry, fish, eggs, vegetable protein, and peanut butter. Meats should be tender and easy to chew; peas and beans, cooked and mashed.	1-2 servings	1-2 oz. or 1/4-1/3 cup	**Breads, cereals, starches** Whole-grain breads and crackers.	4-6 or more servings	1/2-1 slice break 2-4 crackers
			Cereals (fortified with iron for 18 mo. or younger) and starches, e.g., noodles and rice.		1/4-1/2 cup cereal or starches

Plus other foods
Other foods such as fats, butter, margarine, and energy foods such as fruit juice bars, frozen yogurt, sherbets, ice cream, gelatin, fruits, and puddings made with milk may be used to satisfy the child's appetite and to provide energy.

****Adapted from U.S. Department of Health, Education, and Welfare, "Nutrition and Feeding of Children."

Additional Information About the Major Food Groups

Milk and Milk Products

— A child between two and three years of age only needs to drink around 12 oz. a day, plus a small serving of cheese and yogurt. Some may drink less depending on growth rate and size.
— If your child is completely rejecting milk, try substituting foods that are cooked with milk. Good milk substitutes include yogurt, puddings and tapioca or custard. Ice cream is not a very good substitute.
— Low-fat milk (1 or 2%) is recommended rather than no fat or skim, unless your child has other good fat sources. (Whole fat only until 2 years old)
— Mild flavored cheese is liked by most children and is a good source of protein.
— Cheddar cheese is a concentrated form of milk. A 1-ounce slice has about the same calcium as 1 cup of milk. (Fat-free cheese is not recommended for young children.)

Protein Foods

— Two daily child-sized servings of meat, poultry, fish, or other protein food (approx. 2 oz. each time) is important for growing children.
— When serving meat it may be helpful to serve it moist. Most children are less interested in dry meat. Bite-sized pieces that can be eaten with the fingers or a fork are usually easiest.
— Mild-flavored fish appeals more to children than does stronger-tasting fish.
— Peanut butter is a good protein food and popular with children.
— When serving eggs, moisture counts. Try not to let them harden. (Restrictions on eggs are not necessary for young children.)

Fruits and Vegetables

— 4-5 child-sized servings daily are recommended. Orange and grapefruit are the best sources of Vitamin C. Fresh fruit is preferable to canned because there is less sugar.
— Children may show less interest in vegetables because of the way they are cooked. Use a small amount of water, cook fast, serve crisp. Vegetables may be served raw instead of cooked.
— Fruits may be substituted for vegetables.
— Try to offer a wide variety of fruits and vegetables even though your child may not be very interested in them. One day, he may try them.

Cereals and Breads

— Use whole-grain or enriched breads and cereals.
— Cooked whole-grain cereals contain more vitamins and minerals than refined cereals, and they're cheaper. Avoid as much as possible cereals that are sugar coated. Cereals are already high in energy value.
— Avoid too much bran. It may be difficult for your child to digest.

Feeding Guidelines

Small Portions. Small portions are best. A child can always ask for seconds. A rule of thumb for serving sizes is 1 tablespoon of each food per year of the child's life during the preschool years.

Problem Eaters. Don't force or bribe. A child will only eat when he is hungry. A child's appetite usually stays about the same between ages two and three as it was during the previous year.

TABLE 1. INFORMATION ON MILK PRODUCTS AND OTHER PROTEIN FOODS AS GUIDES FOR MAKING SUBSTITUTES IN A CHILD'S DIET*

FOOD	AMT	Calories	Protein (gm)	Calcium (mg)	Fat (gm)	Iron (mg)
DAIRY						
Whole milk (3.7% fat)	8 oz.	157	8.0	290	8.9	.12
2% Fat Milk (Protein Fortified)	8 oz.	137	9.7	352	4.9	.15
1% Fat Milk (Protein Fortified)	8 oz.	119	9.7	349	2.9	.15
Skim Milk (Protein Fortified)	8 oz.	100	9.7	352	0.6	.15
Yogurt, plain (whole milk)	8 oz.	139	7.9	274	7.4	.11
Yogurt (lowfat)	8 oz.	144	11.9	415	3.5	.18
Cheese, American	1 oz.	106	6.3	124	8.9	.11
Cheese, cheddar	1 oz.	114	7.1	204	9.4	.19
Cottage cheese (creamed)	1 TB	29	3.5	17	1.3	.001
Mozzarella cheese (pt. skim)	1 oz.	72	6.9	183	4.5	.001
Cream cheese	1 oz. (2 TB)	99	2.1	23	9.9	.34
Monterey Jack Cheese	1 oz.	106	6.9	212	4.5	.01
NON-DAIRY						
Egg	1 large	77	6.3	25	5.3	.01
Peanut butter	1 T.	94	4.0	5	8.0	.26
Tofu Raw (Soybean curd)	1/4 c.	92	9.9	129	5.5	Not Available
Beans:						
baked, homemade	1/4 c.	95	3.5	39	3.2	1.26
refried, canned	1/4 c.	68	3.9	30	.6	1.1
chickpeas, canned (garbanzo)	1/4 c.	71	3.0	19	.7	0.8
Meat/Poultry						
Beef, gd. lean cooked	1 oz.	75	6.7	2	5.0	.5
Lamb, gd. cooked	1 oz.	79	6.9	6	5.5	.5
Chicken breast, cooked	1 oz.	62	8.0	4	3.0	.3

*Source: Bowes & Church's Food Values of Portions Commonly Used, 16th Ed., 1994

Compiled by JoAnn Hattner, R.D.C.S., M.P.H., Nutritionist, Pediatrics, Stanford University Medical Center, Stanford, California

Try offering a wide variety of foods rather than emphasizing quantity.

Meal Time Routine. It is important to establish a regular meal time routine. An orderly pattern of play, nap, and eating helps many children's appetites. Some meal time rules can be established.

Meal Time Atmosphere. Children learn by imitating, so it is helpful for them to have some meals with their parents (it is often hard eating with a young child, however). Allowances should be made for some messiness and finger feeding. To help the child improve his feeding skills, provide a spoon with a straight, short handle, a bowl with straight sides, a small cup, and a comfortable sitting position.

Snacks. Most children need snacks. To avoid continual eating, try offering a set number of snacks each day (e.g., one morning and one afternoon) and not usually later than two hours before meal time. However, if your child really wants something to eat while you are preparing meals, you could give him a snack from the meal he is about to have. If you are worried about your child's weight, be careful what you buy. Once cookies, cakes, sweets, and the like are in the house, it is very difficult to deny them to your child. A list of snack suggestions is included below. In addition, slices or pieces of cheese are good snack foods along with unsweetened-cereal, bread with cottage cheese or peanut butter, pieces of fresh fruit or vegetables, juices and milk.

Suggestions for Children's Snacks

- Soup, for example, tomato, served in a small cup.
- "Applewiches" made by coring an apple and cutting it into rings, then spreading nut butter between the rings.
- A variety of breads, for example, whole wheat, rye, raisin, pumpernickel, cut with cookie cutters and spread with cheese, yogurt, etc.
- For a special treat at parties, a large apple can be cut into thin slices, peanut butter can be dropped on them and animal cookies stood up on the peanut butter for a "merry-go-round."
- For a nutritious birthday cake, a carrot-raisin-nut cake can be made, frosted with cream cheese icing.
- Cookies can be nutritious. Oatmeal and raisin, molasses, or peanut butter cookies are good energy sources plus suppliers of iron.
- Offer a plate of raw vegetables—cauliflower, green pepper, cabbage, and carrot slices—that children can help arrange. Yogurt or cottage cheese (small curd) can be mixed with a little milk for a dip.
- Children can make their own finger salads with small tomatoes, lettuce and cucumber slices. You can add broccoli (cooked, but crunchy) for color.
- Children can help with an attractive raw fruit plate of orange slices, banana sticks, apple wedges, and berries.
- Frozen "fruitsickles" can be made with orange, pineapple, or apple juice. Pour juice into small paper cups or into ice cube tray. Before juice is completely frozen, place a popsicle stick in the center of each. Try this also with a mixture of plain yogurt and sweetened fruit blended before you freeze it in paper cups.
- "Fruit slushes" can be made by placing crushed ice in a paper cup and pouring concentrated fruit juice over it.
- Children can make their own sandwiches with small squares of a variety of breads, cold meats, and cheese.
- An attractive finger food is a carrot with a prune or other fruit stuck on the end. Cheese cubes can be stuck on pretzel sticks, too.
- For "soda pop," add plain soda to fruit juices.
- "Plumped raisins": Drop raisins into boiling water for 1-2 minutes. Remove with slotted spoon and serve in a small bowl. Raisins will be moist and plump.
- Let your own imagination devise nutritious snacks for children using natural or fresh foods of bright color, good texture, appealing design, and small size.
- Remember, children like to be involved!

PARENTMAKING: A Practical Handbook for Teaching Parent Classes About Babies and Toddlers by B. Annye Rothenberg, Ph.D., et al.
© 1995 Banster Press, P.O. Box 7326, Menlo Park, CA 94026. Can copy for parent classes if this notice is included in full.

TABLE 2. MAJOR NUTRIENTS: THEIR ROLES AND SOURCES *

NUTRIENT	WHY NEEDED	WHERE FOUND
Protein	Promotes growth and repair of body tissues; supplies energy; helps to fight infections; forms an important part of blood, enzymes, and hormones to regulate body functions.	Lean meats; poultry; fish; shellfish; eggs; milk; cheese. Next best are the proteins such as dry beans and peas; nuts; peanut butter; bread; cereals; wheat germ. If served with a complementary animal protein food such as cheese, the combined protein value is high.
Carbohydrates (Starches and sugars)	Supply energy; spare protein for body building and repair; also necessary for bulk and proper elimination.	Breads; cereals; grits; corn; rice; potatoes; the macaroni and noodle families; bananas; sugar; syrup; jam; jelly; molasses.
Fats	Supply concentrated energy; improve taste of food; help body use other nutrients; help maintain temperature; lubricate intestinal tract.	Butter; margarine; whole milk; ice cream; cheese; egg yolk; chocolate; chocolate candy; pies; puddings; vegetable oils.
Calcium	Builds sturdy bones and teeth; helps blood clot; helps to keep nerves, muscles, and heart healthy; aids in healing wounds; helps fight infections.	Milk; cheeses; kale; collards; mustard and turnip greens; salmon; sardines.
Iodine	Helps thyroid gland work properly in regulating energy.	Iodized salt; salt-water fish and shellfish.
Iron	Necessary to form hemoglobin (red substance in blood) which carries oxygen from lungs to body cells. Protects from iron deficiency anemia.	Organ meats; oysters; lean meats; egg yolk; clams; whole-grain and enriched cereals; dry beans; molasses; raisins and other dried fruits; dark green leafy vegetables.
Sodium	Preserves water balance in body.	Salt; meat; fish; poultry; eggs; olives.
Potassium	Keeps nerves and muscles healthy; helps to maintain fluid balance.	Meat; fish; fruits; cereals.
Phosphorus	Essential (with calcium) for bones and teeth; helps fat do its job in the body; aids enzymes used in energy metabolism.	Milk; ice cream; cheese; meat; poultry; whole-grain cereals; dry beans and peas; fish; nuts.
Magnesium	A must for strong bones and teeth; helps muscle contraction; aids in transmitting nerve impulses.	Cereals; dry beans; meats, milk; nuts.

* Reprinted with permission of *Parents' Magazine.*

EATING AND NUTRITION (continued)

TABLE 2 (continued)

NUTRIENT	WHY NEEDED	WHERE FOUND
Vitamin A	Helps maintain eyesight, especially in dim light; aids growth of healthy skin, bones, and teeth; promotes growth; helps resist infection.	Liver; broccoli; turnips; carrots; pumpkin; sweet potatoes; winter squash; apricots; butter; fortified margarine; egg yolk; fish-liver oils; cantaloupe.
Thiamine (Vitamin B_1)	Helps body cells obtain energy from food; aids in keeping nerves healthy; promotes good appetite and digestion.	Pork; lean meats; poultry; fish; liver; dry beans and peas; egg yolk; whole-grain and enriched cereals and breads; soybeans.
Riboflavin (Vitamin B_2)	Helps body use protein, fats, and carbohydrates for energy and for building tissues; aids in maintaining eyesight; promotes radiant skin.	Milk; cheese; organ meats; eggs; green leafy vegetables; enriched cereals and breads; yeast.
Niacin	Required for healthy nervous system, skin, and digestive tract; aids energy production in cells.	Lean meats; poultry; fish; variety meats; dark green leafy vegetables; whole-grain and enriched cereals and breads; peanuts; peanut butter.
Vitamin C (Ascorbic acid)	Aids in building the materials that hold cells together; helps in healing wounds and resisting infection; needed for healthy teeth, gums, and blood vessels.	Citrus fruits; strawberries; cantaloupe; tomatoes; potatoes; Brussels sprouts; raw cabbage; broccoli; green and sweet red peppers.
Vitamin D	Helps body use calcium and phosphorus to build strong bones and teeth.	Fortified milk; egg yolk; salmon; tuna. Direct sunlight also produces Vitamin D.
Vitamin B_6	Aids body to use protein and maintain normal hemoglobin in blood.	Meats; wheat germ; whole-grain cereals; soybeans; peanuts.
Vitamin B_{12}	A necessity for producing red blood cells and for building new proteins in the body.	Meats; fish; eggs; milk; cheese.
Vitamin E	Function is not clearly understood, although it is thought to help form red blood cells, muscle, and other tissue.	Wheat-germ oil; vegetable oils; green leafy vegetables; nuts; dry beans and peas; margarine.
Vitamin K	Promotes normal blood clotting.	Green leafy vegetables; cauliflower; egg yolk; soybean oil.

5

PLAY AND LEARNING[1]

background/preparation

Goals to Work Toward in Presenting This Topic

See the "Goals to Work Toward" section (p. 227) under "Play and Learning" for 15- to 24-month-olds.

Typical Parental Interests and Concerns About This Topic

1. How can I get my child to play by herself more of the time?
2. Ashley can play with books or beads or building blocks for long periods of time but never seems to want to play outside by herself and do more active things.
3. My child is on the move all the time and I can't seem to get him to settle down with any one thing for more than a minute. I'm wondering if there's some way to increase a child's attention span.

4. I'm exhausted after work. How can I play with my child in ways we both enjoy?
5. I think Miranda is getting too interested in television. She asks about it a lot. I know it has some educational value, but how do you decide how much TV to let a child watch?
6. I'm wondering if this is a good age to start crafts activities. What do you start with?
7. How many is too many toys? How do I choose good toys, with so much available?
8. Are there any things I should be teaching my child? She seems very interested in the alphabet letters.
9. Aaron gets frustrated very easily and then he starts to scream or throw things.
10. When can children start putting things away? Chelsea takes everything out but shows no interest in putting things away.
11. My child is forever saying, "Mommy do it." I want to be able to get her to do more of her own play activities.

Areas of Information You Will Need to Learn About to Teach This Topic

- The dynamics between a demanding child and his parents.
- The value and effect of television on pre-school children and the parents' role in its use.

---

1. The primary information for this topic can be found in the 15- to 24-month-old section on play and learning (p. 227). Use that section as a basis and *supplement* with this section for two-year-olds. (Only the "Sample Concern," the "Readings," and the "Homework" sections are complete without the 15- to 24-month play and learning topic.)

- Crafts activities appropriate for two-year-olds.
- Kinds of pre-academic experiences children of this age are interested in.
- The major causes of frustration for two-year-olds.

Family Dynamics—What This Topic Means Psychologically to Parent and Child

Parents of two-year-olds tend to be interested in seeing their children become somewhat more independent in their play. Thus there is interest in having toys, play materials, and other activities in the home that will provide a well-rounded and interesting set of experiences for the child.

Young children, on the other hand, often do not have the cognitive skills necessary for extended periods of play. In addition, two-year-olds—first children especially—are used to having their needs met rapidly so their style is still quite demanding.

Sample Concern of Parents

Concern	Critical Issues
My child and I have some days where we are constantly battling. He wants me to play with him more than I want to. And he becomes very demanding. I feel guilty and then I get angry and sometimes by 5 p.m. I'm wishing the whole day had never happened.	—Battling days.
	—Demanding child.
	—Parent feels guilty and angry.
	—Parent feels disgusted.

Key Questions

1. What is your day and your child's day typically like?
2. What seems to make him more demanding?
3. What have you found that encourages him to amuse himself more?

4. What are you feeling when he continues to be demanding?
5. What message do you think he's getting from what you say and how you say it when he's demanding?

For the group

6. Is there anything others in the group can think of that could change the way demandingness can be handled? What effect do you think that will have?

Readings and Other Resources

Allison, Christine, *I'll Tell You A Story, I'll Sing You A Song* (New York: Dell, 1987).

*Carlsson-Paige, Nancy and Levin, Diane, *The War Play Dilemma* (New York: Teachers College Press, 1987).

*Carlsson-Paige, Nancy and Levin, Diane, *Who's Calling the Shots?* (Philadelphia, Penn.: New Society Press, 1990).

Elkind, David, *The Hurried Child* (New York: Addison-Wesley, 1988).

Galinsky, Ellen and David, Judy, *The Preschool Years* (New York: Random House, 1988), Chapter 2.

*Gonzales-Mena, Janet and Eyer, Diane, *Infants, Toddlers, and Caregivers* (Mountain View, Cal.: Mayfield Publishing, 1989), Chapter 4.

Miller, Karen, *Things to Do With Toddlers and Twos* (Marshfield, Mass.: Telshare Publishing Co., 1984).

NAEYC, *Toys: Tools for Learning* [Pamphlet][2] (Washington, D.C.: NAEYC, 1985).

*Oppenheim, Joanne and Oppenheim, Stephanie, *The Best Toys, Books and Videos for Kids* (New York: Harper Collins, 1994).

Toys & Play [Pamphlet][2] (New York: Toy Manufacturers of America, 1993).

2. For information on ordering the pamphlets, please see p. 236.

teaching/presentation

Homework

The homework for this topic helps each parent focus on her child's play style, her own play style and her spouse's, and any questions she may have concerning the area of play.

Practical Suggestions or Strategies for Teaching This Topic

See the "Practical Suggestions" section of the 15- to 24-month old topic on play and learning (p. 229) and the concerns of parents of two-year-olds (p. 292).

Mini-lecture and Lead-off Questions for Discussion

See the "Mini-lecture and Lead-offs" section (p. 232) of the 15- to 24-month-old topic on play and learning and the "Additional Information" section of this topic.

Additional Information for Parents

• See the handout on p. 298 for information on two-year-old motor development.
• See the information in the "Additional Information" section under 15- to 24-month-old play and learning (p. 232).
• How well children learn to play by themselves is influenced by parents' expectations for themselves and their children. Parents need to be reminded to tap into their own feelings and attitudes about the subject of play. Children pick up their parents' guilt and ambivalence when asked *hesitantly* to play on their own and then find it even harder to stay away from their parents and comfortably play alone. Parents need to remember to consider their child's age and temperament when they ask him to play alone.
• Parents can be encouraged to share how their child's day looks like. Reiterate the importance of balance (from limit-setting discussion), and encourage parents to provide focused attention each day. This helps parents feel less ambivalent about asking the child to play independently as well as satisfying the child's needs so he is more likely to cooperate.
• Sometimes parents can help increase a child's attention span by finding more intriguing materials for him to use; by providing a more conducive atmosphere and adult models for concentration; by inviting friends over to play with their child; or by trying to help their child gain mastery over some of the things he has not been able to concentrate on.
• Most children do need limits on television watching, both in terms of the programs that may be seen and how long they may watch. An hour a day for pre-school children has been suggested as reasonable. Parents may wish to discuss some of the TV programs their children see as well as how they set limits. Even before kindergarten, children can become so absorbed in watching television that some negative after-effects have been observed. (See Marie Winn's *Plug-In Drug* for further information; available in libraries).
• Crafts activities can be introduced at this age but need to be very simple; children's ability to work with craft materials is limited, and frustration with them can cause loss of interest. Some children aren't really interested until age 5 or 6, but tearing and gluing paper, using playdough, pasting stick-on labels, and drawing with felt-tip pens are good initial projects.
• A discussion by the parents about types of toys—the needs they fill and which are most successful—could be very valuable. Most two-year-olds especially enjoy boxes, baskets, tunnels, dress-up clothes, dolls, tools, puzzles, blocks, music makers, a work table and chairs, but prefer whatever the adults near them are

EXPLORING, PLAYING, AND LEARNING

(2–3 years)

1. What are the activities your child enjoys? (Include places, people, toys, and so on.) Think of activities at home as well as at pre-school or day-care.

2. How have the skills that your child has developed recently influenced his/her play?

3. Are there any particular interests or skills that your child tends to focus on more than other children the same age do?

4. Think about what your child did during the last few hours he/she was awake and describe the learning that you think has been going on through that play.

5. What aspects of your child's play or your play with him/her are of concern to you? (i.e., are not going as smoothly as you had hoped)?

6. How does your spouse's way of playing with your child differ from yours?

How does your child handle these differences?

Parent's name _____ Date _____ Child's age _____

using. Housewares and hardwares might therefore be better investments than expensive toys. (See the handouts "Some Examples of Two-Year-Olds' Types of Exploring" and "Types of Play.")

• Most children let parents know that they are interested in and ready to *learn* by the questions they ask and the things they point out. Many two-year-olds start to identify alphabet letters and use color names and a few numbers. Parents often feel that they should launch a program to consolidate these areas quickly and move into an academic curriculum. Generally, however, this approach may put more pressure on a two-year-old than he can handle. A good middle-of-the-road recommendation would be to let the child take the lead in areas of learning with the parent answering and reinforcing what the child asks.

It is believed that a strong preparation for academics comes not from an organized, *academically* focused pre-school curriculum but from experiences in the pre-school years that improve concentration, eye-hand coordination, visual and auditory discrimination, and so on. These experiences come through such activities as pounding, scribbling, looking through books, following directions, and the like. For parents who are eager to do more formal "teaching," sorting, matching, knowing body parts, understanding a few prepositions, some counting, following directions, learning colors, knowing own (street, town) names and copying of simple lines are suggested. (Other suggestions can be found in the handout sections "Some Developmental Motor Skills," "Some Self-help and Awareness Skills of Two- to Three-Year-Olds," and "Some Examples of Two-Year-Olds' Types of Exploring" beginning on p. 294.) Remind parents that it is easiest for two-year-old children to learn "on-the-run" when *they* are interested, *not* when the parents have 15+ minutes for a formal sit-down learning situation.

• Two-year-olds tend to get frustrated very easily. They are becoming more independent in certain ways and want to do a lot of things for themselves. They will at times refuse your help and yet work themselves into a frenzy if they are unable to do what they want, such as buckle their own shoes.

Frustrating times obviously require a great deal of patience on the parents' part, and how well parents and their child get through this stage will depend a great deal on how anger is handled in their family. Some of the *most* frustrating playthings and clothes could be put away for a few months, or parents could attempt to help their child *part* way with something he finds very frustrating, at least when he is not too tired. Parents can share with each other how their families deal with frustration.

• Putting things away is something you can ask a two-year-old to help with. Two-year-olds often have trouble, however, leaving things they just put away, and you will need to work with them on this. Cleaning up is a hard process for pre-schoolers to learn, but if parents persevere, children become more helpful over a period of years.

• Two-year-olds will often ask their parents to make something out of playdough or draw a picture for them. Usually this happens because the child recognizes that what the parents make is far better than what he can do. When children play together, it is often easier for each child to feel good about what he's making, because the standard of comparison is much more at their level. Parents can use materials in a child-like way, which can help children feel comfortable with experimenting. For instance, pounding playdough flat to make "pancakes," or rolling it into a snake allows the child to see what can be done, without the child feeling like she's less competent than the parent.

Handouts

A lengthy general handout for this topic can be found on pp. 237–241 in play and learning for 15- to 24-month-olds. The Play and Learning handout that concerns only two-year-olds has three sections—"Some Developmental Motor Skills," "Some Self-help and Awareness Skills of Two- to Three-Year-Olds," "Some Examples of Two-Year-Olds' Types of Exploring," and "Types of Play"—and can be found on the following pages. You may also wish to recommend or provide a pamphlet on toys and play. See p. 236 for ordering information.

PLAY AND LEARNING

(2–3 years)

Some Developmental Motor Skills*

Gross motor skills

Can jump off a step	by around 2 years
Can throw, catch, and bounce a ball (beginnings)	by around 2½ years
Beginning to hop	by around 2½ years
Pedals tricycle	by around 2½ years
Can walk up and down stairs, one foot per stair	by around 2½ years
Turn somersaults	by around 3 years
Begins to balance on one foot	by around 3 years
Can attempt broad jump	by around 3 years
Can jump over rope raised several inches	by around 3 years
Begins to skip	by around 3½ years

Fine motor skills

Copies circle, cross, vertical and horizontal lines	by around 2½ years
Cuts with scissors	by around 2½ years
Builds 6-block tower	by around 2½ years
Strings beads	by around 2½ years
Winds up toy	by around 3 years
Holds pencil correctly	by around 3½ years
Traces along line	by around 3½ years

Some Self-help and Awareness Skills of Two- to Three-Year-Olds**

Knowledge of family, self

Can identify self by first name	around 2 years old
Tells own sex, full name and age	by 3 years
Can tell the number of family members	by 3½ years

Body parts

Points to hair, hands, ears, head, legs, arms	by 1½ years
Points to fingers, toes, stomach, back, knee, chin	by 2½ years
Points to teeth, heels, fingernails	by 2½ years

Dressing

Removes unfastened garments	by 2 years
Unbuttons front buttons	by 2½ years
Removes pull-down garments (pants)	by 2½ years
Puts on shoes	by 3 years
Dresses with supervision	by 3½ years

---

* There is a wide range of normal development among children.

** By the age listed, most children have accomplished that particular skill. Remember, though, that children differ from each other in their patterns of abilities.

PARENTMAKING: A Practical Handbook for Teaching Parent Classes About Babies and Toddlers by B. Annye Rothenberg, Ph.D., et al. © 1995 Banster Press, P.O. Box 7326, Menlo Park, CA 94026. Can copy for parent classes if this notice is included in full.

PLAYING AND LEARNING

Toileting

Turns faucets on and off	by 2 years
Washes hands (purposefully)	by 2½ years
Flushes toilet (purposefully)	by 2½ years

Some Examples of Two-Year-Olds' Types of Exploring***

Combining	Lacing
Molding	Fitting puzzles
Spreading	Running
Heaping	Throwing
Squeezing, making holes	Jumping
	Climbing
Breaking, mending	Pedaling
Using tools (sticks, etc.)	Pushing
	Pulling
Finger painting	Hitting
Crayoning	Punching
Stringing	Picking
Scissoring	Balancing
	Splashing

***Taken from Sutton-Smith, Brian and Sutton-Smith, Shirley, *How to Play With Your Children* (New York: Hawthorn Books, Inc., out of print).

Types of Play

Large Motor

climbing, sliding: ramps, jungle gym, ladder

jumping: rope stretched out; old mattress, trampoline

ride-on vehicles: tricycle, big wheel, tractor, fire engine, rocking horse

pushing, pulling: wagons, wheelbarrows, lawn mower, vacuum cleaner

running:

building:

tumbling:

swinging: (children learn to pump when they're around 4 years old)

Fine Motor

throwing and catching: ball (Nerf, whiffle or beach ball); foam blocks, bean-bag

put-together: puzzles, lock and key; little dolls that fit in round holes; beads on string, pegboards; Legos; number sorter, Bristle Blocks, waffle blocks

nesting: cans, bowls, round cups

filling and dumping: junk mail—oatmeal carton; large ice cream container; carrying basket or pail of things; emptying drawers

pounding: pounding board

stacking: rings on wooden dowel; round cans

building: blocks—preferably cardboard; Duplos

screwing lids: lids on jars (baby food jars)

sorting: shape sorting box

carrying: boxes and buckets of things

Messy Play

sand: pail, shovel or spoon; cups; a dump truck; use cornmeal in winter

water: sprinkler can, tub (sink inside), hose, funnel, things to wash, sieve, spray bottle, sponge; bubble blowing, bucket and paintbrush

dirt:

Surprise Toys (the unexpected happens)

telephone pop-up; cash register

jack-in-the-box (music box also)

toys with strings where something happens when you pull them

flashlight, bells, buzzers

Imitation-Social Play

dress-up: hats, shoes, clothes; beads; goggles or glasses; gloves

dolls: stroller; stick horse; dishes-pretend play; high-chair

help in kitchen: mop, broom, etc.; setting table; cooking

toy telephone, or discarded real telephone

tools
working in the yard—using a hose or watering can
putting things back in their places
transportation toys: cars, trucks

Dance, Music
rhythm instruments
listening to music; dancing
playing games: Ring Around the Rosy; Pop Goes
the Weasel; London Bridge; Mulberry Bush;
Follow the Leader, etc.
singing:

Crafts (child-sized tables and chairs)
playdough (½ cup salt; 1 cup flour; 1 cup water;
2 T. oil; a few drops of food coloring; 2 tsp.
cream of tartar—Mix over high heat until it
forms a ball; knead it; store in a plastic bag in
refrigerator.)

fingerpaint (1/3 T. cold water; 1 cup powdered
laundry starch; 5 cups boiling water; ½ cup soap
flakes—Mix the starch with enough cold water to
make a smooth paste. Add the boiling water and
cook the mixture until it is glossy. Stir in dry soap
flakes while mixture is warm. Cool & pour into
jars. Cover with tight lid.

crayons or felt-tip pens
chalk
easel or finger painting—big paper
gluing
cutting or tearing
stamps and stamp pads
stickers

Concentration/Language Activities (lots of relating with parents)
reading: catalogs, books, scrapbooks, picture
albums
talking: about opposites (e.g., hot-cold, slow-fast,
etc.); time words; parts of body; quality of objects; sorting and matching

Security Objects
blankets, cuddly animals or dolls; bottles

6

SOCIALIZING AMONG CHILDREN

background/preparation

Goals to Work Toward in Presenting This Topic

Relationships among children are always an important topic for parents of two-year-olds. Many parents are quite surprised and bothered by how two-year-olds relate to other children and often feel, too, that their own child's behavior with his peers is either too aggressive or too passive.

The goals to work on in this topic are: (1) to help parents learn how social development usually occurs in children; (2) to help parents deal with the thorny problem of whether to step in and help children solve conflicts or to let them work it out on their own; (3) to help parents learn some useful techniques for handling conflicts, including working with the "aggressive" and the "passive" child; (4) to help parents learn what being with other children means to a child so that they can determine the sort of play situation—number of children, frequency of play times, ages of other children—that would be helpful to their child; (5) to help parents learn what they can do in their relationship with their child that will affect his behavior when other children are there; (6) to help parents deal with handling conflicts and setting limits when the other child's parents are there as well.

Typical Parental Interests and Concerns About This Topic

1. My child used to be friendly toward other children. Now all I hear is screams of "no" and "mine." And my child is hitting other children. I don't understand what's going on.
2. How much should I interfere in conflicts between my child and the children he has over to play with? Will they grow out of it?
3. What are some of the ways I can help resolve conflicts? I try to get John and his friends to share, but they don't seem to be catching on to that idea. There's so much grabbing, pushing, and hitting.
4. Having other children over is something I'm beginning to dread because of all the hassles. How much contact with other kids is really necessary at this age?
5. Megan is very bossy with other children. I don't know whether to talk to her about it after the other child leaves, or what.
6. How can I help my child be more assertive? What should I tell my child to do when she's hit by another child?
7. My child always ignores the other children he's with. I don't understand why. Does this mean he'll always be a loner? Should I create more social situations for him?

301

8. Brandon is very shy with new children. Is there anything I can do to help him overcome this?

9. Lately, at daycare, my child has started to bite other children when they have what he wants. The staff is trying to set limits but it doesn't seem to be improving. I find I'm really angry with him. What can I do at home to improve the situation?

10. My biggest problem is handling conflicts between Annie and another child when the other mom is there. Everything becomes so emotional. I'm so concerned about what the mother will think and what will happen to our friendship.

Areas of Information You Will Need to Learn About to Teach This Topic

- How social development occurs in the two- to three-year-old period and beyond, and what is reasonable to expect of two-year-olds in social situations.
- Techniques that are useful for parents to learn to help them deal with children's conflicts.
- Specific ways to help children who are at the ends of the continuum in aggressiveness/passiveness.
- The kinds of social situations that are easiest for two-year-olds of various temperaments to handle.
- The effect of parents' relationships with their child on the child's relationship with other children.
- The effect of parents' presence on other parents when children are together.

Family Dynamics—What This Topic Means Psychologically to Parent and Child

Social relations mean a lot to most parents, and where their children's relations are concerned they often have strong feelings and too-high expectations. Many parents feel very personally involved in the way their child treats others. Parents often think their child will learn how to play with other children just as naturally as she learned how to walk, and that if they, the

parents, are nice people, their child will be nice toward others most of the time. When their child treats others in what seems like a cruel or selfish or disinterested way, parents naturally react with disbelief, embarrassment, disappointment, and anger. Parents' strong feelings and mistaken assumptions often make having playmates over a difficult situation for both parents and children.

From the child's point of view, it's interesting to have other children nearby. There's a lot to learn and you never really know what's going to happen next. A child learns about himself as he relates to others and he learns about keeping things he wants, negotiating for what he wants, and handling frustration and disappointments. He also learns a lot about what he can expect from others from his own ongoing relationship with his parents as well as from their showing him ways of solving conflicts with other children.

Sample Concern of Parents

See p. 218 in the 15- to 24-month-old section.

Readings and Other Resources

*Domash, Leanne, *Wanna Be My Friend?* (New York: Hearst, 1994).

Galinsky, Ellen and David, Judy. *The Preschool Years* (New York: Ballantine, 1993).

Gonzalez-Mena, Janet and Eyer, Diane, *Infants, Toddlers and Caregivers* (Mountain View, Cal.: Mayfield Publishing, 1989), Chapters 10 and 11.

Lieberman, Alicia, *The Emotional Life of the Toddler* (New York: Macmillan, 1993), Chapter 10.

*Rubin, Zick, *Children's Friendships* (Cambridge, Mass.: Harvard University Press, 1980). Order by calling (617) 495-2480.

Van der Zande, Irene, *1, 2, 3 . . . The Toddler Years* (Santa Cruz, Cal.: Toddler Center Press, 1986).

teaching/presentation

Homework

The homework for this topic has been planned to help parents develop a better understanding of their child's interaction with other children and to assess their own ability to deal with these situations.

Practical Suggestions or Strategies for Teaching About This Topic

• This topic leads quite naturally into a discussion of early childhood education programs and will work well if scheduled just prior to that topic.
• After a mini-lecture on development, ask the parents to mention the questions they would like to deal with. Then place the questions into an order. Work through the questions with a combination of mini-lecture, discussion, and problem solving.

Mini-lecture and Lead-off Questions for Discussion

Much of the material on socializing found on pp. 221–222 of the 15- to 24-month old section is relevant here. Add to it the handout material on general development found on p. 305.

Additional Information for Parents

Children *do* need to be supervised by parents or caregivers when they play. If playmates seem evenly matched, then parents or caregivers can supervise by just being within earshot. If one child is constantly frustrated, however, parents or caregivers can be of great help by taking a teaching and modeling role and helping the frustrated child by showing him what he can do or say. In this way, the parent can teach both children. Children do need to know what the parents think is acceptable behavior.

When playmates' parents or caregivers are present during their children's play, it is helpful to have the parents agree on who will set limits and handle conflicts. This will avoid having two conflicting sets of rules being handed out at the same time. The parent whose home is being played in is the likely rule maker.

When parents, or parents and caregivers, disagree with each others' rules, it can be very difficult to work out; problems, however, generally are settled over a period of time. Uncertainty on each parent's part, or on the part of the caregiver is often what causes most of the difficulty, and problems usually are less frequent as parenting or caregiving confidence and comfort increases. Keeping communication open by bringing up issues as they arise can be helpful. Setting time aside to discuss rules and expectations for the child, as well as what is and is not working can benefit parents and caregivers.

See pp. 222–224 of the 15- to 24-month-old section for further information. Irene Van der Zande, 1, 2, 3 . . . the Toddler Years is recommended to help parents and caregivers work together.

Handouts

There are three parts to the handout, "Playing with Other Children," for this topic. "General Development" provides information about general social development; "Handling Conflicts" makes suggestions about how to talk to children about their conflicts and settle them in a positive way; "Preparing for Guiding Young Children" discusses ways to handle conflicts and encourage children toward less aggressive behavior. Parents may also be referred to selected pages from the books on p. 309.

SOCIALIZING AMONG CHILDREN

(2–3 years)

1. How often is your child with other children? (Please mention whether he/she gets together regularly with any other children and how old they are.)

2. What is your child like with other children around his age (i.e., how does he/she behave toward other children)? Distinguish between the different reactions your child may have to different kinds of children.

3. Give an example of a conflict situation between your child and another child and also describe what *you* did. (Are there other things you also do when your child is in conflict with another child?) If the conflict was at pre-school or daycare, how it was handled?

4. What kinds of questions do you have about your child's relationships with other children?

Parent's name _____ Date _____ Child's age _____

PLAYING WITH OTHER CHILDREN

(2–3 years)

General Development

• "Two's" begin this stage by being more involved with the adults when both adults and other children are nearby. Slowly they begin to show increasing interest in their peers.

• At the beginning of this stage, there is much more solitary play than parallel or cooperative play. However, solitary play does develop into parallel play and some moments of cooperative play, though the latter does not come for some children until age five.

• Cooperative play often begins on a more physical level (for example, chasing games) but older "two's" do initiate conversation with peers and get responses. The two-year-old's social relations are tentative and experimental.

• Protecting their toys is a very important part of how two-year-olds spend their time with each other. "Two's" often sound far more aggressive than they really are, but they do need to know what you consider to be unacceptable behavior. Around two-and-a-half, children find it more comfortable to begin sharing and trading.

• "Two's" cannot usually stay in a structured group situation for prolonged periods.

Handling Conflicts

Some techniques for handling conflicts are:
• asking the children to take turns
• having the children trade objects
• helping the child to find a substitute toy or object for his playmate
• helping each child know what to say to the other

General guidelines:
• Let children try to work things out *if* they are evenly matched.
• Don't let them hurt each other.
• Consider cooling-off periods of not visiting each other for several weeks for children who are in a constant bitter struggle.
• Have some activities in mind for the children, especially if it's a very argumentative day for them.
• Help your child get ready for his playmate by talking about who is coming, about what the children might enjoy doing, and by putting his "special, too-hard-to-share" toys away.
• Show your child some positive ways of relating to other children.

Preparing for Guiding Young Children*

The following tips on handling children during play are meant to be adapted to your particular parenting or caregiving style and situation.

1. When you want to talk to a child, get her attention first. Address her by name, use a quiet voice when speaking, and be sure to be close to the child. Get down to her level by bending, sitting or squatting.

2. Phrase questions positively. Use direct action verbs, such as, "Keep the sand low" rather than "Don't throw sand."

3. It is helpful to give children advance notice of an upcoming activity so they can finish what they are doing and be prepared to accept the change. You might say, "You need to finish up your project now, it is almost time for juice." Or, "You have time for one more painting, then it will be time to clean up." It is most important that you

have it clear in your own mind whether or not there is a choice for the child. If there is no choice, don't ask, "Do you want to wash up now?" Instead say, "You need to wash now."

4. Expect a child to do what needs to be done if it is important; you can show him an action's importance by the firm tone of your voice.

5. To develop self-reliance in a child, within the limits of his ability, let the child do as much for himself as possible: give help only when it's clearly needed. Try not to *impose* sharing and turn-taking on children unless it is clearly necessary, and encourage children to do their own negotiating for turns: "Ask him if you can have it next, after his turn," or "You will be through soon, won't you? Jacob is waiting for his turn. Will you please tell him when you have finished?" You could suggest taking turns or cooperating in a venture: "Alec can give you a ride, then you can pull him."

At certain times, you may need to step in and limit turns. Try to set the limits at the outset and make sure all children understand whys and hows. You might say, "Since both of you want turns on the silver bike today, we'll each take 10 rides around the circle. You may do 10 times around for your turn, then it will be Alec's turn. I'll help you count." Or, "We are having five-minute turns on the silver bike today because Alec is waiting for his turn. I will watch the clock and tell you when your five minutes are up." Encourage any imposed-upon child to stand up for his rights by helping him say, "It is still my turn," or "You can have it when I have finished."

6. Encourage the children to be more verbal, to substitute verbal for aggressive physical approaches: "Tell him what you want," "You can talk to him. Say . . ." The expression "use your words" often does not provide the child with enough help. We need to model what words to use.

7. For children who are having difficulties, suggest ways to offer and accept compromises, trades, and substitutions, to give something or do something for the other child, and to participate in the other child's activity.

8. Aggression is one of the hardest problems to handle in children's play because it requires immediate attention and may arouse strong emotions. Try to remember that some negative behavior is normal, but be concerned when someone may be hurt or when the frequency and intensity of the aggression make it a real problem.

• Try to discover the aggressor's motive. Does he want to play with the child he is disturbing? Was his negative behavior triggered by something someone else did to him? Does he lack social techniques to get what he wants?

• Encourage the expression of the child's *feelings* while you are helping him to control his *actions*. "Can you tell me about it?" "You are very angry, I know, because he wrecked your building, but you cannot hurt him." "You want to play with him, don't you? It's hard to be friends when you push him like that. Let's bring a wheelbarrow with blocks, maybe you can be the delivery man."

• Help the aggressor to understand the other child's feelings, that pushing hurts, that she doesn't like it, etc.

• Don't ask a child to apologize. You might try "Can you help him feel better?"

• Don't shame him; avoid words like "baby," "bad boy," "bully," etc. The act may be undesirable, but the child is not bad.

• Be ready to suggest special-interest activities to the aggressive child, to forestall trouble, to plan ahead so he will have less chance of reaching a crisis.

• It is important that the aggressive child know you still like him, too, so see that he receives an affectionate pat or smile.

9. Children *feel* more comfortable with adults whom they know have limits beyond which they will not be pushed.

---

* Adapted from information prepared by the Menlo-Atherton Cooperative Nursery School, Menlo Park, California.

7

EARLY CHILDHOOD EDUCATION PROGRAMS

(PRE-SCHOOL AND CHILDCARE)

background/preparation

Goals to Work Toward in Presenting This Topic

The topic of early childhood education programs is one of great interest to parents since they are concerned about what their child's first experience in a school setting with a professional teacher will be like.

The specific goals to work toward on this topic are: (1) to help the parents determine their feelings and attitudes toward early childhood programs; (2) to have the parents learn what can and cannot be expected of early childhood programs; (3) to help parents learn how to look for and evaluate pre-schools and other child-care programs, especially as they relate to their own child; (4) to teach parents how to help their child through his first days in a program.

Typical Parental Interests and Concerns About This Topic[1]

1. What I'm wondering is when and how you should start looking at early childhood pro-

grams. I've heard that some of the best ones are already full for the fall and will only put you on a waiting list.

2. I've visited a few different programs but I'm having trouble trying to figure out how to compare them. How can you tell what's a better school?

3. How much structure does a child need at this age? How often should they attend?

4. I was thinking the other day about all the fuss that people make over pre-schools. When I was little, I never went to one and I turned out all right. Do children really need to go to pre-school? I really don't want to see Alison pick up a lot of bad habits.

5. How can you tell when your child is ready for an early childhood program?

6. What are the different kinds of early-childhood programs and what are their pros and cons?

7. Will my child miss out on important experiences if she's in all-day care?

8. Michael's birth date means he will just miss the public school cut-off for kindergarten. So I have to decide whether to send him to pre-school for two *or* three years. I'm afraid he'll get bored with too much school.

9. Can you recommend some specific early childhood programs that you've heard are good?

---

1. Since children in this age range may not have started an early childhood education program yet, parents have many questions but may not have "concerns."

Areas of Information You Will Need to Learn About to Teach This Topic

- What a child and her parents can expect from the child's attending an early childhood program.
- The kinds of pre-school and child-care programs—cooperative, traditional, Montessori, and so on—that are in your geographical area, and their pros and cons. (You will need to visit and become familiar with local programs, their staff, structure, and costs.)
- The procedures for visiting pre-school and childcare programs and at what time of the year this should be done by parents.
- Some good guidelines for evaluating early childhood programs and ways they can be applied to individual children.
- What parents can expect when their child begins an early childhood program.
- Alternatives to early childhood programs, such as play groups (for information on this area, see p. 223 of the 15- to 24-month-old topic "Socializing Among Children") and community resources like kindergym.

Family Dynamics—What This Topic Means Psychologically to Parent and Child

Many parents have some anxiety about the prospect of their child's attending a pre-school or childcare program. Some concern is usually directed toward the child's starting off in a *good* school and further concern may center around the formal beginning of separation, how well their child may be cared for, the fact that they will no longer know everything that goes on in their child's life. Anxiety can also result if parents find themselves looking forward to the free time pre-school will provide for them; they may feel guilty about their eagerness for the pre-school year to begin. Working parents often feel anxious and guilty about the time they need to be away from their child. Parents may worry, too, about how their child will do in school, particularly how he will adjust to and like the situation. They may be hesitant about the feedback they could get from

the "professional educator," thinking of their child's abilities and personality as a reflection on the job they have done as parents.

From the child's point of view, the *idea* of going to nursery school doesn't have any concrete meaning unless he has visited his friends or older sibling's school many times. However, the *actual starting* of school means a lot to most pre-schoolers, but their reactions vary tremendously both initially and as the school year goes on. Common concerns of pre-schoolers are being left and not picked up; that the teacher and other children are mean; that you must do things you don't want to do; and a fear of the unknown. A child's comfort in an early childhood program depends on many interconnected facts, such as his immediate and ongoing relationship with his parents, his temperament, the teacher, the school setting, the other children, and his experience with being away from home and from parents. Starting school may not be easy for either parent or child, since each may bring fears and concerns into the situation.

Sample Concern of Parents

Concern	*Critical Issues*
How can you tell when your child is ready for nursery school?	—Parent is uncertain if child can deal with nursery school.

Key Questions

1. What makes you feel your child is not ready? (Has he stayed in other group situations without you?)
2. How do you think those areas will be troublesome for him?
3. How do you feel about sending your child to an early childhood program?
4. What are your goals for him for this first school experience?

For the group

5. Do you sometimes wonder if your child is ready for an early childhood program?
6. How do you deal with this?
7. What makes you feel he is or isn't ready?

Readings and Other Resources

Beardsly, Lyda, *Good Day, Bad Day* (New York: Teachers College Press, 1990).

*Bredekamp, Sue, Ed., *Developmentally Appropriate Practice in Early Childhood Programs Serving Children from Birth to Age 8, Expanded Ed.* (Washington, D.C.: NAEYC, 1987).

Eisenberg, Arlene, Murkoff, Heidi and Hathaway, Sandee, *What to Expect the Toddler Years* (New York: Workman Publishing, 1994), Chapter 26.

Elkind, David, *The Hurried Child* (New York: Addison-Wesley, 1988).

Galinsky, Ellen and David, Judy, *The Preschool Years* (New York: Ballantine, 1993), Chapter 8.

*Leavitt, Robin and Eheart, Brenda, *Toddler Daycare,* (New York: Free Press, 1985).

Miller, JoAnn and Weissman, Susan, *The Parents' Guide to Daycare* (New York: Bantam, 1986).

*Read, Katherine, Gardner, Pat, and Mahler, Barbara, *Early Childhood Programs: Human Relationships and Learning,* 9th Ed., (Orlando, Fl.: Harcourt, Brace College Publishers, 1993).

*Van der Zande, Irene, *1, 2, 3 . . . The Toddler Years* (Santa Cruz, Cal.: Toddler Center Press, 1986).

You may also want to refer to the journal, *Young Children,* which deals with nursery schools and young children. It is published by the National Association for the Education of Young Children, 1509 16th St., N.W., Washington, D.C. 20036-1426. Call (800) 424-2460. (They have many useful pamphlets for parents also.)

teaching/presentation

Homework

The purpose of the homework is to encourage parents to think about a pre-school or childcare experience for their child and to think a little about some of their goals for their child. The homework is planned to help parents make better decisions regarding their child's schooling.

Practical Suggestions or Strategies for Teaching This Topic

• When teaching this topic, it is helpful to have the parents tell you what their thinking is as far as early childhood programs are concerned. Groups can range from most parents having decided not to send their children to a program to most members wanting to send their children but not knowing how to find suitable programs, to most members already having enrolled their children for the following year. The amount of time their child spends in a program will also vary widely.

• Once you have determined your group's position, find out the kinds of questions they have and then organize them—on the spot—into an outline for discussion.

• You will find that some group members have information and opinions on many of the questions that are brought up (for example, what a child can realistically expect from going to an early childhood program). Whenever you think participants might have good information, ask them to help answer the questions. Be ready, however, to correct misinformation.

• Parents are often eager for the instructor to recommend specific programs. You will need to think about this before the topic comes up so you can decide whether or not you wish to do so.

Mini-lecture and Lead-off Questions for Discussion

Let's begin the discussion by finding out where everyone is in their thinking about early childhood programs. Let's start with

EARLY CHILDHOOD EDUCATION PROGRAMS
(PRE-SCHOOLS & CHILD-CARE)
(2–3 years)

1. What are some of the skills that you feel your child needs a little extra help on?

2. What would be a few of the most critical elements you'd like to find in a pre-school or childcare program for *your* child?

3. What features in an early childhood program do you think would be wise to avoid for your child?

4. During this next week, observe an early childhood program or talk to the parent of a child in a program of any kind, and try to list some of the pros and cons of what the program might provide for your child.

Pros	*Cons*

Parent's name _____ Date _____ Child's age _____

_____. Try to guide the parents into sharing how far into the process of deciding on a school or deciding against a program they've gotten. If parents raise questions at this point, make a note of them.

Next, summarize the group's position. **From what you've all said, it seems that most people** _____. (The statement could range from "have begun to contact schools and would like to focus on differences among schools and how to evaluate schools," to "have decided that school doesn't make sense for next year and would like to talk about organizing some alternatives such as play groups." Then ask what other kinds of questions the group would like to deal with that day.

When everyone has brought up their questions, organize the questions into categories and then cover them one by one. Following is a suggested order for dealing with areas that are frequently asked about.

1. EXPECTATIONS. Let's first think about what we can realistically expect our children to gain from an early childhood program and what would be unrealistic for us to expect. What are your ideas on this?

2. ATTITUDES AND FEELINGS. Encourage the group to talk further about their attitudes and feelings about early childhood programs. Sometimes these are related to parents' own experiences as very young children.

3. TYPES OF SCHOOLS. Now let's look at the different types of early childhood programs that are available and see how we can describe them. Define the major categories and have the parents bring up any other categories they can think of. Depending on the area you live in, some of the major types of schools could be:

Traditional—primary emphasis on social-emotional development and secondary, on motor skills.
Cooperative—traditional emphasis but with regular participation by parents.
University—usually traditional emphasis but may also have a student training and research focus.
Structured—more emphasis on pre-academic learning; Montessori schools could be included here.

If you think the group already has information on this subject, ask them to talk about each type of school's goals, program, what it will be like from the child's point of view, days-hours, age range of children, and costs.

4. INDIVIDUAL CHILDREN. From the homework you have done for today, do you have any feelings about types of programs that might be especially well suited or poorly suited to your child's skills and needs? Help parents talk about their child and the goals they have for him, and see whether they need guidance in thinking their ideas through.

5. EVALUATING SCHOOLS. Let's look now at the important characteristics of early childhood programs. You can help parents do this by asking the following questions:

- How do you like the teacher? How much confidence do you have in her? Will she be there next year when your child starts the program?
- How does the teacher handle the children and relate to your own child?
- How does the school's philosophy fit with yours?
- When you observed each school, how did the children seem to be feeling? How were their needs being handled? How were their conflicts being handled?
- How many children attend, and what is the age range? What are teacher/child ratios?
- What is the physical setting like?
- What are the equipment and supplies like? Do they include things that your child likes to do?
- How conveniently located is the school? (Long rides to school and to visit new friends can get tiresome if they're undertaken on a frequent basis.)
- If you need it, is there extended care?

The discussion at this point may turn to additional criteria that can be included to evaluate schools. Some parents may want to compare in detail two schools that they are interested in. This could be very beneficial to the whole group since it can show how to apply criteria to this important decision. (See the handout on pp. 309-310 for further criteria.)

6. STARTING SCHOOL. Parents may want to learn about helping their child prepare for school and what to expect in their child's first school days. You can probably best present this information yourself unless some of the parents have had experience with their older children.

Some areas to cover are:
- advance preparation—visiting school, playing with children who will be in the same class;

- first day—telling child about school, how long parent should stay, how parent can help teacher help child.
- early weeks—how child may act upon arrival and departure and after school is over that day; child's inability to "tell what happened." (See the handout on p. 315 for material on this area.)

Additional Information for Parents

- Although the time children spend in school varies widely, it is useful for all parents to learn how to make good decisions about selecting schools.
- It is not unusual for children to be unhappy about school for some period of time during the school year. A parent can work with the teacher and try to find out the cause. Then some reasonable action should be taken, rather than doing nothing about the problem or taking the child out of school.
- It is useful for parents to know the extent to which children's behavior changes from pre-school years to later school years—that is, you should try to put pre-school behavior into perspective for them. (Parents may be concerned whether the way a child feels about pre-school and acts toward the teacher and children are indicative of how things will be for him during his later school years.)
- Parents should try to get in touch with and understand their attitude about their child's being away from them. Feelings about the situation can range from not wanting their child to go to wanting him to be away many more hours than might be necessary.
- Building good communication between parent and teacher is the key to a child's successful experience at school. Parents, particularly those who are working, feel much more comfortable about leaving their child when they know they or the teacher can bring up important issues, or simply share and give feedback about the child's day. Parents can share what has worked for them to foster good communication with their pre-school or daycare program. (See Appendix H beginning on p. 466 for a chapter on classes for working parents.)

Handouts

The two handouts—"Evaluation Checklist for Early Childhood Education Programs" and "The First Days at School"—provide additional pre-school-related information. (The Evaluation Checklist shows what can be expected from the most ideal of early childhood programs. You may want to emphasize only some of the points that would fit the more typical school situation.) The National Association for the Education of Young (NAEYC) has many pamphlets for parents on choosing childcare, developing good caregiver-parent relationships, etc. Call (800) 424-2460 for a catalog of brochures for parents (and books for professionals).

EVALUATION CHECKLIST FOR EARLY CHILDHOOD EDUCATION PROGRAMS

(2–5 years)

The Physical Environment

1. Can quiet and noisy activities go on without disturbing one another? Is there an appropriate place for each?
2. Is a variety of materials available on open shelves for the children to use when they are interested? Are materials on shelves well spaced for clarity?
3. Are materials stored in individual units so that children can use them alone without being forced to share with a group?
4. Are activity centers defined so that children know where to get and where to use the materials?
5. Are tables or rug areas provided for convenient use of materials in each activity center?
6. Is self-help encouraged by having materials in good condition and always stored in the same place?
7. Are cushioning materials used to cut down extraneous noise—rug under blocks, pads under knock-out bench?
8. Are setup and cleanup simple? Are these expected parts of the child's activity?
9. Have learning opportunities been carefully planned in the outdoor area? Painting, crafts, block building, carpentry, gardening, pets, sand, and water all lend themselves to learning experiences outdoors.
10. Is the children's work displayed attractively at the child's eye level?
11. Do the pictures displayed reflect the ethnic and racial variety of our culture? Are women and men shown in nonsexist roles?
12. Do the children feel in control of and responsible for the physical environment?
13. Are staff alert to the health and safety of each child and themselves? (e.g. do the staff wash hands before handling food and after diaper changing?) Are staff trained in first aid?
14. Are indoor and outdoor environments safe for and accessible to children and adults, including those with disabilities?
15. Does every staff member know what to do in an emergency?
16. Is the environment spacious enough to accommodate a variety of activities and equipment (i.e. 35 square feet per child indoors and 75 square feet per child outdoors)?

The Interpersonal Environment

1. Is there a feeling of mutual respect between adults and children; children and children? Do adults listen to children and converse with them?
2. Is the physical environment enough under control so that the major part of the adults' time is spent in observing or participating with children?
3. Can children engage in activities without being disturbed or distracted by others? Are children encouraged to work alone as well as in small groups?
4. Do adults observe children's activities and intervene only when it is beneficial to the child?
5. Do adults have "growth goals" for each child based on the needs they have observed in each child? Is individualized curriculum used to reach these goals?
6. Do children feel safe with one another?

---

*Reprinted, by permission, from *Administration: Making Programs Work for Children and Families*, edited by Dorothy W. Hewes. National Association for the Education of Young Children, (800) 424-2460.

7. Do staff members help children learn gradually how to consider others' rights and feelings, to take turns and share, yet also stand up for personal rights when necessary?
8. Are the adults gentle while being firm, consistent yet flexible in their guidance of children?
9. Are there opportunities for children to play alone, participate in a small group, and participate in a large group?
10. When limits are set, do adults use reasoning and consistently follow through? Are limits enforced?
11. Are the adults models of constructive behavior and healthy attitudes?
12. When children are angry or fearful, are they helped to deal with their feelings constructively?

Activities to Stimulate Development

1. Are activities balanced between vigorous outdoor play and quiet indoor play? Are children given opportunities to select activities of interest to them?
2. Are there many opportunities for dramatic play; large housekeeping corner, small dollhouse, work props, dress-up clothes for boys as well as girls?
3. Is there a variety of basic visual art media: painting, drawing, clay, playdough, woodglue sculpture, fingerpaint, collage?
4. Is music a vital part of the program: records, group singing, instruments, dancing?
5. Is language stimulation varied: reading books, games with feel boxes, flannel board stories, questions and answers, conversation, lotto games, classification games? Are limits enforced through verbal explanation and reasoning?
6. Are there small manipulative toys to build eye-hand coordination and finger dexterity?
7. Are there some opportunities to follow patterns or achieve a predetermined goal: puzzles, design blocks, dominos, matching games?
8. Do children do real things like cooking, planting seeds, caring for animals?
9. Are field trips planned to give experience with the world outside school? Is there adequate preparation and follow-up after trips?
10. Are there repeated opportunities for children to use similar materials? Are materials available in a graded sequence so that children develop skills gradually?
11. Are children involved in suggesting and planning activities? How is free choice built into the program?
12. Are self-help skills such as dressing, washing, eating and toileting encouraged as children are ready?
13. Are new activities developed by teachers as they are suggested by the interests of individual children?
14. Is the range of activities varied enough to present a truly divergent curriculum? Are there opportunities for learning through exploration, guided discovery, problem solving, repetition, intuition, imitation, etc? Is there propvision for children to learn through their senses as well as verbally?
15. Do staff members share with parents the highlights of their child's experiences?
16. Do the staff respect families from varying cultures or backgrounds? Do activities reflect the diversity of staff and children?

Schedule

1. Is the time sequence of the school day clear to both teachers and children?
2. Has the schedule been designed to suit the physical plant and particular group of children in the school?
3. Are long periods of time scheduled to permit free choice of activities and companions?
4. Are other groupings provided for in the schedule, e.g., small group activities, one-to-one adult-child contacts, large group meetings, etc?
5. Is the schedule periodically reevaluated and modified? Are changes in the schedule and the reasons for these changes made clear to both staff and children?
6. Are transition times approached as pleasant learning experiences? Are teachers flexible in handling transition times?

THE FIRST DAYS AT SCHOOL*,**

(2–3 years)

These suggestions for aiding your child's adjustment to his regular experience away from home are all pointed toward one objective: to have your child enjoy pre-school or childcare.

1. Tell your child what to expect, simply and in your own words:

   . . . the teachers's name, that she is there every day.

   . . . you will stay for as long as it seems sensible.

   . . . that "school" is a pleasant and safe place.

Do not, however, paint an extremely alluring or exaggerated picture of fun and joyous times. Do not drill your child in advance on good behavior or ask your child to be a "big boy" or a "big girl." If your child is upset, acknowledge the reality of his or her feelings: "Of course I will stay, as long as I can. Pretty soon you'll be ready to stay at school and have me leave."

2. For an easier adjustment, plan on building up your child's hours gradually. You may be one of the fortunate ones whose child says goodbye cheerfully the first day, but proceed on the assumption that you may need to stay. Your child may need you for only one session, or for several weeks. The teacher can help you decide when to leave, according to your child's individual needs and your own attitude.

When you are remaining at school, here are some suggestions: First, help your child become familiar and comfortable with the surroundings. Greet the caregiver and walk around the room with your child touching and talking about the toys, materials, and people. Pause long enough to actually play in several areas.

Then, sit in the background, as passively as possible. Do not talk more than necessary—to other children or to adults. It is easier for a *child to leave his parent* if the other people and the toys are more interesting than the parent is. If your child asks you for help, do so, then return to the background.

Let your child sit on your lap, cling or stand by you. You may suggest or demonstrate an activity or two; do not continue to press him if he refuses. Observing is a form of participating for him. He may be willing to go through the routines with the other children if you help him with toileting or washing his hands or have a snack near him.

You might say that you have to go to the school office or that you must put your sweater in the car and then come right back. Later you should be able to leave for even a longer time: "I must go to the store and buy some apples. I will be right back." Always do what you say. Sometimes it helps to leave a tangible possession as proof that you will return: a toy, something from your purse, a scarf.

(continued on next pg.)

---

* Adapted from information prepared by the Menlo-Atherton Cooperative Nursery School, Menlo Park, California.

**PETP* has an extensive chapter on separation. Refer to this chapter (pp. 291–318) for information on how to help parents separate, specifically addressing the needs of at-home, part-time, and full-time working parents. Hand-outs include ideas for separation and a look at what children need from home when they are in a group setting for part (or all) of their day.

It is very important to say goodbye before you leave. Always tell the teacher when you are leaving during these first days. Be sure your child has been well briefed on the fact that you will be leaving and when you'll be returning, i.e., after what sequence of school activities.

Continue toward helping your child stay for the whole session himself. If your staying with your child becomes prolonged beyond the first few days, he may come to count on you, not have to really get involved, and find it even harder to separate later.

3. Parents are encouraged to act relaxed, cheerful, and as unconcerned as possible in these first days at school. Your child is very perceptive of your feelings and senses if you are anxious about his reactions to school. Communicate confidence to your child that he will be fine.

8

TOILET TRAINING

background/preparation

Goals to Work Toward in Presenting This Topic

Toilet training is seen as a very important hurdle by most parents, especially first-time parents, and its importance is sometimes blown out of proportion. Consequently, parents feel very strongly about learning all they can about how to toilet train their child.

The goals to work toward on this topic are: (1) to help parents put toilet training in perspective as just a *part* of their relationship with their child; (2) to help parents become familiar with their feelings and attitudes toward both toilet training and toileting in general; (3) to help parents learn to recognize signs of readiness for training that their child may be showing; (4) to present various methods of toilet training, including techniques used by other parents; (5) to help parents work out some of the problems that have arisen in their child's training and to develop guidelines to help their child become successfully trained.

Typical Parental Interests and Concerns About This Topic

Some parents in your group will be in the process of toilet training and others will not yet have started, but most will have interests and concerns about the topic.

1. I'm interested in knowing how to tell when my child is ready to be toilet trained, and what are the steps to train him?
2. In my child's day-care center, the teachers let the parents know when they think the child should be toilet trained? I've heard that the teachers then do the training at child care. Is that OK?
3. Some of my friends feel that I make too much of a fuss about training. They think our boy will just train himself when he's ready and I should stay out of it. Besides, everyone says boys take longer to train.
4. My son is registered at a pre-school that requires the children be toilet trained in order to attend. It's just three months till he's supposed to start. I find myself being very tense with him since this deadline is so near. I just don't know if I can get him trained in time to go.
5. Matt used to be interested in the potty, but no more. I keep trying to remind him to go but even though he knows what to do, he has accidents all the time. What should I do now?
6. I've heard it's good to wait until a child is two-and-a-half years old to start to train them. Is that so?
7. My child is trained for urine but always asks for a diaper for bm's. I am getting angry at having to do this.

8. Emma is pretty well trained but I don't know how to respond to the occasional accidents.

9. How do I work with my sitter to get Zachary trained? She seems to have different ideas.

10. How can you get a child to stay dry all night?

11. I'm going to have a baby in a few months and I'd like to have my older child out of diapers by then. I've heard that trained children regress when there's a new baby, though, and I wonder if it's worth trying to train him now.

Areas of Information You Will Need to Learn About to Teach This Topic

---

• The approximate age range that experienced parents have found to be a good time to begin to toilet train.

• The ways children show interest in the potty before the age of two and what this interest means.

• The signs of training readiness that parents should look for in their child.

• The range of attitudes and feelings that parents generally have toward toilet training.

• The more useful approaches to toilet training and the length of time the process usually takes.

• Helpful hints that experienced parents have learned about toilet training and the equipment that is needed.

• Ways to help parents who are having toilet training problems, including how to guide them into using other approaches and helping them to recognize when they should stop trying to toilet train for a while.

• The age range when parents can expect children to stay dry through the night.

Family Dynamics—What This Topic Means Psychologically to Parent and Child

---

Toilet training can dominate the relationship between parent and child from the time the child is 18 months to the time she is three years or even older. Parents can fear that the outcome of toilet training will affect their child's later personality. They may also fear that this training will be a new ground for a major clash of wills, since parent-child clashes are common in this age group. Parents can feel stress from the need to meet pre-school toilet training requirements, social pressure from grandparents, or parents of toilet-trained children, and frustration from the "never-ending" need to change diapers.

Children, on the other hand, have their own feelings about toilet training. They are being asked to do something that they cannot usually see any reason for—something just to please their parents. Most children are comfortable wetting and soiling their diapers, but all of a sudden they are asked to recognize when they are about to urinate or defecate; to hold it until they reach a toilet; and then to let it go down into a hole. Depending upon readiness, temperament, and feelings about pleasing their parents, children can range from being relatively compliant to being quite resistant to this "unreasonable" and seemingly "purposeless" request.

Sample Concern of Parents

Concern	*Critical Issues*
My child seemed to be ready to be toilet trained and was fairly cooperative for the first week but then started to have accidents. I know she can do it, but I'm not sure what the problem is. Sometimes I think that our life is kind of hectic and then I remember how many of my friends didn't bother and let their children train themselves. I'd like her to be trained, though!	—Parent thinks readiness was there. —Initial cooperative attitude. —Child doesn't seem to have become as "trained" as parent expected. —Parent is uncertain about reasons for accidents. —Parent is busy and ambivalent about need for training. —Parent would like to see child trained.

Key Questions

1. What are the things you noticed that made your child seem ready for toilet training?

2. Can you describe exactly how you tried to train your child?

3. What was different the week following the successful week? What were your expectations about how your daughter would do that week?
4. How important is it to you to have your child toilet trained in the next few months?
5. Let's look at the pace of life in your home and see if it is realistic to expect you'll be able to do what's needed to help your daughter become toilet trained.

Readings and Other Resources

Brazelton, T. Berry, *Touchpoints* (New York: Addison-Wesley, 1992), Chapters 11 and 12.

Galinsky, Ellen and David, Judy, *The Preschool Years* (New York: Ballantine, 1991), pp. 206–213.

Hussey-Gardner, Brenda, *Parenting To Make a Difference* (Palo Alto, Cal.: VORT Corporation, 1992), Chapter 10.

Leach, Penelope, *Your Baby and Child, Rev. Ed.* (New York: Knopf, 1989), pp. 315–320, 401–403.

Mack, Alison, *Toilet Learning: The Picture Book Technique for Children and Parents* (Boston, MA: Little, Brown and Co., 1983). Recommended for the children's picture book only.

Yasgur, Batya S., *Good-bye Diapers* (New York: Berkley Books, 1994).

Azrin, Nathan H. and Foxx, Richard M., *Toilet Training in Less Than a Day*[1] (New York: Simon & Schuster, 1974).

_____

1. This book is included in the list because most parents will expect you to know about it, not because it is recommended for its approach.

teaching/presentation

Homework

There is no homework assignment for this topic. Most parents seem to have all their related questions and concerns at their fingertips.

Practical Suggestions or Strategies for Teaching This Topic

Two- to Three-Year-Olds

• Most parents are very interested in this topic, so it is helpful to plan a full session for its discussion.
• It will be valuable to ask group members before the discussion begins where they are in the toilet training process. (Be certain to ask in a way that reassures them that there are no set expectations on the instructor's part.) With this knowledge and an idea of the questions they have, you will be able to focus the discussion on necessary areas. It will be especially useful to know which parents have already toilet trained their child since these people may be able to help the others.
• It will be valuable to discuss different methods of toilet training as well as different stories of how training went for others. Including personal experiences you had in your own child's training, as well as some humor, will lead to a relaxed, successful discussion. Try to find examples of positive and negative training experiences, and then discuss why each did or did not go well.

15- to 24-Month-Olds

• Parents of toddlers are extremely interested in and concerned about this issue. They want to train their child exactly right and really would like a detailed set of steps. You need to have specific information for these parents, particularly about the signs of readiness for being toilet trained. Parents will want your reassurance that they can do a good job of toilet training in a relaxed fashion. They also need to tell one another that the process is "no big deal."
• You will need to remind parents that it is important for them to watch their child for signs of readiness and to begin toilet training at a slow, well-thought-out pace. *Toilet training before two*

years of age is not usually encouraged because most children do not have enough signs of readiness. Remind parents that most children show a spurt of interest sometime around 1½ to 2 years of age, but are rarely ready at this time.

Mini-lecture and Lead-off Questions for Discussion

Today our major focus will be on toilet training and many of its surrounding issues. For some of you it may be many months before you begin to train so though we're discussing it today, please *don't* interpret this class as pressure on you to begin toilet training later today.

Let's begin with a quick definition of the term so that it will be clear what we're all talking about. Toilet training is the process by which children are taught how to go to the toilet on their own signal and need little outside help with any toileting functions. This whole process can take several years, possibly until the child is about five years old. Most of what is meant by toilet training, however, usually occurs in the first six months after you feel your child is ready for training. Just about the last thing to develop (usually when the child is between ages 4 and 5) is the child's willingness and ability to wipe himself after a bowel movement. Toilet training really is not a major separate issue with your child, but just another aspect of your ongoing relationship.

With that short definition, I'd like to go around the group and have each of you mention where you're at as far as toilet training goes and those areas you'd like to learn more about. Try not to feel that you have to be "in the process of." Parents' experiences have shown that it is often easier to wait to start training until your child is around two-and-a-half years old. This is true despite the initial enthusiasm and interest in toilet training shown by many 18- to 21-month-olds because that eagerness often evaporates as soon as *you* get serious about training.

After each group member has spoken, you should be aware of where in the process each person is and the questions each has about the subject. You should then group the questions for discussion. A useful grouping and order for discussion is:

1. signs of readiness ⎱ use your notes and
2. methods of training ⎰ parents' hints

3. parents' attitudes and feelings about training ⎫ draw on your ex-
4. working on problems parents in the group are already experiencing ⎬ periences as well as those of other parents ⎭

The mini-lecture/discussion usually comes to an end after you have helped parents work through their interests and concerns in these four areas and when the group feels they know what to look for and how to proceed in toilet training.

Additional Information for Parents

It is helpful for parents to think about the kind of child they have, tune in to him, and be respectful during his training because its success will depend a lot on whether *he wants* to be trained. Parents need to work hard to get and keep their child's cooperation, and the process of toilet training can provide a good opportunity for a lot of positive learning to occur between parent and child. (*Note:* Toilet training is very different than training a child to e.g., stop using a bottle and drink from a cup—parents can't simply take away their child's diapers as they may have taken his bottle and expect him to adjust to it.)

Though two-and-a-half seems to be a generally recommended time to begin toilet training, it is better to use several specific criteria rather than just age to determine if a child is ready to train.

Readiness. Some general signs that a child is ready to train are that he/she is:

• Over the excitement of learning to walk and run and is able to sit down and quietly play for a period of time;
• Showing imitative behavior—brushing teeth, shaving, setting the table;
• Showing evidence of wanting to put toys and other possessions where they belong;

- Able to help dress and undress herself;
- Not in a period of great negativism;
- Having bowel movements at regular times every day.
- Takes pride in accomplishments
- Able to understand and follow simple directions

To help determine a child's readiness, parents can ask themselves these questions:

- Is my child showing an interest in the toilet and what it is used for?
- Is my child interested when I or my spouse use the toilet?
- Can my child hold her urine for two hours?
- Does my child seem to have any desire to control her bowel and bladder?
- Does my child have words for urine and bowel movement?
- Does my child not mind a wet or messy diaper or does she want it off?
- Have I begun to talk with my child about the importance of using the toilet so she will be motivated?

To help assess their child's awareness of his bodily functions (often this is a progression and the child is easier to train as he goes from stage to stage), parents can ask themselves these questions:

- Is my child aware *after* he has gone in his diaper? Does he come and tell me? Does he want his diaper changed?
- Can my child tell me *when he is "going"* using words or actions? (Many children hide in a corner or behind a couch when they become aware that they are having a bowel movement.)
- Can my child tell me or can I discern by watching her actions and facial expressions that she is aware *before* she goes? (Children must be able to feel the appropriate muscle control before they are ready to be trained.)

Training. A sensible approach to toilet training is offered by T. Berry Brazelton in his book. Dr. Brazelton suggests parents take the following steps—having the child master each one before going on to the next—when they believe their child is ready to be trained:

- Have your child sit on a potty several times a day with his clothes on. This will get him into the

new habit. Provide him with a floor model that he can use in rooms other than the bathroom.

- When your child has accomplished the first step, encourage him to sit on the toilet with his clothes off. A natural time for this is bath time when clothing is already off. No results need be expected. You may want to have your child do this several times a day.
- Once you have accomplished the first and second steps, begin taking your child to the potty at times when his diapers are dirty. Drop the discards into the potty so your child can get the connection. This step does not take long, perhaps a week.
- After the third step has been successful, put the potty in the child's play area for a period of time—outside, or in the family room or bathroom if this is where your child wants it. (Having the potty in the kitchen or family room can be a helpful step in early toilet training because the potty is more visible and the child doesn't have to separate himself from everyone else to go to the potty.) For a short period of time each day leave your child's diaper off. His ability to "go" when he wishes, by himself, is explained, reiterated, but not commanded.
- When your child has had great success with the fourth step, have him wear training pants. You will need to accompany him to the toilet or in other ways keep toileting visible. Going to the potty is a new habit and often takes several *months* to learn.

Some training suggestions and hints are:
- Keep diapers off as much as possible. This helps children learn or become aware of the fact that urine and bowel movements come from them.
- Keep children in loose clothes they can take on and off by themselves at the toilet. This will help them to feel more independent.
- Children who still drink a lot from bottles will have a harder time being trained because their greater liquid intake causes more frequent wetting.
- It's better not to ask children, "Do you have to go to the potty?" Their tendency is to answer "no." Approaches such as "Let's go to the potty now" meet with less resistance.
- Setting the timer and taking your child to the bathroom can help him develop this new habit of using the toilet approximately six times a day

to urinate and approximately once a day to have a bowel movement.

- Find ways to make going to the bathroom interesting. Providing a special activity just for the potty can be helpful. Examples might be a basket of shells to look at, stickers, reading, or singing a special song.
- If you rush your child to the toilet, chances are he will become tense and not be able to relax on the potty.
- When training a little boy, teach him to urinate sitting down, rather than standing up, which is too difficult for young children. He will need you at first to help him learn how to get his urine into the potty and not all over the bathroom. As he gains confidence with toileting and wants to use the adult toilet, many parents find that having him sit backwards makes it easier for him to balance and keep the bathroom dry.
- Encourage working parents to develop a toileting plan with their day-care provider. Good communication is important to keep the process moving, and to support the child's progress. Children often train quickly when they have other children as models, and parents need to be aware of how training is going at school so they can reinforce these behaviors at home. If the child is being cared for at home, parent and caregiver need to work out a consistent approach.

Parents who face problems during training need to review the methods they have been using to see if the techniques make sense for their particular child.

Parents have to encourage their child's motivation and continue working with her over a period of several months. Some parents stop training after a week and expect their child to continue by herself.

When parents are concerned about how the training is going, some of the following questions may help both you and the parents decide whether it is better to proceed with the training or stop for awhile.

- When did you start training?
- How was the training done?
- How far did your child get, and how long did that take?
- What happened then?
- What are some of the possible reasons this happened?
- When _____ happens now, how do you usually handle it? (Try to find out specifically what and how parents say and do what they do).

Answers to these questions should give you some insights into what is blocking the training. It may also be helpful to find out such things as:

- General degree of conflict and power struggles between parents and child and how these are handled;
- General diet (including liquid intake);
- Regularity of urination and defecation, ability to hold urine; tendency toward diarrhea and/or constipation;
- Child's awareness of how adults and other children use the toilet;
- Motivation level of child and parents;
- Consistency of training and regularity of opportunity for child to be near potty.

Handouts

No handouts have been developed for this topic, but you may wish to develop one on the signs of readiness. You may also wish to refer parents to Alison Mack's book *Toilet Learning: The Picture Book Technique for Children and Parents* which contains a very good storybook for children.

part six

TEACHING ABOUT ONE-MONTH- TO THREE-YEAR-OLDS AND THEIR FAMILIES[1]

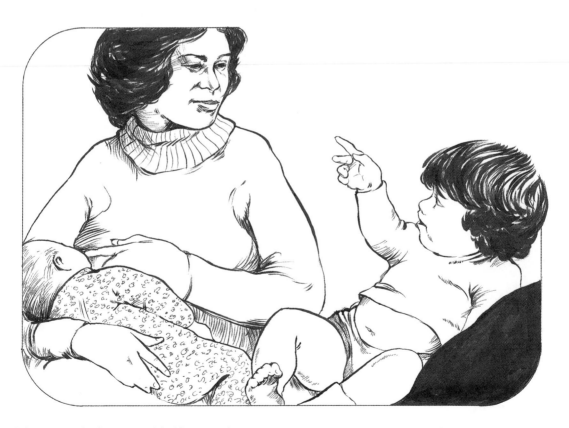

1. *All* the topics in this Part are useful additions to class series for parents of babies and toddlers at least up to three years of age.

1

SICKNESS AND SAFETY

background/preparation

Goals to Work Toward in Presenting This Topic

Although most children encounter minor colds rather than major diseases, thoughts of illness in their child can be frightening for parents. Thoughts about the possible dangers in the home can also be unsettling and parents need support as they begin to explore their own feelings about how to handle sickness and safety. Each family must decide what's best for them; they need to work out a comfortable balance between calling the doctor and caring for their child on their own, and between instituting safety precautions and allowing their child the freedom to explore.

The goals to work toward on this topic are: (1) to help parents learn to recognize signs of illness and to care for a sick child; (2) to teach parents ways to prevent illness in their child and what to keep on hand to deal with illness; (3) to inform parents about ways to safe-proof their home.

Typical Parental Interests and Concerns About This Topic[1]

1. My baby's illness seemed to bother me more than it bothered her. She only had a cold, but I worried the whole time that she might die.
2. I feel like a terrible mother. Jana was sick and uncomfortable but I couldn't stop feeling angry about being cooped up in the house all day and awakened by the crying all night. I'm exhausted and guilty at the same time.
3. I feel so helpless when something's wrong with my baby. I want to help him but I don't know where he hurts.
4. How can I tell if my baby is sick?
5. How should I administer different kinds of medication? I'm worried that I'm not following the doctor's directions correctly.
6. When should I call the doctor (and then call him back)?
7. My pediatrician doesn't answer my questions and I don't know how to handle that.
8. Is my baby sick if his B.M.'s change color (frequency, consistency)?
9. Joshua caught a cold. What did I do wrong?
10. If two babies are near a sick child, why does one get sick and one not?

---

1. Most of the information on sickness relates to young babies but can be adapted to refer to older children as well.

11. I feel so guilty. Noah acted differently for days before his illness was apparent. I should have noticed sooner.
12. What safety precautions should I take in my home before my baby begins to crawl?
13. Should I pad every sharp corner on furniture or should Amanda learn to avoid them?

Areas of Information You Will Need to Learn About to Teach This Topic[2]

How to care for a sick child.
— When to call a doctor and the information to give him.
— Feelings parents often have when their child is sick.
How to prevent illness.
— Equipment to keep on hand (first aid kit, typical equipment often used during illness) and where to buy these items.
— Relevant references (books, pamphlets, local resources, medical records, places to call for help when a parent is sick, how to take a temperature and information to handle fever).
— How to develop a good relationship with a pediatrician and a pediatric nurse practitioner.
Safe-proofing.
— Goals and purposes.
— Accident prevention and toy safety.
— Poison control (poison control center phone number and basic guidelines).
— Equipment for safe-proofing and where to buy it.

Family Dynamics—What This Topic Means Psychologically to Parent and Child

---

Parents are often fearful about their child's first illness. They wonder if they'll be able to tell that he is sick and if they'll be able to help him through the illness; they wonder if they'll know

---

2. Much of this information, for this topic and all others in this part, can be found in the "Additional Information for Parents" sections of the topics.

---

when to call the doctor, and can feel over-protective when they do call or neglectful when they don't. Parental fears about illness can continue through a child's first years, and thoughts about the child's mortality usually underlie the concern.

When children are sick, they are of course uncomfortable, but their parents' manner in handling them can affect their ability to cope with their illness. Children's behavior can temporarily regress or worsen while they are sick.

Sample Concern of Parents

The sample concern for this topic may seem either humorous or tied to the topic of nutrition, but it is included because it is the most frequently raised question in discussions of sickness in the young baby class.

Concern	Critical Issues
My two-month-old baby hasn't had a bowel movement in five days. I don't understand why he's constipated. I feel foolish when I talk to my pediatrician about it—there's not enough time for all my questions—but I'm still worried that the baby is sick.	—Parent isn't sure she knows the signs of illness.
	—Parent needs information—she's uncertain about what's normal.
	—Uncertainty about how to work with pediatrician.

Key Questions

1. How often does your baby usually have a bowel movement? Is there a pattern?
2. How do his stools usually look and smell?
3. What is your child eating?
4. Are there other symptoms your child is showing that concern you?
5. How do you usually feel when you talk with your pediatrician?

For the group

6. What are your children's bowel movements usually like? Are any of you surprised by their appearance or frequency?

7. Would any of you like to comment on your feelings about pediatricians and ways you have established to work with them?

Readings and Other Resources[3]

Burk, Frances Wells, *Babysense* (New York: St. Martin's Press, 1991), Chapters 19 and 20.

*Eisenberg, Arlene et al., What to Expect the Toddler Years (New York: Workman Publishing, 1994) Pt. II and pp. 836–878.

---

3. Readings marked with an * are the most highly recommended. The work of Rose Bromwich is highly recommended for information on the topics in this part and is cited in Appendix A. Articles from *Working Mother, Parents' Magazine, Parenting, Child,* and *American Baby* are often good sources of current information on the topics in this part.

*Green, Martin I. *A Sigh of Relief* (New York: Bantam, 1989).

Jones, Sandy, Guide to Baby Products (Yonkers, N.Y.: Consumer Reports Books, 1991).

Lansky, Vicky and Editors of Consumer Guide, *The Complete Pregnancy and Baby Book* (New York: Plume, 1993).

*Miller, Jeanne, *The Perfectly Safe Home* (New York: Simon & Schuster, 1991).

*Pantell, Robert H., Fries, James F., and Vickery, Donald M., *Taking Care of Your Child* (Menlo Park, Cal.: Addison Wesley, 1990).

*Sears, William and Sears, Martha, The Baby Book (Boston, Mass.: Little, Brown and Company, 1993), Part V on sickness and safety.

Shelov, Steven and Hannemann, Robert, *Caring for Your Baby and Young Child: Birth to Age 5* (New York: Bantam, 1991).

Spock, Benjamin and Rothenberg, Michael, *Dr. Spock's Baby and Child Care* (New York: NAL Dutton, 1992).

teaching/presentation

Homework

The homework for this topic helps parents to focus on their feelings about sickness and safety and on their relationship with their child's pediatrician.

Practical Suggestions or Strategies for Teaching This Topic

• Questions group members ask about sickness and safety tend to be very specific, so you will need to make your presentation complete enough to include broad aspects of the topic that need consideration. When you structure the discussion, let parents know when it will be appropriate for them to ask specific kinds of questions.

• It is important to offer reassurance and understanding. Parents need to know that all children get sick at some time and that they are not failing as parents when their child becomes ill.

• Parents of older babies and toddlers are likely to have concerns not just about safety precau-

tions but about actual placement of furniture, plants, and so on. You will need to help parents gain a basic understanding of safe-proofing without making them feel that their lives will be entirely disrupted.

Mini-lecture and Lead-off Questions for Discussion

The following mini-lecture is an outline of points to cover in your presentation of the topic. Encourage group members to bring up specific points or ask questions after you have discussed the more general areas of concern.

When a child is sick, especially the first time, it can be a very frightening experience for you as parents. Today I'd like to give you some information that might make dealing with illness easier for you.

Caring for a Sick Baby

When a young baby is sick, he may act differently and show any number of symptoms or signs of illness. The following are typical symptoms:

Sickness and Safety

(babies–3 years)

1. Can you describe any feelings that are difficult for you when you think about sickness or safety?

2. What kinds of information would you like to have on these topics?

3. Are you satisfied with the relationship you are building with your pediatrician? Why or why not?

Parent's name _____ Date _____ Child's age _____

- **Cold, clammy skin**
- **Pale, red, rash-covered, hot, dry skin (extensive)**
- **Sleeps a lot or cries a lot (much more than usual)**
- **A higher than normal temperature**
- **Flushed, pale, or perspiring**
- **Noisy, difficult, rapid, or slow breathing**
- **Coughing or sneezing**
- **Irritated eyes**
- **Signs of pain—crying, screaming, or the like**
- **No appetite**
- **Abnormal body movements—twitching, stiffness, or immobility**
- **Vomiting**
- **Abnormal bowel movements—color, consistency, odor, or frequency**
- **Patchy, even, itchy rash**
- **Listlessness, restlessness, irritability**

You may now wish to distribute the handout "Handling Sickness" (p. 332) and then continue.

It's hard to know when any of these symptoms warrants a call to the doctor. When a child is very young and you haven't yet learned her patterns, it's a good idea to call as soon as you're concerned—when you see any physical or behavioral changes. If your baby feels quite warm to the touch, you will probably want to take her temperature. [Despite newer ways to take temperature, most pediatricians feel that the rectal temperature is the most reliable.] **If the temperature is 104 degrees Fahrenheit, 40 degrees Centigrade or above, there is danger of convulsions. Most convulsions usually don't cause brain damage, but they are frightening. You can reduce your child's temperature by giving her a bath in lukewarm water, giving her a sponge bath—take off her clothes and cover her with a blanket, then take one limb out at a time and sponge it off with cool water—or by giving her acetaminophen, such as Tylenol. After about 20 minutes take her temperature again.**

By the time your child is older, you'll know her style of sickness and will probably be more comfortable and confident handling her minor illnesses. You'll call your doctor then only for new things that you aren't sure how to handle.

Parents experience many feelings when their baby is sick, and bringing these feelings out will be important to your discussion. You can ask what kinds of feelings have been difficult for parents as they have dealt with sickness, and bring up the following if they are not mentioned:

Concerned. Am I following the doctor's directions correctly?

Scared. Will my baby die? (It's easy to panic. Acting calm is the best influence on the baby.)

Guilt. I should have noticed sooner . . . I shouldn't have taken her to the _____ .

Frustration. I don't know where he hurts but I want to relieve his suffering.

Uncertainty. How often should I call the pediatrician?

Anger and resentment. My baby can be so difficult to manage.

Cabin fever. I'm tired of being cooped up in my house while my baby is sick.

Exhaustion. Responding to my baby night and day is wearing me out.

Preventing Illness and Equipment to Have on Hand

Direct the parents to the relevant part of their handout. Ask them if they have any questions about any of the points or any information of their own to offer. Then go on to a demonstration of how to take a temperature rectally. Often parents of young babies haven't done this and worry that it will hurt their child.

It's a good idea to practice taking your baby's temperature before he becomes sick. Practice shows you, under comfortable circumstances, how easy it is to take a temperature rectally and how little it disturbs your baby. It also allows you to find out what your baby's normal temperature is ("normal" varies from baby to baby).

You may now ask for a parent to volunteer her child. Demonstrate on the child how to correctly take a temperature, explaining as you proceed. Advice parents that if they use a different method, they should report both the method and the actual reading to the doctor. The following is a good technique to use.

1. Have a watch with a sweep second hand and Vaseline on hand.
2. Shake down the thermometer until the marker falls to around 95 degrees.

3. Lubricate the tip with petroleum jelly, such as Vaseline.

4. Hold the child's legs up with one hand if he is on his back or spread his buttocks if he is on his tummy over your lap.

5. Insert the thermometer a maximum of one inch or just until the silver bulb can't be seen. If the thermometer is held like a cigarette, your fingers and thumb will prevent it from going in further if the baby moves.

6. Keep the thermometer in place for two minutes (20 seconds is usually long enough to indicate the temperature within one-half of a degree).

7. Remove the thermometer and pass it around so that each parent has a chance to read it.

Temperatures fluctuate. They are usually lowest in the early morning and highest between 4 and 6 p.m. (which is why we often find ourselves calling the doctor just before he leaves for the day). When your baby is sick, you can take his temperature about every half-hour to see if it has dropped. It helps to know that a baby's temperature often goes higher than an adult's.

When your demonstration is over, you can discuss with the group any books or pamphlets that are helpful in instructing parents how to handle illness and accidents. You might also wish to mention local people or groups to contact when *parents* become sick and need help caring for their baby. Then continue with a discussion of the parent-pediatrician relationship.

The more we know about health and sickness, the more comfortable we will be handling our child and dealing with medical services. But although we would often like to talk with our pediatrician about developmental and other child-rearing information, his or her primary focus needs to be on the immediate medical needs and problems and time for behavioral guidance *may* be limited. There are things that we as parents can do to work well with our pediatrician. These include:

- **Learning as much as possible about how to care for our child ourselves;**
- **Keeping home medical records—of height, weight, shots, lab tests, or other information the doctor gives us;**

- **Coming to medical appointments prepared with questions or specific concerns—if the doctor hasn't enough time to answer them completely, we should make another appointment;**
- **Exercising our right to choose and refuse—discussing any concern or dissatisfaction with our doctor if at all possible;**
- **Seeking a second opinion if we're not satisfied, especially if it's a real concern;**
- **Being comfortable with our child's pediatrician—personalities differ, but it is necessary to feel confident about a pediatrician so that we can work with him in all aspects of our child's care as well as in emergencies.**

Safe-proofing

The safety of our child is a topic we think about subconsciously almost every day. I'd like to share with you some thoughts on safe-proofing, give you some resource material about the subject, and then open the discussion for any questions and feelings you'd like to share.

We know that most of the accidents that occur during childhood take place in the home and that most of them could have been avoided. All children have some accidents— if they don't, they're really being overprotected—but somehow we need to be aware of potential dangers in their environment and keep our children safe while they taste, explore, and test their world. We need a balance. We need to take intelligent safety precautions, but we also need to keep ourselves from limiting our child's spirit and sense of adventure.

To me, the right amount and kind of safe-proofing does a number of things: (1) it frees the child to learn and grow, (2) it frees the parent from worrying and futile nagging, and (3) it upholds the right of everyone to have a home that's pleasant and comfortable. I'd like to distribute two handouts on safety now ("Safe-proofing Your Home for Children" and "Safety Equipment"—see pp. 334–339), ask you to look through them, and then bring up some of the main areas of safety you'd like to talk about.

If no one volunteers a question, you can ask parents to discuss the safety measures or precautions they feel will be necessary in the next few months.

Additional Information for Parents

• Parents need to think through how much responsibility for child rearing they are turning over to their doctor. Attitudes towards such areas as nutrition, schedules, and behavior patterns may be better based on individual family style and values than on concrete medical information.

Handouts

The handouts for this topic can be distributed during the mini-lecture and will equip parents with sickness and safety resource information to use when needed. The handouts are: "Handling Sickness" which describes when to contact a pediatrician and how to treat a sick child: "Safe-proofing Your Home for Children," which makes suggestions for effective safe-proofing; and "Safety Equipment," which describes various types and purposes of equipment.

You may also wish to request literature from the following excellent resources:

1. U.S. Consumer Product Safety Commission
   Washington, D.C. 20207
   1-800-638-CPSC
   1-800-638-6227

The Safe Nursery—A Buyer's Guide. A booklet that addresses the safety concerns of many types of infant furniture and equipment.

Protect Your Child. Another booklet designed to increase consumer awareness of household dangers, nursery equipment, toys, etc.

Which Toy for Which Child? 0–5. A booklet that combines the issues of toy safety and developmental readiness.

The U.S. C.P.S.C. publishes many other booklets and fact sheets on individual pieces of equipment for consumers. To obtain all of these, send a written request for a full packet of USCPSC publications on infant and child safety to:

U.S. Consumer Product Safety Commission
Washington, D.C. 20207

2. National Highway Traffic Safety
   Administration
   400 7th St. S.W., Washington, D.C. 20590
   1-800-424-9393

Child Safety Seat Package. A packet containing many of the agency's publications dealing with car seat safety (including recalls). You can request this by writing to the address above.

3. American Academy of Pediatrics
   141 N.W. Point Blvd., P.O. Box 927
   Elk Grove Village, IL 60007
   1-800-433-9016

The Academy of Pediatrics offers many articles, fact sheets, etc., on a wide variety of pediatric health issues. Send for a catalog of current publication offerings.

4. C.A.R. (Community Assoc. for the
   Retarded),
   Community Services Division
   525 E. Charleston, Palo Alto, CA 94306

As the lead organization of the "National Safe Kids" campaign, CAR will send out many articles, handouts on injury prevention in children. This is also an excellent resource for pool safety/drowning prevention information. Write to C.A.R. at the above address.

5. Poison Control Centers. While there is no national clearing house for Poison Control Centers, look in the front of your phone book for the crisis or emergency pages where you can find the poison control center nearest you. Many offer written information on prevention and how to respond in the event of a possible poisoning. (They also provide stickers with their phone number to attach to your telephone.)

HANDLING SICKNESS

(babies–3 years)

When calling a doctor:

1. Have paper and pencil ready.
2. Have phone number and name of pharmacy ready.
3. Tell doctor:
   name
   age of child
   weight
   temperature
   symptoms—how long child has had them
4. Find out from the doctor:
   What should I do?
   When?
   How much _____ should I give?
   When?
   When should I repeat medication?
   What should happen?
   When?
   What if this doesn't happen?
   When should I call again?

Call the doctor back if there is:

1. Failure of temperature to drop after administering two to three doses of prescribed medicine for that purpose; a rise in temperature after a period when it has been going down.
2. The appearance of any new symptoms.
3. A head cold that spreads to the chest; the start of a cough that becomes worse.
4. Recurrence of pain, for example, an earache that recurs or spreads to the other ear.
5. Symptoms that might lead to dehydration (vomiting, diarrhea, heavy sweating).
6. A stiff neck, drowsiness, swelling in the neck, abdomen, groin, or any other part of the body.

Administering medication

Nose drops. Put child on his back on your lap; lower his head over your lap (support head).

Put one drop in each nostril. (Use baby nose drops in water, not saline.)

Acetominophen (e.g. *Tylenol*). Use dropper and allow baby to suck the liquid out or gently place medicine to back and/or side of tongue. Don't mix medication with food (you don't know if the child will get it all, and he may not like that food after that). If medication is thrown up within one-half hour, readminister.

Miscellaneous

1. Skin may be cold and clammy or red, hot, and dry, with or without a rash.
2. Have a watch with a sweep second hand available when taking a child's temperature.
3. A temperature of 104 degrees Fahrenheit or 40 degrees Centigrade or above means there's danger of convulsions; administer a sponge bath.
4. Child may regress to younger sleep, eating, or play behavior (e.g., may stop sleeping through the night).
5. A sick baby may sleep a lot but have shorter sleep periods.
6. Sometimes a stuffy baby breathes better when sitting up (in his infant seat).
7. A cold in a baby often lasts up to two weeks.
8. A baby will be more vulnerable for about a week after an illness.

Reducing the likelihood of illness

1. A cool house means an increase in humidity so there's more moisture in the nasal mucous membranes. As a result, receptivity toward illness is lowered.
2. If parent is ill, hands should be washed before handling child.
3. Avoid sick people and crowds, especially during a baby's first six months.
4. Don't overdress a child.

HANDLING SICKNESS (continued)

Equipment to have before your baby is sick

1. Rectal thermometer and lubrication (e.g., Vaseline).
2. Humidifier or vaporizer (turning on the shower and closing the bathroom door produces the same effect). All humidifiers and vaporizers must be cleansed daily in a bleach and water solution to prevent the growth of bacteria. Vaporizers may pose a burn hazard and should be used with caution around children.

3. Syringe (ear or nasal).
4. Acetominophen (such as Tempra, Tylenol, Liquiprin.) Check with your pediatrician first regarding these medications.
5. A dropper.

SAFE-PROOFING YOUR HOME FOR CHILDREN*

(babies–3 years)

Goals of Safe-proofing

Long-range goal

To teach your child caution with and proper use of dangerous objects and products.

Short-range goals

These depend on the ability of the child at each stage of development to exercise his own precautions.

Infancy. You take the whole responsibility of keeping the child's environment safe.

Toddler and pre-school. You expect the child to begin to discriminate between what is all right for him and what is not all right.

Elementary school age. You begin to teach an understanding of why some things are more or less dangerous. Your responsibility and ability to control the environment are diminishing at this stage. The child should be beginning to exercise some of his own safeguards.

Adolescence to adulthood. Your ability to provide protection has diminished even more. Basic skills of evaluating the safety or danger of a situation reside primarily with the child, not with the parent. The adolescent who (a) has been allowed to participate in this learning process since early childhood and (b) who has not been protected from making the necessary mistakes in learning probably will not need to engage in the serious risk taking that is typical of some adolescents.

*Although this information is applicable to all settings that children spend time in such as child care centers, it is most relevant to the safety of homes, including family day care homes. Child care centers have usually been designed with children in mind and do not need to meet the needs of the whole family. Revised with consultation from Larry's Baby Safety Services, Sunnyvale, CA.

General Safety Checks

(The following is not intended to be an all-inclusive checklist, but is simply meant to stimulate your thinking as you inspect your house for possible dangers.)

Electrical wiring, outlets, and appliances

1. Replace worn, frayed cords.
2. Keep electric cords out of reach of children by running them under and behind heavy furniture.
3. Wrap extension cords with electrical tape or use extension cord safety caps to prevent unplugging and insertion into mouth.
4. Protect electrical outlets.
5. Keep bulbs in all sockets.
6. Keep electrical appliances and their cords out of reach so the child can't pull them down on himself.

Floor

1. Put screens or gates around hot floor furnaces, radiators, and fireplaces.
2. Be careful if anything small is dropped on a shag rug. Although it's hard for us to see, a crawling baby finds it easily.
3. Shorten hanging cords for Venetian blinds and drapes so they're out of a baby's reach.
4. Check from time to time to see if any carpet tacks are loose.
5. Be sure that throw rugs are skid proof.
6. Block stairs with safety gates.

Furniture

1. Pad sharp corners on furniture, stairs, and around the fireplace.

SAFE-PROOFING YOUR HOME FOR CHILDREN (continued)

2. Be sure furniture is stable and won't tip.
3. If matches, cigarettes, or foods such as nuts, popcorn, etc., are kept on low tables, move them out of a child's reach.
4. Watch out for breakage of glass shelves or tables when babies bang things on top.
5. Check drawers of coffee tables and night stands to be sure the child can't get hold of dangerous objects or medicine.
6. Paint on furniture that might be chewed should be nontoxic.
7. Keep house plants out of reach. Contact your local poison control center for more information on house and garden plants.

Windows

1. Locks for sliding glass doors prevent opening as well as injury to fingers in closing.
2. Decals on floor-to-ceiling windows warn older children of something in front of them.
3. Make sure window screens cannot be pushed out. Adjustable window guards are a good safety precaution.
4. Avoid placing furniture under windows when children are walking and climbing.
5. Put locks on doors leading to porches, balconies, or decks.

Kitchen

1. Keep pots on the back burners and turn pot handles toward the back of the stove.
2. Have a fire extinguisher on hand.
3. Store plastic bags and cleaning aids in high cabinets or in a locked closet.
4. When the child can reach the stove, a solution is to remove the knobs when they're not in use.
5. Check tablecloths. A child may be able to pull dishes off the table.
6. Secure cabinets and drawers with safety latches.

Bathroom

1. Cabinets under the sink often are used for storage of such dangerous (if swallowed) sub-

stances as shampoo, shaving cream, cologne, nail polish, suntan creams, scouring powder, hair clips, etc. The under-sink cabinet can be used instead for "soft storage" of facial and toilet tissue, towels, washcloths, etc.
2. The combination of water and electricity is dangerous. Cover electrical outlets and keep electric bathroom appliances in safe places.
3. Is it safe to keep medicines in the medicine cabinet? It may be better to keep them elsewhere, especially if your cabinet can't be locked easily after each opening.
4. Use a safety mat or anti-skid devices in the tub. Install a spout guard for the bathtub faucet. Never leave a child alone in the tub.
5. Bathroom door locks can be dangerous since children may lock themselves in and be unable to follow directions to get out. A lock high on the outside keeps him out while a lock high on the inside affords privacy.
6. Plastic or paper drinking cups are safer than glass.
7. Toilet bowl latches provide extra protection for curious children.
8. As glass shower doors reduce access to the child in the bathtub, consider replacing these with tension rods and curtains.

Garage, toolshed, yard

1. These areas often have many objects within reach of a child. Some are safe while others are dangerous. Some areas should be locked or blocked off. Then areas the child may be near can be cleaned of junk.
2. Areas containing gasoline, pesticides, paint, lawn mowers, and other tools should be off-limits to children unless accompanied by an adult.
3. You can minimize risks by storing dangerous materials in simple bins that can be secured with a lock.
4. Block off or fence in a safe area for children to play. Spot and take care of any dangers in this part of the yard.

Some general guidelines

1. A smoke detector should be in place on every level of the house. Check batteries frequently.
2. Parents and other caregivers should have CPR (Cardio-pulmonary resuscitation) and first aid training.
3. Children should never be left alone in or around a bathtub, wading pool, or any container of liquid. Any constantly filled body of water should be treated with caution (hot tubs, pools, ponds, etc.).
4. Consult your local emergency planning guide (located in the front of most phone books) and have a natural disaster plan for your family.

Poisons

Poison control center*

Look up the local poison control center phone number and keep it posted. If the number isn't handy, the operator can connect you with the center. Contact them for any poison question or emergency. The poison control center will be able to assist you with first aid information, symptoms which may develop, or if there is a need to see a physician or go to the hospital.

Some general guidelines

1. Never underestimate what a child can reach by climbing.
2. Consider any substance that can be swallowed as potentially dangerous and any external medicine poisonous in an overdose. Poisonings can occur by many routes such as breathing, skin contact, eye contact, bites and stings.

3. Keep a bottle of Syrup of Ipecac (to induce vomiting) in your first aid kit. It is available without prescription from your pharmacist and usually comes in 1-oz. size bottles. Keep one bottle per child under 6. Never administer Syrup of Ipecac before contacting either your pediatrician or local poison control center.
4. Place the telephone numbers of your doctor, the poison control center, and the closest hospital on an emergency phone list. (In most areas, 911 is also available as an emergency number.)
5. Keep all medicines and common household cleansers in locked cabinets or cupboards. Rinse out all cleanser containers before discarding.
6. Medications kept in women's purses are a frequent source of accidental poisoning. The possibility of a visitor carrying such medication should not be overlooked.
7. Cosmetics can also be hazardous and should not be left out.
8. An especially dangerous time for accidental poisoning is when someone in the family is ill. Medicines are most likely to be left out of their usually safe place during that time and your child may try to imitate the sick person by eating the medication.
9. Before using any medicine, be sure you read the label carefully. Throw away unlabeled medicine. Most medications can be safely flushed down the toilet. Always rinse out the containers before discarding.
10. Call the poison control center immediately even if you just suspect that someone in your family has taken or touched something poisonous. Do not wait for symptoms to appear.

*Revised with the consultation of Edith Studer Rondeau, Ph.D., R.N.

Safety Equipment*

(babies–3 years)

Device	Age	Purpose	Comments
Night Light	From birth	For your own safety during night feedings, etc.	At the age of mobility, a night light in an outlet may be too enticing for a child. Consider using a dimmer switch or a nursery lamp instead.
FOR OUTLETS IN CONSTANT USE **SAFETY PLATE**	From beginning of mobility	Prevents objects from being inserted in outlets.	The type shown is good for outlets used frequently and where plugs do not remain permanently. Outlet is covered automatically if plug is removed. User must slide cover with one hand and insert plug with other hand.
SHOCK GUARDS	From beginning of mobility	Restricts access of child to plugs.	Allows plugs to stay in outlet and restricts access to plug and outlet. Plugs are removable by adults by sliding the guard up, removing plug, and replacing the guard.
PLUG UPS HOLDS TIGHT IN OUTLET UL APPROVED PACK OF 6	From beginning of mobility	Prevents objects from being inserted in outlets.	Good for outlets that are exposed but seldom used. This device should be difficult to remove even for adults. Not convenient if you use the outlet frequently.
SAFETY LATCH CHILD PROOF	From beginning of mobility	Prevents cabinet doors and drawers from opening more than 1-2 inches.	Child can still reach inside. Difficult to install. Adults open door/drawer by depressing the hook to clear the stopper.

*Pictures and information originally printed with permission of Baby News Stores, Hayward, California.

Device	Age	Purpose	Comments
GRIP LOK KEEPS TOTS FROM CABINETS	From beginning of mobility	To keep child out of cabinets and drawers.	Expensive and inconvenient for adults.
NO SPILL DRAWER NO!? STOPS ATTACHES TO REAR OF DRAWER	When able to pull drawers	Prevents drawer from being pulled out and falling on child.	Does not prevent drawer from opening. Can be turned flush with top of drawer to allow removal of drawer from chest.
SAFETY LOCK FOR MEDICINE CABINETS KEEP CHILDREN FROM MEDICINE CABINET	When able to climb	Prevents child from opening cabinet.	May not fit all medicine cabinets.
E-Z DORLOK INSTALLS INSIDE ANY DOOR. PREVENTS CHILDREN USING IT.	When able to manipulate doorknob	For any door you don't want the baby to open.	Installs inside any door and prevents child from opening doors leading outside.
SAFETY KNOBS FITS OVER REGULAR DOOR KNOB	When able to manipulate doorknob	Slips over doorknob and prevents child from turning the knob.	Adults or older children can apply pressure in order to turn knob and open the door.
WINDOW SAFETY LOCK KEEPS CHILDREN FROM OPENING WINDOWS	When able to pull up and climb	Prevents child from opening window.	Can be installed without tools on all modern aluminum windows. Prevents window from being opened all the way.
PATIO DOOR SAFETY LOCK LOCKS GLIDING GLASS DOORS LOCKS IN ANY POSITION	When able to crawl	Prevents child from opening and crawling through patio doors.	When installed, door may be locked or closed in any position.

SAFETY EQUIPMENT (continued)

Device	Age	Purpose	Comments
CORNER GUARDS SELF STICK · PROTECTS FROM BUMPS · SHUR LOK	When able to pull up and crawl	Protects child from sharp corners on low furniture.	Self-stick rubber guards fit over corners that child may run into.
Toilet lid locks 	From the beginning of mobility.	To prevent child from falling into the toilet as well as preventing items from being flushed down the toilet.	Locks in place once lid covers toilet. Requires "know-how" to unlock and lift toilet lid.
Stove guards 	When child can reach onto the stove.	Prevents child from touching heat elements on the stove.	Steel railing around burners prevents fingers from reaching hot burners or pulling hot pots off the stove.

SAFETY GATES

PRESSURE GATE

42. · 50 INCH VINYL COATED WIRE MESH 32" HIGH

SAFETY GATES
4 FEET
5 FEET
8 FEET

Portable pressure gates are adjustable up to four feet and are locked within a door frame by a pressure bar. They will give way if pushed hard enough. Portable pressure mesh gates have smaller openings that prevent a child's hands or head from going through. Since the portables are available in a variety of width sizes, you may want to consider buying a gate wider than necessary for your doorway to keep a maximum of pressure. Probably the most secure is the permanent type of folding gate that is attached by screw and hinge to one side of a door frame. They are available in sizes from 4 to 8 feet. Only the permanent type should be used for areas such as stairways where you need continual security.

General Comments

- Cardboard, wooden, and plastic wedges often do as well as purchased gadgets to keep drawers, doors, cabinets, etc., closed.
- It's better to store dangerous products completely out of reach of a young child than to leave them within reach and try to devise a safety device.
- Any safety device will eventually become an opportunity for problem solving by a child. Be sure to update your devices to match the child's ability when he is older.

2

TEMPERAMENT AND INDIVIDUAL DIFFERENCES

background/preparation

Goals to Work Toward in Presenting This Topic

To parent successfully and be able to solve child-rearing problems that arise, parents need to consider the individual style and temperament differences of each family member. Instead of wishing that a child would act differently and thus alleviate a problem, parents should try to remember that their child is a unique individual and has a certain style that needs to be understood and worked with throughout the child-rearing years.[1]

The goals to work toward on this discussion are: (1) to give parents a framework for understanding children's temperaments and how each child differs from other children;[2] (2) to help parents understand their child according to this framework; (3) to help parents begin to work out their child-rearing problems and questions keeping the individual styles of its family members in mind; (4) to provide parents with a set of non-judgmental terms ("labels") that can be used by them to describe their child's personality characteristics in a positive way.

Typical Parental Interests and Concerns About This Topic

1. How can I incorporate a determined child into our family?
2. Is Ben hyperactive? He never stays still. I wonder how he will ever learn.
3. My child cannot change from one activity to another without getting frustrated.
4. I do not know how to work with my child's persistence.
5. Reed is very quiet in new situations. Some of my friends think he's very insecure.
6. My child is never hesitant to go anywhere and never minds if I leave her. Although that makes some things easy for me, I wonder about her attachment to me.
7. Liz gets up at the same time each morning no matter what time I put her to sleep. To avoid a grouchy day with her, she has to be in bed by 7:30 every night. This schedule makes me really

---

1. Often this is difficult for parents to do. It is only after they learn about different kinds of temperaments that they begin to see why their children and they themselves have certain kinds of interaction problems. Learning about the impact of different children's temperaments is often impossible for a first-time parent to work out on her own.

2. For information on the social-emotional differences of one- to six-month-olds, see pp. 120–128.

tense because it isn't always convenient to get her to bed at that time.

Areas of Information You Will Need to Learn About to Teach This Topic

- Different temperaments found in children and adults. (See Thomas, Chess, and Birch, and Brazelton references in the "Readings and Other Resources" section, p. 342.)
- How to recognize different temperaments in children.
- How to advise parents of different temperaments to work with children in a positive way.

Family Dynamics—What This Topic Means Psychologically to Parent and Child

Parents are often unaware of their child's individual temperament and style. They may be aware of certain components of his style, but often are not sure if these are really a part of him, a part of simply being a child, or something that they have influenced or made part of his style. Parents who don't understand their child's true temperament and their own can feel frustrated in their parenting and uncertain of their parenting skills.

A child whose temperament is not understood or who is not dealt with in a positive way can begin to see himself negatively. He may feel that he is not meeting his own or his parents' expectations of him. A child whose style is understood and respected, however, will be able to grow more confidently and have a better chance for success as an adult.

Sample Concern of Parents

Concern	*Critical Issues*
Cameron is very active and that tends to be our major problem. If we take him	—Awareness of active style.
	—Ways to handle active children.

anywhere where he needs to be quiet, it's a disaster because he cries and has tantrums if we do not let him run around. I get tired of having either my husband or myself standing alone at a gathering because the other is following Cameron around.

—Parent's frustration.

Key Questions

1. What happens, in detail, at a gathering? What do you do? What does Cameron do? What does your husband do?
2. What future benefits can you see of having an active child? What disadvantages do you see?

For the group

3. How do your children behave at gatherings?
4. How do you and your spouse feel when one of you watches your child and the other is with the group?
5. How can parents help an active child to be part of a group?

For examples of how to help parents with "difficult" children, "slow-to-warm-up" children, and with "goodness of fit" differences between parents and children, see Rothenberg, *PETP,* Pt. III, ch. 2, pp. 272–277.

Readings and Other Resources

Berkman, Sue, "Your Baby's Temperament," *American Baby.* (This article is reprinted in its entirety in "Handouts," pp. 349–351.)

*Brazelton, T. Berry, *Infants and Mothers* (New York: Dell Publishing, 1983).

Chess, Stella, Thomas, Alexander and Birch, Herbert, *Your Child is a Person* (New York: Penguin, 1965), (out of print but still available in libraries).

*Chess, Stella and Thomas, Alexander, *Know Your Child* (New York: Basic Books, 1989).

Chess, Stella and Thomas, Alexander, *Temperament in Clinical Practice* (New York: Guilford Books, 1986).

Flexible, Fearful or Feisty: The Different Tempera-ments of Infants and Toddlers (Sacramento, Cal.: Child Care Video Magazine). This 29-minute video-tape can be ordered for $65 (plus tax for Cal. residents) from: Bureau of Publications Sales Unit, California State Dept. of Education, P.O. Box 271, Sacramento, Cal. 95812-0271. [(916) 445-1260].

*Kurcinka, Mary, *Raising Your Spirited Child* (New York: Harper Collins, 1992).

Lieberman, Alicia, *The Emotional Life of the Toddler* (New York: Macmillan, 1993), Chapters 4, 5, and 6.

Rothenberg, B. Annye, et al., *Parentmaking Educators Training Program* (Menlo Park, Cal.: Banster Press, 1993), Part III, Chapter 2 on temperament.

Thomas, Alexander and Chess, Stella, *Temperament and Development* (New York: Brunner/Mazel, 1977).

Turecki, Stanley, *The Difficult Child* (New York: Bantam, 1989).

teaching/presentation

Homework

The homework assignment, "Observation on Individual Differences," asks each parent to take a look at the individual style of her child as a way of gaining insight into the child's behavior. It also provides an opportunity for parents to look at their own temperament and how it affects their parenting. (Parents usually find this information most meaningful when their child is about a year old or older.)

Practical Suggestions or Strategies for Teaching This Topic

The subject of individual differences should be scheduled near the beginning of the series. Talking about different styles and temperaments enables group members to better understand one another as well as their own families.

Particular care should be given to those parents who have a child with a difficult-to-work-with style. These parents can feel that there is no hope; this is not true, but it does mean that they will have more work to do. Encourage group members to understand and help one another and not compete.

The discussion can get tiresome if every parent talks in detail about her child's style. Encourage each parent to talk about some aspect of her child's style, but not all of it. They should also talk about aspects of their own styles. Parents will enjoy and benefit from hearing descriptions of what other parents and children are like.

This topic intertwines itself with every topic you will discuss during the series. The better you know each child's and each parent's style, the more meaningful your work will be with each family.

Mini-lecture and Lead-off Questions for Discussion[3]

Sample mini-lecture

First week. This topic should be covered in two parts. During the first week, the topic should be introduced and copies of the framework for determining a child's style should be presented (see "Handouts"). During the following week, after

---

3. See *PETP*, pp. 272–287 for further mini-lecture information on this topic.

OBSERVATION ON INDIVIDUAL DIFFERENCES

(15 months–3 years)

For next week, please look at your child in terms of his/her "individual style." It is this individuality that makes your child very special. The following observation may give you more insight into your child's behavior.

Specific temperament styles

1. How active is your toddler? (For example, does he/she often run, jump, love to climb, bounce, or is he/she more interested in sitting and looking at books, puzzles, etc.?)

2. Does your toddler have a regular rhythm to his/her behavior? (For example, does your child like to eat at the same time, nap at the same time, and go to bed at the same time—or do you find that one day he/she naps at one time and the next day another?)

3. Is your child enthusiastic about new experiences or is he/she more on the hesitant side? (For example, with a new setting, will your child jump in or stay by you? With a new food, will he/she take a bite or need more experience with it?)

4. What is your child's mood most of the time? (For example, how does he/she wake up from naps and nighttime sleep—happy or crying? Does your child tend to be lighthearted or serious about many things?)

5. How well does your child concentrate? (For example, in his/her usual play style, does play continue for a long time or does any new stimulus get your child going in another direction?)

6. Is your child persistent or not persistent? (For example, does he/she try to master a toy and try until successful or frustrated, or does he/she try and try and if success isn't gained put the toy away for something else?)

More general differences

1. What are some things about your child/s behavior or skills that make him/her easier to handle than other toddlers seem to be?

2. Can you think of some things that make your child somewhat more difficult to handle than other toddlers seem to be?

3. Consider your own temperament styles. What styles do you have that make it easier for you to handle your toddler? What styles do you have that make it harder for you to handle your toddler?

4. Ask your spouse to think about his own temperament. What characteristics does he think he has that make it easier for him to handle your toddler? What characteristics does he think he has that make it more difficult for him to handle your toddler?

Parent's name _____ Date _____ Child's age _____

discussing homework, the framework can be individualized to fit each child, keeping the homework observations in mind. This can best be done by observing the children either through a one-way window or in their playroom; discussion of the various styles works best after the parents have had a chance to meet each other's children.

Children have different styles and temperaments even at birth. Infants will react differently when a cloth is laid over their face and will take different amounts of time to recover after being upset. It is usually hard for the first-time parent to notice temperament differences in very young babies, but the differences become clearer with time and as parents get to know other children. By now most of you have probably noticed some of the distinguishing characteristics of your child's temperament or personality, for example, he or she never gives up; is very active; withdraws in new situations; is passive; sleeps quietly; accepts a new person easily; wakes from sleep crying and unhappy; is easily disturbed.

As parents we sometimes think that if we could only do a better job of child rearing, some of the traits we don't like in our children would vanish. It seems, however, that children are born with certain traits, and each child's and each parent's interaction with these traits helps the child to become what he will be. Everything is not dependent on our child's temperament alone, nor on the way we handle our child, but on a combination of the two. I would like to pass out a handout that describes characteristics that should be noted when individual differences among children are being considered (see p. 348). The handout is based on information contained in *Your Child is a Person* and other books by Chess and Thomas. As we discuss the handout, please ask any questions you may have.

Now discuss the handout, clarifying for the parents what the aspects of temperament mean. Use examples from children you know or from group members' own children. Then you might say:

After looking at the main points of the handout, we can see that it is possible to make many generalizations about ways to

effectively handle our children, keeping the categories of temperament in mind. For example, if a child has difficulty handling new social situations and we push her too hard, most likely the child's tendency will be to withdraw. If we wait and are patient, the child will eventually go forward. If a child has a high activity level, he will have trouble going for long rides in a car without breaks where he can be active. And if a child has difficulty changing from one situation to another he will need time to move slowly or should be given forewarning.

Can you think of something about your child's temperament that is important for you to consider in determining how to handle him better in the future?

After this discussion, pass out the homework "Observation on Individual Differences." Then tell the class:

It is important for you to spend time working carefully on this homework. Every discussion we have for the rest of the series, be it on language, setting limits, socialization, or whatever, will need to take into account your child's temperament. Do you have any questions?

Second week. **Now that we've had a chance to observe our children, let's talk about those characteristics that make them easier to handle and those that make them more difficult to handle. Then we can go on to talk about our own styles—things that we and our spouses do that make it easier and harder for us to handle our children.**

As parents talk about their children, be alert for: (1) parents who have built up negative feelings toward their child—they need some help from you or the group to show them some of the positive qualities their child has;[4] (2) parents who want help with some aspect of the child's temperament (for example, what to do about a child who

---

4. You will find that knowing about the pros and cons of the different aspects of temperament will be of value to you and the parents. *Raising Your Spirited Child* by Mary Sheedy Kurcinka (New York: Harper-Collins, 1991) provides helpful information on the pros and cons of aspects of temperament as does the "Additional Information" section of this chapter. In addition to the focus on temperament in these sessions, you may find that counseling about temperament needs to be continued throughout the rest of the series.

stays on the parent's lap during the whole two hours of play group)—they need general guidance about how they can best help their child; and (3) parents who have an unrealistic picture (positive *or* negative) of what their child is like—they need a gradual introduction to who their child really is.

After guiding the discussion you might wish to summarize the main points of the topic:

Not every parent has a child whose temperament best suits her. Some of us have an active child, but would be more comfortable with a more passive child. Some of us wish our child had a more regular schedule. If we recognize and understand our child's individual temperament and make peace with our own style and that of our spouse, we can work out the best way of parenting for our individual parent-child teams. This takes time, however, and should be a flexible plan.

Additional Information for Parents

When considering children's styles, it helps to look at the plusses and minuses of each style:

Activity Level. If a child has a high activity level, his motor skills will probably develop faster, he'll most likely have a great deal of energy, he will be involved in lots of interesting things, and he may enjoy others very much. Sometimes it is difficult for the adults in a family to keep up with this type of child's pace.

If a child has a low activity level, his large-motor skills may not develop as quickly as those of a high-activity child. By the age of five, however, the more inactive child has usually caught up. It is easy for parents of inactive children to keep up with their children's pace, but they need to think more about guiding their children into some active pursuits.

Pattern. A child who follows a regular pattern is predictable—a parent knows when the child likes to eat, sleep, and perhaps go to the toilet. Having a child with regular habits makes planning the day fairly easy, but it can be hard to work with such a child when traveling or visiting.

It is difficult to determine a daily schedule for a child who follows irregular patterns. Parents will have to work hard to help such children adapt to a routine, but it is easy to take them places and they are generally flexible.

Approach/Withdrawal in New Situations. The child who approaches new situations with ease likes to go places, is easy to include, and often gets positive responses from adults because he is more outgoing.

The more hesitant child will need your consistent, slow-paced help to enable him to get along with new people and new places. He often becomes very comfortable with the new situation in time, as he learns more about it. This child likes and needs repetitive experiences to gain confidence.

Adaptability to Change in Routine. The child who has trouble changing his routine cannot be told to "come on" and "hurry up" without becoming frustrated. She needs to be told ahead of time what will be happening, and it helps the child make the transition more easily if there is an exciting element in the activity that is approaching. Parents can say, for example, "In a few minutes it will be time for your bath. We will make lots of bubbles."

If your child changes routines easily, he will readily go from one activity to the other. It is easy to take advantage of this child, however, and at times expect him to meet your commands too quickly.

Level of Sensitivity. If a child has a low level of sensitivity to his environment, it is likely he does not awaken easily during naps or at night. Little things probably don't bother him.

The more sensitive child probably responds more to noise and may be frightened by vacuum cleaners, loud trucks, and similar sounds.

Quality of Mood. It is easier to be with a child who generally has a happy disposition or style. The happy child smiles and laughs easily.

It is harder to be with a negative child and it is harder for that child to gain positive responses from others. Children with more negative styles do well with a lot of praise, and in calm, repetitive situations.

Intensity. An intense child lets you know what she likes and does not like. This can make adults uncomfortable, but the messages are clear.

When a child is not very intense, it is easy to overlook how he feels. The less intense child is easier to deal with than the intense child in immediate situations, but one must be careful to watch for hidden feelings in later years.

Distractability. When a child has a strong ability to concentrate, it is very easy for him to learn new things but hard for an adult to guide him.

When a child distracts easily, an adult can guide him more easily.

Persistence and Attention Span. The persistent child can become very frustrated if he keeps trying and trying, but can't make something work or happen. He can stay with something for a long time but may need to be taught how to handle frustration and go on to something else.

The not-so-persistent child may be a bit more relaxed but may not have the stick-to-it-iveness required for some activities.

(Additional information on Temperament can be found in *PETP,* pp. 271–289.

Handouts

The handout "Temperament and Individual Differences" describes a concrete way parents can look at their child's style. A second section, "Your Baby's Temperament," is reprinted in its entirety from *American Baby.* In Rothenberg, *PETP,* there are also several handouts for parents, "Your Child's Temperament: Easy, Difficult or Slow-to-warm-up"; "Coping with Your Child's Personality"; and "Suggestions for Parents to Enhance their Young Child's Temperament Style."

TEMPERAMENT AND INDIVIDUAL DIFFERENCES

(older babies–3 years)

The following are descriptions of characteristics that are useful when considering individual differences among children. Each individual child will fall somewhere between the two extremes given for each category. Taken all together, the characteristics form a picture of an individual child's temperament.

Activity level. This encompasses the degree of your child's activity, both waking and sleeping.

Very mobile—"into everything."	Less mobile—remains where he's put.
Wiggles and squirms in highchair.	Sits quietly in highchair.
Much movement during sleep.	Sleeps quietly.

Regularity. This trait deals with how predictable your child is and has been in terms of daily scheduling.

Difficult to schedule as an infant.	Easily scheduled as an infant.
Schedule varies from day to day.	Schedule remains consistent from day to day.
Parent never certain when he will be hungry or sleepy.	Eats and sleeps at approximately same time every day.

Approach/withdrawal in a new situation. This indicates your child's characteristic response to a *new* situation.

In a new place, stays close to parent, observing cautiously.	In a new place, plays and explores happily.
Rejects a new food immediately.	Accepts a new food readily.

Adaptability to change in routine. This describes *how long* it takes your child to adjust to a new or changed situation.

Difficulty in moving from two naps to one.	Moves easily from two naps to one.
Requires repeated interaction with a new person before accepting him or her.	Accepts a new person easily.

Level of sensitivity. This encompasses your child's sensitivity to his environment.

Light sleeper, easily disturbed by noise or movement nearby.	Deep sleeper, undisturbed by moderate noise or movement nearby.
Strong negative reaction to food he dislikes (gags, spits out, grimaces).	Accepts most foods, even if not his favorites.

Quality of mood (negative/positive). This describes the mood that seems most characteristic of your child.

Wakens from sleep crying and unhappy.	Wakens from sleep smiling and content.
Meets most daily situations (meals, naps, bath, etc.) with negative reactions.	Meets most daily situations with positive reactions.

Intensity. This is indicated by the amount of energy your child uses in his characteristic behavior and in reacting to what happens to him.

In play, bangs and throws toys, laughs and vocalizes loudly.	Plays quietly, handling toys gently, observing intently.
When upset, wails loudly—when happy, laughs out loud.	When upset, whimpers softly—when happy, smiles.

Distractability. This describes how easily your child is diverted from an activity.

Easily distracted from a forbidden object.	Returns to forbidden object again and again.
Play is easily interrupted by phone ringing or someone entering room.	Play is usually not disturbed by outside distractions.

Persistence and attention span. This encompasses your child's ability to persist in attaining a goal and to attend to one activity for a period of time.

Tries over and over to get a toy just out of reach or do something difficult.	Gives up after a few attempts.
Plays with one toy for an extended period.	Moves rapidly from toy to toy during play.

PARENTMAKING: A Practical Handbook for Teaching Parent Classes About Babies and Toddlers by B. Annye Rothenberg, Ph.D., et al. © 1995 Banster Press, P.O. Box 7326, Menlo Park, CA 94026. Can copy for parent classes if this notice is included in full.

Your Baby's Temperament: Its Crucial Role in Child Raising

by Sue Berkman

When she was pregnant, Jennifer had it all figured out. Her baby would be born in the spring, and by Labor Day she would be back in full swing as a freelance magazine illustrator. What could be more perfect? The summer months would allow her to establish a routine of child care, and even when she began to take work, she could still be a full-time mother. But that's not the way things turned out.

"What happened," recalls Jennifer, "was that Pamela demanded every instant of my time and every ounce of my energy. When she should have been sleeping, she would often be awake and screaming. Feeding—even if it wasn't time—would sometimes work to quiet her but other times not. During the day I was always so tense and irritated that it was impossible to even think of working. And even in the evenings when my husband was home, I was too tired and depressed to think of anything except crawling into bed."

Jennifer's story demonstrates a fact of life, long overlooked by child-care authorities: to a surpris-

ing degree, the behavior of the baby determines the behavior of his parents. Before 1940, in the belief that a youngster's characteristics are shaped significantly by parental influence, child-rearing authorities emphasized strict rules for feeding and discipline. With the realization that not all children thrived on this regimen, the pendulum began to swing to the opposite extreme. Over the succeeding decades, the authoritative word was *permissiveness.* But in neither case did researchers consider the influence might also run the other way—that a child might act upon his parents and might even be responsible for the kind of parental treatment he receives.

Unique among the investigators who were determined to prove their one-sided child guidance dictums were Alexander Thomas and Stella Chess. He is a professor of psychiatry and she is a professor of child psychiatry at the New York University School of Medicine. For over twenty years they have been working together on a major research problem: the effect of temperament on the mental health of children and of the adults these children become.

As their research demonstrates, science now substantiates what most mothers for thousands of years have probably known—that children differ from infancy onward. Although pediatricians and nurses have, from practical experience, known it too, most have hesitated to act on their intuitive belief that children with basic temperamental differences should be handled differently.

Now, because of the finding of these two experts, parents can take heart in the fact that, from the very beginning, the success of the child-rearing approaches they use depends heavily on the nature of the child born to them, not on some hidden weakness—or strength—buried deep within themselves.

Differences in Children

Thomas and Chess have defined three main groups of temperamental characteristics, which they believe differentiate and define the "easy"

Sue Berkman is a free-lance writer in New York. Reprinted with permission from *American Baby Magazine.*

child, the "difficult" child, and the "slow-to-warm-up" child.

According to Dr. Chess, the "easy" child is just that—easy to live with and to come into contact with. His habits are regular, he responds positively to new situations, and he is quick to adapt to new people, places and things. The easy child tends to be cheerful and contented.

The "difficult" child, on the other hand is, well, difficult. As an infant he has very irregular eating, sleeping and eliminating habits. When exposed to a new stimulus or situation, whether it pertains to foods, clothing, people or places, the difficult child either withdraws noisily or protests vigorously. By three years of age, this type of child will express disappointment "not with a whimper but with a bang"; frustration will usually produce a violent tantrum.

Some researchers working with Drs. Thomas and Chess describe such children as "mother killers." While this may seem a little strong, the difficult child can cause feelings of frustration, guilt and anxiety, turning a normal mother into an abnormal one.

A child who is "slow-to-warm-up" takes a long time to adapt and tends to withdraw from new situations, generally with little or no fuss. "These children can be trying too," Dr. Chess comments. "As babies they are likely to respond to a new food by letting it dribble out of their mouths; in nursery school they remain on the sidelines for several weeks; in kindergarten, when pushed to take part in some activity, they struggle quietly to escape."

Of the hundreds of children studied by Thomas and Chess, two-thirds fall clearly into one or another of these categories, based on the classifications of nine individual behavioral characteristics. These characteristics include:

1. *Activity Level.* Some babies are very active, moving from spot to spot in the crib, kicking off their covers, constantly squirming while being diapered—right on to the moment their eyes shut in sleep. Others tend to be quiet, lying where they are placed and moving both little and slowly. Sometimes such children are almost as still when awake as when asleep.

2. *Regularity.* Some babies are very regular when

it comes to being hungry, needing to eliminate, or being ready for a nap. Others are much less predictable. There is no telling when they will be hungry or how hungry they will be. Naptime may vary from one day to the next.

3. *Adaptability to new situations.* Some babies have no trouble with an initial response to new experiences (the first bath may find them taking to the water like ducks). Others do not splash and kick or coo and play with their mothers. They scream when put into the bath for the first time. Such babies spit out many new foods at first, cry at the sight of a stranger, and react to strange places.

4. *Adaptability to change in routine.* Some babies shift easily and quickly to a changing schedule, altering their behavior to fit in with the pattern the parents want to set. Others fuss and cry or scream and kick when their routines are changed. Shaping the child's behavior is difficult and requires much repetition. Some babies do not adapt at all; it is the parent who often adjusts to the child's pattern rather than continue the unsuccessful struggle to impose preferences.

5. *Level of sensory threshold.* Babies with a high "sensory threshold" are not startled by loud noises, nor are they bothered by bright lights. The texture, fabric, or even the temperature of clothing makes little difference to them. They do not react to being wet or soiled. At the other extreme are the sensitive ones who wake at the slightest sound or change of environment. Some literally shudder at the mere whiff of a disliked food.

6. *Positive or negative mood.* Some children may give no sign that they are either for or against what is happening. They may be classified as neutral. Most babies, however, will show a preponderance of either positive (cooing, gurgling, smiling, giggling) or negative (fussing, crying, sobbing in great gasps) reactions to everything.

7. *Intensity of response.* One child may show hunger by screaming; another may cry softly. One may only open his mouth for food; another may strain toward the spoon. When behavior is characterized by high energy expenditure, it is judged intense, while low energy expenditure is deemed mild. The intensity of response does not relate to whether the baby is showing a positive

or negative mood; it refers to energy expressed in the behavior.

8. *Distractability.* Some babies can concentrate better than others. One child may drink his bottle until he is full, no matter what his environment; another might be diverted by the slightest movement.

9. *Persistence.* In a newborn, persistence can be noticed very early. Some infants will suck diligently at the nipple even when no milk is coming through, while others will give it up quickly. The persistent infant will keep trying to reach a toy that is out of reach, while the non-persistent one will give up after a try or two. A baby with a long attention span can gaze at a cradle gym intently for long periods of time, while one with a short attention span will focus only briefly on any activity or aspect of the environment around him.

Possible Causes

What can explain such basic temperamental differences? Norwegian researchers, using the technique of the New York team of investigators to study both identical and nonidentical twins, indicate that the answer may be found, in part, in genetic differences. One investigator, Anna Marie Torgersen, studied her subjects at two months of age (about the time that a baby's behavior becomes stabilized), and again at nine months. Each time she found that one identical twin (identical meaning having the same genes) was likely to resemble the other in temperament much more closely than did the nonidentical pairs. There seemed to be a genetic component for all the nine traits identified by Thomas and Chess. Evidence for the role of heredity in temperament was strengthened by the results of a study of children of Puerto Rican working class families. These children showed temperamental characteristics similar to the children from middle and upper class families, despite differences in child-rearing practices.

One important point brought to light by these studies is that each type of child can influence parental behavior which, in turn, can influence the child's subsequent development. University of Rochester psychologist Arnold J. Sameroff has found that children with difficult temperaments at the age of four months are the most likely to score lowest on intelligence tests at thirty months.

"The child's temperament at four months of age," Sameroff believes, "influences how the parents are going to treat him in the future. The parent of a child with a difficult temperament can become turned off to that child in some way, and as a consequence may not provide the stimulation and caretaking that would lead to the child's competent performance at 30 months of age."

However, guidance for parents that help them work *with* their child's temperament can go a long way to enhance parent-baby interaction.

This does not mean that a child moves along inevitably in a preordained fashion no matter what the parents do. What it does mean is that a parent is far better off not going by the book. Babies, in short, write their own books. Says Dr. Hilde Bruch, prominent child psychiatrist at Columbia University, "Modern parent education is characterized by the experts' pointing out in great detail all the mistakes parents have made and can possibly make and substituting 'scientific knowledge' for the tradition of the 'good old days'."

Until recently, a mother and father might have concluded that they are not only guilty before proven innocent, but they are also guilty before they even act. They might have believed that every aspect of their child's personality was caused by their child rearing philosophy and skills. Now, with such researchers as Alexander Thomas and Stella Chess leading the way, the pendulum has begun to swing back. With luck it will fall short of a full return, and parents will realize the need to deal differently with different offspring.

Does this imply more responsibility for parents? "Yes," says Dr. Stella Chess, "but, less guilt and more pleasure, too."

3

FAMILY SIZE

background/preparation

Goals to Work Toward in Presenting This Topic

Thoughts about whether or not to have a second child (and, if so, when) can begin for many parents as early as their child's first birthday and can continue for many years. At some point in their first years of parenting, most parents feel the need to discuss this issue, and for those who have already decided, the topic is still of sufficient interest to be included for discussion.

The goals to work toward on this topic are: (1) to discuss information about family size (one-child and more-than-one child families) from the point of view of both parent and child, and to discuss information about the spacing of children; (2) to help parents begin to clarify their feelings about the various decisions possible.

Typical Parental Interests and Concerns About This Topic

1. My husband and I are not at all sure that we want a second child, but we also worry about our son being an only child. What are the drawbacks for him and for us if we decide that one is enough?

2. Is it true that only children are "spoiled" (selfish, lonely, shy)?
3. When is the best time to have a second child? How old should your first child be?
4. We always planned to have two children, but now we just can't believe we could ever love another baby as much as we love our daughter. Is it right to have another one when we feel this way?
5. We can't seem to make up our minds. Our first baby has been a difficult one for us, and, frankly, I'm not sure I could handle it all over again. Is the second child usually an "easier" baby?
6. Can proper spacing eliminate sibling rivalry?
7. My husband wants another child but I don't. How can we begin to resolve this disagreement?
8. What about my career, my age, and the issue of fertility when thinking about more children?

Areas of Information You Will Need to Learn About to Teach This Topic

One-child families.
— Characteristics of the "only child."
— Positive and negative aspects for parents and child.
— Ways of coping with the negative aspects.
— Parents' feelings about this decision.
More-than-one-child families.

— Positive and negative aspects for parents and children.
— Impact of the second child on the family.
— Parents' feelings about this decision.
Spacing of children.
— Medical/physical considerations.
— Meaning of various age differences for the children.
— Meaning of various age differences between children for the parents.

Family Dynamics—What This Topic Means Psychologically to Parent and Child[1]

Whether or not to have a second child is a major decision for most parents. But it differs substantially from their initial decision to become parents because they now have actual knowledge of parenting—what it entails, how they adjusted to it, and their feelings about it. There is also a third person—the first child—to consider this time.

Even though statistics show that parents are having smaller families today, the myths about the "only child" still linger and are of concern to many couples. They wonder if they are being selfish to "deprive" their child of a sibling. They worry about what they consider to be the negative aspects for their child (loneliness, shyness, too much adult attention) and that he will somehow blame them later.

If parents decide they do want a second child, the focus of their concern generally shifts to the first child and the impact of their decision on him. The age range between the children seems critical to most and they try to figure out what they feel will be the best spacing for their children. What they usually discover, after much consideration, is that this is like trying to predict the future—almost impossible and very frustrating. For others the spacing between children may be based almost entirely on maternal age, fertility questions, career concerns, etc. Another major concern to many parents is the need to somehow divide their time and their love between two children. They can see what seem to be disadvantages for both their children and themselves, and they often feel guilty even before the second child is born.

While in the decision-making process, the negative aspects of both possibilities can seem to stand out very clearly. Parents' love for their first child and their desire to do their best for him can actually get in the way of their considering each possibility in a balanced manner, especially since the child cannot be consulted as to his feelings and wishes.

It can be a difficult decision for parents to make, but the best information available to any couple is their knowledge of themselves, their child, and their parenting—what it means to them and how they feel about it. In the last analysis, these factors are the ones that must be weighed so that each couple can make the best decision for their family.

Sample Concern of Parents[2]

Concern: *More Than One Child*	*Critical Issues*
We are really hung up about whether or not to have another child. Our son has been such a good baby—happy, placid, and easy to care for. Things have been so good that I am almost afraid to try again for fear that we could upset the balance and happiness we have now. At the same time, that seems like a pretty selfish reason *not* to have another baby. How can we know whether it's worth the risk?	—Parent's concern about the known vs. the unknown. —Parents' judgment of their own feelings.

Key Questions

1. Can you describe in more depth what you mean by "upsetting the balance"?

---

1. This section will address only the parents' feelings and concerns since the child really cannot take part in making this decision.

2. Since several main issues are involved in this topic, two common concerns of parents are described.

2. How do you think a family might change with the arrival of a second child?

For the group

3. What might be some advantages and disadvantages of an only child to each of you?

Concern: Spacing	*Critical Issues*
How can you decide when the best time is to have a second child? Sometimes I think that it would be better to do it before our little girl is old enough to really comprehend it and be jealous—like before she's three. Other times it seems like it would be better to wait until she's a little older so I can give her all my time and attention while she's little. Then, after she's in nursery school and more independent, maybe she wouldn't mind so much and could enjoy a new baby more. We just can't seem to make up our minds. But we also	—Numerous feelings about the spacing of children with the focus of concern on the first child.

have to consider our age, our careers being put on hold, and will I be able to get pregnant? Help!

—Other factors involved in this decision

Key Questions

1. It sounds like you have really considered how various age differences will affect your daughter. Do you and your husband have any strong feelings about when would be best for *you*? What are they?

For the group

2. Let's spend some time discussing spacing as it affects both parents and children.

Readings and Other Resources

---

*Ames, Louise Bates, *He Hit Me First* (New York: Warner Books, 1989), Chapter 11.

Bank, Stephen P. and Kahn, Michael D., *The Sibling Bond* (New York: Basic Books, 1983).

*Newman, Susan, *Parenting an Only Child* (New York, N.Y.: Bantam Doubleday, 1990).

Roiphe, Anne, "Why Have More Than One?" *N.Y. Times Magazine*. (This article is reprinted in its entirety in "Handouts," p. 358.)

Weiss, Joan Solomon, *Your Second Child* (New York: Summit Books, 1981).

teaching/presentation

Homework

There is no written homework for this topic. Parents, however, should be asked to discuss the topic as a couple during the week before the class and to be ready with questions, concerns, and feelings they wish to share with the group.

Practical Suggestions or Strategies for Teaching This Topic

• The most difficult part of leading this discussion is trying to keep the main issues separate from each other. Careful organization is called for in this topic, since a "free-for-all" discussion usually leaves everyone dissatisfied and concerns unanswered.

• Every group will be composed of individuals who are at different places in the family size decision-making process. You will have parents who already know that they want a second child; their concern will be what spacing is best. There will be parents who know that they do not want another child; their concern will be the one-child family. You will also have parents who are as yet undecided, and you may also have parents who are pregnant with a second child. After finding out where each parent in the group is in the decision-making process, you might suggest that the discussion follow this outline:

— Making the decision about whether to have a second child. In handling this area first, parents who are uncertain can benefit from hearing from those who have already decided. Hearing a variety of experiences and reasons behind decisions brings to light the various aspects of the subject that need consideration and also emphasizes the different approaches that couples may use to problem solve.

— One-child families and concerns about the "only child."

— More-than-one-child families and the spacing of children.

• As the leader of the group, your opinions and ideas may carry more weight in this area than you might expect. You can, of course, share with the parents your personal decisions and opinions, but be careful to emphasize that they are yours, not necessarily either universal or expert.

• Family size and the spacing of children are areas in which many people have strong beliefs and opinions. Since the topic is often scheduled toward the end of the series, parents by then will probably have developed mutual respect and support. Despite this you may still need to work to keep the discussion positive and helpful, and to guard against judgmental or critical remarks about any parent's beliefs or feelings. This subject is a very personal one, and many parents may feel vulnerable.

• Try to help each parent separate her own feelings from others' expectations of her. This effort can help group members recognize that people are often easily swayed by others' opinions or expectations, and it emphasizes how individual a

decision this particular one is for each couple represented in the group.

• The discussion of this area tends to be long. Try to leave enough time in the series to discuss it fully.

Mini-lecture and Lead-off Questions for Discussion

With brief opening remarks, you can set a tone of openness and respect for each parent's opinions. You might begin by saying:

Although biological considerations such as age, difficulty in becoming pregnant or "surprise" pregnancies often remove the decision from us, the question of whether or not to have a second child is a very personal and intimate one for each couple represented here. Some of you have already made a decision in this area and some have not. I hope that those of you who have will feel able to share the reasons for your decision with the group. Your experiences can be a help to those who are still searching for the best answer for themselves.

There are many feelings that come to bear on this question, not the least of which are your feelings about your own childhood, the feelings you have about the time you've had with your first child, and your feelings about the impact of parenting on your relationship with your spouse. The goal of our discussion today is to help each parent in the group clarify her thoughts and feelings so that she can make the very best decision—with her spouse—for herself and her family, or be comfortable with the decision she has already made. With that goal in mind, let's go around the group and have each of you share where you are in the process of making this decision. Let's keep in mind as we discuss and listen that we're talking about where each of you stands today. You may change your minds many times during the next several months or years.

After the parents have shared their situations, you can begin the discussion as outlined in "Practical Suggestions for Teaching This Topic" (p. 354).

Additional Information for Parents

Making the Decision

• Everyone is influenced to some degree (positively and/or negatively) by their own childhood and the characteristics of their parents and siblings. Sometimes it helps to look at these feelings more closely to see how they might be influencing the decisions being made as adults. Sharing feelings about positions held in a family (only child, oldest, youngest) can help parents to know how others felt as children.

• As a couple, parents have a lot more information to work with when confronting the question of a second child than they did before their initial decision to become parents. But the big unknown is the temperament of the second child. Having a second child to be a friend or playmate for the first-born is probably not the best reason for having a second child at all. Parents' feelings and desires (or lack of same) for another child *must* take precedence. The best reason to have another child is because both parents want one.

• Parents are often concerned that they may not be able to love a second child as much as their first. But love does not need to be divided—the more that's expressed, the more there is. Whether parents have one child or six, their goal should be the same—to recognize and nurture the developing individual.

One-Child Families

• At the present time, society's views of family size and purpose are changing and evolving. In the not-so-distant past, large families were necessary for biological and economic survival. This no longer holds true in our culture, but the feelings about small or one-child families being somehow inadequate still linger in many minds. Approximately 20% of the current population are only children, and the percentage is rising. The one-child family is, therefore, no longer that unusual.

• If parents decide to remain a one-child family, they can work on ways to see that their child frequently comes in contact with other people. They can plan to have their child be with other children in a variety of situations, and if no other relatives are in the area can work to create a "family" of close friends and their children with whom to share holidays, vacations, and birthdays.

• The "only child" is a child like any other.

Spacing of Children

• The spacing of children is a very individual decision. There are many considerations, including both parents' temperaments and that of the first child. There are also a lot of unknowns that cannot be planned for. For example, parents may decide that they'd like to have their children two years apart, but the woman may not become pregnant according to the plan. It helps to be somewhat flexible in planning and to be aware of possible pitfalls in a very rigid timetable. There are advantages and disadvantages to every age difference between children. Recognizing this can help parents be more open to the reality of their situation.

• Second children are sometimes considered easier to care for. This is undoubtedly due more to the parents' accumulated knowledge and experience than to any inherent quality of second children. Because every action and activity (bathing, diapering, and so on) is not new for the parents, they tend to be less tense, more confident. Their assurance communicates itself to the new baby, and everyone benefits.

Handouts

The handout "Considerations About the Spacing of Your Children" can be used in conjunction with or as a summary of the discussion of spacing. A second handout, "Why Have More Than One?", is reprinted in its entirety from the *New York Times.*

HANDOUT

CONSIDERATIONS ABOUT THE SPACING OF YOUR CHILDREN

(1–3 years)

1. How did you feel during your last pregnancy? You won't be able to "pamper" yourself as much during another pregnancy since you'll have an older child.

2. How much help (with older child, housework, etc.) can you count on from your spouse and/or other nearby family members? Consider both the periods before and after the new baby arrives.

3. How much physical care does your older child require (lots of lifting or carrying, diaper changes, etc.)?

4. How are you feeling about your relationship with your child? How much independence does he show? How is your spouse's relationship with the child?

5. Consider your feelings about permanently regaining some freedom away from home through a career, volunteer work, hobbies, or school. The closer in age your children are, the shorter the span of time that encompasses the pre-school years.

6. Also consider your feelings about the demands that two children will make on you physically and emotionally. The farther apart children are spaced, the more individual attention you will be able to give each child.

7. How relaxed is your attitude toward housekeeping and other non-child-related responsibilities that you have? Two children close in age may mean you'll have to relax some of your standards or rearrange your priorities for a while.

WHY HAVE MORE THAN ONE?

by Anne Roiphe

Images of man's future that have us standing on our allotted one square foot of space or waiting on infinite lines for a cup of desalinated water; women's new-found drive for self-realization, for doctoral degrees and executive secretaries of their own; concern about holocaust, revolution, depression—these cause many young couples to pause before conceiving a second child. What rational reason could there be for having another baby? The first, after all, has made them parents, has given them the experience of process, of wonder, of exhaustion, of change in life style. Their first-born has succeeded in muting their egotism and shifting the marriage from mere romance to the earnest discipline of baby sitters, tuition plans and Saturdays spent at the zoo. What more could the second child do or be? What vacuum remains for it to fill? Isn't *one* of nature's miracles and all the complications that follow enough? Apparently not. For nearly 50 percent of the parents in the labor rooms in New York Hospital last month, one child was only the beginning. There may be fewer new families being started in America nowadays. Many more young people are delaying or deciding against having children altogether, but for those young Americans who have decided to become parents, the majority still plan on that second baby and maybe more.

The most frequent reason given for the second baby, prior to its birth, is that it will be company for the first, that the first child needs a friend, needs a competitor, should not be the only apple of its parents' eye—it's more normal for the child to have a brother or sister. This reason for conception is one of those harmless rationalizations we use as we climb about our lives. Without dwelling on how ungrateful the first child usually is for this particular gift of normality, it's hardly a decent thing to bring a life into the world in order

to make another life better, happier, more normal. Furthermore, it's an idea that only exists while the second child remains a vague suggestion without particular form. Once the second baby has arrived, its need to be burped, have an allowance and attention paid to its nightmares, its clay ashtrays, will erase all previous considerations of its worth as a companion for the first child. For better or worse, 'til death do us part, it is a life unto itself.

Several young couples expecting a second baby said that they wanted to be sure that at least one of their children would survive. These couples were pushed by some drive toward the immortality of their DNA, some stake in the endurance of their personal helixes. Of course, with infant mortality down so dramatically since the turn of the century and the common childhood illnesses all but defeated, the odds of any particular American child surviving to adulthood are so enormous that one really doesn't have to take a double flier for one success. In actuality, the second child doubles the jeopardy of suffering the incredible pain a loss through birth defect, cancer, or accident can bring. The parent of two or more children is more exposed—double the odds—to the haunting visions of catastrophe that, realistic or not, lie dormant just beneath the gay nursery wallpaper.

It used to be, when people had children to help on the farm or to bring in money, that parents thought of their children as some form of high-premium insurance against future isolation and poverty. Now, of course, most of us know that this land of mobility may very well take our children into universes, psychologically or culturally or physically far distant from ours. Therefore, very few are counting on a second child to increase the chances of a comfortable old age.

Some of the expectant young couples I spoke to were hoping their second child would be of a different sex from their first. They expressed a real desire for a child of each gender. However, they were all quick to say they wanted a healthy baby. They were not having the baby just for sexual variety among the offspring. They would welcome a child of either sex. Since there are as yet no foolproof methods of guaranteeing a baby's sex, one would have to be mad to conceive that second child for reasons of sexual diversity. The chances of disappointment are too great, and while a spouse who turns out in an unexpected or unpleasant way can be discarded, a child is a commitment of another sort.

So then, if none of the reasons people give each other for that second birth seem in and of themselves very convincing, there must be some other, perhaps not entirely conscious, reason that explains it. It must after all have to do with an image of family, an almost unconscious expectation of what that word "family" means—an expectation that goes quite beyond anything a man and woman can reasonably discuss over their afterdinner coffee. Maybe it comes from images of Dick and Jane and Spot in those influential early readers. Maybe it comes from all the weight of the stories of the past, from fairy tales where brothers and sisters vied for the crown, from Bible stories of inheritances stolen, of coats of many colors, from lists of names of sons and daughters that rumble through the Old Testament, the "Odyssey," the "Iliad," the stories of Roman gods. Maybe, on the other hand, our sense of what a family should be comes from some unconscious connection of ourselves with the rest of the animal world, where lion and lioness are standing in the veld, surrounded not by cub but by cubs. Maybe our need to create family comes not only from some need to make life, but to test our quality, our worth, in nurturing it. Or it could be that the second child is a peculiarly unconscious act of faith, a religious act on the part of the parent who says, "If God made more than one living creature, I should, too."

Whatever is valid among these speculations, the fact is that families continue to be created at as fast a rate as they fall apart, and a disappointment and a sense of personal failure racks almost every divorced parent as he anguishes over the end of a not even clearly articulated dream of what the family meant to him.

What really happens when the second child is

born? Immediately, most parents experience guilt for having created the jealousy quickly apparent in the first child. That marks the beginning of the balancing of the needs of one against the other and the tensions that are routine in family life. Soon after the new arrival is absorbed into the fabric of the household, the parents become involved in the truly fascinating game of watching the similarities and differences in their offspring. Late at night they begin discussions on nature versus nurture that may last 40 years. They begin to worry if this one's crankiness, that one's allergies, this one's fear of spiders and that one's resistance to dinner are outward manifestations of something wrong in themselves. Equally, they soar with exultation when one child learns to read prematurely and another has perfect pitch.

There is a kind of family joy when one's offspring is talking back to "Sesame Street" and the neighbor's only babbles to his bottle. This has already been experienced with the first, but with the second comes an additional risk of failure and an additional chance to buttress one's self-pride and self-worth. Perhaps the second will be an athlete or a ballet dancer or a tough guy or a poet, fulfilling some parental ambition that the first didn't. Of course, it's equally possible that the second will be thrown out of school for pushing dope, will wash out, be laid-back, drop out or drift away. The game is played for emotionally high stakes because we are not birds that nudge our young out of the nest and then forget. We know we can be held, we hold ourselves, responsible.

Within the larger family, patterns of behavior can have more variety. The several children of the family, whether of the same sex or not, take into their separate psyches the differing, sometimes conflicting character traits and childhood experiences of their parents. This one is always good and conforming, his anger like nuclear waste buried underground. That one is just like her mother, defiant, courting catastrophe at every turn. In the making of their new family both parents bring a mixed bag of memories from their old. Unconsciously and consciously they repeat patterns of the past. The son is better loved or the daughter always sickly. Sometimes parents try to undo what was done to them as children, often creating traumas in the opposite direction:

"I give my youngest a lot of attention because my older sister was preferred."

The children also shape themselves in response to each other. This one gives up violin lessons because her brother is so good at the cello. That one loves to cook because his sister hates it, and each eyes the other with that mixture of rancor and love, opposition and imitation that becomes, like orange juice and Oreo cookies, the daily fare of family life. In cases where the balance of love and hate dips way to the negative side, the terrible Cain and Abel drama is recreated, to be chewed over and over and regretted endlessly in later years.

When the children reach adolescence, the family dream is subjected to its greatest strain. The children are pulling away and the parents are adjusting both to the ending of their nurturing years and the reality of what they and their genes have wrought. Some may see their own faults, their own failures imitated in their children's gestures. They may have hoped for some degree of human happiness in their children that unfortunately has not been achieved. They repeat through their children the anguishes of their own uncertain acne days. Two children increase the risks all around. No matter what feelings of love and compassion bind the family together, they are strained by the new elements of disenchantment. Illusions fade and expectations (Johnny will pass math next year), (Dad will curb his temper), (Mom will understand me), (Sister will be a tennis champion) die. The wonder that was family life can turn to wormwood, to rue, to ulcers, to compromise, to prune instead of plum. With two children, more possibilities exist that the family playroom can turn into a storage space full of albums never looked at because of painful memories.

On the other hand, if there is only one child, the drama is heightened, the pulling away is more difficult and more terrible. In the multichild family, each child will feel less pressure to stay, but the odds are one or the other will keep some emotional closeness. Sister may be a revolutionary after daddy's heart while brother is a Wall Street lawyer whose name is never spoken. Second sister may be kind or vicious, whatever is the opposite of her sibling, and parents can patch up the

family dream being bewildered, bemused, ashamed and proud at the same time.

Ridiculous as it is, the idea of family stays with us and lurks even in those who would change its form, or outward shape. It is absurd, this giving of love to beings that can never return it because family relationships become tainted with such complex psychological interactions that love itself becomes a word to hide behind.

To father and mother a family is to expose one's most vulnerable flank to certain attack. The hurt when one's child is hurt is unlike any other torture extant. To find oneself even momentarily hating one's own child is a terror of the highest order. To be the object of the anger of one's child, to experience the occasional coldness of his or her eyes, is to be in a special circle of hell. No one can marshal rational arguments against those young people who steer clear of the family encounter entirely, saving their money for skiing weekends in Vermont and their psyches for work and pleasure that depend only on themselves. For the rest of us, who have cornered ourselves into creating families, which may split and re-form in different ways, who, in this way, have dared fate to humiliate us with pain or defeat—we have to recognize that this two-parent, multichild family image at the core of our lives, while preposterous, is still amazingly dear.

There are grand things to say about the sanctity of birth and the grace of nature. I could go on about the bravery of the human spirit that risks disaster in searching for an ideal of family, of generational responsibility. But the last impenetrable line of defense is in certain images shared in a variety of forms by most of us, images that are a part of the parenting experience whether there is one child or many, but if there are more than one, they occupy more internal space, reflect more external time and account for more of what we might call our individual souls. Images of balls thrown in the park, of wheels turning, bikes, skates, hoops, the thumping of jump ropes, the call at dusk of moving shadows, "allee, allee in free," images of a tone-deaf mother hearing her daughter sing at the school assembly, of a father teaching a child to swim, comforting a child crying over a broken bicycle or a lost friendship, of nights spent worrying about a child's school failure, about a sore throat that wouldn't go away, images of a man and woman trying to find the money for a scout trip, or medical school, images of hours spent in the pediatrician's waiting room, in the dentist's waiting room, in the shoe store, at the barber's, of games of Monopoly and Walt Disney movies. Image after image floats up of time spent enmeshed in the seemingly trivial work of family life which, if things go well enough, can make us less alone, can hide from us the vastness of the universe and the insignificance of our individual place in it.

The conventional family dream will have to do some changing. Too many of us don't stay married. Too many of our children end up repudiating our life styles and selected goals. Too many children grow up damaged or abused and pass on

this damage to the family of their own making. But the care of children, the dream of family life must be repaired. We may be riding in a blimp that leaks and is highly flammable, but at the moment we have no other transportation.

I spoke the other day to a man in his 60's who had eight children, one after another, right after World War II. "I had a need," he explained, "to replace the lives that were lost in the war, to replenish the globe." "Now that your children are grown," I asked, "would you do it all over again? Would you have all eight?" "Of course," he replied. "They've made me the man I am." "What about overpopulation," I asked, "aren't you concerned?" "Oh, you're right," he answered. "If I were young today I would really only have two children. But which two?" He looked bewildered. "I could never choose!"

4

NEW BABIES AND SIBLING RIVALRY

background/preparation

Goals to Work Toward in Presenting This Topic

Most people who have had one child give some thought to what it would be like to have a second. Parents who are considering having another child or those already pregnant want to try hard to fully prepare their child for the arrival of a new baby, and have a lot of concerns about what a new baby will mean to the whole family. Parents who already have two or more children usually wish to keep the sibling rivalry to a minimum and thus are very interested in this area as well. Parents who have made a firm decision to have only one child have less interest in the discussion than the others but are curious enough that the session is still worthwhile.

The goals to work toward on this topic are: (1) to help parents become more aware of what is worrying them while they are pregnant with another child; (2) to teach parents some of the things they can do to help their child anticipate a new baby; (3) to give parents a chance to consider what getting adjusted to the new baby could mean for them and their child; (4) to help parents look ahead to their older child's continuing adjustment as the new baby becomes able to move around and really starts to show his own personality.

Typical Parental Interests and Concerns About This Topic

1. What can I do to prepare my two-year-old for the new baby?
2. Lauren has been getting into a lot of things she shouldn't be lately. I think it's because I've been so tired during this pregnancy. I'm not much fun and don't pay as much attention to her.
3. When the new baby is born, I'm probably going to be in the hospital for one to two days. My son and I have never been separated and I'm afraid he's going to be very upset. Should I have my husband bring him to the hospital each day so we can visit?
4. Since our new baby was born about two weeks ago, my older child has become very clinging and nagging. I feel terrible because I can't give her the kind of attention I used to and I feel she is really being deprived.
5. Elizabeth sometimes seems interested in the baby but she is too rough with him. She doesn't seem to understand about being gentle. I'm not sure how to handle this.
6. Michael didn't seem to show any real adjustment problems when our second child was just born, but since the baby has started to crawl, walk around holding on to furniture, and reach

362

other people's things, Michael is constantly angry with him. He pushes him over, hits and teases him. Is this normal?

Areas of Information You Will Need to Learn About to Teach This Topic

- Feelings that family members typically have when the mother is pregnant for the second or later time.
- Things that can be done to prepare a young child for a new sibling.
- Useful techniques that can ease separation difficulties during the mother's hospital stay.
- Things that parents can reasonably expect of themselves during the first few months after a second or later baby is born.
- What can be expected from a young child adjusting to a new baby.
- All about sibling rivalry: how it develops, why it exists, and some guidelines for dealing with it.

Family Dynamics—What This Topic Means Psychologically to Parent and Child

Most parents look forward to the birth of their second child but tend to have several reservations. They may wonder about the impact the baby will have on their older child and on their relationship with each other. Parents sometimes wonder if they'll be able to love their new baby as much as they do their first child. They also wonder if they can guide the older child and new baby into a loving relationship with each other. Parents have memories of their own sibling relationships and may want their own children's relationship to be different and/or more successful.

From the child's point of view, it is nearly impossible for him to grasp the idea that he will be having a new baby brother or sister *until* it actually happens. Young children, however, do respond to changes in their mother's behavior during pregnancy, for example, her tendency to become more introspective and her decreased energy level; and they do respond to changes in the household and the availability of the parents after the baby is there. Since children, especially one- and two-year-olds, are very concrete and very "here and now" in their thinking, they may find it difficult to wait for attention and those other things that were more readily available before the new baby arrived. This is part of why parents usually see some negative reactions in their child after the new baby is born. Many children feel for a while that they have only lost by having a new sibling, not gained.

Sample Concern of Parents

Concern	*Critical Issues*
Our older child is two-and-a-half and our new baby is just five weeks old. We spent a lot of time preparing our older child for the new baby, and since the baby was born we have spent a lot of individual time with our older child. We have been very understanding and accepting of her negative and mixed feelings for the baby and us, and relaxed a lot of our demands because we know this is such a hard time for her. We can't understand why she's becoming more difficult and doing things she shouldn't.	—Older child has been "prepared" for new sibling. —Parents have given much attention and understanding to older child since baby was born. —Parents have asked very little of her. —Child is being more difficult and more negative.

Key Questions

1. What kinds of preparation did you do? What do you think your child was anticipating just before the baby came home?
2. What have you been trying to do with your older child since the baby has been home?
3. What has been the general atmosphere in your home this last month? How hard do you and

your husband have to work to be understanding and available for your older child?

4. What are your feelings about how things are going for you as you try to incorporate your new baby? What are your feelings about your older child at this time?

5. How are things different for your older child than they were before the baby was born? How are the expectations, rules, and limits different from her point of view? Do you think she could be floundering and needing to test limits again because you've cut down your expectations for her and bent over backwards to help her adjust?

Readings and Other Resources

Bank, Stephen P. and Kahn, Michael D., *The Sibling Bond* (New York: Basic Books, 1983).

Colman, Arthur and Colman, Libby, *Pregnancy: The Psychological Experience, Rev. Ed.* (New York: Farrar, Straus & Giroux, 1991).

*Crary, Elizabeth, *Kids Can Cooperate* (Seattle, Wash.: Parenting Press, 1984).

*Dunn, Judy, *Sisters and Brothers* (Cambridge, Mass.: Harvard University Press, 1985).

Eisenberg, Arlene, Murkoff, Heidi and Hathaway, Sandee, *What to Expect the Toddler Years* (New York: Workman Publishing, 1994), Chapter 24.

*Faber, Adele and Mazlish, Elaine, *Siblings Without Rivalry* (New York: Avon Books, 1988).

Rothenberg, B. Annye, et al., *Parentmaking Educators Training Program* (Menlo Park, Cal.: Banster Press, 1993) Part III, Chapter 5 on Sibling Relationships.

*Zweibach, Meg, *Keys to Preparing and Caring for Your Second Child* (Hauppauge, N.Y.: Barron, 1991).

teaching/presentation

Homework

Although homework is not necessary for this topic because parents readily remember their interests and concerns, and discussion generally begins easily on these areas, *PETP* has two homework sheets. In the Sibling Relationships chapter of *PETP* on pp. 378 and 379, one is on Second Baby and the other on Sibling Relations.

Practical Suggestions or Strategies for Teaching This Topic

The topic of new babies and sibling rivalry seems to fit in well with the other topics that deal with the self, the family, and interpersonal relation-

ships, such as meeting your own needs, family size, and husband-wife relationships. These topics generally work well if they are presented toward the end of the series.

Before discussing this topic, be aware of the family constellation and expectations of the parents in your group, for example, which parents have other children, which are pregnant and how many months, and which are expecting to have only one child. It is also important to be aware of which parents are divorced, unwed, possibly much older. Since having another baby is not an option open to all parents in the class, it is important that you not appear to be advocating another child for everybody. Try to find ways to make all parents in the group comfortable during the discussion.

The entire discussion needs to be handled diplomatically so that group members can learn what to expect but not be urged in any direction. Parents who are trying to decide about a second child will usually listen hard, and pregnant women should not be made to feel anxious or more ambivalent.

Note: This is one of the few topics during whose discussion you may feel that you're teaching to a *too diverse* group (parents with a baby and a pre-school-aged child; parents with a pre-schooler and a school-aged child; pregnant women; divorced or unwed parents; parents of adopted children; parents who want only one child; women dealing with the pain of infertility; and so on).

Mini-lecture and Lead-off Questions for Discussion[1]

This topic can be started with a brief introduction and then followed by the parents bringing up and discussing their interests and concerns. There are only a few main areas to be dealt with—tuning into feelings and concerns during pregnancy, techniques for preparing a young child for a sibling, and considering what adjustment to a new baby will mean to family members. As each comes up, it is useful for you to try to get the group to deal with it deeply and fully.

Today, we'll be talking about preparing for a new baby and adjusting after the baby comes home. This is an area that I know is of importance to many of you. What are some of the issues you'd like to talk about?

As an example, a parent may mention her concern about what she can do to prepare her child for the new baby. You can give some background on what the child (depending on his age) can understand and encourage the other parents to make suggestions. When this area seems thoroughly covered, you can summarize it for the parent who brought it up. Work through each new area in that way.

Note: It is common for parents *not* to bring up their own fears or concerns but to focus on the older child's adjustment. If you gently guide each parent into looking at herself as well as her child, the discussion will be more complete and useful.

---

1. See *PETP* Pt. III, ch. 5 Sibling Relationships for extensive information on having a second child *and* on enhancing sibling relationships.

Additional Information for Parents

Preparing for a New Baby

When a second or later child is soon expected, most parents tend to be concerned about their older child's adjustment to the new baby and want to help him prepare for the arrival. When the older child is two years old or younger, it is usually quite difficult for him to be very well prepared. However, telling a child about a coming baby and showing how his family will be like some other families with new babies that he knows can be helpful. Very simple books on the subject can also help, as can setting up the nursery ahead of time. Parents should try to answer any of their child's questions as simply as possible. They should also emphasize positive aspects of the sibling's arrival, but not make unrealistic promises about the new baby. An unrealistic promise is, for example, that "You're going to have someone to play with." A two-year-old would tend to expect to be able to play with the baby immediately.

Children also need to know that their mother will be away for a day or two when the baby is born (unless, of course, there is a home delivery). Parents should try to encourage in advance a closeness between their child and whoever will be taking care of him during the mother's hospital stay (if the father will not be available full-time).

Mothers and fathers have their own, often unspoken, concerns during a second pregnancy about the changes that may occur in them and their family when the new baby arrives. During this pregnancy, mothers can be preoccupied, tired, and irritable, and their child will certainly be aware of that. Most mothers feel they can't lie down when tired as they did during their first pregnancy, but must keep going.

During the Hospital Stay

Most young children do best if they stay with a familiar, warm, and loving person while their mother is in the hospital. Daily contact with their mother, perhaps on the telephone if hospital visits are not permitted, can be valuable, but some children become upset with short talks or visits because they really want to have all of their mother, not just a quick view or a few words from her. Sometimes a calendar for hospital stays longer than a day or two or some other concrete way of explaining time is useful. Mostly, however, a familiar place where the older child's questions can be answered and his father can be with him is helpful.

Getting Adjusted to the New Baby at Home

Some of the more surprising things that parents notice in the initial months of a new baby's presence is that their feelings and expectations are often very strong and sometimes quite unexpected. Parents may find themselves resenting the older child, may feel a need to settle into a one-to-one relationship with the new baby, and may see the older child as intrusive.

Parents may also feel guilty—because they are not spending the same amount of time with their older child as they used to, because the baby isn't getting what the first child got, because the husband is involved with the older child out of necessity, because the couple has little time for each other or for all of those reasons. Their guilt over the older child may encourage them to bend over backwards to make things easier on him, but they may end up removing so many of the usual limits that the child becomes unsure of himself and starts testing limits. This can cause the parents to become very angry with the older child.

Instead of feeling guilty or bending over backwards, parents can involve their older child in the care of the baby. Children do need to be taught gentleness with a baby and most children under three need a lot of supervision and reminders about this. Parents can stress the positives of the baby but also the specialness of being the older child who can do things the baby can't. Depending on the nature of the child, special time with him can be helpful; gifts for him when gifts are given to the baby may also be of some use.

Parents should expect some anger and regression from their older child and try to be understanding. They should not allow most limits to be bent, however. Parents should also expect times when they'll be torn in too many directions, but should remember that *if THEY feel what they're doing is expected and all right, their child will not feel short-changed.*

Sibling Rivalry as Both Children Get Older

As both children grow older and adjust to some of the initial changes, it is helpful for parents to remember that:

• Sibling rivalry is inevitable; parents waste a lot of emotional energy trying to *prevent* conflict;
• Parents' guilt over what each child is missing can add to the conflict;
• It's not possible to always treat two or more children equally;
• Children learn a lot about compromises by living with their siblings, and that's a valuable experience;
• Parents often take sibling conflicts more to heart than children do. In fact, parents sometimes see and feel relationships between their children in the same ways they saw and felt them between themselves and their own siblings. This can add a lot of confusion and conflict to their children's relationship, and needs to be sorted out by the parents;
• Parents should strive for some individual time with each child. They should also learn to deal with them positively when they're together;
• How the sibling relationship develops depends a lot on the temperaments of the two children involved;
• Parents should try to model good ways for the children to relate to each other based on the children's temperaments. They should eventually aim at not being in the center of the children's *every* dispute, when each is trying to convince the parents that he is right and the other wrong;
• It's natural for children to compete with each other for their parents' favor.

Handouts

Reprinted articles on second-babies and sibling relationships can be found in Rothenberg, *PETP* pp. 374–377 in the "Sibling Relationships" chapter. However, handouts are not necessary because usually parents are *very* helpful to each other when discussing these interrelated topics.

5

BABY-SITTERS[1] AND RETURNING TO WORK

background/preparation

Goals to Work Toward in Presenting This Topic

Most new parents don't anticipate that finding and using baby-sitters will be a difficult or emotionally charged issue. When they actually start to need or use a sitter, however, they may wonder why they have so many questions and doubts about leaving their child with one. More questions arise when a parent is faced with the decision of whether or not to return to work, since one of the biggest factors in the decision is who will watch the child. With more and more mothers of young children returning to work and more and more outside pressures for and against working to contend with, it's important that every parent be given the opportunity to consider her own ideas and feelings.

The goals to work toward on this topic are: (1) to help parents learn more about their own needs for time away from their child; (2) to help parents identify their feelings about leaving their child with a sitter; (3) to give parents suggestions for ways to find and evaluate different kinds of sitters; (4) to help parents establish routines to make the use of sitters simpler and more comfortable; (5) to give parents the opportunity to consider all issues involved in the decision to return or not return to work.

Typical Parental Interests and Concerns About This Topic

1. I'm worried that Julia will feel abandoned if I leave her with a sitter.
2. Which kind of child care provider is best to use: a younger person, an experienced person; a licensed day care home, a day care center; a person who comes to my home, or someone who sits in her own home?
3. How do I find a good sitter? And after I find someone, how can I tell if she's doing a good job?
4. How much should I pay a sitter?
5. What are the positive and negative effects of leaving my child with a sitter?

---

1. This chapter deals mostly with the use of occasional babysitters. Some of this is applicable for the *regular* caregiving situation as well. Returning to work issues are also discussed in this chapter. See pp. 307–316 for the chapter on Early Childhood Education Programs, both pre-schools and childcare centers.

6. Caitlin screams when someone else holds her. This makes me feel guilty. Maybe I'm doing something wrong and maybe I shouldn't leave her at all now.

7. Can my husband and I go away for a weekend soon or should we wait until our baby is a certain age before leaving him overnight?

8. I can't decide whether or not to go back to work.

9. How often and for how long should I leave my child?

10. How can I return to work (or school) and still be a good mother?

11. I'm concerned that if I return to work, someone else will be raising my child instead of me.

12. If quality time is more important than quantity, how can I maximize my time with my child once I go back to work?

13. What are the effects on children when mothers work?

Areas of Information You Will Need to Learn About to Teach This Topic

Parents' needs.
— Necessity for time alone.
— Necessity for time together as a couple, away from the child.
— The need to maintain a sense of individual identity apart from the role of parent.
Parents' feelings.
— Ambivalence of separation.
— Range of feelings that bother parents about leaving their child.
Effect of sitter care on a child.
— Ways sitters can help children and parents.
— Stages of stranger anxiety and how parents can handle them.
Finding and evaluating sitters.
— Sitting options available in your community—co-ops, colleges, day-care centers, and so on—and their costs.
— Places to contact to locate sitters.
— Considerations about which kind of caregiving situation to use.
— How to evaluate a sitter—questions to ask before and after she cares for the child.
— Importance of a child's reaction and parents' feelings about a particular caregiver.

Routines to make the use of sitters simpler and more comfortable.
— Information to leave with caregivers.
Issues involved in returning to work.
— Questions parents can ask themselves as they make their decisions.
— How continuous child care differs from more short-term sitting arrangements.
— Ways home life can change when a parent returns to work.

Family Dynamics—What This Topic Means Psychologically to Parent and Child

Parents can feel so personally responsible for the care of their child that they experience guilt at just the thought of using a baby-sitter. They often want to avoid the guilt and attempt to make their child feel "secure" by always being nearby, but they can't give up their individual lives or their life with their spouse just because they've become a parent. Parents can feel a powerful conflict between their desires and responsibilities, and confusion about who they are as individuals.

Uncertainty can also be a strong emotion to deal with. Parents may wonder about what will happen when they're away from their child—will the child give the sitter a difficult time? Is he or she old enough to be involved in this kind of arrangement? Will the sitter give the child the proper care? (If the parent herself doesn't feel competent caring for her baby or young child, she may wonder if anyone else can do it correctly.) Arranging for a sitter for a few hours' time may seem like a major effort, and concerns can multiply when long-term day care is involved.

From the child's point of view, a sitter is someone new who is taking care of him. If the sitter is well-informed and prepared, the child will learn to enjoy her. He will also learn that though his parents go away, they will soon return. Contact with sitters provides children with first-hand knowledge of the different qualities, strengths, and weaknesses different people have.

Sample Concern of Parents

Concern	Critical Issues
When we left Michael with a sitter for the first time last week, he screamed so hard that we're reluctant to leave him again. It was the first night out for my husband and me since Michael was born three months ago. Although I wanted to feel like a couple again, I couldn't even enjoy the evening because I missed Michael and worried about him. When we called home to check on him, the sitter said he was fine. But I was still upset.	—First experience using sitter. —Baby very upset. —Parents have rarely gone out. —Desire to be a couple. —Hard to enjoy evening. —How to handle upset feelings.

Key Questions

1. How did your husband feel about leaving and about the evening?

2. How did you feel about the quality of the baby-sitting and about how your baby was when you returned?

3. If you are considering not going out in the future, what would this mean for you and your husband?

4. Do you think your feelings might change with continued experiences of leaving your baby?

For the group

5. How have some of you felt about leaving your baby, especially when he was screaming?

6. Why do we feel guilty when we leave our child?

Readings and Other Resources

Brazelton, T. Berry, *Working and Caring* (Reading, Mass.: Addison-Wesley, 1985).

*Burck, Frances Wells, *Babysense,* Rev. Ed. (New York: St. Martin's Press, 1991), Chapters 15-17.

Cardozo, Arlene, *Sequencing* (New York: Macmillan, 1986).

*Eisenberg, Arlene, Murkoff, Heidi and Hathaway, Sandee, *What To Expect The Toddler Years* (New York: Workman Publishing, 1994), Chapter 26.

*Hobfoll, Stevan and Hobfoll, Ivonne, *Work Won't Love You Back* (New York: W. H. Freeman and Co., 1994).

*Hochschild, Arlie, *The Second Shift* (New York: Viking Penguin, 1989).

*Rothenberg, B. Annye, et al., *Parentmaking Educators Training Program* (Menlo Park, Cal.: Banster Press, 1993). Part III, Chapter 3 on separation.

teaching/presentation

Homework

The homework for this topic helps parents begin to think about their own attitudes and feelings about baby-sitters.

Practical Suggestions or Strategies for Teaching This Topic

• It may be hard for some parents in the group to know where to begin a discussion of childcare. They may need to discuss their own difficult and ambivalent feelings about leaving their child before they can consider ways of finding and using the occasional sitter or more long-term childcare.

BABY-SITTERS

(babies–3 years)

Having someone else care for your child can often bring up unexpected thoughts and feelings. As a prelude to our next discussion, please think about and respond to the following questions.

1. When you think about having a baby-sitter for your baby or young child, what do you feel would be the advantages?

2. What do you think might be difficult about it? What might be some of the disadvantages?

Parent's name _____ Date _____ Child's age _____

• Sharing your own feelings about using a sitter—both pros and cons—and why you think you feel this way will encourage group members to talk about their own feelings.

• After presenting your mini-lecture you may wish to follow the subheadings in "Additional Information for Parents" (p. 371) to guide the discussion.

• When you discuss techniques for finding and using sitters, ask the parents to add any tips they may have, such as questions they ask when interviewing a sitter.

• Be careful that a parent who is not ready to leave her child is not made to feel uncomfortable about it. Help her to acknowledge her feelings and encourage her to think about separating in the future.

Mini-lecture and Lead-off Questions for Discussion

Sample mini-lecture[2]

A major concern for many parents is finding time for themselves. It's helpful to be able to count on some time alone, since this can help us become better parents and better individuals, but arranging time away through the use of baby-sitters is not always easy. Many of us wonder how to find good sitters. How should we choose them and decide if they're good? Are there routines that make the whole process of using sitters easier? What will be the effects on our child? How will we handle our own feelings about leaving our child with a sitter? How will child care influence our decision about whether or not to return to work? Let's first consider our own needs and feelings regarding these issues, then move on to the mechanics of finding and using sitters, and finally to the decision about returning to work.

You may now wish to give a personal example of a concern you had about using a sitter, for instance:

---

2. See Appendix H for the chapter on Working Parent classes for suggestions on talking to working parents about child care and family time issues as well as difficult feelings.

Before our daughter was born, I didn't think twice about baby-sitters as an issue. However, when the time came to call one, I was surprised to find that it seemed like a huge hurdle, something that was easier to avoid than attempt. I wasn't prepared for my sweaty palms and the knot in the pit of my stomach when I left my daughter for the first time. Have any of you experienced feelings of anxiety at the thought of leaving your baby or young child? Why do we often have such problems when we leave our children in the care of others?

Lead-offs

• What are some feelings you have had about leaving your child with a sitter?

• What are some advantages of having time to yourself or with your husband?

• What are some of the benefits you think your child would receive from getting to know a sitter?

Additional Information for Parents

Parents' Need for Time Away from Their Child

• Parents are individuals as well as parents and have strong needs of their own. If these aren't recognized, repression can distort them so that they affect the child in a negative way.

• Parents can't affirm their child's life if there is no corresponding confirmation of their own needs. It may be hard to meet personal needs in the early months when babies make so many demands, but parents need to remember that they can meet more of their own needs as their child gets older.

• If parents can respect their own needs over the long run, it will help their child learn to respect the needs of others.

• Parents can feel more giving and loving after they've had time away or time for themselves.

• No parent can feel good about herself if she is "on call" 24 hours a day. But how much time away each parent needs will differ with each individual.

• Although it often seems like too much trouble to make child-care arrangements, the goals of time away are important ones—for the parent to have time for thinking and doing things just for herself, for the child to learn to trust others, and for the husband and wife to maintain their relationship as a couple.

• When both parents work outside the home, parents are usually less able to take the additional time to meet their personal needs.

Parents' Feelings About Leaving Their Child

• For many, being a parent is a continuous struggle to balance ambivalent feelings. Parents want love and closeness with their child but also personal freedom and individuality. At one moment they can love their marvelous baby and the next moment feel angry and trapped. They want time to themselves but also want time to be with their child and their spouse. Parents know it's not easy to find a balance among several roles and desires, but they need to know that their feelings are very normal.

• Some parents have the unpleasant feeling that they're involving their baby in a business arrangement when they employ a sitter. They need to remind themselves of the benefits their child will receive from getting to know a sitter.

• New parents often feel uncertain and a little incompetent. They're not sure what to tell a sitter about what their child will do or need, and are unable to give instructions. They think that if they're not sure what to say, the sitter won't be able to handle the situation.

• Being very nervous about leaving a child is a common feeling.

• A parent may have strong feelings about being left with babysitters, etc. when he or she was a child. Positive or negative, these experiences influence a parent's attitude about leaving their child.

The Effects of Baby-sitter Care on a Child

• Rather than believe she's avoiding a responsibility to her child when she leaves him, a parent can learn to be aware of the benefits her child will gain from a sitter. A child will gain some independence and learn trust for others; to respect the needs of others by seeing her parent respect her own needs; become acquainted with different personalities; and learn about the many different qualities people have. In addition, comments from a caring and competent sitter can help a parent view her child from a new perspective and give her new insights on how to handle problems.

• Even newborns react to their parents' feelings. The screaming that can occur when parents leave their child may indicate the child's awareness of the parents' fear and anxiety. Babies establish their attitudes about new people and separations based on their parents' responses to those situations. Parents need to watch what kinds of messages they're sending as they leave their child.

• Sitters are new and different people to children, and babies and young children usually do fine with them. While parents may be tired and uncertain, a sitter is rested and enthusiastic. Most children react favorably to the enthusiasm and attention given them by a new person.

• In the United States, mothers tend to be the primary day-time contact of children, and children therefore are greatly influenced by their mother's personality. Sitters provide a healthy alternative to this exclusive contact with the mother.

Ideas for Finding and Evaluating Different Kinds of Sitters and Childcare Providers

To find sitters and/or childcare providers, contact:

• Sitting agencies—Check the phone book for listings.

• Friends with sitters—Often friends will share sitters they use or ask their sitters if they have friends who also want to baby-sit.

• High school and junior high school guidance departments—Some schools keep lists of students who want to baby-sit.

• Girl Scout troops—Check with local leaders for Scouts who wish to sit.

• Churches—Often churches will post requests for child care on their bulletin boards.

• Colleges—Check with the part-time student employment office.

• Friends—Friends with children may wish to exchange sitting.

• Baby-sitting co-ops—Check with friends for names and information.

• Other parents you met in neighborhood parks—Arrangements to switch children can come from these contacts.

• The local paper—Parents can place an ad for a sitter or find one a local sitter has placed.

• Child care resource and referral agnecies—Their

role is to provide names of child care centers for you to evaluate. Also ask about family day care homes where one mother cares for several children in her home.
• Nanny or inhome daycare location agencies—Check the phone book for listings.

When evaluating a sitter, parents should consider:

• Age—Is an older, experienced person wanted, or is a local teen-ager who can be trained more appropriate for your family?
• Experience with other children of the same age—Though it can have some bearing, this qualification may not be extremely important to every parent. (However, for a regular childcare arrangement, experience and education should be considered carefully.)
• Personality—Is the person affectionate, understanding, sensible, self-confident? How does your baby or child react to this person? How do you feel about her?
• Chemistry—Are the feelings between parent and sitter and sitter and child comfortable? It may take several sitting experiences to get a good idea.
• Transportation—Does the sitter have a car, or will the parent have to drive?
• References—Parents should ask the sitter for references and then check them.
• Having the sitter over once before leaving her with the child—Parents can meet, interview, and have the sitter play with the child before having her babysit on her own.
• How things went while the sitter took care of the child—Does the sitter talk about the time she spent with the child when the parents return? Can she tell in detail what she did or can she respond with accuracy to questions? What impression does she give about how much she knows about child care? Where are the diapers and dirty clothes? How does the house look? Parents should think about their own feelings about the experience—do they feel good about leaving their baby with this sitter?
• Availability—Will the sitter be free at appropriate, necessary times?
• Cost—Does the sitter charge a reasonable fee?

Routines to Make the Use of Sitters Simpler and More Comfortable

• Parents can ask the sitter to come a half-hour early to leave time to explain instructions and to give the child time to get adjusted to a different person.
• Parents should leave written instructions for the sitter so she knows the child's usual routine and what methods usually work to comfort and care for the child. (See "Information to Be Left With Baby-sitters" on p. 376 for pertinent information.)
• Parents can check to see if a close friend or a neighbor will be home while they're out. Sitters can be told to contact this person if they need help.
• A regular weekly time to have a sitter can be established. This sets up a pattern for the child and allows the parent to be able to count on time out. It can also avoid last-minute problems of finding a sitter.
• Parents should think of ways to make their sitters comfortable: leave food they will enjoy, explain how to use the stereo, and so on. If a sitter enjoys the experience, she'll most likely agree to come again if asked.
• Using one or two regular sitters will keep the baby or young child from having to get used to many strangers.

Issues Involved in the Decision to Return or Not Return to Work

Points to consider:

• If a parent doesn't have to work for financial reasons, her decision will be purely personal and based on how satisfied she is staying at home. A parent with home-oriented skills or creative interests and with friends who have remained home with babies may be oriented toward staying in the home. A parent without these skills or others that can be put to use with a young child around may be oriented toward returning to work.
• If a parent doesn't enjoy staying home, she may first wish to try to develop domestic skills so that she will enjoy being home. Some parents may find they change and become more satisfied at home once they view their problem with flexibility and become aware of what makes them happy. Parents should try to avoid "either-or" thinking and not make a decision too quickly. As awareness develops, parents can ask themselves:
— What is it I'm missing in my life?
— What skills am I not using that I know can bring me satisfaction?
— How can these skills be expanded little by little?

— What do I like to do?

— How can I arrange to do some of the things I like?

— How can I share ideas with other parents? How can I get involved and avoid feelings of isolation?

• Parents' attitudes toward returning to work are largely formed by the experiences of their own upbringing and the expectations they have of their role as parent.

• No matter what decision is made, difficult feelings are likely to be experienced. If a woman goes back to work she may have feelings of guilt toward her family, and business and home pressures to contend with; if she stays home she may be bored, depressed, feel worthless or guilty about spending money when she doesn't earn any.

• Individual differences among parents are as important as individual differences among children, and no one should be made to feel bad for the choice she makes. However, every parent needs to think through the decision very carefully so she can deal with the opinions and feelings of others that will bombard her later. Each parent should make her own decisions.

• Whether working or not, all parents need a special time for themselves—enough to satisfy them without putting too much pressure on the rest of their life.

• Attitude is crucial to each parent's decision. If a woman is bored at home, she may be bored at work, too. Work may not be a "way out," and going to work may be as unsatisfying as staying home. A woman has to deal with herself first— find out what feels right to her—before rushing into a decision.

• Parents need to be reminded that decisions don't have to be permanent—parents can always change their minds.

• As pressures to work have increased, women can benefit from developing key friendships with others who have also chosen the same option to work or not outside of the home at this time.

Some Difficult Feelings Working Women May Have to Deal With

• Working women often get the feeling that their child comes last when he should come first— especially at times when he seems to need his mother emotionally or during sickness. A working mother may feel that she's leaving her child with someone else because she doesn't like him, or may fear that the child will think she doesn't like him.

• Working mothers may feel negative attitudes from their child's teachers or sitters and from friends who care for the child. These people may feel mothers should remain at home or be ambivalent about the working woman's career. Feelings of others can make a parent feel guilty, selfish, or that she doesn't really love her child.

• Women who work outside the home generally are responsible for the housework as well. Equal sharing of housework between husband and wife is still the exception. Statistics all over the world show that working women with children still do more of the housework. A husband may be pleased if his wife works outside the home, but he may resist doing the traditional household chores himself. A husband's attitude toward housework can have a bearing on the woman's decision regarding work.

• Working women may feel guilty that they aren't around their child all day. They may not even feel like a mother when their child slips and calls the sitter "Mother." Mothers may feel they have to spend as much time as possible with their child, but they can't give all their free time to him. Other things need to be done and when they are, the child can begin to demand more attention.

• A working woman may feel that *every* moment has to be spent in a worthwhile way. A tight schedule, however, will leave less time to spend with her child and less for social life.

Some Difficult Feelings Women Who Remain at Home May Have to Deal With

• Women with few outside interests or who are unable to take time for themselves may feel depressed or bored with their lives. They will need to take responsibility for meeting their own needs to avoid depending on other people for their happiness.

• Women who remain at home may be exposed to negative feelings from friends or society in general. Other people can be jealous of the nonworking parent's status or upset at the fact that the parent is not actively pursuing a career. Feelings like these can make parents feel guilty or worthless.

• Personal feelings of the woman at home can also make her feel guilty. She may be upset by evidence of frustration, boredom, or a desire for time away or alone.

Handouts

There is one handout for this topic. The first section, "Baby-Sitters," provides guidelines for parents, for sitters, and for young sitters' parents; it is reprinted from "Health Tips," a publication of the California Medical Education and Research Foundation. The second section, "Information to Be Left," lists a number of points a sitter needs to know about a child. The list is quite comprehensive but is meant to be a guideline, a way to help parents think of what to tell their sitter (often this is hard, or hard to put into words).

For handouts of early childhood education programs, see pp. 312–316.

1 month–3-year-olds

BABY-SITTERS*

(babies–3 years)

To an increasing extent, the responsibility of childcare is being shared with baby-sitters—many of them teenagers. Most young baby-sitters can cope splendidly with the requirements of the job and find that they learn much in assuming the responsibilities of being in charge of a small child.

In the interests of the child's safety and well-being, everyone involved—the child's parents, the sitter and the sitter's parents—should keep the following pointers in mind.

For the child's parents

• Know your sitter. Be sure that the sitter knows where you will be, how you can be reached and what time you are expected home. If you are delayed, phone.
• Tell your children in advance that you are going to be gone and that a sitter (identify by name) will be in charge.
• When the sitter arrives, take time, particularly if he/she is new to your home, to show the sitter around, introduce him/her to the children and give any special instructions.
• Put in writing any instructions about medications a child may require during your absence.
• If the children are to be fed in your absence, it is preferable that you prepare the food. If the sitter is to prepare the food, tell him/her exactly what to serve the children. It is much safer to ask the sitter to heat a casserole you have prepared than to ask him/her to prepare anything which must be fried or boiled; there is always the danger of grease fires getting out of control or of scaldings from steam or boiling water.
• Warn the sitter of any hazardous conditions in the house—broken steps, slippery surfaces, equipment in need of repair, etc.—so that the children will be kept away from them. Show the sitter how to turn on and off all appliances he/she may need.
• Give your sitter information about whom to call in case of emergency. This means not only the phone number at which you can be reached, but also the numbers of the child's doctor, the police and fire departments, a nearby relative or friendly adult neighbor, and the number at which a working parent can be reached.
• Write and sign a note authorizing emergency medical treatment for each of your children.
• If the sitter is working at night, one of the parents should escort him/her home. If you are driving the sitter home, do not drive off until he/she is safely through the home door.

For the sitter

• Arrive on time, in a cheerful mood, looking clean and neat.
• Do not take a baby-sitting job while you have a cold or any other contagious disease.
• Listen carefully to all instructions about when and what to feed the children, if and when to bathe them and when to put them to bed. Make notes you can refer to later.
• Do not bring food from your own home for the children. Feed them only what you are told to . If you bring toys for them to play with or books to read to them, ask their parents' approval.
• Keep matches, knives, scissors, open safety pins, broken glass and all other hazardous articles away from the children.
• If you give a baby a bath, be sure the water is not too hot. Test it with the underside of your forearm. Under no circumstances leave the baby in the tub or on the bath table while you answer the phone or doorbell. Either wrap the child and take him with you or let the ringing continue until the child has been put in a safe place.
• At the end of the evening's play—just before bedtime—pick up all the toys or, if the children

---

*Taken from *Health Tips, Index 386*. Reprinted with permission from the California Medical Association.

BABY-SITTERS (continued)

are old enough, get them to pick them up. This will not only restore the house to order for the returning parents but it will also prevent them, you and the children from tripping over toys and injuring yourselves.

• When you put a small child to bed, be sure that the sides of the crib are securely fastened. Do not leave in the crib any toys which have small parts which can be pulled off and swallowed or inhaled.

• When the children are asleep, listen alertly for any sounds from them. This means that the TV or radio should not be loud, you should not be so involved in a phone conversation that you are not listening for the children, and you should not be entertaining friends who might take your mind off your responsibilities. In addition to listening for sounds from the children's bedrooms, check them personally from time to time.

• Have a flashlight on hand in case the lights go out.

• When the parents return, report fully everything that happened during their absence—any injury, no matter how minor; any symptoms a child has complained of; any abnormal behavior; any mechanical failure.

For the sitter's parents

• Know the family for whom your son or daughter is sitting. Be sure you have the phone number and address. If it can be arranged, talk with the parents before you send your youngster into their home.

• Help your youngster learn all he/she can about childcare, first aid and good safety practices. It will not only help him/her to be a good baby-sitter but will contribute to being responsible and ultimately a good parent.

• Do not let your youngster work too much or too late. Do not let baby-sitting interfere with study time or time for recreation. Do not let him/her accept jobs which mean late hours and deprivation of needed rest.

• Be sure that both you and the employer agree as to whether or not the sitter is permitted to entertain friends while working.

• Insist that an adult escort your youngster home after working at night.

Information to Be Left*

Because there is so much information a sitter needs to absorb and remember, we feel the following should be left in writing or on an audio or video tape for the sitter to refer to. Some of the information will need to be updated periodically.

Diapering

1. Location of clean diapers; what to do with soiled ones
2. How often to change baby
3. Use of oil, powder, lotion, etc., and general diapering procedure (a demonstration would be most helpful)
4. How many diapers should be used (whether baby wears double cloth diapers at bedtime)
5. Any special instructions, for example, if the baby has a diaper rash

Feeding

1. How often baby is usually hungry
2. How much he usually eats
3. How often to burp
4. Type of milk used; how to prepare it; use of sterilized bottles; whether to warm milk or not
5. Whether baby can hold bottle on his own
6. How much spitting up is typical

Sleeping

1. Which end of the crib the baby faces and whether she sleeps on her back or stomach

---

*The first three areas pertain mostly to sitters of young babies; the rest pertains to sitters of babies and young children.

2. Whether blankets are used
3. Whether bedroom door is left open or shut, curtains pulled, light on or off
4. How baby usually goes to sleep (rocked, with pacifier, fed first, cries self to sleep, etc.)
5. When bedtime is
6. Whether baby is a light sleeper or not (should sitter go in and check on baby or would this wake her?)
7. How long baby usually sleeps and what should be done if she wakes up soon after put down
8. How to soothe the baby if she cries

Phone numbers

They should be taped on the wall by phone or be in an easy-to-find-and-read location that you've *shown* the sitter.
1. Police department
2. Fire department
3. Pediatrician
4. Nearby neighbor
5. Spouse's work number, if appropriate
6. Number where you can be reached
7. Home address (in an emergency, a sitter might forget the street address)
8. Cross street
9. Poison control center

Helpful Facts

The sitter will find it helpful if you tell her the following facts:
1. The toys and games your child likes
2. If he can go outside; what to wear; how far to go
3. What *she* can eat (and how to turn on the oven or stove, if appropriate)
4. When you expect to return
5. How to turn on the TV, VCR and stereo
6. Where changes of clothing and bedding for the baby are
7. The location of a spare key in case the sitter locks herself out.

6

MEETING YOUR OWN NEEDS

background/preparation

Goals to Work Toward in Presenting This Topic

Often parents are so busy taking care of their child's needs that they forget to take care of themselves. They also forget how important taking care of themselves is, both to them, their spouse, and to their child, in the present as well as the future. The topic of meeting personal needs is an important one since it helps parents begin to think about finding a better balance in their family life.[1]

To help parents become better able to meet their own needs, the goals to work toward on this topic are: (1) to help parents define their needs; (2) to help them become aware of how satisfied they are or how balanced they feel in terms of their own needs versus the needs of their family; (3) to help group members to see to what extent they need to reorganize their priorities so that their needs can be satisfied.

Typical Parental Interests and Concerns About This Topic

1. I hardly use a baby-sitter. I feel rather oppressed by Jill. I feel we would get along better

---

1. For information on this topic relating to the first months after a baby is born, see "Adjusting to Parenting" on pp. 90–103.

if we spent less time together but is that OK?
2. My son demands so much attention!
3. I need to know how to get through the rough times—how to have time for everyone.
4. My daughter is up until 9:30 every night. My husband says she should be in bed by 8:00 p.m. She cries if I put her to bed sooner. I need time in the evening, but it makes me nervous to hear her cry.
5. Always being with my family drives me up the wall.
6. I don't even know who I am or what *I* like any more. If I unexpectedly have a few free hours, I don't even know what to do for myself.
7. I seem to get irritable a lot with Emily even when I've been at work all day but it doesn't seem right to hire a baby-sitter just to get away after she's already been in child care.

Areas of Information You Will Need to Learn About to Teach This Topic

- How to help parents be able to talk about their real needs for at-home, part-time working, and full-time working parents.
- Your own needs. Try to define them and see how difficult this is to do. What ways you are finding to meet some of your own needs?
- How the ways you and others have found to meet your own needs compare.
- The needs that child-rearing books state are typical of new parents.

• Specific actions or things parents can do to help them feel more satisfied with their lives and relationships.

Family Dynamics—What This Topic Means Psychologically to Parent and Child

Parents seldom say that they are not meeting their own needs, but often this can be the case. And when parents are not meeting many of their own needs, they can feel fatigue, resentment, anger, guilt, tension, and lack of confidence. When these feelings occur, the time parents spend with their child usually becomes a ritual rather than an exciting experience.

When a child has a parent who gives and gives, he simply demands that she give more, and offers no positive feedback for her efforts. When a child has a parent who feels guilty when she tries to get time for herself at home, he can sense her concern and will demand more of her time. A child senses his parents' confused feelings and becomes less sure of himself and thus wants to be closer to his parents and becomes more interruptive.

Sample Concern of Parents

Concern	Critical Issues
I am mainly concerned about two things: safety and guilt. Why am I not enjoying motherhood as much as I thought I would? How much do I have to change my life style to accommodate my daughter? Why don't I enjoy playing with her more? Why do I blame myself if she gets hurt? I often feel lonely and trapped. Is this normal? She's darling, normal, smart, etc., but I'm tired and need a new	—Parent's feelings. —Parent's expectation about parenthood. —How her life changed when she became a parent. —Parent's need for time for herself. —Parent's positive feelings for her child.

hobby! I love her, but when will my house be clean again?

—Establishing realistic expectations as a parent.

Key Questions

1. What do you think are the reasons behind your disenchantment with the role of mother?
2. What did you expect motherhood to be like?
3. What things in your life or self have you changed to be a mother? Which of those do you like? Which do you dislike?
4. What things are you doing just for yourself?
5. What do you feel are some things you need to do for yourself?
6. What kinds of things did you do for yourself before you had a child?
7. What do you feel you can do to change your way of living so that you are able to meet more of your own needs?

Readings and Other Resources

Burck, Frances Wells, *Babysense,* Rev. Ed. (New York: St. Martin's Press, 1991), Chapter 13 and 14.

*Cardozo, Arlene, *Sequencing* (New York: Macmillan Publishing Co., 1986).

Eisenberg, Arlene, Murkoff, Heidi and Hathaway, Sandee, *What To Expect the Toddler Years* (New York: Workman Publishing, 1994), pp. 751–784.

*Friedland, Ronnie and Kort, Carol (Eds.), *The Mother's Book: Shared Experiences* (Boston, Mass.: Houghton Mifflin Co., 1981).

Galinsky, Ellen and David, Judy, *The Preschool Years* (New York: Random House, 1988), Chapter 6.

Hochschild, Arlie, *The Second Shift* (New York: Viking Penguin, 1989).

*Kelton, Nancy, "A New Mother's Confession of Ambivalence, *San Francisco Chronicle.* First appeared under the title, "Am I Glad I Decided to Become a Mother?" (This article is reprinted in "Adjusting to Parenting," pp. 97–98.)

*Lindbergh, Ann Morrow, *A Gift from the Sea* (New York: Random House, 1978).

Reese, Sarda, "Reflections of a Father Who Became a Mother," *Redbook* (this article is reprinted in its entirety in "Adjusting to Parenting," pp. 99–103).

*Rich, Adrienne, *Of Woman Born* (New York: W. W. Norton & Co., Inc., 1976).

*Wolfson, Randy and DeLuca, Virginia, *Couples With Children* (Order by calling (800) 443-9942).

Also see books listed on p. 92 of this book.

teaching/presentation

Homework

There are two homework assignments for this topic. One, "Feelings and Needs of Parents," has as its goal helping parents pinpoint their needs and find ways to meet some of them. The other, "Feelings and Needs of Mothers," can be used in a class for women only.

Practical Suggestions or Strategies for Teaching This Topic

The topic "Meeting Your Own Needs" should be scheduled for a time between the middle and the end of the series. The group should be supportive and understanding of one another before this topic is presented.

A powerful and meaningful introduction to this topic will be necessary to help the group members give more than surface thought to it. Sharing some of your personal feelings and experiences will be particularly helpful.

To make the discussion of this topic effective and worthwhile, you need to be aware of your own needs and feelings and read a variety of resource materials that deal with the needs and feelings of parents. Such preparation will give you a more genuine feeling for the topic.

Be certain your group environment is safe, warm, and supportive as each parent talks about herself.

Mini-lecture and Lead-off Questions for Discussion[2]

Sample mini-lecture

Material written by new parents about meeting their own needs provides the best introduction to this topic. The article reprinted on p. 389 is a good example. Look through magazines and other resources you can read to the group or distribute and use as a focus for the discussion.

Lead-offs

• After reading an article that talks about needs and feelings, ask the group how they feel about what was said.

• Restate a paragraph or thought from an article you have read to the group and show how it has helped you in some way. Then ask the parents if any of them has felt or acted in a similar way.

• Use the homework (see pp. 382–387) as a framework for your discussions. Have the parents talk about what they stated were experiences that made them feel good or bad during the last few days and things they feel they can change to bring about more good experiences. Then help them to dig deeper by asking them why they think certain things make them feel better. Does something happen to their body? To their emotions?

• Let the parents talk about the things that concern them. Guide their discussion, but give them the freedom to help each other. If you are willing to share your own feelings and experiences you will find that the group is more open.

• When summarizing the discussion, offer some suggestions of things parents can do to help themselves feel better.

Additional Information for Parents

• Everyone has some specific needs that must be met to enable him or her to function well. Meeting these needs should be given the highest priority possible.

• The needs of children must be met, but to help them in a willing and constructive way parents must also help themselves.

• Many parents often expect too much of themselves as parents.

---

2. Further information for conducting the discussion can be found in "Additional Information for Parents."

FEELINGS AND NEEDS OF PARENTS

(1–3 years)

For next week's class, we will focus on feelings and needs of both you and your spouse—especially those you experience being the parent of a young child. This homework observation will be the guide for our discussion, so we would like you to take time this week to think about your answers.

1. What experiences or incidents were you involved in during the past few days that made you feel GOOD? Consider the smallest moment of satisfaction as well as the greatest, for example, a phone call from a special friend, rocking your child, sitting down at the dinner table with no interruptions from the rest of the family, seeing sunshine in the morning, playing tennis, getting your guitar out again.

2. Mention any other kinds of experiences that made you feel GOOD—the "highs" of your days.

3. What experiences or incidents were you involved in during the past few days that made you feel BAD? For example, your child hanging on your leg, cleaning spilled food off the floor, your inability to get your hair washed and to take a shower, someone's negative comment about your child, your spouse's departure for the day or for a business trip.

4. Mention any other circumstances that occurred that made you feel bad—the real "lows" of your days.

5. Looking at what makes you feel good and what makes you feel bad, what do you think you would have to change in your life to get more "feeling good" times?

6. Which of these changes would be comfortable for you to make? Why? Which of these changes would not be comfortable for you to make? Why?

7. What are some of your spouse's needs that he/she is finding hard to meet now that he/she is the father/mother of a young child?

8. What would make his/her life as a father/mother and husband/wife more comfortable for him/her? What would make him/her "feel good"?

9. In what ways are you and your spouse working on the development of your marriage and your changing relationship as a couple?

Parent's name _____ Date _____ Child's age _____

PARENTMAKING: A Practical Handbook for Teaching Parent Classes About Babies and Toddlers by B. Annye Rothenberg, Ph.D., et al. © 1995 Banster Press, P.O. Box 7326, Menlo Park, CA 94026. Can copy for parent classes if this notice is included in full.

FEELINGS AND NEEDS OF MOTHERS

(1–3 years)

For next week's class, we will focus on you and your role as a mother and wife.

1. Your role as a mother
   - List three or more expectations you had for yourself as a mother before you had a child.

   - Have you met all these expectations? Why or why not?

   - What gives you pleasure in mothering? What gives you displeasure? Knowing these things, can you make any changes?

2. Your role as a wife
   • List three or more ways your relationship has changed with your husband since you had a child.

   • Are you comfortable with these changes? Why or why not?

3. Yourself
   - What do you need to do for yourself daily, weekly, and monthly to feel good?

   - Have you given up any activities since you had a child? Why? Would you like to incorporate any of these back into your life?

Parent's name _____ Date _____ Child's age _____

- Parents are models for their children. If parents meet their own needs, their children will most likely follow their example.
- Parents need time alone—time to renew their spirits and to be with themselves. The time that is necessary will depend on each parent and each child.
- There are some basic needs that all adults should meet regularly:
  — To follow a healthy diet.
  — To obtain adequate rest. If a parent is getting up at night with her child, she should nap when he does during the day.
  — To exercise. Walk, dance, jump rope, ride a bicycle, jog, play tennis—these are all good tension releases.
  — To spend time alone each day, even if it is only a few minutes.
  — To do something each day that they enjoy.
  — To have contact with other adults.
  — To have a new learning experience or some form of intellectual stimulation.
  — To have diversion, doing something away from home that is not related to child care.

- This is important for all parents—married and single; at-home, part-time working, and full-time working; and so on. Even the busiest and the most "bored" of parents can benefit from the sharing in this discussion and also from the suggestions that might be made to help each other. (See Appendix H beginning on p. 466 for a chapter on classes for full-time working parents.)

Handouts

No handouts have been developed for this topic; however, articles written by parents that share their feelings would be useful to distribute. The following article, "Getting to Know You," by Suzanne Massie, contains valuable information. You may also wish to refer to other articles (and books) listed in "Readings and Other Resources" (p. 380).

GETTING TO KNOW YOU*

by Suzanne Massie

When life is busiest, you must remember to take some time from being wife and mother—to concentrate on your own individuality.

Every living thing needs space to breathe and grow. Plants need air and a clearing around them so that rain and sun can encourage the roots to spread. A tree growing straight and tall needs to be free of clinging vines or else it suffocates and dies. In the same way, we humans need to preserve within ourselves a clearing, an inner space we keep exclusively for ourselves, a space for breathing and growing that is nourished and fed in our own individual way.

Most often, it's women who neglect this need. I thought about this the other day while trying to get back to writing. For several weeks the days had been crowded with children at home for vacation: running to the supermarket, the shoemaker's, the cleaner's; doing mountains of laundry—all the ordinary busywork of the household.

Finally, things were quiet. But I kept wandering around the house, plumping up the pillows, trying to find excuses not to face myself with the loneliness of the clean, white page. Oh, there was a lot to do around the house—there always is—and it was easy to tell myself I wasn't getting to my typewriter because of the limp pillows and the dirty floor. But what had really happened was that during those weeks I had gotten out of the habit of spending any time with myself. I was out of practice. The spirit was flabby. Once again the old fear was upon me—if I stopped all the busywork and faced my soul squarely there might be less there than I expected.

What's more, I was feeling guilty. Should I take all that time for myself? Wasn't I being selfish, when there were others who needed my time? If I don't clean the closets, who will? Isn't that more important than my scribbling? Those other things "had" to be done, and concentrating on myself seemed less important and necessary. By now I have learned to cope with my guilt, but how strange, I thought, that it still lingers so close to the surface and has to be fought, over and over.

This time I decided to see if other women felt the same way. I was astonished at the instant response, the relief they seemed to feel that someone had asked them. Each believed that, somehow, time didn't really belong to her. It belonged to others—to children, bosses, husbands, lovers—but not to her, and there was something a little selfish, akin to vanity, to claim it for herself. One said, "We're taught not to sit and look into mirrors and commune with our thoughts. We must be constructive. If anyone wants you, you must be there. You must give others what they need. If you don't, it's as if you're valuing yourself more than you should." And all of them, young and not-so-young, said, "I don't know why, but if I think of myself, I feel guilty."

Why do we have so little sense that time belongs to us? Is it because, from our earliest days, subtly and not so subtly, we are trained to believe that our mission in life is to think of others, to serve others? Men, who are encouraged, as a matter of course, to develop their own personalities, never question their right to call time their own. Women, however, approach this "masculine" concept tentatively, almost ashamed to admit that it's a need. We worry about our faces, our hair, our complexions. We worry more about losing our outer appearance than we do about losing ourselves, forgetting that the spirit, too, can lose fiber and tone unless we accord it at least the same careful concern that we usually reserve for our thighs and waistlines. Why is worrying about appearance and "staying attractive" approved and even pressed on us by society, but the need for attention to our emotional well-being is not?

I think what surprised me most was that after consciousness-raising and all the strides of women's liberation, even young girls feel this way. They still seem to accept the old idea that "behind every great man there is a woman." I have yet to meet a man of any age who thinks one of his primary missions in life is to see that the woman in his life achieves *her* maximal potential as an individual. A woman is still, unconsciously, perhaps, expected to look after others first and then, only if there's any time left over, "be herself."

The trouble is that during the years of child-raising there is so little time left over. Life is full of diapers and sniffles, dishes and Christmas presents, trips to the store, washing machines spilling over . . . and exhaustion. I remember that sick-to-the-stomach feeling of bone-tiredness at night. Too tired to read, too tired to do anything except collapse in a chair and watch television.

Retaining the Individual

How to retain the individual among all the demanding pressures that disperse and distract? Men come home after work and feel free then to take time for themselves, but work and free time are not so clearly defined for women. There is so much to do for others that taking time for ourselves comes low on the list of priorities. All creative effort demands isolation—even loneliness—and most of all, the discipline of regular attention. Developing the inner self is a creative effort. We put it off until that "someday" when life will be quieter. Yet it is precisely then, when life is so busy and fragmented, when the demands on us from others are greatest, that it is vital to remember that this one need is unfulfilled, and to begin to systematically budget time for *you*—and only you.

Otherwise we start to become dependent on others for life. Our inner self is eroded, and we begin to lose the sense of where we begin and others leave off, of who *we* really are. Then, when suddenly left on our own, we feel weak and helpless. It happens more quickly than we realize. I remember when, after a few years as the mother of young children and the wife of a busy journalist, I went away for my first trip without them. I had lost the habit of being alone, of spending any time with myself—and there was nothing but a deafening silence. I was frightened; I felt insecure without all the familiar demands of others which had become my life. Sue, the individual, as opposed to Sue, the wife and mother, had grown weak from lack of practice. I knew then that I had to do it more often, and from then on, whenever I felt that I was afraid to leave, I made every effort to go.

We teach our children to be independent and self-reliant, to develop their own personalities—but do we follow our own lessons? For although children have a way of making us feel guilty if we take time from them, is it they who are making us feel guilty, or is it our own uncertainty about our right to be ourselves? I think that deep down, especially as they grow older, children are worried and dismayed to feel that they are their mother's whole life. Nothing is heavier than the weight of another human being who is utterly dependent on us for fulfillment and happiness. Why burden our children with ourselves and our unaccomplished dreams as well as with their own problems of growing up?

It's good for them to learn that they must sometimes make sacrifices of their own time in order for another to be free. For them to know that mother also values herself as does Nancy or Joan and that Nancy or Joan is not always mother, that she has feelings and aspirations that have nothing to do with them. That there is time that is hers alone, for her to do with as she likes, even if it means leaving them on their own. It's good for them to learn that love can give strength, and independence and support, without binding. If they understand this, they'll feel proud that they, young as they are, can contribute significantly to the growth and contentment of the important person on whom they depend.

When a woman has cultivated her inner self and feels whole as a person, then the departure of children for lives of their own is a joyous occasion for all, a source of satisfaction at a job well done, and not of bereavement and emptiness.

So set aside time just for you. Be alone, think about yourself and yourself alone. Hold onto the dreams you had when there was no husband, no children; replenish those dreams in your own special way. Because the day does come when life is not so full of the needs of others, when the children go away and the floor seems to stay clean all the time. Then you wake up and say, "Now that I have time, whatever happened to *me*? I'd like to get to know myself again." And you may find that the person you once were, or wanted to be, has left—gone somewhere, disappeared, and that there is nobody left where she once lived.

Find her before she leaves. Give her space to breathe and grow. Remember that she's absolutely unique and that she belongs to no one else except you—and to God.

7

HUSBAND-WIFE RELATIONSHIPS

background/preparation

Goals to Work Toward in Presenting This Topic

The marriage relationship is the foundation of family life yet it is often overlooked by parents as they strive to raise their children, manage their jobs, maintain their home, and have some outside friendships.

The goals to work toward on this topic are: (1) to remind parents of their marriage relationship and the nurturing that it needs to keep it healthy; (2) to help parents understand where their relationship began and where it is today *and* to help them understand how it developed to its present point; (3) to inform parents of beginning techniques they can use to help increase closeness in their marriage; (4) to give parents the opportunity to learn about other couples with young children and what paths these couples' relationships have taken; (5) to give parents the opportunity to talk with other couples about what they do to continue working on their relationship.

Typical Parental Interests and Concerns About This Topic

1. My husband and I have found it very hard to be alone together since our child was born.
2. We try to have a set date once a week but I miss the spontaneity of the way things used to be between us.
3. When my husband comes home at night, I'm so happy to see him. I hate to say this but it's mainly because I know I'll get some relief from taking care of our daughter.
4. My wife doesn't want to go out until she's put our child to sleep. Our evenings get started so late.
5. We never seem to have time to really talk any more. Our son interrupts so much that my husband and I can barely tell each other the essentials. By the time he's asleep, we're too exhausted and frustrated to really talk.
6. With both of us working, any free time we have is spent with the children. We're finding it hard to make time for ourselves as a couple. Help!

Areas of Information You Will Need to Learn About to Teach This Topic

- How marriages often develop after children join the family.
- The kinds of things parents can do to work on their marriage, and why these steps are so hard to take.
- How marriage and family dynamics are affected when both parents work outside the home; when one parent remains "at home."

Family Dynamics—What This Topic Means Psychologically to Parent and Child

The marriage relationship tends to backslide after the first child is born. Just when there is less time to spend on it, this relationship needs more work than ever. When husbands and wives become parents they develop another whole side of themselves that has little to do with their "coupleness." As parents, they each bring new expectations about their spouse and themselves that are seldom possible to meet. Couples do not decide to marry on the basis of how they behave as parents, yet many of their post-child hours are spent with each functioning in a parental role. It is common for work loads to increase and communication time to decrease. Much is never said. Different responsibilities may make the husband and wife grow apart.

Until recently, many parents—especially mothers—paid little attention to the weakening husband-wife relationship because of their involvement in the child/parent world. However, with the increase in the number of divorces, most parents are motivated to look at what's happening and try to work on their relationships before the point—which is reached by some—where there's little to salvage.

From the child's point of view, a solid and growing relationship between his parents is a strong foundation for his feelings of confidence and security. [For information concerning children's reactions to separation and divorce, see *Helping Children Cope With Divorce* by Edward Teyber (New York, N.Y.: Lexington/Macmillan, 1992). See also Appendix A for other books on this topic.]

Sample Concern of Parents

Concern	Critical Issues
My husband and I both seem to spend so much time working that we're exhausted at night. Even though I always look forward to the weekend, it doesn't have any really free time because we have our child to care for and household work to do. It seems like we have little free time together and I'm worried that we're growing apart.	—Husband and wife busy. —Both exhausted. —Even weekends don't provide fun or close times. —Wife fearful of growing apart.

Key Questions[1]

1. What are the demands on you that are causing both you and your husband to work so hard?
2. Have you decreased your demands on yourself about such things as writing individual letters with your Christmas cards, having a clean house at all times, and so on?
3. What are your expectations about how much time parents get for themselves, both as individuals and as a couple?
4. What are your feelings about using baby-sitters or getting help from friends and relatives?
5. How would you like your home life to be on evenings and weekends? How could some or all of these ideas be made possible?

---

1. The parent whose concern you're dealing with needs input from you or other parents before you deal with her concern.

Readings and Other Resources

*Brazelton, T. Berry, *On Becoming a Family* (New York: Dell, 1982).

*Cowan, Carolyn P. and Cowan, Philip A., *When Partners Become Parents* (New York: Basic Books, Harper Collins, 1992).

*Dorman, Marsha and Klein, Diane, *How to Stay Two When Baby Makes Three* (Buffalo, N.Y.: Prometheus Books, 1984). To order, call (800) 421-0321.

Gochros, Jean S., "Why Fathers Get Jealous," *American Baby* (this article is reprinted in its entirety in the "Handouts" section, pp. 399–401).

Greenberg, Martin, *Birth of a Father* (New York: Avon Books, 1986).

*Hochschild, Arlie, *The Second Shift* (New York: Viking Penguin, 1989).

Rosenblum, Constance, "Men and Women May Speak Different Languages," *Peninsula Times Tribune* (this article is reprinted in its entirety in the "Handouts" section, pp. 402–403).

Rothenberg, B. Annye, et al., Parentmaking Educators Training Program (Menlo Park, Cal.: Banster Press, 1993). Part III, Chapter 1 on Husband-Wife relationships.

*Tannen, Deborah, *You Just Don't Understand* (New York, Ballantine, 1990).

*Wolfson, Randy and De Luca, Virginia, *Couples with Children* (out of print; to order, call (800) 443-9942).

teaching/presentation

Homework

The two homework assignments for this topic are for both spouses. The first, "Parenting and Family Relationships" is used in the "Learning More About Older Babies" class (from 7 to 14 months) and gives both parents an opportunity to ask themselves some *beginning* questions about being parents. The second, "Feelings and Needs of Parents," has as its goal helping parents get back in touch with themselves as individuals, then as parents, and then as a couple.[2] It is most helpful if you can encourage *both* husband and wife to think about, discuss, and complete the homework.

There are two additional homework sheets in the *PETP* chapter on Husband-Wife Relationships. On p. 260 of *PETP*, the homework focuses on being more caring and on p. 265 of *PETP*, the *focus* is on what you expected of each other as parents.

Practical Suggestions or Strategies for Teaching This Topic

The subject of husband-wife relationships tends to be more openly and fully discussed when it is presented toward the end of the series and group members have gotten to know each other.

When the topic is being discussed just among mothers, it almost always comes up or can easily be brought up after the subject of meeting your own needs—usually during the same session.

The most valuable way to work on this topic is to discuss it in a couple's class (six or seven couples is a good size).[3] Most participants find it easier to focus on the couple relationship if both spouses are present. Even if some of the class members are single parents they need to be

---

2. This homework is also used in discussing the topic "Meeting Your Own Needs." For that topic, the emphasis is on the first part and for this topic the last homework questions are particularly relevant. See "Meeting Your Own Needs" (p. 382) for a copy of the homework assignment.

---

3. The couple's class should be preceded (no more than two weeks) by a father's class during which the fathers have an opportunity to discuss child rearing. (See Part I: 8 beginning on p. 38 for information about a father's class.)

PARENTING AND FAMILY RELATIONSHIPS

(7–14 months)

This homework observation deals with the feelings and expectations you and your spouse have about parenting and family life. We will use the homework as a basis for our discussion next week. Please spend some time thinking about the questions and discussing them with your spouse. Bring this with you to refer to during the discussion.

You and your spouse have been parents for about a year now and you are aware that it is not just a job with a given set of rules that you can follow. It is interplay and interaction among three people and it requires an ongoing series of adjustments as your child develops and situations change. Now that you two have moved through the initial excitement and upheaval that the birth of a child causes, consider what parenting and family life are like for each of you now.

1. What do you enjoy most about your role as a parent?

2. What do you find most difficult about being a parent?

3. Did you expect that the roles and relationships within your family unit would be different than you find they are today? Please discuss.

Parent's name _____ Date _____ Child's age _____

involved in the discussion because they are likely to be developing couple relationships too. How to include them depends on the circumstances and planning you can do.

It is important that you remain impartial during the discussion and not see things mostly from the mothers' or the fathers' point of view. Try to be a balanced advocate of the couple relationship.

Mini-lecture and Lead-off Questions for Discussion

(See *PETP,* pp. 247–253 for more suggestions.)

The suggested format that follows is for a couple's class but it can be easily modified for a mothers only or fathers only group discussion. (However, when only mothers or only fathers are to meet, it is important that they brainstorm about their spouse's needs and try to see things, in terms of their coupleness, from their spouse's point of view as well as their own. Husbands should fill out the homework prior to a "mothers only" class as well as prior to a couple's class.) Your goals are to emphasize both parents' needs and to have class participants go home and discuss this area with their spouse.

Tonight we will be focusing on the effects of parenting on ourselves as individuals and on our couple relationship. Parenting is a fantastic mixture of great things and hard things. The great things are so reinforcing they hardly need a class devoted to them but the hard things *can* use some time devoted to them. When you're raising young children it can be hard to be aware of your own self and your coupleness and to know if what you're experiencing is anything like what other families are going through. I hope as we discuss the effects of parenting that you'll try to be open, honest, and especially supportive of each other. It's not easy to talk about personal feelings, but if you extend yourselves in the discussion others will too, and you'll find tonight to be a worthwhile evening.

Let's begin by introducing ourselves and then take a look at some of the changes in our lives since we became parents. Being a parent brings many changes for each of us. What are some of the changes you've experienced and how have they affected you?"

(Give personal examples as needed.)

Now direct the discussion to the needs of the mothers in the group. If the women have been meeting regularly in your class, they will find it easier to share and might make it easier for their husbands to participate when it's their turn. You might want to start with a personal example: **One of the hardest things for the mother of a young child to do is stay in touch with herself as a person and as a changing person. I find myself needing to be up for my whole family but I can't stay up at all unless I've been able to get in touch with and meet some of my own needs.**[4]

After the mothers have brought up their needs, ask the fathers to talk about their needs as parents. Then, depending on where the discussion tends to be going, try to relate both parents' needs to the husband-wife relationship. Usually, someone has brought up something in the earlier part of the evening that can lead into this area.

Continue by talking about the evolution of the husband-wife relationship. You can describe a little about courtship, its romanticism and the need to be together. Then go on to talk about the early years of marriage when perhaps both partners worked and had free time on the weekends. Move on to the current years of new parenting, bringing in some of what was said at the beginning of the evening. You may prefer to describe the course of your own marriage relationship instead of speaking in a general way. No matter which course you follow, the main point is to give couples a chance to step back and look at what's happening to them in their relationship.

Now you may wish to hand out a brief article that deals with stress, such as, "Why Fathers Get Jealous" (see the "Readings" [p. 394] and the "Handouts" [p. 398] sections). Let each couple read it together silently and then have them respond to questions on another sheet of paper by writing a caring letter to each other. (If some parents attend without their spouse, they can still write a caring letter to him or her.) If there are rooms available, have each couple go to one to write and discuss their letters. If rooms are not

---

4. The topic of needs is dealt with in detail on pp. 379–391 but is included here because it is a good way to begin the class on couple relationships.

available, couples can find corners and other places in the meeting room to use together.

You may prefer to give the couples questions other than the ones provided, but here are a few suggestions:

- How has our relationship changed since courtship days?
- How do I expect our relationship to be?
- What do I expect of you and of myself in our marriage?
- What are some of the hard issues in our relationship now?
- What's possible to change? How would I feel about that? How do I think you would feel about that?

Depending on the questions that you choose, you will need to decide on the amount of time the couples need to answer them. One or two questions in about 20 minutes should be sufficient.

After the writing time is over, ask each couple to exchange letters, read them silently, and then share their thoughts and feelings about them with each other. Again, 20 minutes is a good amount of time for this sharing.[5]

After they've had time alone, ask all the couples to come back to the group and encourage them to share some not-too-revealing aspect of their discussion—such as what they learned about their expectations for each other, or what were their feelings about the letters they just read.

A very positive way to end the evening is to bring up for discussion things that couples can do to strengthen their relationship during the early parenting years. Try to encourage the group to go beyond the level of saying they ought to "go out together one night a week."[6]

---

5. The idea of spouses writing caring or loving letters to each other in response to selected questions and then exchanging the letters and discussing them as a couple has been adapted from the Marriage Encounter program, which provides a weekend marriage enhancement experience for couples.

6. A separate, ongoing couple's class may be useful in your program with an evening, perhaps six-week, format. This would enable you to do more than just help catalyze things.

Additional Information for Parents

- Parents should learn that the early parenting years usually produce a great deal of work and fatigue for both parents. Fathers often feel an increased sense of responsibility that drives them to work harder.
- Mothers usually want help with child care and household chores and husbands often don't meet their wives' expectations. Each parent can silently feel that the other partner has the easier job, even if they both work.
- Children's needs and demands tend to be very interruptive and it is usual for parents to be unable to communicate at any length. In fact, after several years of being a parent and having little time to really talk, share and learn about each other, many parents find it hard to communicate when they suddenly have a few hours alone. This situation results from parents getting out of the habit of talking and listening rather than anything else.
- Parents may be disappointed because their spouse is not meeting their needs as he or she used to. They may have to learn how to better understand the strains of the early parenting years and make time for themselves as individuals and as a couple.

Divorce, Single Parenting, Step Parenting

- In most parenting classes, some parents are divorced, some are single parents, and some are stepparents. To understand their situations better, read some of the suggested books in this category found in Appendix A.
- Since child development and behavior and many parent reactions are quite similar in married and divorced families, parenting classes do not necessarily have to be separated along marital lines. However, divorcing parents, single and step parents all need additional support focussed on the "end of marriage" or "new marriage" issue. Married couples in parenting classes can often be quite helpful to these families.

Handouts

Two articles are included here as possible handouts: "Why Fathers Get Jealous," reprinted here from *American Baby,* or "Men and Women Speak Different Languages," reprinted from the *Peninsula Times Tribune.* In addition, in Rothenberg, *PETP,* handouts include: The Newborn Mother: Stages of her Growth, pp. 256–258; "Using 'I' Messages," p. 259; and Diary of a Very New Father, pp. 261–264.

WHY FATHERS GET JEALOUS

by Jean S. Gochros

"Imagine! A grown man competing with a tiny baby! I feel as if I have two infants instead of one!"

Mark flushed and hotly defended himself against a long list of crimes. According to his wife, Barbara, he was sexist, selfish, immature, lazy and demanding. He "used" his wife as a sex object, treated her like a maid, and did not love either her or the baby. That was only for starters. After a long harangue, she concluded, "The trouble with you is that you can't stand seeing anyone else get any attention. You're just jealous!"

Mark retaliated by hurling a few accusations of his own. Barbara was the selfish one. She was incompetent, insensitive, bossy, petulant and manipulative. She was overprotective of the baby, cared only about herself and the baby, "used" him only to bring home money and do her chores, and on top of everything else, she was frigid!

Only in a private interview could Mark admit, with great shame, that he was indeed jealous of the baby. He'd always wanted children, but he'd never expected to feel like an intruder in his own home, completely replaced by a baby. Was it true? Was he just an immature, jealous child?

"Jealousy" of one's offspring is not a unique problem. It is, in fact, quite common among new parents, especially during the first few months with the baby. The basic theme is usually this: the baby completely disrupts the couple's lives, and they each experience a sense of loss. There is loss of freedom—time and ability to choose recreation and to express affection spontaneously, time to get work done, and time in which to be alone. There is loss of energy, plus loss of self-esteem and self-confidence, related to the anxieties of caring and providing for an infant. There is loss of the romanticism of each being the center of the other's universe. There is the loss of companionship, and finally, there can even be the loss of individuality as each begins to feel defined by his or her roles and functions, rather than by individual personality. The "gain" of a squalling, demanding infant hardly compensates for losses that, combined, deprive each person of the very human need to know that he or she is a worthwhile, capable, and well-loved person.

In the case of Barbara and Mark, when "jealousy" was redefined as resentment and anxiety about such losses, the difficulties seemed more understandable, and Barbara was feeling them just as keenly as Mark.

Who is to blame?

The basic problem usually lies not in a couple's feelings, but in the way in which they handle such feelings. Barbara and Mark were ruled by romantic myths about how "mature parents" are "supposed" to feel, so they labeled any feelings that did not seem to fit the mold as "immature" or "silly." Guiltily they had tried to hide or erase feelings, and when this did not work, they had looked around and tried to assign blame for unacceptable thoughts. Since they obviously could not blame an infant, they vacillated between silently blaming themselves and noisily blaming each other. In the process, they succeeded only in cutting themselves off from each other. Once they stopped worrying about who was at fault and began to let themselves be vulnerable by sharing feelings honestly, they were able to treat specific issues as puzzles to be solved together. Here are some examples:

Fatigue

Barbara had automatically expected Mark to realize how fatigued she was, and hence assumed that he would automatically help with the housework and baby. But the only time she told him how tired she was occurred when she was angry at him or when she was refusing sexual advances.

*Reprinted from *American Baby*, with permission of the author, Jean S. Gochros.

Hence he heard only the attack on him, not her plea for help, and he reacted accordingly. At the same time, he was having problems at work, and the strains of having an infant at home were fatiguing him, too. He badly needed a few minutes of relaxation before he could think of giving the help he was quite willing to provide. But he, too, expressed his fatigue only when defending himself against complaints, and hence his needs were never understood. Once they both sat down and honestly confronted the problem of fatigue, they were more able to work out changes in schedule and work load, experimenting with different solutions, and changing them as the need arose.

Help with infant care

Barbara saw Mark's unwillingness to help with the baby as a sign of laziness, sexism, and the lack of love for the baby. She did not realize that Mark was terrified of doing the wrong thing and she misinterpreted his slowness and ineptitude as deliberate. Her impatient, "Never mind! I'll do it myself!" responses, coupled with her unwillingness to share her own past and present anxieties, made him feel incompetent and worthless. Small wonder he gave up quickly with an irritable, "Yeah, you're so good at it—you do it!" or "That's your job! Why do I have to do it?"

Of course, she could not read his mind any more than he could read hers. Once they both shared their worries about handling a tiny baby, they were able to provide mutual help and support; Barbara shared tips she had already learned, and as Mark gained in confidence and expertise, he gladly gave more help.

Companionship

Barbara was starved for companionship and adult conversation. She could hardly wait for Mark to return home and was hurt that he never confided in her anymore about work, didn't chat with her, and didn't seem to see her as a "person." She did not realize that she was engrossed in the baby and that her first words when he returned home were a demand for help, that her questions about work often seemed cursory rather than interested, or that Mark often needed time to relax before he could recount the day's events. Mark, on the other hand, did not realize that what he saw as "protecting" Barbara from his own worries was in actuality shutting her out of an important part of his life. Yet he, too, sorely missed the companionship they had formerly given each other, and he was just as hurt as she was. Again, honest comparing of notes helped them not only to correct misinterpretations, but also to find solutions.

Love, affection, and sex

When it came to expressions of love, especially where sex was involved, the fear of sounding foolish interfered with communication so severely that Barbara and Mark's original request for help had been based on the fear that they had stopped loving each other.

Each felt that the other had stopped all expressions of affection, and consequently both felt hurt and rejected. Barbara felt that any expression of affections would lead to intercourse, which she did not always want. Consequently, she was afraid to ever kiss or hug Mark or to let him show affection toward her unless she wanted intercourse. Conversely, he saw her stiffening whenever he caressed her as a sign of rejection, and he misinterpreted lack of willingness for intercourse as lack of love; often he led her to the bedroom after a kiss merely because he thought that's what he was supposed to do, thereby adding to her feeling that his expressions of affection were given only when he wanted sex.

Once in the bedroom, other miscommunications occurred. Barbara was both distracted by baby noises and embarrassed about having intercourse while the baby was in the room. Self-conscious about her figure, she stiffened whenever Mark touched her stomach. She had always enjoyed his caressing and kissing her breasts. But now she found his touch too rough and was embarrassed about leaking from the nipples. Hence she often pulled away; when he responded with anger, she did not tell him that she suddenly felt her body was no longer her own property but that it was being claimed by both baby and husband.

She did not realize that Mark saw this as a sign that her body was now forbidden territory to all but the baby and that he had been "replaced." Mark, too, had sometimes felt rather foolish while caressing her breasts, but he'd never told her. In general, each had assumed that because he or she had never heard certain thoughts expressed by the other, such thoughts must be too foolish to dare mention. Consequently, they avoided the very expressions of affection that each needed so badly.

It's easy to see that while treated as separate issues, the problems were often interrelated. The solution to any one problem, then, often automatically helped solve others. Increased help in the kitchen and nursery led to less fatigue and more interest in sex. More time to relax and chat provided more companionship and recreation. More cooperative ventures in infant care led to greater ease and fun; more caressing with or without intercourse stopped the unrealistic separation between "sex" and "love," and conversely, lack of desire for intercourse was not misinterpreted as lack of love.

Not all problems were solved, of course. No amount of communication can find time that isn't there, change a three-way relationship back to a two-way one, or remove the hassles of infant care.

In short, as they learned to approach problems with honesty, humor, and understanding, and to consider "jealousy" as one way of expressing their love for each other, Barbara and Mark were able to change jealousy into a process of sharing both the woes and joys of parenthood. It took courage and work, but the process itself made their new relationship stronger than it had ever been before.

MEN AND WOMEN MAY SPEAK DIFFERENT LANGUAGES

by Constance Rosenblum

So you think you talk like a man just because you've mastered the language of the locker room and the battlefield, just because you throw around terms like "ballpark estimate" and "game plan" and figured out that the Knicks isn't a First Avenue singles bar.

Don't kid yourself. The differences between the way men and women talk are various and subtle, and you couldn't conquer them all even if you moved in with the chairman of the board.

Stimulated in part by the women's movement, linguists have recently made some surprising discoveries about women's speech. Studies show that:

Women often express statements as questions. When he asks, "When's dinner?", she'll reply, "Six o'clock?" as if adding parenthetically, "Is that OK with you?" And when women do make flat-out statements, they're often blunted with tag-end questions, as in "It's a boring movie, isn't it?"

When a man and woman talk to each other, the man is far more likely to interrupt the woman than vice versa. In mixed-sex conversations, men also talk more than women. So much for the "women who never shut up" stereotype.

When a man gives a direct order—"Pass the salt"—a woman is more likely to ask an indirect questions—"Is there some salt at your end of the table?"

Women tend to speak in italics, and not just in *Cosmopolitan* magazine. It's a way of expressing uncertainty with your ability to express yourself, suggests Robin Lakoff, a Berkeley linguist and one of the leading experts on women and language. "Italics say something like: Here are directions telling you how to react, since my saying something by itself is not likely to convince you."

Women use certain words—cute, charming, lovely, adorable—that men shy away from. Have you ever heard a man gush, "It's to die!"? And when was the last time you heard a man describe anything as mauve?

Women tend to hedge. "That speech was sort of interesting," they'll say; then, if anyone disagrees, they've got an out. And if they say, "I guess it's going to rain," they can't be held responsible if it doesn't.

"They're all ways of avoiding or diluting responsibility for what you're saying," says Lakoff. "If you don't have confidence in yourself, you'd prefer to put the responsibility for what you say elsewhere. And, if you don't want responsibility, you'll certainly never get it."

Others suggest that women have little choice, especially in such areas as interruption; they insist the men call the shots in conversation just as they do in most other areas.

In fact, suggests Mary Richie Key, a University of California linguist who's an expert on women's speech, the real issue may be power—"a woman with money or power won't be interrupted"—but since, for the most part, men are the ones with the power, it amounts to the same thing.

You won't find the rules of girltalk and boytalk in any textbook, but we get the message. For every Katharine Hepburn, giving as good as she gets from Spencer Tracy, there's a simpering Marilyn Monroe, hedging her way into men's hearts. For every forthright Jane Fonda, there's a giggly Annie Hall, a walking question mark.

And heaven help the woman who breaks the rules. Expletives deleted didn't cost Richard Nixon his job, but as Casey Miller and Kate Swift point out in their book, "Women and Words," a New Jersey schoolteacher lost hers in part because she referred to school board head William Bell as "Dong Dong Bell"—clearly no way for a lady to speak.

A woman may never realize exactly what signals she's sending, and a man may never realize—consciously—that he's receiving them. But the effect is potent.

And a woman unaware of these dynamics can send badly mixed messages. Her gray flannel suit,

---

Reprinted from the *Peninsula Times Tribune.*

briefcase and firm voice may shout out, "I'm strong. Hire me." But when the boss asks how long she has worked, she replies, "Three years?", and when she asks, "Would you mind passing me the ashtray, please?", she's saying, "Don't trust me, I don't trust myself."

It's believed that every child starts out learning girltalk because of early exposure to mothers and female teachers. Then, when boys develop a taste for rough language, girls are discouraged from direct speech, a process that may become ingrained as early as age 10.

"Society teaches little girls to talk like ladies while little boys learn to be conversational bullies," says Rae Moses, a Northwestern University linguist with a special interest in children's language.

And the patterns persist. A sampling of New York City teachers said they noticed that male students tend to answer questions with a blunt, "It's so-and-so," while female students more often suggested, "Maybe it's this or that."

One area where grown women talk a lot of girltalk is in marriage. Pam Fishman, a Queens College sociologist, taped 54 hours of conversation by three couples in their homes, to analyze male-female power relationships in everyday conversation.

She found that women asked nearly three times as many questions as the men (to draw them out), used twice as many attention-getters like, "this is really interesting" and "did you know that . . ." (to flag interest in what they were saying), interspersed their conversation with the phrase "you know" 10 times as much as the men (apparently to hold the men's interest), and were largely the ones who studded the conversation with phrases like "oh, really?" and "uh-huh"—to help keep the talk perking along.

Fishman also found that women initiated almost twice as many topics of conversation as the men.

But, while all the topics raised by the men turned into conversations, only a third of those raised by women did.

"It's women doing the support work of conversation," she says. "This is just another job women have to do." You might call it conversational housework, and, like all housework, it's invisible until you stop.

Says Fishman, "If a woman goes on strike, if she refuses to do this support work, the man will get very upset. I think that's what arguments are about."

Many marriage counselors agree, "If this system of the woman lubricating the conversation breaks down, the man may not understand what's happening," says Dr. Charles Smith, a Manhattan marriage counselor who sees this problem in his work. "He may relate it to something else, but he doesn't see that she's stopped the conversational housework."

Most people notice when one sex talks like the other. Something clicks when we hear a woman uttering commands instead of questions. And something clicks even louder when we hear a man use the word "lovely."

Though neither girltalk nor boytalk is intrinsically good or bad, we invariably favor the masculine approach. Ironically, assertiveness training, a cornerstone of feminism, teaches women to forego waffling uncertainty in favor of male bluntness.

"Many people say male speech is more desirable," says Barrie Thorne, a Michigan State University sociolinguist whose speciality is gender and language. "But there are real values to the way women speak. Women's speech allows for more ambiguity; everything doesn't have to be stated in black and white."

Ideally, say the experts, we'd all speak a sort of middle-ground language that drew on the best of both forms. And a man who used the word "mauve" wouldn't seem weird.

8

COMMUNITY RESOURCES

Most parents are interested in knowing more about the community resources—for both themselves and their children—that are available to them. In a small community, many people will already know what these are, but in a large, more diverse community it may be necessary to search out and compile this information. You can start by contacting community agencies and organizations—park and recreation departments, school districts, libraries—and then check into any private organizations that are relevant—those that offer classes on parenting, nutrition, baby care, first aid, gymnastics, pre- and post-natal fitness, swimming, or any other subjects you feel may interest the group. Bring to class any catalogs or brochures these groups offer and let the class read through and discuss them. If you include a discussion of community resources in a class toward the end of the series, parents will be able to share additional ideas for outings or local activities that they have discovered and enjoyed and which have provided them with a break from long days at home with a young child or can be used as outings for children by their child care providers. Parents may know about (or libraries can help you locate) books or compiled information about local places to take young children. When you talk about community resources, the following questions can open up the discussion:

- What are some outings or activities you have enjoyed with your child?
- Have you discovered any helpful community services you would like to tell the group about?
- Are there some good parks in your neighborhood?

As the discussion moves forward, you can guide it to deal with questions the parents bring up.

9

READING LISTS

Parents are usually interested in knowing what books are considered helpful for learning about child rearing. People are used to turning to books for information about many kinds of things. Parenting, however, is far more personal and interpersonal than many other subjects. An understanding of its numerous concepts is gained in many ways—through experimenting, talking with other parents, thinking, developing and revising personal theories—*as well as* reading books. There is no scientific answer to the question "How should I raise my child?" The decision, like every parent-child relationship, is unique and is based on feelings and values as well as on fact.

Books on child rearing, however, can be helpful to many parents if the information is read, discussed or thought about, and then fitted to the needs and philosophies of the reader. Books can:

- provide information to enable parents to see and listen to their child more fully;
- help parents better understand their child's development and behavior;

- help parents better understand their own responses and actions as parents;
- help parents see the discrepancies between the values they profess and the actions they take;
- help parents think about and determine their long-range parenting goals; and
- provide suggestions about how to realize those goals.

Because books can be helpful in these ways, lists of books that have proved to be insightful and useful in a variety of parenting areas have been compiled. A separate list is available for each of the four age ranges this book covers (lists overlap in many areas), and each provides a brief description of the individual books. You may wish to hand out copies of the pertinent list toward the end of your series so parents don't consider it to be assigned reading. As you emphasize those you feel are the best books, ask the group to comment on any of these or other books they have found to be especially helpful. Parents may also want information on bookstores or libraries that carry copies of the books.

READING LIST

(1–6 months)

Care of Baby

Penelope Leach, *Your Baby and Child*
An excellent guide for parental interests and concerns in the newborn to five-year-old period.

Benjamin Spock and Michael Rothenberg, *Dr. Spock's Baby and Child Care*
Excellent source of help for all kinds of baby-care concerns.

Child Development

T. Berry Brazelton, *Infants and Mothers*
Deals with the first year of life—month by month—comparing babies of three different temperaments.

Frank Caplan, *The First Twelve Months of Life*
A thorough month-by-month description of baby's development. More systematic than the Brazelton book that precedes this entry but with no emphasis on individual differences among babies.

The Growing Child (order by calling: (800) 927-7289)
A monthly pamphlet on child development that devotes one issue to each month of a child's life, newborn through 6 years. Your subscription can begin with the issue that describes your child's current age. A subscription is $15.00 for the first year, $20.00 for each year following.

Arlene Eisenberg, Heidi Murkoff, and Sandee Hathaway, *What to Expect the First Year*
Very thorough month-by-month format of baby's development; parents' issues and questions makes this a favorite for parents.

Emotional Development

Polly Berends, *Whole Child, Whole Parent*
With comments ranging from the philosophical to the practical, this book covers influences on emotional development.

Dorothy Briggs, *Your Child's Self-esteem*
Useful book of guidelines for parents to use in helping their child develop good feelings about himself.

Selma Fraiberg, *The Magic Years*
Looks at a baby' behavior from the baby's point of view.

Louise Kaplan, *Oneness and Separateness*
Describes the development of infants and toddlers in wonderful detail and is very helpful in understanding what young children need.

Playing with Your Baby

Jean Marzollo, *Fathers and Babies*
This book contains many good ideas for playing with your baby, along with some practical information on baby development and care.

Marilyn Segal and Don Adcock, *Your Child at Play: Birth to One*
The first book in an age-divided series that covers many aspects of child's play in a very thorough way.

Child Care and Nursery Schools

T. Berry Brazelton, *Working and Caring*
A sensitive and helpful presentation of babies and parents' needs in child care and ways of getting them met when parents work.

Sue Bredekamp, *Developmentally Appropriate Practice in Early Childhood Programs Serving Children From Birth Through Age 8* (order by calling: (800) 424-2460)
Now the standard for appropriate child development practices with young children for early childhood educators, this book is also useful for parents to develop more age appropriate expectations of their children.

Janet Gonzalez-Mena and Diane Widmeyer Eyer, *Infants, Toddlers and Caregivers*
This book addresses the needs and the "curriculum" for infants and toddlers, and what can help create a better relationship between young children and their caregivers.

Joanne Miller and Susan Weissman, *The Parent's Guide to Day Care*
This comprehensive book covers the questions to ask and the information needed to select, begin and monitor child care.

Safety/Medical/Illness

Sandy Jones, *Guide to Baby Products (Consumer Reports Books)*
A valuable guide for evaluating the many products used by babies.

Martin I. Green, *A Sigh of Relief*
A first aid handbook for childhood emergencies that includes simple instructions and illustrations for handling injuries.

Robert Pantell, James Fries, and Donald Vickery, *Taking Care of your Child*
A thorough medical guide that enables parents to participate in a more educated way in the medical care of their children.

Nutrition/Nursing

Marvin Eiger and Sally Olds, *The Complete Book of Breast Feeding*
Much information on nursing.

Kathleen Huggins, *Nursing Mother's Companion*
Comprehensive manual on all aspects of breast feeding, highly recommended by lactation specialists.

Sheila Kitzinger, *Breastfeeding Your Baby*
An excellent book filled with photographs, enjoyable to read.

Ellyn Satter, *Child of Mine: Feeding with Love and Good Sense*
A comprehensive book on feeding and nutrition from infancy through toddler years.

Sleep

Joanne Cuthbertson and Susie Schevill, *Helping Your Child Sleep Through the Night.*
Very helpful advice for dealing with all common sleep issues from infancy to age 5.

Richard Ferber, *Solve Your Child's Sleep Problems*
A very good guide on sleep problems; simpler to use, but does not offer as much age-based help as Cuthbertson and Schevill.

Parents

T. Berry Brazelton, *On Becoming a Family*
An excellent book detailing infant behavior and development and differences in mothers' and fathers' behavior and feelings during the early attachment and bonding as a family

Arlene Cardozo, *Sequencing*
An excellent book to help mothers become comfortable with putting their careers on hold while they focus on mothering.

Marsha Dorman and Diane Klein, *How to Stay 2 when Baby Makes 3*
This book helps couples develop new ways to be with and communicate with each other as they enter the world of parenthood. Contains many enjoyable exercises and activities to do together. (Order by calling: 800-421-0351)

Andrea Boroff Eagan, *The Newborn Mother: Stages of Her Growth*
Very helpful during the early months of motherhood. Based on her interviews of a large group of first-time mothers, the author suggests a fascinating process of development that takes place for women as they become mothers.

Martin Greenberg, *Birth of a Father*
Of the books available for fathers, this is considered one of the best. Some chapters are especially helpful (including the chapter specifically for mothers!)

Arlie Hochschild, *The Second Shift: Working Parents and the Revolution at Home*
An outstanding book that deals with the work

that needs to be done by men and women at home—house management and childcare. Provides a thoughful and realistic look at how parents work out these arrangements and what is behind those problems and inequities.

Renee Magid, *When Mothers and Fathers Work*
This is a very practical book on common problems and feelings of both mothers and fathers with many helpful suggestions. The information is based on personal experience and interviews of working parents.

Randy M. Wolfson and Virginia DeLuca, *Couples with Children*
An outstanding practical and experiential book describing the major stresses on couples as they adjust to being parents. (Order by calling: (800) 443-9942)

READING LIST

(7–14 months)

Care of Baby

Penelope Leach, *Your Baby and Child*
An excellent guide for parental interests and concerns in the newborn to five-year-old period.
Benjamin Spock and Michael Rothenberg, *Dr. Spock's Baby and Child Care*
Excellent source of help for all kinds of baby-care concerns.

Child Development

Louise Bates Ames and Frances L. Ilg. *Your One Year Old*
One in a series of books that are very helpful in the area of development.
T. Berry Brazelton, *Infants and Mothers*
Deals with the first year of life—month by month—comparing babies of three different temperaments.
Frank Caplan, *The First Twelve Months of Life*
A thorough month-by-month description of baby's development. More systematic than the Brazelton book that precedes this entry but with no emphasis on individual differences among babies.
The Growing Child (order by calling: (800) 927-7289)
A monthly pamphlet on child development that devotes one issue to each month of a child's life, newborn through 6 years. Your subscription can begin with the issue that describes your child's current age.
Arlene Eisenberg, Heidi Murkoff, and Sandee Hathaway, *What to Expect the First Year*
Very thorough month-by-month format of baby's development; parents' issues and questions makes this a favorite for parents.

Emotional Development

Polly Berends, *Whole Child, Whole Parent*
With comments ranging from the philosophical to the practical, this book covers influences on emotional development.
Dorothy Briggs, *Your Child's Self-esteem*
Useful book for parents to use in helping their child develop good feelings about himself.
Selma Fraiberg, *The Magic Years*
Looks at a baby's behavior from the baby's point of view.
Louise Kaplan, *Oneness and Separateness*
An excellent book that describes the development of infants and toddlers in wonderful detail.

Playing with Your Baby

Jean Marzollo, *Fathers and Babies*
This book contains many good ideas for playing with your baby, along with some practical information on baby development and care.
Marilyn Segal and Don Adcock, *Your Child at Play: Birth to One*
The first book in an age-divided series that covers many aspects of child's play in a very thorough way.

Child Care and Nursery School

Lyda Beardsley, *Good Day, Bad Day*
An excellent book comparing the same group of young children at a poor child care center and at a good center. Helps parents understand what is a quality center and what to look for. (Order by calling: (800) 575-6566)
T. Berry Brazelton, *Working and Caring*
A sensitive and helpful presentation of babies and parents' needs in child care and ways of getting them met when parents work.
Sue Bredekamp, *Developmentally Appropriate*

Practice in Early Childhood Programs Serving Children from Birth Through Age 8 (Order by calling: (800) 424-2460)
Now the standard for appropriate child development practices with young children for early childhood educators, this book is also useful for parents to develop more age appropriate expectations of their children.

Janet Gonzalez-Mena and Diane Widmeyer Eyer, *Infants, Toddlers and Caregivers*
This book addresses the needs and the "curriculum" for infants and toddlers, and what can help create a better relationship between young children and their caregivers.

Joanne Miller and Susan Weissman, *The Parent's Guide to Day Care*
This comprehensive book covers the questions to ask and the information needed to select, begin and monitor child care.

Safety/Medical/Illness

Consumer Guide, *The Complete Baby Book*
A valuable guide for evaluating the many products used by babies.

Martin I. Green, *A Sigh of Relief*
A first aid handbook for childhood emergencies that includes simple instructions and illustrations for handling injuries.

Robert H. Pantell, James F. Fries, and Donald M. Vickery, *Taking Care of Your Child: A Parents' Guide to Medical Care.*
Provides practical information on the most common medical problems of childhood.

Nutrition/Nursing

Marvin Eiger and Sally Olds, *The Complete Book of Breast Feeding*
Much information on nursing.

Kathleen Huggins, *Nursing Mother's Companion*
Comprehensive manual on all aspects of breast feeding, highly recommended by lactation specialists.

Ellyn Satter, *How to Get Your Kid to Eat . . . But Not Too Much*
An excellent book on eating issues—deals well with the nutritional and psychological aspects of food from the infant, child, teenager, and parent point of view.

Sleep

Joanne Cuthbertson and Susie Schevill, *Helping Your Child Sleep Through the Night*
Very helpful advice for dealing with all common sleep issues from infancy to age 5.

Richard Ferber, *Solve Your Child's Sleep Problems*
A very good guide on sleep problems; simpler to use but does not offer as much age-based help as Cuthbertson and Schevill.

Parents

Arlene Cardozo, *Sequencing*
An excellent book to help mothers become comfortable with putting their careers on hold while they focus on mothering.

Marsha Dorman and Diane Klein, *How to Stay 2 when Baby Makes 3*
This book helps couples to develop new ways to be with and communicate with each other as they enter the world of parenthood. Contains many enjoyable exercises and activities to do together. (Order by calling: 800-421-0351)

Andrea Boroff Eagan, *The Newborn Mother: Stages of Her Growth*
Very helpful during the first year of motherhood. Based on her interviews of a large group of first-time mothers, the author suggests a fascinating process of development that takes place for women as they become mothers.

Martin Greenberg, *Birth of a Father*
Considered one of the best books for fathers. Some chapters are especially helpful (including the chapter specifically for mothers!)

Arlie Hochschild, *The Second Shift: Working Par-

ents and the Revolution at Home
An outstanding book that deals with the work that needs to be done by men and women at home—house management and child care. Provides a thoughtful and realistic look at how parents work out these arrangements and what is behind those problems and inequities.

Renee Magid, *When Mothers and Fathers Work*
This is a very practical book on common problems and feelings of both mothers and fathers with many helpful suggestions. The information is based on personal experience and interviews of working parents.

Randy M. Wolfson and Virginia DeLuca, *Couples with Children*
An outstanding practical book describing the major stresses on couples as they adjust to being parents. (Order by calling: (800) 443-9942)

READING LIST

(15–24 months)

Care of Toddlers

Penelope Leach, *Your Baby and Child*
An excellent guide for parental interests and concerns in the newborn to five-year-old period.

Benjamin Spock and Michael Rothenberg, *Dr. Spock's Baby and Child Care*
Excellent source of help for all kinds of baby-care concerns.

Child Development

Louise Bates Ames, Frances Ilg, *Your One Year Old*
Useful book on normal changes in development, behavior, and habits.

Frank Caplan and Teresa Caplan, *The Second Twelve Months of Life*
A detailed description of toddler development from 12 months to 2 1/2 years.

Fitzugh Dodson, *How to Parent*
Helpful in developing a philosophy of child raising.

Arlene Eisenberg, Heidi Murkoff, and Sandee Hathaway, *What to Expect the Toddler Years*
The authors continue their month-by-month format with parents issues and questions about children from 13 to 36 months.

The Growing Child (Order by calling: (800) 927-7289)
A monthly pamphlet on child development that devotes one issue to each month of a child's life, newborn through 6 years. Your subscription can begin with the issue that describes your child's current age.

Emotional Development

Dorothy Briggs, *Your Child's Self-esteem*
Useful book for parents to use in helping their child develop good feelings about himself.

Selma Fraiberg, *The Magic Years*
Looks at a child's behavior from the child's point of view.

Louise Kaplan, *Oneness and Separateness*
An excellent book that describes the development of infants and toddlers in wonderful detail and is very helpful in understanding what young children need.

Temperament

Stella Chess, A. Thomas, H. G. Birch, *Your Child is a Person*
Deals with particular stages or issues in infant and child development and how children of different temperaments are helped or hindered by their parents in getting through these stages. (Out of print, available in libraries)

Mary Kurcinka, *Raising Your Spirited Child*
This is an excellent book on raising children with "difficult" temperaments.

Limit Setting

Clare Cherry, *Parents, Please Don't Sit On Your Kids*
An outstanding book on limit setting for parents of children starting at toddler age. It emphasizes the best in early childhood development.

Elizabeth Crary, *Without Spanking or Spoiling*
A very helpful book for helping parents set limits with toddlers and preschoolers. (Includes written exercises)

Adele Faber and Elaine Mazlish, *How to Talk So Kids Will Listen and Listen So Kids Will Talk*
An excellent book to help parents deal with their own and their children's feelings and to encourage cooperation and independence in their children.

READING LIST (continued)

Siblings and Only Children

Meg Zweibach, *Keys to Preparing and Caring for Your Second Child*
Offers concise guidelines for parents anticipating the birth of a second baby.

Children's Play

Jean Marzollo, *Fathers and Toddlers*
This book contains many good ideas for playing with your toddler (from 18 to 36 months), along with some practical information on toddler development and care. (Not just for fathers.)
Marilyn Segal and Don Adcock, *Your Child at Play: One to Two Years*
The second book in an age-divided series that thoroughly covers many aspects of child's play.

Child Care and Nursery Schools

Sue Bredekamp, *Developmentally Appropriate Practice in Early Childhood Programs Serving Children From Birth Through Age 8* (Order by calling: (800) 424-2460)
Now the standard for appropriate child development practices with young children for early childhood educators, also useful for parents to develop more age appropriate expectations of their children.
Janet Gonzalez-Mena and Diane Widmeyer Eyer, *Infants, Toddlers and Caregivers*
This book addresses the needs and the "curriculum" for infants and toddlers, and what can help create a better relationship between young children and their caregivers.
Joanne Miller and Susan Weissman, *The Parent's Guide to Day Care*
This comprehensive book covers the questions to ask and the information needed to select, begin and monitor child care.
Irene Van der Zande, *1,2,3 The Toddler Years*
This is an easy-to-read book useful for parents and caregivers of toddlers; helpful ways to handle typical toddler behaviors that will bring parents and caregivers into closer accord with each other and benefit the toddlers.

Safety/Medical/Illness

Martin I. Green, *A Sigh of Relief*
A first aid handbook for childhood emergencies that includes simple instructions and illustrations for handling injuries.
Robert H. Pantell, James F. Fries, and Donald M. Vickery, *Taking Care of Your Child: A Parents' Guide to Medical Care.*
Provides practical information on the most common medical problems of childhood.

Nutrition

Ellyn Satter, *How to Get Your Kid to Eat . . . But Not Too Much*
An excellent book on eating issues—deals well with the nutritional and psychological aspects of food from the infant, child, teenager, and parent point of view.

Sleep

Joanne Cuthbertson and Susie Schevill, *Helping Your Child Sleep Through the Night.*
Very helpful advice for dealing with all common sleep issues from infancy to age 5.

Parents

Mitch and Susan Golant, *Finding Time For Fathering*
Good book for dads; deals with many of their difficult role and time issues.
Martin Greenberg, *Birth of a Father*
Considered one of the best books available for fathers. Some chapters are especially helpful (including the chapter specifically for mothers!)
Arlie Hochschild, *The Second Shift: Working Parents and the Revolution at Home*
An outstanding book that deals with the work that needs to be done by men and women at

home—house management and child care. Provides a thoughtful and realistic look at how parents work out these arrangements and what is behind those problems and inequities.

Renee Magid, *When Mothers and Fathers Work*
This is a very practical book on common problems and feelings of both mothers and fathers with many helpful suggestions. The information is based on personal experience and interviews of working parents.

Randy M. Wolfson and Virginia DeLuca, *Couples with Children*
An outstanding practical book describing the major stresses on couples as they adjust to being parents. (Order by calling: (800) 443-9942)

READING LIST

(2–3 years)

Child Development

Louise Bates Ames and Frances Ilg. *Your Two-Year-Old: Terrible or Tender*
Another good Gesell book, specifically discusses two-year-olds.

Ellen Galinsky and Judy David, *The Preschool Years*
A helpful and comprehensive book on issues that most of today's parents experience in raising preschoolers.

The Growing Child (Order by calling (800) 927-7289)
A monthly pamphlet on child development that devotes one issue to each month of a child's life, newborn through 6 years. Your subscription can begin with the issue that describes your child's current age.

Arlene Eisenberg, Heidi Murkoff, and Sandee Hathaway, *What to Expect the Toddler Years*
The authors continue their month-by-month format with parents issues and questions about children from 13 to 36 months.

Penelope Leach, *Your Baby and Child*
An excellent guide for parental interests and concerns in the newborn to five-year-old period.

Emotional Development

Dorothy Briggs, *Your Child's Self-esteem*
Useful book of guidelines for parents to use in helping their child develop good feelings about himself.

Selma Fraiberg, *The Magic Years*
Looks at a child's behavior from the child's point of view.

Temperament

Mary Kurcinka, *Raising Your Spirited Child*
This is an excellent book on raising children with "difficult" temperaments.

Limit Setting

Clare Cherry, *Parents, Please Don't Sit on Your Kids*
An outstanding book on limit setting for parents of children starting at toddler age. It emphasizes the best in early childhood development.

Elizabeth Crary, *Without Spanking or Spoiling*
A useful handbook with exercises to practice a wide range of useful discipline techniques.

Adele Faber and Elaine Mazlish, *How to Talk so Kids Will Listen and Listen so Kids Will Talk*
An excellent book for parents to help them deal with their and their children's feelings and to encourage cooperation and independence in their children.

Children's Play

Jean Marzollo, *Fathers and Toddlers*
This book contains many good ideas for playing with your toddler (from 18-36 months), along with some practical information on toddler development and care. (Not just for fathers.)

Zick Rubin, *Children's Friendships,* Harvard University Press, *The Developing Child* series, (Order by calling (617) 495-2480)
An excellent book to help parents understand more about children's friendships.

Marilyn Segal and Don Adcock, *Your Child at Play: Two to Three Years*
The second book in an age-divided series that thoroughly covers many aspects of child's play.

Child Care and Nursery Schools

Sue Bredekamp, *Developmentally Appropriate Practice in Early Childhood Programs Serving Children From Birth Through Age 8* (Order by calling (800) 424-2460)
Now the standard for appropriate child devel-

opment practices with young children for early childhood educators, this book is also useful for parents to develop more age appropriate expectations of their children.

Janet Gonzalez-Mena and Diane Widmeyer Eyer, *Infants, Toddlers and Caregivers*
This book addresses the needs and the "curriculum" for infants and toddlers, and what can help create a better relationship between young children and their caregivers.

Joanne Miller and Susan Weissman, *The Parent's Guide to Day Care*
This comprehensive book covers the questions to ask and the information needed to select, begin and monitor child care.

Irene Van der Zande, *1,2,3 The Toddler Years*
This easy-to-read book is useful for parents and caregivers of toddlers; helpful ways to handle typical toddler behaviors that will bring parents and caregivers into closer accord with each other and benefit the toddlers.

Siblings and Only Children

Elizabeth Crary, *Kids Can Cooperate*
Helps parents understand sibling relations and explains a problem-solving approach that parents can teach their children.

Adele Faber and Elaine Mazlish, *Siblings Without Rivalry*
This useful book focuses on relations between siblings; also discusses parents' relationships with their children. It offers many techniques for preventing and managing sibling conflicts.

Susan Newman, *Parenting an Only Child*
This book offers guidance for successfully raising an only child and presents a thorough discussion about the issues involved. It is strongly supportive of having only children.

Meg Zweibach, *Keys to Preparing and Caring for Your Second Child*
Offers concise guidelines for parents anticipating the birth of a second baby.

Sleep

Joanne Cuthbertson and Susie Schevill, *Helping Your Child Sleep Through the Night*.
Very helpful advice for dealing with all common sleep issues from infancy to age 5.

Richard Ferber, *Solve Your Child's Sleep Problems*
A very good guide on sleep problems' simpler to use, but does not offer as much age-based help as Cuthbertson and Schevill.

Nutrition

Ellyn Satter, *How to Get Your Kid to Eat . . . But Not Too Much*
An excellent book on eating issues—deals well with the nutritional and psychological aspects of food from the infant, child, teenager, and parent point of view.

Safety/Medical/Illness

Martin I. Green, *A Sigh of Relief*
A first aid handbook for childhood emergencies that includes simple instructions and illustrations for handling injuries.

Robert H. Pantell, James F. Fries, and Donald M. Vickery, *Taking Care of Your Child: A Parents' Guide to Medical Care*
Provides practical information on the most common medical problems of childhood.

Parents

Arlene Cardozo, *Sequencing*
An excellent book to help mothers become comfortable with putting their careers on hold while they focus on mothering.

Mitch and Susan Golant, *Finding Time For Fathering*
Good book for dads; deals with many of their difficult role and time issues.

Arlie Hochschild, *The Second Shift: Working Par-*

ents and the Revolution at Home
An outstanding book that deals with the work that needs to be done by men and women at home—house management and child care. Provides a thoughtful and realistic look at how parents work out these arrangements and what is behind those problems and inequities.

Renee Magid, *When Mothers and Fathers Work*
This is a very practical book on common prob-lems and feelings of both mothers and fathers with many helpful suggestions. The information is based on personal experience and interviews of working parents.

Randy M. Wolfson and Virginia DeLuca, *Couples with Children*
An outstanding practical book describing the major stresses on couples as they adjust to be-ing parents. (Order by calling: (800) 443-9942)

part seven

APPENDICES

resources, information and forms

A

READINGS AND OTHER INFORMATION FOR INSTRUCTORS*

*Books on Group Guidance Techniques***

*Auerbach, Aline, *Parents Learn Through Discussion* (Malabar, Fl.: Krieger Publishing Co., 1980).

*Braun, Linda, Coplan, Jennifer, and Sonenschein, Phyllis, *Helping Parents in Groups* (Boston: Wheelock College Center for Parenting Studies, 1984; order from Redleaf Press, phone [800] 423-8309).

*Curran, Dolores, *Working With Parents* (Circle Pines: Minn.: American Guidance Service, 1989).

*Rothenberg, B. Annye, *Parentmaking Educators Training Program: A Comprehensive Skills Development Course to Train Early Childhood Parent Educators (Birth to Five)*—a book and videotapes package (Menlo Park, Cal.: Banster Press, 1993).

*Books on Child and Parent
Development and Behavior*

Ames, Louise Bates and Ilg, Frances L., *Your One Year Old, Your Two Year Old, . . . Your Nine Year Old* (New York, N.Y.: Delta/Bantam Doubleday Dell, 1980's). This series is very helpful in the area of development.

Brazelton, T. Berry, *On Becoming a Family* (New York: Dell Publishing Co., Inc., 1982). An excellent book detailing infant behavior and development and differences in mothers' and fathers' behavior and feelings during the early attachment as a family.

Brazelton, T. Berry, *Infants and Mothers* (New York: Dell Publishing Co., Inc., 1983). An outstanding book that deals with the first year of life—month by month—comparing babies of three different temperaments.

*Bredekamp, Sue, *Developmentally Appropriate Practice in Early Childhood Program, Birth to 8* (Washington, D.C.: National Association for the Education of Young Children, 1987). This book is now the standard for quality child care practices with young children. Very useful information.

Briggs, Dorothy, *Your Child's Self-Esteem* (Garden City, N.Y.: Doubleday and Company, Inc., 1975). Useful book of guidelines for parents to use in helping their child develop good feelings about himself.

*Bromwich, Rose, *Working With Parents and Infants* (out of print, but available by sending a check for $15 to Child Rearing, CHC, 700 Sand Hill Road, Palo Alto, Cal. 94304). This is the best resource for providing thorough guidance to parents on more than 60 common issues for parents of children from birth to age three.

Caplan, Frank, ed., *The First Twelve Months of Life* (New York, N.Y.: Berkley/Perigree Books, 1993). A thorough description of a baby's development, month by month. More systematic than *Infants and Mothers* but with no emphasis on individual differences among babies.

Caplan, Frank, ed., *The Second Twelve Months of Life* (New York: Bantam, 1982). (Also, *The Early*

---

*This list for parent educators contains some very important books that provide a good foundation. See *Readings and Other Resources* in all the chapters in Parts II through VI and the Parenting Reading Lists beginning on p. 405 for additional suggestions on general and specific topics such as nutrition, language, safety and illness, sleep, etc.

**Books marked with an * are recommended for parent educators and not especially for parents.

Childhood Years (2 to 5), (New York: Putnam Publishing, 1983). Similar in approach to Caplan's *First Twelve Months of Life;* a helpful guide on behavior and development.

*Chess, Stella and Thomas, Alexander, *Know Your Child* (New York, N.Y.: Basic Books, Inc., 1989). This is must reading for parent educators and is basically a review of developmental psychology for the parenting guidance professional.

Cherry, Clare, *Parents, Please Don't Sit On Your Kids* (Carthage, Ill.: Fearon Teacher Aids, 1985). An outstanding book on limit setting for parents of children beginning at toddler age. It emphasizes the best in early childhood development.

*Cowan, Philip and Carolyn, *When Partners Become Parents* (New York, N.Y.: Basic Books/Harper Collins, 1992). A research-based book on the changes for couples as they become parents.

Crary, Elizabeth, *Without Spanking or Spoiling* (Seattle, Wash.: Parenting Press, 1993). A very helpful book for helping parents set limits with toddlers and preschoolers (includes written exercises).

Cuthbertson, Joanne and Schevill, Susie, *Helping Your Child Sleep Through the Night* (New York, N.Y.: Doubleday and Co., Inc., 1985). Very useful developmentally-based guidance dealing with all the common sleep issues from infancy to age 5.

Faber, Adele and Mazlish, *Liberated Parents, Liberated Children* (New York, N.Y. Avon/Hearst, 1990). Also, *How to Talk So Kids Will Listen and Listen So Kids Will Talk* (New York: Avon/Hearst, 1982). Excellent books to help parents deal with their and their child's feelings and build better communication and cooperation.

Faber, Adele and Mazlish, Elaine, *Siblings Without Rivalry* (New York, N.Y.: W. W. Norton and Co., 1987). This useful book focuses on the relations between siblings; also discusses parents' relationships with their children and offers parents help preventing and managing sibling conflicts.

Fraiberg, Selma, *The Magic Years* (New York: Macmillan, 1966). Looks at a child's behavior from the child's point of view.

Galinsky, Ellen, *The Six Stages of Parenthood* (Reading, Mass.: Addison-Wesley Co., 1987). An excellent book about parenthood and its impact from your child's birth to adulthood.

*Greenspan, Stanley and Greenspan, Nancy, *The Essential Partnership* (New York, N.Y.: Viking Penguin, Inc., 1989). Helpful for parent educators to learn in detail about the emotional development of young children and the role of the parents.

The Growing Child (Lafayette, Ind.: Dunn & Hargitt, 1995 updated annually; order by calling [800] 927-7289).

A very good monthly series on child development that devotes one issue to each month of a child's life, newborn through 6 years.

Jones, Molly Mason, *Guiding Your Child from Two to Five* (New York: Harcourt, Brace & World, Inc., 1967). Covers discipline, play, and most other situations you encounter in child rearing. Helps a parent gear her focus toward pre-school and less toward her child as a baby. Outstanding. (The book is out of print but may be available through your library.

Kurcinka, Mary Sheedy, *Raising Your Spirited Child* (New York, N.Y.: Harper-Collins, 1991). This is an excellent book on raising children with "difficult" temperaments; the guidance is quite helpful.

Leach, Penelope, *Your Baby and Child* (New York, N.Y.: Knopf, 1989). An excellent guide for parental interests and concerns in the newborn to five-year-old period.

Satter, Ellyn, *Child of Mine: Feeding with Love and Good Sense* (Menlo Park, Cal.: Bull Publishing Co., 1986); also *How to Get Your Kid to Eat But Not Too Much* (Menlo Park, Cal.: Bull Publishing Co., 1987). Both are excellent books on nutritional and psychological aspects of food from child's and parent's point of view; the first book focuses on infancy through toddlers; the second from infancy through teen years.

Wolfson, Randy M. and DeLuca, Virginia, *Couples with Children* (Available only by calling Birth and Life Bookstore (800 443-9942). An outstanding practical and experiential book describing the major stresses on couples as they adjust to being parents.

Books on Working Parent Families

See Appendix H for reading list

*Books on Divorce, Single Parenting, and Stepparenting****

Anderson, Joan, *The Single Mother's Book* (Atlanta: Peachtree Publishers, 1990).

Bernstein, Anne C., *Yours, Mine, and Ours* (New York, N.Y.: W. W. Norton and Co., 1989).

Cerquone, Joseph, *"You're A Stepparent. Now What"* (Far Hills, N.J.: New Horizon Press, 1994).

Gardner, Richard, *The Parents' Book About Divorce* (New York: Bantam Books, 1977, 1991).

***The Children's Rights Council, Inc. in Washington, D.C. ([800] 787-KIDS) can provide parent educators with information on parenting groups for divorced and divorcing parents to be able to continue to work together in their child rearing.

Lansky, Vicky, *Divorce Book for Parents* (New York, N.Y.: Signet/Penguin, 1989).

Teyber, Edward, *Helping Children Cope with Divorce* (New York: Lexington/Macmillan, 1992).

Visher, Emily and John, *Stepfamilies: Myths and Realities* (New York: Carol Publishing, 1979, 1993).

Wallerstein, Judith, *Second Chances* (New York: Ticknor and Fields, 1989).

Warshak, Richard, *The Custody Revolution* (New York: Poseidon Press, 1992).

Books on Prematurity and Multiple Births

Clegg, A. and Woolett, A., *Twins: From Conception to Five Years* (New York, N.Y.: Ballantine Books/Random House, 1988).

Gromada, Karen and Hurlburt, Mary, *Keys to Parenting Twins* (Hauppauge, N.Y.: Barron's, 1992).

Jason, Janine and Van der Meer, Antonia, *Parenting Your Premature Baby* (New York: Delta/Bantam Doubleday Dell, 1989).

Manginello, Frank and DiGeronimo, Theresa, *Your Premature Baby* (New York, N.Y.: John Wiley and Sons, 1991).

Books on Adoption

Melina, Lois, *Raising Adopted Children* (New York, N.Y.: Harper Perennial, 1986).

Melina, Lois, *Making Sense of Adoption* (New York, N.Y.: Harper Perennial, 1989).

Books on Ethnic Minorities****

General Readings on Ethnicity and Families

Davis, L. E. (Ed.), *Ethnicity in Social Group Work Practice* (New York: Haworth, 1984).

Gonzalez-Mena, J., *Multicultural issues in infant care* (Mountain View, Cal.: Mayfield Publishing, 1992).

Lynch, E. and Hanson, M., *Developing Cross-Cultural Competence: a guide for working with young children and their families.* (Baltimore, Md.: Paul H. Brookes, 1992).

McAdoo, H. (Ed.), *Family Ethnicity: strength in diversity.* Newbury Park, Cal.: Sage Publications, 1993.

Mindel, C. H., Habenstein, R. W., and Wright, R. (Eds.), *Ethnic Families in America: Patterns and Variations,* 3rd edition (New York: Elsevier, 1988).

Storti, C., *The Art of Crossing Cultures* (Yarmouth, Me.: Intercultural Press, 1990).

York, S., *Roots and Wings: affirming culture in early childhood programs* (St. Paul, Minn.: Red Leaf Press, 1991).

African-American Families

Books

Hale-Benson, Janice, *Black Children: Their Roots, Culture and Learning Styles* (Baltimore: Johns Hopkins University Press, 1986).

Hopson, Darlene Powell and Derek, *Different and Wonderful: Raising Black Children in a Race-Conscious Society* (New York: Fireside/Simon and Schuster, 1990).

McAdoo, Hariette Pipes, ed., *Black Families* (Newbury Park, Cal.: Sage Publications, 1988).

Parenting Educator Resources

The Guide for Choosing African American Parenting Curricula by Robin Wingo and Carol Mertensmeyer, 1994. A complete description and evaluation of the known curricula. Order from the Parent Link Connection Center (314) 882-7321.

Working with African-American Families: A guide to Resources by Carolyn Ash, 1994. Order from Family Resource Coalition (312) 341-0900.

Latino Families

Moore, J. and Pachon, H., *Hispanics in the United States* (Englewood Cliffs, N.J.: Prentice-Hall, 1985).

Rothenberg, B. Annye, *Understanding and Working with Parents and Children from Rural Mexico: What professionals need to know about child rearing practices, the school experience, and health care concerns.* (Menlo Park, Cal.: The CHC Center for Child and Family Development Press, 1995). Order by calling (415) 326-5575.

Williams, N. *The Mexican-American Family: Tradition and Change* (New York, N.Y.: General Hall, 1990).

Parenting Educator Resources

The Guide for Choosing Hispanic/Latino American Parenting Curricula by Robin Wingo and Carol Mertensmeyer, 1994). (See African-American families for ordering information).

****The Parent Link Connection Center in Missouri (314) 882-7321) and the Family Resource Coalition in Chicago ([312] 341-0900) are both excellent sources of additional information on parenting education curricula designed for specific ethnic minorities.

Asian Families

White, Merry, *The Japanese Educational Challenge* (New York, N.Y.: Free Press/Macmillan, 1987).

Chen, J., *The Chinese of America* (New York, N.Y.: Harper and Row, 1981).

Bond, M. H. (ed.), *The Psychology of Chinese People* (Hong Kong: Oxford Press, 1987).

Hurh, W. M. and Kim, K. C., *Korean Immigrants in America* (N.J.: Associated University Press, 1984).

Takaki, R., *Strangers from a Different Shore: A History of Asian Americans* (Boston: Little Brown, 1989).

Native American Families

Hoffman, F. (Ed.), *The American Indian Family: Strengths and Stresses* (Isleta, N.M.: American Indian Social Research and Development Assn., 1981).

Morey, S. M. and Gilliam, O. L., *Respect for Life: Traditional Upbringing of American Indian Children* (Garden City, N.Y.: Waldorf Press, 1974).

Olson, J. S. and Wilson, R., *Native Americans in the Twentieth Century* (Chicago: University of Illinois Press, 1984).

Parent Educator Resources

The Guide for Choosing Native American Parenting Curricula by Robin Wingo and Carol Mertensmeyer, 1994. (See African-American families for ordering information.

Catalogs and Reviews[1]

All of the following are excellent sources of information on childbirth and parenting books including reviews of new and recently published books. Published several times each year.

Birth and Life Bookstore, Inc., *Imprints* (141 Commercial Street, N.E., Salem, Ore., 97301; call 800-443-9942.)

International Childbirth Education Association, *Bookmarks* (P.O. Box 20048, Minneapolis, Minn. 55420; call 800-624-4934.)

Redleaf Press (450 N. Syndicate (Suite 5), St. Paul, Minn. 55104; call (800) 423-8309.)

ORGANIZATIONS INVOLVING CHILD-REARING EDUCATORS AND EDUCATION

American Society for Psychoprophylaxis in Obstetrics, 1200 19th Street NW (Suite 300), Washington, D.C. 20036; call (202) 857-1128.

Family Resource Coalition[2], 200 South Michigan Avenue, 16th Floor, Chicago, Ill. 60604; call (312) 341-0900.

International Childbirth Education Association, P.O. Box 20048, Minneapolis, Minn. 55420; call (612) 854-8660.

National Association for the Education of Young Children, 1509 16th Street N.W., Washington, D.C. 20036; call (800) 424-2460.

National Center for Clinical Infant Programs (NCCIP), 2000 14th Street North, (Suite 380), Arlington, Va. 22201; call (703) 528-4300.

National Council on Family Relations (NCFR), 3989 Central Avenue N.E. (Suite 550), Minneapolis, Minn. 55421; call (612) 781-9331.

Journals

Children Today, The journal of the Administration for Children and Families, Department of Health and Human Services; call (202) 401-9215.

CFLE Network, The newsletter for certified family life educators of the National Council on Family Relations; call (612) 781-9331.

FRC Report, the newsletter of the Family Resource Coalition; call (312) 341-0900.

Young Children, The journal of the National Association for the Education of Young Children; call (800) 424-2460.

Zero to Three, The newsletter of the National Center for Clinical Infant Programs; call (703) 528-4300.

Magazines

American Baby, 249 West 17th Street, New York, N.Y. 10011.

Parenting, 301 Howard Street (17th Floor), San Francisco, Cal. 94105

Parents' Magazine, 685 Third Avenue, New York, N.Y. 10017.

Working Mother, 230 Park Avenue, New York, N.Y. 10169.

---

1. This and the following entries are only a sampling of the many journals, organizations, and magazines that are available.

---

2. The Family Resource Coalition offers many books, listings, and technical support to parent educators. One of their publications, *Programs to Strengthen Families* tells about model parenting programs and their various curricula.

B

SAMPLE PUBLICITY AND REGISTRATION FORMS

Boxed Display Ad to Advertise for Instructors

CHILD-REARING/PARENT EDUCATOR

Quarter-time position available for a parent with very young children who has the professional background, experience and interest to help develop and teach well-organized classes on child rearing and child development information, techniques, and observation skills to parents of "normal" babies and toddlers at a mid-peninsula children's services agency. Send details of background to [*P.O. box number or address*].

Newspaper Publicity Article

CHILD-REARING CLASSES SLATED

Classes at the [*name of program or agency*] in [*name of city*] will begin in [*name of month*] and continue for [*number of weeks*] until [*name of month*]. Scheduled classes are: "[*series' title*]"

([*age range of children involved*]), taught by [*instructor's name*], beginning [*day of week, date*], from [*time period*]. [*Additional classes should be listed following the same format.*]

According to [*program head or instructor's name*], the purpose of the classes is to help parents understand more about their relationship with their child as they learn about their child's development as well as their own needs. Through the use of lectures, discussion, and observation of the children, parents learn more about the meaning of their child's behavior and how the world looks from a child's point of view. Each course, [*program head or instructor's name*] says, focuses on one particular age range and is appropriate for parents when their child is in that range.

Although the topics covered are different in each class, typical topics include play and stimulation, setting limits, social relationships among children, nutrition, establishing or improving existing routines such as sleeping, what it means to be a parent, and relationships between husbands and wives [*or list your topics here*].

Emphasis in all the courses, [*program head or instructor's name*] says, is on helping parents learn problem-solving and observation skills and on recognizing their child's uniqueness and their uniqueness as parents.

Children come regularly to the program with their [*mothers or parents*] and a specially designed "playcare" program is provided for each age group. The youngest babies, however, stay with their parents. Fathers also have an oppor-

425

tunity to come to the program with the children during the series [*include if applicable*].

Instructors in the program are [*list instructors' backgrounds*]. All are also parents of young children.

Further information or registration details may be obtained by contacting [*list name, address, and phone number*]. There is a fee [*or no fee if applicable*] for the classes.

Informational Flyer for Parents

[*name, address, and phone number of program or agency*]

Purpose: When parents become involved in the job of raising a child, they often realize how little training they have had for such an important and demanding profession. There are so many new experiences and feelings during the years of child rearing that most parents have found that they would like to have more support.

The classes offered by [*name of program or agency*] have been a valuable support to parents since the program began in [*date*]. The major goals of these classes are to help parents become more knowledgeable about child rearing and more comfortable with their role.

Schedule of Classes: [*Number of classes*] covering the [*age range of children involved*] are offered [*number of times a year*] beginning in [*date*]. Each class meets for [*number of hours*] [*number of times a week*] during the [*day or evening*] for [*number of weeks*] and is appropriate for parents to take when their child is within any of the following age ranges:

[*list titles of series and age ranges*]

Fathers participate in the program by attending an extra class with the children held [*day of week*] during the series. During this session, fathers work on issues that are important to them in their new role and have an opportunity to observe their child and other children of a similar age [*include this information if applicable*].

Content: The classes offer education about the behavior and development of children as well as the adjustments and challenges facing parents. The topics that are important naturally differ in each age group, but some of the most typical areas that are covered are normal development; play and learning; setting limits; social relationships among children; nutrition; establishing or improving existing routines such as sleeping, eating, etc.; individual differences among children and parents; and needs and feelings of parents [*or list your topics here*].

The presentations and discussions are structured, yet humor, warmth, and informality are encouraged as parents share ideas with each other, hear information presented by the instructor, receive practical handouts, and observe the children.

All the material presented is a combination of the most "tried and true" aspects of child psychology as well as parents' "on-the-job" learning. Emphasis in all classes is on developing the necessary skills for the long-term role as a parent: learning problem-solving skills, learning observation techniques, and recognizing and dealing with the child's and parent's individuality while harmonizing the two.

Playcare: While parents are attending classes, a playcare program is provided for the children at a nominal fee. The children benefit from being with other children in a special play area with appropriate activities and toys while they are cared for by concerned and involved adults. During each class the parents observe the children [*mention one-way observation window if available*] to develop a better understanding of their behavior and development.

In the Young Baby Class, the babies stay with their [*mothers or parents*] during the classes, but there is help in caring for the babies on an "as-needed" basis.

Staff: The staff of instructors in this program consists of [*list backgrounds of leaders*]; all are also parents of very young children. The instructors are: [*list names and degrees or positions*].

Fees: [*Note titles of series and fees if applicable.*]

Enrollment: Classes are open to all parents of "well" young children. Each class is limited to [*number of families*]. If you are interested in these classes or [*note additional services if available*], please call [*name of program or agency*] at [*phone number*] or fill out and return the detachable form.

Additional Services [List (if available) any additional services such as child rearing counseling, telephone warm line, parent resource library, etc.]

Here is an example of a description of one of the additional services:

- *Child Rearing Counseling*—The staff also meets with parents of "well" children [*age range*] in [*length of session*] to help them work on child-rearing areas that they have questions about. Topics that are frequently dealt with are: how much to expect from your child, what kind of discipline to use to encourage cooperation, handling sleep problems, working with aggression or shyness in your child, parents' feelings, etc. There is a fee [*or no fee*] for this service.
- *Location:* [*Note address of meeting place and any well-known buildings or areas it is close to.*]

We would be glad to tell you more about our services. Please call [*name of program and phone number*] and we will call you back or send you more information.

Initial Information Request Form

To be notified of: [*list class series*]

Date: _____ Time: _____

Parent's name: _____

Child's name: _____

Birth date: _____ Age: _____

Address: _____

_____

Phone: _____

Comments:

Guidelines for Answering Telephone Inquiries

Instructions and Answers to Frequently Asked Questions About the Classes

Please ask the person's name and the age of his or her child as soon as you can in the conversation. This will help you give the appropriate answers to the questions.

Purpose of the classes: To help you learn more about your child and about yourself as a parent. You will also learn some techniques that are very useful to parents of young children.

How are the classes taught? (What do we do in the classes?) You will learn through the three parts of our classes that take place each week:

- Lecture and handouts on the main topic of that week;
- Group discussion on the main topics of the week as well as on other questions raised;
- Observation of the children.

Who teaches the classes? Instructors with backgrounds in [*list backgrounds*] who are all also mothers or fathers of young children.

What is the length of the series? [*Note number of weeks, length of each class, and if there is an additional class for spouses.*]

How many are in the class? Usually the group is limited to [*number of people*] so there can be enough time for everyone to be involved in the discussions.

What class should my child be in? Start when your child is:

1-6 months	for	Young Baby class
7-14 months	for	Older Baby class
15-23 months	for	Toddler class
2 years- 2 years 11 mos.	for	Two-Year-Old class

[*substitute your age ranges and names of classes above*]

How can I register? Describe registration procedure—phone, fax, mail or in person—and when it takes place.

NOTE: You may also want to provide specific information on: what is taught, who the teacher is, what the cost is, when the class meets, and how the children are cared for, since most of this information is different for each class.

Parenting Program Brochure

We have developed a brochure which we send out to all families currently on our mailing list about six weeks before the beginning of classes. The brochure begins with a description of the philosophy and purpose of the Child Rearing Program and a letter of welcome from the program head.

Included in the opening page is a brief listing of the class series, indicating the age ranges for those classes, the days and times they are offered and the beginning date, and whether or not playcare is available. This listing also includes the page of the brochure where more information for each class can be found.

On subsequent pages there are descriptions of each class and an explanation of the playcare program. (See examples)

The brochure also includes information on the umbrella agency, background information on the instructors and descriptions of other services available. Finally there is information on registration procedures and a registration form.

Sample Program Philosophy and Purpose for Parenting Program Brochure

When parents become involved in the job of raising a child, they often realize how little training they have had for such an important and demanding profession. There are so many new experiences and feelings during the years of child rearing that most parents have found that they would like to have more guidance in the learning and many adjustments that there are to make. The [*name of program*] was started because many parents from the community as well as many of our staff felt the lack of help and support for this extremely challenging job of being a parent.

The class series offered by the [*name of program or agency*] have been a valuable resource to parents since the program began in [*year*]. The major goals of these series are to help parents become more knowledgeable about child rearing and more comfortable with their role and to enable parents to try to meet their own and their child's needs more satisfactorily so that their understanding, respect and enjoyment of each other can be increased.

The classes at the [*name of agency or program*] offer education about the behavior and development of children as well as the adjustments and challenges facing parents. The presentations and discussions are structured, yet encourage humor, warmth and support as parents share ideas with each other, hear information presented by the instructor, receive practical hand-outs, and observe their children through a one-way window [*include if available*].

Emphasis in all classes is on developing important skills such as learning how to problem solve and recognize and deal with each child's and parent's individuality and both of their needs and perspectives. Parents will have much opportunity in the series to share experiences and feelings and to begin to develop an overall set of guidelines for their own family's approach to child rearing.

Sample Description of a Class Series for Parenting Program Brochure

[*Title and age range of series*]
[*Number of classes in series and beginning date*]

Content: includes information on the development and needs of children and the meaning of their behavior; play and stimulation; setting limits; nutrition; problems that new parents experience; helping parents find ways to make themselves and their relationship with their children more comfortable. [*substitute other topics for the above as appropriate*].

Method: Presentation, group discussion, and observation of the children.

Time: [*Day and time*]

Instructor: [*Name and degree or title and phone number.*]

The brochure would typically contain a description of each class series.

Sample Description of Playcare for Parenting Program Brochure

A special "playcare" room (indoors and outdoors) is provided for your child to have a good experience being with other children the same age and with caring adults while you attend classes. Parents observe their children for part of each class through a large one-way window. Playcare for your child has become a valuable and integral part of our program. (In the Young Baby class, the babies stay with their parents, but there is help caring for the babies on an 'as needed' basis.) This year, playcare is ready 15 minutes before the parenting classes begin so you have time to get your child settled.

Our parenting education and our playcare staff are willing to help you and your child with most separation issues should they develop. If this is anticipated by you, please talk to the parent educator at least a week before the series begins so we can help you and your child lay any special groundwork. Some additional individual sessions may be necessary to help families with more difficult separation issues.

Registration Form

The top of the registration form should include the name and mailing address for the program. The rest of the registration form will be made up of spaces for the parents to fill in the following information:

Both parents' names and a way to indicate who is attending.

Home phone number and address.

Work phone numbers.

Child's name and birth date.

List of classes with space to check off which one(s) they are registering for.

A space to indicate whether or not the child will be attending playcare [if applicable].

Fees for the classes.

Fees for playcare.

The total amount enclosed or to be charged.

Credit card number, expiration date and signature [if applicable].

Sample Policy Statement for Program Registration

Registration send-outs by [name of program or agency]. All "current" families listed in the card file or data base whose children are within the age range of the class will be sent a brochure approximately [number of weeks or months] before the class begins. (The "age ranges" are [list ranges].) *No priority is given to old or new people.*

Registration response by parents. All registration will be handled by [telephone, fax, mail or in person].

Filling a class. Registration is on a first come first served basis. All registration forms will be timed and dated as they are received.

If registration forms are received from one or two families whose child's age is at the opposite end from others in the group, the instructor is responsible for discussing this point by phone with the parents and recommending a later or older class or whatever is appropriate. *The parent's decision, however, is binding.*

Parents will receive a postcard confirming enrollment in the class.

OR

Parents will receive a letter informing them that the class is full, and that they will be on a priority mailing list for future classes.

Payment. No one can begin a child-rearing class without having paid for the class in full prior to its start.

Refunds. A full refund less a [dollar amount] administrative charge will be available up until three full working days before the start of the class.

Confirmation Letter and Attachments

[name, address, and phone number of program or agency]

[date]

Dear Parents:

We have received your reservation form and payment for [number of sessions] series "[name of series]" which will be held at [location] beginning [day and date] from [time]. We're glad you'll be able to join us.

We are located at [address and pertinent directions]. We will meet in the [specific room or area]. Please arrive 10 minutes early.

During the orientation, we'll be talking more about the series and what your major child rearing interests and questions are. We'll also be giving the children and you a chance to get familiar with the "playcare" room and their "teachers" and giving people a chance to know each other better. We'll all be staying with the children for a while to help them get comfortable.

For your child's care here, please bring [list necessary equipment such as diapers]. You can put the equipment in a bag with *your child's name on it*. You will also be able to write down special instructions for the "teachers" when you get here. There will be a list of the children and their "teachers" on the door of the "playcare" room.

Please pack [lunch or snack, if applicable] for your child. [OR we will provide crackers and fruit for snack time.] We think the children will really enjoy eating together.

In preparation for our first class, please fill out the attached forms. Knowing your child-rearing interests and concerns will help us to make up a series outline that will be more meaningful for you; it will also help us to get to know you better.*

Please return your completed forms in the envelope provided, by [date], or you may FAX them to me at [FAX number].

We look forward to seeing you and your [baby, toddler or child] on [day, date, and time].

Sincerely yours,

[staff member]
[title]

---

*In addition to interests and concerns forms, parents may also be asked to fill out other forms concerning their birth (or adoption) experience and their child's separation experiences. (see the following pages for samples).

CURRENT CONCERNS

Please describe the concerns you are having now with regard to your child. Include some detail on how you're handling these concerns at home.

Parent's name _____ Date _____ Child's age _____

PARENTMAKING: A Practical Handbook for Teaching Parent Classes About Babies and Toddlers by B. Annye Rothenberg, Ph.D., et al.
© 1995 Banster Press, P.O. Box 7326, Menlo Park, CA 94026. Can copy for parent classes if this notice is included in full.

PARENT'S INTERESTS
YOUNG BABIES

Besides your concerns, what areas are you especially interested in discussing during this series?

Please rank order the ten topics of interest to you using #1 to show the one of most interest, etc.

_____ Understanding the stages of infant development (physical, social/emotional, intellectual, language)

_____ Playing and learning with your baby

_____ Nursing, feeding, and nutrition

_____ Handling baby's crying

_____ Sleep issues/"Schedules"

_____ Coping with your sick baby

_____ Safety and common accidents

_____ Leaving your baby with a baby-sitter

_____ Local programs and community resources for infants and parents

_____ Adjusting to parenthood

_____ Changes in the husband-wife relationship

_____ Spouse-baby relationship

_____ Your child's behavior or development—how normal it is

_____ Return-to-work issues

_____ Child care concerns

_____ Other:

Comments:

Parents' names _____ Child's age _____

PARENT'S INTERESTS

OLDER BABIES

Besides your concerns, what areas are you especially interested in discussing during this series?

Please rank order the ten topics of interest to you using #1 to show the one of most interest, etc.

_____ Limit setting and discipline

_____ "Child-proofing" and safety

_____ Nutrition and eating habits (what and how your child eats)

_____ Weaning from breast or bottle

_____ Baby's patterns and schedules

_____ Cognitive and motor development

_____ Play and learning

_____ Social development (interaction with other babies, etc.)

_____ Language development

_____ Baby's needs and demands

_____ Emotional development (temperament, behavior, etc.)

_____ Habits (thumb sucking, crib rocking, etc.)

_____ Handling a sick baby

_____ Traveling with your baby

_____ Dealing with difficult feelings that parents have

_____ Roles and relationships within the family

_____ One-child and more-than-one child families/spacing of children

_____ Your child's behavior or development—how normal it is

_____ Other:

Comments:

Parents' names _____ Child's age _____

PARENT'S INTERESTS
TODDLERS

Besides your concerns, what areas are you especially interested in discussing during this series?

Please rank order the topics of most interest to you using #1 to show the one of most interest, etc.

_____ Limit setting (discipline)

_____ Socializing among children

_____ Sleeping (naps, bedtime)

_____ Nutrition (eating habits)

_____ Development and expression of emotions

_____ Toilet training

_____ Language development

_____ Play and learning

_____ Local programs and Community resources (for toddlers and parents)

_____ Individual differences in temperament and their impact on the family

_____ Husband-wife relationships

_____ Your child's behavior or development—how normal it is

_____ Continuing your growth as a parent and meeting your needs

_____ Babysitting and childcare

_____ Other:

Comments:

Parents' names _____ Child's age _____

PARENTMAKING: A Practical Handbook for Teaching Parent Classes About Babies and Toddlers by B. Annye Rothenberg, Ph.D., et al. © 1995 Banster Press, P.O. Box 7326, Menlo Park, CA 94026. Can copy for parent classes if this notice is included in full.

Besides your concerns, what areas are you especially interested in discussing during this series?

Please rank order the ten topics of interest to you using #1 to show the one of most interest, etc.

_____ "Terrible two's"—what is going on inside the child and how to deal with this stage

_____ General discipline guidelines

_____ Socializing among children

_____ Nursery school programs

_____ Play groups

_____ Learning and play

_____ Language development

_____ Children's fears

_____ Day-to-day hassles (eating, sleeping, etc.)

_____ Toilet training

_____ How two-year-olds differ from each other

_____ How parents differ from each other

_____ Continuing your growth as a parent; meeting your needs as a person, spouse, and parent

_____ Spouses and their role as parent

_____ Husband-wife relationships

_____ Incorporating a new baby into your family

_____ Your child's behavior or development—how normal it is

_____ Other:

Comments:

Parents' names _____ Child's age _____

SEPARATION EXPERIENCES

Please describe briefly the separation experiences you and your child have had. Include ages at time of separation, frequency, length of time (½ day, 2 hours, etc.), who were the caregivers. If your separation experiences have been numerous, just list the most consistent or important ones.

How has your child reacted to being separated from you recently?

How have you felt about these recent separations?

What are your beliefs about what may make a separation difficult or easy for you and your child?

What feelings do you have about the separate playcare set-up in our program?

What specific ways/things comfort your child? (e.g., pacifier, lovey, blanket, toy, bottle, etc.)

Parents' names _____ Child's age _____

CHILD CARE AND SEPARATION EXPERIENCES
WORKING PARENTS' SERIES

1. Describe your child's childcare history (i.e., at what ages has she/he received care—from what center or in family day care or at home?)

2. What is your child's current childcare arrangements?

3. Are you planning to continue with these arrangements for the foreseeable future?

4. How comfortable is the separation now for you and your child at your child's current childcare?

5. How has your child reacted to being separated from you recently in other circumstances (e.g., your going out on the weekends, etc.?)

6. How have you felt about these recent separations?

7. In regard to your child's upcoming playcare experience, is there anything you'd like us to know, for example, what specific ways/things comfort your child? (e.g., pacifier, "lovey", blanket, toy, bottle, doll, etc.)

(On this and all of our questionnaires, we welcome hearing from both parents, whether or not you are both able to attend all of the classes. We hope that you will each feel free to express your views.)

Parents' names _____

Child's name _____ Child's age _____

Birth or Adoption Experiences

The following information would help me in both understanding your child and in learning about your early parenting experiences with your child.

The comments can be as brief or as detailed as you wish. Please use the back of this page as needed.*

1. How would you describe your pregnancy with your child?
   (e.g., "Wonderful! I never felt better"; I had to go to bed for the last two months because I was spotting. It was a terrible time!", etc, or ——)

2. How would you describe the birth of your child?
   (e.g., "A classic textbook labor and birth"; "I had a Caesarean because he was too big for my pelvis", etc.)

3. What were the early weeks (or months, years) like with your child?
   (e.g., "As an infant he had colic and was very difficult to comfort. As he got older the crying diminished", etc.)

4. If you have become a parent through the adoption of your child, please comment on the steps leading to this decision and the adoption process. (e.g., "We received a call one day and the next day we were parents"; "We waited two years with an agency and then another two years before we independently adopted".)

Parent's name _____ Child's Age _____

*Adoptive mothers, please answer the third and fourth questions.

PARENTMAKING: A Practical Handbook for Teaching Parent Classes About Babies and Toddlers by B. Annye Rothenberg, Ph.D., et al. © 1995 Banster Press, P.O. Box 7326, Menlo Park, CA 94026. Can copy for parent classes if this notice is included in full.

C

SAMPLE ORIENTATION FORMS AND SERIES OUTLINES

General Information Form

[name of umbrella agency]
phone number

Description

The [Name of Program] supports the healthy emotional and physical development of today's families and provides parenting class series and individual child rearing consultations [if applicable] for parents of children from birth through 3 years.

In addition to the quarterly, comprehensive series, in-person child rearing counseling sessions and calls are readily available [if applicable, or you may list other services you offer] to all community families:

The *Child Rearing Counseling* is an individual face-to-face consultation to work on a child rearing question or concern in depth. Topics that are frequently dealt with are: handling sleep problems, separation issues, setting realistic limits, toileting difficulties, working with children's demandingness, sibling rivalry, helping children get along with their peers, guiding children to become more responsible, parents' difficult feelings, etc. [Fee]. [Length of consultation] Appointments are usually in the daytime. (Home sessions and evening ap-

pointments are possible.) Many medical insurance carriers will cover these fees.

The *Child Rearing Counseling Call* is a telephone consultation for questions or concerns that are more limited and clear-cut. [Fee]. [Length of call]. (evening calls are possible.) These calls are also made by appointment.

The parent and the parent educator decide together which service is more appropriate.

Class Information

Missing classes. Please call if you and/or your child won't be able to come or will be late for a class. If you miss a class, call one of the other parents in the class to find out what was discussed since each class tends to be built on the previous one. (We'll save any handouts and give them to you the next week; we'll also mail you any "homework" observations that are due for the next class.)

"Homework". Almost every week during the series you will be asked to do some thinking and writing at home during the week on your own child rearing and your child's development. Since each class has a specific focus, parents tend to get more out of the series if they prepare ahead of time for each topic, relating it to their own family situation. We know being a parent is time-consuming, but please try to work on the homework/observation sheets you are given.

"Welcome to Our Child-Rearing Series" Form

[name of program or agency]

Please fill out this form and return it before you leave.

Date: _____

Mother's name: _____ Age: _____

Father's name: _____ Age: _____

Child's name: _____ Age: _____

Pediatrician's name: _____

Phone no. or address: _____

1. Do you have other children?
   If so, what are their names and ages?

2. How long have you and your spouse been married?

3. Are you working now outside of your home? If yes, what kind of work are you doing?

   If not, what kind of work have you done in the past?

   Are you planning to return to work in the next few months?

4. What kind of work does your spouse do?

5. Are you getting any regular help at home (baby-sitting, housecleaning, etc.)?

6. Has your family been experiencing any unusual stresses lately (e.g., moving, remodeling, financial, job loss, illness, etc.)? If so, what are the stresses?

7. How did you hear about this series?

8. If you know of any classes you'll be missing during the series, please mark down approximately when and how many classes you will miss.

Sample Series Outlines* (all age groups)

SERIES OUTLINE
(1-6 months)

Orientation: introduction; parents' interests; labor and delivery (or adoption) experiences.
*Other classes***
   Crying: reasons babies cry; dealing with periods of fretfulness; ways to comfort babies and things to do if they can't be comforted; how to handle the frustration and guilt feelings that come with letting/not letting your baby cry.

Patterns for sleeping and feeding: (what patterns??!!) helping babies develop patterns; how much sleep babies need; how you can find some time for yourself in the midst of all the changes.

Feeding and nutrition: breast- and bottle-feeding; introducing solid foods; the feeding relationship-developing good attitudes and feelings about feeding your baby; how to prepare baby food; allergies.
Pacifiers.
*Teething.****

Motor and cognitive development.
Play and learning: spending time with your baby; parents' roles in guiding their baby's development; attention span; importance of play to baby's understanding of his/her world; stimulation and overstimulation.

Baby-sitters: how to find them; how to evaluate them; information to leave with them; parents' feelings about leaving their baby with a sitter.

---

*This and many of the other forms used in this program usually have the agency or program name at the top of the form, the name of the class and its age range just below that, and then the name of the form.
**Discussion of the question "How did the week go?" is an important and regular part of each class in this series, in addition to the topics listed here.
***Topics grouped together are usually covered in one session.

Coping with a sick baby: dealing with parents' feelings; ways to make baby more comfortable; when to call the doctor.

Adjusting to Parenthood: coping with times of low self-esteem, fatigue, and identity changes; how to be fair to your child and still do things for yourself; feelings about returning to work or staying home.

Changes in the husband-wife relationship: feelings about cooperation with spouses; husband-baby relationship; how things look from the husband's point of view; time for each other.

Safety and common accidents.
Equipment for babies.
Local programs and community resources related to infants.

Language and development.

Social development: nurturing the spirit of your child; what benefits a baby emotionally; differences among babies; influencing your child's characteristics; developing a child-rearing philosophy.

SERIES OUTLINE
(7-14 months)

Orientation: introduction; playcare plans for the children; parents' interests.

Other classes.

Nutrition: transition to table foods; developing adequate eating habits; individual eating style ("picky" eater, "overeater," food as a "pacifier"); concerns about breast-feeding, bottles, cups, pacifiers, and weaning.

Limit setting: setting consistent boundaries without stifling curiosity; effects of your baby's increasing maturity and mobility; coping with your baby's negative reactions and frustrations.

Child-proofing and safety precautions: first aid; providing protection without being overly restrictive.

Social and emotional development: dependence-independence issues; baby's needs and demands; fostering self-esteem.

Baby's patterns and schedules: daily routines of sleeping, eating, and play; encouraging your baby to sleep through the night.

Individual differences among babies: variations in temperament, behavior, and development and how these influence parenting styles.
Finding quality child care.

Adjusting to parenthood: what to expect from yourself; deciding what you really need for yourself; dealing with difficult feelings such as irritability, frustration, and guilt; growing as an individual and as a parent.

Play and learning: intellectual and motor development; providing a good play environment; selecting toys; parents' roles in the child's play; amount of quality time spent one-to-one.

Family relationships: communication, cooperation, and sharing responsibilities; balancing time alone, couple time, and family time, and work; how things look from your spouse's point of view.

Language development: communicating with a pre-verbal child.

Looking ahead: returning to work; one-child and more-than-one-child families; spacing of children; sibling rivalry; development of a child-rearing philosophy.

SERIES OUTLINE—A SECOND EXAMPLE
(7-14 months)

Orientation: introduction; playcare plans for the children; parents' interests.

Other classes.

Emotional Development: relationship between baby's unique temperament and issues such as separation anxiety, fears of new people and situations; increasing independence.

Patterns and Schedules: establishing a family life style that works for parents and baby; daily routines, eating and sleeping, night wakefulness.

Nutrition: getting established on solids and finger food; developing healthy eating habits; emotional aspects of feeding; weaning; teething, dental health.

Discipline: what and how to childproof; when and how to say "no"; coping with baby's reaction.

Play and Learning: how babies learn; providing good play environment, appropriate toys, "quality time"; how to stimulate without pressuring. Cognitive Development. Motor Development.

Language Development: developmental sequences; encouraging communication; activities to stimulate language development; good first books.

Adjusting to Motherhood: dealing with difficult feelings of anxiety, irritability, time-pressure, guilt; growing as individuals and mothers; going to work; getting in touch with pre-baby interests.
Husband/Wife Communication.

Siblings and Spacing: one-child and multiple-child families; spacing of children.
Child Care: selecting quality day care; communicating with care providers.
Toward a Personal Child Rearing Philosophy: setting priorities for family tone; developing family traditions.

SERIES OUTLINE
(15-24 months)

Orientation: introduction; playcare plans for the children; parents' interests.

Other classes.
Your child's temperament: studying your child's style; accepting and living with your child's uniqueness.

Emotional Development: how to help toddlers recognize and express their emotions; how to respond to temper tantrums, whining, anger willfulness; how to foster high self-esteem; awareness of our own emotions in parenting and how to deal with them on good and bad days; pacifiers, thumbs, loveys and bottles.

Setting limits: what to expect; developing a limit setting philosophy; how to know if you are too controlling or too gentle; how to set limits for a child while encouraging good self-esteem; good limit setting techniques; husband and wife differences in limit setting; specific limit setting issues: sleep issues, feeding issues; problem solving techniques.

Nutrition: what toddlers eat; vitamins and health; sweets; poor eaters; how to present new foods.

First-aid: emergencies.

Parents: encouraging your growth as a person, wife, and mother; husband-wife relationship

changes and growth since children; roles in the marriage as father, husband, provider, and mother, wife, and provider—how we feel about our roles—what do we like and what do we want to change.

Socializing: what to expect; sharing; how often does a toddler need to be with other children?; how involved should the parent be in children's play; toy disputes; hitting other children.

Toilet Learning: how to know if your child is ready; methods of toilet training.

Language: what to expect; how to encourage language development in a toddler.

Early Childhood Education programs: what to look for in a nursery school or child care setting; types of nursery schools and child care centers

Play and Learning: when to teach; how to teach; should you teach? Toys and other play materials; encouraging your child to play alone.

Spacing: "do I want an only child?"; "Do I really want a second child?"; spacing; how to handle the arrival of a new child.

SERIES OUTLINE
(2-3 years)

Orientation: introduction; playcare plans for the children; parents' interests.

Other classes.
How two-year-olds think.

"The difficult two's": what is going on inside your child and how to deal with this stage; "spoiling" a child; setting limits; encouraging cooperation; handling intense feelings—yours, your spouse's, and your child's; handling other people's attitudes about your child rearing.

Expectations: how much your child can be in charge of, how much you should be in charge of (eating and nutrition, bottles, dressing, etc.).
Fears, dreams, sleeping.

Skills: language, cognitive, motor.

Socializing among children: peer relationships.

Play and learning.

Continuing your growth: dealing with guilt; husband-wife relationships; your spouse as a parent; issues concerning work.

New babies, sibling relationships, one-child families.

Early childhood education programs, play groups, resources for young children.

Toilet learning.

Differences among children and among parents (this topic is actually discussed *throughout* this series).

SERIES OUTLINE
Working Parent Series*
(15-24 months)

Orientation: introduction; playcare plans for the children; parents' interests.

Other Classes.
Emotional Development: helping your child and you through separations; the importance of routine; smoothing out transitions.
Cognitive Development: how toddlers think: concrete, egocentric and in the here and now.

Temperament: understanding and learning more about your child's and your own unique styles.

Limit Setting: what's hard about setting limits; reasonable expectations; preventive and limit setting techniques; problem solving.

Language Development: what to expect; how to encourage language development in a toddler; good books for toddlers.

Socializing: sharing; helping toddlers in conflict; how much socializing does a toddler need?
Child Care: in home care, family day care or center-based care? Finding quality care; communicating with your child care provider.

Nutrition and Eating: vitamins and health; good foods for toddlers; avoiding food battles; mealtime behavior.

Toilet Learning: signs of readiness.
Siblings and Spacing: one child or more? Adjusting to a new sibling.
Crib to Bed Transition.

Working and Parenting: what are the stresses and how do we cope? Finding time for ourselves, our partners, and our children; maximizing the good times.

---

*See Appendix H beginning on p. 466 for the chapter on teaching classes to full-time working parents.

D

SAMPLE CLASS FORMS

Class Session Outline*

2- 3-YEAR-OLD CLASS, 4TH SESSION

Schedule	Notes	Schedule	Notes
(9:20) Help children get settled in "playcare" room.	Help Sara and Matt and their mothers in their separation.	(10:45 - 11:20) Problem solving.	Work with the group to help a parent solve a common problem that came up during discussion.
(9:30) Go with parents to parent room.			
(9:30 - 10:15) Topic: limit setting (finish).	Continue with next subtopic left over from last week. Work toward a summary of limit-setting techniques.		
(10:15 - 10:45) Observation.**	Limit setting: Watch for examples of limit-setting in the "playcare" room. What limits are being set. What techniques are the caregivers using.	(11:20) Discuss and hand out homework for next week. (see next page for sample)	Socializing. Make sure all of last week's homeworks have been collected.

**There is a one-way observation window in one wall of the parents' room that looks into the "playcare" room.

*We find it very important in the Young Babies series to start every week with a check-in time. Some of you may wish to do this in the older classes also.

Homework Assignment

SOCIALIZING AMONG CHILDREN
(2-3 years)

1. How often is your child with other children? (Please mention whether he gets together regularly with any children and how old they are.)

2. What is your child like when he is with other children around his age (i.e., how does he behave toward other children)? Distinguish among the different reactions your child may have to different kinds of children.

3. Give an example of a conflict situation between your child and another child and also describe what *you* did. (Are there other things you sometimes do when your child is in conflict with another child?

4. What kinds of questions do you have about your child's relationships with other children?

E

SAMPLE PARENT GUIDE

PROBLEM-SOLVING GUIDE

(older babies-3 years)

This is a guide to help you focus on any conflicts you are having with your child.

1. What is one of the repeated problems that you are experiencing with your child? *Describe it in detail.*

2. How do you think he should behave in this situation? Is this realistic for his or her stage of development and temperament?

3. What problem-solving techniques are you using now and how are they working to stop the behavior?

       Technique   *Child's response*

(a)

(b)

(c)

(d)

4. Do days go by when you do not have this conflict? Can you explain why?

5. Is there a particular circumstance that always leads up to this behavior? For example:

a. Does this problem occur at any specific time of day?

b. Where does it occur?

c. Does it happen when your child seems particularly tired, sick, irritable, demanding, etc.?

d. What people are usually involved? (Does the same problem occur if different people are involved?)

e. Does this happen when you've been *particularly* abrupt, busy, inconsistent, daydreaming, etc.?

f. What is usually going on just before this behavior occurs?

6. What is the mood of your child, family, and self before this behavior occurs? When the behavior occurs? After the behavior occurs?

7. At the present time, what is your overall feeling about your child? Are you feeling pleased, confident, worried, frustrated, etc.?

After thinking about your answers to the previous questions:

a. Describe anything that you think might be fostering your child's inappropriate behavior.

b. List any changes you might like to try in handling the conflict, and describe why you think they might work.

F

SAMPLE PLAYCARE FORMS

Guidelines for Parents about Playcare*

*(15-24 months)***

Following are several procedures we found to be helpful for making things a little easier for you and your child.

1. Arrive a few minutes before your class begins so you can settle your child without rushing and still be in class on time.

2. At the orientation, each child will be assigned to a *special playcarer*. There will be a list on the door to tell you his or her name. He or she will also be wearing a name tag. (Any changes in playcarers will be posted on the door.)

3. When you arrive in the playcare room, give your child's playcarer any items your child may need—a diaper, coat, or sweater or whatever is necessary. *Please write your child's name in bold letters on your diaper bag. Also give the playcarer any special instructions*—written or verbal.

4. You do not need to bring food for your child—it will be provided at snack time. The children will be asked to eat at a table for two reasons: (a) to have them together as a group; and (b) to keep "spills" to a defined area. In nice weather the children may have snack outside.

5. After meeting the playcarer, you may want to sit with your child a few minutes and then tell him you are leaving to go to a class. Some ways of parting that might be helpful are: "See you in a while." "I'm going to class," or "I'll be back after my class."

Be *confident*!! If you sound assured and look assured, we think you'll both feel better.

6. Please try to leave the playcare room before the time class begins.

7. We have found that if parents are late and keep entering the playroom through the main door, the children are disrupted. At class time the door to the playcare room will be closed. If you are late, please bring your child in through the yard.

8. If your child is having a very hard time adjusting to the playcare room, the playcarer will bring him to you. If he has a hard time each week, the parent educator, head teacher and your child's playcarer will be happy to work with you and your child to help both of you become more comfortable. If your child is very tired or asleep, you may bring him to the parents' class and take him later to the playcare room.

---

*See Appendix H for a description of playcare in Working Parent classes.

**Guidelines for parents of other age groups will vary according to the stage of the children's development.

Objectives for Students

The following are the overall objectives of the students' program:

1. To become more comfortable with children by learning how to talk to, play with and take care of them.

2. To learn about normal young children's behavior and development and its variability.

3. To learn, by hearing and reading information about family life on a day-to-day basis, about the reality of the impact of parents on young children and the impact of young children on the parents.

4. To learn how to function with other students as a team in meeting the goal of providing a good group experience for children.

5. To learn how to observe and report on selected aspects of child development and behavior, such as emotional development, language, play, and social skills.

6. To learn to talk with parents about their children in an objective and ego-supportive manner.

7. To learn how to observe and interpret parent-child interaction.

Information for Playcarers*

Attitude

You will be considered a professional in this situation. When a parent is present in the room, please do not discuss any child or parent. Your job is to help every toddler and parent feel comfortable in this program. They all need warmth and understanding.

Physical environment

- Prepare the snack for the children. (The head teacher or parent educator will provide the snack.) Be sure that there are enough napkins and cups for all the children.

- Put a clean sheet on the changing pad. Check for wipes, gloves and plastic bags. Extra supplies are in the closet at the end of the hall.

- Remove those toys that are not applicable to the age group, turn the dollhouses around, put away those toys with many manipulative parts.

- See that the room environment is appealing— put out those toys children of this age enjoy (pull-toys, push-toys, puppets, and anything else you have observed them using). Do not leave all the toys stacked on the shelves.

- Be prepared to introduce new objects to the play room as the session goes on. It is not necessary to have all the toys out as soon as the children enter the room.

Parents' and toddlers' arrival

- Greet each parent and child with a smile and show that you are confident in this setting.

- As you get to know the parents and their children, try to call each of them by name. This is very important.

- Each week you will be assigned two toddlers, most likely the same ones each time. Each week those parents whose children are assigned to you will describe the needs of their toddlers. If you feel you cannot remember everything, write it down. A parent's concern may not always sound valid to you, but it is to her.

- Help your toddlers to get interested in the activities about the room. Encourage the parents to leave, and say "good-bye" and "See you later."

- When a toddler is upset about separating, try to comfort him and interest him in another activity. Weather permitting, taking the toddler outside immediately after his parent leaves helps him to get over the tearful farewell.**

- Turning on the record player will often help an upset toddler to calm down and feel better.

Toddler care

- It is not necessary for you to follow your assigned children about the room. It is better to take a zone approach, with some playcarers staying in the main room and someone outside

---

*These instructions are for the care of 15- 24-month-olds and would need to be modified for use with other age groups.

**See Separation Practice Session on page 454 for helping families with more difficult separations.

at all times if the door is open. It is important to watch all the children all the time. Keep your eyes moving. The trick is to give one toddler attention, and yet know what the others are doing at the same time. This takes practice!

- In working with the children, gentleness, calmness, and firmness are words to keep in mind. Observe the children to determine what each individual needs when upset. Some need a hug or holding while some need a moment to "pull together" alone.
- When disagreements between children arise over a toy, substitution of a toy can be a successful technique. If you are aware that a "push-pull" match is about to begin, it would be helpful to interest the children in something else before they become very upset.
- When a child has inappropriate behavior, use a positive approach. Let him know what you want him to do. Don't dwell on the wrong.
- When children are making inappropriate use of materials in the room (e.g., throwing heavy things), you can show them how to use the particular toy, find an appropriate toy for them to bang or throw in an appropriate place, or try to redirect their interests.
- Disputes over toys are often settled by the toddlers themselves. If this does not occur, allow the first child to keep the toy and help the other(s) get busy with something else.
- Some toys should not be used outside, either because they are easily lost or because they can be ruined by sand or moisture. Some "outside" toys should not be brought in because they usually are sandy. Help the children to distinguish between "inside" and "outside" toys.
- Pick up and put away toys not in use. Though this is an unending process, it's not only safer but also renews the toddlers' interest in toys discarded earlier.
- Keeping books on a high shelf helps make them "special." Reading to the toddlers for short periods gives them a chance to have a little quiet time.
- When several children are using the slide, encourage everyone in the group to climb the ladder, not the slide, before they slide down.
- Seat the toddlers at the table for snack. This is not only easier for you but the children enjoy the structure.
- Please be aware of the children's diapers. It

works well to check and change all the children a half-hour before the session ends. Wash your hands after each diaper change.

- Deal with the children at eye level—sit or squat to play, to demonstrate, or to comfort.
- Hugging, touching, cuddling, and holding the children gives them a sense of love, warmth, and security. Tender loving care works wonders.

Daily schedule

9:15-9:30   Parents arrive with children.
9:30-10:30   Allow the children to have free time. This would include children playing or observing. Remove any toys that children are not using.
10:30-10:45 Snack time, consisting of juice and cheese, crackers, and fruit. The period will go more easily if one of you prepares the snack ahead and places it on the table before the children sit down. The children should stay at the table with the snack to prevent a sticky, dirty room.
10:45-11:15 Allow the children more free time and also provide some activities in which the children can participate if they desire. These could be:

- music activities—"Ring Around the Rosie," playing an instrument with a record, listening to a record, dancing or clapping to music, listening to a guitar
- reading a story to those few who might be interested
- rolling balls with children
- sliding
- using the ramp

11:15-11:30 Allow the children to continue their free time. *Check the diapers of each child and be sure each child's things are ready for the trip home.*
11:30   Parents pick up their children.

Parents' and toddlers' reunion and departure

- Many toddlers may cry or act up when their parent returns. This is normal.
- Try to give each parent a very objective report of what her toddler has done. It is best to begin with the positive points, such as one of his favo-

rite activities for the day or the story you read to him. If he was upset at any time, let the parent know. You might tell her how you handled the child, for example, "He spent a long time going up and down the slide. He cried a few minutes after you left but I got him interested in the music box and he relaxed."

- If a parent tries to get you to make value judgments about her child, or get advice on how to solve a problem, refer her to the parent educator or the head teacher.

Series Curriculum for Playcarers*

A Ten Session Outline

1. Orientation: emphasis on how the playcare is managed, questions students have about the experience, and talking about how to help parents feel comfortable.
2. Students will care for the children and make careful observations. Special attention will be given to parent and toddler needs. Students will take into consideration their own style in working with the children. Are they comfortable with this style?
3. Emotional development of the children and their parents will be the focus. The kinds of things that should be expected in toddlers' emotional development and the types of emotions parents experience will be discussed. A written observation will be completed describing how parents separate from their children and return to their children.
4. This session will focus on how each child, and his family, is unique. The students will complete an observation about one or two children and compare it to one the parents have completed.
5. The students will discuss how the young child plays and learns. Special attention will be placed on what skills toddlers develop as they play as well as on styles of play. Each student

will observe a portion of the room and how it is used by different children.
6. Language development of the toddler will be discussed. Each toddler's receptive language will be the focus for the observation.
7. The topic will be what to expect from toddlers in their social skills, including what parents expect and what actually occurs. The students will observe how different children make their needs known in this setting.
8. Students will discuss in detail each child in the group, considering his individual temperament, activity level, interests, emotional development, how he makes his needs known, social development, physical skills, fine- and gross-motor coordination, and any general comments that seem important.
9. A continuation of 8.
10. Students will evaluate their experience.

Possible Observations for Playcarers

Some of the student observations that have been useful in the one- to three-year-old classes are described in this next section. Students should have an opportunity to see and discuss the assignment before being with the children. The students can then take turns leaving the playcare room to fill out their observation forms—ideally, observing the children through a one-way window. If it is not feasible for the students to leave during the care of the children, the observations can be completed after the children have gone.

Student assignments for the observation of younger or older children can be adapted from the following suggestions. Additional observations for students can be adapted from the homework assignments for parents that have been developed for each age group and topic. (See the "Homework" section in each topic in Parts II-VI.)

Parent-child separation. Assign early (see the form on p. 455).

Making children comfortable. Assign in the first weeks. This observation shows what students have learned about how to make the children feel comfortable (e.g., structured activities, cuddling, a particular toy, being outside, etc.).

Description of child. This observation asks

---

*This example of a curriculum would be useful for students working with one to three year olds. Modification would be needed for use with other age groups.

students to think of their two assigned children and then write down descriptions of them in all the ways they can think of—physical, behavior, language, emotions, interests. This observation should be assigned early on and the students may wish to share some of their observations during discussion.

How does the child make you feel? This observation asks students to write about how being around each of their assigned children makes them feel. It's a chance to understand about different "chemistries" and not feel guilty about not enjoying or even disliking certain children.

Students' goals for child. This assignment should be scheduled about one-third of the way through the series. At that point students will have some basic understanding of their assigned children and the rest of the children. The parent educator, head teacher and students may wish to brainstorm goals together.

Language observation. This observation should be scheduled around mid-series (see the form on p. 456). By then students will be more involved in the children's language.

Children's thinking. Use this observation after the language observation (see the form on p. 457). The assignment helps students to see things from the children's point of view.

Individual differences. This observation should be used toward the end of the series (see the form on p. 458). It provides a good opportunity to contrast children on the basis of their temperaments.

What you'd like the parent to know. After their observation of individual differences, students may have some useful input that you'd like to give the parents.

Separation Practice Session*

When a separation problem is anticipated or encountered in this program, we may schedule a separation practice session. The parent educator will call the parent and discuss separation with her, including helpful separation techniques and how to say goodbye to the child. Then she invites the parent and child to come to the playroom, at a time when other children are not there, for a separation practice session. The parent educator, head teacher and, possibly, the child's student caregiver are all in the playroom so that the child has a chance to become comfortable with the room and the people who care for her. When the parent and child are ready, the parent can leave for a practice separation. The parent educator and the parent go to the parent room so that they may watch the child through the one way window. The parent educator helps the parent see how the child uses her own coping skills and how the caregiver(s) helps the child with the separation.

Head Teacher/Caregiver

In addition to the students working in the play-care room, it is a good idea to hire a head teacher/caregiver. The head teacher is responsible for overseeing the students and children while they are in the playcare room. When possible we try not to assign children to the head teacher so that she can help out wherever needed and keep the schedule of the day flowing. She is a resource to the students in the play care room, modeling appropriate ways to work with the children and good communication with the parents. The head teacher also shares responsibility with the parent educator for the student discussions. Because of her presence in the play room, she can help the students link the discussions to their work with the children. In some classes of twelve children you may wish to have both a head teacher and another "junior" teacher along with the students.

The head teacher/caregiver needs the following qualifications:
•experience working with children the same age as those in the class.
•experience working with groups of children.
•able to communicate well with parents.
•able to guide college students.
•have good references or have been observed by a staff member.

You may find head teacher/caregivers through local child care programs, community colleges or universities. Also students who show great skill in working with the children, and parents, can be asked to work, perhaps as a "junior" teacher first, then eventually as head teacher.

*For more information on teaching about separation, please refer to Pt. III, chapter 3 in the Parentmaking Educators Training Program (Menlo Park, CA: Banster Press, 1993).

STUDENT OBSERVATION ON PARENT-CHILD SEPARATION
(1–3 years)

Today let's observe how children and parents separate and reunite. Choose one family to observe.

1. Observe the family. Note what the parent and child do before parting.

2. How does the parent separate? What does she say? What does her body say?

3. What does the child do as his parent leaves?

4. What does the child do when his parent returns?

5. How does his parent respond to him?

Student's name _____ Date _____ Child's name and age _____

1. *Listen* to the children. Comment on any language or lack of language among the children.

2. *Receptive language.* As you're working with your assigned children, try to find out how much they understand. Note how they respond to what you say.

3. *Expressive language.* Talk with and listen to your assigned children. What do you think about their vocabulary development?

Student's name _____ Date _____ Children's names and ages _____

STUDENT OBSERVATION ON
CHILDREN'S THINKING

(2–3 years)

1. What are the children thinking and talking about today? (Let's see if we can begin to get some feeling about what's on their minds—how they see the world.)

_____ Your child's name and age.

_____ Your other child's name and age.

_____ Choose any other child in the group, if time allows

Student's name _____ Date _____

This week, please look at one of your two children in terms of his "individual style." It is this individuality that makes him very special. The following questions may give you more insight into his individuality.

Specific temperament styles

1. How active is the child? (Does he often run, jump, love to climb, bounce, or is he more interested in sitting and looking at books, puzzles, etc.?)

2. Is he enthusiastic for new experiences or is he more on the hesitant side? (With a new setting, will he jump in or stand back? Does he join the group or play alone?)

3. What is his mood most of the time? (Does he tend to be generally light-hearted or serious about many things?)

4. How well does he concentrate? (In his usual play style, does he play for a long time or does any new stimulus get him going in another direction?)

5. Is this child persistent or not persistent? (Does he try to master a toy and try and try until successful or frustrated, or does he try and if he can't be successful, put it away for something else?)

More general differences

1. What are some things about this child's behavior or skills that make him easier to handle than other children seem to be?

2. Can you think of some things that make him somewhat more difficult to handle than other children seem to be?

Student's name _____ Date _____ Child's name and age _____

EVALUATING PLAYCARERS

Learning Outstanding	Learning Satisfactory	Needs More Work	
			OBSERVATIONS
____	____	____	1. Learned how to observe and record descriptions of children and/or parent-child behavior and development.
			CHILD DEVELOPMENT AND BEHAVIOR
____	____	____	1. Increased knowledge about the norms of child development and behavior as well as the variability.
			CARE OF CHILDREN
____	____	____	1. Increased ability to ascertain children's needs in this group setting.
____	____	____	2. Established and maintained a good play and learning environment for the children.
____	____	____	3. Helped develop and implement an age-appropriate curriculum (e.g., nature of projects, records, toys, etc.).
____	____	____	4. Became aware of own child-care style and areas that need attention.
			PARENT-STUDENT RELATIONSHIP
____	____	____	1. Was able to relate to parents as instructed.
____	____	____	2. Was able to help the parent be comfortable with the playcarer.
____	____	____	3. Was able to help parent and child separate, if help was necessary.
____	____	____	4. Was able to review the child's "playcare" experience with the parent in a supportive, honest, but non-judgmental manner.

Learning Outstanding	Learning Satisfactory	Needs More Work	
			UNDERSTANDING OF PARENT-CHILD RELATIONSHIPS
___	___	___	1. Broadened interpretations of parent-child interactions.
___	___	___	2. Increased understanding of the impact of parents on young children and vice-versa, particularly as it is described within the home setting.
___	___	___	3. Used this understanding in own interpretations and ideas about guidance of parent-child relationships.
			SEMINAR PARTICIPATION
___	___	___	1. Learned how to share actively as a member of a team in a group learning experience.
			2. Learned how to work as a team member in the care of the children and the room.

Student's Name_____ School _____ Date _____

Parents' Observations of Playcare*

During the weekly playcare observations, we have learned that parents are fascinated by watching their children play. They do not want to fill out observation forms as they observe but prefer to simply look at the children most of the time. The following observation suggestions help parents learn more about their child in relation to other children and about themselves as parents, but they allow parents to learn through watching, thinking and listening rather than through written assignments. The observation should be a positive experience for those involved. It is important for the parent educator to encourage and model diplomacy and positive ways of describing the children. The procedures for making each observation are described in detail.

Initial observation

• Watch for a while and have parents identify their child for the group.
• Tell the group what can be observed—activity level, play interests, etc.
• Ask parents, "When you know you're going to have a chance to watch your child, what's your own personal question about him or her?" Give parents examples, for instance, "Does he seem comfortable without me?"

Separation

• Watch as a group immediately after parents leave children in the playroom.
• Have parents notice what their child is doing to adjust to their separation.
• Have parents talk in pairs to discuss their children's history of separation (what has each child used to adjust in the past and now; what are the critical factors in how he adjusts). Observe each other's child briefly.
• Have the whole group discuss what has been discovered. Summarize as a group the main critical factors involved in successful vs. "less than successful" separations.

_____

*Most of these observations can be used with parents of older babies to three year olds.

Feelings about your child vs. others

• Watch for a while as a group.
• Have parents observe and talk in pairs. Ask each parent to watch for a few minutes any child in the group that is not her own, keeping track of how they feel when they watch the child. Then have them watch their own child and keep track of those same feelings. You might talk about how _you_ would feel during those two observations if one included your own child.
• Ask parents to focus just on their feelings and any differences they felt when they watched the two children. Have them describe their feelings to their partner.
• Summarize for the whole group what some of the different feelings are.

Free time

• Let parents observe and then comment on or ask about anything that occurs to them. (This can also be a good time for parents to have a chance to chat in an unstructured way.)

Individual differences

Ask any of the following questions:

• What characteristics does your child have that make him easier to handle? What characteristics does your child have that make him more difficult to handle?
• What things about your child describe you as well? What things describe your spouse?
• What about your style makes it easier for you to handle your child? What about your style makes it harder for you to handle your child? (Parents are usually quite interested in learning about their temperaments in relation to their child and in learning what other families experience in raising children of different temperaments.)

Early childhood program atmosphere

This observation goes well at the end of a series, dovetailing with the discussion of nursery schools and childcare. Its intent is to enable parents to see what they like and can learn about from the playcare experience. Have parents talk about the pros and cons of the playcare situation, especially in relation to future nursery school or day care situations for their individual child.

Observing other children

• Watch for a while as a group.
• Have parents watch another child and note his or her attention span and play interests.
• Have parents watch their own child for the same things.
• Ask parents to share with the group what they noticed.

Difficult emotions

• Ask parents to think of some of their child's difficult emotions (whining, fussiness, anger) and begin a discussion on handling these. Ask parents to observe what causes their child to change his response to a more negative or more positive level (adult contact, a new toy, etc.).

NOTE: The key to developing good observations for parents is if the instructor can remember back to what she would have liked to talk about when *her* child was that age.

G

SAMPLE EVALUATION FORM

SERIES EVALUATION

Names of class series: Starting date of series:

1. Overall, were you pleased with this series? (Place an x along the scale below.)

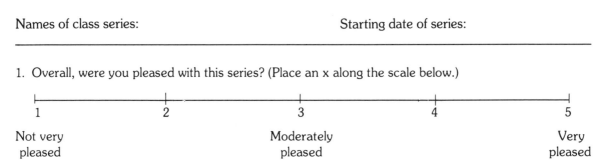

1	2	3	4	5
Not very pleased		Moderately pleased		Very pleased

2. What do you feel you have gained from this series?

3. What would you say was *most valuable* about the series?

4. What bothered you or what didn't you like about this series?

5. What would you like to change about this course that would have made it more helpful to you?

6. How did you find the playcare experience for your child?

_____

Parent's Name - Optional

H

CLASSES FOR FULL-TIME
WORKING PARENTS*

Providing parenting classes that address the needs of working parents are now a necessity in our work as parent educators. During the last twenty years, increasing numbers of mothers have joined the workforce due to changes in economic and social demands. While many women still choose to stay home and become the primary caregiver, many other mothers are choosing to enter the workplace. With greater economic pressures on the family and ever-widening roles for women, more and more mothers are combining the challenges of parenthood with those of paid employment. This generation of women (of child-bearing age) has grown up knowing they have a choice about work and parenthood and many expect that if and when they have children, they will continue their paid employment.

These women who are choosing to combine the responsibilities of family life and work are no longer a small minority. In 1990, 40% of all mothers whose youngest child was under age one were employed—15% part-time and 25% full-time. By the time their youngest becomes a toddler, 52% were employed (18% part-time and 34% full-time). In the mid-90's, these numbers continue to stay the same. This rate of employment grows as the age of the youngest child increases. Sixty-nine percent of mothers of 6 to 9 year olds work (47% full-time and 22% part-time). However, to look at this another way, as their youngest children become elementary school age, about half the mothers work full-time and the other half either don't work outside of the home or work part-time.

In families where both parents work and share more of the financial responsibilities, the husband is more likely to share in more of the family work. When the father is more involved in parenting and household responsibilities and the mother is working outside of the home, the roles of mother and father are necessarily redefined. These parents struggle to change their definition of the family to fit the new reality of two working parents. Parenting classes for working parents, therefore, must try to be sensitive to the different set of needs, experiences, conflicts and feelings of families where both parents are working parents, especially when both are full-time or nearly full-time employed. This chapter will address the ways in which a class for full-time or nearly full-time working parents might be organized and presented, taking into account the very different daily realities and family life of working parents.

In our experience, we have found that the full-time or nearly full-time working parents' needs are different enough—especially when all the parents in the family (single parent or married couple) are working full-time—that we wanted to offer an option for them to have those needs met in classes designed just for them. Weekday daytime classes

*We would like to thank Cynthia Wilcox-Rittgers, M.A., for her work in preparing the first draft of this chapter. Additional helpful suggestions were provided by Julie Kelsey, B.S. and Karen Friedland-Brown, M.A. All three are parent educators experienced in teaching "Working Parent" classes.

466

are mostly attended by at-home and part-time working parents. Full-time working parents with flexible or non-traditional working hours sometimes attend the weekday daytime classes but may not feel satisfied with them as their needs can be quite different.

Being a Full-Time Working Parent

Full-time working parents with young children have a *very* busy life. They often report a high level of stress as a result of the many demands placed on them in their varying roles as a worker, a marital partner, and a parent, among others. Some complain of a typically fast pace common to the work world but less suited to the "relationship world" of parenting and being with young children. Some working parents experience a sense of guilt as they rush through this routine without enough opportunity for enjoyment of the quality of time they would like with their child. After a long work day, they reunite with a tired child who may demand more than they are able to give just then. Some working parents face the doubts, guilt, anxiety, questions, and separation issues that leaving a child in child care can create. Lack of time leading to doing tasks quickly, incompletely *or* not at all is a major source of the parents' stress.

The trade-off for many working parents, despite these challenges, is greater financial stability and the opportunities that women enjoy to develop themselves creatively and intellectually outside of their parent role. For many families, the opportunity to share with their children new images of mother and father, free from rigid sex roles, is another dividend enjoyed as a result of both parents working outside the home. Many working mothers argue that they have more to offer their children as a result of their greater satisfaction with themselves and their involvement outside the home. And many couples, as a result, learn to share the responsibilities of house and family, relieving at least a share of the burden of these tasks from the traditional domain of the mother. Some parents have work and caregiving situations that are not as stressful and can feel very satisfied

with the balance of time between work and child rearing. In addition, some families feel very positive about the quality of their child's caregiver—both in terms of their child's development and what they are learning about their own child and about child rearing in general.

There is much for parent educators to learn about what working full-time means to a parent. As you think about developing classes for working parents, it is most important to understand more about what their lives are like, what are their perspectives, and needs. Through this chapter, through the books listed at the end of the chapter, and through talking to these parents, we can become better prepared to teach supportive and meaningful classes for them.

Publicizing These Kinds of Classes

Classes for working parents should be publicized in all the traditional ways such as through newspapers, pediatrician's and obstetrician's offices, childbirth education classes, libraries, and through public service announcements (PSA's) on radios (see p. 13). In addition, mailings should be sent to child care center directors and to the attention of Human Resource managers at corporations. You might also be able to access an appropriate computer bulletin board concerned with children or parenting issues. Sometimes, there are parent networks at companies through which information can be disseminated.

Scheduling Working Parent Series

Parenting classes for working parents can be offered to couples, parents attending without their spouse, and divorced and otherwise single parents. Working parents balance many different roles and in doing so usually have a very busy schedule. Classes should be offered at times, therefore most convenient to the schedules of these parents, such as evening, weekends, and minor holidays. Working parents prefer shorter series of classes, usually four, six or eight weeks.

If children are not coming, classes could start at 7 or 7:30 p.m. on weekday evenings or possibly be held on weekends. If children are coming with their parents, early evenings or weekend days are generally the best. Of course, naptimes for the children of these parents must be considered when choosing an appropriate class time. Some working parents prefer weekends but just as many find that a weekday evening is optimal. Between 6:00 and 8:00 p.m. seems to be a good time for a 2 hour class, although babies and toddlers may often get tired and cranky around 7:30 or 8:00. Parents can bring children's pajamas for the child to be changed into so that he is more ready to go to sleep when they get home.

When parents attend evening classes, they bring a particular set of needs with them. After a long work day and after picking up their child, the working parents typically arrive to class tired and hungry, and generally worn-out. This does not lend itself to the most optimal learning environment. The parents need time to slow down, relax, and if care is provided for children, play with their child in an unrushed and unpressured setting. For parents who arrange to attend the class as a couple, each parent may also need to reunite with the other spouse who may have arranged to meet them at the class. They may need to feel a part of their family again and to begin to feel a sense of comfort in sharing their family with other families. Allowing time to be together in a playroom or "family room" setting is very helpful. When an evening series is offered to working parents, dinner needs to be ready for the children (if they are attending) and parents appreciate having dinner available for them as well when they arrive to class.

If the class is offered on a weekend day, the families may arrive to class a little less stressed, but sometimes still tired after a long work week. They usually have already had some time to re-unite and play together, to relax and rest as a family. In general, the mood during the weekend classes tend to be a little more relaxed and easygoing because the parents have already had some time to transition from their jobs to being together with their families.

Registration

The process of registration is described on pp. 14–15. Appendix B contains information and sample forms such as a Confirmation Letter, a Current Concerns and Interests form. For working parents' classes, we add to these forms more topics for parents to choose from such as balancing parenting/work/spouse relationship; child care; dealing with morning and evening transitions; and co-parenting. There is also a form dealing with Child Care and Separation Experiences for the parents to fill out. This is generally useful in understanding the parents and child better—even if child care is not being provided at the parenting class. (Also see Appendix B).

Nature of the Working Parent Series

Typically, working parents prefer more structured classes than the at-home and part-time working parents who are not usually as time-stressed. This means presenting more content in the form of lectures and short well-organized handouts. These parents tend to bring in many questions for which they want immediate answers and prefer less time to process feelings and experiences.

The challenge for the parent educator is to provide much of the information but try to help build relationships among the parents—both for learning and support. Many working parents feel an urgent desire to get an answer to a pressing concern, such as how to get their child to get to sleep at night or how to handle recurring temper tantrums because these problems are interfering with the family's daily routine. Parent educators who are used to teaching parents who are at-home or working part-time, usually have to change their style to one that has the feel of a business meeting because that is the setting that the parents will feel more comfortable in and more confident that they will learn from. Each group will vary in terms of the level of structure with which they are comfortable and the degree of group support and sharing that they desire.

Because married *couples* often attend the class series for working parents, the dynamics of the group can be very different from groups with mothers and fathers but not couples. As with any other parent group, the parent educator must be aware of and facilitate dynamics between individual group members. But, in this case, there is also the dynamic between each of the couples, as well as within each couple relationship. There can be tensions that develop between all the men and women in the group, as gender differences in parenting styles emerge during discussions. In addition, if there is a couple that is experiencing a high level of marital dissatisfaction and conflict, this can be an ongoing problem that affects the whole class series. For example, a pattern may emerge in which one parent reports each week how her spouse failed as a parent, attempting to blame him and to align the group with her. If marital conflicts such as this begin to emerge during the class series and your discussion with these parents before or after class does not change how they act in class, you may have to ask them to meet with you in a private session to address their concerns. In leading parenting groups, the needs of the larger group are usually considered the most important. Consultation or a referral for marital counseling may be necessary.

In working parent classes, instructors should set a clear and written agenda for the class, provide information on child development and behavior that is solidly supported and lead a focused discussion that does not allow people to go on tangents. Specific problem solving should be provided. It is important to weave into the classes discussion of family time, quality time, getting to really know their child, and the struggle to create a balance. Working parents are often worried that the limited time with their children is having negative effects on their child. By being with other similarly-oriented parents, their needs for validation and reinforcement of what they are doing have a greater chance of being met.

Important Issues to Cover in Teaching a Working Parents Series

---

Working parents share many concerns regarding parenting with other parents. They wonder how to feed their children properly, struggle with how to get their child to sleep through the night, and have real concerns about how to discipline and teach their child. Working parents, like other parents, tend to value information regarding individual differences. They like to learn more about child development, particularly cognitive, motor, language, and emotional development. Many working parents are interested in approaches to limit-setting and discipline. Of course, other issues related to the particular developmental stage of the child are also of great interest to all parents, such as when to begin to toilet train your child.

There are other concerns related to parenting that usually are of special interest to many working parents. Because working parents have less time with their child overall, the quality of time they spend with their child is critical. Yet, often these parents reunite with their child at the end of a work day, when their energy level is low and their availability to their child is a minimum. Often dinner needs to be prepared; bathtime and bedtime follow quickly in succession. These parents can often benefit from the opportunity to discuss these challenges with other parents who struggle with the same concerns. Of high interest are the issues of when, how often, and how to play with their child. Playtime can be framed as a tool to facilitate reconnecting with their child after being apart.

Parents may also have less time to learn about children in terms of appropriate expectations and child rearing methods and sometimes need a great deal of basic information about children. With less time to spend with their child, generally, working parents tend to have less understanding of the child overall, compared to a parent who stays home and cares for the child all day. Sometimes they have additional difficulties in limit-setting because they have less *time* to engage their child's cooperation. As a result, child development is an area that this group of parents often needs to spend more time learning, most particularly, how much to expect of their children and what do situations look like from the child's perspective—the psychology of the child. Opportunities through the parenting class or at day care to play with and observe their children and other children can be enormously helpful to working mothers and fathers. As they watch the different children interact and play, they learn about the developmental and personality differences and similarities of the particular age group. They may also learn about new ways to talk to, play with, and set limits with children.

Schedules and routines can be a difficult topic area for working parents for many reasons. First of all, the family schedule may vary each day, depending on any changes in the parent(s)' work schedule. Secondly, the parents may have difficulty keeping to a routine because of their sense of guilt that they have been gone so much. Third, the weekday schedule may vary a great deal from the weekend schedule, causing difficulties in the child's adjustments to these changes. Finally, working parents have the added challenge of having to work out an arrangement between their routine and schedule and that of the caregiver or child care environment. When a conflict exists between the two routines and the parents and the caregiver(s) are not communicating openly, there can be resulting problems in the child's behavior. Schedules and routines are a useful topic for working parents in the classes to discuss with each other.

Time management issues are also of high concern for working parents. Many of these parents are performing multiple roles each day as parent, worker, homemaker, and spouse/partner among others. If they compare themselves to a "Superwoman" or "Modern Man" image as portrayed in the media or have otherwise high expectations of themselves, this can add another layer of stress to an already stressful lifestyle. Time in class can be used to address their expectation of themselves as they juggle these multiple roles and tasks each day and to discuss priorities and coping strategies.

Time management issues often can be discussed alongside issues concerning co-parenting, because the two topics are so interrelated. The couples and individuals in the group can be encouraged to share with other parents how they share the parenting responsibilities. Often, during a discussion on co-parenting, common themes regarding typical conflicts, their own time management and stress reduction techniques emerge. Sometimes there are also general problems in child rearing because neither parent has taken on the role of "psychological parent"—i.e., the parent who keeps track in an overall way of the child's development and the child's needs such as haircuts, clothes, doctor's appointments as well as the child's problems—even if they are minor.

If single parents are members of the group, it is a good idea to briefly address the challenges that they may be facing that differ from those of the couples. Some single parents have extended family members that perform the same "co-parenting" tasks that a spouse or partner would perform. Some of the issues regarding communication and cooperation between divorced mothers and fathers or between single parents and their extended family are similar to those for married couples. If a single parent does not share the parenting with a partner or a family member, it is important to empathize with the "double-load" that this parent has indeed taken upon him or herself and to underscore the importance of seeking community support services, such as single parent support groups. If the single parents are a small minority of the class, it is best to check in with them after the class on co-parenting and discuss any individual issues that were raised but not addressed fully for them. An individual consultation or a referral might be offered. Parent classes can work very well for married and single parents and separate groups for each is not generally needed or recommended.

A common theme among working couples is that the mother feels a greater burden of responsibility for the parenting and household tasks than does the father. During the class discussion on co-parenting, this concern must be addressed sensitively so as to validate both the mothers' and fathers' perspectives. You may want to offer an explanation of the origins of this in terms of the way the sexes have been socialized to traditionally "share" the different roles within the family and the fact that we are in a period of transition, involving more choices and added benefits for both men and women. Stress the importance of working out together the division of the different tasks so that both partners can live comfortably with the arrangement. For some couples, this involves a 50-50 sharing of parenting and household tasks, while for others it is divided much differently. The important thing is to encourage them to agree to a plan that they can live by and support with actions on a daily basis. Then, if the plan is not working, encourage them to re-evaluate and have another planning meeting until the division of labor works better for both partners. Continual re-evaluation of the division of labor is critical to avoid falling into patterns that may not necessarily work for either or both parents.

Finding time to be together as a couple is another pressing concern for many working parents. Information regarding marital satisfaction and frequency of divorce can sometimes help to provide a catalyst to challenge working couples to make their relationship become a higher priority. It is essential to underscore the importance of the strength of the marital relationship in supporting the child's emotional growth, so that the couples view their commitment to spending time alone with each other as involving more than just the pleasure they both derive. Help them to view this time as a form of an investment in their child's growth. A child benefits from seeing his or her parents happy with each other. Unfortunately, though, for many working parents, time alone together often falls to the bottom of the priorities as other demands take precedence.

Another whole area of concern relates to child care. Working parents must rely on child care arrangements while they are away at work. Leaving one's child in child care can bring up many feelings and questions. There are many sub-topic areas that would be helpful to cover:

1. Searching for child care
2. Different options for child care
3. Differences among models for curriculum in child care and preschools
4. Individual differences in children and goodness of fit with the child care arrangement
5. Developmental needs of the child in child care
6. Evaluating the quality of child care and deciding on child care
7. Communication with the child care provider(s)
8. Working out plans with the child care provider(s) regarding toilet training, naptimes, mealtimes, and the consideration of individual differences in needs
9. The effects of child care on the child

What is most critical in teaching full-time working parents is for the parent educator to have some understanding of the issues that many working parents face and not to be judgmental about the choices that have been made. It can be particularly difficult for parent educators to be supportive of full-time working parents because these parents do not have as much time with their children as parent educators may believe is necessary for their child's well-being. These are often the same feelings that the child's child care providers

have about the parents. The parent educator of full-time working parents has the opportunity to have a key role in supporting these parents in solving some of these difficult problems in healthy and positive ways, while continuing to help them to re-evaluate present values and future choices that will continue to effect the quality of their lives together as a family. Sometimes this means one or both parents changing or decreasing their work hours or changing their child's care arrangements.

Many of the topics that are important to cover in working parent classes can be seen on p. 444 in the sample series outline for working parents of toddlers. Mini-lecture with handouts, discussion, and observation of the children, if that is possible, are all important elements of these classes.

Playcare

In classes for full-time working parents, the children have usually been away from their parents some or most of the day. For every parenting program, a well-considered decision has be to made about offering care for the children. See Part I, Chapter 7 for some of the considerations. The child's caregivers while the parents are at work may be relatives, friends, Nannies or Au Pairs, part-time sitters, family day care providers, or child care center staff. The children may vary, too, in terms of the degree of consistency of primary caretakers and their experiences of coping with separations from their parents. These must all be taken into consideration when planning if and how to provide care for each child while the parent attends the parenting class.

Because of all these factors, if you are going to have child care, it is very important to provide a consistent caregiving environment during the class series. It will be helpful to explain to the caregivers the critical role they play in helping both the parents and the children feel comfortable during each class. If the child is in distress, the parent most likely will be unable to enjoy and learn in a parent class. A commitment from the playcare caregivers to be available for every class (barring illness or emergency) is really essential.

For an evening series, the child will arrive with many needs. Especially with young children, they may come to class tired and hungry. Perhaps Mom or Dad were rushed. Very young children may be needing a diaper change and a bottle. Toddlers and older children usually will need a dinner soon after they arrive. Early serving of dinner helps hungry young children and also may decrease the strains of separation if the children are busy eating and experiencing sitting around a table as a group when it is time for the parents to depart to the parent class. Then after the children eat, the stage is set for a comfortable playtime. For weekend classes, too, bottles or snacks may be provided for the children, depending on the age of the group.

Besides needing to be fed, all children usually need just simple playtime with each parent before the parents go to the class. They also need time to adjust to the play environment, to get acquainted with the caregiver and to become familiar with the other children. A short "family playtime" before the parenting class begins provides a nice settling in period for all involved. As the weeks go by and children become increasingly comfortable, this transition time often becomes shorter.

In general, the mood of the group of parents and children who arrive to attend a working parents' class differs from other parent groups. Their stress level is higher. The parents arrive feeling more fatigued and rushed. And the children may be feeling particularly needy after being away from their parents that day. Encourage the caregivers to be prepared when the parents and their children arrive. The caregivers need to understand it is their job to provide a warm and soothing environment when the families arrive. The environment, including food should, of course, be prepared for the children in advance so that the caregivers are fully available to attend to the children and their parents.

Observations of the Children

Observation periods during the class provide useful opportunities for the working parents to learn more about their child. A one-way observation window is enormously helpful if it is available in your parenting class facility. However, even if it

is not, ways for parents to observe and participate within the child's playroom are very helpful to parents.

Because most working parents leave their children when they go to work, they separate from their child on a regular basis. They can learn a great deal about the child's behavior and coping style following the separation by observing the child immediately after leaving him or her to go to class.

If the parent experiences a high level of anxiety regarding each separation from the child, the other parents and the parent educator can support her or his efforts to learn how to confidently say goodbye to the child and to manage this anxiety. The other parents can also provide some feedback about how the child appears to be responding to the initial separation so the parent can evaluate more clearly the child's separation anxiety apart from the parent's anxiety. There is the opportunity to problem-solve with the rest of the parent group regarding how to support the child before, during, and following each separation. This is helpful information to take home and to provide to the caregiver(s) who cares for the child while the parent is at work.

The parents may also learn more about how to evaluate the skills of a caregiver and the quality of a child care environment during these observation periods if the parent educator shares her or his own perceptions of the individual children, the group dynamics among the children, and the interactions between the caregivers and the children.

Finally, another benefit of these observation periods that are particularly relevant to working parents is that the parent can learn through watching their child in this setting how he or she is playing, learning, relating to others, cooperating, etc. Parents also will see how other children play, how they respond to limits, how they relate to other children and adults. These observations help parents develop more appropriate expectations of children and often enhanced skills in child guidance.

The length of the observation depends on the purpose of the observation. Observations can last for as little as two minutes to check in on the children, especially with infants and toddlers, to 20 to 30 minutes to observe peer relations and play skills.

Evaluation of Series

After the final class of the series, as with any other parent series, it is always useful to ask for written feedback through formal evaluation forms. This may provide useful information about the changing needs of working parents and be useful in planning of the next series of classes. See p. 41 for a discussion of this subject and Appendix G for a sample class evaluation form. Teaching full-time working parents, although different, is extremely important. Reaching these parents and helping them find a time and place for parenting education is an enormous challenge. Some corporations support lunch-time parenting programs. Some parent networks support evening or weekend parenting education at each other's homes. Guiding busy parents of young children is a challenge for both the parents and the parent educators. The benefits to the families make this challenge worth meeting.

Readings About and for Working Parents**

Ashery, Rebecca and Margolin, Michele, *Guide for Parents with Careers* (Washington, D.C.: Acropolis Books, 1986)

This book deals entirely with the practical issues of child care and home management largely from an efficiency and time management point of view. It is helpful for those who need organizational strategies but it does not deal with parents' feelings nor children's needs and feelings.

Berg, Barbara, *Crisis of the Working Mother* (New York: Summit Books, 1986)

This is a helpful book—especially—for mothers. It covers most all the issues including historical ones that working mothers deal with all the time. It talks about many other mothers' experiences and is supportive and helpful.

Brazelton, T. Berry, *Working and Caring* (Reading, Mass.: Addison-Wesley, 1985)

This book deals in depth with difficult feelings and choices that working parents experience from returning to work after the birth of the baby to difficult times in their children's early years. Brazelton follows three very different families through those years with thoughtful commentary and suggestions. (Helpful except for the idealistic solutions in child care that some of these families eventually find).

Brooks, Andre, *Children of Fast-Track Parents* (New York, N.Y.: Viking Penguin, 1989)

This book provides insights and suggestions to busy, professional families who need to know what "the good life" looks like from their children's point of view.

Grollmen, Earl and Sweder, Gerri, *The Working Parent Dilemma* (Boston: Beacon Press, 1986)

This book tells what it is like to have working parents from *the child's point of view*. The children are elementary school through high school age and this book covers nearly everything you would want to ask your child. It is extremely helpful to parents—even those with very young children—to know how children view themselves and their working parents. This book is very valuable and strongly recommended.

Hobfoll, Stevan and Hobfall, Ivonne, *Work Won't Love You Back* (New York, N.Y.: W. H. Freeman and Co., 1994)

This excellent book helps you evaluate and problem-solve your life as a working parent and offers many personal experiences to learn from. Strongly recommended.

Hochschild, Arlie, *The Second Shift: Working Parents and the Revolution at Home* (New York: Viking Penguin, 1989)

This is an outstanding book that deals with the work that needs to be done by men and women at home—house management and childcare. This author has gone beyond the others in her thoughtful and realistic look at how mothers and fathers work out these arrangements and what is behind those problems and inequities. This book is not at all gender biased. Strongly recommended.

Magid, Renee, *When Mothers and Fathers Work* (New York: Avon Books, 1987)

This is a very practical book on common problems and feelings of both mothers and fathers with many helpful suggestions. The information is based on personal experience and interviews of working parents.

**For additional readings on "working parents" and on "child care", see p. 31, 92, 309, 369, and 381.

Index

Adjusting to parenting, 90–103 (*see also* Baby-sitting, Needs, parental, and Temperament and individual differences)
  difficult feelings and experiences during, 91, 94–96, 97–98, 99–103
  expectations during, 95, 99–103
  needs during, 94, 95, 96, 101–103
Advertising (*see* Publicity)
Advice (*see* Counseling)
Agenda (*see* Series outline, and Instructors, weekly preparation for teaching)
Assessment (*see* Evaluation)

Baby-sitting, 367–378
  baby-sitters
    finding and evaluating, 372–373
    hints for working with, 373
    instructions for, 376–378
  parent's feelings about, 368, 371–372
  value of, for child, 368, 372
  value of, for parent, 371
Books (*see* Readings)
Brazelton, T. Berry, 56, 59, 69, 126, 321
Breast- and bottle feeding (*see also* Nutrition)
  of young babies
    allergies associated with, 68–69
    effect of, on sleep, 58
    milk, types and amounts of, 67, 73
    supplementary bottles for breast-fed babies, 70
    using a cup, 69
    weaning, 77, 163
Budget, 15

Chess, S., Thomas, A., and Birch, H. G., 125, 349–351
Child care (*see* Nursery schools)
Child-rearing classes (*see* Parenting classes)
Child Rearing Education and Counseling Program, 4
  children's involvement in (*see* Playcare)
  class size of, 8
  class structure of, 7–8
  description of, 4
  evaluation of, 4
  goals of, 4

length of series, 8
other services, 42
  child-rearing counseling, 42
  Warm-line, 43
participants in, 8n
philosophy of, 5–6
Children (*see also* specific topics throughout Parts II-VI)
  differences among (*see* Temperament and individual differences)
  involvement of, in parenting classes (*see* Playcare)
  point of view, 9 (*see also* Family Dynamics sections throughout Parts II-VI)
  of two-year-olds, 259–264
Children's Health Council
  description of, 4, 4n
Class outline (*see* Series outline, and Instructors, weekly preparation for teaching)
Cognitive-motor development
  of older babies, 166–170
    areas of learning in, 169, 170
    how they learn, 168
    meaning to baby, 167, 168
    parent's influence on, 167, 169
  of toddlers
    areas of learning in, 232–233, 237, 238–239
  of two-year-olds
    areas of learning in, 298–300
  of young babies, 80, 83, 84, 86
Costs (*see* Budget)
Counseling (*see also* Sample Concern, Family Dynamics, and Additional Information sections throughout Parts II-VI)
  by telephone, 42–43
  individual conferences for, 43
Couples' classes (*see* Husband-wife relationship)
Crying and schedules, 51–62
  changing sleep patterns affecting, 57–58, 60–61
  conflicting advice about, 52
  reasons for (crying), 56
  sleeping through the night, 59
  working with (baby's schedules), 58–59

Differences, individual (*see* Temperament and individual differences)

Discussions, leading (*see* Leadership techniques)

Early childhood education programs, 307–316
Eating (*see* Nutrition)
Emotional development (*see also* Social-emotional
   development, and Temperament and individual
   differences)
  of toddlers, 193–202
    handling difficult behavior during, 200–201, 202
    parent's feelings about, 194, 201
    parent's needs during, 200–201
    self-esteem during, 201
    separation difficulties during, 199–200
    toddler's behavior during, 194, 198, 202
Equipment
  basic, 104–110
    types and uses of, for babies, 106–110
  for treating sickness, 333
  safe-proofing, 337–339
Ethnicity, 423–424
Evaluation
  of Child Rearing Education and Counseling Program,
    4
  of each class, 22
  of leadership skills, 29
  of orientation class, 18–19
  of parenting series, by parents, 41
    sample form for, 464–465
  of playcarers, 34
    sample form for, 460–461

Facilities, 11
Family size, 352–361
  multi-child families
    preparing for siblings in, 362–366
    spacing of children in, 352, 353–357
  one-child families, 356, 357–361
  parent's concerns about, 353, 356
Fathers' classes (*see also* Husband-wife relationship)
  format of, 38–40
  further types of, 40
  pre-class preparation for, 38
  purpose of, 8
  techniques of teaching, 38–40
  typical concerns of fathers in, 39
Fears and nightmares (*see also* Sleep, and Social-emo-
    tional development
  child's view of, 276
  parent's concerns about, 276
  parent's techniques for dealing with, 278
First class (*see* Orientation class)
Foods (*see* Nutrition)
Foundation of child-rearing program (*see* Philosophy of
    child-rearing program

Goals, teaching (*see* Goals to Work Toward sections
    throughout Parts II-VI)
Groups, parenting
  beginning and ending (*see* Parenting classes)
  problems with, 29–30

Handouts (*see* Handouts sections throughout Parts II-VI)
Homework (*see* Homework sections throughout Parts
    II-VI)
Husband-wife relationship, 96, 392–402
  communication differences in, 402–403
  couples' classes, for supporting, 8, 389n
    leading of, 392–397
    problems with, 8n, 40
  importance of, for child, 393
  stresses on, 393, 397, 399–401
    handling of, 399–401

Inquiries, parent (*see* Registration)
Instructors (*see also* Leadership techniques)
  ongoing emotional support for, 24
  organizing resource information for, 22
  pre-series preparation for teaching by
    class content, 8–9
    leadership techniques, 9–10
    self-nurturing, 23–24
  qualifications and hiring of, 11–13
  sample ad for, 425
  weekly preparation for teaching (developing a class
    outline)
    areas to learn about (*see* Areas of Information sec-
      tions throughout Parts II-VI)
    current week's topic, 22
    handouts, 22 (*see also* Handouts sections through-
      out Parts II-VI)
    last week's topic, 21
    next week's homework, 22 (*see also* Homework sec-
      tions throughout Parts II-VI)
    observation of children, 22

Leadership techniques (*see also* Instructors)
  co-leading, 9, 23
  developing a class outline, 21–22
    sample for use in, 445
  establishing ground rules, 25–26
  for difficult group situations, 29–30
  for fathers' classes, 38–40
  for keeping discussions going, 27–28
  for leading off discussions, 26–27
  for problem solving, 27–28
    sample parent guide, 447–449
  mini-lectures, 26 (*see also* Mini-lecture and Lead-off
    Questions sections throughout Parts II-VI)
  practical hints (*see* Practical Suggestions or Strategies
    sections throughout Parts II-VI)
  self-evaluation, 28–29
  sharing labor and delivery experiences, 17
Learning, child's (*see* Play and Learning, and Thinking,
    child's)
Lectures (*see* Leadership techniques, mini-lectures)
Limit setting
  for older babies, 131–138
    definition of, 134, 136
    parent's concerns about safety in, 136, 137–138
    parent's feelings about, 132
    techniques for, 136–137

understanding and viewpoints on, 132, 136, 137
for toddlers, 203–213
  difficulties in, 209
  guidelines for, 210
  parent's expectations, 213
  parent's feelings about, 204, 209
  parent's needs during, 211–212
  techniques for, 210–211, 212, 213
  understanding and viewpoints on, 204, 210
for two-year-olds, 265–274
  child's skills to consider during, 266
  parent's guidelines for, 271, 272, 274
  parent's problems with, 266, 272
  purpose of, 271

Marriage relationship (see Husband-wife relationship)
Milk (see Breast- and bottle feeding, and Nutrition)

Needs, parental, 381, 388, 389–391
  child's reactions to, 380, 389–391
  effects of not meeting, 380, 389–391
New babies (see Siblings)
Nightmares (see Sleep, and Fears and nightmares)
Nursery schools, 307–315
  child's reactions to, 308, 312
  evaluating, guidelines for, 311, 313–314
  first days at, guidelines for, 311–312, 315
  parent's concerns about, 304, 308, 312
  types of, 311
Nutrition (see also Breast- and bottle feeding)
  of older babies, 156–165
    feeding hints for, 161, 162
    finger foods, 68, 162, 165
    foods, dangerous, 163
    growth patterns related to, 161
    meaning of food to, 157, 161, 162
    nutrients, purpose and sources of, 290–291
    parent's concerns about, 157
    parent's awareness of, 161, 162
    recommended daily meal plan, 164
    weaning, 163
  of toddlers, 214–216, 280–291
    dietary substitutes, guidelines for, 288
    eating behavior guidelines, 216
    feeding abilities, 285
    nutrients, purpose and sources of, 290–291
    parent's guidelines for handling, 287–289
    recommended daily meal plan, 286
    snack suggestions, 284, 289
  of two-year-olds, 280–291
    child's feelings about, 281
    dietary substitutes, guidelines for, 288
    feeding abilities, 285
    growth patterns, 283
    nutrients, purpose and sources of, 290–291
    parents feelings about, 281, 284
    parent's guidelines for handling, 284, 287–289
    recommended daily meal plan, 286
    snack suggestions, 284, 289
  of young babies, 63–77
    allergies, 68–69
    changes in eating patterns, 58–59, 70, 71–72

growth patterns related to, 67, 74
milk, types and amounts of, 67, 73
solids, 67–69, 74–76

Observation
  for information gathering, 8–9
  of children, by parents, 32, 39–40 (see also
      Homework)
    of older babies, toddlers, and two-year-olds, 35
    of young babies, 34–35
    techniques for, 462–463
    topics for, 35–36, 462–463
  of children, by playcarers
    topic suggestions and samples for, 453–459
  problems of, 36
Only child (see Family size)
Orientation class
  developing a series outline for, 19–20
    samples for, for all ages, 441–444
  format of, 17–18
  goals of, 16
  instructor's assessment of, 18–19
  instructor's preparation for, 16–17
    sample demographic information form, 441
    sample program information form, 428–429
  parent's feelings during
    about labor and delivery experience, 17
    about playcare, 17
  parent's pre-orientation forms for
    birth or adoption experiences, 439
    confirmation letter, 430
    current concerns, 431
    parent's interests, 432–436
    separation experiences, 436–438

Parenting (see also Temperament and individual differ-
      ences, and Husband-wife relationship)
  adjusting to, 90–103
  nurturing of self during (see Needs, parental)
  problems of, 3
  support for
    baby-sitting, 367–377
    books, 4, 405–417
    classes, 4
    friends and relatives, 3–4
    pediatricians, obtaining help from, 3
Parenting classes (see also Child Rearing Education and
      Counseling Program, and specific topics through-
      out Parts II-VI)
  beginning
    developing an affiliation for, 11
    fees for, 15
    finding a facility for, 11
    hiring staff for, 11–13
    publicity for, 13–14
    registration for, 14–15
  children's involvement in (see Playcare)
  ending
    encouraging further group interaction, 41–42
    evaluation of series, by parents, 41, 464–465
    providing additional services for individuals, 42–43
  goals of (see Goals to Work Toward sections through-

out Parts II-VI)
inquiries about, handling (see Registration)
leaders of, 8–10 (see also Instructors)
orientation class, 16–19
reason for, 4
types of, to offer, 7
Parents (see Adjusting to parenting, Needs, parental, and other specific topics throughout Parts II-VI)
  concerns of (see also Sample Concern of Parents sections throughout Parts II-VI)
    adjusting to parenting, 90, 379
    baby-sitters and returning to work, 367–368
    cognitive-motor development, 166
    crying and schedules, 51–52
    equipment, 104
    family size, 352
    husband-wife relationship, 392
    language development, 111, 180, 242
    limit setting, 131–132, 203–204, 265
    nursery schools, 307
    nutrition and eating behavior, 63, 156–157, 214, 280–281
    patterns and schedules, 149–150
    play and learning, 78, 171, 227, 259, 292
    siblings, 362–363
    sickness and safety, 325–326
    sleep, 275
    social-emotional development, 120, 139–140, 193
    socializing among children, 217, 301–302
    speech (see language development)
    temperament, 340–341
    toilet training, 317–318
Patterns and and schedules (see also Temperament and individual differences)
  older babies, 149–155
    changes in (baby's patterns), 150
    effects of growth on, in babies, 150
    parent's ability to affect, 154–155
Pediatricians, 3 (see also Sickness)
Philosophy of child-rearing program, 5–6
Play and learning (see also Nursery schools)
  of older babies, 166–170, 171, 179
    skills needed in, 175, 178–179
    parent's involvement in, 175–176, 179
    parent's understanding of, 172
    purpose of, 172, 175, 178
    toys, types and uses of, 176, 178–179
  of toddlers, 227–241
    parent's expectations of, 228
    parent's involvement in, 233–235, 240
    play environments for, 237–238
    purpose of, 228, 232, 235
    skills needed in, 237, 239, 240
    toys used in, guidelines for buying, 239
    types of, 233, 238–239
  of two-year-olds, 292–300
    crafts, 294, 297, 300
    how they think, 259–264
    parent's involvement in, 253, 294, 297, 298–300
    pre-academics, 294, 297, 298–300
    skills needed in, 298–299
    television viewing, guidelines for, 294

toys, types and uses of, 294, 297, 299–300
  types of play, 299–300
  of young babies, 78–89
    concerns about development of, 84
    growth and development in, 80, 83, 86
    parent's involvement in, 83–84, 88
    purpose of, 79
    toys and stimulation in, 87–88, 89
Playcare
  dealing with parent's feelings about, 17
  for older babies, toddlers, and two-year-olds, 31–32
  for young babies, 31
  guidelines for parents about, 450
  parent's observations of, 462–463
  purpose of, 8, 31
Playcarers
  curriculum for, 33–34
    objectives of, 451
    sample observations for, 453–454, 455–459
    sample outline for, 453
  evaluation of, 34
    sample form, 460–461
  head teacher/caregiver, 454
  hiring of, 33
  training of, 33
    sample written instructions for, 451–452
Preparation, instructor's
  pre-series, 8–10, 23–24
  weekly, 21–23
Problem solving, 27–28, 447–449 (see also Sample Concern of Parents sections throughout Parts II-VI)
Publicity, 13–14
  community distribution, 13
    sample flyer for, 426
  newspapers and other media, 13–14
    sample article for, 425
  problems with, 13
  professional contacts, 13
  word-of-mouth, 14

Readings
  for instructors (see also Readings and Other Resources sections throughout Parts II-VI)
    on adoption, 423
    on child and parent development, 421
    on divorce, single parenting and stepparenting, 422
    on ethnic minorities, 423
    on group guidance techniques, 421
    on prematurity and multiple births, 423
    on working parent families, 473
    reviews and current literature, 424
  for parents, 405–417
    about older babies, 409–411
    about toddlers, 412—414
    about two-year-olds, 415–417
    about young babies, 406–408
Registration
  enrollment, 15
    post-enrollment sample forms, 429
    pre-enrollment sample forms, 428
  inquiries
    handling, 14

sample answers to, 427–428
keeping records, 14
sample form for, 427
policy
sample statement of, 429
Resources, community, 404
Resources, teaching (*see also* Readings)
organizations for parenting educators, 424

Safety, 325–339
choking, handling, 163
parent's concerns about, 136, 137–138
safe-proofing homes
areas to check, 334–335
equipment for, 337–339
poison prevention, 335–336
purpose of, 330, 334
Schedules (*see* Crying and schedules, and Patterns and
schedules)
Separation anxiety (*see* Social-emotional development)
Series outline
developing, 19–20
samples of
for older babies, 442–443
for toddlers, 443
for two- to three-year-olds, 443
for working parents, 444
for young babies, 441–442
Sibling rivalry, 362–366
guidelines for parents about, 366
parent's concerns about, 363
Siblings, 362–366
child's reactions to, 363, 366
guidelines for adjusting to, 366
guidelines for preparing child for, 365
parent's concerns about, 363
Sickness, 325–339
medication during, administering, 332
parent's fears and feelings about, 326, 329
pediatricians, sharing care with, 329, 330, 331, 332
preventive measures for, 332
supplies for treatment of, 333
symptoms of, 327, 329, 332
temperature during, taking and interpreting,
329–330, 332
Single parents, 422
Sleep
for older babies, 154
changes in patterns of, 60–61
through the night, 59
for two-year-olds, 275–279
child's problems with, 276, 278
effects of child's growth patterns on, 278
parent's problems with, 276
parent's techniques for handling problems with,
278–279
for young babies, 56
changes in patterns of, 57–58, 60–61
effect of breast- and bottle feeding on, 58
through the night, 59
Social-emotional development (*see also* Temperament
and individual differences)

of older babies, 139–148
baby's behavior during growth, 140, 142, 144–145,
148
baby's self-esteem, 146–147
parent's understanding and handling of, 140, 146,
147, 148
separation anxiety during, 144, 145–146
of young babies, 120–128
growth patterns, 123–125, 128
individual differences, 125
parent's encouragement of, 126
parent's self-care during, 126–127
Socializing among children (*see also* Nursery schools)
toddlers, 217–226
growth in skills, 218, 221, 225
parent's expectations of, 218, 222
parent's feelings about, 218
play group experiences, 223–224
problems of, 222–223
techniques for channeling, 223, 225–226
two-year-olds, 301–306
growth in skills, 305
parent's expectations of, 302
parent's feelings about, 302
purpose of, 302
techniques for channeling, 303, 305–306
Spacing of children (*see* Family size, Sibling rivalry, and
Siblings)
Speech and Language development
of older babies, 180–190
checking baby's hearing during, 118–119
growth patterns in, 113, 115–116, 117
parent's stimulation of, 116, 118
of toddlers, 242–255
articulation during, 246n, 250
growth patterns in, 246, 248
parent's feelings about, 243
parent's involvement in, 246–247, 248–250, 252
problems with, 247, 251–252
of two-year-olds, 242–255
articulation during, 246n, 250
growth patterns in, 250
parent's involvement in, 246–247, 252, 253–255
problems with, 247, 251–252
of young babies, 111–119
growth patterns in, 185, 186–188
parent's feelings about, 181, 182
parent's stimulation of, 182, 185, 186–190
Staff
instructors (*see* Instructors)
playcarers (students), 32–34 (*see also* Playcarers)
program head, 12–13
secretary, 143
teacher/caregivers, 454
Students (*see* Playcarers)

Teachers (*see* Instructors)
Teaching techniques (*see* Leadership techniques)
Temperament and individual differences
of young babies, 125
of older babies-three-year-olds, 340–351
aspects of temperament, pros and cons of, 346–347

definition of, 345, 348–351
value of understanding, 341, 345, 346, 349
Thinking, child's
 two-year-olds, 259–264
  areas of interest, 263
  parent's feelings about, 260
  parent's techniques for working with, 263
  skills involved in, 260, 261, 263, 264
Toilet training, 317–322
 child's reactions to, 318
 child's readiness for, 320–321
 hints for, 321
 parent's concerns about, 318
 parent's guidelines for, 320, 321

problems of, handling, 321–322
process of, 320
Toys (*see* Play and learning)
Training
 of instructors, 11–12
 of playcarers, 33

Work, returning to (*see also* Baby-sitting)
 making the decision, 373–374
 parent's feelings concerning
  not working, 374
  working, 374
Working parent classes, 466–473

About the Authors

B. Annye Rothenberg, Ph.D. (Cornell University) is a Child/Parent Psychologist and the Founder/Director in 1973 of the Child Rearing Education and Counseling Program at the Children's Health Council (CHC) in Palo Alto, California. She is a nationally recognized expert on parenting education and guidance of parents of young children and has taught parenting classes covering all the ages in this handbook.

Dr. Rothenberg is also a leader in training professionals in education, health care, and social services to provide more effective guidance to parents and help increase parents' skills in understanding and raising their children. In addition to being the senior author of **Parentmaking,** she is also the senior author of **Parentmaking Educators Training Program: A Comprehensive Skills Development Course to Train Early Childhood Parent Educators (birth to 5).** Her newest book is **Understanding and Working with Parents and Children from Rural Mexico** (Menlo Park, CA: CHC Center for Child and Family Development Press, 1995). This book is

the first in what is expected to be a series of contributions to the important area of ethnic minority family and child rearing practices. Dr. Rothenberg lives in Woodside, California with her son Bret.

Sandra L. Hitchcock, M.A. (University of Washington), was a parent educator at CHC from 1975 to 1980, teaching the "Learning More About Toddlers" class. Her background is in early childhood education. She lives in Palo Alto, California, with her husband Art, son Peter, and daughter Nicole.

Mary Lou S. Harrison, M.Ed. (University of Rochester), an experienced high school teacher and counselor, was a parent educator at CHC from 1975 to 1979, primarily leading the "Learning More About Young Babies" series. She lives in Los Altos, California, with her husband Doug, daughter Daryl, and son Craig.

Melinda S. Graham, M.Ed. (Kent State University), previously a counselor and a parent educator at CHC from 1975 to 1978, now lives in Canton, Ohio, with her daughters Erin and Meredith. She is a parent educator and training consultant in the northeastern Ohio area. During her association with the Child Rearing Program, she was the instructor of the "Learning More About Older Babies" classes.

Dr. Rothenberg and her colleagues from the Child Rearing Education and Counseling Program at CHC have developed a new professional education program to train instructors of early parenting classes. The program and accompanying videotapes **Parentmaking Educators Training Program: A Comprehensive Skills Development Course to Train Early Childhood Parent Educators (birth to 5)** is available as a self-administered on-site training program. Contact: Banster Press, P.O. Box 7326, Menlo Park, CA 94026 or call (415) 369-8032 for more information.

Additional Contributors to the Second Edition of *Parentmaking*

Jomary Hilliard, Ph.D.
(University of California at Los Angeles)
Dr. Hilliard, a clinical psychologist, has taught and counseled in the Child Rearing Program at the Children's Health Council since 1987. She has taught the Parenting Older Babies and Two Year Old series. Most recently, she has been teaching the Parenting Kindergarteners and First Graders series. She lives in Mountain View, California with her husband, Robert Bolles and their three sons, Stephen, Philip, and John Paul.

Karen Friedland-Brown, M.A.
(University of California, Berkeley)
Part of the Child Rearing Program staff since 1991, Karen teaches Parenting Older Babies, Parenting Two Year Olds, and the Working Parents of Pre-schoolers series. She is also a child rearing counselor. Her primary training is as a resource specialist in education. Karen and her husband, Mark Brown and their son Jordan live in Mountain View, California.

Rebecca Beacom
(University of California at Los Angeles)
A childbirth and parenting educator who became part of the Child Rearing staff in 1987, Becky has taught the Parenting Young Babies class series and classes for expectant parents. She and her husband James live in Palo Alto, California with daughter Jeanne and son Jack.

Julie Kelsey
(Santa Clara University)
Julie's background is in child care and early childhood development. She has been part of the Child Rearing Program since 1993. She teaches class series to Working Parents of Toddlers. Julie lives in San Jose, California with her husband Matt, daughter Emma and son Vincent.

Doreen du Celliée, M.S.
(San Francisco State University)
Doreen, a speech and language clinician, was on the Child Rearing Staff from 1989 to 1994 teaching the Parenting Toddlers series and providing parent counseling. She now lives in Sebastopol, California with her husband Jeff Muller and daughters Ariel and Julia.

Second Edition

PARENTMAKING

A Practical Handbook for Teaching Parent Classes About Babies and Toddlers

B. Annye Rothenberg, Ph.D. with the staff of the
Child Rearing Program at the CHC Center for Child and Family Development

Parenting educators have struggled alone to develop their own curriculum and group leadership style so they could help new parents learn about their youngster's practical day-to-day development and behavior and their own new roles as parents.

This **just-revised** and still **unique-in-the field** handbook fills the gap for a needed training and curriculum resource. **PARENTMAKING** enables parent educators to help new parents learn about their youngster's practical day-to-day development and behavior and their own new roles as parents.

Revised by Dr. Annye Rothenberg, child/parent psychologist and her colleagues after two decades of teaching new parents, **PARENTMAKING** covers every major topic usually raised by parents in new parenting groups such as crying and schedules, play and learning, limit setting, feeding and nutrition, socializing among children, adjusting to parenting, etc. **Each topic, presented in age-divided sections, includes teaching goals, parents' most common questions,** *sample lectures,* **homework,** and *handouts to give to parents,* **guidelines to help parents analyze and solve their child-rearing concerns,** and *further suggested readings.*

PARENTMAKING also provides techniques for presenting information to groups, insight into parent group dynamics and management, and strategies for providing both education and emotional support in a group setting. Through these features, parenting educators with their diverse backgrounds and skills (such as nurses, educators, psychologists, and counselors) have a resource that meets their various needs. New information on teaching "working" parent families is also included along with resources for those working with ethnic minorities, single parents, etc.

This handbook emphasizes practical information and is based on the "tried and true" experiences of thousands of families integrated with basic psychological and developmental principles. It focuses on both children and parents, emphasizing the balance necessary for the healthy growth of the family.

Consistently highly acclaimed by leading authorities such as Brazelton, Dodson, and Ames, *PARENTMAKING* is a *MUST* for all professionals in this field. Its thoroughness will save even the experienced group leader hundreds of hours in research and preparation time. The detailed information on the topics of frequent concern to parents also makes this a valuable resource for providing **individual** guidance to parents of babies and toddlers.

512 pages • Quality paperback • 8¼" x 10½" • ISBN 0-9604620-2-3

$29.95 for a limited time (Publisher's list price $35.95)

Banster Press • P.O. Box 7326 • Menlo Park, CA 94026 • (415) 369-8032